CONVENTS AND THE BODY POLITIC
IN LATE RENAISSANCE VENICE

WOMEN IN CULTURE AND SOCIETY
A series edited by Catharine R. Stimpson

CONVENTS *and the* BODY POLITIC

JUTTA GISELA SPERLING

in late RENAISSANCE VENICE

The University of Chicago Press / Chicago and London

Jutta Gisela Sperling is assistant professor at Hampshire College.

The University of Chicago Press, Chicago 60637
The University of Chicago Press, Ltd., London
© 1999 by Jutta Gisela Sperling
All rights reserved. Published 1999

08 07 06 05 04 03 02 01 00 99   1 2 3 4 5
ISBN: 0-226-76935-6 (cloth)
ISBN: 0-226-76936-4 (paper)

Library of Congress Cataloging-in-Publication Data

Sperling, Jutta Gisela.
   Convents and the body politic in late Renaissance Venice / Jutta Gisela Sperling.
      p. cm. — (Women in culture and society)
   Includes bibliographical references (p.) and index.
   ISBN 0-226-76935-6 (cloth : alk. paper) — ISBN 0-226-76936-4
(pbk. : alk. paper)
   1. Monasticism and religious orders for women—Italy—Venice—History—16th century.   2. Women—Italy—Venice—Social conditions—16th century.   3. Nobility—Italy—Venice—History—16th century.
4. Venice (Italy)—Social conditions—16th century.   5. Monasticism and religious orders for women—Italy—Venice—History—17th century.   6. Women—Italy—Venice—Social conditions—17th century.
7. Nobility—Italy—Venice—History—17th century.   8. Venice (Italy)—Social conditions—17th century.   I. Title.   II. Series.

BX4220.I8 S64 1999
271′.9′009453109031 21—dc21   99-042787

JUTTA GISELA SPERLING

in late RENAISSANCE VENICE

The University of Chicago Press / Chicago and London

Jutta Gisela Sperling is assistant professor at Hampshire College.

The University of Chicago Press, Chicago 60637
The University of Chicago Press, Ltd., London
© 1999 by Jutta Gisela Sperling
All rights reserved. Published 1999

08 07 06 05 04 03 02 01 00 99   1 2 3 4 5
ISBN: 0-226-76935-6 (cloth)
ISBN: 0-226-76936-4 (paper)

Library of Congress Cataloging-in-Publication Data

Sperling, Jutta Gisela.
   Convents and the body politic in late Renaissance Venice / Jutta Gisela Sperling.
     p. cm. — (Women in culture and society)
   Includes bibliographical references (p.) and index.
   ISBN 0-226-76935-6 (cloth : alk. paper) — ISBN 0-226-76936-4
(pbk. : alk. paper)
   1. Monasticism and religious orders for women—Italy—Venice—History—16th century. 2. Women—Italy—Venice—Social conditions—
16th century. 3. Nobility—Italy—Venice—History—16th century.
4. Venice (Italy)—Social conditions—16th century. 5. Monasticism
and religious orders for women—Italy—Venice—History—17th century. 6. Women—Italy—Venice—Social conditions—17th century.
7. Nobility—Italy—Venice—History—17th century. 8. Venice
(Italy)—Social conditions—17th century. I. Title. II. Series.

BX4220.I8 S64 1999
271'.9'009453109031 21—dc21   99-042787

♾ The paper used in this publication meets the minimum requirements of
the American National Standard for Information Sciences—Permanence of
Paper for Printed Library Materials, ANSI Z39.48-1992.

For Jim Kan

Contents

List of Illustrations

List of Tables

Foreword

Sometime between 1640 and 1650, a protofeminist and literary nun in Venice, Sister Arcangela Tarabotti, decided to write about convent life. She contrasted the lives of two sisters, one a wealthy wife, the other an impoverished nun. The second sister had not entered the convent out of devotion but was placed there involuntarily, in the name of family honor and the republican "ragion di stato." Her story reflects that of thousands of European women. For them, Hamlet's orders to Ophelia, "Get thee to a nunnery," might well have been echoes of their own experience.

Tarabotti's work, in English *Hell of Nuns*, was finally published in 1990, one sign of our contemporary interest in women's history, gender, and the various forms of women's spirituality. Now Jutta Sperling has written a formidable book about Venetian convents that deepens our understanding of all of these subjects. Her setting is the Republic of Venice, the legendary and beautiful place that has generated myths of its perfection, nobility, and splendor. Her focus is the last century before the republic's decline, which set in with full force in the decade in which Tarabotti was writing her pungent critique of "the tyranny of fathers," the dowry system, and coerced monachizations. At the same time Venice's ruling elite, the patriciate, began to sell memberships instead of reserving them exclusively for its blood sons, another sign that the age of republican purity and perfection had come to a close. Working with a vast array of historical and archival materials,

Sperling opens up the profound relations between the republic and its convents.

Some of these relations were imaginary. Here nuns were powerful metaphors, repositories of the foundational values of purity and the integrity of the patriciate. Their virginity was increasingly deployed as a symbol of true nobility and Venice itself. As virgins, they were linked to the Virgin Mary, who was a keystone to the structure of the republic's symbolic life. Venice's myth of origins dated its founding to the A.D. 421 commemoration of Mary's Annunciation, when the archangel Gabriel told the young virgin that she was to bear the infant Jesus. Because of the Virgin's importance to the republic, the convent Santa Maria delle Vergini was under direct ducal jurisdiction, and, in a major civic ceremony, each new abbess underwent a ritual of marriage to the doge, the Venetian chief magistrate. During the late sixteenth century, when the Catholic Church in Rome was seeking to extend ecclesiastical authority over secular governments, Santa Maria delle Vergini became "a showcase of republican sovereignty" (p. 213). A Venetian could easily, even automatically, construe a nun's life as supremely honorable, because of the many metaphoric associations of virginity with the republic's spiritual and political values. To be sure, the goddess Venus was also a great Venetian symbol, contrasting sharply with that of the Virgin. During the sixteenth century, as Venice lost dominance as a sea-trading power and turned to land as a source of wealth, associations with Venus became decadent rather than celebratory.

Nuns were also an integral part of Venetian social and cultural life. Many belonged to the ruling oligarchic families. As a result, convents constituted a political network no less influential for lacking a constitutional mandate. They also served the republic. Not only did they raise and educate the daughters of the elite, but they also provided women with socially palatable and ideologically exalted alternatives to marriage. In 1581, Sperling estimates, over 50 percent of Venice's patrician women lived in convents. Sperling's major project is to explain this phenomenon as a crucial element of Venetian history. For the most part, neither piety nor a cheerful rejection of marriage put women into convents. Venetian families did. Sperling rightly refuses to oversimplify the causes of these "coerced monachizations," but three are crucial.

First, the Venetian patriciate practiced endogamy. That is, husbands and wives were to come from the same class. Some men married down, often to women from wealthy, social-climbing families, a pre-cursor of the marriages of rich American girls to titled Englishmen and Europeans in the late nineteenth and early twentieth centuries. In contrast, the restrictions on women against marrying outside of their class were stringent. To do so would diminish a family's honor. This obviously lowered the pool of potential husbands. Second, the deeply ingrained dowry system demanded that wealth accompany a bride. The higher the dowry, the more prestige it carried. Third, gifts called for countergifts and costly, showy reciprocity among families. This wasteful spending also characterized the marriage ceremony itself. Venetians commented on the money associated with marriage, but split on whether to blame men or women for the lavish extravagance. Sperling argues that sending a daughter to a nunnery, although an apparent money-saver, was the most ostentatious part of "the nobility's game of conspicuous gift-giving and consumption" (p. 71). A nun's family indicated that no worldly groom could be found whose relatives were worthy to receive and reciprocate the gift of this noble virgin, whose symbolic value surpassed the dowry her parents were willing to spend. Also, the nobility as a class exhibited a capacity so large and a concern with exclusivity so pronounced that it preferred to waste its daughters' reproductive capacities, resources on which its very survival as a body politic depended, rather than invest them in mismatched marriages to commoners. Suggestively, Sperling applies anthropological theories— Marcel Mauss on gift-giving and the potlatch, Claude Lévi-Strauss on the exchange of women—to place Venetian practices in an even larger context.

Cui bono? Who benefited from these practices? Court cases that Sperling cites reveal how greedy a nun's relatives could be. Most often, a brother profited from a sister's enforced monachization. This was part of an agnatic strategy to pass estates down through the male line, which harmed widows, spinster sisters, and disinherited brothers as well as nuns. For a generation or two, the use of convents helped to maintain the structure of the republic. However, the practice was ultimately so self-destructive that Venetians were unable to see their own behavior clearly. One pressing and depressing consequence was demographic: the reduction in the birthrate of the elite. Demographic shrinkage meant a political shortfall of men eligible to govern Venice, which, in turn, forced the patriciate to sell itself in 1646.

Interacting with enforced monachization was a second historical development, the reforms in the Catholic Church that the Council of Trent mandated in 1563 and that Pope Pius V reconfirmed three years later. They represented an ecclesiastical effort to break the power of monastic orders and private families and, Sperling argues, an ecclesiastical and secular effort to police all women. Seen through modern eyes, these reforms were horrendous for convents and nuns—although some convents had become sexually relaxed and although many needed better financial management. One of Sperling's most rigorous chapters is about Venetian convent finances and the economic distinctions among houses. After Trent, strict encloisterment (clausura) was imposed on female religious communities. Nuns were to keep within the walls of their convents. Social welfare activities were to cease. So were economic transactions conducted in public. Vows of obedience were stressed. Dress and speech were placed under gimlet-eyed, eros-fearing surveillance. Abbesses were to serve three-year, not life-long, terms. As compensation, nuns were shrouded in rhetorical reassurances that they were the brides not of men but of the far more glorious Christ. The clausura movement coincided with an increase in Venetian monachization rates between 1580 and 1620. The latter guaranteed a supply of nuns who had to accept the claustrophobic rigors of the former.

Venetian nuns resisted. At times, the secular authorities supported the Catholic Church; at times, if secular authorities were themselves struggling with the church for power, they might support the nuns. Some convents explicitly protested the loss of traditional rights and powers. Despite restrictions, some convent parlors became a form of salon. Some nuns continued to give dramatic and musical performances. Some escaped and fled. Despite absolute prohibitions on sex, some nuns had sexual relations with men or other women. And life, needy and unruly, could overwhelm regulations. As Sperling writes ironically, the authorities "did not anticipate the potential for disorder in an enclosed environment" (p. 163). Moreover, the walls of the convent had to be breached. Young boarders had to enter in order to be educated. Some stayed, but some left in order to marry. Servant nuns had to go out and about on errands. Married women entered for periods of retirement and respite. Relatives visited. Despite resistance, despite these breaches and violations of the stern constrictions of the ideal female community, the weight of authority lay with both enforced monachization and clausura.

Sperling's last sentence carefully delineates the scope of her book: "The Venetian potlatch was therefore a unique, and perhaps the most spectacular, manifestation of a problem that to varying degrees plagued elite women all over Catholic Europe at the end of the six-teenth century." The word "plague" is resonant. For plagues are dis-eases that have drastically affected the past, including the European past, and do affect the present. Arguably, "monachization" and "clausura," these grave and weighty words, did some good. Neverthe-less, they appear to have done greater harm—to women, to the princi-ple and practices of local authority, and to spiritual life itself. Like a loving marriage, a rich spiritual life cannot be coerced, only chosen in full awareness of its rigors.

Catharine R. Stimpson
New York University

Acknowledgments

This study owes much to the persons and institutions that have supported my research. First, I would like to thank my former mentor Volker Hunecke (Technische Universität Berlin), who suggested the topic to me and helped me to get started on what was to become a much more protracted project than either of us anticipated. I would also like to express my gratitude to Heide Wunder (Gesamthochschule Kassel) and Rudolf Vierhaus (Max-Planck-Institut für Geschichte, Göttingen) for their support and useful advice. In the United States, Geoffrey Symcox and Lauro Martines (both at UCLA) offered constructive criticism on my project at an early stage. Monica Chojnacka and her father, Stanley Chojnacki, whom I met in a coffee bar in Venice a decade ago, supported my research through their generous encouragement and kindness more than either of them can imagine. I wish to thank them both most warmly.

My very special thanks go to my adviser at Stanford University, Judith C. Brown. Without her keen scholarly advice, practical support, encouraging kindness, and—last but not least—her patience in helping me to overcome the difficulties the English language can pose to a nonnative speaker, this book would not have been written. She was the most helpful academic mentor possible, and continues to be a source of inspiration and advice. Also at Stanford, Mary-Louise Roberts and Keith M. Baker taught me the conceptualization of historical data. Their intellectual rigor, precise thinking, and systematic interpretative approach to the study of history made a lasting impression on me. I also wish to thank the participants in the Early Modern History Workshop and the Workshop on Women and Gender at Stanford University for their comments and criticism. Among the most insightful readers were my fellow graduate students Patricia Mazón, Josh Feinstein, Christophe Lécuyer, and Amir Alexander. Colin Jones also gave me most useful advice on early drafts of the manuscript.

My research in Venice was supported by several generous grants from the Centro Tedesco di Studi Veneziani/Deutsches Studienzentrum in Venedig. Discussing the intricacies of Venetian history on the terrace of "our *bello* palazzo" might have given my research its peculiar flavor. I would like to thank my co-fellows and friends from the Archivio di Stato di Venezia, especially Alfredo Viggiano and Daniela Hacke, for their interest in my work.

I also want to thank Anna Pizzati and Victoria Primhak for sharing their unpublished work with me, and Francesca Medioli for her comments and hospitality. The Istituto Storico Italo-Germanico/Deutsches Historisches Institut in Rom, the Stanford History Department, the Andrew W. Mellon Foundation, the Stanford Humanities Center, the Georg-August-Universität in Göttingen, and the University of California also contributed to my work financially. I would like to express my gratitude to each of these institutions and foundations for their generous support.

Edward Muir read previous versions of the manuscript and gave most useful advice. Diane O. Hughes, Elissa B. Weaver, and Patricia Mazón provided me with the opportunity to discuss my work with other Venetianists and Renaissance historians. Gabriella Zarri, John Najemy, Julius Kirshner, Charles Stinger, Stephanie H. Jed, Margaret Rosenthal, and Robert Davis, among many others, made valuable suggestions. My friends and colleagues at Hampshire College also supported my work. Equally helpful were the staff at the Stanford University Libraries, the Archivio di Stato di Venezia, the Archivio Patriarchale di Venezia, and the many other archives and libraries I visited during the course of my research.

Finally, I would like to express my gratitude to Jim Kan. This book is dedicated to him.

List of Abbreviations

APV	Archivio Patriarchale di Venezia
ASV	Archivio di Stato di Venezia
AV	Archivio Segreto del Vaticano
BNM	Biblioteca Nazionale Marciana
BSP	Biblioteca del Seminario Patriarchale di Venezia
CC	Codex Cicogna
CL	Compilazione Leggi
CX	Consiglio de' Dieci
MCC	Museo Civico Correr
m.r.	more romano; calendar year starts on January 1
m.v.	more veneto; calendar year starts on March 1
PsM	Provveditori sopra i Monasteri di Monache

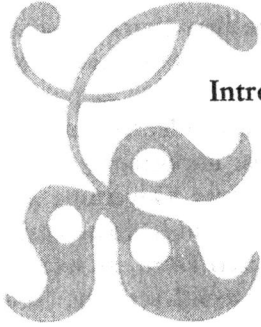

Introduction

> At one time, the Corinthians had an oligarchic constitution. The clan of the Bacchiadae governed the city, intermarrying among themselves. But one of these men, Amphion, had a lame daughter—in fact, her name was Labda. None of the Bacchiadae wanted to marry her, so she was taken by Eetion . . . who was from the village of Petra. . . . He had no children by this wife . . . so he went to Delphi to ask about getting offspring. Just as he was entering the oracle, the Pythian priestess greeted him with these verses:
> Eetion, no one honors you, honorable though you are.
> Labda is pregnant and will give birth to a stone
> That will roll over the oligarchs and pass judgment on Corinth.[1]

As usual, the Oracle of Delphi proved right. The Corinthian oligarchy was overthrown by Labda's son and replaced by a tyrannical regime. Intermarriage, Herodotus seems to suggest, is fundamental to oligarchic governments. Downward female marriages threaten aristocratic regimes; children born from female misalliances are prone to be frustrated by a constitution in which political rights are legitimized by "honorable" patrilineal descent. They are like stones "that will roll over the oligarchs."

No such avalanche ever threatened the Republic of Venice. The city, the constitution, and the nobility of Venice were, as every contemporary of the sixteenth century knew, of divine foundation, miraculous perfection, and timeless stability. Combining the best characteristics of all possible forms of government, the republican constitution was well-balanced, stable, and, as "history" seemed to suggest, of potentially eternal duration. All the patriciate had to do to let the miracle unfold was to protect the constitution and, most importantly, itself against the corruption of time and outside influences. Governing according to the laws and reproducing the patriciate as an enclosed caste were two complementary tasks. After all, as Marco Ferro, an expert on Venetian statutory law, declared in the late eighteenth century, "the Venetian noblemen . . . are the state itself."[2] Patrician rule was legitimized by the grace and special virtues that God conferred upon the nobility at the time of the city's foundation, and needed to be passed along to future generations in a pristine state.

Paradoxically, it was only after Venice was almost conquered by the League of Cambrai in 1509 that the myth of its longevity and immaculacy gained currency. And it was not until the Venetian patriciate, a formerly urban merchant class, had transformed itself into a land-based aristocracy that it fashioned itself as a "noble" body politic. The theory of Venetian perfection and stability was elaborated at a time when the experience of change, vulnerability, and crisis had become a common, and threatening, feature in politics and society. In an Italy occupied by foreign powers, pressured by either the French, the Spanish, the pope, or the Turks, the republic was in a precarious military situation. Internally, the patriciate's ongoing differentiation in wealth and status threatened to erode the supposedly homogeneous republican body politic. Fueled by the importation of feudal ideals from the *terraferma* and neighboring Italian states, hierarchical models gradually supplanted the egalitarian concept of the Venetian patriciate as a legally defined ruling class; notions of a nobility based on descent coexisted uneasily with the older version of a constitutionally legitimized body politic.

And yet the oligarchy of Venice was never overthrown, neither by internal nor external enemies. Unlike the Florentine ruling class—too permeable, dynamic, and volatile to avoid factional strife, popular uprisings, and feudal tendencies before falling prey to domestic tyrants and territorial monarchies on the rise—the Venetian patriciate successfully defended its collective claim to power. As the government gained full sovereignty from the emperor and the pope, colonized the eastern Mediterranean, and extended its rule to surrounding cities of the *terraferma,* its republican body politic gradually transformed itself into a hereditary class.³ Observing ever more strictly the rules of intermarriage and tightening the laws defining legitimate patrician descent, Venetian noblemen jealously guarded their self-appointed political privileges against interlopers, a process known as *serrata*. Marriage legislation issued in the fifteenth and sixteenth centuries turned the patriciate's endogamous reproduction behavior into a constitutional principle.⁴ The competitive display of "magnificence" accompanied the patriciate's refusal to marry "down," making the social construction of a legally defined ruling class appear to be the natural outcome of the nobility's wealth, generosity, and sophistication.

Women in particular were discouraged from marrying commoners, since they, unlike their male counterparts, could not pass on their aristocratic title to sons born of mismatched marriages. In order to avoid kindling the political ambitions of nonpatrician in-laws and descendants, and to prevent patrician wives from claiming undue authority over their husbands of inferior status, the vast majority of Venetian noblemen refused to offer their daughters to outsiders or men of inferior status.⁵ As Herodotus's story seems to suggest, women's downward marriages challenged the principles of both patriarchal and oligarchic rule. Had she lived in sixteenth-century Venice, Labda would not have been allowed to marry a stranger; rather, she would never have married at all. In contrast to ancient Greek oligarchies, early modern elites had recourse to a prestigious, relatively cheap, and altogether convenient means to protect themselves against the subversive effects of female misalliances. Unable to find a groom within her class, Labda would have been honorably withdrawn from the marriage market and placed in one of the city's numerous convents. Praying for the longevity of her family and republic while keeping her reproductive capacities in check, she would have dutifully contributed to the perpetuation of patrician rule.

This was the kind of patriotic service the majority of patrician women rendered their republic at the end of the sixteenth century (as we shall see in chapter 1). As Patriarch Giovanni Tiepolo pointed out in his letter to the Senate in 1619, "more than two thousand patrician women . . . live in this city locked up in convents as if in a public tomb."⁶ Justifying his lenient attitude in supervising the many nuns under his jurisdiction, he reminded the government that "they are noblewomen, raised and nurtured with the highest delicacy and respect so that if they were of the other sex, they would command and govern the world . . . they have confined themselves within those [convent] walls, not out of piety, but obedience to their family, making of their own liberty . . . a gift not only to God, but to the fatherland, the world, and their closest relatives."[7] Tiepolo spelled out what had become a common source of concern among his contemporaries: the skyrocketing rates of coerced monachizations among patrician women. Aside from the disciplinary problems that forced vocations caused, the sorrow and distress of involuntary nuns—a commonplace topic in popular songs and literature—moved many of his fellow noblemen to compassion. Despite the fact that the Council of Trent had reconfirmed the principle of voluntary consent as the basis of its sacraments and ruled that every novice must undergo an examination of her spiritual disposition before pronouncing the holy vows, the practice became even more frequent in the post-Tridentine period.[8] Like Patriarch Tiepolo, who declared that the nuns' sacrifice served a political purpose, most patricians preferred to rationalize the inevitability of the problem instead of looking for possible solutions.

Although it addresses the problem of forced vocations with provocative bluntness, Tiepolo's letter suggests a number of questions: What exactly were the circumstances that demanded that patrician women "confine themselves within convent walls," even if they lacked piety and personal vocation? Why was it that women "raised and nurtured with the highest delicacy and respect" were asked by their families to spend their lives "locked up in convents as if in a public tomb?" And why did they obey, given that "if they were of the other sex, they would command and govern the world"? In what sense was their confinement a "gift"? And how exactly did this gift benefit "not only . . . God, but . . . the fatherland, the world, and their closest relatives"?[9]

Venetian noblemen as well as modern historians have tried to explain the peaking rates of coerced monachizations in the late sixteenth and early seventeenth centuries as a result of individual families' financial constraints caused by dowry inflation.[10] Faced with the rising costs of weddings, the reasoning goes, more and more fathers persuaded their daughters to become nuns, because convents demanded "spiritual dowries" well below the marriage portion any upper-class bride could expect. The assumption that dowries became "too expensive" to marry all daughters honorably, however, does not explain why brides required a certain amount of money in the first place, why sons were entitled to higher shares of their fathers' patrimonies, and why, finally, unmarriageable patrician girls were pressured to sacrifice themselves as "gifts" to God and the world. The argument lends itself to viewing the practice of coerced monachizations as if it were a problem not only *of* women, but *caused* by women, as late-eighteenth-century Venetian historians, eager to find scapegoats for the patriciate's loss of power and prestige, cunningly claimed. (According to this misogynist "theory," women's luxurious desires had precipitated not only dowry inflation, but the ruin of most patrician families and, as a consequence, the decline of the Venetian empire itself.)[11] Most importantly, the argument does not elucidate why the patriciate chose to "save" money by wasting the reproductive capacities of its women— a practice that, in a political system legitimized by descent, rapidly developed a self-destructive dynamic. Rather than dowry inflation and its financial effects on individual families, it was the very *system* of dowry exchange and its social function within the ruling class that triggered rising rates of monachization among patrician women.

A dowry was a woman's share of her father's patrimony, which she received at the time of her marriage. Upon signing the marriage contract, she had to renounce any further claim to her family's fortune. Dowries rarely consisted of immobile properties, tended to be lower in value than the inheritance portions of sons, and were managed by the daughter's husband. Only a widow had the right to retrieve her dowry from her husband's estate, in order to either return it to her father's family, invest it in a second marriage, or bequeath it to her children, friends, and relatives.[12] Excluding women from the bulk of their fathers' patrimonies and denying them full possession of their properties while married, the dowry system served to establish patrilineal inheritance patterns[13] and to rid the economy of female entrepreneurs. Its revival in the Middle Ages after centuries of neglect was an instant success. Dowry transfer became the sign of a proper marriage even among the virtually propertyless. A variety of meanings and purposes quickly proliferated around this ancient Roman institution. In addition to guaranteeing brothers' exclusive claims to their deceased fathers' immobile patrimonies and supporting husbands financially in their careers as merchants, artisans, or large-scale manufacturers,[14] dowries represented female honor, and initiated the type of open-ended, reciprocal exchange of women that united members of the same social class in a web of mutual ties of obligation. They also functioned to guarantee parents' control over their children's choice of spouse, and prevented the kind of random social mobility that "love marriages" tended to promote.[15]

The main advantage of the dowry system, however—next to fostering patriarchal principles in politics, law, and the economy—was its effect of infusing all social relationships among the men between whom women were exchanged with the notion of *credit*. Dowry exchange served as a model for relationships based on mutual obligations among members of the same social class and, possibly, even for patronage relationships formed by persons of different rank and status. While wedding gifts of previous ages such as *morgengabe* and brideprice marked the transfer of women as complete once the marriage was consummated,[16] dowries were returned, though never instantly. Only when the bride's father or brother acquired an equally well endowed daughter-in-law—ideally, a better-endowed one—did the dotal investment pay off. Bridal dowries functioned like loans that men took out as grooms and paid back as fathers or brothers. The time lag accounted for the inflationary trend dowries were subject to, and signaled the trust as well as the hope for gain that men placed in the validity of in-law relations. In lengthening the cycle of return of bridal exchange, dowries also widened it—that is, they invited a theoretically unlimited number of families of comparable rank to form in-law relations, provided they observed the rule of endogamy. Only endogamy guaranteed the reciprocity of the exchange, which was realized over time by different generations of members of the same social group.[17] Given the specific social dynamic that the dowry system promoted, that is, upward social mobility within a closed circle, it comes as no surprise that complaints about dowry inflation, especially among the upper class, were as old as the dowry system itself.

The far-reaching effects of the dowry system in shaping social relations in early modern society, especially among the elites, rendered the relationship between dowry inflation and coerced monachizations more complex than is intuitively obvious at first sight. The argument that more and more patrician daughters were sent to convents because their fathers were unable or unwilling to pay for their weddings becomes circular once it is revealed how both dowry inflation and coerced monachizations were complementary parts of the same system of exchange. Forced vocations were the result of a particular type of bridal exchange to which Venetian patricians had committed themselves in order to legitimize and perpetuate their political prerogatives. They were the ultimate expression of a system in which women and dowries had to be returned "with interest" or else be offered up as brides of Christ. They were both the result and the precondition of an increasingly hypergamous marriage behavior, the competitiveness of which not only prohibited women from marrying "down," but encouraged them to marry "up." They signified the conspicuous destruction of gifts too precious to be properly returned, and protected the system of bridal exchange against paralysis. While temporarily suspending the rule of reciprocal gift-giving, the nuns' sacrifice constituted yet another—even infinitely more noble—form of exchange itself. By dedicating their virginity to Christ, the nuns were promised the bliss of an afterlife in close proximity to their celestial spouse, while their families and state received forgiveness for their sins and protection against God's wrath.

In a marriage market torn between dowry inflation and the prohibition of female misalliances, the convent option provided temporary relief to families anxious to place their women honorably, but it magnified the groom shortage for the following generation of marriageable girls.[18] The rapid decline in patrician marriage rates and birthrates was an effect of female patricians' massive religious retreat,[19] thus revealing the paradoxical character of a marriage behavior whose criteria for selecting spouses protected the nobility against interlopers only at the price of threatening the body politic with physical extinction. Tiepolo and his contemporaries were understandably concerned about the fact that the vast majority of noblewomen—willingly or unwillingly—entered convents. The rapid increase in patrician vocations revealed a crisis caused by the very principles upon which the Venetian state, literally embodied by the patriciate, was built. When, because of the rapid demographic decline of the patriciate, the elaborate election procedures for political offices became unworkable, eighty-two families from among the citizenry of Venice and the nobility of the *terraferma* were granted patrician status for the price of 100,000 ducats each—a measure that irrevocably "polluted" the body politic but helped replenish the ranks of the Maggior Consiglio (Great Council) at least temporarily, as well as raising money for yet another Turkish war.[20] The complex political, social, economic, and cultural implications of the patriciate's reproductive crisis suggest that coerced monachizations, as well as the marriage behavior that triggered it, functioned like a *potlatch*[21] and represented an early modern version of the type of "total social phenomenon" Marcel Mauss investigated in his famous *Essai sur le don (The Gift)*.

The literal meaning of the term *potlatch* is "to feed, to consume." Mauss used it to refer to a particular kind of gift exchange that he observed among peoples as diverse as the Tlingit and the Haida of the

American Northwest and the Trobriand Islanders of Polynesia, and of which he found traces in ancient Roman, Greek, and Germanic legal sources as well. According to Mauss, the exchange of gifts in archaic societies accompanied a variety of social interactions—remnants of which persist in modern times—such as "banquets, rituals, military services, [the exchange of] women [and] children, dances, festivals, and fairs, in which economic transaction is only one element, and in which the passing on of wealth is only one feature of a much more general and enduring contract."[22] What gave such interactions a contractual nature was the obligation to "voluntarily" return any gift received with an item of equivalent or higher value. Mauss located the origin of this obligation in the assumption that part of the owner's soul resided in the gift given, exerting a "magic hold" over the recipient until it was returned to its place of origin or replaced by an item of equivalent value (p. 12). In addition, matter itself was believed to be animate. The ritual destruction of objects enabled their souls to return to their true owners, the spirits of the dead, which is why sacrifice by destruction can also be seen as "an act of giving that is necessarily reciprocated" (p. 16).

According to Mauss, the "totality" of gift exchange as a social phenomenon is constituted by the fact that during a potlatch, religious, juridical, moral, political, economic, and social institutions are "given expression at one and the same time" (p. 3). Likewise, the ownership one obtains through gift exchange is "ownership of a certain kind" (p. 24), in which different legal concepts such as ownership, possession, pledge, rent, usufruct, purchase, deposit, mandate, and legacy are fused. The prevailing function of the gift is credit, however, since "time is needed in order to perform any counter-service" (p. 36) and because a "potlatch must be reciprocated with interest" (p. 42).[23] Although gift exchange creates unity and fosters alliances, its nature is deeply competitive. Because of the imperative to return more than one has received, a "principle of rivalry and hostility . . . prevails in all these practices [of gift exchange]" (p. 6). Among the native inhabitants of Northwest America, political status, social rank, and marriages for their children were gained in a "war of property" (p. 37), that is, in "a competition to see who is the richest and also the most madly extravagant." "Everything is conceived of as if it were a 'struggle of wealth' " (p. 37). In certain cases, Mauss remarks, the "notion of honor . . . is . . . really destructive," when "it is not even a question of giving and returning gifts, but of destroying, so as not to give the slightest hint of desiring your gift to be reciprocated. . . . In this way one not only promotes oneself, but also one's family, up the social scale" (p. 37).

Gift exchange is by its very nature wasteful and competitive, Mauss asserts, but it serves an important social function: it ties different social groups, families, or individuals together in a form of constant interaction, of which the passing on of wealth is the external signifier. It promotes solidarity and channels hostilities and struggles for power and prestige into nonviolent forms of contest. It facilitates the exchange of goods in pre-market economies and helps to rationalize gain. As a sacrificial offering, it establishes communication with God or the spirits. It is as basic, archaic, and ubiquitous a form of social interaction as language; and, like language, it follows a strict set of rules. In its most fully developed and rarest form, the potlatch, it performs a variety of different functions simultaneously. A potlatch structures and pervades all social relations and is the medium in which—or the foundation upon which—juridical, political, economic, religious, and social institutions are built. In this sense, it is an encompassing—that is, "total"—social and cultural phenomenon, of which traces have survived into modern times.

Following Mauss, Claude Lévi-Strauss investigated the complexity and internal mechanisms of different systems of bridal exchange in his study *The Elementary Structures of Kinship*. He postulated that the prohibition of incest established the rule of exogamy as a primary form of exchange, in which women themselves are "the supreme gift[s]."[24] Adopting Mauss's idea that gifts have to be returned with "interest," Lévi-Strauss concluded that generalized exchange—that is, the nonprescriptive circulation of spouses within a particular social group[25]—"establishes a system of operations conducted 'on credit' ":

> A surrenders a daughter or a sister to B, who surrenders one to C, who, in turn, will surrender one to A. . . . There must be the confidence that the cycle will close again, and that after a period of time a woman will eventually be received in compensation for the woman initially surrendered. The belief is the basis of trust, and confidence opens up credit. . . . the whole system exists only because the group adopting it is prepared, in the broadest meaning of the term, to speculate. (P. 265)

Generalized exchange, according to Lévi-Strauss, "presupposes equality . . . since the theoretical condition for the application of the elementary formula is that the operation, c marries A, which closes the cycle, is equivalent to the operation, A marries b, which opened it in the first place.[26] The speculative character of the system," however—"the widening of the cycle, the establishment of secondary cycles between certain enterprising lineages for their own advantage, and, finally, the inevitable preference for certain alliances" (p. 266)—leads to hypergamy, that is, to marriage between spouses of different rank and status. In Lévi-Strauss's opinion, it is "the very fact of the formula of exchange" that triggers social differentiation (p. 474), which is why "generalized exchange seems to be in particular harmony with a society with feudal tendencies" (p. 266). Applied to a society with dowry exchange, the "formula" shows how bride c would have to offer a higher dowry to groom A than bride b (whose previous marriage to another groom from the A family had opened the cycle), because of the inflationary trend of a system built on the notion of credit and because of her position at the end of a cycle of exchange. If, in the meantime, family A had lost in social status, bride c might prefer to look for a more suitable spouse elsewhere, thus widening the cycle; or, if greater exogamy were not an option, she might not marry at all. Such "accumulation of women at some stage of the cycle" is one of the "factors of inequality, which may at any moment force a rupture . . . and lead to [the] downfall [of the system]" (p. 266). In order to avoid such "paralysis of the body social" caused by the lack of placement opportunities for upper-class women, different societies propose different solutions, real and mythical: polygamy among the wealthy; "swayamvara" marriages, in which princesses are offered to strangers provided that the latter perform extraordinary deeds; "free choice" relationships, consisting of the "gift of the woman by herself" (p. 475); or, we might add, the sacrificial engagement of nuns to their celestial groom.

Despite the universalist claims of Mauss's *The Gift* and Lévi-Strauss's *Elementary Structures of Kinship,* their insights into the dynamic aspects of gift exchange are applicable to our historical investigation. Their definition of gift exchange as inherently competitive and speculative resonates well with the questions at hand: Why did the number of patrician nuns in Venice reach unprecedented heights between 1550 and 1650? What kinds of political, economic, social, religious, and, in the broadest sense, cultural factors induced the majority of patrician women to take the veil? And what does the phenomenon of coerced monachizations reveal about the society that practiced it, despite the many personal, religious, social, and political problems it caused?

Lévi-Strauss can help us understand how, in a patriarchal society such as Renaissance Venice, women were exchanged as gifts; how the dowry system facilitated the circulation of brides among men of similar rank and status; how dowries, as gifts, engendered the notion of credit; how the reciprocal and competitive character of bridal exchange led to dowry inflation, hypergamy, and the "accumulation of [unmarried] women" at the upper echelons of society;[27] how monachizations themselves constituted a form of exchange; and how, finally, the competitive character of gift exchange promoted social mobility within a theoretically homogeneous body politic. Mauss's concept of the potlatch as an encompassing social phenomenon contributes to broadening our perspective and to seeing coerced monachizations as a problem of more than economic relevance. It enables us to view forced vocations within the context of conspicuous consumption, that is, the pressure to display aristocratic magnificence among the elite, and highlights the destructive effects of struggles for honor and prestige. It helps us analyze the political dimensions of coerced monachizations as an integral part of the patriciate's strategies to reproduce itself as a pure and immaculate, that is, "virgin," body politic. It shows, finally, how forced vocations as a social practice seem to enact what political theorists demanded from a noble ruling class in order for it to be truly noble. In short, Mauss's notion of the potlatch as a "total service" contributes to locating the practice of forced vocations at the center of republican politics and ideology, and to theorizing the importance of a phenomenon long relegated to the very end of a causal chain of arguments.

In addition to highlighting the dynamic, transformative, and even destructive aspects of the potlatch, aspects that both Mauss and Lévi-Strauss neglected in favor of emphasizing the stabilizing functions and universal structures of gift exchange, respectively, any historical application of their theories has to take into account the question of gender. While Lévi-Strauss's categorical pronouncement "it is men who exchange women, and not vice-versa" (p. 115) might provoke deserved protest among those who prefer to ponder why, when, and how women acquired their object status,[28] his insistence on the inherent gender asymmetry of bridal exchange nonetheless proves useful for an investigation of the particular imbalances of the Venetian patriciate's marriage behavior. Marriage strategies that encouraged women to marry "up" but limited their choice of partners to a steadily diminishing pool of candidates aggravated the destructive aspects of the patriciate's "war of conspicuous consumption" against outsiders and lesser members of its own class, a war in which marriage strategies played an important part. With respect also to the question of women's agency, the benefits that wives drew from dowry inflation, and the advantages of convent life over marriage—problems recently debated among feminist historians of Renaissance Italy[29]—Mauss's and Lévi-Strauss's studies seem to offer little if anything, because of their disregard for individual choices and the manipulability of power structures. What they offer instead is a conceptual framework for the analysis of those legal, political, and social structures that, in limiting individual agency, also made it possible, and within which struggles for power took place.

While the patriciate, at the cost of political credibility and prestige, could not but engage in the morally questionable and self-destructive practice of forced vocations, virginity became a pervasive metaphor in political theory (chapter 2). The image of an "immaculate" female body governed not only the discourse of female encloisterment, but also the rhetoric and politics of aristocratic closure and republican perfection. It gave meaning to, but also reinforced, the socially problematic but politically indispensable practice of coerced vocations. At the same time that monachization rates peaked, the innate purity and fragility that a woman's untouched body stood for became the symbol of "true nobility." Like the potlatch—a paradoxical and therefore deeply problematic practice—the virgin metaphor was inherently ambiguous. While the exclusivity of the body politic, socially constructed through the competitive and restricted exchange of patrician women, was iconographically represented by the Virgin Mary, the miraculous nature and divine origin of the city and the constitution of Venice were expressed by the simultaneous use of two contradictory images: the Virgin Mary and Venus Anadyomene. The conflation of paradoxical metaphors, a rhetorical device denoting paralysis, lack of change, and the absence of worldly conditions, was instrumental in representations of the miracle of Venice's timeless perfection. Likewise, the marvel and awe the city's sight aroused in foreign travelers was couched in terms of a paradoxically structured trope.[30]

Gradually, the Virgin-Venus paradigm fell out of favor, while the inherently paradoxical body of Mary, virginal mother of God, became the sole representative of the city. In political theory, the concept of nobility was associated with the innate perfection of an immaculate female body, which was to be defended against the corruption of time and matter and cherished as a naturally given but extremely fragile state of purity and virtue. In political practice, the metaphor of the republic's inviolate body was employed whenever issues of territorial sovereignty, independence, and military safety were discussed. When the first "anti-mythical" treatises appeared in the aftermath of the Interdict of 1606, attacking the republican patriciate's ideology of perfection, the emphasis on historical reality versus myth was accompanied by a polemical reversal of the virgin metaphor.[31] Especially after the sellout of the patriciate in 1646, when wealthy citizens and mainland aristocrats bought membership titles to the Great Council, Venice, in the eyes of its critics, turned into a prostitute. The use of paradoxical tropes and body metaphors to represent the miracle of Venetian perfection thus backfired in the long run, just as the logic of "preserving" the patriciate by "wasting" its reproductive resources proved dysfunctional within a few generations.

Metaphors of enclosure did not only inform the way by which the patriciate reproduced and represented itself in and as a "virgin" caste; they also structured the convents' institutional, administrative, and economic development (chapter 3). In the eyes of both the government and the curia of Venice, only a thorough disciplinary reform, epitomized by the imposition of *clausura* (strict encloisterment), could secure the nuns' monastic observance in an era of rapidly rising rates of coerced monachizations. The policy of subjecting all nuns to total seclusion—a program initiated by the Venetian government well before the Council of Trent—was one feature of a more general phenomenon that Michel Foucault might have called the "renfermement des femmes." The categorization of women by sexual status and their confinement in special institutions were part of an encompassing project to contain social chaos by reordering public space. In several Italian cities, lay and church authorities founded institutes for penitent prostitutes, badly married women, or spinsters at risk, while the post-Tridentine papacy defined strict encloisterment as a standard requirement of female religious life.[32] After centuries of libertinage, when nunneries had allegedly turned into public brothels, convents were now to become enclosed oases of the sacred in sinful urban environments. Clausura laws and the tight surveillance of unruly nuns were intended to promote convent life as a safe and honorable alternative to marriage when, because of the "war of conspicuous consumption," fewer and fewer women entered the sphere of competitive exchange. Since coerced monachizations increased the threat of disorderly behavior among nuns, convents were subject to the legislative authority and executive power of both the government and the curia of Venice; only the criminalization of the nuns' social and sexual relationships with outsiders could, in the eyes of the reformers, secure the function of nunneries as safe-deposits of patrician women.

The concept of clausura held the potential for a catastrophic reversal, just like the potlatch dynamic and the virgin metaphor. Perfect seclusion was a guarantor of chastity only given the premise of a heterosexual scenario; sexual contact within the convent walls was either too outrageous or too self-evident a crime for convent reformers to worry about. Love affairs among nuns were largely exempted from prosecution,[33] despite the fact that same-sex intercourse was conceived to be a greater threat to a nun's virginity than certain forms of heterosexual intercourse: according to canon lawyers, men had the option of protecting a nun's hymen by penetrating her "posterior vessel," while a lesbian woman either was endowed with a clitoris large enough to deflower her lover or else used a dildo. Thus, even if realized perfectly, strict encloisterment did not completely eliminate the possibility that a nun might lose her virginity; instead, it generated temptations and risks of its own.

But apart from the possibility that the nuns' seclusion might favor particularly dangerous crimes, clausura was never entirely realized. Although the close surveillance of convents by state and church authorities made it more dangerous for nuns to cultivate relationships with outsiders, the political, social, and cultural importance of monachization practices inevitably connected them to the civic world at large. Despite the clausura prohibitions, convent parlors developed into salonlike gathering places for young patrician males, musicians, and women of dubious reputation, and served as clearinghouses for marriage contracts, political alliances, and business transactions of the nuns' relatives.

In trying to subject the convents to strict encloisterment, state and church followed a two-pronged approach. The criminalization of the nuns' social and sexual relations with outsiders was intended to protect their virginity. Mortmain laws and the limitation of "spiritual dowries," in connection with an emphasis on profit maximization and rational management, were designed to establish convents as economically self-sufficient entities (chapter 4). Only if convents were rich enough to live off their revenues, without depending on charitable donations and private subsidies, could strict encloisterment be successfully imposed. And only if convents were prohibited from accumulating further capital could the influence of private families be reduced. Likewise, the embezzlement and waste of convent resources by corrupt abbesses, estate managers, and legal agents had to be contained in order to sever the nuns' ties with the outside world, as well as to protect their patrimonies against loss. In short, the rationale of economic self-sufficiency, aiming to abolish both loss and gain, translated the principle of enclosure into a theory of economic management.

The project failed, however, partially because it was based on erroneous assumptions—no economy exists without exchange and circulation—but mainly because the government's executive power lagged behind its legislative activities. As a close analysis of the convents' tax records from 1564 to 1769 shows, most of the convents increased their landed properties as well as their urban real estate holdings in defiance of the mortmain laws. Neither did the introduction of a standard dowry seem to influence the development of the convents' patrimonies tangibly. While the poor convents displayed the fastest growth rates, the gap in income distribution between the super-rich and the virtually propertyless convents remained unaltered over the course of two centuries.

As did the imposition of strict encloisterment, the loss of economic freedom caused great resentment and sometimes open resistance on the part of the nuns. The limitation of "spiritual dowries" was perceived to be a particularly painful intervention when, because of the high demand for monachizations at the beginning of the seventeenth century, convent fees rose rapidly. The nuns of San Lorenzo—and, to a certain extent, those of Santa Caterina—openly defied the government, extending their fight for unlimited spiritual dowries into a defense of their ancient privileges and exemptions from superior rule (chapter 5). The government, which only a few years earlier had successfully defended its absolute authority in "temporal" ecclesiastic affairs against the pope and the Venetian curia, proved unable to force the nuns' obedience without the collaboration of the patriarch of Venice. This incident not only demonstrated the limited practical relevance of the concept of "absolute" state sovereignty in early-seventeenth-century Venice, it also revealed the degree to which the nuns of San Lorenzo and Santa Caterina were politicized during the Interdict of 1606, having close contact with Paolo Sarpi, Fulgentio Micanzio, Nicolò Contarini, and other main protagonists of the jurisdictional conflict with Rome.

Because of the eminent political function convents assumed in the context of the patriciate's endogamous and competitive reproduction patterns, the Venetian government extended its jurisdictional authority correspondingly and relegated the patriarch to the role of an executor of state laws. Subject to both secular and ecclesiastic rule, convents—as essentially hybrid institutions—became prime objects of contention during the many jurisdictional conflicts between Venice and Rome in the aftermath of the Council of Trent. But because the government firmly rejected outside interference in what it defined as its internal affairs, the papacy was cautious in asserting its authority over the nunneries of Venice.

While Venetian convents in general symbolized the integrity, purity, and thus legitimacy of the nobility—in connection with their social function of preventing mismatched patrician marriages—the convent of Santa Maria delle Vergini assumed a particular metaphoric significance: allegedly founded by Pope Alexander III and Emperor Frederick I in 1177 in homage to Venice for negotiating their peace settlement, it symbolized the republic's formal recognition as an independent state. In 1613, the Venetian Senate decided to honor the convent with a yearly procession, reviving the memory of the republic's ascent to its position as an equal partner among Europe's medieval superpowers and emphasizing the convent's role as a sign of Venetian sovereignty, authority, and independence. This happened immediately after the government's narrow victory over Pope Pius V and the Interdict of 1606, a conflict during which the republic proclaimed its "absolute" power over all its subjects, ecclesiastic and lay persons alike.

The Venetian state and, albeit for different reasons, the Venetian curia were relentless in their efforts to silence those nuns whose protests against strict encloisterment and spiritual dowry laws jeopardized the smooth performance of the potlatch at the height of its reign. The introduction of the government's annual procession to Santa Maria delle Vergini signaled that no occasion would be missed to publicly celebrate the republic's mythical perfection. The invention of yet another occasion to magnificently display the patriciate's charisma, as well as the many jurisdictional conflicts between state, church, and convents at the beginning of the seventeenth century, shows that the issues of convent policy and monachization practices had reached the peak of their importance in the patriciate's struggle for power and prestige.

Nunneries were battlegrounds of the aristocracy's self-destructive "war of conspicuous consumption," until the decline of monachization rates following the sale of memberships in the patriciate in 1646 marked the irrevocable slide of the Venetian ruling class into "moral decay" and political irrelevance. Only a few generations after coerced monachizations had peaked, the potlatch dynamic led to the demographic erosion of the body politic and its consequent "contamination" by citizen and *terraferma* families. Once virgin Venice had, in the eyes of its critics, turned into a "prostitute," the patriciate's reproduction patterns became more flexible, and involuntary nuns less numerous. Unlike the Corinthian clan of the Bacchiadae, the Venetian ruling class survived, but only at the cost of gradually losing its influence and authority.

Despite their largely peripheral status in modern historiography, convents offer a perspective from which to revise the *grand récit* of Venice's decline.[34] Virgin metaphors structured political discourse, monachization practices fulfilled the "figure" of a noble body politic, and convents symbolized the republic's quest for territorial sovereignty and integrity. Although temporarily stabilizing a political system in crisis, the project of "enclosure" ultimately failed, largely because of the paralyzing effects of a policy based on paradoxical assumptions. Combining the methods of structural anthropology, discourse analysis, and institutional and economic history, this study is an attempt to analyze the complex relations between convents and the Venetian body politic on the brink of the republic's decline.

One

POTLATCH ALLA VENEZIANA:
COERCED MONACHIZATIONS IN THE
CONTEXT OF PATRICIAN INTERMARRIAGE
AND CONSPICUOUS CONSUMPTION

In the fifteenth century, monachization rates among upper-class women all over Italy began to rise steadily, reaching an unprecedented peak in the late sixteenth and early seventeenth centuries. Studies on patrician monachization strategies in fifteenth-century Florence,[1] high female celibacy rates in early-seventeenth-century Milan,[2] restricted marriage patterns among Venetian, Florentine, and Neapolitan elites in the sixteenth and seventeenth centuries,[3] and skyrocketing convent populations everywhere[4] suggest that between 1550 and 1650, aristocratic girls were more likely to become nuns than wives. While in earlier centuries the term "brides of Christ" had been used to explain the virginal status of nuns in terms of marriage, in sixteenth-century Venice a reversal occurred: secular brides were called *novizze*.[5] Among upper-class girls, marriage—that is, departure from the convents where most of them were raised[6]—had become the exception, religious service the norm. On the basis of census data and various convent records, I have estimated that close to 54 percent of Venice's patrician women lived in convents in 1581, with a rising tendency in the early seventeenth century (see table 2 later in this chapter). Despite the incomplete and scattered nature of my evidence, the figures of my estimate are corroborated by data from R. Burr Litchfield's and Dante Zanetti's studies on the Florentine and Milanese aristocracies.[7] As recent scholarship on the endogamous (or homogamous) marriage patterns of urban patriciates and feudal aristocracies in Italy suggests, the phenomenon of peaking monachization rates at the end of the sixteenth century has to be approached in the context of the nobility's restricted and competitive marriage behavior, of which entailment strategies (primogeniture in the south) and dowry inflation were the defining coordinates.

In early modern Venice, the rate of upper-class intermarriage seems to have been exceptionally high: according to Volker Hunecke, the endogamy rate of patrician men in the second half of the seventeenth century lay between 75 and 80 percent—in his opinion, a low rate compared with previous centuries. In the fifteenth century, more than 90 percent of patrician grooms chose a patrician bride, and roughly 83 percent did so in the early seventeenth century.[8] These rates are, to my knowledge, among the highest ever ascertained for early modern European elites; Thomas H. Hollingsworth calculated only 37.5 percent for the male British peerage in the seventeenth century,[9] and Anthony Molho established 64.5 percent for Florentine upper-class males in the fifteenth century.[10] While both Hollingsworth's and Molho's calculations result in slightly lower endogamy rates for women (31.7 percent and 61.9 percent, respectively),[11] my sample study suggests that in sixteenth- and seventeenth-century Venice, marriages within the same class were more frequent among brides than grooms: of 111 patrician women who married between 1569 and 1640 in Santa Maria Formosa—a parish with a high percentage of noble residents—fewer than 10 percent chose nonpatrician husbands. Several of their grooms were foreigners; in only two cases did the records mention explicitly that the groom was a *mercatante* (merchant) or *cittadino* (citizen).[12] In a "marriage market"[13] kept artificially tight by high endogamy rates, this gender differential reduced women's chances of finding suitable partners even further, and may have partially caused men's increasing acceptance of lower-class brides.

Hunecke shows that the strong pressure on nobles to marry within their rank was accompanied by a rapid decline in officially registered patrician marriages. Between 1560 and 1574, approximately forty patrician marriages were concluded each year, compared with only twenty-eight a century later.[14] In roughly the same period, between 1550 and 1650, the number of members of the Great Council shrank by more than a third, from twenty-five hundred to fifteen hundred—a decline that in 1646 led to the first massive extension of patrician membership rights to wealthy citizens and mainland aristocrats since the late fourteenth century.[15] Although the patriciate gradually became aware of the self-destructive side effects of its endogamous reproduction patterns, it was unable to devise marriage strategies that would allow for the survival of both individual families and the body politic as a whole. As Bernardo Nani complained at the end of the eighteenth century, only the *barnabotti* (poor patricians) "multiply, all of them marry, all of them have children"—in contrast to rich patricians, "of whom only rarely more than one per family [marries] to preserve the patrimony undivided."[16] Nani's theory that the tightening of inheritance rules for males—a practice that became popular all over Italy in the second half of the sixteenth century[17]—caused rich families to shrink is still regarded as a valid explanation.[18] In my opinion, the explosion of upper-class monachization rates was at least as important a factor in the patriciate's failure to reproduce as were entailment strategies.

Hunecke also documents that the decline in officially registered marriages coincided with an increasing tendency among male patricians to engage in "secret" marriages with lower-class women.[19] If, upon request, the local bishop agreed to waive the Tridentine publication requirement, a valid marriage could be celebrated "secretly" by a priest in the presence of only two testimonies. Such marriages were not recognized by the state, but they were sanctioned by the church, for which a couple's consent continued to be the only constitutive element of the marital sacrament even after the Tridentine reforms.[20] Any secretly married couple was thus in the predicament of not being able to produce legitimate offspring, despite the fact that their relationship was recognized as indissoluble by the church. Consequently, no "honorable" woman would engage in such a relationship; most secret marriages took place between aging upper-class men and their concubines. The gender gap among secretly married patricians was indeed extraordinary: from a sample of one hundred secret marriages registered with the Venetian curia between 1633 and 1672, thirty-five were concluded between noblemen and lower-class women, but only one between a patrician woman and a commoner. In no case were both partners of noble descent.[21]

The ways in which the tightening of the marriage market affected men and women were thus diametrically opposed: while men who chose (or were chosen) to engage in a formal marriage gradually lowered their standards and started to consider rich nonpatrician girls as suitable partners, or else married secretly and thus opted to drop out of a system that either denied them marriage or drastically limited their options, women did the opposite. Between 1550 and 1650, most patrician girls withdrew (or were withdrawn) from the marriage market in order to avoid misalliances. The two trends seem to have been mutually reinforcing: as more women refused to marry "down"—that is, to consider nonpatricians as well as patricians of lower prestige and wealth as possible partners—more men were forced to look for partners among the citizenry. And as more noblemen were forced to remain bachelors, lived with concubines in secretly sanctified unions, or married richly endowed commoner girls, fewer patrician women were successful in making a proper match. Since entering a convent was the only honorable alternative to a high-status marriage, upper-class monachization rates rose rapidly, and contributed significantly to the decline in marriage rates.

Recently, historians have concluded that the pressure to display "honor" through the reciprocal and conspicuous exchange of gifts, rather than modern, rational economic thinking, shaped the marriage behavior of Italy's ruling elites.[22] Lorenzo Fabbri is of the opinion that despite the "mercantile" spirit pervading fifteenth-century Florentine marriage patterns, nonpecuniary criteria such as female honor and beauty were at least as important in choosing a bride as a girl's dowry and family connections.[23] Christine Klapisch-Zuber has argued that the wasting of a considerable portion of bridal dowries on marital counter-trousseaus—instead of allowing grooms to invest the entire sum in a start-up business[24]—symbolically fulfilled the requirement of reciprocity fundamental to every system of exchange.[25]

The "honorable," that is, reciprocal, exchange of gifts and favors accompanied all sorts of social relationships—not just marriage alliances. Mario Biagioli has shown that the patronage system of court societies, which Galileo so masterfully exploited for the purpose of promoting both himself and his scientific discoveries, was based on the obligation to return gifts "with interest."[26] The axiom that "we must give back more than we have received" was coined by Marcel Mauss, who argued that it was the competitive nature of all systems of gift exchange that required Trobriand Islanders and the native inhabitants of the American Northwest to conspicuously destroy the gifts they deemed too precious to be properly reciprocated.[27]

Mauss's theory that in gift-giving societies, prestige and honor are challenged and maintained by returning gifts "with interest" resonates neatly with discussions by Venetians of the early modern period on the performative character of "true" nobility. Giovan Maria Memmo, for example, author of the *Dialogo . . . , nel quale . . . si forma un*

perfetto Prencipe, & una perfetta Republica (Dialogue, in which . . .
a perfect prince, and a perfect republic are being formed; 1563), perceived that in an egalitarian, republican ruling class, the imperative to
outspend others could have politically disruptive effects. The dilemma
was that "honorable citizens who govern the city" should—naturally—be "as magnificent . . . as possible," but "citizens who, in building their palaces, spend fortunes on ornaments and superfluous pomp,
and . . . who spend on one banquet enough to feed their families for
an entire year, are worthy of . . . not little reprehension." In Memmo's
eyes, excessive spending "not only damages . . . private families, but
corrupts entire cities: because many who are moved [to envy] by these
examples but lack the means to do the same . . . lose every scruple in
making money . . . and this corruption finally ruins . . . cities and
republics."[28]

Not all of Memmo's contemporaries shared his scruples regarding
the adoption of aristocratic spending habits by a republican ruling
class. In his apotheosis of aristocratic governments entitled *Della perfettione della vita politica* (On the perfection of political life; 1579),
Paolo Paruta affirmed that, next to construction projects and banquets, weddings were among the prime occasions when "it is proper
to spend without considering the price, but only the grandeur and
beauty of the enterprise"—when, in short, "magnificence . . . as a noble virtue . . . has the opportunity to display itself."[29] Frugality and
profit-oriented investment strategies might once have been indispensable means for a mercantile elite to acquire wealth and status, but a
republican patriciate turned "nobility" had to consolidate its power
through conspicuous consumption and aristocratic waste. Paruta's
maxim that wedding celebrations in particular required the display of
true magnificence was popular among patricians until the very end of
the republic,[30] illustrating—besides the vanity and self-absorption of
a languishing elite—that for a hereditary ruling class, marriage was
an issue of prime political, even constitutional, significance. In a recent
article, Stanley Chojnacki has argued that the closure of the patriciate
was a gradual process, achieved through marriage legislation during
what he calls the "second *serrata*" between 1414 and 1422.[31] In this
period, the government defined legitimate descent from a member of
the Great Council as a prerequisite for participation in the *barbarella*,[32]
introduced a standard dowry for noblewomen,[33] and excluded the offspring of patrician men and "vile" women from office. These laws,
all of which were aimed at fixing the body politic by regulating its

reproduction, were, in Chojnacki's opinion, the first to define "uniformity within the patriciate and its differentiation from the rest of society" as essential characteristics of the Venetian nobility.[34]

As the nineteenth-century historian of culture Pompeo Molmenti pointed out, the first *serrata* had already been accompanied by rules that encouraged patrician intermarriage and by sumptuary laws that aimed at containing the excessive display of wealth on the occasion of weddings.[35] First, male members of ducal families were prevented from marrying rich women of feudal descent, in order to avoid conflicts of interest and to curb the doges' possible dynastic aspirations. Women's "upward" marriages to foreign aristocrats were initially regarded as a sign of Venetian respectability, but high-ranking patrician brides were gradually also encouraged to marry within their class. The ban on men's and women's hypergamous marriages outside the patriciate was considered to be crucial for the construction of a republican—that is, close-knit and egalitarian—body politic. While the prohibition of marriage alliances between ducal families and mainland aristocrats was an essential element of the first *serrata*, the closure against newcomers from below took another century to develop. But even the second *serrata* did not preclude the possibility of social mobility altogether: an asymmetrical gender arrangement provided for a certain degree of permeability. While the patriciate guarded its own women jealously, discouraging all marriages with men of both higher and lower social status, the government explicitly invited rich commoner girls to choose their grooms from among the political elite. The dowry law of 1420, designed to keep patrician dowries low, encouraged *popolani* (commoner) brides to compete with their blue-blooded sisters by allowing them to pay 25 percent more for a patrician groom.[36]

At all stages, the process of closure of the patriciate was gender-specific: the purity of the body politic was defined by not letting patrician women marry out, while lower-class women were allowed to marry in, *if* they could compensate for their lack of prestige with higher dowries. This discrepancy between male and female endogamy threatened the constitutional principle of equal exchange: the construction of a hereditary, republican ruling class based on female endogamy implied that the legal definition of equal political rights among patrician men rested upon the social practice of exchanging patrician women *as if* they were of equal value. Asymmetrical inheritance laws, which allowed patrician men, but not women, to produce patrician offspring with "misallied" partners, upset this balance.[37] Dowry inflation was thus a direct result of asymmetrically gendered, patriarchal inheritance laws, which prevented men from marrying into the patriciate but institutionalized upward female social mobility. In addition, it accelerated the differentiation in wealth and status among noblemen, whose "uniformity" was never more than a constitutional ideal.[38]

The "honorable" and competitive exchange of women as well as gifts—the display of "magnificence" on the occasion of weddings, as it were—and the interplay between aristocratic closure and agnatic inheritance patterns were at the root of the patriciate's increasingly restricted marriage behavior. Dowry inflation and monachization practices were complementary effects of this dynamic: patrician honor required all women who could not be returned "with interest" to be withdrawn from circulation.

Traditionally, historians have seen monachization practices as a means to preserve family patrimonies threatened by dowry inflation, echoing contemporaries' apologetic explanations.[39] This theory does not explain, as already pointed out, why fathers agreed to pay inflated dowries in the first place, why they never considered reducing the inheritance portions of sons, or why they prevented their daughters from marrying commoners with lower dowries if money was all they needed to avoid "burying" their daughters in "public tombs." If, as has been claimed, patriarchal "honor," not Weberian economic thinking, shaped the marriage behavior of early modern elites,[40] monachization strategies have to be explained on the basis of the same parameters. The overwhelming refusal of rich and poor patrician girls to marry "below" their state at a time of peaking monachization rates suggests that the logic of honorable waste inherent to all gift-giving systems also shaped the convent rush in late-sixteenth-century Venice.[41]

Recent studies on aristocratic women in Sicily and Naples have confirmed that monachization strategies were an integral part of the conspicuous consumption patterns of newly fashioned nobilities.[42] Sara Cabibbo, Marilena Modica Vasta, and Elisa Novi Chavarria have argued that, especially among the higher echelons of south Italian aristocracies, monachization strategies were adopted less for reasons of frugality than because they signaled dynastic aspirations through the display of "magnificence."[43] Among the nobility of Venice, the conspicuous consumption of women took other forms. No patrician tried to impress his fellow noblemen by founding a convent for his daughter and bribing the pope into canonizing her, as did Giulio Tomasi, Baron of Montechiaro.[44] However, the Venetian republic adamantly defended its jurisdiction over convents against the post-Tridentine papacy, insisting that a "foreigner" should not have access to the "deposits of its [the patriciate's] blood and viscera."[45] Convents were of prime civic significance in a state whose religious head praised patrician women's encloisterment as a patriotic act of sacrifice.[46]

But what about religion? Couldn't the convent rush have been the result of a post-Tridentine surge in female piety, rather than the ultimate expression of the patriciate's infatuation with wasteful "magnificence?" And what about girls who preferred the independence of a spiritual life among women to the burden of childbearing in arranged marriages to men twice their age?[47] Recently, historians have started to question contemporaries' claims that convent life was "dreadful" by comparing it with "the almost unbearable conditions under which some married women suffered."[48] After all, nuns were free from the dangers of continuous childbearing and seem to have been less likely to contract bubonic plague and other epidemic diseases; they also lived longer beyond the childbearing years, regardless of epidemic mortalities.[49]

Of course, groom-hunting under conditions of artificial scarcity and parental supervision could hardly have been a romantic experience; childbearing did account for high mortality rates among women; and the overwhelming majority of girls who entered convents were indeed devout Catholics and took their vows seriously. But, in contrast to the situation a century earlier, no female religious movement swept through Venice in the post-Tridentine era;[50] nor did the majority of patrician nuns reject the institution of marriage as such, as did many medieval saints.[51] Therefore, neither the religious argument nor the proto-feminist or heroic model is a valid framework of analysis. Although by no means every teenager destined to take the veil was held at knifepoint by her father, as was Chrestina Dolfin (see case study 1 below), I insist on calling monachization rates of over 50 percent the result of coercion. In most cases, it was women's endemic dearth of choices that forced them to enter convents. The reasons for patrician women's rapidly shrinking range of alternatives in the period between 1550 and 1650 were structural. Rather than trying to determine how many nuns actively chose convent life over marriage, how many rebelled against their fate, or how many resigned themselves quietly, my

intention is to unearth the social and cultural mechanisms that produced the phenomenon of involuntary monachizations, a practice that
even the Venetian curia found deplorable.

Monachization Rates of Patrician Women, 1550–1650

"More than two thousand patrician women . . . live in this city locked
up in convents as if in a public tomb," Patriarch Giovanni Tiepolo
had declared in his letter to the Venetian Senate in 1619 expressing
his concerns over the rapid increase in patrician monachization rates.[52]
Although this figure may have been exaggerated, his remarks suggest
that the traditional practice among early modern upper-class families
of "depositing" a large proportion of their female offspring in convents had reached worrisome dimensions during his patriarchate. As
far back as 1553, the government was complaining that it was impossible to find eligible candidates for the office of Provveditori sopra i
Monasteri di Monache, a magistrate charged with the delicate task of
supervising the city's convents, because Venetian law disqualified all
patricians who counted a nun among any of their daughters, sisters,
nieces, or cousins.[53] According to estimates I have made based on convent records listing nuns with their family names, around three-fourths
of the 2,408 *monache*[54] in Venetian convents in 1586 were aristocratic.
By 1642, the ratio had decreased to about two-thirds, while the absolute number of nuns rose to 2,905 (see tables 1 and 2).

While the number of nuns was increasing, the patrician population
decreased considerably, a phenomenon that accentuated the simultaneously growing rate of patrician monachizations.[55] The widening
discrepancy between the number of brides and the number of nuns
indicates that in the seventeenth century, patrician women were more
likely to enter a convent than to marry within their class.[56] Between
1590 and 1670, 2,440 patrician brides married patrician men. In the
same period, 1,434 patrician nuns were documented as living in Venetian convents (see appendix, table A2). Since only 41 percent of the
convents produced records listing nuns by surname, the real number
of patrician nuns must have been much higher.[57] After 1650, the number of nuns declined steadily, especially in the eighteenth century; for
example, there were 1,732 nuns in 1766 but only 1,555 in 1780 (see
table 2 and the appendix, table A1). The rise in monachization rates
was accompanied by a decline in officially registered patrician mar-

TABLE 1   How Many Nuns Were Patrician? (1591–1670)

	1591–98[a]	1600–18	1620–28	1656–70[b]
Nuns with listed surnames[c]	240	766	476	1,072
Patrician nuns among the above[d]	176	569	331	685
Percentage of nuns who were patricians[e]	73.33	74.28	69.54	63.90
Number of convents that list surnames	10	14	9	30
Average number of patricians per convent	18	41	37	23

Sources: APV, Visite Priuli (1592–96); Visite Vendramin (1609–18); Visite Tiepolo (1620–27); Elenchi Elezioni Abbadesse (1656–70); Decretorum et Mandatorum Monialium, c. 12r; Torcellania Criminalia Monialium (1600–1689) (Tarli); ASV, Provveditori sopra Monasteri, busta 263, fascicolo 19; busta 268, fascicolo 36; busta 270, fascicolo 5; busta 347, fascicolo 1; Corpus Domini, busta 8, fascicolo "Pro Ven.o Mon.o Corporis Christi, S. Lucretia Morosini"; Santa Croce di Venezia, busta 2, fascicolo 2.

[a] These lists were compiled to register nuns who had private revenues; patrician nuns who did not dispose of personal income were not included.

[b] Only consecrated nuns over age 25.

[c] These lists of names derive from diverse convent records, such as visitation protocols, criminal investigations, chapter decisions, and inventories of nuns who disposed of personal income. Because of the scattered nature of the evidence, the numbers are inexact and can serve only to indicate trends.

[d] Because the lists give only the nuns' family names, never their fathers' names, it is impossible to reconstruct their precise family background. A considerable proportion of them might have been the illegitimate daughters of patrician fathers and thus, strictly speaking, not of noble descent.

[e] Because convents with a high percentage of noblewomen were more likely to record the family names of their inmates, it is probable that my table overcounts patrician nuns. This unfortunately inevitable statistical error is to a certain extent offset by the fact that patrician nuns who lived in convents on the Lido or the mainland were not included.

riages. At the same time, endogamy continued to be high, especially among women.[58] Although the proportion of patricians among Venetian nuns and that of nuns among patrician women seem to have been highest in the second half of the sixteenth and the first half of the seventeenth century, the phenomenon of steadily rising monachization rates among upper-class women started at least 150 years prior to its peak around 1600. In the fifteenth century, numerous convents were founded all over Italy, many of them belonging to the mendicant orders. In Venice, the number of convents rose from twenty-eight to forty-one between 1448 and 1505. (For a list of convents in Venice and Torcello by year of their founding, see appendix, table A3.) In Florence, the rate of religious professions among girls enrolled in the Monte delle Doti rose from 1.81 percent between 1437 and 1489 to 15.76 percent between 1520 and 1560.[59] However, the development of these institutions in the fifteenth century was not a predominantly aristocratic phenome-

TABLE 2   How Many Patrician Women Were Nuns? (1581–1656)

	1581	1586	1642	1656	1766	1780
Nuns[a]	2,508	2,408	2,905	2,508	1,732	1,555
Percentage of nuns who were patricians[b]	73.33	74.28	69.54	63.90		
Number of patrician nuns (projected)[c]	1,839	1,788	2,020	1,602		
Patrician women[d]	3,418	3,577	2,476	1,778[e]		1,976
Percentage of patrician women who were nuns (projected)[f]	53.80	49.98	81.58[g]			

Sources: APV, Visite Priuli (1592–96); Visite Vendramin (1609–18); Visite Tiepolo (1620–27); Elenchi Elezioni Abbadesse (1656–70); Decretorum et Mandatorum Monialium, c. 12r; Torcellania Criminalia Monialium (1600–1689) (Tarli); ASV, Provveditori sopra Monasteri, busta 263, fascicolo 19; busta 268, fascicolo 36; busta 270, fascicolo 5; busta 347, fascicolo 1; Corpus Domini, busta 8, fascicolo "Pro Ven.o Mon.o Corporis Christi, S. Lucretia Morosini"; Santa Croce di Venezia, busta 2, fascicolo 2; Daniele Beltrami, Storia della popolazione di Venezia dalla fine del secolo XVI alla caduta della Repubblica (Padua, 1954), pp. 72, 73, 79; Volker Hunecke, Der venezianische Adel am Ende der Republik (1646–1797): Demographie, Familie, Haushalt (Tübingen, 1995); Francesca Medioli, ed., L'inferno monacale di Suor Arcangela Tarabotti (Turin, 1990), p. 132, n. 24.

[a] Figures deriving from census data (for 1581, 1586, 1642, 1766, and 1780: Beltrami; for 1656: Medioli).

[b] See table 1, line 3. My estimate that 63.9 percent of nuns were patricians in 1656 is derived from lists of consecrated nuns with identifiable names from the years 1656 to 1670. Since during those years the percentage of patrician nuns was 63.9 percent of the nuns listed, I calculated the number of nuns in 1642 using the same proportion. The calculations for the year 1586 were done in a similar manner. My estimate of 74.28 percent of patrician nuns in 1586 is derived from lists of nuns with identifiable names from 1600 to 1618.

[c] Inferred from lines 1 and 2.

[d] Calculated on the basis of census data given by Beltrami for the entire patrician population (for the years 1581, 1586, 1642, and 1766); since, according to Hunecke, the gender ratio of Venetian census data is 100 males/80 females for the seventeenth century, my figures are adjusted for a gender ratio of 100:100. The same could not be done for Medioli's figures, which seem a bit low compared with Beltrami's.

[e] The figure reported by Medioli is disproportionately low.

[f] Derived from lines 3 and 4.

[g] This figure is too high to be realistic, but it indicates a clear trend.

non. Scholars attribute the proliferation of convents to several causes, among them the general population growth, a strong religious movement among middle- and upper-class women, and dowry inflation.[60]

In Venice, the fifteenth-century wave of convent foundings was an almost exclusively urban phenomenon; also, it was socially mixed in character.[61] Many of the newly founded nunneries resulted from middle-class women's initiatives aimed at transforming their already existing, Beguine-like communities into proper convents.[62] Although patrician women played a significant role in endowing and promoting these new convents, only relatively few of them entered as nuns. Among patricians, who preferred the Benedictine and Augustinian or-

ders to Franciscan houses, the nunneries of San Daniele, Santa Giustina, and Santi Cosma e Damiano became popular; the other new convents were too poorly endowed to attract patrician girls. Of the few
nunneries established in the sixteenth century, only San Giuseppe
housed noblewomen. Most of the other newly established religious
institutes were semi-secular asylums for penitent prostitutes, spinsters,
and other "women at risk."[63]

The increase in patrician nuns around 1600 did not lead to an
institutional development comparable to that in the fifteenth century.
Although new forms of monastic devotion stimulated the foundation
of several convents in the aftermath of the Counter-Reformation, patrician women for the most part did not participate in these initiatives.
The nunneries founded in Venice in the seventeenth century belonged
almost exclusively to the Carmelites, Capuchins, and Servites—all of
them strictly observing orders, whose female branches insisted on an
austere and contemplative life in perfect seclusion. They were therefore
unattractive to the majority of aristocratic girls, who were used to a
certain degree of comfort and luxury and were eager to keep their relationships with the outside world. Other types of Counter-Reformation
orders with an emphasis on women's education—the Ursulines and
other "female Jesuits"—were more popular on the mainland than in
the capital.[64] One of these institutions, Santa Maria delle Dimesse, was
founded as a third-order community for lower-class women in Murano in 1593.[65]

As a consequence, the majority of patrician nuns who took their
vows in the late sixteenth and early seventeenth centuries crowded into
the exclusively or predominantly aristocratic convents of early medieval foundation,[66] transformed formerly "citizen" convents such as
Santa Caterina dei Sacchi di Venezia into purely patrician nunneries,[67]
or colonized the "mixed" convents.[68] Apart from the new, poorly endowed, and extremely strict convents, only a few nunneries retained
a purely "citizen" or middle-class character in the period from 1550
to 1650.[69]

Inflated Dowries: "Involuntary Nuns" and Their "Lucky Sisters"

In the absence of a strong religious movement among Venetian aristocratic women during the Counter-Reformation, it is obvious that the
increasing rate of patrician monachizations was triggered by other,

more worldly concerns. Contemporaries, including ecclesiastical authorities, justified the development by pointing to the financial difficulties of many patrician families due to dowry inflation. Modern historians have so far tended to offer the same explanation:[70] the melodramatic scenario in which an unjust rationale forces unlucky girls to renounce their inheritance so that their sisters might be happily married has informed feminist as well as traditional scholarship.[71] As has already been suggested, a much more far-reaching explanatory model is needed to account for the complexity of the phenomenon. Rather than seeing coerced monachizations as an unfortunate but inevitable by-product of truly "crucial" factors such as economic constraints, I argue that monachization practices themselves were at the center of a complex political, economic, social, and cultural transformation. After all, what counts as a valid economic explanation is culturally determined. Some expenses are deemed necessary, others dispensable. Since whatever financial constraints Venetian patricians complained about cannot be regarded as objectively valid and transparent factors of historical change, contemporary discourse surrounding coerced monachizations has to be approached with caution. Nonetheless, an analysis of the dowry-monachization paradigm might reveal why the patriciate so readily accepted coerced monachizations as an inevitable sacrifice, and why the dowry explanation in particular was able to calm the conscience of even those who otherwise might have hesitated to "bury their daughters alive."

In 1580, Nuncio Alberto Bolognetti informed the pope, who was eager to have Venetian convents inspected for their compliance with post-Tridentine clausura rules, that a stricter discipline in nunneries would deter many patrician girls from taking the veil, and that this would "cause the ruin of many [patrician] families because of the excessive dowries noblemen usually give their daughters who marry."[72] Since the reintroduction of the dowry system in the Middle Ages, dowry inflation had been a matter of constant concern to upper-class families.[73] Monachization strategies were generally seen as protection against the threat of financial ruin caused by the cost of women's marriages. Whether daughters destined to take the veil had any religious vocation mattered little.

The "involuntary nun," forced into a convent by an avaricious father, brother, or even mother, was already a firmly entrenched topos in popular literature in the sixteenth century. The contemporary song "Barzelleta dele Monacelle" comically describes the tragic fate of "imprisoned little nuns" tricked into entering a convent by flattering and deceiving parents. The "nuns' joke" is a humorous account of nuns escaping the convent and "returning to the world"—only to be chased out of their family home a second time, as if they were the "mortal enemies" of parents "who say that they have too many troubles endowing the other sisters."[74] The song goes on to complain about the unjust and meaningless workings of fortune, "this blind, deaf, adverse, and deceitful Goddess reigning over the world, who is mother to the one, stepmother to the other, who gives and takes as she likes."[75] The motif of fortune and its arbitrary effects is elaborated by juxtaposing the destiny of several sisters, as one sister is allowed to "sit in fortune's lap [while] the other ones are chased away . . . the one is always in pain and tears, the other in joy and feast, the one has jewels and rich garments, the other is veiled in black!"[76] The nuns lament the "sweet time that we are losing" when "locked up in our cells, we, all naked, often look at our white and beautiful bodies, crying . . . [and saying] how much delight must follow the holy dictum 'go forth and multiply.' "[77] The song closes with the escaped nuns' vow "to use every strength, idea, and art, to take the vilest jobs rather than return to the convent, [since] we are determined to live joyful lives with husbands in the world," if—and this is the punch line—"you help us with a dowry."[78]

The dowry as the key to a woman's worldly life and happiness was also a focus for women writers engaging in the Venetian *querelle des femmes*.[79] Arcangela Tarabotti, a nun and writer of proto-feminist treatises against "paternal tyrannies," developed the topic in great detail from the point of view of an "involuntary nun." Like the composer of the tragicomic "nuns' joke," she structured her writings by juxtaposing opposites: the innocence of girls versus the deception of their fathers; the nun's poverty and imprisonment versus her married sister's rich life in the world. By highlighting these contrasts, Tarabotti illustrates the injustice done to involuntary nuns. Starting with a depiction of how young girls are lured into convents before they are old enough to realize the extent of their sacrifice, her *Inferno monacale* (Hell of nuns; written 1640–50, first published 1990) goes on to discuss the "unjust partiality of parents . . . whose malice . . . generates marvel and compassion."[80] The parents marry off one daughter lavishly and prestigiously, marking her worth with jewels and precious garments, while condemning the other to a life of poverty and seclusion. While the lucky sister is endowed with "tens of thousands of ducats," the unfortunate one is forced to enter a convent "accompanied by a sum between nine hundred and twelve hundred ducats—according to the customs of those most miserable places—or by an annual pension between fifty and one hundred ducats, only to hear the reproaches of her parents for these excessive and superfluous expenses." In Sister Arcangela's eyes, this practice is illegal, because "there is no law that allows married daughters more reasonable claims to their parents' inheritance than daughters put into convents, if they are both of legitimate birth."[81] Ultimately, it is the government that is to blame: "That private persons out of their own interest . . . commit such monstrosities is an abominable practice; but that the authorities and the princes allow this to happen is a fact arousing horror in insensitivity itself; the Prince's eye has to watch not only over the *ragion di stato* [reason of state], but also over the welfare of souls, and should not let so many die miserably."[82]

Almost in the fashion of the Enlightenment, Tarabotti demands that the government take care of the (spiritual) welfare of its citizens instead of tolerating such a cruel practice as forcing girls to take the veil. In Tarabotti's opinion, coerced monachizations are doubly abominable: in addition to wasting innocent women's earthly lives, their souls are put into jeopardy, because involuntary nuns cannot live up to the rules of the monastic life to which they have committed themselves in the eyes of God. Nuns without devotion are continually on the verge of falling into the devil's claws. Coerced monachizations should thus be prosecuted by the state, especially since the patriciate praises its government as just and tolerant. But instead of contradicting the Venetian *ragion di stato,* in Tarabotti's view involuntary monachizations are—unfortunately—in perfect agreement with it. They lie at the core of the political system of the Venetian republic, "because, if all the [aristocratic daughters] got married, the nobility would grow too much in number, and the families would become impoverished because of the expenses of so many dowries."[83]

In detecting inconsistencies between the myth of Venice as a free and justly governed city and the authorities' connivance with a criminal practice, Sister Arcangela implicitly denounces the republic as tyrannical. She sarcastically dedicates the *Inferno monacale* to "that republic where, more frequently than anywhere else in the world, daughters are forced to enter convents." Her treatise is also dedicated to "your grand Senate, which hopes to eternalize you, beautiful Virgin, Queen of the Adriatic, by imprisoning virgin girls so that they may

chastise themselves, recite psalms, and pray for you in return." The
bitter irony in Tarabotti's dedication brings her political critique to
the point: the mythical republic's eternal duration is in reality based
on a tyrannical practice, justified and disguised only superficially by
its metaphorical relation to the city's patron, the Virgin Mary, who
allegedly protects the city's legendary longevity. The cynicism of endangering so many innocent women's access to paradise in the name
of the Virgin shows that the republic's traditional values—justice, liberty, and piety—have been perverted.

In revealing the fundamental paradoxes of the Venetian *ragion di
stato,* Tarabotti suggests that the much-praised liberty of Venice is a
chimera, just as "convents represent a theater where the darkest tragedies are performed. . . . everything is vanity, perspective and shadow
deceiving the eye."[84] In her view, the government's tolerance of crimes
that jeopardize the souls of innocent girls reveals the arbitrariness of
the judicial system; and the patriciate's custom of sacrificing many of
its women on the altar of economic interests is in reality a power game
favoring a small elite. If the government were seriously concerned with
solving the financial problems of private families, it would simply abolish the dowry system altogether.[85]

A revolutionary thought. Already in the sixteenth century, writers
such as Giovan Maria Memmo and Giovanni Botero had spoken ad-
miringly of ancient Sparta's King Lycurgus, who, in order to encourage
marriages and population growth and to prevent marriages from being
concluded for monetary reasons alone, abolished the institution of the
dowry.[86] Of course, no patrician ever seriously proposed to follow Lycurgus's example. The endogamous exchange of upper-class women
and their dowries was too intricately connected to the way the nobility defined and reproduced its prestige and political power for such
"spartan" measures to gain currency. Instead of abolishing the dowry
system, the government tried to contain the inflation of dowries and
thereby prevent some of the system's worst consequences. In 1420,
1505, 1535, 1551, and 1575, the Senate defined upper limits for dowries "so that thereby this bad and harmful custom, which was introduced among our nobility and citizenry, of spending exorbitant
amounts of money when marrying daughters off [will be abolished, a
custom] that brought great damage to the fathers, and dissatisfaction
to everyone."[87]

The government's efforts to fight dowry inflation, however, were
unsuccessful. Like other sumptuary laws, dowry legislation continued

to be violated, often by citizen fathers eager to buy their daughters' entry into patrician families in need of money.[88] In the sixteenth century, when a skilled artisan's annual income was approximately fifty ducats, patrician dowries could easily consist of tens of thousands of ducats; in the early seventeenth century, the highest dowries reached up to forty thousand ducats.[89] In its attempts to keep up with the inflation rate of dowries, the Senate repeatedly adjusted the legal maximum—from three thousand ducats in 1505 to six thousand in 1575. Yet these laws were impossible to enforce: between 1564 and 1575, dowry laws were suspended altogether because of the frequency with which they were violated. Fines could not prevent rich and ambitious fathers from paying high dowries. Given the logic of conspicuous consumption patterns, the payment of a fine became part of the expense of a dowry and only enhanced the prestige of a costly wedding. The reintroduction of a legal limit in 1575 hints at the possibility that dowry laws were needed less to set an upper limit than to define an acceptable minimum for an honorable patrician marriage. This might also explain why the proposal to raise the upper limit to ten thousand ducats in 1575 was defeated.

The competition for prestige and power involved in the exchange of women proved to be damaging to the body politic as a whole, while it was advantageous to very rich families and to individual social climbers. One of the preambles to the dowry law of 1535 stated, "When these dowries are excessively and inordinately large, the great power of the rich causes resentment in the middling sort, and they want to compete with them beyond their own means to the great detriment of their houses, and this disorder produces many undesirable results in forcing a large part of their children to be made nuns and also in excessive expenditure on weddings."[90]

As these various statements from lawmakers, songwriters, "feminist" nuns, and ecclesiastical authorities illustrate, the assumption that coerced monachizations were caused by the dowry system was firmly rooted in public discourse. They also indicate a widespread uneasiness about a social custom that was perceived to be both indispensable and subversive. On the one hand, dowries were an essential part of marriage, not only among the elite. A common type of charitable legacy, for example, was to leave money to confraternities for the purpose of endowing dowries for "deserving" poor girls who might otherwise fall into prostitution.[91] On the other hand, dowry inflation was seen as detrimental to the cohesiveness of the body politic because it promoted hypergamy, forced prestigious families to compete financially with social climbers, and thereby aggravated the concentration of wealth among a small elite.[92] In this context, the growing number of patrician monachizations was seen as another unfortunate, and ultimately destabilizing, by-product of a social institution whose dynamic gradually eroded its original function of preserving noble families.

This was the dilemma Patriarch Tiepolo hinted at in his letter of 1619 to the Venetian Senate, in which he complained that family concerns, not devotion, were responsible for the high number of patrician nuns.[93] In arguments of which Arcangela Tarabotti certainly would have approved, Tiepolo drew attention to the moral problems involved in semi-voluntary monachizations among members of his own class, who, "if they were of the other sex," would "command and govern the world." He spelled out the distress many a patrician must have felt with regard to a social practice that caused widespread dissatisfaction and resistance among upper-class women. His answer to the touchy issue of involuntary monachizations and their consequences (such as disciplinary problems and frequent violations of the monastic rules) was a lenient attitude in imposing convent discipline. The purpose of his letter was to plead with the government to indulge his policy. Tiepolo allowed the nuns to cultivate an aristocratic lifestyle, within acceptable limits—to wear fine fabrics instead of rough woolen cloths, to mitigate the schedule of nighttime prayers, and to disregard certain dietary restrictions. Acknowledging the fact that many nuns did not freely choose their profession, he meant to ease the burden of the honorable sacrifice they were making for the welfare of their families and their state.

On this point, however, Sister Arcangela's and Tiepolo's opinions differ considerably. Whereas Tarabotti insisted on strict enforcement of the Tridentine decrees according to which no novice should be allowed to pronounce her vows unless ecclesiastical examiners made sure she was truly devout,[94] Tiepolo deemed the gift made by patrician girls, despite their reluctance, to be a patriotic and, in a broader sense, religious act. Sister Arcangela would later denounce ecclesiastical authorities like him as accomplices of the secular elite's immoral practices.[95] In her eyes, coerced monachizations were doubly reprehensible: not only did they condemn many women unfit for religious service to eternal damnation, their suffering was also entirely useless, because "the King of Heaven does not favor, but abominates, victims offered to him who are not voluntary, but forced."[96] Whereas she implied

clearly that the existing sociopolitical system had to be changed, starting with the abolition of the dowry system and coerced monachizations, Tiepolo praised the nuns' "sacrifices" precisely because they
allegedly helped to preserve the status quo. Had these noblewomen
refused to make a gift of their freedom and liberty, "had they wanted
to dispose of themselves otherwise, what confusion! what damage!
what disorder! what dangers! what scandals! and what bad consequences would have occurred for the families, and for the city!"[97]

But dangers lurked nonetheless, even behind convent walls. Both
ecclesiastical and secular authorities charged with supervising convent
discipline knew that involuntary monachizations were a constant
source of disorder and scandal. As Tarabotti herself proclaimed, "fathers and relatives of these girls . . . know very well how many of them
. . . have dishonored both their house and that of God."[98] In criminal
trials over illicit relationships between nuns and their lovers, one of
the nuns' strategies of defense was to arouse the judges' compassion
by claiming to be "involuntary," forced into the convent by avaricious
family members. During a lay tribunal's investigation of Sister Serafica
Balbi's love affair in 1604, her mother superior, the prioress of San
Daniele, defended the suspect by saying, "she is a good girl, but may
God forgive those who force their daughters into convents." Sister Serafica herself burst into tears during the interrogation: "I was betrayed
by my own relatives. . . . I wish I had been born the daughter of a
servant."[99]

The investigating magistrate was entirely unimpressed by Sister
Serafica's tragic situation. The following case studies illustrate that the
topos of the "involuntary nun" was by no means an entirely fictive
concept. Many nuns seem to have indeed been pushed or persuaded
to enter convents against their will; whether the reason was financial
constraints caused by dowry inflation, however, remains to be seen.

Case Study 1: The Rebel Nun

Sister Chrestina Dolfin's case is the "classic" drama of a girl's abuse
by a tyrannical father. Chrestina was the daughter of Benedetto Dolfin
and his second wife, Sagreda Sagredo; besides her brother, Alvise, she
had three half-sisters and two half-brothers from her father's first marriage.

Forced into the convent of Spirito Santo at age eleven, Sister Chrestina escaped from the nunnery after the death of her father and one
of her half-brothers. Outraged over this violation of family honor, her

Andrea Dolfin
|
Benedetto (1504–58)
1. m.: Isabella Contarini di Piero di Matthio di Girolamo
(1522)

Andrianna m. Giov. Balbi (1550)	Piero (b. 1532) m. Fontana Orio (1558)	Andrea (b. 1534)	Marina nun	Angela *pizzochera*

2. m.: Sagreda Sagredo
(1540)

Alvise (b. 1542) m. Cecilia Pesaro/Pizzamano? di Piero (1562) | three sons	Chrestina nun in Spirito Santo

The family of Chrestina Dolfin

brother Alvise and her brother-in-law Giovanni Balbi formally denounced Hieronimo Ferraruol for abducting her.[100] The convent magistrate instituted legal proceedings against Ferraruol and others who
helped her escape, charging them with contravening the *clausura* (enclosure) laws. The Dolfins suspected Sister Chrestina and Ferraruol of
having been lovers. During the investigations, the abbess rejected these
claims, testifying that "Sister Chrestina did not leave for any dishonest
reason, but because she did not want to stay, especially after the death
of her father and her brother."[101] Chrestina's servant, Sister Monacha
conversa, stated that Sister Chrestina had always cursed her deceased
father and her brother for having made her take the vows.[102] Apparently, Chrestina's father had forced her to enter the convent at age
eleven by threatening her with a knife and keeping her locked up.[103]
According to several testimonies, Sister Chrestina was determined to
achieve a formal dissolution of her vows and to retrieve her share in
her family's inheritance—a task Ferraruol, as a canon lawyer, helped
her with. She hid in the countryside, expecting a *breve* from Rome.
Neighbors and friends who offered Chrestina temporary shelter after
her flight from the convent indicated that she suffered from nervous
disorders, possibly hysteria and anorexia nervosa.[104] After interrogating several witnesses, the convent magistrate decided to abandon the
trial; nobody seems to have been sentenced. It is uncertain whether
Sister Chrestina ever obtained a formal dissolution of her vows. She

probably left Venetian territory, and definitely never returned to the convent.

The precise reasons for Chrestina's abuse are impossible to ascertain. It seems likely, though, that her father's economic considerations played a role. Benedetto Dolfin had three sons to take care of; only one daughter from his first marriage—Alba (Andrianna), the "lucky" one—married, endowed with the substantial sum of four thousand ducats. Another daughter, Marina, entered the modest convent of San Martino di Burano, and Angela became a *pizzochera*. Chrestina's monachization was thus a "normal" and systematic—even though violent—procedure in the Dolfin family, aimed at excluding all but one of the daughters from their inheritances and dowries.

Case Study 2: Devilish Temptations

The case of Sister Laura Querini, a nun in San Zaccaria, is an illustration of Tarabotti's argument that nuns without devotion often lacked the spiritual strength to resist worldly temptations. Diana Querini (Sister Laura's secular name) was born in 1570, the only child of Giulio Querini di Girolamo and Beatrice Battagia di Michele. Her father was poor and died in prison while she was still a child.[105] Her mother's dowry was modest—consisting of twenty-four hundred ducats and precious jewels—but could have been sufficient for Diana's marriage. In 1574 Beatrice appointed Diana her universal heir,[106] but in her revised testament of 1579, she decided to leave only fifteen hundred ducats to Diana and a thousand to her niece, Lauretta.[107] Eventually, Diana became a nun in San Zaccaria, the city's most elegant and prestigious convent, where she joined her aunt, Sister Hortensia, the illegitimate daughter of her maternal grandfather. She lived there quietly and inconspicuously until 1614, when her abbess informed the patriarch about her and her servant's love affairs with two young men, illegitimate sons of patricians. Sister Laura and Sister Zaccaria had hidden the men for two weeks in the convent's basement, providing them with food and joining them at night. They were found out after someone discovered the loose bricks through which their lovers sneaked in. Sisters Laura and Zaccaria had worked for more than a month to dig this hole in the convent walls.[108]

Interrogated by the patriarch, Sister Laura confessed her serious offense immediately. Oscillating between repentance and an attempt to justify her behavior, she told him about her life:

I came to this convent as a small girl during the plague [i.e., between 1574 and 1575, when she was four or five years old], like all the girls, and then I was educated in [the convent of] San Vito di Burano, where I stayed for five or six years until I was accepted as a nun in this convent, when I was about fifteen years old. I became a novice, and then I professed with my mouth, but not with my heart. I was always tempted by the devil and close to breaking my neck, and I always had affairs in the past, provided by Donna Cipriana [a matchmaker], who is now dead; but during these affairs I never committed any bad thing, that is, I never lost my virginity. Finally, it must have been six years ago, Donna Cipriana introduced me to Zuanne Cocco, a young man of about 20 years, who came occasionally to see me in the parlor in such a way that I fell in love with him, and I got him to love me also; I used every art, even magic, that is, incantations, conjurations, and invocations of the devil, to get him to love me, and I achieved these things with the help of Donna Cipriana by offering money to Cocco; and I invited him to come and see me.[109]

If the trial proceedings in the case of Chrestina Dolfin reveal the violence involved in some involuntary monachizations, Sister Laura's case illustrates how inconspicuously smooth and normal the procedure of "depositing" daughters in a convent often was. As soon as they could walk, speak, and eat on their own, most patrician girls were sent off to convents, where they grew up and received a rudimentary education. If their parents decided against a marriage, the girls simply stayed in the environment in which they had grown up, where they had friends and, often, female relatives to rely on. A teenage girl accustomed to convent life did not necessarily object to taking the veil any more than she might have protested against marrying a stranger twice her age.[110] Only when they were old enough to understand the extent of their sacrifice did nuns such as Sister Laura experience doubts and conflicts regarding their profession. Although it was theoretically possible for "involuntary nuns" to achieve a dissolution of their vows from Rome, the Venetian government did not allow nuns to make such a request.[111] In Sister Laura's case, given the particular situation of her family, the convent option was almost mandatory: she had neither a close male relative who could have arranged a marriage for her nor her mother's support and inheritance.

Case Study 3: The Wronged Orphan

The case of Sister Cecilia Malombra concerns an orphaned girl who was cheated out of her inheritance and her rightful claims to a dowry worth more than six thousand ducats by deceitful relatives. In order

Gerolamo Malombra
m. Teodosia Marin
|
Zorzi
|

Bortolo Catarina Anzolo Lugretia Bernardo Polo Gerolamo Mattio Giacomo Zorzi
| |
Piero   Mattio

Iseppo Bortolo   Zorzi (d. 1606–9)   Gerolamo (d. 1626)
                              | m. Maddalena Andriani
                           Cecilia
                       nun in Corpus Domini

                                    Matteo Cecilia Paulina Felicita Alba

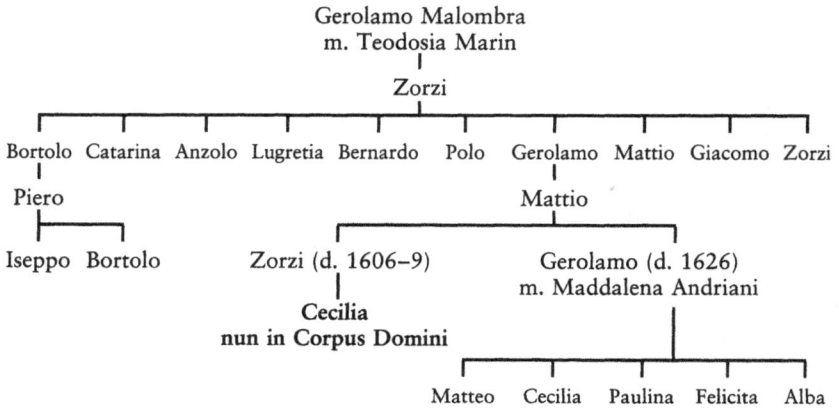

The family of Cecilia Malombra

to claim missing annuity payments, Sister Cecilia initiated legal proceedings against her deceased father's sister-in-law. Her lawsuit shows how claims of "spiritual" as opposed to bridal dowries were negotiated and resolved in Venetian courts.[112]

Cecilia was the only child of Zorzi Malombra, who belonged to a citizen family of high repute.[113] Her paternal uncle, Gerolamo, disregarded his deceased brother's testamentary provisions to marry her honorably and kept the inheritance for himself after "depositing" her in the convent of Corpus Domini. In his testament of 1606, Zorzi had left Cecilia three thousand ducats in cash, furniture worth thirty-two hundred ducats, and the entire dowry of her mother. His universal heir and trustee was Gerolamo, whom he encouraged to stay together with his wife and to take proper care of his daughter.[114] However, three years later, in 1609—probably after the death of Cecilia's mother—Gerolamo signed a contract with Corpus Domini, pledging to pay sixty ducats annually and four hundred ducats in cash for Cecilia's monachization. The source of this money was income from houses that Teodosia Marin had donated to Zorzi's ancestors in 1541. When Gerolamo died, his widow, Maddalena Andriani, initiated legal proceedings with the Offizio sopra Datij (office for the collection of customs and excise duties) in order to confiscate the houses as part of the properties she wanted as a substitute for her dowry.[115] The convent magistrate, charged with protecting the convents' patrimonies, entitlements, and credits of unpaid annuities, ordered that the decision in Maddalena's favor be suspended. In 1628, the Avogadori di Comun (state attorneys) confirmed the convent's request against Maddalena's claims; by now, the Malombra family owed 296 ducats to Corpus Domini. In order to resolve the impasse resulting from the mutually exclusive decisions by different courts, the Avogadori suggested that Sister Cecilia's claim be satisfied from the confiscated patrimony of a certain "Giuseppe *bandito*," an exiled relative of hers.[116] One year later, Maddalena gained a confirmation of her own claims through the Giudici del Proprio, a court devoted to protecting the rights of wives and widows and helping them to recover their dowries.[117] Eventually, Maddalena agreed to pay the convent dowry from Teodosia's houses until her father-in-law, Mattio, successor to the properties of his exiled cousin Iseppo, died. After Mattio's death, Iseppo's brother, Bortolo, was to be responsible for the annuity payments, to be recovered now from Iseppo's properties. Maddalena thus managed to receive the houses originally pledged with Sister Cecilia's pension as a compensation for her own dowry.[118]

Maddalena herself was burdened with having to provide for a son and four daughters. In her (unopened) testament of 1617, she ordered that her property be divided equally among her children while favoring her daughters' monachizations. If they did not want to enter a convent, they had to wait for their inheritances until age twenty-four; if they wanted to become *pizzochere*, they had to wait until age twenty-eight.[119] Thus it seems likely that part of the inheritance of which Gerolamo deprived his niece Cecilia was employed to support yet another generation of nuns.

Arcangela Tarabotti was right in claiming that nuns without devotion were often victims of "tyrannical" family patriarchs, and that involuntary nuns tended to disregard the monastic rules more than others. But she was wrong in assuming that involuntary monachizations were a direct effect of dowry inflation. Sister Laura Querini, who could not resist Zuanne Cocco's charms, was an only child; the nieces of orphaned Sister Cecilia Malombra were indiscriminately encouraged to become nuns themselves, according to their mother's testament; and although Sister Chrestina's half-sister Alba was the only "lucky" one among Benedetto Dolfin's four daughters who was able to marry, her brother Alvise was at least as interested in preventing Chrestina from claiming her inheritance as was her brother-in-law, Giovanni Balbi. The last case in particular suggests that if involuntary monachizations were the effect of economic considerations, these considerations tended to favor the nuns' brothers more than their "lucky sisters."

Entailed Patrimonies: "Involuntary Nuns" and Their Lucky Brothers

My case studies suggest that "involuntary nuns" populated Venetian convents in large numbers indeed—an impression that the numerous criminal investigations against nuns who either tried to escape from their convents or cultivated illicit relationships within them seem to confirm (see chapter 3). The case studies do not indicate, however, that coerced monachizations of "unlucky" daughters paid for the inflated dowries and lavish weddings of their "lucky sisters." Of course, only a quantitative analysis of how monachization rates and dowry payments affected individual families' patrimonial development could precisely answer the question of whether coerced monachizations helped parents save the money that they then squandered on inflated dowries. Because Venetian convent records rarely identified nuns by their fathers' and grandfathers' names, however, such an analysis appears impossible to conduct. But no matter what the exact financial effect of rising monachization rates might have been, the topos of the "involuntary nun" and her "lucky sister" is inadequate because it deflects attention from the fact that the real winners from coerced monachizations were the nuns' lucky brothers. Both the dowry system and monachization strategies have to be seen as complementary parts of the asymmetrically gendered inheritance patterns of a patriarchal society designed to facilitate the agnatic transfer of family fortunes.

Monachization strategies were the last stage in a centuries-old movement to exclude women from the family patrimony. The medieval reintroduction of the Roman dowry—defined as a daughter's compensation for renouncing her inheritance—was the first step in this direction.[120] Although upper limits for dowries had been legislated in Venice since the thirteenth century, no law protected daughters from getting too little. A dowry had to be "congruous" with the family patrimony, but the relation between a girl's dowry and her brothers' shares in the inheritance was—to my knowledge—nowhere specified.[121] Employed as a means to institute agnatic inheritance patterns, dowries were usually considerably lower than the inheritance portions that brothers could expect, despite the increasing pressures of dowry inflation.[122] Monachizations favored male heirs further, since daughters destined to enter a convent were paid off with even less than their "lucky sisters": according to ecclesiastical and secular decrees issued in 1593 and 1602, a nun was entitled to only one-fifth of the legally defined maximum—that is, the standard amount—for a bridal dowry (see chapter 4). As the numerous lawsuits initiated by nuns and convent chapters in the seventeenth century show, male relatives would frequently refuse or neglect to pay even those sixty annual ducats.[123]

From this perspective, the economic rationale of peaking monachization rates consisted of an intensified expropriation of daughters' inheritance portions in favor of agnatic entailment. Dowry inflation did not necessarily upset this trend, since to an increasing extent large dowries tended to be raised by the bride's mother and her female relatives.[124] The commonplace assumption that coerced monachizations were caused by (other women's demand for) exorbitant dowries—a theory that by the eighteenth century had gained currency[125]—is thus entirely misleading: it suggests that the nuns' suffering was caused by other women, whereas in reality it was the families' universal heirs in whose favor *all* women's portions were curtailed.[126]

When, in the sixteenth century, Venice lost its place as a major international center of trade and became the hub of a regional, land-based economy, fathers started to curb their sons' inheritance rights in addition to increasingly dispossessing their daughters. Although primogeniture was rarely practiced in Venice—where the brothers' joint ownership of the family patrimony *(fraterna)* was too firmly rooted as a legal institution—entailment strategies of a more "egalitarian" kind were increasingly practiced. From the sixteenth century on, the "conditioning" of patrimonies in the form of testamentary *fidecommessi* became a widespread custom.[127] A *fidecommesso* was a rather flexible form of entailment: its prime function was to exclude illegitimate sons from the inheritance and to prevent all future heirs from alienating the patrimony, which could be left to all sons indiscriminately or just to a favored one. Given the logic of agnatic inheritance patterns, it is necessary to see monachization strategies, the dowry system, and the entailment of patrimonies as interdependent means of preserving the wealth of noble families in a period of economic change.[128] The following case studies exemplify how two families emphasized different components of this multifaceted strategy to accumulate patrimonies by restricting inheritance. Both cases reveal the marked gender asymmetry of patrician inheritance patterns, although not all of the male heirs were equally "lucky." The Morosini family (case study 4) practiced primogeniture—that is, the strict exclusion of all children but the firstborn son from the family patrimony—in one generation, unrestricted inheritance for males and marriage of all sons and daughters in the next. The Pesaro family (case study 5) was committed to a disproportionately high rate of monachizations over several generations while leaving their sons' inheritance rights untouched.

Case Study 4: Entailing Patrimonies, Dividing Siblings

The lawsuit of Sister Lugretia Morosini against her family for the omission of annuity payments reveals the problems that arose from the entailment of her father's patrimony. Lugretia, one of ten children, was born in 1584 to Piero Morosini di Andrea and Chiara Corner di Gerolamo di Fantin. Four brothers died at an early age. Her surviving siblings were Andrea, firstborn son and universal heir of the family fortune; Francesco and Giacomo, who never married; Paulina, who did not marry until she was past childbearing age; and Morosina, who remained a spinster.

Lugretia was born the same year her father died; she was one year old when her oldest brother, Andrea, married Laura Memmo. Her mother died before she came of age. In 1600, Andrea concluded a contract for her "spiritual dowry" as a nun in Corpus Domini.[129] He as-

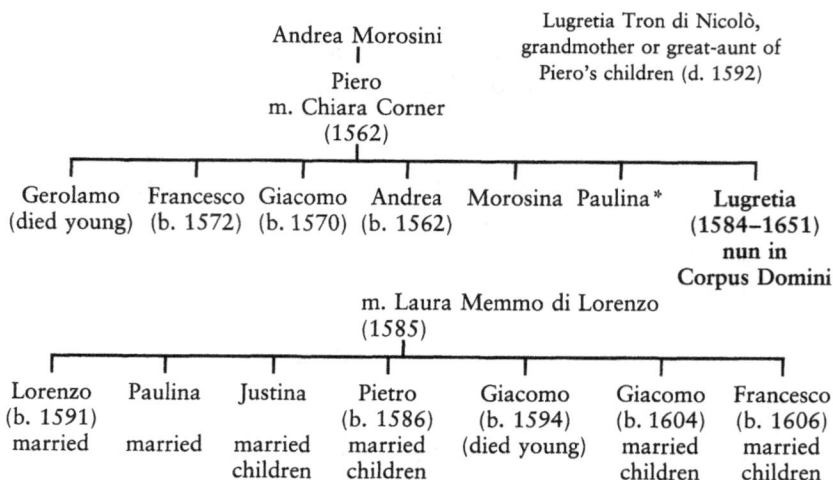

Andrea Morosini
|
Piero
m. Chiara Corner
(1562)

Lugretia Tron di Nicolò,
grandmother or great-aunt of
Piero's children (d. 1592)

Gerolamo (died young)	Francesco (b. 1572)	Giacomo (b. 1570)	Andrea (b. 1562)	Morosina	Paulina*	Lugretia (1584–1651) nun in Corpus Domini

m. Laura Memmo di Lorenzo
(1585)

Lorenzo (b. 1591) married	Paulina married	Justina married children	Pietro (b. 1586) married children	Giacomo (b. 1594) (died young)	Giacomo (b. 1604) married children	Francesco (b. 1606) married children

* Paulina married sometime before 1639.

The family of Lugretia Morosini

signed her the usual sixty ducats annually by pledging the rent of three houses, one of them located in San Marcuola and the other two in San Gregorio. In exchange, she signed a *quietanza* (quitclaim) before taking her holy vows in 1601.[130]

The financial condition of the Morosini family was mediocre. According to their tax declaration of 1582, the combined income of Piero Morosini and his aunt, Lugretia Tron di Nicolò, amounted to 325 ducats per year.[131] Piero's firstborn son Andrea, however, got a substantial dowry from his wife, Laura Memmo, consisting of a pearl necklace worth 1,000 ducats, furniture worth 300 ducats, 300 ducats in cash, 1,500 ducats in cash after her mother's death, 16 fields *(campi)*, and income of 46 ducats annually from 28 fields that remained in her father's possession.[132] The entire family seems to have been committed to a policy of strict entailment. For example, Andrea's great-aunt, Lugretia Tron di Nicolò, left all of her territories in Villa di San Bruson to Andrea while recommending to his siblings that they obey his orders. The rest of her property was to be divided equally among Andrea, Giacomo, Francesco, Paulina, Morosina, and Lugretia. The girls who decided to enter a convent would lose their portions to Andrea; otherwise, they were free to do with them as they pleased.[133]

Gradually Andrea gained control of these properties as well. In 1605, after Gerolamo's death, Andrea's five remaining siblings signed a contract of division regarding territories in Polesine, Mira, and San Bruson; income from tax farming; and the houses whose rent paid for Sister Lugretia's pension. Gerolamo's share was divided by his brothers Andrea, Giacomo, and Francesco.[134] Giacomo, indebted to Andrea for five hundred ducats, sold his share to his oldest brother right away. Francesco, Paulina, and Morosina appointed Andrea as trustee and manager of their shares and all their mobile properties without asking for any interest payment until another legal settlement was found.[135] A contract that these three siblings signed in 1628 with Andrea's six remaining children was a further step in their gradual exclusion from the family patrimony. The parties agreed to sell a property in San Bruson held in common (of which Andrea's children owned six shares, his siblings three shares) for thirty-three hundred ducats. Part of the cash Paulina, Morosina, and Francesco received was immediately consumed by settling their debts to Giacomo's (illegitimate?) son Polo.[136]

Sister Lugretia seems to have been paid regularly until 1623. By 1627, however, the Morosini family owed 226 ducats to the convent.

The two spinster sisters had moved into the house in San Marcuola, whose rental income was assigned to Sister Lugretia. A contract of 1625 shows that Paulina and Morosina leased the house for 250 ducats yearly to Antonio Reniero. From then on, Lugretia's annuities were paid only partially and at irregular intervals.[137] In 1639, the children of Andrea Morosini claimed property rights on the house in San Marcuola as part of their mother's inheritance.[138] Francesco, the last of their paternal uncles who had previous rights on this house, had apparently just died. Their paternal aunts agreed—or were forced to agree—to sell their remaining shares in the house to their niece Paulina, daughter of Andrea.[139] These contracts were the last in a series of notarial documents tracing the gradual transfer of the properties Piero Morosini had distributed among all of his children to his firstborn son, Andrea, and his offspring.

In 1651, Sister Lugretia died, still creditor of some four hundred ducats. Because of her death, the second husband of Paulina Morosini (Lugretia's niece) ordered the renters of the house in San Marcuola to stop paying their rent to Corpus Domini. In 1654, Paulina's brother Pietro sued the convent after it officially requested the confiscation of the house, a decision affirmed in 1656.[140]

The litigation documents concerning the Morosini family's debts give insight into a classic—and apparently successful—case of accumulation and preservation of the family patrimony through entailment. Of Piero Morosini's seven surviving children, only the firstborn son married. None of his daughters got a dowry; Lugretia, orphaned at an early age, probably grew up in a convent before she took her vows. The two older sisters, who remained spinsters,[141] were even worse off than Lugretia, who was well provided for in a prestigious convent. Like their brothers, Paulina and Morosina eventually lost all their properties to Andrea.[142] Although Andrea profited enormously from being the universal heir and manager of his father's and his great-aunt's fortune, he himself does not seem to have entailed his patrimony. Since all of his four sons and two daughters got married, he apparently distributed his possessions evenly and without conditions—at least among his sons. Perhaps Andrea learned from experience that entailing patrimonies tears families apart.

Case Study 5: Excluding Women Only

The legal proceedings instituted by Sister Elena da Pesaro against her relatives reveal a strong tradition of monachizations within a politi-

Marin Pesaro
m. Lugretia

Alvise   Zuanne   Antonio   3 nuns   Giacomo   other
m. Isabetta Morosini   in San   daughters
(widow Contarini)   Lorenzo

Carlo Contarini   Andrianna
(from Isabetta's first marriage)   nun in San Lorenzo

Lugretia   **Elena**   Marino Cavaliere   Giacomo
m. Paolo Correr di Vettor   **nun in San**   (b. 1594)   (1598–1634)
(1602)   **Lorenzo**   m. Laura Giustinian
m. Bernardo Polani   (1622)
(1610)

Vettor Correr (b. 1605, exiled 1655)   Giacomo   Gerolamo
(from Lugretia's first marriage)

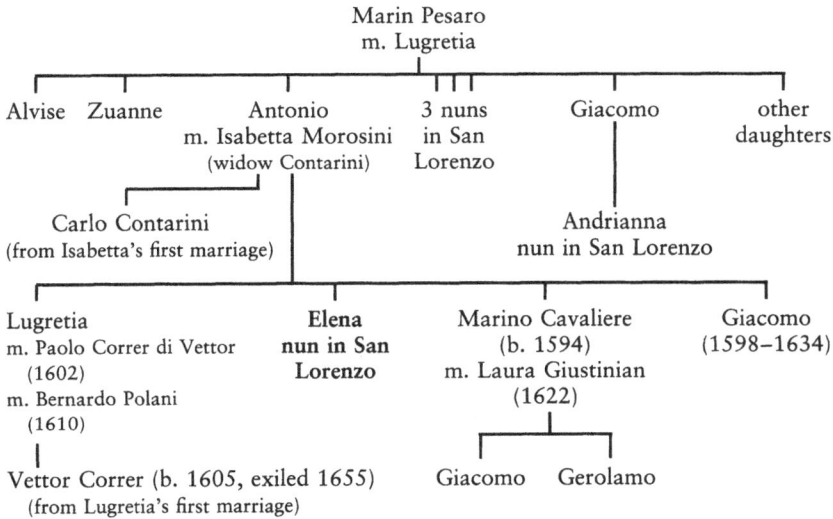

The family of Elena Pesaro

cally successful and wealthy family. Sister Elena was one of four children of Antonio Pesaro (son of Marin) and Isabetta Morosini, widow of Carlo Contarini. She had an older sister, Lugretia, who was supposed to have become a nun but married instead; a brother, Marino, who continued the family line by marrying Laura Giustinian di Giovan Battista; and another brother, Giacomo, who never married and died prematurely at age thirty-six.

Sister Elena's father, Antonio Pesaro, concluded her dowry contract in 1599; her annuity was to derive from a house in San Giovanni Decollato.[143] Three years earlier, he had given one thousand ducats to San Lorenzo as a spiritual dowry for Lugretia, who left the convent shortly thereafter and married Paolo Correr in 1602.[144] San Lorenzo functioned as an extended family for the female offspring of the Pesaro: in addition to Elena and her cousin Andrianna, three of the girls' paternal aunts were already living there.

Elena's family was the wealthiest among the families under consideration: according to the 1582 tax declaration of her grandfather Marin Pesaro,[145] his annual taxable income in cash amounted to 650 ducats, not counting large amounts of income in kind.[146] In his testament of 1581, Marin Pesaro mentioned that he had also been engaged—unsuccessfully—in long-distance trade. He encouraged his son-in-law, to whom he owed money, to sue the Pisani-Tiepolo bank for a recovery of one thousand ducats he had invested in a failed occidental voyage. His other debts were to be paid off by selling his ceremonial garments.[147] For "her servitude which she did in this house," his wife was to receive some land—the "jewel" of his patrimony—worth nine thousand ducats, as a restitution of her dowry. Since she had to bequeath this possession to their sons, however, his assignment was in reality a usufruct—qualitatively very different from the full restitution of a dowry, which a widow could usually dispose of as she wished.

The status of his family's women seemed fragile in general: Marin Pesaro encouraged his sons not to chase their mother out of their house, and explicitly stated that his married daughters, as well as his three daughters in San Lorenzo, would not receive a penny more than the dowries they had already been paid. Despite his frugality with regard to his wife and daughters, he did not put a *fidecommesso* on his property. His real estate was to be divided equally among his sons, his mobile properties among all his heirs.[148]

The formidable standing of the Pesaro family was displayed also by the dowry that Elena's mother, Isabetta Morosini, brought into her marriage with Antonio Pesaro in 1584: she gave him four thousand ducats in cash, furniture worth four hundred ducats, five hundred ducats in Monte Vecchio shares, and 130 fields in Vigiruol, in the territory of Padua.[149]

Like her father-in-law, Isabetta Morosini neglected her daughters financially in favor of her sons; in addition, she entailed her dowry. In 1617, she had temporarily given her entire dowry, worth eleven thousand ducats, to her sons. A year later, however, she demanded it back, along with the legacy her aunt Lugretia Pieggia had left her.[150] In her testament of 1631, she asked her daughter Lugretia to renounce the two thousand ducats she had promised her, because "the family is suffering from financial difficulties, as everybody knows," and "because I have sons." She appointed her son Marino as her universal heir, left nominal sums of four and three ducats annually to her daughter Elena and her niece Andrianna, respectively, and did not even mention the son from her first marriage, Carlo Contarini, or her last-born son, Giacomo.[151] Giacomo might have been dead by 1631. He died sometime before 1634, when Marino requested the official partitioning of his deceased brother's properties into three equal shares, of which he would get two, his sister Lugretia one.[152]

Lugretia was apparently the only one to leave Sister Elena some

Marin Pesaro
m. Lugretia

- Alvise
- Zuanne
- Antonio
  m. Isabetta Morosini
  (widow Contarini)
  - Carlo Contarini
    (from Isabetta's first marriage)
  - Lugretia
    m. Paolo Correr di Vettor
    (1602)
    m. Bernardo Polani
    (1610)
    - Vettor Correr (b. 1605, exiled 1655)
      (from Lugretia's first marriage)
  - **Elena
    nun in San
    Lorenzo**
  - Marino Cavaliere
    (b. 1594)
    m. Laura Giustinian
    (1622)
    - Giacomo
    - Gerolamo
  - Giacomo
    (1598–1634)
- 3 nuns in San Lorenzo
- Giacomo
  - Andrianna
    nun in San Lorenzo
- other daughters

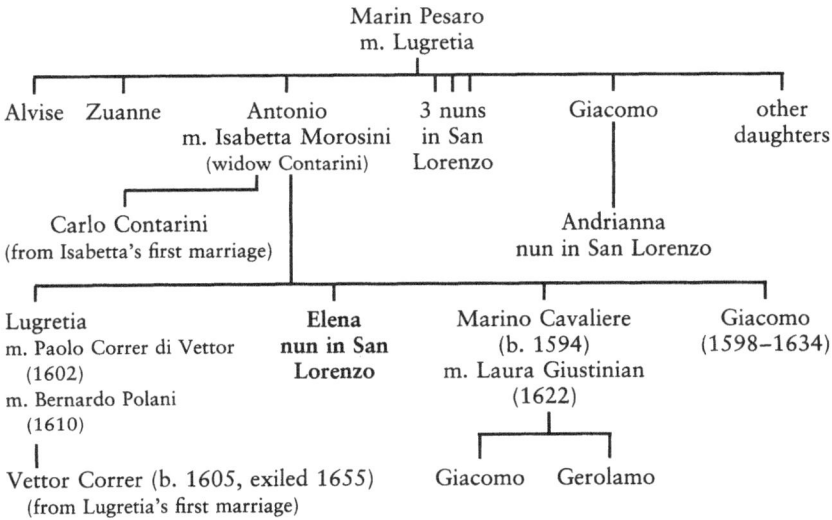

The family of Elena Pesaro

cally successful and wealthy family. Sister Elena was one of four children of Antonio Pesaro (son of Marin) and Isabetta Morosini, widow of Carlo Contarini. She had an older sister, Lugretia, who was supposed to have become a nun but married instead; a brother, Marino, who continued the family line by marrying Laura Giustinian di Giovan Battista; and another brother, Giacomo, who never married and died prematurely at age thirty-six.

Sister Elena's father, Antonio Pesaro, concluded her dowry contract in 1599; her annuity was to derive from a house in San Giovanni Decollato.[143] Three years earlier, he had given one thousand ducats to San Lorenzo as a spiritual dowry for Lugretia, who left the convent shortly thereafter and married Paolo Correr in 1602.[144] San Lorenzo functioned as an extended family for the female offspring of the Pesaro: in addition to Elena and her cousin Andrianna, three of the girls' paternal aunts were already living there.

Elena's family was the wealthiest among the families under consideration: according to the 1582 tax declaration of her grandfather Marin Pesaro,[145] his annual taxable income in cash amounted to 650 ducats, not counting large amounts of income in kind.[146] In his testament of 1581, Marin Pesaro mentioned that he had also been engaged—unsuccessfully—in long-distance trade. He encouraged his son-in-law, to whom he owed money, to sue the Pisani-Tiepolo bank for a recovery of one thousand ducats he had invested in a failed occidental voyage. His other debts were to be paid off by selling his ceremonial garments.[147] For "her servitude which she did in this house," his wife was to receive some land—the "jewel" of his patrimony—worth nine thousand ducats, as a restitution of her dowry. Since she had to bequeath this possession to their sons, however, his assignment was in reality a usufruct—qualitatively very different from the full restitution of a dowry, which a widow could usually dispose of as she wished.

The status of his family's women seemed fragile in general: Marin Pesaro encouraged his sons not to chase their mother out of their house, and explicitly stated that his married daughters, as well as his three daughters in San Lorenzo, would not receive a penny more than the dowries they had already been paid. Despite his frugality with regard to his wife and daughters, he did not put a fidecommesso on his property. His real estate was to be divided equally among his sons, his mobile properties among all his heirs.[148]

The formidable standing of the Pesaro family was displayed also by the dowry that Elena's mother, Isabetta Morosini, brought into her marriage with Antonio Pesaro in 1584: she gave him four thousand ducats in cash, furniture worth four hundred ducats, five hundred ducats in Monte Vecchio shares, and 130 fields in Vigiruol, in the territory of Padua.[149]

Like her father-in-law, Isabetta Morosini neglected her daughters financially in favor of her sons; in addition, she entailed her dowry. In 1617, she had temporarily given her entire dowry, worth eleven thousand ducats, to her sons. A year later, however, she demanded it back, along with the legacy her aunt Lugretia Pieggia had left her.[150] In her testament of 1631, she asked her daughter Lugretia to renounce the two thousand ducats she had promised her, because "the family is suffering from financial difficulties, as everybody knows," and "because I have sons." She appointed her son Marino as her universal heir, left nominal sums of four and three ducats annually to her daughter Elena and her niece Andrianna, respectively, and did not even mention the son from her first marriage, Carlo Contarini, or her last-born son, Giacomo.[151] Giacomo might have been dead by 1631. He died sometime before 1634, when Marino requested the official partitioning of his deceased brother's properties into three equal shares, of which he would get two, his sister Lugretia one.[152]

Lugretia was apparently the only one to leave Sister Elena some money. In her testament of 1639, she bequeathed her twenty ducats annually—a legacy the nun never received.[153] To make matters worse, Elena's annuity payments ceased. In 1650, San Lorenzo demanded the payment of outstanding debts.[154] Marino Pesaro, as the remaining heir, refuted this claim; instead, he demanded a payment of five hundred ducats from the convent, claiming that it had never returned the thousand ducats his father had paid for Lugretia, the sister who left the convent before taking holy vows.[155] Four years later, the convent magistrate decided the case in favor of San Lorenzo, creditor of eleven hundred ducats. The inheritance of Antonio Pesaro and Isabetta Morosini was to be confiscated for the purpose of paying off Marino's debts.[156] Two years later, a convent magistrate claimed several possessions from the inheritance of Antonio Pesaro for the liquidation of the convent's credits—which meant in practice that the farmers on the family's land were now obliged to pay their annual rents to San Lorenzo.[157] But the farmers refused to do so, so that other ways of accommodating the convent's claims had to be found.[158] In the meantime, Lugretia Pesaro's son Vettor Correr was exiled from Venice for fraud.[159] Vettor owed Sister Elena money as well: 280 ducats, a debt deriving from his mother's legacy to Elena of twenty ducats annually. After Vettor's ban, his son Paolo was made responsible for liquidating this debt.[160]

Marino Pesaro's social status was apparently incompatible with his taking the decisions of the convent magistrate seriously. Instead, he appealed directly to the doge for liberation from what were, in his eyes, the convent's unjust claims. However, the government affirmed the magistrate's decision, and Marino was forced to apologize publicly for the bad impression he had made in rejecting the convent's justified demands.[161] In 1665, twenty-eight fields in Villa di Gorzo were sold in a public auction for the liquidation of Marino Pesaro's debts.[162] That same year, Sister Elena died. In 1666, sixteen additional fields in Gorzo and ninety fields in Villa di Tarasta were confiscated for the payment of the rest of the debts, which by now amounted to 2,775 ducats.[163] Finally, Marino's sons Giacomo and Gerolamo asked for an informal settlement of the case. They offered to pay five hundred ducats in cash right away, the rest in annual installments of eighty ducats.[164]

Thus a painful lawsuit was brought to an end. It showed how in a prestigious, fairly rich, and politically successful family, patrimonies were protected by rigidly excluding women. Although the dowries of his daughters and of his granddaughter Lugretia could well have been high, Isabetta Morosini's canceling of Lugretia's inheritance in favor of her brother indicates a strong commitment to agnatic entailment. Marino's incomprehensible refusal to pay his sister's convent pension also hints in this direction; financial problems as such could not have played a role, since his sons agreed to settle the affair immediately in 1666. In appealing to the doge, he only embarrassed himself publicly. We will never know the motivation for his obstinate behavior: he might have been anticlerical, or found the convent settlement too high, or hated Sister Elena; or perhaps he was just a snob. No matter what his precise reasons might have been, they were certainly shaped by the prevailing assumption among the Pesaro that fathers and sons were the rightful owners and heirs of the family patrimony and that daughters' inheritance rights had to be curtailed as much as possible.

Frugality or Waste? The Patricians' Dilemma of Reproducing the Body Politic

As the case studies of the lawsuits by Sister Lugretia Morosini and Sister Elena Pesaro demonstrate, nuns—whether they were "involuntary" or not—cannot be regarded as the only victims of a patriarchal family economy: widows fighting for their dowries, unaccommodated spinster daughters, and disinherited brothers were equally subject to the mechanism of exclusion prevailing in the patriciate's reproduction patterns around 1600. Therefore, the perception of nuns as the ultimate victims of Machiavellian fathers' economic greed has limited explanatory power as a category of historical analysis, in spite of the undeniably tragic quality of forced monachizations. Coerced monachizations, the dowry system, and entailment strategies were inseparable components of the patriciate's restricted reproduction patterns,[165] and as such they were social practices of economic and political significance. They acquired their meaning from cultural constraints requiring the patriciate to maintain the genealogical purity of its class as a prime source of prestige and power. Each of the three components functioned in the context of the other two; all of them ultimately derived from agnatic inheritance patterns designed to preserve the family patrimony for legitimate male heirs. The extent to which these practices did indeed promote frugality is, however, debatable. My hypothesis is that restricted marriage and inheritance patterns functioned like a prisoners' dilemma.[166] They were of short-term advantage to individual families' patrimonies but of long-term damage to the body politic as a whole. The withdrawal of women from the marriage market has to be seen as part of a multifaceted phenomenon that defies any one-dimensional explanation.

The endogamous, competitive, and reciprocal exchange of women and dowries was an important way of circulating wealth among noble families, while the entailment of patrimonies guaranteed the safe transfer of accumulated capital to subsequent generations within one family.[167] Patrician marriage patterns were designed to preserve the exclusivity of the ruling class, to perpetuate the "purity" of its blood, and to limit the circulation of its capital within the elite. Yet the endogamous exchange of brides, as the nobility's primary form of conspicuous consumption, did not only foster cohesiveness within the body politic. Given the built-in competitiveness of the dowry system, it was also an instrument of upward social mobility.[168] Since patrician status was defined by agnatic descent, the endogamous marriage pattern excluded unworthy grooms from elite families among which brides circulated, but it also offered an opportunity for highly endowed daughters of social climbers to enter top families threatened by impoverishment. Although prestige was ultimately determined genealogically, female hypergamy flourished because aristocratic honor had to be displayed by conspicuous spending and consumption habits. Dowry inflation was therefore the result of rich brides' hypergamy and the resistance of ancient families against it.[169] By promoting social mobility, the competitive dowry system served to circulate money among the upper classes while also fostering and increasing the gap between wealthy and impoverished families among the patriciate.[170]

The increasing social differentiation by wealth among the patriciate was perceived as a serious problem by politicians, who usually blamed dowry inflation for eroding the cohesiveness of the body politic.[171] Vettor Sandi, a Venetian historian writing in the eighteenth century, was of the opinion that in the sixteenth century, a "considerable crowding of evils derived from the . . . excessively large dowries given to women when marrying them off." The bad consequences were, among others,

> The serious damage done to the families from which the women leave; the incapacity of many [families] to marry their daughters because of the excessive dowries given to women of equal or inferior status . . . the pressure [to engage in] exorbitant expenditure for luxury items on those families who receive excessively endowed women whose hearts— because of the natural arrogance of this sex—are pierced by the arrows

of high dowries; the fatal ruin of the families who receive them, because when these wives are widowed, lawsuits almost always arise for the restitution of the dowries, which have to be given back entirely, since Venetian law allows women to bequeath their dowries also to strangers, that is, to persons of their [the women's] descent, diminished only by the husband's expenses for the counter-trousseau *[corredo]*.[172]

In Sandi's view, women's high dowries jeopardized both their fathers' families when they married and their husbands' families when they were widowed. Inflated dowries corrupted the dowry system, which had been instituted to preserve, not squander, patrimonies. Because of the "natural arrogance of this sex," women not only demanded large dowries from their fathers, but forced their husbands to match the "gift" they were bringing into their families by spending exorbitant amounts of money for luxurious countergifts. And, once widowed, women would finally ruin their husbands' families by retracting their dowries from their children's estate and bequeathing them to their own kin, that is, "strangers." Sandi bitterly concluded: "Truly rare are those cases . . . in which a rich dowry provides relief for families, because once the ready money is consumed, the burden remains . . . to pay it back with interest."[173]

In contrast to Sandi, who in the eighteenth century identified women's abuse of the dowry system as one of the prime causes of Venice's decline and degradation over the previous two centuries, observers in the sixteenth century still hoped to find a remedy for what they perceived as the devastating effects of inflated dowries and women's subsequent economic power. Lodovico Dolce, for example, one of Venice's most prolific authors on issues of gender, insisted that a woman's chastity and virtue were the most precious treasures she could possibly possess, while her dowry should irrevocably belong to her husband: "But the prudent wife should not think that the dowry, the money, the beauty, the nobility, or related things that she brings into the house of her husband belong to her; only the honesty, the chastity, the goodness, the virtue, the obedience, the diligence in running a household, and similar treasures [belong to her], by which, if she has them in abundance, she is richly endowed of every good."[174]

The perfect woman according to Dolce was dispossessed not only of her dowry, but of her beauty and nobility as well. In Aristotelian fashion, Dolce interpreted a woman's beauty and prestigious ancestry not as intrinsic characteristics, but as paternal qualities merely attached to her person. Like a high dowry, they were her father's markers of her body's worth. A girl's beauty and nobility belonged to the men between whom she was exchanged; they were qualities enhancing her father's prestige in giving her away and her husband's prestige in receiving her. "The wife has no power over her body: it is entirely in the power of her husband," Lodovico affirmed.[175] A woman could claim ownership only of those "treasures" that were the opposite of the riches her men were so proud of: modesty, obedience, and chastity.

The celebration of a wedding was a prime event for engaging in conspicuous consumption; therefore, a bride's beauty, prestige, and dowry were important attributes for the public display of patrician families' wealth and status. Since the very concept of "nobility" was defined genealogically and circularly, that is, by the "noble" marriage and descent of one's parents, wedding celebrations were crucial in displaying and reaffirming the nobility of the bride's and groom's families. Without the reciprocal exchange of women, Venetian patricians could neither claim nor represent their newly fashioned status as noblemen of quasi-feudal habits.[176]

According to Francesco Sansovino, a sixteenth-century writer and expert in matters of aristocratic self-fashioning and Venetian mythology, the conspicuous display of a bride was at the core of a patrician wedding. After signing the marriage contract—that is, after agreeing on the dowry and countergifts—the bride was presented to the groom and his male relatives and friends in her father's house:

> After the marriage is settled by a third party, . . . the groom—without having seen the girl—goes . . . to the Government Palace, where the marriage is registered. . . . Then the friends are invited to the house of the bride's father, . . . where the Avogadori [state attorneys], and the Savi, and the Capi del Consiglio de Dieci [all major government officials] . . . go to enjoy themselves. . . . As soon as they are seated in the *sala* [main hall], where one sees nobody but men, the Paraninfo [master of dance and ceremonies] leads the bride out of a room, dressed, according to an ancient custom, in white, her hair falling down to her shoulders, embellished with golden threads. After pronouncing the nuptial vows, she is conducted all over the *sala,* accompanied by the sound of flutes, trombones, and other harmonic instruments, gracefully dancing and bowing to the guests. After having been presented in this manner and seen by everybody, she retires.[177]

While the bride, gracefully dancing under the gaze of an exclusively male spectatorship, displays her beautiful and precious body, she reconstitutes the prestige and nobility of the two families between whom she is exchanged. Aristocratic weddings were frequently discussed in treatises on nobility, with respect to their function of marking the social status of the two families through the exchange of women between them. Lodovico Domenichi, for example, discussed "femininity" and "nobility" in terms of each other; he praised women as more "noble" than men and emphasized that "nobility" was most importantly represented by the conspicuous exchange of beautiful (and noble) women. The "royal and sumptuous wedding" of the Marchese Sforza with Francesca Sforza, his "most beautiful and lovely" bride, provided the setting for Domenichi's Neoplatonic treatise *La Nobiltà delle Donne* (The nobility of women; 1551). While a "beautiful and rare couple is joined in matrimony," the interlocutors feast on a "magnificent dinner, a royal banquet"; afterward, they casually gather, led by the bride's mother, to converse about the worth and value of women.[178]

Giuseppe Passi, on the other hand, a bluntly misogynist author of Aristotelian imprint, ridiculed the conspicuous consumption of luxury goods as one of the many "feminine defects" that his book, published in 1601, lists in great detail. "If a woman marries, and is endowed with five hundred scudi, she spends six hundred on dresses, jewelry, and embellishments; and . . . because women have a natural craving for splendor, they are never sufficiently adorned."[179] Like Vettor Sandi in the eighteenth century, Passi attributed dowry inflation as well as the ruinous spending habits of the upper classes to women's insatiable vanity—a theme taken up also by Francesco Buoninsegni. Buoninsegni's satire *Contro 'l Lusso Donnesco* (Against the luxury of women; 1644) was published together with an *Antisatira* by Sister Arcangela Tarabotti, in which she defended women's delight in luxury items as compensation for a lack of true affection on the part of their husbands, whom they provided with a high dowry:

> All these complaints of married men [about women's spending habits] are mere nonsense, even slander by those who, after having obtained a rich dowry with artful means, refuse to make the necessary expenditure for those [women] who have shown themselves to be precious things by bringing with them an abundance of treasures; all the more so since [the same men], before they achieved their aim of marrying them, professed to desire and love them, and now want them to dress in the manner of our first mother, in order to squander their money even more generously on prostitutes. This is where men's deafening complaints about women's dressing and pomp come from.[180]

All of the authors cited agreed that the squandering of treasures was at the core of a patrician marriage, although their opinions as to how to evaluate this fact differed: Domenichi suggested that money spent on women displayed the nobility of the spender, while Passi, Buoninsegni, and Sandi declared conspicuous consumption to be a female vice with ruinous consequences to agnatically organized families. Tarabotti agreed with her misogynist opponents in criticizing the dowry system as such, but located the vice of luxurious waste in men. Dolce proposed to strengthen men's eroding authority by stripping women of their nobility and riches, and thereby turn into legitimate ownership what otherwise would have been waste. Everybody seemed to have been of the opinion that by the sixteenth century, the dowry system had exceeded its original function of instituting agnatic inheritance patterns and preserving individual families' patrimonies. It was perceived that the patriciate's marriage practices had become a danger to the body politic as a whole, since more and more patrician families were unable to engage in "aristocratic" consumption habits. Rich and hypergamous social climbers threatened to diversify the social composition of the ruling class, a theoretically egalitarian and homogeneous body. While many contemporary writers held women responsible for turning patrician weddings into a major battleground of sumptuous spending, the patriciate itself tried to find pragmatic ways of mitigating the harmful effects of wasting its resources.

Monachization and entailment strategies were intended to preserve and consolidate individual family fortunes in the context of dowry inflation and shrinking economic opportunities. They aimed to restrict the number of marriages of both sons and daughters; too many dowries and too many future male heirs threatened to dissipate even large family fortunes. In his seminal study *The Decline of the Venetian Nobility as a Ruling Class,* James Cushman Davis paraphrased the explanation given by Giovan Antonio Muazzo, a Venetian nobleman, of the reproduction patterns of his class in 1680:

> The custom of only one of a group of brothers marrying was introduced in the latter half of the sixteenth century as a means of keeping a family rich even when its income had declined. After Western nations had cut into Venetian commerce with the East . . . the nobility saw that it was difficult to become rich in trade and turned to landholding on the Venetian mainland. Even though land provided a fairly sure income, the returns were smaller than those provided by trade. Unable to increase their wealth, the families elected to decrease their size.[181]

According to Muazzo, restricted inheritance became an attractive means to accumulate capital while the patriciate shifted from mercantile activities to landed investments and money lending. In a period when long-distance trade was struck by recurrent crises, investments in land, *livelli*,[182] and state funds were essential in preserving the nobility's wealth.[183] Some families profited enormously from agricultural investments by accumulating huge landed estates in the sixteenth century that served as a power base for centuries to come.[184] They represented what Gaetano Cozzi has called a new type of nobility, emerging from the dialectic encounter between the mercantile patriciate of Venice and the feudal aristocracy of the *terraferma* in the sixteenth century.[185]

But most noble families did not adapt as rapidly to the exigencies of an economy in transition. Landed investments accelerated the concentration of wealth among a small elite and contributed to widening the gap between the very rich and the "shamefully poor" among the patriciate.[186] In contrast to international sea trade—a risky but lucrative business that small capital holders could also successfully engage in—landed investments offered fewer possibilities for impoverished patrician families to improve their condition; agriculture offered profitable investment opportunities mainly for already-accumulated capital. Properties in the form of real estate and land had the advantage of a guaranteed return (except in years of bad harvest), but land was a limited resource, and income deriving from agriculture was certainly lower than the profits previously earned in sea trade. The government was aware of these problems and tried to revitalize trade in the hope of luring patricians back into commercial activities—but without much success.[187]

Although they were constructive responses to a mercantile economy in crisis, the patriciate's new investment patterns had damaging political side effects in the long run. Entailment strategies served to protect individual patrimonies from disintegrating in a period of economic instability; yet contemporaries as well as modern historians suggested that they contributed to a contraction of the marriage market and to the numerical decline of the patriciate.[188] Giovanni Botero was, to my knowledge, the first to warn of the ongoing demographic erosion of the body politic. In his *Relatione della Republica venetiana* (Report on the Venetian Republic; 1605), he pointed out that "the number of noblemen reached forty-five hundred in the beginning, but hardly comes to three thousand today, as many families have become extinct."[189] This was a fatal development. In his view, population growth was one of the factors by which to measure the power of cities and states. The numerical decline of the patriciate had politically destabiliz-

ing effects, since it threatened to subvert the system of political representation; after all, the nobility physically embodied the republic's
constitution.[190] Within a couple of generations, a shrinking patrician
electorate rendered the rather intricate system of election procedures
dysfunctional. This was a serious problem, given the crucial significance that Venetian political theorists such as Gasparo Contarini had
attributed to the republic's "well-balanced" system of lot drawing,
bottom-up elections, and top-down choices, all of which required a
considerable number of candidates and voters for each of the numerous, semiannual election procedures.[191] In addition, the disintegration
of the patriciate seemed to tangibly represent the irrevocable decline
of the Venetian empire, because of the intricate connection between
governing elite and political system that theorists and propagandists
of earlier times had so proudly proclaimed. Faced with these problems,
the government decided to add eighty-two families (citizens and aristocrats from the *terraferma*) to the Venetian patriciate for the price of
100,000 ducats each, starting in 1646; this was also a way to finance
the War of Crete (1645–69). Thus the Senate planned to replenish the
defense budget as well as the ranks of the Great Council. Far from
recuperating its mythical unity and purity, however, the nobility, already torn by inner differences and weakened by the extinction of
prestigious families, became—in the opinion of contemporaries—a
"monstrous" and "grotesque" body once its virgin-like enclosure was
violated (see chapter 2).[192]

This demographic trend shows that the patriciate's complex reproduction patterns were caught between the mutually exclusive demands
of economy and politics: successful in preserving individual families'
wealth in times of shrinking economic opportunities, *fidecommessi*
and monachizations squandered the nobility's reproductive capacities.
The dowry system exceeded its original function of protecting agnatic
inheritance once it became closely linked to the patriciate's increasingly exorbitant consumption habits. Dowry inflation promoted wom-
en's social mobility through hypergamy; it also accelerated the concentration of wealth within a small elite that was eager to protect its
exclusivity against newcomers by raising dowries even further. By fostering social differentiation among the patriciate, inflated dowries and
entailment strategies ultimately helped to undermine the mythical homogeneity and cohesiveness of the body politic.[193] Thus, the rapid decline of patrician marriages and births can be seen as a direct effect
of the patriciate's combined reproduction patterns, that is, entailment

strategies, high monachization rates, and inflated dowries. The nobility's demographic decline was a result of practices deriving from cultural constraints that pressured the patriciate to reproduce itself in and as an enclosed and hierarchical system—practices that, in the context of contracting economic opportunities, developed a self-destructive dynamic.

The nobility's strategies for preserving wealth were thus inherently wasteful; although the entailment of patrimonies was a means of thrift, it served to accumulate capital to be spent on inflated dowries, among other things. Saving and squandering went hand in hand: the aristocracy's conspicuous consumption habits were expensive and required large patrimonies. Ultimately, the discrepancy between the economic constraints of individual families and the sociocultural and political demands of a republican ruling class undermined the patriciate's strategies to reproduce itself in and as an enclosed system. Among patricians, the price of frugality was high.

The Potlatch

The increasing rate of patrician monachizations around 1600 was certainly the most conspicuous symptom of the patriciate's restricted inheritance and reproduction patterns, which preserved wealth by squandering human resources. Contemporaries were unable to solve this dilemma: they unanimously perceived the depositing of daughters in convents as a measure of frugality, but complained about the injustice and ostensible irrationality of wasting innocent women's lives. The fictive juxtaposition of "involuntary nuns" with their "lucky sisters" was a rhetorical device that couched a disturbing dilemma in melodramatic terms; it was a way of rendering a paradox intelligible. Although monachization rates were not directly—or not exclusively—linked to the economic constraints of inflated dowries, the commonplace assumption among contemporaries that there was such a linkage hints at a possible clarification of the issue while simultaneously obfuscating it. Arcangela Tarabotti, for example, was wrong in assuming that coerced monachizations had the prime function of mitigating the financial constraints faced by individual families as a result of dowry inflation. Yet she was right in suggesting an intimate connection between dowry inflation and monachizations as components of the patriciate's restricted marriage behavior.

In my view, inflated dowries and high monachization rates were connected in that they constituted complementary parts of the patriciate's most conspicuous form of consumption: the competitive exchange of women. The endogamous exchange of women, as well as the withdrawal of girls from circulation, assumed their financial significance as essential parts of the patriciate's economy of honor and prestige. Sixteenth-century observers writing on issues related to gender, such as Dolce and Domenichi, conceived the dowry as a monetary marker of the bride's precious noble body; a high dowry signified, though did not constitute, the prestige of the couple's families.[194]

In contrast to contemporaries' apologetic explanations of monachization strategies as a necessary means of containing costs, as a Machiavellian practice justified by the patriciate's *ragion di stato*, "involuntary nuns" should be seen as the result of an inherently wasteful, self-destructive, and "irrational" phenomenon. If, in Mauss's terms, the most highly developed and most noble form of competitive gift-giving is the conspicuous destruction of wealth, the ritual waste of patrician women's reproductive capacities can be seen as a potlatch.[195] According to Mauss, in gift-giving societies prestige is challenged and maintained by returning gifts "with interest." Competitive gift-giving is a domesticated form of aggression; it is a mechanism of exclusion, offering at the same time limited opportunities for advancement and integration. Following Lévi-Strauss, Gayle Rubin has argued that the exchange of women and dowries is the most fundamental system of competitive gift-giving.[196] The Venetian patriciate's endogamous and competitive circulation of women can be seen as such a system of reciprocal gift-giving, in which aristocratic spending and reproduction habits were practiced by returning women "with interest."

Christine Klapisch-Zuber was the first to investigate how Renaissance upper-class marriage systems fulfilled the necessary condition of reciprocity. In her opinion, a husband's countergift functioned symbolically as a counterweight to the dowry.[197] In my view, the reciprocity of the system has to be sought elsewhere, since marital countergifts never even pretended to equal the value of bridal dowries. The reciprocity—that is, the promise of a return of gifts of equal or higher value—was constituted by receiving daughters-in-law and their dowries through the future marriages of sons and grandsons. Every wedding carried the notion of credit, of an investment expected to bear fruit in future times. Only if dowries were assumed to be returned "with interest" in future generations did dowry inflation and endogamous marriage patterns make economic sense in an agnatic inheritance system.

Any withdrawal of women from circulation in the marriage market had the effect of temporarily suspending the law of reciprocity and equal exchange that usually governed the transfer of gifts. If the sole function of a gift is to be returned, the conspicuous "destruction" of a daughter by fixing her destiny as a nun signaled either that she could not be expected to be replaced by a future daughter-in-law of equivalent value (because her prestige and wealth were too high), or that she could not return the value of an existing daughter-in-law (because her prestige and wealth were too low). In other words: patrician nuns did not necessarily enter convents because they did not have appropriate dowries, but because they could not find appropriate grooms. A marriage could not take place if a girl was too valuable or not valuable enough.[198] The key to understanding the pressure to destroy "inappropriate" gifts lies in analyzing the political and cultural meaning of a "proper" match.

The case of the Cornaro girls, documented in 1684 by the anonymous author of a manuscript entitled *Distinzioni segreti che corrono tra le Casate Nobili di Venezia* (Secret distinctions among the noble families of Venice), might offer a first clue. "Some families practice the custom of the most sublime princes, that is, to give or take women only from their own blood," were the opening lines of the author's digression on the marriage practices of some illustrious Venetian families. As the anonymous observer reports, Procurator Cornaro della Casa grande di San Maurizio, who was the Venetian ambassador to Emperor Leopold, had recently married his three daughters to close relatives, two of them blood kin; and one of his sisters had finally agreed to marry an "outsider," a nephew of the deceased Doge Sagredo, although she had originally insisted on entering a convent, as her sister had. The account continues:

> And when I investigated whether her monachization was [due to] true vocation, an informed person told me confidentially that she wanted to enter a convent to avoid suffering a man's dominance, because she only found men who merited nothing more than to serve her. . . . And the other sister, who was already destined to celibacy, declared with feminine inconstancy that she wanted to marry, news that seemed strange to her brothers, who already believed themselves to be exempt from the obligation of this dowry; but when confronted with the decision of their sister, they assigned her 30,000 ducats . . . and gave her to the nephew

of Doge Sagredo, who did not even care for any . . . dowry, knowing and admitting the superiority of [her] blood.[199]

As the high dowry amount indicates, financial problems did not shape the Cornaro girls' wish to enter a convent. Rather, they were aware that no other family could reciprocate a gift as precious as that of their blood and bodies. Given the uncontested superiority of their family's prestige, the marriage of a Cornaro woman to anyone but a Cornaro man would be a misalliance. The offer of the procurator's sister was a gift extraordinary enough to theoretically subvert the logic of conspicuous consumption patterns: as the groom declared, his bride's descent was a treasure precious enough to replace the money that usually indicated rank and prestige. (Practically, of course, this was unthinkable; no family could "afford" to marry a daughter without publicly demonstrating her worth in cash value.)

When interpreted as a recognition of the impossibility of properly reciprocating any gift given *or* taken, monachizations of daughters from less illustrious families can also be perceived as a potlatch. As we will see in case study 6, an impoverished but equally illustrious branch of the Corner family had to "waste" their daughters' bodies just as their rich cousins, the Cornaro, had. While their sons capitalized on their prestigious family name by attracting hypergamous brides, their daughters had to either withdraw from circulation or else marry downward. Theirs was the classic case of patrician girls who lacked dowries commensurate with their status. This case also illustrates that the real problem behind dowry inflation was not the rise in expenditures for weddings, but, as Vettor Sandi said, "the incapacity of many [families] to marry their daughters because of the excessive dowries given to women *of equal or inferior status*" (my emphasis). In his report on Venetian-Roman relations at the end of the sixteenth century, Nuncio Alberto Bolognetti also explained that many patrician women were forced to enter convents by their fathers, who, "lacking the necessary means, [are] unable to marry them to their peers, and *unwilling to marry them to inferiors* in order to not diminish the splendor of their families" (my emphasis).[200] Similarly, the "involuntary nun" of Baltassare Sultanini's libertine novel *Il novo parlatorio delle monache* (The new parlor of nuns; 1677) complained that "the policy of my father required that I come to this place to be safe . . . because his birth and his ambition did not allow him to marry me to a person of unequal condition."[201] In contrast, a contemporary of Sultanini, the anonymous author of the *Discorso aristocratico sopra il governo de'*

Signori Venetiani (Aristocratic discourse on the government of the Venetian gentlemen; 1675), proposed that "one could prevent many evils and lamentations if one agreed to degrade poor noblewomen by giving them to rich citizens, as is common practice for needy noblemen, who gladly take opulent commoner brides."[202] His remarks suggest that in the second half of the seventeenth century, female misalliances slowly began to be accepted as a remedy for both coerced monachizations and inflated dowries.[203]

It was thus the discrepancy between a girl's prestige and the measurable marker of her worth that made many patrician women and their families choose the convent option. Balance sheets of incoming and outgoing dowries show that families sought to match the size of dowries given and received if the brides were of equal standing. Alexander F. Cowan interprets the fact that a certain branch of the Tiepolo family steadily offered and received the flat amount of forty thousand ducats as "a strong indication of their position among the highest-ranking families of the patriciate."[204] The rapid increase in status of social climbers such as the Pisani dal Banco and Moretta is also reflected in dowry amounts: both families offered higher dowries than they received until roughly the end of the sixteenth century, when they seem to have gained permanent access to the most prestigious women of the elite. Afterward, the balance between incoming and outgoing dowries stabilized at the top level of forty to fifty thousand ducats.[205] In contrast, a branch of the Contarini family seems to have capitalized on their ancient descent and attracted hypergamous brides for many generations. The value of the dowries paid to Contarini daughters was only five-eighths of what Contarini men received from their wives between the end of the sixteenth and the middle of the eighteenth centuries. Given this considerable discrepancy, it is likely that Contarini girls married into families of lesser prestige.[206]

According to Mauss, the custom of returning a gift "with interest" was an effect of the competition for power among the elite. The patricians' increasing complaints about dowry inflation show that the nobility was unable to reconcile its image as a homogeneous and cohesive body politic with the differentiating effects of dowry inflation. A republican body politic was supposedly egalitarian; its prestige and the legitimacy of its rule rested upon the assumption that every single member of the Great Council was endowed with special qualities and virtues that nonpatricians lacked. In this sense, every patrician bride was ideally of equal value. The gift-giving patterns of a republican ruling class should have required that received goods be reciprocated with items of equal value. Sumptuary laws, particularly the continual but unsuccessful efforts to define a legal maximum for dowries, can only be understood under this premise. In practice, however, Venetian patricians did return gifts "with interest," thereby accelerating the social differentiation within their class. The patriciate's competitive and restricted marriage patterns not only distinguished the nobility as a separate caste, but reflected and established a ranking system of power and prestige among noblemen themselves.[207]

Since a gift could not be exchanged for an item of lower value, a girl's inappropriately low dowry could potentially have been compensated for by the prestige of her family. Many families, however, avoided marrying their daughters if they were not able to display their intrinsic worth in cash value. Women did not own their nobility or prestigious descent, as Dolce declared; since they could not raise the status of their husbands, poorly endowed girls of illustrious descent were not necessarily a good match. Nonpatrician men who married "up" could not expect to gain anything except wives endowed with a bothersome feeling of superiority; and patrician fathers offering their daughters to commoners squandered their credit on unworthy sons-in-law unable to pay a proper return on the gifts they received. Ideally, patrician marriages were well-balanced, contracted either between equals or between hypergamous wives and impoverished noblemen of prestigious descent; neither bride nor groom was supposed to sink in status. Frequently, however, the marriage market did not offer the opportunity for a well-balanced match: a family's prestige and wealth could be too high to find an appropriate groom; a prestigious family of modest means might refuse to marry their daughters downward; a rich family of little prestige had to compensate for their daughters' relatively low social status by inflating their dowries; a poor family without any special merit might try to upgrade their daughters' status by sending them to a convent.

The inability to reciprocate the gift of a bride "properly" with a bride of equal or higher prestige and wealth revealed inadmissible imbalances within the republic's supposedly homogeneous body politic and threatened to paralyze the system of endogamous circulation. The potlatch offered a solution. Any impasse resulting from the discrepancy between alleged status and available dowries could be smoothly resolved by removing unreciprocable women from circulation. Those women who could not function as gifts were conspicuously sacrificed to their celestial groom in a religious ceremony, by engaging them in yet another form of bridal exchange (see chapter 3). Only a formal monachization procedure could disperse the embarrassment resulting from a gift-giving system in paralysis without tarnishing a family's honor; keeping spinster daughters at home did not have the same social and symbolic significance.

The exorbitant number of nuns among patrician women between 1550 and 1650 was thus a phenomenon of high political significance. Without the possibility of withdrawing women honorably from the marriage market, the fragile system of balances within an extremely differentiated and enclosed elite could not have been sustained. What remains to be explained is the fact that contemporaries and generations of historians alike have persisted in causally linking dowry inflation to involuntary monachizations. My hypothesis is that the structural wastefulness of conspicuous consumption and the self-destructive elements of the patriciate's reproduction patterns could not be revealed without threatening the system with collapse. The waste of necessary resources was at the core of the patriciate's strategies of self-preservation—an unresolvable paradox, unintelligible for contemporaries who struggled to resolve the dilemma without risking destabilization of the social order.[208] By insisting that dowry inflation caused coerced monachizations, writers of the time misrepresented the phenomenon as a "women's issue," thereby camouflaging the fact that both problems derived from the competitive and endogamous exchange of women under agnatic inheritance laws. By turning women into scapegoats, contemporaries avoided looking too closely at the source of the problem, while they simultaneously drew attention to it through the very mechanism they applied to obscure it. Among all the contemporary writers to ponder the question, only Arcangela Tarabotti came close to answering it, with her uncompromising critique of the "paternal tyranny" that in her eyes had perverted all moral values.

The following two case studies show in greater detail how a potlatch served to avoid mismatches between girls of prestigious but impoverished families and men of lower status.

Case Study 6: High Prestige and Poverty

In contrast to the sisters and daughters of Procurator Cornaro, whose combined wealth and prestige reduced their chances to marry honorably, the two daughters of Giacomo Corner and Chiara Morosini faced the problem of lacking dowries commensurate with their pre-

Giovanni Corner di Marco (d. 1582)
m. Cecilia Corner di Gerolamo
(1553)

Marco	Gerolamo	Giacomo	Nicolò	Fantino
(b. 1553)	(b. 1558)	(b. 1559)	(b. 1560)	(b. 1563)

m. Chiara Morosini di Piero

Cornelia	Marco	Isabetta	Gerolamo	Giovanni	Piero
(b. 1586)	(b. 1591)	(b. 1595)	(b. 1598)	(b. 1600)	(b. 1604)
nun in San		nun in San	m. Angiola		
Lorenzo		Lorenzo	(1628)		

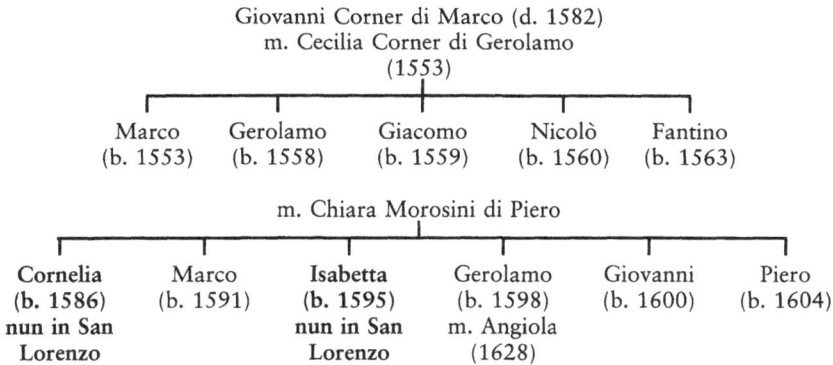

The family of Isabetta and Cornelia Corner

cious family name. Giacomo Corner and his wife could barely pay for their daughters' religious profession. They also had four sons; only Gerolamo, the second-born, married.

Although Isabetta and Cornelia were accepted in San Lorenzo at a considerably reduced rate, their annuities were never paid regularly or completely.[209] In 1623, the Giudici del Mobile (civil law court) ordered that the entire fortune of Chiara Morosini be used to pay the family's debt to the convent, a sentence confirmed by Doge Giovanni Corner in 1628.[210] But payments were never made, probably because the entire family lived off Chiara's dowry. In 1635 and 1636, she divided her allowance among her four sons—some of whom were in debt—while reserving one hundred ducats annually for herself and a total of sixty ducats for her daughters' pensions.[211] Her sons must have neglected the latter part of her provision, because the amount they owed to San Lorenzo rose continually. The convent received another ducal confirmation of the debt for Isabetta's and Cornelia's missing annuities in 1641.[212] A year later, San Lorenzo decided to retrieve the missing 1,320 ducats from Chiara Morosini's mill,[213] but Isabetta and Cornelia were never paid off during their lifetimes.[214] In 1661, the Corners' debt still amounted to 1,252 ducats, a sum finally paid after Gerolamo's possessions were sold in a public auction.[215]

Isabetta and Cornelia clearly came from an extremely prestigious, though impoverished, family. Their illustrious descent is evidenced by the fact that the courts that usually handled dowry settlements (the convent magistrate, the Giudici del Proprio, the Giudici del Mobile, etc.) lacked the necessary authority to deal with this case; instead, the convent twice appealed directly to the doge as a means to lend weight to its claim. And yet the Corner family got away with lagging behind on its dowry payments for more than half a century before serious measures—a public auction—were taken. The Corners' main sources of income were well-endowed daughters-in-law: Isabetta's and Cornelia's mother, Chiara Morosini, brought a dowry into the marriage that supported the entire family for the next generation. Their brother Gerolamo collected a dowry of 5,665 ducats from his wife, Angiola.[216] Since their father was poor, these gifts of women and dowries that the family received could not be reciprocated. In contrast to the sisters and daughters of Procurator Cornaro, whose combined wealth and prestige proved to be an obstacle to marriage, Isabetta's and Cornelia's problem was the discrepancy between their illustrious descent and their poverty. In such a case, taking the veil was virtually mandatory.

Case Study 7: Sons Living off Their Father's Name and Hypergamous Daughters-in-Law

Cornelia and Maria Dolfin were daughters of a similarly impoverished but prestigious family. Cornelia was the oldest daughter of Marco Dolfin di Zorzi, a patrician of ancient descent, and Isabetta Maldotto di Agostin, who came from a reputable citizen family. Cornelia had one brother, Zorzi, who died shortly after his marriage; a sister, Marina, who died young; and a second sister, Maria, who was not provided for until she joined the *pizzochere* of San Martino di Burano in her late forties. All the women in the family entered religious life. When Cornelia became a nun in San Lorenzo, she joined her paternal aunt Sister Maria. Her father's second sister was a nun in Santa Croce della Giudecca, an equally prestigious convent.

Family members were open about their serious financial problems. In her testament of 1600, Sister Cornelia's paternal grandmother, Cornelia Corner, explained why she appointed her son Dolfin universal and sole heir of her estate: whereas her other five sons had married advantageously and lived off their wives' dowries, Dolfin never capitalized on his descent by making a good match. He was in the embarrassing situation of not being able to "live as a gentleman." In an addition to her testament, Cornelia even canceled the modest provisions she had originally made for her daughters, Sister Maria and Sister Maria Grazia, and her granddaughter, Sister Cornelia, in order to leave every single ducat to Dolfin.[217]

Lunardo Dolfin

Vettor	Zuanne	Zorzi	Zuan Francesco
m. Betta Molin		m. Cornelia Corner	
(1542)		(1551, 15 Feb.)	
m. Marietta Donado			
(1546)			

Marco	Zorzi	Zuan	Dolfin	Vettor	Lunardo	Maria Grazia	Maria
(b. 1557)		Francesco				nun	nun in San
							Lorenzo

m. Isabetta Maldotto di Agostin
(1594)

Zorzi	Cornelia	Maria	Marina
(1600–1640)	nun in San	*pizzochera*	(d. early)
m. Giulia Priuli di Giulio	Lorenzo		
(1639)			

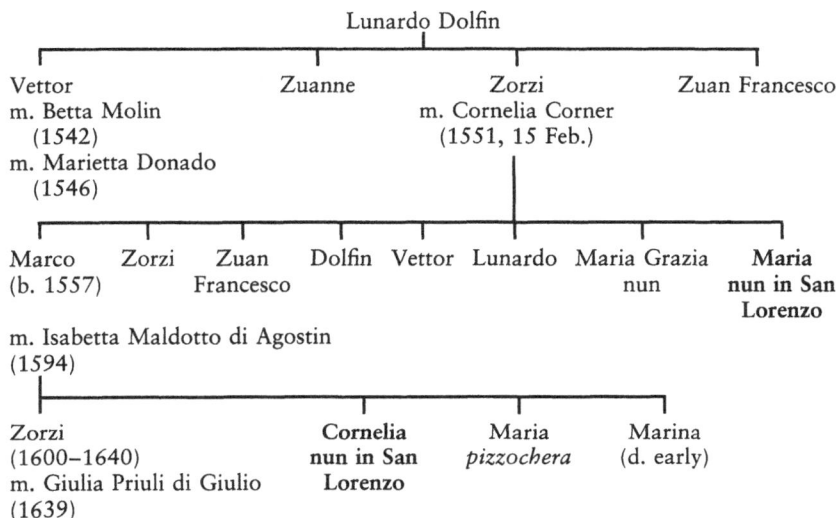

The family of Cornelia Dolfin

Sister Cornelia must have been the first child of Marco Dolfin and Isabetta Maldotto. Her parents married in 1594, and by 1609 her dowry contract with San Lorenzo was already concluded. In 1614 her by now widowed mother had already missed five annuity payments of seventy-nine ducats each.[218] Isabetta was forced to pledge her dowry, but in 1622 the debts had still not been discharged. The Giudici del Mobile consequently confirmed the notarial agreement of 1614 in favor of San Lorenzo.[219] A document mentioned that in 1622 Cornelia's maternal aunt Vittoria Maldotto bequeathed her part of a possession from which the convent pension could be paid.[220] This possession consisted of half a house that Vittoria left to the children of her sister Isabetta. In 1627, Cornelia's siblings sold the house for 2,450 ducats to their tenants, to whom they were already indebted. As part of the sales agreement, the buyers obligated themselves to invest five hundred ducats for Cornelia's convent dowry.[221] In 1628, Sister Cornelia signed a quitclaim, renouncing all further claims against the inheritance of her aunt Vittoria in exchange for her pension.[222] For the next ten years, Cornelia received thirty ducats annually from the new owner of her aunt's house (the other half of her allowance seems to have come from a vineyard in Burano).[223] When the payments ceased again in 1638, the convent immediately requested that the convent magistrate confis-

cate the house.[224] But Marc'Antonio Prezzato, the new and independent owner of the house, refuted the convent's claims.[225]

The Dolfin family was insolvent, and the money impossible to retrieve. In 1640, a document stated that Sister Maria Dolfin and her
niece, Sister Cornelia Dolfin, had rightful claims against the inheritance of numerous deceased relatives: Dolfin Dolfin, Cornelia Corner
Dolfin, Zuanne Dolfin di Marco, and Zorzi Dolfin di Marco. The
nuns, however, were not the only creditors; Giuda Camis, for example,
had prior claims. The convent's procurator promised to start retrieving
the money, which would then be divided among the creditors,[226] but
debts were all that was left of the meager Dolfin patrimony. A contract
drafted in 1643 between Cornelia's sister Maria, heir of their deceased
brother Zorzi Dolfin's "fortune," and Anzolo Marcello di Antonio,
one of Zorzi's creditors, showed that Maria was persecuted by creditors. She renounced the entire inheritance in exchange for being able
to settle as a *pizzochera* in San Martino di Burano. Anzolo Marcello
agreed to pay her three hundred ducats in cash and ninety ducats annually; in return, he got Zorzi's entire fortune, consisting of some forty
campi and three small houses, diminished by about fourteen hundred
ducats in debts.[227] No further document shows that Cornelia's convent
dowry was ever paid.

This case presents once more the problems of an impoverished
family of ancient patrician descent that was unable to endow its
daughters. Cornelia, honorably settled in a prestigious convent such
as San Lorenzo, was lucky compared to her younger sister Maria, who
had to live unprovided for until she exchanged her deceased brother's
inheritance for a pension among the *pizzochere*. Joining the middle-
class third-order community of San Martino was definitely a large step
down on the scale of social honor compared to being a professed nun
in the city's second-best nunnery.

In the absence of any substantial patrimony to be handed down,
sons' marriages were not restricted: on the contrary, marriage became
the prime source of income for poor sons of a prestigious family. As
Cornelia Corner, widow of Zorzi Dolfin di Lunardo, explained, all six
of her sons except Dolfin managed to make an honorable living by
attracting hypergamous wives. Given the agnatic organization of families, the same strategy of capitalizing on a prestigious family name was
not a viable option for women. The Dolfin daughters lacked the external representation of their worth: a substantial dowry.

The Political Dimensions of the Potlatch:
More Paradoxes

Conceived as both an important complement to the entailment strategies of individual families and as the ultimate expression of the patriciate's conspicuous consumption habits, monachizations lay at the heart of the political order in late Renaissance Venice. Functioning as a potlatch, monachizations intensified—rather than mitigated—the constraints of the patriciate's competitive marriage patterns. "Involuntary nuns" of the kind Sister Arcangela Tarabotti described certainly did populate the convents in large numbers; but the argument that patrician nuns were victims of Venetian patriarchs' economic rationale and frugality fails to explain the paradoxical dynamic of conspicuous gift-giving in the context of dowry inflation, entailment strategies, and shrinking economic opportunities. Moreover, the convent option was by no means a cheap alternative to marriage, as the last two case studies have shown.[228] Apart from their economic significance in the context of entailment strategies, coerced monachizations were a social practice through which the nobility sought to maintain the prestige as well as the unity of the body politic.[229]

The physical marginalization of patrician nuns did not preempt their conspicuousness in political discourse and popular literature, as the topos of the "involuntary nun" suggests. Nuns inhabited the outskirts of the city or distant islands in strict seclusion; they were said to be "dead to the world" and "buried alive."[230] And yet, patrician nunneries were the repository of values that the nobility as body politic claimed for itself. Patrician convents and the bodies of nuns were the sites where the honor, purity, and distinction of the nobility as a class resided. Noblewomen "deposited" in convents quite literally embodied the immaculate and inviolate state of the body politic and of "virgin" Venice (see chapter 2). The sacrifice of noblewomen to the service of God could be seen as the countergift the patriciate made over and over again in recognition of the divine grace God had conferred upon the city in 421 on the day of Mary's Annunciation, the day Venice was founded.[231] Patrician nuns were, so to speak, living metaphors of the nobility's mythical qualities:[232] they exemplified the enclosure, purity, and integrity of the patriciate as a distinct and powerful class endowed with political rights and special privileges. They represented the aristocracy's autonomy, heroic virtue, and spiritual superiority, attributes associated with the virgin bodies of nuns.[233] The withdrawal of patrician nuns from circulation enhanced the prestige of the body politic, in that every monachization was a potlatch reenacting the law of competitive gift-giving. The nuns' virginity and seclusion preserved the enclosure and immaculateness of the nobility. The conspicuous "waste" of women's reproductive capacities was thus a social practice of metaphorical significance. Monachizations "fulfilled" the "figure" of the nobility as a virgin body;[234] they transposed cultural demands into social reality.

But despite these apparent tautologies, the relationship between monachizations as a social practice and the metaphorical value of the nuns' virginity was not without contradictions. The relation between the social significance of monachizations as "waste" and the semantic value of seclusion and virginity as a means of "preservation" was entirely paradoxical. Only if one conceives of monachizations as a profoundly ambiguous practice can one understand the discrepancy between the perception of "involuntary nuns" as marginalized victims on the one hand and the high prestige they enjoyed by being living proof of the "virginity" of the body politic on the other. Although contemporaries such as Tiepolo and Tarabotti felt uneasy about the irrationality and injustice of coerced monachizations as a wasteful practice, its paradoxical quality was not apparent to them.

Social practices such as the endogamous and competitive exchange of women, coerced monachizations, and the entailment of patrimonies were meaningful as long as the patriciate convincingly fashioned itself as "nobility," that is, as an impermeable caste, as a mythical body endowed with special virtues and legitimized by divine grace. Only insofar as the patriciate had to preserve its distinct qualities and immaculate state did the restricted marriage and inheritance patterns make sense. Throughout the sixteenth and the first half of the seventeenth century, the conception of the ruling class as an ancient nobility of Roman descent, representing and physically embodying the longevity and stability of the republic and city of Venice, was a vigorous political ideology. But in the middle of the seventeenth century, once the reproduction of the patriciate as a "pure," self-sufficient body stopped being necessary and advantageous, endogamy and potlatch fell out of favor. In fact, when the patriciate's political power and cultural significance started to wane in the context of Venice's "decline"—especially after the "sellout" of the nobility in 1646 by the opening of its ranks to newcomers—the continuing decrease in the patriciate's marriage rate was accompanied by an increasing number of female misalliances and patricians' refusals to register their marriages in the "Golden Book."[235] Correspondingly, the number of patrician monachizations decreased rapidly (see tables 1 and 2).

This development leads us to confirm the hypothesis posed initially: that patrician monachizations were not just a deplorable result of economic constraints, and therefore of peripheral significance to the *grand récit* of Venice's "decline." Rather, given the tight coupling of the patriciate's social, economic, and political practices, monachizations were a crucial phenomenon. In portraying "involuntary nuns" as marginalized and passive victims of a morally corrupt and tyrannical system, one dismisses the central role they played in the economy of prestige and honor underlying the logic of aristocratic self-representation and reproduction. Patrician girls were not just forced into convents to make possible their sisters' splendid marriages; when seen as a potlatch, monachizations played an active part in the nobility's game of conspicuous gift-giving and consumption. Granted, whether a girl became a nun out of poverty or a sense of social superiority ultimately makes no difference in assessing the "waste" of women's lives resulting from the dowry system. The distinction is vital, however, to the proper conception of the important political role monachizations played in the Venetian patriciate's last attempts to preserve the prestige and cohesiveness of its body politic. Seen from the perspective of enforced monachizations, the narrative of Venice's "decline" and the erosion of its "myth" unfold as a complex process in which the conjuncture of mutually exclusive requirements developed a self-destructive dynamic. The waste of patrician women in potlatch fashion was the most conspicuous symptom of a political system in crisis.

Two

Marvelous Venice: A Virgin City and Its Noble Body Politic

The patriciate's complex language of self-fashioning—commonly referred to as the "myth of Venice"—achieved its classic form shortly after the republic had emerged "miraculously" unscathed from the War of the League of Cambrai (1508–10).[1] The unrivaled masterpiece of Venetian myth-making was Gasparo Contarini's treatise *Della republica, e magistrati di Venezia* (On the republic and magistrates of Venice; written between about 1525 and 1535, published in 1543), presenting the unique survival of the republic as an effect of its "perfect" constitution. This book served as an indispensable point of reference for generations of political theorists. Contarini combined various elements of the city's complex foundation myth with a functional analysis of its republican government inspired by Aristotle, Plato, and Polybius.[2] His premise was that the republic's founding fathers had successfully aspired to "fashion [their commonwealth] in the highest degree of perfection."[3]

Rendering Venice's supranatural "perfection" intelligible had been the aim of both religiously inspired historians and political theorists trained in classical scholarship since the beginning of Venetian mythography. The earliest "evidence" of Venice's miracle was identified by artists and writers in the thirteenth century, a formative period for the republic in both political and economic terms. Three "historical" events—the city's foundation in 421 on the day of Mary's Annunciation, the translation of Saint Mark's relics in 828–29, and the peace treaty concluded between pope and emperor under the leadership of republican diplomacy in 1177—were regarded as certain signs of the city's privileged place in redemption history.[4] Even after Florentine and Venetian humanists had begun to theorize Venetian perfection in a more "rational," that is, secular manner, historians such as Marino Sanudo, Marc'Antonio Sabellico, and Thomas Diplovatazio continued to insist that the republic, singled out by God's grace and thus immune to the corruption of time, prefigured apocalyptic truth.[5] In the post-Tridentine era, Cardinal Agostino Valier rehashed the theme by arguing that Venice's longevity was due to her "steadfast devotion to the Christian religion and loyalty to the pope."[6]

Friends of Francesco Barbaro, an early-fifteenth-century Venetian humanist, were the first to analyze the republic's political stability on the basis of ancient philosophy. Pier Paolo Vergerio, a Florentine writer, characterized the republic as a particularly well constructed aristocracy, since it contained monarchical and democratic features as well. In a preface to his translation of Plato's *Laws,* George of Trebizond, a refugee from Greece, claimed that Venice conformed to the ideal of Plato's utopian republic.[7] In contrast to Florence, relentlessly victimized by internal revolutions and wars, the Republic of Venice seemed blessed with exemption from the whims of fortune. In the eyes of humanist intellectuals, her unique stability derived from a perfect distribution of political power. The secret of Venetian success, some writers argued, lay in the republic's well-balanced and "mixed" constitution; others hailed the "immaculate" nobility of its ruling class.[8] Gasparo Contarini was the first to ingeniously combine the two arguments. In his opinion, it was the very combination of paradoxes that made Venice perfect. On the one hand, he presented the republic's constitution as the utopian mixture of monarchic, aristocratic, and democratic elements ancient writers had recommended.[9] On the other hand, he praised the republic's founding fathers for having denied political rights to commoners.[10] Access to the Venetian ruling class, Contarini proudly declared, had always been based on the "nobility of lineage" alone.[11]

How exactly a "pure" aristocracy was able to metaphorically embody and functionally represent the principle of "mixture" was a tricky problem for Contarini to explain. He resorted to body imagery, comparing Venetian society with a well-balanced, functionally differentiated "living creature." But in attributing the republic's "eyes" to the ruling class and identifying his ancestors' "wisdom and vertue" with the pure "mind" and "reason" inherent to law-based governments—gifts of both "heaven" and "nature the mother of all things"[12]—he located the concept of material "mixture" outside the government and enhanced the nobility's pristine moral and intellectual qualities. It was only by highlighting the functional differentiation of the body politic itself that Contarini could argue for the existence of monarchic and democratic features in what he implicitly praised as an aristocratic constitution. But even in analyzing the distributive power of the Great Council, repository of the republic's sovereignty, the only "popular" element he discerned was the procedure of selecting magistrates by lottery; this observation, however, was immediately followed by a reassuring remark that important positions were always filled on the basis of "noble" criteria such as merit and qualification.[13] In order to lend some credibility to his far-fetched claim that the Great Council "representeth" the "forme of a popular state," Contarini chose to call its members "citizens," without clarifying that he was actually referring to the Venetian patriciate of "noble lineage."[14] The tension between purity and mixture as two mutually exclusive yet allegedly complementary principles of perfection was repeated and reaffirmed every time the author attempted to resolve it. Despite its inherent logical inconsistencies, Contarini's interpretation of Venice's ability for the "preservation of civill concorde" as deriving from a well-balanced mixture of opposites proved extraordinarily persuasive to future Venetian political theorists who attempted to conceptualize their republic's unique stability.[15]

In contrast to Venetian writers, who experimented with ways to express the "miraculous" lack of corruption through time in Venice's history, Florentine political thinkers had to confront their republic's "temporal finitude."[16] According to Machiavelli, *fortuna*'s moves were, to a certain extent, predictable: he advised princes to anticipate her whims by studying how power struggles effected historical change. The wheel of fortune, a necessary condition of human experience, could not be kept from turning; however, a "virtuous" ruler's planned innovation could dictate their direction.[17] Machiavelli embraced the particularity and changeability all republics were subject to, deemphasizing stability in favor of military expansion. With regard to new principalities, he devised rules aimed at enhancing their life span. In distinguishing between states and the societies they governed, he introduced the concept of a necessarily dynamic relationship between the two; people inevitably changed, and constitutions had to be adapted to meet their needs. Although obsessed with disarming *for-*

tuna, he turned away from the principle of divine causation inherent in late medieval political thought. In his eyes, the succession of earthly events occurring in human time was not entirely meaningless, as medieval eschatologists had claimed, but subject to rules of change intelligible to men here and now.

Venetian political thought seems to have developed in direct opposition to Machiavelli, stubbornly holding on to medieval notions of earthly manifestations of grace and ancient utopias of perfection. Contarini, for example, intent on mending the psychological damage the near disastrous outcome of the Italian Wars had caused among the patriciate, celebrated Venice's survival as proof of the city's preordained uniqueness. While not denying that other republics might have suffered from a condition of finite particularity, he did not bother to adopt the analytical framework that Florentine writers had developed to decipher what were in his view meaningless contingencies. Instead of explaining predictable ruin, Venetian observers revealed their republic's miracle of longevity. Machiavelli's principle of binary distinctions, introduced to conceptualize change over time, was antithetical to the purpose of myth-making.[18] The republic's well-balanced constitution displayed cosmic harmony, and its various members were as perfectly combined as the parts of a human body. No class struggle divided rulers and citizens; as a *pars pro toto,* the functionally differentiated patrician government represented the entire city and republic of Venice, exemplifying the harmonious integration of all components of society. In order to figure the timeless perfection and wondrous beauty that the republic and city of Venice stood for, mythographers postulated the mysterious combination of opposites as a stable balance of oscillating parts, a dynamic equilibrium of opposing forces. As Niklas Luhmann has remarked, paradoxes express—and cause—paralysis. Collapsing opposites into sameness, they obstruct the capacity to differentiate; in the manner of Gorgons, they hinder the description of reality: "The Gorgons had thus the same effect as paradoxes. For paralysis means immobility; and immobility, to be unable to observe."[19] Theseus succeeded in slaying Medusa only by breaking her gaze in a mirror; such change in perspective, such removal from the scene of action, was also a precondition for Machiavelli's disarmament of fortune.[20] In contrast, Venetian writers thrived on the blinding effect of paralyzing paradoxes, used to arouse the immobilizing stupor, marvel, wonder, and amazement that foreigners allegedly experienced when gazing at the city's supranatural beauty.[21]

After the publication of Contarini's spellbinding classic, only outside observers such as Donato Giannotti, Jean Bodin, and, to a certain extent, Giovanni Botero dared to adopt a more critical or "realistic" language in analyzing the Venetian republic. Patricians writing in the wake of Contarini, such as Giovan Maria Memmo and Paolo Paruta, or authors either employed by or sympathetic to the republic, such as Luigi Groto or Francesco Sansovino, capitalized on the marvel effect of mythical oxymorons, whose resilience to the onslaught of analytic dissection following the ruptures of war was just as miraculous as the survival of the republic they were supposed to immortalize.[22]

On the level of policymaking, the same decidedly un-Machiavellian spirit prevailed. In the aftermath of Venice's defeat by the League of Cambrai at Agnadello in 1509, ambitions for further territorial expansion succumbed to a more realistic policy of peace and neutrality; preserving the status quo became the maxim of foreign policy until the end of the republic.[23] Nonetheless, the picture of static perfection Contarini presented did not correspond to reality. During the very years in which he was writing *Della republica* (ca. 1525), the Venetian government went through a major period of *renovatio* (renewal). Hostile to any kind of heroic innovation, Venetian politicians preferred the idea of reform, literally understood as the return to an originally perfect shape. The closest a Venetian politician ever came to resembling Machiavelli's modernizing prince was Doge Andrea Gritti, whose influence on Venetian Renaissance architecture and urban planning Manfredo Tafuri has so masterfully discussed.[24] Despite his charisma and the enormous prestige he enjoyed at home as well as abroad—or perhaps because of it—Gritti failed to implement many of his ideas, accused by his *pares* (peers) of "behaving like a lord."[25] As Tafuri has shown, Gasparo Contarini was one of Gritti's most faithful supporters, as was Francesco Zorzi, abbot of San Francesco della Vigna—a monastery Tafuri has called the "pantheon of Gritti's circle of power"—and author of hermetic tracts inspired by Neoplatonism and the kabbalah.[26] The close ties connecting Andrea Gritti, energetic politician and promoter of classical architecture, Gasparo Contarini, diplomat and evangelical church reformer, and Francesco Zorzi, hermetic philosopher and impresario of Chiara Bugni's mystic marriage, underline the peculiar characteristics of Venetian "renewal" in political theory and practice.[27] If Neoplatonism and mystic spirituality were as pervasive as is suggested by Gritti's choice in turning Zorzi's monastery into the first showcase of Renaissance Venetian architecture, Contarini's refusal to adopt the type of analytic methods developed by Florentine historians has to be understood in this context. Apart from the conservative, restorative purpose that his apotheosis of the Venetian patriciate clearly had, *Della republica* might have been intended as a contribution, perhaps corrective, to Gritti's policy of renewal; from this perspective, the treatise appears to be less "outdated" than has been suggested by modern scholars.[28] In a political climate pregnant with oligarchic tendencies, Contarini's endorsement of the Great Council as the site of republican sovereignty and his cautious, if unconvincing, attempt to present it as an assembly of quasi-popular appearance were important contributions to Venetian reform politics after Agnadello.

Many of the characteristically traditional features of Venice's *renovatio* seem to have been anticipated in Domenico Morosini's essay *De bene instituta re publica* (On the well-ordered republic), written between 1497 and 1509. Gaetano Cozzi has pointed out that this unusually independent-minded patrician had recommended putting an end to territorial expansion long before the republic was defeated by the League of Cambrai and substituting a policy of imperial peace for military conquest. Following Cozzi, Tafuri has argued that Morosini's demand for a strategy of deterrence based on economic success and exterior magnificence inspired Gritti's program of urban renewal.[29] Morosini declared that the splendor of a city's public and private buildings testified to its might—in contrast to Machiavelli, who refused to rely on anything but a well-equipped citizen army. According to Morosini, the capacity to impress by displaying wealth and beauty would be a sufficient safeguard against exterior—and possibly interior—enemies. Morosini's proposition that the patriciate engage in conspicuous consumption as a nonviolent means to demonstrate its power and legitimize its rule—to practice the potlatch, in other words—gained great currency in the course of the sixteenth century. Although he believed that private buildings should not lag behind public ones in elegance and luxury, the display of individual magnificence continued to be regarded with suspicion throughout the first half of the sixteenth century. Andrea Gritti's private palace, for example, begun in 1525, obeyed the rule of "significant *mediocritas*," intended to express this most charismatic doge's "adherence to the ideology of an egalitarian patriciate celebrated by Cassiodorus, imitating the evangelical and angelic simplicity of the Franciscan community it [the palace] faces."[30] By 1562, values had changed. Lodovico Domenichi declared

Paolo Veronese, *Pax Veneta* (Hall of the Great Council)

Paolo Veronese, *Pax Veneta* (detail)

that "nowadays, Venetian noblemen are called magnificent, [because they] win all comparisons in the grandiosity and pomp of their public and private buildings with ancients and moderns alike."[31] A year later, however, Giovan Maria Memmo warned of the politically destabilizing effects of ostentatiously outspending one's peers in building palaces.[32] The first to unabashedly demand that the patriciate display magnificence as a proof of true nobility was Paolo Paruta in 1579.[33]

Morosini's proposal to move away from republican modesty and to politicize conspicuous consumption as a form of domesticated aggression accompanied his plan for an oligarchic restructuring of the republic. He proposed to elect senators for life and to enhance the executive and legislative power of the Collegio.[34] This plan was never realized as such, although the tendency to concentrate power in fewer and smaller government organs characterized the constitutional development of the republic in the following decades.[35] In reaffirming the authority of the Great Council as the repository of republican sovereignty, Contarini opted for a different strategy of renewal, aimed at enhancing the prestige and dignity of the ruling class as a whole. In 1506 and 1526, marriage and inheritance laws were passed to "keep our nobility . . . immaculate," which Contarini firmly supported "so

Paolo Veronese, *Justice and Peace Pay Homage to Venetia* (Hall of the Collegio)

that our assembly of noblemen should not pollute itself [non s'imbrat-tasse d'alcuna macchia]."[36] The tension between oligarchic "innova-tion" and republican "re-form" characterized Venetian politics up to the end of the sixteenth century and beyond. Sumptuary laws and the endemic neglect of them, as well as two "corrections" of the almighty Council of Ten (constitutional amendments by which the competencies of this council were reduced), testify to this process of political contes-tation on the level of legislature.[37] Despite considerable political resis-tance against legalizing the oligarchic redistribution of power, the in-creasing pressure to "display magnificence" fostered elitist trends, which effectively denied "noble" status to all patricians who were less than super-rich. Paradoxically, Contarini's efforts to promote the dig-nity of the ruling class as a whole and Paruta's recommendation that individual patrician families compete for prestige against one another rested upon the same imperative of aristocratic distinction. The two

Jacopo Tintoretto, *The Provinces Submit to Venice* (Hall of the Great Council)

trends both reinforced and paralyzed each other simultaneously: the definitive closure of the Great Council in 1506 drew a clear line between noblemen and the rest of society, postulating that the patriciate collectively possessed an innate capacity to rule; but the potlatch ideology first formulated by Morosini worked to erode ruling-class solidarity and the concept of republican equality.

Claudio Donati has argued that in Italy, the discussions on how to define "true" nobility passed through three stages of development: between the end of the Italian Wars and the beginning of the Council of Trent, heated debates about the respective merits of "small" versus "large" governments took place, while some city councils began to exclude merchants. Such diversity of opinion was replaced by a certain "homogeneity" toward the middle of the century, when duels ceased to be outlawed, primogeniture and entailment practices curbed inheritance rights, and land investments replaced commerce as a more "noble"—and profitable—economic activity. Near the end of the century, this exclusivist ideology was consolidated.[38] The Venetian discussions roughly follow this periodization. Some fine-tuning of Donati's scheme is nonetheless necessary: despite the patriciate's increasing differentiation in wealth and the cultural demand for "aristocratic" wastefulness, the republican constitution remained firmly entrenched; according to Bouwsma, anti-oligarchic governments celebrated their last triumph during the crisis of the Interdict of 1606.[39] Individual "virtue" as a measure of nobility never ceased to be a criterion in scholarly debates. In short: rather than resulting in the "consolidation" of a "homogeneous" ideology, the Venetian debates on nobility displayed an ambiguity between rival concepts. This situation persisted until the end of the sixteenth century, when Paolo Paruta dismissed Contarini's carefully crafted oscillation of opposite forces in favor of a tautologically defined concept of innate nobility.[40]

But back to the myth. The Venetian nobility, as Contarini and others before him pointed out, was descended from lawgivers as excellent and wise as founders of ancient states. Venice, as we recall, was "born" in its perfection on the same day that the Virgin Mary immaculately conceived.[41] Taken together, the secular and religious variants of the city's foundation legend suggest that the patriciate was endowed with God's grace at precisely the moment when the city was "conceived"; without such special, intrinsic qualification, its accomplishment of creating a "perfect" constitution was hardly imaginable. The belief in innate virtues also explains the patriciate's growing reluctance to grant outsiders membership privileges to the Great Council and its vigilance over the proper transmission of political rights to legitimate heirs. The creation of the Golden Book in 1506 implicitly defined the "immaculate" reproduction of the body politic as a constitutional duty.[42] Just as the city had for over "twelve hundred years preserved its virginity intact,"[43] the patriciate had to guard its purity, lest the republic's original perfection be corrupted.

Venice's state of inviolate virginity was all the more "miraculous" in light of the city's unprecedented beauty: while her "wondrous site" afforded protection from attacks,[44] the city's "most beautiful bosom"[45] and similar charms could not but attract her enemies' possessive desire. But as Morosini had predicted, the "stupor and admiration"[46] that Venice, this "new Venus born naked in the midst of the sea,"[47] aroused among those who gazed at her seemed to have a disarming effect. Morosini's maxim was peace through splendor; the building boom begun under Andrea Gritti would have certainly satisfied his wildest dreams. Once it became commonly accepted that "it is proper for a magnificent man to construct theaters, temples, squares, loggias, and palaces," urban planning commissions and private builders rapidly turned Venice into a truly splendid city.[48]

Ennio Concina states that Venice's urban body was modeled to mirror the state[49]—not only in terms of its architectural language (of perfection), one should add, but with respect to the paradoxical image it conveyed. A city built in the sea, "defying the laws of nature," a human artifice so complete as to suggest divine intervention, resembling both Mary, mother of Christ, and Venus, daughter of Zeus— where else would a republic as perfect as the Venetian one and its noble body politic reside?

Perfect Bodies, Impossible Paradoxes

Sixteenth-century political discourse in Venice was governed by two mutually exclusive female body images. The virginal body of Mary expressed the closure and original perfection of the city, the republic, and the patriciate portrayed by Contarini. The sensual, inviting body of Venus, goddess of love, represented the city's beauty and riches gained through commerce. Standing in direct opposition to each other, the two allegories displayed the ambiguities of patrician identity, oscillating between egalitarian republicanism and aristocratic distinctiveness, openness and seclusion. The combination of the two body

metaphors produced the marvel effect typical of paradoxical constella-
tions as employed in Venetian mythographic discourse.

David Rosand has shown that the iconographic tradition of "Venetia figurata" reached back at least to the early fifteenth century, acquiring several different political connotations in the course of its formation. By 1550, four iconographic traditions were fully developed:
Venice was allegorized variously as Justice (Justitia), Goddess Rome
(Dea Roma), the Virgin Mary, and Venus Anadyomene.[50] In Rosand's
opinion, the fourfold figure of Venice was intelligible only by reference
to the political myth of Venice, each allegory personifying different
aspects of the republic: Justice represented the highest value in a state
where political power was defined in terms of law;[51] Dea Roma signified the transfer of imperial power from Rome to Venice; the Virgin
alluded to the conferral of divine grace upon a city founded in 421 on
the day of Mary's Annunciation, as well as to the immaculate, that is,
inviolate state of the city; and Venus, like Venice, was born of the sea.[52]

In the sixteenth century, the Virgin Mary and the pagan goddess
Venus gained importance over Justitia and Dea Roma, who were particularly popular in the preceding period of Venetian conquest. While
Justice and Rome complemented each other in denoting the develop-
ing imperial aspirations of the republic, Venus and the Virgin Mary
seemed to be mutually exclusive images. Among the associations
evoked by the metaphor of virginity were containment, purity, autonomy, and impenetrability, but Venus stood for traffic (in love) and
procreative capacities. The two images were used alongside each other
without embarrassment, as if they were similes rather than opposites.
Luigi Groto, a state-employed orator and author of panegyric texts,
repeatedly declared: "I would say that Venice is Venus, [in that] both
of them [are] heavenly, both [are] mothers, and nutrients of holy love.
. . . Venice has always preserved the flower of her virginity."[53]

While Groto depicted Venice as both generative and immaculate—as a kind of "Marian" Venus—Pompeo Caimo, an Aristotelian
thinker and professor of medicine at Padua, proposed a comparison
of Venice with Danaë. Caimo gave an equally Christian twist to the
Ovidian story of Jupiter's love affair with the mortal Danaë. In
Caimo's fashioning of Venice as the object of divine love (and desire),
Jupiter's "golden shower" became the flow of God's grace that helped
Venice preserve her virginity: "These vapors truly produced a golden
cloud, which descended then in the form of precious rain in the lap
of this Virgin, but not in order to corrupt her, and stain her, as did

Filippo Calendario, *Venetia* (west facade of the Ducal Palace)

the golden cloud descended in Danaë's lap according to some poets' fiction, but in order to conserve and distinguish her, according to the testimonies of all the historians."[54]

In conflating the account of Jupiter's mortal desires with Venetian mythography, Caimo adds a somewhat subversive dimension to the foundation myth of Venice, according to which God's grace was con-

ferred upon the city on the day of its foundation. Caimo's reference to Dante's version of the legend of Danaë and her encounter with the divine was probably intended to cleanse the notion of "golden treasures" of its sexual connotations. While gold stained the lap of Jupiter's lover, the riches of Venice helped *preserve* the city's immaculate state.

In trying to grasp the cognitive value of the Virgin-Venus (or, as in Caimo, Virgin-Danaë) paradox in its reference to both the city and the republic of Venice, another, more basic question has to be settled first. What exactly is the semantic foundation of a trope that allows a political system (republic) to be represented by a beautiful woman, who in turn stands for the whole city? What are the components in this process of metaphorization that Rosand subsumes under the expression "the iconography of a myth?"

The missing link in this otherwise confusing chain of associations is the body image, a devouring metaphor capable of subsuming the most disparate images under its rule and thereby rendering them compatible.[55] Although employed to denote the stability, unity, and homogeneity of the signified concept, body metaphors derive their rhetorical

Jacobello del Fiore, *Triptych of Justice* (Galleria dell'Academia)

power from their structural instability, from their capacity to generate (other metaphors), and from the principle of gendered differentiation that they promote. The relationship between the city, the republic, and the government of Venice was thus conceived of in a variety of ways: by synecdochical replacement, by reference to the Aristotelian antagonism between form and matter, or by way of a maternal allegory. In Contarini's opinion, the doge represented and metaphorically constituted the unity of the city through the uniqueness of his quasi-regal body.[56] Pompeo Caimo, less ingeniously, envisioned the republic as a masculine soul that gave form and shape to an amorphous, female urban matter.[57] In a speech delivered to mourn and honor the patricians who died in the battle of Lepanto, Paolo Paruta declared that Venice's sons had proven themselves to be worthy of their noble mother.[58]

One of the prime qualities of the body image is its ability to denote unity while simultaneously generating differences. Because virgin Venice could assume imperial as well as jurisdictional associations, the allegories of Justice and Rome were conceptually subsumed under the Virgin Mary. Venus, however, was its paradoxical complement, representing a differentiation of Venice's female body into polar opposites.

Giovanni Pietro Birago (?), *Oratio Panegyrica* (British Museum, London)

Reverse side of a coin of Doge Francesco Foscari.

Anonymous, *Venice as Justice* (Loggetta).

The double metaphor of Venice as Virgin and Venus seemed to replicate and emphasize the function of the body image itself, focusing on containment and stability while alluding to the possibility (and danger) of violating and transgressing the boundaries of virgin Venice. The virgin metaphor had ambiguous connotations itself, when, for example, it was used to praise the political status quo while implicitly warning of decay. Given the mythical perfection of Venice, change inevitably meant decadence and disintegration. None of the treasures of virgin Venice—that is, her immaculate territory, constitution, and nobility—could be touched without running the risk of conquest, plundering, and internal dissolution.

Any major crisis could be perceived as a disruption of Venice's

Paolo Veronese, *Venetia Receiving the Graces* (Hall of the Council of Ten).

virgin body. For example, the devastating plague of 1575–77 turned the once immaculate city into a "horrible monster" torn by "open and voracious wounds," as the poet Maffio Venier phrased it. The plague was perceived by contemporaries as God's punishment for the immorality, corruption, and "luxuria" prevailing in Venice: in losing her virtue—and virginity—the city had turned from a "lovely nymph" into "a monster that wails and weeps."[59] The grotesque decay of an urban body formerly characterized by immaculate perfection was the main theme of Venier's poem on the plague of 1575; the author elaborated the topic by juxtaposing numerous antagonistic (body) images:

> Already the earth swells its belly
> Without any reason pregnant with death
> Women and girls full of love tear apart
> Their blond braids with innocent hands
> And their profound inner
> Wounds make them weep bitterly
> And cover with radiant pearls
> Their bleeding countenance.[60]

Less sophisticated poets, such as the anonymous author of "Sopra la peste" (About the plague) interpreted the plague bluntly as a result and symbol of the city's transformation from an "intact virgin" into a "dirty whore."[61] In this way, the Virgin-Venus paradox was rendered intelligible and meaningful through semantic associations with salient topics in contemporary discourse, which in turn were shaped and structured by the pervasiveness of this allegory.[62]

Paradoxical images appeared frequently in Venetian mythology; one might even say that the miracle of Venice was constructed as a paradox. For how could perfection—by human standards beyond description—be expressed other than through rhetorical figures denoting a structural impossibility? A government's perfection meant absence of change; perfection could not develop over time—it had to exist from the beginning, and it would last forever. Perfection meant the collapse of past and future. What rhetorical configuration could render the sense of perfection better than the simultaneity of antagonistic concepts resulting in reciprocal paralysis? This is precisely how Contarini explained the perfect state of Venice's constitution: in his opinion, it was produced by combining mutually exclusive forms of government into a well-balanced mixture of coexisting paradoxes.

As the Republic of Venice was conceived as inherently paradoxical in its perfection, so was the city: "She [Venice] . . . is entirely of divine making. . . . To me it seems very important, because I have seen the impossible in the impossible," said the foreign visitor in Nicolò Doglioni's dialogue *Le cose notabili, et maravigliose della città di Venetia* (The noteworthy and marvelous things of the city of Venice; 1602).[63] Similarly, a German traveler called Venice the "miracle within a miracle."[64] If the immutability and perfection of the Venetian constitution was rendered intelligible rhetorically by the use of paradoxes, the paradoxical structure of Venice as a city was a visible phenomenon. Foreign visitors never tired of recalling the sensation of wonder and amazement aroused as they marveled at her. Her miraculous nature was displayed before everyone's gaze; her perfection was signified by beauty. In travel accounts and tourist guides, the beautiful urban body was presented as the visible sign of a perfect government. Just as visual representations of beautiful virgins "figured" the city, so the entire city of Venice "figured" the republic's abstract perfection. The visible impression of the city as a figure of the republic was structured according to the paradoxical foundation of the government's perfection. Playing with paradoxes was a standard way of talking about Venice—a city built on water, defying the laws of nature, unprotected yet invincible.

Descriptions of Venice as an urban phenomenon often borrowed their imagery from the allegory of Venice as Virgin and Venus. As Luigi Groto phrased it, Venice was a "new Venus born naked in the midst of the sea," yet she was a virgin city "without walls."[65] In his speech of 1569, given in honor of Doge Pietro Loredano, Groto resumed his play on Venus's nudity, that is, Venice's lack of protective city walls. Here he asked, "who does not wonder . . . whether [Venice], which through the grace of Heaven preserved an uncorrupted virginity for eleven hundred and forty-six years, is not of Sibylline nature?" To Groto "this city is . . . not without walls, but surrounded by threefold walls," consisting of the patriciate's love and counsel and of God's protection.[66] The stability of the city was also due to "her broad liberty, and her public generosity"; Venice was "a public market, a continuous fair. . . . an open theater."[67] Thus it was her paradoxical character—of being open and naked like Venus as well as confined and protected like a virgin—that constituted Venice's miraculous stability. This miracle could only be described by adding paradox after paradox: "Thus the greatness of Venice is that in so bitter a sea lies a city so sweet, in a sea so unstable a republic so firm."[68] Venice was able to maintain her enclosure and immaculate sovereignty *because* she was a figure of openness, "an image of the earth, dissolved in all its parts, and a figure of heaven, open at every side."[69]

The paradoxical images that prevailed in Venetian mythology were employed to arouse sentiments of wonder and amazement, to achieve a certain "marvel effect."[70] The portrayal of Venice in her threefold persona as republic, city, and nobility was supposed to provoke awe and admiration. Just as the seductive paintings of female Venetian allegories by Giorgione, Titian, and Veronese were to be gazed at in wonder, so too was the fantastic urban space intended to arouse amazement—a sensation also produced by the "impossible" perfection of the state.[71] Thus it was not only the rhetorical "corporeality" of these allegories and their paradoxical features that marked them as metaphorically similar to the republic, the city, and the patriciate of Venice; all individual constituents of the "mystical body of Venice" also shared the same aesthetic effect of giving rise to marvel among those who gazed at her perfection.

Public festivities, rituals, and processions constituted the apex of Venetian marvel-production. Magnificent urban spaces such as Saint Mark's Square or the Grand Canal provided a stage on which the entire city could present its splendor and periodically reenact the mystery of its inner harmony. "Tourist guides" such as Francesco Sansovino's treatise *Delle cose notabili che sono in Venezia* (On the noteworthy things of Venice; 1561) sought to give an insider's account of the Venetian "theater" to an international audience, focusing on civic celebrations as a way of popularizing the myth of Venice to a nonscholarly readership.[72] Sansovino's treatise became an instant classic, updated and extended periodically up to the middle of the seventeenth century.[73] Instead of pedantically emblazoning the city's many miraculous sites in proper Petrarchist fashion, minutely describing each of its important relics, churches, and palaces, as Marc'Antonio Sabellico had done half a century earlier,[74] Sansovino gave a refreshing account of— in this order—Venice's "ancient customs, clothes, magistrates, important victories, famous senators, intellectuals, dukes and their lives, all the patriarchs, music of various types, construction projects and palaces, sculptors and their work, painters and paintings."[75] His top three subjects underline once again the extent to which contemporaries saw as inseparably intertwined the city's urban body (the stage for civic rituals, or "customs"), the nobility (fashioning itself quite literally through its clothes), and the constitution (consisting of its system of magistrates). His idea of combining the portrayal of government officials, the outfits they wore, and the festive occasions for which they wore them was picked up by fashion experts and engravers such as Cesare Vecellio and Giacomo Franco, whose beautifully illustrated books were important contributions to late Renaissance Venetian mythography. Vecellio's historical account of the different types of robes worn by doges, senators, and other dignitaries was interlaced with well-researched information—often taken from Sansovino—on Venice's constitutional development and foreign affairs.[76] His commentary on the earliest ducal robe, of which he discovered a depiction in one of San Marco's mosaics, shows how closely he related myth and "fashion": "This coat [of the *doge antico*] truly represents the felicitous and well-founded greatness of this most Christian Republic, founded on the firm rock of the Holy Faith . . . as can be seen clearly [from the fact] that up until today she has preserved herself as an intact Virgin. The coat shown above is of great decor, and [attests to the] greatness of this most Serene Republic."[77]

Giacomo Franco's collection of etchings gives a similarly politicized view of patrician clothing. He drew an even closer connection between Venice's urban body, its government institutions, and its well-dressed noblemen performing their functions like actors on stage. His series of illustrations, entitled *Outfits of Venetian Men and Women with the Procession of the Most Serene Signoria and Other Details Such as Triumphs, Festivals, and Public Ceremonies in the Most Noble City of Venice* (1610), starts with a bird's-eye view of the city, followed by an image of the Great Council in session, a portrait of a doge, and a view of Saint Mark's Square; it then shows other important magistrates, as well as outfits of noblemen, merchants, and artisans. Charmingly detailed illustrations of public events ranging from the feast of the Ascension to fistfights and women's regattas constitute the core of the series; they are interspersed with portraits of noblewomen, ordered by marital status. Female aristocrats also figure prominently in his etchings of state festivities: in a close-up, Franco depicted Dogaressa Morosini riding the state galley, and he showed "balls that the Most Serene Republic gives for its Noblewomen, richly embellished with jewels, to honor Princes who visit Venice."[78]

The extraordinary pomp of Dogaressa Morosini's coronation ceremony was among the most "noteworthy and marvelous things" Nicolò Doglioni added to Sansovino's account of Venice in the updated version published in 1602. Following a brief overview of the city's noble origins and recent history, Doglioni gave a minute description of Doge Marino Grimani's election festivities in 1595 and the unusual "coronation" procedures for his wife two years later. According to Doglioni, Marino Grimani's election was met "with so much jubilation, and so much happiness of the whole city that this merriment was clearly shown in an extraordinary way. . . . And because this prince had a wife, called Morosina of the family Morosini, he ordered that she was to be crowned as dogaressa, which was done with more pomp and pageantry [*apparati*] than ever."[79]

In grandeur and elegance, Morosina Morosini's coronation festivities surpassed by far those of her husband.[80] Her "investiture" was performed on the day of the Bucintoro, lending her ceremony special symbolic and political significance. This most important of Venice's many holidays coincided with the feast of Mary's Ascension. Its core ritual was the doge's "marriage" to the sea, performed from the Bucintoro (the republic's ceremonial galley) by throwing a ring into the water.[81] It symbolized Venetian supremacy over other Adriatic cities and the republic's imperial aspirations in the Levant[82] and commemorated the peace treaty that Venetian diplomats had helped negotiate between Emperor Frederick I and Pope Alexander III in 1177. Because of Venice's important role in achieving this settlement between the two medieval powers, Venetian historians interpreted the treaty as an official recognition of the republic's sovereignty and its independence from imperial and papal dominance (see chapter 5). The combining of the republic's highest state holiday with Morosina's coronation hints at the extraordinary political significance Doge Grimani attributed to his wife's festivities.[83] According to Doglioni's account, the processions in honor of Morosina displayed core features of Venetian mythography. In addition to the pageants, painted images of Venice (as Virgin, Venus, Justice, and Rome), heraldic signs, and floats designed especially for the occasion embellished the numerous processions, banquets, and dances.

Festivities such as this one were recurrent opportunities for the body politic to constitute itself in front of the public, to display its dignity and power visibly, and to mark out the symbolic space of the city through processions. On the occasion of Morosina's coronation, the nobility presented itself in an overwhelmingly female—even virginlike—manner. After the dogaressa was formally crowned in her husband's private palace, she handed golden coins stamped with her likeness to the senators and members of the Signoria (the inner government circle), mounted the Bucintoro, and was carried to Saint Mark's Square, accompanied by three hundred selected patrician women. Upon arrival at the square, the women formed a procession:

> Two of them in a row, dressed in white with fans of white quills, walked, supported by some young patricians adorned in a noble manner. They had a bouquet of flowers with golden frill, which was carried by these youngsters, because their [the women's] hands were occupied. . . . And in this manner one saw one hundred forty-two, all of them very young, beautiful, well made up, and with a pearl necklace for each

of them, and a golden chain, which was tied to the fan of excessive value. . . . Then one saw fifty [women] older in age, dressed partly in green and partly in peacock color. . . . Then fifty matrons [followed,] dressed in black with broad sleeves, the wife of the Great Chancellor, and the wives of the Procurators of Saint Mark's. . . . Behind them came the dogaressa in her golden Ducal coat, and the *corno* on her head in the manner of the doge, only smaller, and she stood between two Councilors.[84]

The dogaressa's entourage of 142 young noblewomen dressed in white, adorned with white feathers and pearls, points to the peculiarities of patrician self-fashioning at the turn of the century. Morosina Grimani's virginal procession enacted the allegory of Venice, a gorgeous and attractively immaculate woman exempt from the corruption of time, in a live performance. The overwhelmingly virgin-like image the body politic conveyed on the day of Morosina's coronation festivities—praised by contemporary observers as one of the most splendid civic rituals ever performed—corresponded to the frequent use of virgin metaphors in political discourse and their crucial significance to the myth of Venice.

Entailing Treasures, Defending Boundaries, Remaining Immaculate: A Virgin Body Politic

In associating Venice with a virgin body, mythographers praised her immaculate state and uniqueness while at the same time stressing the improbability, or even impossibility, of such a perfection under human conditions. Venice, born Venus-like of the sea, naked, rich, and beautiful, was extremely vulnerable;[85] having received the grace and attributes of the Virgin Mary, however, the city was invincible and eternally persevering.

Toward the end of the sixteenth century, the semantic associations of the Virgin-Venus paradigm underwent a profound change: Venus ceased to carry positive connotations and started to function as a dangerous counter-image to the mother of Christ. As Dogaressa Morosini's coronation procession indicates, allegories of Venice eventually assumed unequivocally virgin-like attributes. Half a century earlier, Venus, the goddess of love and beauty, had still signified the commerce, prosperity, and liberty of Venice. The frequency of business encounters, the exchange of money and goods in this metropolitan city, were explicitly couched in terms of Venus's traffic in love. Luigi

Groto addressed Venice in a speech given in 1559 as a "lap open to the commerce of [with?] all men; O new world, O earthly paradise."[86] In his speech of 1569 in honor of Doge Pietro Loredano, Groto had listed the advantages of Venice's peculiar site, again in terms of her physical openness; like Venus, she lacked the protecting garment of city walls: "The fact that Venice has neither material walls that surround her nor gates that seclude her nor keys that lock her proves her broad liberty, and her public generosity; it witnesses that she is a public market, a continuous fair, an open court, an open theater, a general port, and the universal mother of the whole world."[87] Venice's liberality as a site inviting commerce and trade carried here the connotations of maternal generosity and a carnivalesque public life; in Groto's speech, the city's Venus-like attractions and openness were the preconditions of her wealth and freedom.

At some point during the 1570s, associations of commerce with traffic in love ceased to be employed to praise the greatness of Venice. This happened at a time when the patriciate definitely abandoned the crisis-prone sea trade in favor of more secure landed investments and money lending, when polemics against prostitutes and courtesans increased, and when—as already mentioned—the diseased body of a whore came to signify the devastation of a plague-ridden city, of an urban body punished for having indulged in luxury and debauchery.[88] If half a century earlier Pietro Aretino could have Antonia choose prostitution as the only honest status for a woman, "because a whore cheats neither convents nor husbands; she is like a soldier who is paid for doing evil, and she does not pretend to be virtuous, because her shop sells what she has to sell," toward the end of the century the venality of love came under serious attack. That government and church authorities should polemicize and take action against prostitution in the immediate post-Tridentine period does not surprise, but even unorthodox writers such as Sperone Speroni and Veronica Franco criticized the "venereal" profession harshly in their writings from about 1575 on. Whereas Aretino sarcastically stated that "the gardeners sell herbs, the drugstores sell spices, and the bordellos sell . . . syphilis,"[89] Speroni condemned a whore's traffic in love as devilish and evil. In his moralizing "Orazione contra le cortegiane" (Speech against courtesans)—a treatise that he seems to have written for political reasons in self-defense[90]—he attacked the belief that exchange of money rendered a prostitute independent: "You free, you a lady, you miserable woman? while not having one body part that is not subject to the common people [*populo*]. Perhaps you pretend to dominate them, because they come to your house every night with hands full of gold and silver? You are no less crazy than wicked. . . . The gold and silver [given to you] . . . is no tribute, but payment for buying you: thus you serve, not dominate."[91]

In contrast to the more relaxed attitude of former times, in which cultured courtesans enjoyed if not respect then at least recognition among aristocrats, artists, and intellectuals, Speroni's polemic of 1575 was bluntly misogynist. He mercilessly ridiculed the opinion that prostitutes could ever receive an equal or higher monetary value for what they offered; selling one's body meant servitude by definition. Veronica Franco, a courtesan herself, problematized the venality of a prostitute's body in more complex ways, although she agreed with Speroni that the power structures established between a prostitute and her client were always asymmetrical and worked in most cases to the advantage of the latter. In one of her "Lettere familiari" (Familiar letters), she vehemently discouraged a mother from planning her daughter's career as a courtesan. She emphasized a courtesan's dreadful fate by describing the injustice and violence to which the girl would be subject:

> It is a most wretched thing, contrary to human reason, to subject one's body and industriousness to a servitude whose very thought is most frightful. To become the prey of so many, at the risk of being despoiled, robbed, killed, deprived in a single day of all that one has acquired from so many over such a long time, exposed to many other dangers of receiving injuries and dreadful contagious diseases. . . . What greater misery? What riches, what comforts, what delights can possibly outweigh all this?[92]

Franco's idea was to establish the girl in the newly founded spinsters' asylum, the Zitelle, or else marry her off; in reminding the addressee "you know how often I begged and admonished you to take care of her virginity," she spoke with contempt of the mother's efforts to dress and make up her daughter so that "the commodity may find high currency in spending it" (that is, so that her virginity might receive a high price).[93] Like Speroni, Franco also described a young girl's venality as undignified; her virginity was to be protected like a treasure in a spinsters' asylum, or else invested honorably in marriage.

As Margaret Rosenthal has shown, Franco at times defended the exchange of money in her profession as a sign of honesty, and she insisted on her freedom in rejecting a certain well-paying man she did not love. She could easily have cheated him, a "gentleman of great quality," with the "artifice of flattery" in order to receive help and protection—as courtesans ordinarily did, one might add; but, she told him, "I decided not to do so because I did not want to deceive you since I am unable to return your love."[94] In portraying herself as an admirable exception, Veronica Franco seemed to agree with contemporary polemics against the deceitfulness and undignified servitude of a common prostitute's business. In her writings, Franco was preoccupied with protecting her personal dignity, but she also portrayed the abuse and humiliations a prostitute typically had to endure. Selling one's body was not like selling spices and herbs, as Aretino ironically posited: a successful courtesan often had to deceive well-paying gentlemen who demanded love and admiration, but in principle, every prostitute's body was exploited. Only in rejecting a man's offer could Franco preserve her honesty and freedom.

Thus the innocence with which Luigi Groto compared Venice to the open lap of Venus or to a carnivalesque marketplace was gone by the time Veronica Franco encouraged young girls to enter spinsters' asylums[95] and Sperone Speroni was forced to publish his "abjuration." Instead of playing with explicit ambiguities and contrasts, authors following Francesco Sansovino now emphasized the "inviolate and immaculate" state of the city's "excellent government" while avoiding references to Venus.[96] Moreover, the emphasis on Venetian trade and commerce as such—even without hints at "venereal" connotations—ceased to be a sign of the city's mythical excellence. Selling (one's body) meant servitude, as Speroni's and Franco's concerns over prostitution illustrated. Just as traffic in love sealed the courtesan's subjection to tyrannical clients, traffic in goods guaranteed the "servitude" of merchants in times of crisis.

Contemporaneously with the devaluation of Venus and commerce, agricultural activities gained esteem in the eyes of a formerly mercantile patriciate. Treatises such as Agostino Gallo's *Le tredici giornate della vera agricoltura & de' piaceri della villa* (The thirteen days of true agriculture and of the pleasures of residing in the countryside; 1564) became widely popular during the general upswing of land investments and grain prices in the second half of the sixteenth century.[97] Gallo, a nobleman from Brescia, presented agriculture as an economic activity that was not only profitable and pleasurable, but also genuinely noble and virtuous.[98] He did so by contrasting the "inferno" of city life with the "paradise" of country dwelling.[99] It was the simplicity, peacefulness, and sanity of country life, the freedom from social constraints and intrigues, that made one of the interlocutors in Gallo's book, the nobleman Giovan Battista Avogadro from Brescia, abandon the city. He described his new life "in villa" as an innocent, pastoral idyll: his days were more serene, the people were more polite, his pleasures were honorable, his social life was free of concerns for prestige and power;[100] but most importantly, country women were domestic, chaste, and virtuous. He felt liberated from such constraints of urban life as dressing up and observing a strict social etiquette, but women "were even happier than we [men] to lead a positive life, to enjoy gracefully with us a precious liberty, rather than to live as matrons busy with social obligations in the city."[101] At this point his interlocutor and visitor, Cornelio Ducco, gets carried away with a somewhat disconnected digression on "vain women." In Ducco's opinion, city women had too many liberties:

> [Many women] . . . always want to go wherever they please, well dressed, made up, perfumed, puffed up with a thousand vanities, so that they are all the more admired and flattered by every man who sees them. Always thinking of going everywhere they want, showing up where one dances, sees comedies, tragedies, jousts, revelries, and tournaments; or standing for most of the day in the doorway, or at the window in the manner of crazy women, and without the least bit of shame; they are and always will be the scandal of the entire city.[102]

The blurring of boundaries between inside and outside, between the realm of domesticity and the public realm of politics, seems to be what Ducco was mainly concerned about.[103] Standing at windows and in doorways, immodest city women corrupted the basic differences of a well-ordered society. As many contemporary Aristotelian as well as Neoplatonic treatises on women stressed, assigning a proper place to women was vital for the maintenance of the autonomy, independence, and power of the upper classes. Just as women should be enclosed in their homes, their bodies should be impermeable to all but their husbands. Lodovico Dolce, one of Venice's prime authors on issues of women, compared an unmarried girl's body to a ship "floating in a sea of many dangers, all the orifices of which have to be closed so that [these dangers] cannot penetrate into the inner parts . . . in such a way that [the body] drowns in them."[104] In Dolce's eyes, adultery by a married woman came close to treason:

> I certainly do not know whether those who ruin their fatherland, destroy the laws, kill their fathers, and profane sacred things commit higher crimes [than adulterous women]. And how can an immodest wife

rely on God's defense and the friendship of men? The laws, the fatherland, the father, the relatives, the children, and the husband condemn
her, and punish her harshly. God the just judge castigates her with just
revenge.[105]

Gallo also judged women's promiscuity to be a capital crime. Although it is unclear whether Ducco was talking about prostitutes as
an urban phenomenon or about adulterous wives and immodest
daughters, the topic unleashed Avogadro's fury against "bad women"
and those fathers and husbands who were unable or unwilling to chastise them:

> What's even worse is that this disease increases every day due to blind
> husbands and dumb fathers who are the cause of this reprehensible cus-
> tom: and there could not be a better remedy to terminate this pestiferous
> germ than the execution of that just sentence pronounced exclusively
> against all bad women. As one has to give a bad daughter death as a
> dowry, worms as a garment, and the tomb as a house, so one has to
> dig out the eyes of an infamous wife, cut off her tongue, and hack off
> her hands; or even . . . burn her alive.[106]

Ducco tried to pacify Avogadro's wrath, but adultery and prostitution symbolized everything Avogadro hated about city life. Raging
against women's promiscuity triggered his more ferocious remarks
about "ambitious, envious, proud, deceitful, disloyal, and murderous"
city people in general.[107] Gallo conceived of the innocence and freedom
of country living as being epitomized in the chastity of women,
guarded by their husbands' and fathers' tyrannical regime. In the manner of a circular argumentation based on the initially posited antagonism between "infernal" cities and a "paradisiacal" countryside, he
drew the following analogies: city women are as lecherous as country
women are chaste; city life is as sinful and libertine as country life is
innocent and truly "free"; and, one might add, commerce is as vile as
agriculture is virtuous. The rhetorical play with analogous opposites
conflated the attack against prostitution with a devaluation of commerce, since the vices of prostitution *and* commerce were equally antithetical to the virtues of country women and land investments.

One might expect that once the advantages of country dwelling
and agriculture were couched in terms of women's chastity, the reputation of Venice as a figure of virginity would vanish. Miraculous Venice,
however, was not Brescia, was not just any hellish city. Despite its
traffic, prostitution, and plague, Venice remained—according to the
city's most prominent courtesan and poetess, Veronica Franco—"a

truly maiden city, immaculate and inviolate, without the stain of injustice, and never shattered by foreign forces, by wars nor earthquakes, in every revolution not only entirely preserved through miracles, but also never tempted by oppositional forces, as she is miraculously founded in the midst of water, and with marvelous tranquility standing firm . . . for infinite periods of time."[108]

Why did Venice remain—figuratively speaking—a virgin in spite of its commerce and many "bad women?" What are the semantic connotations of the virgin metaphor that secured its intelligibility at a time when "Venus" became gradually discredited?

Despite the devaluation of urban spaces as "sinful," Venice retained its status as an "immaculate city" because of the "noble" body politic it signified. Veronica Franco connected the perseverance of virgin Venice to the justice of patrician rule. In Sansovino's popular tourist guide, it was the government that, in remaining immaculate, secured the city's freedom from foreign domination. In paraphrasing Contarini, Sansovino emphasized that the government's inviolate liberty was a direct result of the city's noble origin. The city's founders were the "most noble inhabitants" of the nearby *terraferma*, who held the rank of "citizens, and then Senators of Rome."[109] The government's nobility, which was distinguished by justice and liberty, qualified it to rule wisely. In Venetian mythology, the city's virginity became a sign of the patriciate's aristocratic virtues. Venice remained immaculate because of the perfect government with which it was allegorically identified. In addition, the epithet "virgin city"—an oxymoron, given that urban spaces were increasingly defined as sites of decadence—underlined once again the miraculous uniqueness of Venice.

"Virginity" came to denote "nobility" in a variety of ways. In reevaluating agriculture and country dwelling as a "most noble" activity by emphasizing country women's chastity and virtue at a time when commerce and mercantile activities were in crisis, Agostino Gallo expressed an encompassing cultural trend. By the time "Venus" was vanishing, the Venetian patriciate was increasingly fascinated by the idyllic innocence of a life "in villa"—a tendency accompanying the patricians' abandonment of trade and their preference for profitable and secure land investments. As Gaetano Cozzi has pointed out, the Venetian colonization of the *terraferma* has to be understood as a process of reciprocal influence during which the ruling patriciate gradually absorbed the values and the lifestyle of the mainland aristocracy.[110] Thus the virgin metaphor retained its intelligibility as a signifier of virtue and nobility in a period of transition, during which a formerly mercantile patriciate refashioned itself after models deriving from the *terraferma* nobility. Virtue was no longer connected with commerce and international trade—activities through which Venice and its patriciate had once become rich and powerful—but with agriculture and the isolated life on a country estate. This change was especially marked during the last quarter of the sixteenth century, when the patriciate definitively abandoned sea traffic in exchange for more secure and profitable economic activities, and when the last attempts of the government to revive long-distance trade failed.

New theories of aristocratic virtue also gained currency in political discourse. Gasparo Contarini's complex rhetorical strategy of presenting a formally aristocratic state as a mixture of three different forms of government was gradually abandoned; while Contarini had been careful to camouflage the aristocratic (or even oligarchic) character of the government by calling the members of the Great Council "citizens," the new generation of political writers theorized openly the republic's aristocratic form. In so doing, supporters of Venice such as Paolo Paruta (a patrician himself) and critics of the republic such as Jean Bodin continued Contarini's line of thought rather than contradicting it; for Contarini did not recommend any political participation of nonpatricians.[111] On the contrary, he justified the institution of a hereditary political caste, that is, a "nobility of blood," in the name of "public reason."[112] Contarini also proclaimed that Venice had been founded by late Roman aristocratic refugees from mainland cities.[113]

Later writers such as Paolo Paruta developed Contarini's rather sober theory into an apotheosis of aristocratic rule based on virtue. In his "Orazione per i Nobili Veneziani morti a Lepanto" (Speech for Venetian noblemen fallen at Lepanto; 1571), he represented the republic's victory as a rare example of divine heroism; he addressed the young noblemen killed in action as "most courageous men," "perfect in every sense," and emphasized the "nobility of their descent." Moreover, he presented the battle as a turning point in Venice's and all of Italy's recent history, as a divine sign of fundamental renewal: "The public reputation declined . . . the ancient glory faded . . . but are we so blind as not to see the radiance of divine grace that has revealed itself so clearly by descending to these men, in order to save them through their virtue?"[114]

This renewal of political life was to be based on virtue enhanced by grace—a theme that he developed further in his book *Della perfetti-*

one della vita politica (On the perfection of political life). In Paruta's opinion, virtue was the cornerstone of civic life in a republic governed by noblemen. Furthermore, virtue was practically synonymous with nobility.[115] Paruta characterized virtue as the capacity to contain one's passions through reason, as a gift that humans possess to obtain felicity and perfection—that is, firmness and constancy. These qualities legitimized the nobility's power to rule and to enjoy the privileges of political independence and economic autonomy. In a circular line of argument, Paruta's interlocutors collapsed effects with causes and presented the nobility's moral perfection—rendered visible through magnificence—and its legal privileges as inseparable features. The aristocracy's virtue, its political rights, and its riches were timeless qualities conferred upon this distinguished class; the nobility's riches were not the result of work or exploitation, but a moral necessity. Without economic independence, virtue and nobility did not exist:

> Riches are of high importance to the nobility, responded Ambassador Ponte, because they are of great help to both the inner disposition and the outer workings of virtue: the rich man eats good food that renders the constitution delicate, and more disposed to discipline. . . . the rich man can provide his sons with good teachers, in order to develop their good inclinations [i.e., to become virtuous] with studies. . . . I regard somebody as rich who possesses enough to be a good father, and a good citizen: that is, somebody who, without anybody's help, can raise a family on his own income; who, abandoning any vile work, can attend to the government of the republic, to literary studies, to a military career, or to any other honorable and noble occupation.[116]

Financial independence and freedom from work characterized the nobility in economic terms. The source of its political privileges was equally self-evident: the earthly representation of divine hierarchies— that is, a legitimate government—was, in Paruta's eyes, "the most noble and most perfect [aspect] of our humanity." Domination did not derive from violations of the laws of nature, as a young participant in the debate suggested; on the contrary, natural differences distinguished between more or less noble, dignified, and virtuous men and established the divine order of things on earth. Not only was a legitimate government per se a noble institution, but it was legitimized insofar as it consisted of noblemen. This masterpiece of circular and hermetic reasoning, enhancing the status of aristocratic governments as intrinsically virtuous and perfect, culminated in a discussion of the Republic of Venice. Here Paruta paid homage to Contarini's theory of the republic as an aristocracy "representing" and combining three different forms of government.

But what does Paruta's discussion of nobility have to do with the increasing popularity of virginity as a metaphor in contemporary discourse, alluding, as we have posited, to a revised understanding of the patriciate as a ruling class? Virginity, according to Paruta, is a heroic virtue, characterized not by temperance and moderation, but by the complete eradication of unruly passions. It is a form of purity not unlike nobility itself. Virginity "lifts man above his own humanity"; it is the highest form of spirituality a human can achieve.[117] Apart from this brief exposition by the interlocutor Uberto Foglietta, virginity pervades Paruta's text as a hidden master metaphor—semantically as well as structurally. His key concepts show a remarkable affinity with the notion of virginity as a form of closure, purity, and stasis. In Paruta's definition, nobility *alias* virtue is a moral category justifying and rightfully demanding political and economic powers; it cannot be acquired through work or any other means; it is an innate, timeless quality that can only be lost or kept; it is a state of perfection, evidenced by firmness and constancy; it can be passed along only as long as it is contained and its exclusivity maintained. Like virginity, nobility is defined as a state of perfect purity existing *ab origine;* it has to be defended from corruption; it signifies autonomy and intransigence, and thus power and freedom from tyrannical rule. Tyranny is understood as being in opposition to the "natural" hierarchies of an order reflecting God-given differences among men. It is the usurpation of others' legitimate powers, the violent undoing of a primordial state. In Paruta's text, nobility, virtue, and perfection are polysemic concepts whose meanings overlap with "virginity" in many instances. Virginity functions as the invisible vanishing point for the reciprocal semantic relations Paruta establishes between his main concepts, the many connotations of which virginity, as a master metaphor, secretly subsumes under its rule.

Apart from semantic affinities, Paruta's rhetorical style shows traces of "virginity" on a strictly formal level. As much as virginity suggests the hermetic enclosure of a "truth" that would be destroyed if "penetrated" by a linear argumentation unmasking the "cause of causes" in an Aristotelian fashion, so can nobility be circumscribed only in a cyclical arrangement of references and metaphors: "Nobility generates several worthy virtues, that is, magnificence and magnanimity"; but "virtue combined with honor gives birth to nobility."[118] Nei-

ther virginity nor any of its equivalents—nobility, virtue, and magnificence, notions around which Paruta's Neoplatonic and hermetic
dialogue gravitates—would have resisted the attack of an analytic
search for origins, causes, and developments. The rhetorical power of
Paruta's ideological concepts derives from their very vagueness, their
mysteriously impenetrable point of reference, always already existing
in complete perfection. In earlier versions of the "myth," Venus and
the Virgin—two paradoxical images in oscillation—conveyed the
sense of Venice's uniqueness, her miraculous balance and ahistorical
stability; the same effect is achieved by Paruta's system of tautological
references. Eliminating Venus, the antithesis of virginity, Paruta pic-
tures nobility as a self-referential value that he can only encircle, never
fully grasp; as a magic quality whose inner core must remain untouched by reason lest it dissolve into nothing. Apart from its semantic
affinities to nobility, virginity functions as a structural requirement and
model image in Paruta's discourse on "perfection."

In Paruta's *Discorsi politici* (Political discourses; 1599), the topics
of containment, stability, and the preservation of independence are discussed more explicitly with reference to the Republic of Venice and
recent events in Venetian history. Paruta explains that Venice can preserve its independence and territorial integrity only through efforts to
secure peace; accordingly, he supports the republic's policy of strict
neutrality, aimed at preserving the existing balance of power in Italy
and Europe. In his eyes, the catastrophic foreign invasions during the
first decades of the century were ultimately due to the imperial aspirations of some Italian states (notably the Republic of Venice) and to
the weakness of others. Only a concentration on defense could secure
the survival of states in the current situation.[119] In stressing peace and
stability, Paruta explicitly rejected Machiavelli's opinion that for any
contemporary Italian state to be called great, it would have to conquer
the rest of Italy and reestablish the Roman Empire.[120]

The emphasis on defense and security was a common reaction to
the trauma of the Italian Wars, during which many states—with the
exception of Venice—lost their independence. Donato Giannotti, a citizen of Florence but an admirer of the Venetian republic, had proclaimed as early as 1540 that "the welfare of a state does not consist
of the greatness of its empire, but of a life in tranquility and universal
peace."[121] In his opinion, the perfection of Venice was proven not only
by its stability, but by the "excellent nobility" of its ruling class. The
Venetian aristocracy descended directly from late Roman senators and

had succeeded in "maintaining the purity of its blood" in the absence of revolutions and wars.[122] According to Giannotti, the formation of the patriciate as a hereditary political caste and the increasing power of the republic went hand in hand.[123]

Like Paruta and Giannotti, numerous other writers attributed the miraculous longevity of the Venetian republic to the immaculate state of its noble body politic. Because of the metaphorical relationships established between the patriciate, the city, the republic, and the figure of Venice, characteristics such as stability, independence, and immaculacy were freely interchangeable between these entities. Paruta's apotheosis of the republic's perfectly virtuous and immaculate nobility was popularized in a variety of ways. In his 1627 treatise, Pompeo Caimo attributed the longevity of the republic to the nobility's immaterial purity by elaborating the gendered opposition he envisioned between the amorphous matter of a female urban body and the masculine government as its form and soul. Mixed governments—that is, those stained with popular elements—are subject to revolutions; only purely aristocratic republics, as the only governments capable of embodying abstract moral values, last forever:

> And it truly appears to me that one can observe a beautiful similarity between republics and natural bodies, in that . . . those [bodies] which are not mixed with matter . . . as is true with regard to celestial bodies, according to the doctrine of Aristotle . . . are exempt from any alteration, and free of any danger of corruption; but those which are material and have not been able to flee any contact with matter—cause of every imperfection—are subject to a thousand variations. . . . and so the republics formed solely of noblemen without the participation of the common people are so well founded that they almost never suffer any alteration, and last in a certain way permanently; but those which consist of noblemen and commoners suffer a thousand mutations, by which they finally are overcome.[124]

As late as 1651, an English traveler to Venice named James Howell illustrated the miracle of how the republic remained inviolate by calling Venice "a pure Virgin, and Independent. . . . No forren Prince could come nere her privy parts all this while."[125] He also transcribed a document, supposedly preserved in the Hapsburg imperial archives, according to which the Venetian ambassador pronounced vows of allegiance to Emperor Maximilian I as part of the peace treaty of 1509.[126] Howell mitigated the disgrace of this sensational disclosure by insisting on calling Venice a virgin republic nonetheless, because " 'tis known that Mayds have teares at will, therefore most men thought these words were not cordiall but meer complements."[127]

Howell's coquetry with the myth of Venice's maidenlike state hints at the fact that in the seventeenth century, the belief in the city's mythical virginity gradually faded away. Open critiques of the republic—commonly referred to among modern historians as the "anti-myth"—began to appear. Piero Del Negro dates those writings back to the War of Crete (1645–69) and the aggregation of new noble families in 1646;[128] according to Franco Gaeta, it was the Interdict of 1606 that triggered the first substantial criticism.[129] In those writings, the Virgin-Venus paradox was often the point of departure for critics contrasting "myth" with "reality." Traiano Boccalini, a political satirist, ridiculed the Republic of Venice for "being a pure aristocracy and therefore the most perfect form of government that a free people could create," and he poked fun at

> our Senators, [who] neatly resemble those young girls who with chaste souls and virgin bodies get married. Like the neglected husbands who, in sending them to all the parties, throw them right into the balls of whorish affaires, so the free fatherlands thoughtlessly throw their civil-and well-minded senators into the abyss of tyranny through public praises, which elsewhere serve commonly to acquire a popular charisma and the following of the common people.[130]

Boccalini's harsh criticism of the blinding effects of Gorgon-like mythography marked the beginning of the end of the patriciate's pluri-secular tradition of self-fashioning and republican ideology. The representation of the nobility by a procession of patrician virgins during Dogaressa Morosini's coronation festivities in 1597 was perhaps the last, and most spectacular, allegorization of the body politic as immaculately noble. Soon afterward, the ruling class began to lose its purity, prestige, and power. In seventeenth-century "anti-mythography," the once well-protected, virgin body politic degenerated into a diseased, whorish monster.

Virgin Venice in Decay

Tommaso Campanella was probably the first to slander Venice as a whore. Desperate to please the pope,[131] he attacked the republic vehemently during the crisis of the Interdict, proclaiming that only her father in Rome could efficiently protect the city's virginity.[132] In his eyes, a young girl could not exist alone without falling prey to the machinations of corrupting powers: any ally Venice might seek in the upcoming war would violate her sovereignty, subject and rape her.[133] She might also leave "her monastery" and become a Lutheran whore; or else the *terraferma* inhabitants might rebel against her as they did during the Interdict of 1509, when Venice was at the mercy of Pope Julius II.[134]

While the government of Venice trumpeted the republic's inviolate state in order to foster cohesion in a moment of existential crisis, Campanella's text drew attention to the fragility of Venetian sovereignty.[135] However, although it polemicized against the myth of unstained independence, the influence of Campanella's *Antiveneti* as one of the first "anti-mythical" texts should not be overestimated. After the peaceful resolution of the Interdict, it clearly lost its momentum; moreover, the manuscript was banned from Venice and published rather late.

A more provocative treatise was published clandestinely and anonymously a few years later, the *Squitinio della libertà veneta* (The vote for Venetian liberty; 1612), in which the mythical claim of Venice as an originally independent and free city was debunked by an excellently informed insider. The author obviously knew the magisterial works of Contarini, Paruta, and other Venetian historians and—unlike Campanella—had insight into Venetian policymaking. Through a critical historical analysis, quoting from charters, chronicles, and other sources, he refuted constitutive elements of the myth point by point. He replaced the timeless and ahistorical quality of the Venetian myth with a genealogical model of development. The author argued that Venice was initially a vassal of the Holy Roman Empire, until around 1300; the period of undisturbed independence lasted for only about two hundred years, when Venice was forced to swear allegiance to Maximilian after her clamorous defeat at Agnadello. Also, her constitution was not always as immutable and perfect as her mythographers would have it. Originally, the doges were representatives of the emperor and enjoyed quasi-monarchical powers, until the Great Council was instituted as a representative assembly of the citizens of Venice. This assembly was democratic until membership became hereditary after a coup d'état in 1297, provoking serious unrest among the populace as well as among the ancient nobility. In this sense, neither the republic nor its body politic could be called immaculate: the republic, independent only since 1300, had been violated by invading troops in 1509; and the "nobility" of Venice was neither homogeneous nor of ancient descent—it was a legally defined group of mixed social origin endowed with hereditary political rights since the *serrata* of 1297, which arbitrarily restricted membership in the Great Council to those families who were elected that particular year. The author concluded his treatise by asserting that "liberty is the republic's government and rule, and resides in the nobility alone, while all the other inhabitants are deprived of it." [136]

For the Venetian patriciate, the year 1606 was the apex and turning point of mythical self-fashioning: while the government presented its policy during the Interdict as a defense against outside intruders in domestic affairs, as an affirmation of secular and state sovereignty in "temporal" ecclesiastical affairs, and, ultimately, as a battle for republican independence and liberty,[137] the crisis triggered critical investigations of Venice's self-proclaimed mythical nature. Although gradually fading from its central position as an ideology that legitimized a republican government in an age of rising absolutism, the myth was definitively discredited and abandoned only after the War of Crete. The glorious victory at Lepanto (1571) was not repeated; Venice lost its most important colony to the Ottoman Empire; and, most importantly, the government financed the war by selling privileges of membership in the Great Council—that is, aristocratic titles—to rich citizens of Venice and gentlemen from the *terraferma*.

Starting in 1646, the addition of new families to the Great Council in exchange for 100,000 ducats each provoked a lively discussion among the patriciate. The supporters of this proposal stressed that Venice needed money to finance the current war. Should the Turks win, not only the colonies would be lost, but Venice's independence and its patriciate altogether. Those who defended the patriciate's ancient "nobility of blood" against the pragmatists' viewpoint expressed their outrage at the proposal. In their eyes, the sale of membership titles to the Great Council would politically ruin the aristocracy, whose prestige resided in the purity of its blood and body. As Angelo Michiel put it: "this immaculate virgin, the honor of the republic, the lamp of the world, is proposed to be prostituted so cheaply to the vilest people who desire her?"[138]

In the opinion of many, policymaking after the sellout of 1646 became "grotesque,"[139] since the formerly homogeneous body politic degenerated into a "monster" consisting of various opposing factions. Because the newcomers were consistently denied important government positions, they formed an alliance with an increasing number of impoverished noblemen by buying their votes.[140] But rich parvenus were not the only ones who engaged in bribery. The Austrian ambassador to Venice and likely author of the "Relazione della Serenissima Republica di Venezia," Cesareo Della Torre, described the republic's entire political class as corrupt. After having sold its only true treasure—its purity—the nobility neglected to preserve its legendary virtues. Members of the ancient patriciate started to cater to the new nobility's demands in order to secure their prominence and positions: "It is most noteworthy that the ancient Nobility has become an admirer of their [the new noblemen's] manners . . . in order to secure their favors and their votes; because those, as practitioners of commerce, don't want to sell their favors if not for the high price of offices, and flattery."[141]

The sale of the aristocracy's virginity changed the practice of policymaking irreversibly; once the purity of its blood and body was exchanged for money, all political and juridical decisions became a matter of negotiation and commerce. Not only the virgin republic, but Justitia itself became a prostitute: "There are two evil scandals: the first consists in conceding grace instead of rendering justice, the second in conceding grace for a price . . . and thus turning her, who should be a maid [i.e., Justice], into a public prostitute."[142]

The most devastating undoing of the myth of Venice was probably Saint-Didier's travel account *La Ville et Republique de Venise* (The city and republic of Venice), published in 1670. In contrast to sixteenth-century writers, he stressed the many changes the republic and its constitution experienced before it reached its classical state. After a fair and sober presentation of the government's magistrates, his style became polemic when he discussed the highly praised liberty of Venice. In his opinion, one should rather speak of political libertinage: "One sees once in a while a Venetian nobleman living in the first floor of a house and a courtesan . . . in the second, without causing any trouble to the nobleman: this is the essence of Venice's liberty. . . . The famous liberty of Venice attracts foreigners in high numbers, and the distractions and pleasures make them stay and empty their wallets."[143]

Saint-Didier then described the patricians' extramarital affairs with courtesans, their debauchery and lasciviousness, and proclaimed their lifestyle to be an indicator of their general state of corruption. Syphilis had irreversibly corroded Venice's once immaculate body politic:

> In this sort of disorder, and in this sort of general corruption, one should not wonder that the disease that usually follows such a lifestyle is very

widespread; I don't mean to say among the courtesans, who are almost all infected, but also among the married women, and more so among noblewomen than among commoners' wives; and the reason is that . . . not only the youth, but also the married patricians have fallen into debauchery . . . and the result is a general corruption.[144]

Thus Venus made a late but clamorous and pervasive comeback in the second half of the seventeenth century. It marked the definite defeat of virgin Venice: the rhetoric of carefully balanced paradoxes aiming to speak the unspeakable was gone and discredited. Contemporary writers did not "deceive" their readers; their intent was to unmask mythical commonplaces as chimeras. Liberty was in "reality" libertinage, the republic's perfect and most virtuous government was in "reality" corrupt and unjust. In unveiling the mystique of a political discourse that, Gorgon-like, had resisted analytic dissection for so long, seventeenth-century anti-mythographers exposed the metaphor of immaculate perfection as a clever means to disguise dirty politics. Slaying Medusa's allegedly immortal Venetian sisters,[145] they demonstrated that virgin Venice was in reality a whore. A patriciate that had allowed its immaculately noble body to be stained by unworthy elements had proven to be unworthy of the awe and respect it had formerly commanded. As a consequence of the nobility's loss of innocence, the myth of Venetian perfection became entirely untenable.

The patriciate was aware of the destabilizing effects of adding new families to the Great Council in 1646. In giving up the principle of immaculate reproduction as the basis of its claim to power, however, the nobility was anything but thoughtless or purposefully suicidal. As already discussed in chapter 1, its decision to let outsiders stain its virgin body was triggered by an existential threat that outweighed the problem of ideological incoherence: apart from its financial needs in a time of war, the government was plagued by the steady numerical decline of the ruling class. This phenomenon endangered the constitutional procedures of the republic, in which a highly differentiated system of magistrates and offices was run exclusively by patricians. As another French observer, Amelot de la Houssaie, put it: "With regard to the sale of the nobility, it is absolutely necessary, given that the ancient families are becoming extinct day by day, and because the government would decline into an oligarchy if one did not replace them with others."[146]

Vettor Sandi, an eighteenth-century historian of Venice, defended the extension of the Great Council in 1646 (which would not be the last expansion) in similar terms: the constitution of the republic was threatened by an inevitably shrinking body politic.[147] Thus it was not the aristocracy's voluntary sellout that caused its political downfall after the War of Crete. Neither was the deflowering of its virgin body the main problem. In stressing the patriciate's reproductive deficiencies, the above-mentioned authors alluded to a long-term development for which the addition of new members to the Great Council was supposed to be a pragmatic remedy. The problem itself reached back to a period when the myth was still in full bloom, when the virgin metaphor was still in exclusive command of political discourse. Metaphorically speaking, the problem was virginity itself. Theories such as Paruta's, which emphasized the nobility's exclusivity and purity, had been successful in legitimizing the patriciate's claim to power, but developed a paradoxical dynamic when transposed into concrete social practice. Since the nobility existed as a morally distinguished class only as long as it remained hermetically enclosed, only a strictly endogamous marriage behavior (among women) could guarantee the survival of the body politic as a privileged class, securing the unstained transfer of its God-given virtues to the next generation. On the other hand, it was precisely the patriciate's restricted marriage behavior in the context of dowry inflation and monachization strategies that caused the number of noble marriages to decline rapidly and jeopardized the survival of the body politic in the seventeenth century.

The patriciate's game of immaculate reproduction—shaped, as we have seen, by conspicuous consumption and patriarchal family structures—derived its meaning from political theories about what constituted "true nobility." The increase in patrician monachization rates at the end of the sixteenth and the beginning of the seventeenth century was the most vivid symptom of an ideological dilemma: permanent celibacy among women became a fashionable alternative to marriage—and, increasingly, a requirement—only insofar as the emphasis on aristocratic distinction made misalliances between patrician women and nonpatrician men undesirable. Coerced monachizations were the result of cultural constraints that identified the "nobility" of Venice's ruling class with its morally and physically unpolluted state, that is, the enclosure of its body and the purity of its blood. They were the most painful expression of a self-destructive social practice, generated by the paradoxical and circular logic of the myth of Venice and the republic's allegorical representation as a virgin. Accelerating the decline in patrician marriages, peaking monachization rates only temporarily preserved the exclusivity and distinction of the nobility; in the long term, they were, ironically, the very cause of its pollution. In 1646, the patriciate's uniquely restrictive reproductive system collapsed, after its endogamous and competitive marriage behavior had preserved the "immaculacy" and timeless "perfection" of the body politic for more than one and a half centuries.[148]

As Venetian mythographers had repeatedly pointed out, paradoxes, perfection, and paralysis were indeed antithetical to the human condition. No longer serving as a sign of God-given grace and miraculous wisdom, the "impossibility" of virgin Venice had finally become real. Once Venus was back in command of public discourse, monachizations among patrician women ceased to be mandatory for those who did not find a proper match. Although they continued to offer an honorable and prestigious lifestyle until the end of the republic and beyond, their appeal as a social practice that guaranteed the purity of the body politic was gone. The evolution of Venetian political discourse from myth to anti-myth unfolded as the creation and subsequent undoing of the paradoxical assumptions and circular logic on which the myth was based. The initial triumph and then collapse of coerced monachizations as a "total social fact," designed to realize the ideal of an "immaculate" body politic, displayed the same dynamic. Reaching a peak at the end of the sixteenth century, virginity and exclusivity as master metaphors in political discourse and as organizing principles in society collapsed into their opposites half a century later.

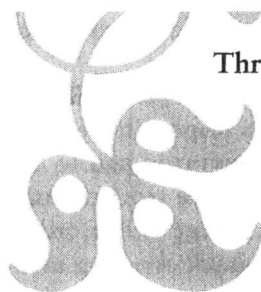

Three

THE THEOLOGY AND POLITICS OF CLAUSURA

In 1563, the Council of Trent decided to systematically impose strict encloisterment *(clausura)* on all female religious communities independently of their individual rules, privileges, and exemptions.[1] Three years later, Pope Pius V reconfirmed this decree. Stressing the nuns' vows of obedience, he abolished the rule according to which no monastic could be forced to observe a stricter discipline than the one she had professed to follow; he also disregarded the economic constraints of mendicant and tertiary communities, who relied on outside contributions for their very survival.[2] In order to expedite the new decree, all convents were made subject to local episcopal authorities; apostolic visitors would have to periodically check the extent to which strict encloisterment was enforced. Suppressing the demand of many religious women to actively participate in the work of reconstructing the Catholic Church and evangelizing nonbelievers, Pope Pius V defined clausura as the sine qua non of post-Tridentine female monasticism.

Since the late fifteenth century, monastic reformers had repeatedly tried to subject female religious communities to strict encloisterment. In some cases, nuns and *pizzochere* (tertiary nuns who had not professed holy vows)[3] willingly agreed to obey a harsher rule, but most chapters refused to be "reformed," insisting on their ancient privileges and exemptions. Some convents rejected clausura out of principle, claiming that their dire financial situation and charitable activities made relationships with the outside world necessary.[4] Order generals, bishops, and civic authorities justified their repeated interventions in convent affairs by accusing the nuns under their jurisdiction of constant violations of monastic discipline—most particularly neglect of chastity.

Morals had indeed loosened in the pre-Reformation period; itinerant preachers held unruly nuns' sexual escapades responsible for the many manifestations of God's wrath that contemporaries had to endure. City governments all over Italy started to enforce strict encloisterment as part of an encompassing program to restore public order. Purging the public sphere of "wayward" nuns, miracle-working mystics, prophetesses, and *pizzochere* became paramount to the kind of spiritual and moral reform that lay and church authorities envisioned for nuns and the rest of society as well.[5] Clausura was supposed to protect the sacred enclosures of Christ's virgin brides from the danger of pollution, but it was also supposed to solve concrete problems in convent management. The privatization of convent properties had been a dangerous trend since the beginning of female monasticism.[6] Isolating the nuns from powerful friends and relatives was meant to reduce outside pressures on abbesses and chapters and to restore collective self-government under the tutelage of civic authorities and local bishops. The abolishment of lifelong terms for abbesses in favor of triennial elections usually accompanied the clausura reform and was aimed at preventing individual families from manipulating the management of convents that they had come to regard as secure dependencies for their female offspring.[7]

The attempts of lay and ecclesiastic authorities to reform individual convents remained by and large unsuccessful, however, unless accompanied by the zeal of reform-minded abbesses and the nuns themselves.[8] Dominican and Augustinian nuns were usually the first to embrace voluntary "observance." The inmates of Benedictine convents, most of whom were unmarried female aristocrats eager to maintain as comfortable a lifestyle as possible, usually disposed of enough family connections, money, and influence to appeal to Rome whenever city governments, bishops, or order generals attempted to infringe upon their ancient "rights." Their resistance was hard to break. Only when city governments and church leaders gained papal approval and coordinated their efforts, as happened in early-sixteenth-century Venice, was it possible to confine religious women whose public appearances were increasingly perceived as improper, transgressive, or "scandalous."[9]

Following the groundbreaking work of Gabriella Zarri, Italian historians of gender and religion have stressed the importance of strict encloisterment in the confinement of other women as well.[10] Disorderly nuns and "living saints" were not the only women locked up behind convent walls; currently active as well as "converted" prostitutes, "badly married" women, orphans, and spinsters were categorized by sexual status and permanently or temporarily confined in closed institutions run by lay patrons or by the church.[11] In her seminal synthesis of two millennia of female monasticism, Jo Ann Kay McNamara confirms that in the age of what Michel Foucault has termed "the Great Confinement,"[12] "poor women, begging women, abused women, and immoral women were a source of increasing anxiety. Controlling them became the key to the whole fabric of social control *and the cloistered convent became the model for that control*" (my emphasis).[13]

The introduction of clausura gained exemplary significance in the process of the social, cultural, and institutional transformations that other historians have analyzed from the perspective of "confessionalization," "modern" identity formation, and the imposition of "social discipline." Wolfgang Reinhard has argued that all post-Reformation churches were forced to outline "clear criteria of orthodoxy and membership to distinguish themselves from each other," and to supervise their members' adherence to these norms.[14] The dissemination and interiorization of these norms through books and school education, the prohibition of counter-propaganda, and the criminalization of deviators were parts of a complex program to achieve "confessional discipline." This process required, but also helped to develop, the bureaucracy and institutions typical of early modern territorial states; the "politics of confessionalization" fostered the creation of territorial or national identities among a "homogeneous" citizenry. In addition to the centralized efforts of state and church in imposing confessional standards from above, the "decentralized processes . . . governed by new cognitive methods," as analyzed by Michel Foucault, contributed to the process of confessionalization, which, according to Hans Schilling, culminated between 1580 and 1620 in the Empire but declined as a result of "irenic impulses" during the Thirty Years' War.[15]

Until the sixteenth century, "discipline" was understood as the "exterior expression of an interior state of mind," as a form of modesty and restraint practiced in monastic communities and aimed at promoting harmony. A properly disciplined body and mind allowed reason to rule over passions and enabled monastic as well as urban communities to cultivate "civilized" intercourse.[16] In post-Tridentine

Catholic societies, discipline became synonymous with the normative observance of monastic rules.[17] Gabriella Zarri has argued that both the introduction of clausura and the foundation of new female orders were integral parts of the reformers' efforts to "discipline" and "confessionalize" Catholic believers. The Dimesse, an order that was founded in 1585 by Antonio Pagano in Vicenza and that rapidly spread all over the Veneto,[18] were in her eyes a typically post-Tridentine female religious community. They aimed at achieving "perfection" through communal living arrangements and mutual "corrections," and served church and society through the education of young girls and assistance to the sick.[19]

Despite—or, rather, because of—many religious women's attempts to contribute to the program of reconstruction and reform, the Catholic Church obstructed the foundation and dissemination of new female orders unless they renounced their active engagement in the world and emphasized contemplation under the condition of strict encloisterment. In France, where the Council of Trent was not recognized until the early seventeenth century and, as a consequence, strict clausura did not immediately become mandatory, communities of "female Jesuits" such as the Visitandines, Ursulines, and Daughters of Charity mushroomed. In Italy, the papal decree of 1566 demanding the observance of strict enclosure by all female religious communities indiscriminately had a devastating effect on nuns eager to help "evangelize" the masses. The Ursulines, founded by Angela Merici in 1525 as a company of religious women who continued to live at home but were committed to chastity and who collectively ran schools and hospitals, escaped clausura and permanent vows only because of bishop Saint Carlo Borromeo's special protection. The Jesuit-like Institute of Mary Ward, which immediately after its approval in 1616 opened dependencies all over Catholic Europe, was less fortunate: initially supported by Pope Paul V, the congregation was dissolved after its founder came under attack by male competitors and was condemned as a heretic.[20]

One of the effects of strict monastic enclosure was a resurgence of female mysticism. Since the secular clergy claimed a "monopoly over the channels of grace," women mystics' ecstatic encounters with God were perceived to be almost as threatening to the newly reconstituted church as other nuns' plans for a *vita activa* (active life). As long as women endowed with prophetic gifts and the power of miracle-working did not fall prey to devilish obsessions, attract public interest, or disseminate heresies, however, Catholic authorities tolerated their asceticism and devotional practices.[21] The subjection of all female convents to episcopal authority and the suppression of religious women's public appearances were intended to eliminate the "scandalously" worldly behavior of nuns as much as their extravagant manifestations of faith. Strict encloisterment was supposed to turn convents into the "enclosed gardens" of paradise, into hermetically sealed oases of the sacred in the midst of bustling urban centers, into living metaphors of the inviolate and soon-to-be-unified church triumphant.[22] Gradually, these ideals were put into practice, but only over the vehement resistance of nuns who had never vowed to observe clausura and at the cost of suffocating the most vibrant expressions of female religious activities, which in the late fifteenth and early sixteenth centuries had shaped the devotional practices of aristocrats and the urban middle classes alike.[23]

The clausura taboo also obstructed the nuns' literary and artistic activities. Although religious women never entirely ceased to write plays and compose music, for example, the prohibition against performing in front of lay audiences, cultivating relationships with writers and musicians outside the convent, taking singing lessons, or reading secular literature severely limited their productivity and accomplishments.[24] With the publication of the Index of Forbidden Books in 1555 and the subsequent inspection and purging of convent libraries, the nuns' lack of access to even religious books that were deemed dangerous or unfitting similarly curtailed their intellectual development.[25] Nuns were encouraged to read monastic rules, the lives of saints, and "how-to" books intended to guide them on their path to spiritual perfection. Gabriella Zarri has argued that the explosion of publications on Catholic piety after Trent, addressed to both lay and religious women, promoted the type of female identity formation aimed at interiorizing the ideals of chastity, obedience, and retreat from the public sphere that the institutional reforms sought to impose from above.[26] Most of the religious texts authored by nuns were mystical in nature, in contrast to the more learned, theological writings produced in convents during the late Middle Ages.[27]

While father confessors, authors of guidebooks for virgins, and other such counselors did the "capillary" ideological work aimed at rendering clausura if not desirable or even acceptable, at least intelligible to the increasing numbers of involuntary nuns subjected to it, an efficient bureaucracy and well-functioning executive organs were employed to supervise, coerce, and criminalize those who resisted it. In Venice, state governments had since the early sixteenth century collaborated with episcopal authorities in enhancing monastic discipline for the purpose of turning convents into civic institutions; that is, through the very observance of monastic rules such as clausura, triennial abbess elections, "democratic" property management, and communal living arrangements, the state sought to "liberate" convents from the influence and manipulation of private families, out-of-state order generals, and papal legates, in order to substitute for them government-run magistrates. The reconstruction of the nuns' collective self-government was achieved through the concerted interventions of city governments and episcopal authorities, and served to develop the executive institutions characteristic of "modern" states.

Clausura was at the center of a complex process of restructuring society: it functioned to subject women in "liminal" states to systematic surveillance, to express Catholicism's firmest values, to produce docility in female bodies and minds, and to accelerate the development of efficient, functionally differentiated, "modern" bureaucracies. In late Renaissance Venice, the most immediate pressure to impose clausura derived from the potlatch dynamic as analyzed above. Venetian convents, some of which were compared to public brothels in early-sixteenth-century apocalyptic preaching, were gradually transformed into the safe-deposits of patrician blood and bodies that the state depended upon for the reproduction of its aristocracy. Convent reform became an issue of paramount political importance especially after the Council of Trent, when patrician monachization rates reached unequaled heights and reinvigorated church hierarchies competed with secular magistrates in managing convent affairs.

Sacred Enclosures

As Marino Sanudo reports, Patriarch Gerolamo Querini and a delegation of senators inspected the convent of Santa Maria della Celestia in 1525, "because those very immodest nuns wear long hair and other things . . . and when they saw a certain daughter Taiapiera with braids, the patriarch took hold of her and cut her hair off with his own hands."[28] The nuns' worldly hairstyles and clothing would preoccupy generations of patriarchs to come. In 1578, Patriarch Giovanni Trevisan outlawed the Venetian nuns' habit of wearing "blond and curly hair," as well as "shoes of the Roman type" (platform shoes), "pleated

Choir habit of the nuns of San Zaccaria, ca. 1500. From Helyot,
Histoire des ordres monastiques, 6:314, fig. 2. (Courtesy of
Department of Special Collections, Stanford University Libraries.)

and elaborate shirts in the fashion of secular women, and fine handkerchiefs to hold in one's hands."[29] In 1579, he excommunicated the nuns
of Santa Lucia because they refused to wear their black veils.[30] In 1592,
Patriarch Lorenzo Priuli admonished the nuns of Sant' Andrea de Zirada "to wear honest and modest clothes, underneath as well as on top
so that neither the breast nor any other body part should be exposed
. . . [the nuns] should not show their hair but wear their headbands
low over their foreheads."[31] When visiting the same convent seventeen
years later, Patriarch Francesco Vendramin ruled that the nuns' dresses

Benedictine du Monastere de S.ᵗ
Zacharie a Venise en habit ordinaire dans la maison

Informal habit of the nuns of San Zaccaria, ca. 1500. From Helyot,
Histoire des ordres monastiques, 6:314, fig. 1. (Courtesy of
Department of Special Collections, Stanford University Libraries.)

"should not be colored nor extraordinarily refined, their hair should
be low without *fonghi*[32] on their temples or *zuffi* [bangs] on their foreheads, the headbands . . . low, simple, unpleated; nor should anyone
wear a silk dress; the dress should be high-necked, the veils abundant,
so that they entirely cover breast and shoulders . . . the wearing of
platform shoes is totally prohibited."[33] Inspecting the convent of San
Zaccaria, Patriarch Vendramin requested that the nuns veil their heads
"so that one sees nothing of the hair" and that "the veils of the shoulders be wide and ample so that they cover the flesh entirely, [and that

Habit of the nuns of Santa Maria delle Vergini, ca. 1500. From Helyot,
Histoire des ordres monastiques, 3:50, fig. 2. (Courtesy of
Department of Special Collections, Stanford University Libraries.)

they be] fine, but not transparent."[34] In 1619, he issued a general ordi-
nance prohibiting "the use of sleeves of fine fabrics . . . of fishnet stockings, of shoes of the Roman kind with silk strings . . . [of] earrings
. . . [and] brooches of silver or gold, or with any other kind of embel-
lishment like enamel or pearls . . . one should not see long hair hanging
down from the temples, nor curls in the form of *fonghetti* and *monticelli* [little mountains] on the forehead."[35]

    As this random selection of quotations illustrates, Venetian nuns
were as tenacious in wearing fancy hairstyles, barely veiled décolletage,

and high-heeled shoes as Venetian patriarchs were in trying to prevent them from doing so. The nuns' fashions were a prominent issue among "reform" legislators in the decades before the Council of Trent and especially afterward, when just about every aspect of the nuns' lives was subject to regulation and close surveillance by both episcopal and—as far as the nuns' interactions with persons outside the convent were concerned—state authorities. After centuries of negligent observance, a reinvigorated church specified the proper monastic forms of the nuns' most basic everyday activities, from their sleeping and eating habits[36] to their forms of communication and musical activities;[37] unnecessary visual sensations and affective attachments of any sort were to be completely eliminated.[38] What Marcel Mauss would have called the nuns' proper monastic "bodily techniques" or "habits" were to become—in the eyes of monastic reformers—points of departure, exterior signs, and results of their spiritual renewal.[39] As Dionisio Certosino proposed in his "Dialogo . . . della Riforma delle Monache" (Dialogue on the reform of nuns; 1576), strict bodily discipline characterized by sensual deprivation and containment would strengthen the nuns' fight against temptations.[40] Since lack of resistance to even minor sensual pleasures was supposed to trigger a chain reaction of desires jeopardizing the nuns' chastity,[41] post-Tridentine patriarchs aimed at eliminating every imaginable source of pleasure and temptation, ranging from colored wall fabrics, backrests, and footstools to "magnificent and splendid beds" covered with lace blankets, cushions, and pillows.[42] More dangerous distractions, such as the exchange of letters and gifts, the reception of non-related visitors, or even gondola tours and parties outside the convent, were strictly forbidden and increasingly prosecuted.

Following the logic of a presumed hierarchy of temptations, the entire body of laws issued by the Venetian government and curia regarding the nuns' bodily discipline was instrumental in preserving their virginity. Since coerced monachizations were a widespread practice, protecting the nuns' immaculacy required increasingly close surveillance by the authorities. The persistent but unsuccessful efforts of state and church to police the nuns' bodies, to provide for their spiritual welfare *malgré elles,* showed the cynicism of a policy in which power was contested metaphorically over issues of gender. While the post-Tridentine church was particularly interested in safeguarding the nuns' fragile state of angelic perfection because their virginity signified the (lost but soon-to-be-recovered) unity and integrity of the church,[43] government authorities saw violation of the nuns' purity as a danger to social order. After the military defeat of Venetian troops at Agnadello in 1509, the republic's political instability was presented as the result of a collapse of essential distinctions in society. Next to prostitutes and sodomites, sexually active nuns were seen as the most conspicuous symptom of a spreading social disorder. When in 1514 the Council of Ten (the highest legislative, executive, and juridical government office in Venice at the time) issued a comprehensive law against fornication with nuns, the government explained its previous ineffectual handling of the issue by declaring that "the contamination of the sacred virgins dedicated to God" was a crime too horrible for former legislators to have conceived. It was referred to as a "plague" and a sign of contemporary society's decay:

> When our forefathers of the first government of our city took care that due punishments be inflicted on the perpetrators of every sort of crime except for the heinous vice and sin of sacrilege, that is, the contamination of the virgins consecrated to God, they testified that . . . because such dastardliness had been unknown for hundreds of years . . . those holy forefathers of our republic thought and took it for granted that such a loathsome crime, that is, the violation of the brides of Christ our Lord and God, could never come to mind in any Christian.—Such did they judge the horror and abomination of this sin.—But in the knowledge that for many years since then such a plague has been teeming and . . . growing, different provisions were taken to eradicate it, which, mostly limited to the punishment of the result . . . [proved ineffective].[44]

The intrinsic "horror" of the crime could be alluded to only metaphorically. Sex with nuns had a theoretically unspeakable meaning, because it constituted the threefold crime of "sacrilege . . . spiritual adultery (insofar as it violates the bride of Christ), and incest (because a nun is the bride of God, who is our Father, and consequently she is our blood relative, because we are all God's children)."[45] According to modern anthropologists, a taboo is instrumental in symbolizing and safeguarding the three most fundamental prohibitions in human culture (prohibitions regarding the sacred, other men's wives, and blood-related women); its violation signifies the collapse of all distinctions in society.[46] The drama and apocalyptic quality of the legislators' rhetoric in 1514 indicated a new emphasis on the dangers of sex crimes against God—in contrast to the fifteenth century, when fornication with nuns was regularly referred to as incest and adultery.[47] Stressing the plaguelike effects and contagious nature of such crimes justified

the intervention of the republic's most powerful council and legitimized the tightening of punishments and jurisdictional procedures.

Even before the precarious outcome of the Italian Wars had sharp-
ened the government's sense for identifying the erratic forces of political and social dissolution, sex with nuns was conceived to be miasmic.
Sexually active nuns did not just create a plaguelike disorder; "nuns-
turned-whores" literally caused the plague as a manifestation of God's
wrath. During his Christmas sermon in 1497, Fra Thimoteo of San
Francesco della Vigna denounced the convents as public brothels, as
sites where sins more horrible than blasphemy, usury, and sodomy
were committed. He exhorted the doge, who was among the audience,
to prevent the current plague epidemic from spreading by disciplining
the nuns:

> My Lords, you close the churches out of fear of the plague; you act
> wisely; but if God will, closing the churches won't do. If you want to
> counteract the causes of the plague, they are the horrible sins that are
> being committed; the blasphemy of God and the saints; the schools of
> sodomy; the innumerable contracts of usury closed at Rialto; and above
> all, the sale of justice in favor of the rich and against the poor. And
> worse: whenever a [foreign] lord comes to this country, you show them
> the convents of nuns, not convents but public whorehouses. Most serene
> prince! I know that you are not ignorant, and that you know everything
> better than I. Make provisions . . . against the plague.[48]

In corrupting and perverting fundamental symbolic distinctions,
sex with nuns was perceived to be both cause and manifestation of a
contagious disease. Hygienic measures had to be taken: the law of
1514 against fornication with nuns was inspired by the government's
decision "to purge our country of such a horrible vice."[49] It aimed to
redraw and stabilize the boundaries between the sacred and the profane, between brides of Christ and women "of the world." It not only
prohibited sex, but ruled that nuns were to live in perpetual seclusion;
only close relatives were allowed to talk to them, such as "fathers,
brothers, uncles, nephews, and cousins, that is, sons of brothers and
sisters of fathers and mothers, and in-laws, and only at the bars of the
parlors and not anywhere else."[50] Exceptions for physicians, servants,
father confessors, and other employees were specified. The law tried
to restore "order" by manipulating the nuns' bodies through the re-
arrangement of social space. Inner spaces within the city were created
by prosecuting and punishing those who transgressed the newly defined boundaries: Venetian convents were to be turned into arrange-

ments of interlocking interiors, into "enclosed gardens" hiding the "enclosed gardens" of virginal bodies.[51] To the same extent that virginity signified the purity of an interior bodily space, convents were to become oases of purity and sacred enclosures in the midst of Venice; disorderly nuns "wandering about the city" scandalized the public. Bodily discipline required separation from the world. The Benedictine rules, translated for the newly reformed nuns of Santa Maria della Celestia in 1527, distinguished four types of nuns according to the principles of seclusion and discipline:

> [There are] the cenobites, that is, those who live in convents . . . the hermits, who . . . go to the desert . . . in solitude . . . the Beguines . . . who . . . work in the world . . . and, not secluded in the harems of God, but in their own rooms, have as a rule their own desires, and their own will . . . the vagabonds [i.e., mendicants] . . . [who] live all throughout their lives in different provinces . . . always wandering around, never stable, and succumbing to their own desires and to gluttony.[52]

The "vagabond" nuns who upset the authorities in the early sixteenth century, however, were not the above-mentioned mendicant and third-order nuns (who were "unruly" per se), but the "non-observant" cenobites who had left their "harems" by way of papal exemptions. In 1501, the Senate asked the pope to revoke and annul these exemptions because "the nuns . . . who have left their convents under the pretext of papal briefs . . . are roving around the city and countryside as they please, with great scandal, and universal murmuring."[53] Eventually, the coerced encloistering of all types of nuns that was decreed by the Council of Trent in 1563 toned down the apocalyptic rhetoric of secular legislators. Whereas pre-Tridentine reformers had demanded that society be purged of disorderly nuns, post-Tridentine governments supervised the nuns' seclusion so that "the sacred sites where virgins dedicated to the service of our Divine Majesty are secluded, as well as the virgins themselves, should be preserved and guarded from the profanations and contaminations of the world."[54] In 1604, when the Council of Ten reissued the law of 1514, the problem of how to keep the nuns inside—now being dealt with by church authorities—was replaced by the problem of how to keep intruders out. In this respect, the purification and reordering of society did not seem to have made significant progress, in spite of the fact that episcopal and papal reformers had defined the nuns' clausura as the essential characteristic and general prerequisite of female monasticism.

The nuns' compulsory seclusion under the Tridentine decree of

1563—which was reconfirmed by Pius V in 1566 and Gregory XIII in 1572—was met with strong resistance and continued to create disciplinary problems even after it was recognized as a general norm. Clausura was not required by most of the monastic orders, nor was it part of the nuns' vows;[55] and although the contemplative orders had always insisted on the nuns' retirement from the world, special papal privileges had formerly granted exemptions. In many cases, perfect seclusion was practically impossible to realize. Mendicant nuns and *pizzochere,* for example, depended financially on begging or work.[56]

Female monastic life changed drastically after perpetual encloistering became obligatory; byzantine rules specified not only how the convents' interior spaces were to be rearranged, but also how, where, when, and with whom nuns were allowed to communicate.[57] Architecturally, convents were to be transformed into panoptical spaces. When visiting a convent, post-Tridentine patriarchs would carefully inspect every single one of the building's orifices for their "safety" and function. They usually ordered that all doors except for one opening "to land" and one opening "to sea" be walled up or locked with multiple keys, and that "superfluous" windows, balconies, and *ruote* (revolving drawers through which things could be passed in and out) be covered with Venetian blinds, wooden boards, or bars.[58] The locks and doors of the nuns' cells, in contrast, had to be removed so that any "private" interior to which the abbesses did not have immediate access was eliminated.[59] Nuns were subject to the inspection of superiors at any time, but could not see or be seen by people "of the world"—climbing up the campanile, for example, was strictly forbidden.

Another important aspect of the program for enclosure was protecting the nuns' patrimonies from alienation through corruption, mismanagement, debts, and squandering. The convents' financial management was reorganized in order to prevent the powerful relatives of individual nuns or corrupt estate managers from usurping convent property. The abbesses' powers were curtailed by transforming their formerly lifelong governments into triennial appointments[60] and by restoring the authority and decision-making powers of the convents' chapters. The nuns' resolutions, however, were subject to the approval of state magistrates, the patriarch, and three elected procurators.[61] Formal authorities were supposed to contain the influence of private families.[62] Also, the convents' indiscriminate distributions of "charities" in the form of food and wine—which in fact were often bribes for servants and go-betweens or gifts for friends and relatives—were entirely forbidden, because they squandered important resources.[63] The idea was to transform convents into economically self-sufficient entities whose possessions were shielded from dissipation; mortmain laws, on the other hand, prevented ecclesiastical patrimonies from growing.[64] Since restoring order meant drawing boundaries, the nuns' properties as well as their bodies were to be fenced in (see chapter 4).

Given the nuns' active and passive resistance, the project of reducing all nuns to a life in perpetual seclusion was extremely difficult to realize. Arguments, threats, and force were variously applied to make them observe the new rule. In 1594, the abbesses and vicars of two Franciscan convents were imprisoned after the nuns went on "clausura strike." According to the nuncio, they "tore down the wall of the cloister, entered the exterior churches, opened the doors, and stayed there for a whole day, walking about the church, and returned to their seclusion only after the government threatened them . . . in order to be obeyed without uproar, it was necessary to employ the [secular] authorities and [executive] organs."[65] More frequent than conscious acts of protest, however, were inadvertent transgressions of the clausura law. Bishop Antonio Grimani reported to the nuncio that in his diocese of Torcello, many nuns had fallen into automatic excommunication because they "allowed female relatives, particularly girls who have been educated in the convent, to enter the seclusion, not, however, with bad intentions nor with scandal, but rather because of the ignorance or bad customs of those villages."[66] Customs worsened and ignorance increased the more peripheral and remote a convent was. In Feltre, shepherds grazed their sheep in convent gardens;[67] the nuns of Aquileia "live entirely as they please" because they "have never deigned to obey the patriarch, nor to care about ecclesiastic censures."[68] This patriarch's laxity was fatal in a period when Tridentine hard-liners in Rome evaluated a bishop's competence by his ability to impose the clausura rule effectively. Judging it necessary "that Our Lord should know of the state in which most of these miserable people of Aquileia live, who have out of ignorance entered the seclusion of the nuns," the papal emissary gave a disastrous report of the discipline in this diocese; two months later, the patriarch resigned "because of old age."[69] But it was not only the ignorant villagers, libertine nuns, and negligent bishops of the republic's periphery who were reluctant to accept or unable to understand the full implications of clausura as defined by Tridentine reformers. Even the doge's granddaughter had to request the pope's absolution for briefly entering a convent when visiting the nuns she had grown up with, not knowing—or pretending not to know—of the prohibition.[70] And only months before his colleague from Aquileia was forced to retire, Patriarch Giovanni Trevisan declared that he himself would have to resign if the government continued to refuse its support in implementing the nuns' general clausura. He frankly admitted his lack of authority:

> I have not failed . . . to make provisions against the many abuses, disorders, and scandals that have happened, and continue to happen daily in the convents of nuns. . . . I have talked about this often in the Most Excellent Collegio, and many times also to His Serenity and the Most Illustrious Signoria . . . with the intervention of the . . . Deputies over the Convents and my Vicar, [and] I have discovered the many evils, and requested that I should be given the help of the secular authorities in order to cope with them. . . . Individual punishments, although helpful, are not sufficient, since there is practically no clausura in the convents . . . which . . . could be easily imposed if there were a corresponding decision in the Excellent Council of Ten. . . . Otherwise I will resign . . . and I am hurt, because the particular scandals . . . are reported . . . to Rome, where I am perhaps deemed negligent . . . although without being guilty.[71]

The refusal of the nuns (and their secular relatives and friends) to accept the clausura decrees was certainly motivated in part by the patriarch's lack of prestige and authority in a city with strong antipapal and anticlerical traditions. In Venice, successful attempts to "reform" the convents required the close collaboration of secular and ecclesiastic authorities. However, a rule that prohibited everyday activities such as praying in the convent's exterior church or embracing female relatives who stopped by for a visit was difficult to promote among the many "involuntary nuns" of the city.[72] Permanent encloisterment and total separation from the outside world were not what they had had in mind when sacrificing themselves to a life of poverty, chastity, and obedience. In particular, those who had taken their vows before the Council of Trent did not feel obligated to observe such a harsh and seemingly arbitrary rule.

In order to persuade the nuns that their souls would be in serious jeopardy unless they completely retired from the world, didactic treatises such as Giolito's *Avvertimenti monacali* (Advice for nuns) were on every reading list that bishops recommended when censoring the nuns' secular books. It was a collection of contemporary and early Christian texts emphasizing the value of virginity, this "most precious treasure . . . hidden in a fragile vase . . . [which] one has to guard with the utmost diligence," according to Dionisio Certosino in his text "Della lodevol vita delle Vergini" (On the praiseworthy lives of virgins).[73] Paraphrasing Saint Jerome and Saint Augustine, Certosino declared that only virginity offered liberation from the "stinking dung of dirty libido" (in the words of another author in the same volume),[74] freed the body and senses from the "stench of carnal desires" (p. 20), and defined the nuns' very "nobility and lucidity" (p. 23); it was a sign not only of purity, but of perfection and beauty, which had to be preserved by "guarding the eyes" (p. 24), "despising laughter" (p. 25), refraining from any "license of the tongue" (p. 28), and the like. Cleansing oneself of temptations required a bodily technique guided by the principle of sensual deprivation. This discipline was most easily achieved when "shunning the public squares and staying at home" (p. 30). Virginity was discussed not only in terms of bodily hygiene, discipline, and confinement; it was also understood as both the means and the end of a lifelong battle. Any victory in the fight against the stain of carnal desires would be rewarded by an aureole "given . . . for the achievement of a very difficult, excellent, and privileged task, such as virginity, martyrdom, and delivering effective sermons" (p. 35). Another incentive to win the battle was the "fear of offending that celestial Spouse," but also the possibility of obtaining the sweetness of Christ's embraces, which would be the eventual reward of every intact nun: "Christ . . . is a beauty immense in every aspect, and he is infinitely more beautiful, more pleasant, more joyful to look at than every other creation; similarly, he is infinite sweetness. . . . All the sweetnesses of all the things created gathered together . . . would be less sweet than his delightfulness. . . . It is more than happiness to be spiritually embraced by him" (p. 45).

The anthropomorphization of God as the most desirable of all grooms was carried to the extreme in the author's second didactic treatise, "On the Reform of Nuns," set up as a dialogue between the celestial Spouse himself and one of his spiritual brides. In this dialogue, Christ reminds the nun that she has renounced the world because all flesh is "decaying matter, food for worms, stinking dung" (p. 72). He tries to convince his skeptical bride that only a life in perpetual seclusion can preserve her virginity, not only because sensual stimuli can best be avoided in perfect retirement from the world, but mainly because "women are particularly, and naturally, unstable, fragile, soft, and weak in reasoning" (p. 54). Since "a man's tongue can hurt a woman like the devil's arrow" (p. 56), she should recognize "how use-

ful and necessary perpetual seclusion is for all of you, and how fragile
the feminine sex is, and how deficient the feminine characteristics generally are" (p. 57).

Christ's attempts to inform the nun of the nature of women "so
that you can understand yourself" (p. 54) were instrumental in obscur-
ing the fact that clausura was hardly justifiable in terms of canon law
and the monastic tradition. When asked "Why did you say that I
should stay in the convent in perpetual seclusion—which is not included in the rule [of my order]—and why do the nuns have to be
more secluded than the monks of the same order?" (p. 50), Christ eva-
sively refers to her vow of obedience, obligating her to observe any
papal decision indiscriminately. He adds that the Tridentine clausura
decree, reconfirmed by Pius V and Gregory XIII, was not without precedent in the ecclesiastic tradition, but went back to Boniface VIII's bull
Periculoso, issued in 1298 (p. 51). The nun, however, is not yet satisfied. She insists, "I want to know whether the nuns were locked up
and obligated to live in perpetual seclusion before Pope Boniface's constitution" (p. 52)—a delicate question that momentarily embarrasses
her divine interlocutor. In trying to deflect his bride's attention, Christ
ridicules her for being frivolously curious ("you ask me many things
very usefully, although partially out of feminine curiosity") before so-
phistically trying to circumvent her question: "The nuns were enclosed
a long time before him, but several years before Boniface they had
abandoned *that* [form of] encloisterment" (my emphasis).[75] Christ's
answer obscures the fact that the voluntary seclusion nuns observed
in the early Middle Ages was qualitatively very different from the strict
encloisterment that Tridentine reformers imposed as a standard requirement on all nuns regardless of their vows and orders.

His strategy of arguing in terms of gender in response to the nun's
poignant inquiry about the juridical validity of clausura is successful
at last: once informed of her female curiosity, fragility, and other deficiencies, his bride surrenders. No longer questioning clausura as a general concept, she only wonders how—in practical terms—those nuns
who currently enjoy certain liberties could be reeducated. Christ, having regained his confidence, somewhat arrogantly remarks that "they
should carefully consider the severity of divine judgment" (p. 58).
When explaining the value of her sacred vows in terms of marital fidel-
ity, however, he loses his self-control a second time. Carried away by
his pain at having been cuckolded so many times, he reproaches her
for "having despised and stained our most noble and celestial mar-

riage, like an adulteress you engage in illicit, repulsive, vile, and abominable fornications of the mind, and perhaps even of the body" (p. 67). Calmed temporarily by his bride's submissive behavior, he resumes his talk on questions of monastic discipline, only to burst out again: "Am I not infinitely and incomparably better than any other creature, more lovable, more tender, more noble, more beautiful, intelligent, potent, rich, more faithful, and in every perfection, happiness, and glory more excellent? What exactly do you [nuns] dislike in me, that you have abandoned me and turned your hearts to vain, transitory, and carnal things?" (pp. 75–76).

In representing the dilemma of disorderly nuns and clausura as a melodramatic tearjerker, in which Christ complains about being cuckolded by unappreciative fiancées despite his many qualities, Dionisio Certosino could hardly have been more explicit in depicting the logic of the nuns' potlatch-like sacrifice. In his and other reformers' experience, only strict encloisterment would enable the nuns to preserve their virginity—the precious gift they had promised, but not yet delivered, to their celestial spouse. Involuntary nuns in particular were in constant danger of losing their hymen, without which their engagement to Christ as the most noble of all kinds of bridal exchanges could not be effected. Only if a nun died "intact" could her sacrificial marriage to Christ be consummated and render its return: eternal bliss for herself and protection from God's wrath for the living. Clausura was often compared to a safe-deposit device, which would guarantee that the virgins' immaculate bodies, invested in an exchange with the longest possible return cycle, would preserve their value forever.[76] Keeping the nuns' posthumous reward in mind, Tridentine convent reformers felt justified in imposing strict encloisterment even on those nuns who claimed to be "involuntary," or to have professed their vows before the new rule took effect.

In contrast to reform activists, canon lawyers regarded the issue of clausura as a precarious and somewhat embarrassing topic to discuss. When analyzing the concept from a legal point of view, Francesco Pellizzari, author of a compilation of church law regarding monastic communities, could not gloss over certain inconsistencies as easily as Dionisio's Christ did. In his *Manuale Regularium,* he frankly stated that although "the observance of clausura most befits the status of nuns . . . no ecclesiastic law provides that claustration belongs to the intrinsic definition of the religious status of nuns . . . and therefore one must say that it is not necessary for the religious status of nuns."[77] This juridical assessment was precisely what Christ tried to conceal in Dionisio's popularizing discussion of perpetual seclusion; instead of giving a fair account of the equivocal legal tradition, he promised a happy end for those willing to repent, retire in perpetual seclusion, and reconcile with their celestial groom. Pellizzari even specified that clausura was "introduced not by the natural, or the divine, law, but by the human and positive law of the church."[78] He nevertheless affirmed its legal validity: given the nuns' vow of obedience, clausura, like any other papal or episcopal rule, had to be strictly observed. But if the nuns' perpetual seclusion was not a requirement of natural law nor of monasticism, why—the nun of Dionisio's dialogue might have asked—did church legislators so vehemently insist on its indispensability? This was a simple and obvious but far-reaching question, which Pellizzari anticipated by considering, just like the nun's offended celestial spouse, "the natural condition and fragility of the female sex."[79] Forced to abandon temporarily the realm of precise juridical analysis, he concluded: "the seclusion of nuns is morally necessary in order to [preserve their] status of purity . . . [not only] for the observance of chastity."[80]

Clausura was thus a circular concept, defined by reference to the other "enclosed gardens" it was intended to guard. Its justification consisted in replacing the concept to be explained by a metaphorically related one already accepted as sacrosanct: clausura was legitimized by analogy to virginity. In material terms, it referred to the walls surrounding the convent. As an additional hymen, it prevented humans from accessing the nuns' sacred interior spaces;[81] it was a fortification of their delicate bodily enclosures.

In order for clausura and virginity to function in terms of law—that is, as prohibitions whose transgression was subject to penalty—the boundaries of these interlocking enclosures had to be unequivocally defined. This is where Pellizzari's analytical capacities unfold again, only to dissolve in obscure casuistry when faced with the slipperiness of the concepts in question. Purity, virginity, chastity, and clausura were—in addition to being fragile states—rather ambiguous terms. Clausura, for example, was defined as "that space which lies beyond the entrance door of the convent, which is always locked";[82] entering or leaving the convent through this door or any other orifice was thus prohibited. But what about borderline cases—for example, if "a nun, when climbing up a tree of the convent garden, reaches a branch that is jutting over the convent wall, and stays there for fun?"[83]

According to Pellizzari, this would be a clear violation. More difficult to decide were the following cases:

> Is it against the law of clausura if a nun, through magic arts, succeeds in being transported through the air above her convent? . . . It is not if she is transported by such means only within the perimeter of the clausura . . . just as she does not violate the clausura if she sleepwalks on the roof of her convent . . . unless she transgresses the boundaries of the roof of her convent. . . . It is considered a violation of the clausura, however, if a nun [floats] at such a high altitude over the roofs of her convent that . . . she could be reached neither with the help of a ladder nor through any other human art.[84]

Thus, the boundaries of the nuns' spatial enclosure were perceived to be anything but stable; they were in fact quite volatile. Equally difficult to define were cases of unchastity that could constitute an impediment to a nun's consecration. In principle, any violation of the hymen—whether through rape or consensual sex—prohibited her from receiving the black veil, "because when consecrating a virgin it is of no importance whether she committed a fault before consecration, but whether virginity exists, in bodily and material terms, which is signified by this consecration . . . and [which] represents the integrity of the church triumphant."[85] The same principle did not apply, however, if the hymen was broken during a medical exam. A borderline case was a nun "who is polluted through a voluntary effusion of semen, while keeping her enclosure *(claustro)* intact."[86] Pellizzari deemed it possible to consecrate her, "because the church only requires the integrity of the flesh when receiving the veil of consecration . . . and it is nowhere stated that the nun has to be interrogated about any contamination. . . . She is not a virgin in terms of her virtue, but in terms of her [bodily] status."[87] According to the same principle, it was possible to consecrate a nun "who was carnally known by a man in the preposterous orifice," but not a nun "who was carnally known by another woman." In the latter case, if "the nun is known by another woman by means of a wooden or glass instrument in her natural orifice" or if she has sex with a "woman who has a large clitoris . . . and is able to deflower her," her hymen is usually lost, and she must not be consecrated.[88]

As Pellizzari's numerous hypothetical cases show in great detail, violating the vow of chastity did not necessarily imply the loss of virginity. While indulging in sexual pleasures constituted a grave offense to God, only a broken hymen rendered a nun unable to function as a signifier of the church united and triumphant. On the other hand, the strict physical definition of virginity did not presuppose unchastity when diagnosing a nun's bodily corruption. This seemingly precise criterion for establishing whether a nun could be consecrated or not could theoretically lead to paradoxical situations: in cases of ambiguity, only a medical exam—itself thought to be extremely dangerous to the hymen—could establish whether a nun had been deflowered or not. This rather dysfunctional method of gaining certainty was therefore exempted as a cause of bodily corruption prohibiting a nun's consecration; and in order to avoid confusion, it was decided that a nun could be denied her consecration only if her corrupted state was public knowledge. If she had been deflowered secretly, she could hide the fact and receive consecration in good conscience.[89] While it was difficult to state in legal terms when and how a nun lost her virginity, transgressions of her vow of chastity could occur in a variety of even more vaguely defined circumstances: if they "take delight in matters of love . . . hold or listen to obscene speeches, read filthy books on topics of love; if they keep obscene images . . . take delight in kisses and embraces," or even "get close to violating the vow of chastity," nuns engaged in activities that could constitute a violation.[90]

Enclosure, chastity, and virginity were thus ambiguous and negotiable concepts. The boundaries they signified were supposed to be precisely fixed, but they appeared to be increasingly volatile as Pellizzari's analysis progressed. The notion of "woman" was also quite unstable. It referred to an extremely vulnerable and degradable kind of human being whose bodily integrity and gender seemed to be in constant jeopardy. Whether widows or other "corrupted" women could enter convents, for example, was a juridical problem discussed by Pellizzari. He also presented the hypothetical question of "whether and when hermaphrodites could be received in the order of nuns." They could, "if according to physicians and midwives the female sex prevails." If, however, after pronouncing her holy vows, a hermaphrodite "erupts into a man," he "can stay in the world and get married."[91]

The instability of core concepts surrounding the virginal bodies of nuns appears to be a systematic feature of the discourse on convent reform. The determination of church (and secular) authorities to subject all nuns to perpetual seclusion contrasts starkly with the problems they had in defining clausura as a juridical concept—to say nothing of their difficulties in overcoming the nuns' resistance and in realizing clausura as a project of profound architectural, social, and economic change. Since the boundaries surrounding the nuns' interlocking enclo-sures—their seclusion and their virginity—were structurally unstable, they could only be preserved by being constantly redrawn. Although virginity, chastity, and seclusion were static concepts denoting closure, order, and purity on the semantic level, they were discursively em-ployed as ideals promoting progress toward perfection. In the eyes of the church fathers, the vow of chastity obligated a nun to wage a life-long battle for the preservation of her virginity; and Bishop Antonio Grimani declared that his reform decrees were inspired by his wish "that the regulated monastic state should go on acquiring merit in the exemplarity of its progress, and should pass . . . from perfection to perfection."[92] It was the very tension between the static nature of seclu-sion and the impossibility of realizing it "perfectly" that mobilized the reform movement. In punishing those who transgressed the strictly drawn boundaries protecting the nuns' sacred interiors from the profa-nations of the outside world, church and state gradually sought to im-pose their authority over nuns and laity alike. While the transgression of these boundaries was the focus of Tridentine reformers—in the form of regulation, supervision, and criminalization—the entrance into the monastic enclosure itself was staged as a spectacular rite of transition.

Contemporary liturgy celebrated the girl's entrance in two ceremo-nies: the *vestizione,* during which a prospective novice was "dressed," and the *professione,* during which an approved novice pronounced her holy vows.[93] The dressing ceremony consisted of two acts, the first staging the girl's transition into perpetual seclusion, the second mark-ing the sacrificial nature of the ceremony. The girl's passage was framed by two processions that mirrored each other, describing a full circle: the first proceeded from the main altar of the exterior church to the convent gate, the second returned through the interior church to the window near the main altar, which connected the nuns' part of the church with the public part.[94] An entourage of friends and relatives accompanied the girl to the entrance door of the convent, where she was received by the abbess and nuns. These two processions not only highlighted the girl's transition, they also connected the two parts of the dressing ceremony dramaturgically.

The first procession, which culminated in the entrance scene, was preceded by the last—and probably most outstanding—of the girl's worldly appearances: her recital of the psalm "Quemadmodum desid-erat cervus," describing the longing of a thirsty soul for the soothing encounter with God, a text also set to music as a passionate love mad-rigal for secular performances.[95] Bishop Grimani complained that this recital, as well as the subsequent procession, had turned into an osten-tatious spectacle; he prohibited the girls from "enter[ing] with great pomp, [wearing] silk dresses, jewelry and pearls, accompanied by many people,"[96] and also considered it an "unbearable corruption" that the prospective novices "learn some verses from their chaplains . . . in order to recite them on the day of their *vestizione* . . . wasting many months' worth of time in this most superfluous vanity. . . . Some-times they lose themselves in reciting them shamelessly . . . turning a sacred and pious act . . . into a vain performance."[97] Also, the recurrent attempts of several generations of patriarchs to prevent the nuns from practicing to sing the *canto figurato* (melodic songs) indicate that the girls' recital of Psalm 42 was an important part of female monastic culture.[98] After the recital, the procession, headed by priests carrying the cross, led the girl to the convent entrance; on the other side, abbess and nuns waited to receive the novice. The moment of passing the doorstep was highlighted and delayed by a brief question-and-answer part between priest and novice, accompanied by the nuns' recital of an antiphon and followed by the girl's blessing. Once the girl crossed the threshold, the door was closed, and the first act was over.

The procession through the nuns' part of the church opened the second act. Its pivotal scene, the girl's "dressing" and tonsure, was preceded by prayers, the nuns' recital of the hymn "Veni Creator Spir-itus," and the celebration of a mass. A dialogue between father con-fessor and novice was meant to illustrate the voluntary nature of her sacrifice. The girl had to answer the priest's question "What do you desire?" with quotations from different psalms, among others "to be one with the Lord . . . [and] to inhabit the house of the Lord every day of my life" and "I will voluntarily sacrifice myself to God."[99] Then gown and veil—which "the female sex should wear as a sign of subjec-tion, humility, and honesty, because of the angels"—were blessed.[100] The veil, to be worn "in memory of the disgraceful death of your sweet groom," marked her widowhood.[101] The novice also received a belt from the abbess as a "sign of temperance and chastity," wishing that "the Lord may gird the loins of my body and circumscribe the vices of my heart."[102] Afterward, the father confessor would pray to Christ "for this servant of his, who hurries to discard her hair out of love for Him."[103] Each nun, starting with the abbess, would then cut off a strand of the novice's hair. Once this sacrifice of love was completed, the abbess would fasten the girl's veil as a sign of "modesty, sobriety, and continence."[104]

Each detail of the dressing, veiling, and tonsure scene had a distinct but thematically connected metaphorical significance. While the girl's change of dress was a sign of humility and *imitatio Christi*, her tonsure was performed as a sacrificial rite, in which the community of nuns offered the voluntary victim's beauty as a sign of love. Since the cord was meant to "circumscribe" the girl's vices, the girding scene was likewise reminiscent of a sacrificial offering; the belt was supposed to metaphorically contain her desires. The veil surrounded her virginity like an additional hymen, protecting her body by hiding its charms, while also signifying her sacrificial widowhood. Sacrifice and enclosure, or rather enclosure as sacrifice, were the overarching themes of the entire ceremony. The prayer immediately following the dress-and-tonsure scene underlined this connection: "Accept and protect, we beseech you [our Lord], your servant . . . so that she may keep the cloister of her modesty as a sign of truth, like an enclosed garden, a sealed fountain."[105] The ceremony ended, but not before the novice had neutralized the violence done to her by a reconciliatory "kiss of peace" offered to abbess and nuns.

The theme of sacrificial enclosure was reaffirmed in the liturgy of the "ceremony of profession," during which an approved novice committed herself irrevocably to convent life by pronouncing the three holy vows (chastity, poverty, and obedience). The actual *professio* was staged as a love scene anticipating the novice's promised encounter with God and resembling a sacrificial offering. At the window separating the interior and exterior parts of the church, the novice had to lie face down, entirely covered with a black veil. When the priest told her, "Get up, my daughter, and light *[orna]* your lamp, your spouse is coming, go and meet him,"[106] the nuns would remove the novice's veil. She would then get up, step toward the priest, and answer, "Here I come to you, my sweetest Lord, whom I loved, whom I desired, whom I always wanted."[107] This scene was repeated three times. The novice would then pronounce her vows in front of the abbess and immediately afterward approach the altar of the interior church, embrace it for a few minutes, and declare, "I offer and sacrifice myself entirely as a living host."[108] As a sign of her "contempt for the world" and in order for her "never to accept another lover after Him," that is, after this ritual embrace, the professed nun would receive her new veil from the abbess.[109] The profession was thus a rite of sacrifice and love, during which the nun ritually anticipated the union with her celestial spouse and celebrated God's acceptance of her offering.

This liturgical script, approved by Patriarch Vendramin, was not the only contemporary text to emphasize the sacrificial character of the nuns' seclusion.[110] Arcangela Tarabotti, for example, praised the pacifying function of "voluntary" nuns, who, sacrificing and encloistering themselves out of real devotion, were able to "contain the divine wrath, because if they did not hold back the flagellations owed to the sins of the world, the flames of a fire extending into the universe would be seen incinerating mankind, and water [would be seen] overcoming the highest towers and most sublime mountains."[111] Even Pietro Aretino acknowledged in a letter to a devout nun that "with your prayers you ensure that God does not correct us with his anger nor castigate us with his rage."[112] The nun in Ferrante Pallavicino's satire *Le divorce céleste, causé par les dissolutions de l'Espouse Romaine* (The celestial divorce, caused by the dissolute life of the Roman Spouse; 1649), on the other hand, complained about being condemned to hell, because as an "involuntary nun," she was offered to God unpurged of her sensual desires:

> One always observed the custom of cutting the victims' throats before sacrificing them to God, because it was apparently thought—since blood is the principal site of bodily affections—that it would be improper to offer any victim to his divine Majesty that was not first purged of any worldly passion through bleeding; but our fathers and mothers have no consideration for this fact with respect to us. We are consecrated to God with all of our affections, and all of our passions. So how could we believe that we could please God?[113]

Offerings had to be pure in order to please God: the corruption of a nun's body not only invalidated the metaphorical relevance of virginity and caused essential social distinctions to collapse, it also annulled the sacrificial value of the nun's claustration. Likewise, the seclusion of nuns was not only an important fortification of their fragile hymens, or a necessary measure for the reordering of society: living in and as an enclosed garden constituted the sacrifice itself. Without clausura, the potlatch in its double meaning of conspicuous waste (of the nuns' reproductive capacities) and sacrificial offering (as a ritual engagement with Christ) could not be performed. Strict encloisterment was functional, in that it supported the nuns in their struggle to keep their fragile bodies unpolluted. But it also had a normative meaning:

as Patriarch Tiepolo had pointed out, the nuns' gift consisted in the very renunciation of their freedom.

In this sense, the Venetian patriarchs' expert knowledge of women's fashions, of which there was a brief display earlier in this chapter, was instrumental in more than one way: the detailed prohibitions regarding the nuns' frivolous hairstyles and transparent veils aimed to prevent a chain reaction of sinful desires and to impose a bodily discipline striving for sensual deprivation, but most of all they tried to correct sacrificial signifiers gone astray. If a nun's tonsure and veil served both to represent her sacrifice and to defend it by hiding her charms, curls of blond hair peeping out from under barely visible veils could not but completely undo the symbolic offering. The insistence of many nuns that they were "involuntary" threatened to erase the sacrificial value of their supposedly voluntary vows. Their black veils, commanding reverence and awe for their consecrated bodies, were furthermore intended to shield the virgins against lay men's wantonness. The transparent lace veils of Venetian nuns, however, attracted rather than deflected the gaze of male desire, and tangibly represented the dilemma of "perfect seclusion." How permeable the convent walls, grilles, and doors could become from time to time—with or without the help of magic arts—seemed to be captured emblematically by those veils. The instability of boundaries, be they hymens, veils, or clausura demarcations, was, after all, not just the result of circularly defined metaphors' being pierced by analytic reasoning, but of recalcitrant nuns' protests against coerced confinement as well. It was precisely because so many "involuntary nuns" were either unable or unwilling to maintain the immaculacy of mind and body required of them as sacrificial victims that sumptuary laws were issued, the nuns' bodily discipline supervised, and their social practices curtailed. Clausura became mandatory at a time when, because of the rising numbers of involuntary nuns, its violence was felt most painfully.

The Institutionalization of Surveillance

The most intensive phase of the clausura reform movement coincided with the peak in patrician monachization rates between 1580 and 1620. The practice of coerced monachizations and the imposition of perpetual seclusion were two interdependent and mutually reinforcing policies: rising numbers of "involuntary"—that is, potentially disor-

derly—nuns seemed to require and justify an intensification of surveillance. Only by imposing a more rigid discipline could the notoriously
scandalous lifestyles of "unreformed" nuns be abolished and female
monasticism revaluated as a prestigious and honorable alternative to
marriage. Strict encloisterment aimed to upgrade the status of virginity
and thereby undo the damage that non-observant nuns of the early
sixteenth century had caused when their behavior threatened to turn
convent life into a form of open prostitution. Enforced seclusion was
perceived to be both precondition and result of the patriciate's extensive monachization practices, just as coerced monachizations were the
precondition of a successful clausura reform: only because many prospective nuns lacked alternatives to convent life could Tridentine reformers define the contemplative and strictly encloistered form of female monasticism as the only acceptable one. Had the supply of nuns
not been secure for generations to come, ecclesiastic authorities would
have hesitated to impose the extremely unpopular clausura requirement and to suppress several noncontemplative women's movements
at the same time. The policy of implementing clausura sought to preserve the status quo of both secular and ecclesiastic establishments; it
was also the vanishing point at which the religious duties and the secular functions of an essentially hybrid institution converged. The double
function of nunneries in general and clausura in particular resulted in
the close collaboration between state and church in matters of convent
reform, despite the fact that the relationship between Venice and Rome
was traditionally tense, and often adversarial.

Popular discourse seemed to reflect the convergence of peaking
monachization rates among patrician women and their intensified
surveillance. The tragicomic and melodramatic trope of "involuntary
nuns" accompanied, complemented, and gradually supplanted the
burlesque mode of ridiculing the unruly, yet-to-be-disciplined nuns
who turned convents into bordellos.[114] Victim and rebel nuns stood
side by side. Modern (secular) historians also tended to study mainly
the licentious aspects of sixteenth-century convent life and the repres-
sive aspects of enclosure reform,[115] until Gabriella Zarri opened up the
topic for an encompassing reinterpretation. In her view, subjecting all
nuns to perpetual seclusion was not only at the core of the Tridentine
convent-reform program, but crucial for the establishment of a new
economy of power within the church:

> The imposition of clausura on the nuns is part of a more general process
> of the repression of religious movements. . . . Clausura appears to be,

at the same time, a measure to police, to repress suspicious religious ideas, to discipline cults, and, more generally, the first methodical and capillary application of the criterion of "renfermement," subsequently turned against the margins of society.[116]

The nuns' enclosure and confinement required not only collaboration between episcopal authorities and powerful state magistrates, but the development of new executive institutions capable of breaking the power of monastic orders and eliminating the influence of private families.[117] In other words, the imposition of clausura was an encompassing political project in which traditional powers, discredited by scandals and corruption, were gradually dismantled and replaced by reinvigorated bishops and newly established government organs. Although it culminated several decades after the Council of Trent (1545–63), this process dates back to the beginning of the sixteenth century.

In Venice, the pre-Tridentine reform movement started in the late fifteenth century, when, in light of recurrent scandals involving nuns, both the Senate and the patriarch repeatedly asked the pope to revoke the exemptions and privileges his predecessors had granted to various convents.[118] Also, several convents traditionally under papal jurisdiction were now subjected to the immediate authority of the Venetian patriarch.[119] In 1514, the Council of Ten itself intervened, issuing a detailed law concerning the nuns' clausura, the reception of visitors, and the punishment of perpetrators.[120] This law became an instant classic: reissued by the Venetian government until the end of the seventeenth century,[121] it was reaffirmed by Tridentine hard-liners such as Patriarchs Lorenzo Priuli and Francesco Vendramin.[122] Although it partially summarized previous decrees (the Great Council and the Senate had already prohibited the violation of clausura in 1486 and 1509, respectively), the law was a novelty because it was issued by the Council of Ten and because of its attention to detail, enforcement procedures, and anticipation of papal legislation. In claiming primary legislative authority in convent affairs while leaving some of the executive competence to the patriarch, it was the prototype for a new form of government intervention in matters of convent reform for years to come.

More specifically, the 1514 law was a prelude to the ambitious and politically precarious project to transform eight "open" convents of Venice (including two of the most prestigious houses, San Zaccaria and Santa Maria delle Vergini) into observant communities. After declaring on 4 May 1519 that the reform of non-observant nuns "was an issue worthy of the government's attention," the Council of Ten ordered that nuns from recently founded "observant" convents be introduced into the nunneries of San Zaccaria, Santa Maria delle Vergini, Santa Marta, Santa Anna, Santi Biagio e Cataldo, Santa Maria della Celestia, San Secondo, and Santa Chiara.[123] A papal brief supporting the government's policy was requested and obtained. The observant nuns were endowed with the patrimonies and governance of non-observant convents; those convents that refused to accept the new rules lost their right to accept novices and to participate in chapter decisions. The nuns affected by the reform perceived it as the presumptuous interference of an unauthorized agency in their "private" affairs.[124] Since vested interests were at stake, they protested vehemently: on 25 June 1519, the nuns of Santa Maria delle Vergini tore down the wall that had been built to partition the convent into two halves; the next day, they celebrated the arrival of a papal brief supporting their wish "to reform themselves."[125] On 31 July, the nuns of San Zaccaria succeeded in having Patriarch Antonio Contarini summoned to the Rota (a papal court) in Rome "to see whether it is legal to introduce novelties in this convent."[126] On 26 August, the nuns of Santa Maria della Celestia were reported to have escaped from the convent and to have sent their belongings to relatives.[127]

Nonetheless, the reform proceeded as planned. In order to consolidate its results, the Council of Ten reissued its parlor and clausura rules of 1514 on 11 February 1519 (m.v.), and in 1521 an ad hoc commission of three patricians was elected whose task it was "to listen together with the patriarch to the complaints and litigations of the non-observant nuns with respect to their livelihood."[128] This commission was formed after the abbesses and former abbesses of San Zaccaria, Santa Maria delle Vergini, Santa Maria della Celestia, and Santa Marta made a spectacular appearance in the Collegio on 21 August 1521, accompanied by an entourage of relatives. After the abbess of Santa Maria delle Vergini addressed the doge in Latin, the nuns' relatives complained not only about the degrading effects of the reform in convents such as San Zaccaria, "where everybody used to be aristocratic, and now there are . . . Greek bastards and commoners among the nuns," but also about the nuns' poverty after they had been deprived of their revenues.[129] The three patricians "sopra le monache" were charged with providing for the expropriated non-observant nuns; they also had to extend the reform to the diocese of Torcello. One month after this commission was created, Pope Leo X retroactively legalized the project to "subject the non-observant nuns to perpetual seclusion"; he supported the reform in all its details.[130]

The attempt to transform some of the most prestigious convents into "observant" communities was the first concerted effort of the Venetian state and curia to undo the nuns' traditional networks of power and to abolish intermediate agencies. A permanent executive institution was created, "since there are still many things that need to be dealt with in this issue of nuns." In 1522, the ad hoc committee "sopra le monache" was reappointed and its jurisdiction extended to "the limitation of the expenses of both observant and non-observant nuns in this city and in Torcello." This was an audacious mandate, because in supervising the nuns' financial management, powerful private interests would have been infringed upon. Presumably because nobody wanted to risk his political career over such a delicate issue, the government had to explicitly prohibit elected patricians from rejecting their appointment before a new commission could be constituted.[131] Although it seems unlikely that the commission ever interfered with the financial management of individual convents prior to the late seventeenth century, the government continued to issue ordinances in this respect: in 1528, the Provveditori sopra i Monasteri di Monache (convent magistrate) became a permanent magistrate, charged with "checking the accounts of the convents' agents and estate managers."[132] Given the convents' allegedly disastrous economic situation, the Council of Ten passed various decrees aimed at preventing the alienation of convent properties through embezzlement and mismanagement.[133] In addition, the patriarch declared that only rich convents could continue to accept novices without limitation, since "the abbesses have reduced the convents to extreme poverty by accepting new nuns without having the means to provide for them."[134] In 1536, state regulations concerning church property culminated in a comprehensive mortmain law.[135]

The government's convent reform "from above" thus followed a two-pronged approach: on the one hand, the convent magistrate was to supervise the nuns' discipline by collecting evidence against transgressors of the clausura laws and by delegating their cases to the Avogadori di Comun (state attorneys) for trial; on the other hand, it was to sue corrupt estate managers and administrators.[136] Designed to both enclose the nuns and prevent their properties from being dissipated, the convent reform was part of an encompassing policy aimed at containing the growth of ecclesiastic real estate and subjecting the existing patrimonies to secular taxation.[137] Nuns, convents, and church institutions in general were to be fenced in by state regulations. In this broader context, the implementation of clausura appears to have been a strategically important measure intended to weaken the convents politically and institutionally; once the nuns were deprived of their traditional support system ("private" connections to the papacy provided by influential relatives and friends; their monastic congregations) and subject to clausura by episcopal and state authorities, the way was paved for a more incisive intervention in the convents' financial management. In this sense, clausura was not only a metaphor for a pure and well-ordered society; it was the means to impose a "capillary" system of power through the establishment of institutions designed to confine and to exclude.

In the first half of the sixteenth century, government and episcopal authorities lacked the power to thoroughly reform the convents' finances and the nuns' morals. In the aftermath of the Council of Trent, they resumed their abandoned project with renewed vigor. Since the Republic of Venice and the Roman Curia collaborated successfully at the level of high diplomacy, the auspices for a continuation of the reform were good: Pius IV agreed to have Venetian church properties reestimated for tax purposes, and in recompense the republic was the first state to recognize the Council of Trent, in 1564.[138] A wave of legislation in convent matters followed. In 1566, the Council of Ten reissued a tightened clausura law.[139] In 1569, it reconfirmed the parlor rules of 1514;[140] it also passed two laws intended to restructure the convents' financial management. These latter decrees curbed the abbesses' self-rule, reinstituted the chapters as decision-making agencies, and subjected chapter decisions to the approval of each convent's three procurators, the Provveditori sopra i Monasteri, and the patriarch. Instead of targeting embezzlement by estate managers, the laws of 1569 were directed against corrupt abbesses who contracted loans *(livelli)* to the advantage of private moneylenders.[141] The reestimation of church properties conceded by Pius IV provided the government with detailed information about the debts of individual convents. Thus, the reintroduction of ecclesiastical tithes in 1564 proved to be useful for taxing as well as reform purposes.

Patriarch Giovanni Trevisan supported the government's efforts by complementing the laws of 1569 with detailed ordinances and adjusting them to the specific needs of particular convents. When inspecting the nunneries of his diocese, he collected information about individual convents' income and expenses,[142] forbade excessive giving of alms and gifts,[143] and exhorted the nuns to negotiate the highest dowries possible when admitting novices.[144] While the government curtailed the power of abbesses and prioresses by subjecting their decisions to outside authorities, Trevisan attempted to "democratize" the convents from within: the rotation of all offices became mandatory;[145] the personal and secret vote was introduced to eliminate election fraud and the sale of votes;[146] cash deposit boxes were provided with a triple lock, with the abbess (or prioress), the treasurer, and the secretary (or storage keeper) each possessing a key;[147] "expense" committees were required to keep separate books and render a regular account to the chapters;[148] and a council of older nuns was instituted to assist the abbess in all decisions.[149] In accordance with the two-pronged approach of the government's reform program, Trevisan's decrees against corruption and mismanagement were accompanied by his efforts to adapt the clausura rule to the nuns' everyday life, and to impose a stricter discipline wherever necessary. Among other things, he admonished the nuns to dress properly, to receive only authorized visitors,[150] to stay within the confines of their clausura,[151] to have every door walled up except for one "to land" and one "to sea,"[152] to prevent masked revelers and musicians from entering the parlors during the carnival,[153] to stop washing the laundry of monks and priests,[154] to build walls around the convent, and to secure the windows and balconies with bars.[155] Complying with the Tridentine policy of promoting the cult of the Eucharist, Trevisan also inspected the altars of convent churches to make sure the Holy Sacrament was "well preserved."[156]

In addition to state legislation and ecclesiastic supervision, a systematic criminalization of transgressors was employed to enforce the nuns' seclusion. By assuming jurisdiction over lay offenders in 1566, the Council of Ten upgraded the seriousness of crimes against nuns and centralized the prosecution.[157] One of the most spectacular cases was tried in 1568, when five noblemen, among them Zuan di Lorenzo Priuli, son of a doge, were accused of having entered several Venetian convents in order to meet their lovers.[158] Two of the nuns involved became pregnant as a result of these encounters, and four escaped from their convent after the scandal became public. The Council of Ten almost subjected Sister Anzelica Pisani to torture to find out who had fathered her child. The suspect was Zuan Priuli. While his case was delegated to the Collegio, the other defendants were acquitted except for Francesco Corner, who was fined sixteen hundred ducats and deprived of his vote in the Great Council for four years.

After a series of cases involving commoners, citizens, and priests, another trial against noblemen was initiated in 1587. Marco Corner di Andrea, Francesco Querini detto Stampalia, and Francesco Contarini di Domenego were exiled for having entertained their lovers from Santi Rocco e Margherita in an apartment adjacent to the convent. Three other defendants were acquitted of the charges against them, while the lovers' go-between, the servant Santa Gucchiadora, was sentenced to prison for life. The nuns were handed over to the patriarch for trial.[159]

To engage in illicit sex (inside or outside the convent) was the most spectacular form of violating the nuns' clausura, but love affairs were not always at the center of trial proceedings. In the years 1555 to 1566 and in the first half of the seventeenth century, the convent magistrate instituted numerous proceedings against fugitive nuns.[160] Each of these nuns had a different reason for leaving: Sister Faustina escaped from the convent of San Giovanni in Laterano in 1556 to reach her fiancé, whom her father and stepmother had forced her to abandon. An "involuntary nun," she had always dreamed of leaving the convent and had been imprisoned several times for bad behavior.[161] In 1558, Sister Raphaela Balbi fled from the convent of San Bernardo di Murano after quarreling with the abbess. Sister Raphaela had asked that her girlfriend Laura be permitted to enter the convent and visit her, but the abbess refused. During her flight, she received help from Laura's brothers and from various women with whom she had grown up during her time as an *educanda* (boarder educated in a convent).[162] In 1618, Sister Isabella fled from the penitentiary Santa Maria Maddalena (Le Convertite) after she had unsuccessfully requested that her vows be legally annulled.[163] The same year, Sister Gratiosa Raspi left the convent of San Sepolcro to join the friars of Rua, disguised as a man. Inspired by the legends of Saint Marina and Saint Eufrosina, she wished to lead the "most austere life possible, believing that this mortification of the body could please the Lord."[164]

The prosecution of clausura delinquents and the criminalization of sensuality[165] were instrumental in renegotiating existing hierarchies of power among monastic orders, episcopal authorities, papal legates, and the city government. In 1556, for example, Nuncio Aloysius Scorta asked the convent magistrate to intervene in the case of San Giovanni in Laterano. To prevent "great inconveniences," the nuns were forced to readmit Sister Gratia *conversa* after they had expelled her for quarreling with the abbess and the confessor. During the interrogations, Sister Gratia denounced Father Stefano for entertaining nuns at his house and inviting them to stay overnight; in return, he accused her of wearing a courtesan's attire—*zoccoli da cortesana* (platform shoes) and the *velo deshonesto* (a veil worn by courtesans and prostitutes)—of working as a go-between, and of having an affair with the nuncio's chancellor. Surprisingly, these transgressions were of little concern to the prosecutors; neither did they care to know that Sister Gratia had once seduced the father confessor of her former convent and that Father Stefano kept a concubine. What mattered to them most was that Stefano had instructed the abbess to disregard the patriarch's orders to replace the door of the confessional and to supply its window with bars. Interrogated by the convent magistrate for his reasons, Stefano boldly stated that the convent was subject solely to its Roman congregation and that neither episcopal nor papal—much less state—authorities could interfere with its government. He even admitted to having bribed several persons in Rome to get hold of certain documents testifying to the convent's ancient privileges. Stefano's fight for the convent's independence cost him his career; on 6 March 1556, the Council of Ten ordered the removal of Father Stefano from all his positions.[166]

Some fifty years later, the trial of several nuns of San Daniele and their alleged lovers revealed how a community of nuns, backed by a monastic congregation, tried to resist state and episcopal interventions—until inner power struggles led one nun to collaborate with the authorities. In 1604, the convent magistrate received two letters of denunciation from nuns at San Daniele regarding a scandalous affair involving high-ranking patricians and citizens. Since the nuncio himself seemed to be involved (Sister Serafica Balbi apparently possessed his portrait), and since the superiors of this convent's monastic congregation (Padri della Carità) tried to downplay the affair, the Provveditori sopra i Monasteri required that the convent be subjected to the jurisdiction of the patriarch.[167] Once this was achieved, legal action was taken against Francesco Badoer, governor of Vicenza, and Piero Pellegrini, state secretary, for having illicit affairs with Sisters Lodovica Vico and Anzelica Soranzo. Five other nuns were to be interrogated as witnesses. The prosecutors experienced "great wonder," however, when they realized that neither the two accusers nor the prioress nor any other witness would make relevant statements.[168] Before resuming the interrogations, the Provveditori ordered the abbot of the convent's congregation to appoint an extraordinary father confessor,[169] hoping that the nuns would stop lying after having been confessed and communicated. They also tried to intimidate the prioress:

> The Sublime Council of Ten, which, as you should know, has the highest authority over all creatures living in this Most Serene Dominion, was very surprised and outraged [to hear] that you . . . [having been] elected to govern this sacred place well, and to remove those scandals . . . that could stain the honor of the convent . . . instead of disclosing the plagues and errors so that they can be cured and corrected, hide everything, and deny not only the delicts that have been committed secretly, but also the public ones. . . . We are confident that you now, after having received the sacraments, and understanding the determination of the Council of Ten, will tell us everything you know, to protect your soul from damnation, and to prevent these Excellencies from using other means to discover the truth.[170]

Neither the moralizing admonitions nor the threats of torture and eternal damnation, however, could move the prioress to talk about the convent's dubious affairs. The other witnesses likewise insisted that they knew nothing. One of the accusers, however, Sister Innocentia Ottobon, hinted at a conspiracy: "I don't want to die a sudden death."[171] A few weeks later, the Provveditori returned to the convent. They had asked the patriarch to accompany them, hoping that his spiritual authority would persuade at least some nuns to surrender. Indeed, after the patriarch celebrated a mass and read the pope's brief to the nuns,[172] they all "kneeled down . . . sighing, many of them groaning, and crying, and said they would obey His Holiness, but requested that they be given father confessors from among the friars [of their congregation] . . . and that the Most Reverend Patriarch allow their old father confessor . . . to reconcile and admonish them."[173] But since the old confessor had tried to obscure and downplay the affair in the first place, the patriarch refused to let the nuns get back in touch with him. By the time the prosecutors resumed their interrogations, the nuns had changed their strategy. They still pretended to know nothing of duplicated keys, sawed grilles, and secret rendezvous between Francesco Badoer, Piero Pellegrini, and their alleged lovers, but some nuns deflected the investigators' attention by accusing Sister Serafica Balbi of illicit relations with a certain Giulio da Molin. Sister Serafica was outraged and denied the allegation.

The next time the members of the commission returned, they were accompanied by State Attorney Bellegno. Desperately, they complained to the prioress: "This is the fifth time that this delegation of the Most Sublime Council of Ten comes to your convent."[174] Again, none of the witnesses budged. Eventually, Sister Serafica herself broke the deadlock by informing the prosecutors that no witness would ever dare to tell the truth unless protected by anonymity, and that every single member of the community had to be interrogated.[175] Sister Serafica might have wanted to redirect the magistrates' attention away from her lover back to Badoer and Pellegrini, hoping that some nuns might incriminate them.[176] The prosecutors took her advice, and after interrogating the sixty-eight nuns of San Daniele one by one, the commission had enough evidence to release arrest warrants for Badoer and Pellegrini. Because of the length of the proceedings, however, the two defendants had had enough time to inquire about the charges against them, prepare an alibi, and find defense witnesses.[177] On 11 September 1604, they were acquitted of all charges. Giulio da Molin, already prohibited in 1601 from visiting San Daniele, was also accused but did not stand trial; he was sentenced in absentia to ten years of exile.[178]

The initial resistance of the nuns of San Daniele against state and episcopal investigators was unique in the history of clausura proceedings. Most likely, their old confessor encouraged them to boycott the investigations. Collective silence was the most effective means to undermine the punitive power of the convent magistrate and the patriarch, based entirely on their ability to extract confessions and encourage denunciations. The nuns' silence puzzled the Provveditori, who usually had the opposite difficulty of distinguishing, among a plethora of mutual recriminations, false from true testimonies. In the magistrates' experience, nuns frequently employed calumnies and reciprocal denunciations as a means to settle private feuds. Personal animosities and factional power struggles were seething also in San Daniele, where they were initially targeted against Sister Lodovica and Sister Anzelica but in the end caused the fall of Sister Serafica.[179]

Denunciations often backfired, as the case of Sister Diodata, a nun in San Giuseppe, suggests. She anonymously informed the convent magistrate that the prioress would publicly kiss her father confessor and entertain him and his brother in her cell. She also illegally appointed him the convent's procurator. Mother Cipriana defended herself by pointing out that Sister Diodata was obsessed with taking revenge on the confessor, who forbade her to receive visits and love letters from a certain Friar Bassan. The patriarch soon recognized that Sister Diodata was generally regarded as a chronic grumbler (she was repeatedly imprisoned by the prioress for quarreling with her); he abandoned the investigations and left Sister Diodata to her fate among the nuns.[180]

Since the criminalization of the nuns' sexual and social relationships depended on the solicitation of denunciations, the distribution of power within individual convents became highly susceptible to manipulation. Single nuns such as Sister Diodata were easily isolated, but groups of nuns often aimed to renegotiate inner hierarchies of power through abusive denunciations, bribes, and threats. Convent employees were in an especially precarious situation. In 1652, the procurator of San Giovanni Evangelista di Torcello had to defend himself against an unspecified allegation regarding his frequent visits to the convent. He explained that he often came to see his daughter, who was a boarder in the convent, and that he was employed to catalogue and transcribe some twelve hundred parchments and other ancient documents (the convent was founded in 640) in order to compile a cadastre. His appointment was part of the convent's plans to stop the dissipation of patrimonies due to negligence and ignorance concerning its property titles, contracts, and revenues. The procurator was upset to see "how mismanaged such a rich convent is." Wine and grain spoiled every year, and the estate manager was entirely corrupt: in collaboration with several notaries, he had contracted unauthorized loans and embezzled the surplus revenues after favorable lease contracts had been negotiated. Therefore, the procurator concluded, he himself might well have become the enemy of certain people: "The Most Excellent Sirs have to understand that this is an imposture perhaps of those who manage the revenues of the convent, and who are perhaps bothered by the fact that I handle these affairs, and fearing that I deprive them of their interests and bribes, they did not have anything better to do than to suggest to the Most Illustrious Bishop that I frequently come to this convent [to socialize with the nuns]."[181]

Personal animosities between nuns also often ended in criminal trials. A long-lasting enmity between Sister Anna Marchi and Sister Colombina of San Vito di Burano, for example, caused the vicar of Torcello to initiate three trial proceedings. In 1607, Sister Anna informed him that she and Sister Cherubina had picked up a love letter thrown into the garden for Sister Colombina. A servant nun testified that she had once caught Father Zuane, the alleged author of the letter, in Colombina's cell. The defendant had an airtight alibi, however, and the trial ended in a mild punishment.[182] Five years later, the vicar had to intervene again: Sister Cherubina had stopped attending chapter sessions, "because Sister Colombina offends me in every possible way."[183] In 1621, Anna Marchi, by now abbess of the convent, struck a definitive blow against Colombina. She caught her enemy having sex with Gasparo Muraro, a convent employee. She gave a colorful and detailed account of how she spent an entire night spying on the two lovers. As in 1607, when Anna had read Colombina's mail, her moralistic attitude proved to be tinged with voyeuristic curiosity and jealousy. After cornering Gasparo, she said, "I reproached him vehemently. . . . He wore only a shirt, a red woman's shirt, and he held a pair of red pants in his hands; I saw it because I carried a light in my hand. As he wanted to put on his pants, I turned away out of modesty. . . . He had told me earlier that he was 36 years old, but I think he is younger, he is a handsome youth, red, white, curly-haired, corpulent, though somewhat short."[184]

While nuns and convent employees manipulated trial proceedings in matters of clausura for private reasons—and thereby threatened to undermine the judicial authority of state and church—government and episcopal magistrates tried to affirm and concentrate their powers. In the period between 1580 and 1620, the Provveditori's institutional jurisdiction was significantly extended, the surveillance of convents intensified, and the punishment of transgressors tightened. After the government successfully avoided the planned apostolic visitation of Venetian convents in 1581—insisting that outsiders (i.e., papal legates) should not have the right to inspect the "deposits of the patriciate's blood and viscera"—the Council of Ten was determined to have the convent-reform legislation executed more closely. The Provveditori sopra i Monasteri "should meet with the patriarch at least twice a week" to find ways of imposing obedience and thereby "avoid the great inconvenience of having an apostolic visitor take charge of this affair."[185] In 1584, the convent magistrate was granted independent judicial powers; the government authorized the Provveditori to sentence transgressors to up to five years, and from 1589 on to ten years, of imprisonment or exile.[186] After two major affairs were uncovered in 1604 and 1608 involving several nuns of two convents and dozens of high-ranking patricians,[187] the clausura laws were tightened again: under the new law, transgressors had to face decapitation.[188] The government expanded the authority of the convent magistrate by declaring that "the function of our Provveditori sopra i Monasteri is of such eminent importance . . . that they should come from among the principal Senators of our republic,"[189] and by extending its penitentiary competences to include all punishments *citra poenam mortis* (except the death penalty).[190] In 1609, the nuncio wrote to Rome that "the secular authorities have imprisoned many people, and nobody wants to enter [convents] any more, but the nuns . . . threaten to leave them."[191]

The Venetian curia worked hard to prevent that from happening. After Patriarch Giovanni Trevisan—like Patriarch Antonio Contarini before him in 1519—admitted that he needed the government's explicit support to implement the clausura decrees, the government appointed Lorenzo Priuli, a Tridentine hard-liner, as his successor (1591–1600). Priuli did not have authority problems. He began his tenure by issuing detailed decrees regarding the nuns' clausura and supervised their implementation closely. When visiting the convents of his diocese, he followed the post-Tridentine standard procedure of staging his visitations as awe-inspiring events with grandiose processions. Priuli would approach the convent in the company of selected priests and administrative assistants. He would bless bystanders before entering the church, kneel in front of the Eucharist, celebrate a mass, and venerate the Eucharist a second time. He would give detailed instructions as to how the tabernacles and oil flacons should be embellished (with silk embroidery, velvet, silver, etc.) and check whether all the altars were consecrated, neatly kept, and sufficiently decorated. Wooden altars were to be replaced by stone altars. Afterward he would enter the convent, explain his regulations to an assembly of completely veiled nuns, and proceed to inspect every single door, window, *ruota,* and balcony. He had his secretary take note of those doors and windows that needed to be walled up or supplied with bars or Venetian blinds, and dictated minute regulations regarding convent life. The patriarch also requested the nuns to compile inventories of church apparel, relics, and books, as well as lists of priests celebrating requiem masses. Before leaving, he would interrogate every single nun in private to ferret out secret love affairs, corruption, and other violations of monastic discipline.[192]

The visitations performed by Priuli's successor, Francesco Vendramin (1605–19),[193] were characterized by even greater pomp, attention to detail, and intimidating procedures. He reproached the nuns whenever they had neglected his predecessor's regulations, and he added his own.[194] Besides clausura issues, Priuli and Vendramin also paid close attention to the convents' financial situation. Priuli reconfirmed Trevisan's rules regarding the responsibilities of elected treasurers, secretaries, and abbesses (i.e., exact bookkeeping and the rationalization of the convent's financial management);[195] he also kept records of individual nuns whose relatives supplemented the convent rationing in the form of personal pensions. Vendramin, in addition, kept lists of the yearly revenues and expenses of convents in difficult economic situations. Priuli was the first patriarch who tried to guarantee all convents a regular income by standardizing the amount of money that incoming nuns were required to pay. "Considering the state of convents in this city, which for the most part are very needy, and unable to provide for the nuns' clothing and even livelihood, so that every nun needs many things from outside the convent, thereby endangering her soul," he ruled in 1593 that every nun should receive a yearly pension of sixty ducats—that is, the interest on one thousand ducats invested by her parents in secure funds—plus four hundred ducats in cash to furnish the cell and to pay for the festivities following the dressing, profession, and consecration ceremonies.[196]

During the jurisdictional conflicts between Venice and Rome at the beginning of the seventeenth century, Priuli's pension decree developed an unforeseen dynamic. The Senate, concerned with both the inflation of "spiritual dowries" in some convents and the lack of available funds in others, took an interest in Priuli's theretofore poorly implemented decree. This decree, it was realized, could solve two problems simultaneously: it would guarantee poor convents a regular income and thereby help preserve the nuns' clausura;[197] secondly, it would protect individual families against the devastating effects of inflated convent dowries. A spiritual dowry à la Priuli would burden private patrimonies only temporarily, since the invested capital was to be returned upon the nun's death. It would prevent private patrimonies from shrinking and convents' patrimonies from growing; it would also enlarge the government's budget by increasing the number of investments in state funds. In short, Priuli's decree was a mortmain law.

Between 1602 and 1620, the government passed a series of laws restricting ecclesiastical properties, of which Priuli's pension decree was an important part. In accordance with the traditional two-pronged approach aimed at containing and preserving convent property as well as enclosing the bodies of nuns, various clausura laws accompanied the dowry legislation of the early seventeenth century. Sexual "commerce" with nuns became a capital crime in 1605 (reconfirmed in 1616);[198] the law of 1585 prohibiting serenades and aubades under convent windows was reissued in 1611 and reconfirmed in 1626;[199] also in 1611, prostitutes were banned from convent churches and parlors;[200] in 1613, banquets were outlawed;[201] in 1615, a special police force was created, charged with raiding convent parlors and arresting illicit visitors;[202] in 1625, women living temporarily in convents became subject to the nuns' clausura laws.[203]

In addition, the government expanded and modified the functions and jurisdiction of the convent magistrate. Beginning in 1628, the Provveditori intervened in convent-reform issues statewide, that is, outside the city of Venice and the Dogado.[204] In 1637, male monasteries were for the first time subjected to the magistrate's authority. In collaboration with the Sopraintendenti alle Decime del Clero (collectors of the ecclesiastic tithe), the Provveditori audited the account books of several monasteries suspected of tax evasion and alienation of church property.[205] This shift in emphasis indicated that by 1620, the peak of the convent-reform movement in Venice had passed.[206] After having established the structures for supervision and criminalization of Venetian nunneries, the convent magistrate was now busy imposing its authority on convents and monasteries statewide.

The Provveditori's criminal records suggest that in the early seventeenth century, the surveillance of Venetian nuns had become a routine affair; the prosecution of individual scandalous affairs gave way to the extensive policing of convents in an attack on petty crime. To take a random sample, in the year 1611 the convent magistrate investigated the following cases: Father Iseppo Tagiapiera, a priest in San Martino di Burano, tried to convince Sister Diodata to escape from her convent, San Vito di Burano;[207] a bricklayer was accused of building two cells in Santa Anna without permission;[208] a certain Camillo, pimp and *gondoliere,* pressured his wife, who was also a prostitute, to return to him after she had taken refuge in the convent of Santa Maria Maddalena;[209] Veronica di Rosi talked to a nun without permission;[210] a bricklayer was accused of working without permission in Santa Caterina;[211] two Jews talked to a nun of Corpus Domini;[212] two young men sang obscene songs under the windows of Santa Anna;[213] a servant of Santa Marta lost her license to enter the nuns' clausura for talking to musicians;[214] Pasqualigo *sonador* (musician) was convicted of exhibitionism;[215] a well-known prostitute went to the church of Sant' Andrea de Zirada, "facendo molti giasi" (making a lot of fuss) and quarreling with a noblewoman;[216] Piero Antonio Ciola, a physician, talked to nuns in the garden of San Gerolamo.[217]

While the prosecution of small offenders became a routine procedure in Venice, especially after the Provveditori's special police began raiding convent parlors at night, convents in the upper lagoon were less well guarded. Several important trials in the diocese of Torcello between 1650 and 1658 indicate that the practice of systematic surveillance of nuns and the criminalization of clausura offenders was only now spreading to the periphery of the lagoon and to the mainland.[218] Nuns in the upper lagoon got pregnant and cultivated long-term relationships as late as 1658.[219] Even Venetian nuns still managed to be taken out to parties and on gondola tours in 1623, like Francesco Capello's lover—dressed in green stockings and a purple overcoat[220]— or to escape the convent in 1634, like Sister Candida Corner, wrapped in a bedsheet.[221] Despite these incidents, the institutional surveillance of nuns in Venice was well established at the beginning of the seventeenth century, compared with the lack of recognized authorities a hundred years earlier; accordingly, the lifestyles of non-observant nuns prior to the reform were significantly more licentious than the clausura boycotts of "involuntary" and "rebel" nuns fifty years after the Council of Trent. It was thought that once the center was under control— and the authority of the convent magistrate sufficiently recognized— the Provveditori could successfully claim jurisdiction over convents in remote areas and male monasteries.[222]

The efforts to implement a stricter discipline and seclusion, however, never entirely prevented nuns from cultivating social, and sometimes sexual, relations with outsiders. Not only was clausura a structurally volatile concept, as shown earlier, but as a political project, it was almost impossible to realize. Nuns were continuously and necessarily in contact with persons belonging to the outside world: convent priests, physicians, and other employees were exempted from the clausura rule; upper-class girls were educated in convents before entering either convent or marriage; married women often retired to convents in crisis situations; servant nuns had to go to the city on errands; and authorities such as the doge and dogaressa had special visiting rights in the convents under their jurisdiction. If the nuns' perfect seclusion was an ideal impossible to realize; if convents could, for practical reasons, never become the enclosed gardens of paradise that church and state reformers envisioned; and if, therefore, the nuns' virginity was essentially as fragile after the Council of Trent as before, then clausura—like virginity—functioned as a battleground for the contestation of power. It aimed at illusory results in order to spur a powerful and dynamic movement. As the church fathers said, the preservation of the nuns' virginity (and, by extension, their clausura) was "a very difficult task" to fulfill; an aureole would crown their "triumphant struggle," and therefore they "should never get tired of making a strong effort."[223] In this sense, the process of implementing the clausura rule was as important as the preservation of achieved results; the surveillance of possible offenders was as crucial as the punishment of convicted delinquents; the constant redrawing of new boundaries was as meaningful as the fortification of existing ones. The goal of the convent reform was to establish and stabilize new relationships of power through the process of confining and excluding.

Borderline Cases

Despite the efforts of state and church to transform Venetian nunneries into sacred enclosures of upper-class virgins, convent parlors developed into salonlike gathering places for people of all kinds of social background. The increased surveillance of the nuns' seclusion seemed to attract rather than deter visitors; messy urban crowds populated the antechambers of the nuns' confinement. Parlors became the sites where a sacred interior met the outside world, where order confronted chaos, where purity faced the perils of corruption, and where the consecrated brides of Christ watched the profanities of a world they had lost. While convent interiors were transformed into the most secret of urban places, the convent's external spaces attracted the general public. Parlors were legally reserved for the nuns' relatives, but foreigners, ecclesiastics, musicians, and courtesans were regular visitors as well. In 1617, a Father Gerolamo was sentenced to two years in prison "for having scandalously frequented several convents," where he performed madrigals he had composed; he also sent gifts and love letters to various nuns.[224] In 1625, a prostitute was caught in the church of Ognissanti "making *chiassi* [fussing around] with some nuns" while the mass was celebrated.[225] The same year, Moisé Coppio, "Jew, but now Christian of appearance," was denounced for having "noisy," "licentious," and "scandalous" conversations with several nuns of Santa Maria Maddalena, to whom he sent letters and gifts.[226] A patrician, a merchant, and a prostitute—"young people of bad reputation"—entertained the nuns of San Matteo di Murano by singing the litanies backward.[227] In 1627, a barber had some prostitutes perform a dance in the parlor of San Vito di Burano.[228] In 1642, "licentious" patrician youngsters (male and female) would stay in the parlors of San Lorenzo until late at night, playing music and singing "undignified

Anonymous, *The Parlor of San Lorenzo*

Master of the Ridotto, *The Parlor of San Zaccaria* (Ca' Rezzonico)

songs."²²⁹ Musicians also performed "mattinate con musica" (musical matinees) in the canal of San Lorenzo, accompanied by many people in gondolas.²³⁰ In the carnival of 1658, some Venetian patricians and a certain Count Gambara arranged a costume ball in the parlor of Santa Caterina.²³¹ While some performances were meant to be recreational, others were deliberately offensive: the nuns of San Vito di Burano, for example, notorious for having "secret" affairs, were ridiculed in a *chiarivari* during the midsummer night of 1658. Lit by a full moon, Piero Bon and Mazolo Vio sang and danced stark naked in front of the nuns' balconies; they also rang the bells to draw attention to a straw puppet and its oversized penis dangling from the campanile.²³²

Venetian nuns were not only spectators of the profane entertainments arranged by visitors in the exterior parlors; sometimes stage and audience switched sides, when nuns gave concerts or performed tragedies from behind the grilles. The *canto figurato,* for example, was widely practiced, although strictly outlawed. Some nuns were excellent singers. In 1622, the abbess of Santi Marco e Andrea di Murano had to justify why she had Sisters Gratiosa and Regina sing for the Princess of Rondel; recitals in front of secular audiences had been repeatedly forbidden in previous years. Apparently, the princess had come to Murano especially to hear the two famous nuns.²³³ In 1596, Patriarch Priuli wrote to the abbess of San Sepolcro when he heard "that people talk to the nuns until late at night behind locked doors, delivering fabrics and other things for the performance of tragedies and similar shows with great confusion inside the convent, and great scandal outside."²³⁴ Despite many admonitions, the nuns refused to renounce what they considered an "honest recreation," as Bishop Antonio Grimani complained; he allowed performances of holy representations, but prohibited the wearing of masks and of secular, especially male, clothes.²³⁵ Costumes, however, were essential to the theater, and nuns who acted in plays never stopped wearing them. Priuli feared that the exchange of clothes, a rather personal affair, either presupposed or would lead to an intimate friendship between lender and borrower. Furthermore, dressing up as a man required the wearing of stretch pants—a daring garment for a nun. On "fat Wednesday" of 1660, the abbess of San Giovanni Evangelista di Torcello dressed one of her favorite nuns, the "most beautiful Sister Eletta Querini," in men's clothes and presented her to Father Domenigo from Naples. He was so enchanted that he would not leave the convent for days.²³⁶ Count Antonio Martinengo, bishop of Torcello, apparently suspected a similar chain of events when interrogating Sisters Angela Amai, Eccelsa Falier, and Vittoria Amai of San Mauro di Burano. The three nuns, accused of having sexual relations with local priests, were known not only to wear fancy feminine clothes and hairstyles, but to have appeared in men's trousers during a theater performance.[237] To attract the gaze of outsiders was regarded as particularly dangerous for a nun, no matter whether she displayed herself in tight pants or in a décolleté dress, during a recital, theater performance, or regular parlor hours.

Aside from arousing men's desires, nuns in trousers were assumed to attract other nuns as well. When accusing Sister Colombina of having slept with Father Zuane, Sister Clara of San Vito di Burano could not give a convincing description of the delinquent; in response to the vicar's request for clarification, however, she insisted that "it could not have been another nun dressed up [as a man]."[238] The vicar's question, as well as the many episcopal admonitions that two nuns should not sleep in the same bed, suggests that love affairs or strong affective attachments between nuns or between nuns and boarders were quite frequent.[239] The case of Sister Raphaela Balbi, for example, who escaped from her convent to join her friend Laura, hints at a very close relationship between the two young women; Raphaela and Laura had grown up as boarders in the same convent. Although never subject to criminal investigations, these relationships preoccupied episcopal authorities because they violated monastic discipline and disrupted convent life. During his visitation of Santa Marta in 1594, Patriarch Priuli discovered that

> The *putte a spese* [boarders to be educated] greatly disturb the convent. . . . There are some who sleep in the cells of the nuns themselves, and they run around in the dormitory and wherever they wish without any rule, and they play cards late at night with great scandal. And there are significant love affairs between Sister Lorenza Capello and Orsetta Zorzi, and between Sister Marina Bragadin and Andriana Corner, so that provisions had to be made that they go neither to the choir, nor to the dormitory together, nor to any other common location without the necessary guardians.[240]

As long as relationships between nuns remained secret, the patriarch usually did not interfere, as in the case of San Giuseppe, where it was reported in 1620 that "Sister Chiara del Calice . . . wears a *zuffo* [bangs], plucks her eyebrows, uses face lotions, and sleeps every night with Sister Fiorenza, and never obeys, and sometimes Sister Lucietta Zen sleeps also with her. . . . They use perfumes. . . . Sister Bianca is

Sister Perpetua's friend, she is one being with her, and locks herself up with her."[241] Only "scandalous"—that is, public—relationships with outsiders were prosecuted. Sister Chiara, for example, lover of Sisters Fiorenza and Lucietta, was incriminated a couple of years later for having an affair with a nobleman. While sex between nuns was never prosecuted in Venice, "border" violations were regarded as serious crimes: "Several times nuns were found in the parlors . . . with noblemen who had their hands in their bosoms and nuns having their hands in the pants of those men and other things."[242]

In order for the nuns' clausura and virginity to remain intact, affective and sensual relations with persons inside the convent as well as without had to be avoided. As Francesco Pellizzari explained, intercourse with women put the nuns' hymens in even greater jeopardy than sodomitic relations with men. He also maintained—like everybody else at the time—that sensual desires were preceded and aroused by visual attraction. Dressing up in either male or female fashion was thus extremely dangerous to nuns. Showing their legs in stretch pants could attract outside visitors as much as exposing their breasts through low necklines and transparent veils. The same attires, however, could also incite the nuns' mutual attraction and lead to erotic relationships; affairs between nuns were potentially more disruptive of convent discipline than affairs with men, sodomitic or not, because they were impossible for outside authorities to control. Since denunciations by other nuns were the only source of information on those affairs—the truth of which was difficult to assess—neither episcopal nor state authorities ever dared to prosecute them.

Nuns were thus prohibited from engaging in any kind of "gazing." Posing in plays and other performances was as much of a temptation as watching them; glances that transgressed the boundaries of their confinement were as dangerous as those that circulated within; arousing either men's or women's desires in either male or female disguise was similarly offensive. Nuns were not to participate in anybody's gaze, whether as object or subject, whether in male or female attire. They were required to deflect desire by wearing a "neutering," awe-inspiring monastic gown. By cutting their hair and hiding their female bodies, they displayed their status as sacrificial victims. Nuns were removed from the realm of the living and "buried alive" as fiancées of a dead God. They were consecrated offerings to Christ, living examples of the afterlife, anticipating the state of redemption in a quasi-paradisiacal setting. Theirs was a neutral status, "post-female" and as such "post-worldly," signified by virginity, retirement, and veiling. The nuns' veils hid their feminine beauty, replaced it, but reminded viewers of it. Accordingly, virginity and clausura both emphasized and denied the nuns' femininity. To renounce sexuality and procreation was the sacrifice of a woman who had renounced a woman's worldly life. Nuns were angelic, genderless beings. Given their "neutered" and "post-secular" perfection, dressing up as either a man or a woman was a kind of drag, an illicit transgression of their ideally ungendered state.

Although "immodest acts" between nuns were theoretically as harmful to their virginity as violations of the clausura law, corruption within the walls was a secondary issue for convent reformers. Busy trying to confine the nuns within firm boundaries by criminalizing transgressors, state and church authorities did not anticipate the potential for disorder in an enclosed environment. In 1622, Patriarch Tiepolo got a taste of a paradise turned hell: lesbian nuns, a schismatic sect, and the practice of "diabolic arts" threatened to transform the convent of San Giuseppe into a satanic site.[243]

As already mentioned, the nuns' perfect enclosure was a battle concept, fictive, but instrumental for the project of gradual exclusion. The borderlines shielding the nuns' sacred enclosure from worldly contaminations had to be constantly redrawn and renegotiated: aside from being breached by mutual attractions between nuns and outsiders, convent walls were—for practical reasons—never as impermeable as would have been necessary in order to seal off the nuns hermetically from the surrounding secular environment. Convents were inhabited not only by professed nuns, but also by young boarders, married women temporarily retiring from the world, and servant nuns who went out on errands; ecclesiastic and, in some cases, secular authorities had permanent access to the nuns' enclosure; father confessors, physicians, and other employees were exempt from the clausura rule. Ideally, convents were oases of purity; in reality, the unruliness of city life often encroached upon the nuns' gardenlike enclosure.

In 1656, the nuns of San Mauro di Burano refused to readmit the noblewoman Betta Bianchi, who was sent to live in this convent whenever her brother was absent from Venice; while the nuns told the convent magistrate that "never again shall this type of woman be among us," Betta Bianchi took revenge by denouncing her many enemies in the convent. Among others, she was offended by Marietta, called Cicerana, who "used [to be] a public whore, and who is now a boarder in this convent . . . she is so scandalous that she is constantly in the parlor, pompously dressed, receiving priests, friars, and seculars, and she is also a very close friend of the abbess."[244] Betta Bianchi was a friend of the two Amai sisters, imprisoned at the time by the bishop for having had sexual affairs with locals. Betta nonetheless regarded them as "good nuns." *Donne a spese* (married boarders) such as Betta Bianchi or Marietta, who were usually living temporarily in convents because of a crisis situation—an impending divorce, for example— were often met with hostility by the nuns.[245] Boarders, especially adult women, insisted on certain liberties that nuns did not enjoy. Among other things, it was difficult to subject them to the clausura and parlor rules;[246] as Patriarch Trevisan mentioned in 1589, the "fiole à spese" (unmarried boarders) in Sant' Andrea de Zirada often caused "confusion in the parlors."[247]

Whenever secular authorities suspended the clausura rule—or had it suspended—for their own purposes, they displayed its arbitrary and negotiable character. In 1578, the dogaressa asked the nuncio for papal permission to visit her sister, a nun in Santa Maria degli Angeli di Murano, and to spend some time in this convent in the company of two or three other noblewomen.[248] After a long political quarrel over the reception of novices in San Lorenzo and, most of all, over the spiritual dowry they were supposed to pay, some councilors and several principal senators entered the convent in 1610 "to check whether it is true what the nuns say, that they need to construct more cells for those young girls."[249] In 1612, the doge and an entourage of noblewomen entered the convent of Santa Maria delle Vergini, celebrating and reconfirming this convent's ducal jurisdiction, a privilege conceded by Pope Alexander III.[250]

A source of great disturbance in convents were the servant nuns *(converse),* who, for practical reasons, were exempt from the clausura rule. During Patriarch Priuli's visitation of Santa Maria Maggiore in 1594, the professed nuns denounced several *converse* for going out on walks, eating outside the convent, and even traveling as far as Udine.[251] In Santa Maria dei Miracoli, another Franciscan convent, the *converse* also abused their privileges. The choir nuns complained about the servant nuns' arrogance and power: they would "manage the revenues of the convent, conclude lease contracts, and collect income as they please"; they would guard the keys to the parlor and the exterior *ruote,* spend the three summer months in the countryside, introduce friends and relatives into the convent, steal bread, offend the nuns' relatives, and neglect their work. In short, the chapter nuns had no authority

Gianantonio Guardi, *Parlor of Nuns* (Ca' Rezzonico)

Anonymous, *The Convent Parlor* (formerly in London, Sundin Collection)

over the *converse,* who practically governed the convent's affairs. As Priuli recorded, "some of the [choir] nuns wish that they [the *converse*] would be reduced to observing the clausura, so that they could not spend as much, and help the nuns a bit more, who now do all the work."[252] In order to contain the disorder caused by servant nuns' traveling about the *terraferma,* the patriarch ruled that every convent should appoint four servant nuns over age forty who would be permitted to go as far as the center of town.

Mostly, however, it was the *educande* who disrupted convent discipline. Aside from occasional love affairs between these teenage girls and their *maestre* (teachers), and aside from the "confusion" they created in parlors and dormitories, they provoked great jealousy among "involuntary nuns" when getting engaged to be married. In 1554, Patriarch Francesco Contareno recommended that "novices [i.e., secular brides] before their matrimony, or transferal, should not appear in the parlors or elsewhere in the convent in bridal attire."[253] Since those "novices" apparently insisted on wearing the customary bridal attire while still living in clausura, Patriarch Trevisan ordered that "weddings should not be celebrated in convent churches, that marriage contracts should not be negotiated in convent parlors or at church windows, and that the novices should not be shown for contracting those matrimonies."[254] These rules seem to have been widely ignored. Since the majority of upper-class girls were educated in convents until they reached the proper age for either marriage or monachization, many parents negotiated their dowry contracts before taking their daughters back home. Considering the parents' wish to keep their daughters in a safe place until their career was settled while also trying to prevent the envy and animosity of those girls destined for convent life, Patriarch Vendramin and Bishop Grimani modified their predecessors' rules. Girls engaged to be married were to leave the convent immediately so that they would not "dress up as brides and receive their fiancés at the windows with scandal."[255]

While the prolonged mixing of bridal and religious "novices" inside the nuns' clausura intolerably blurred the distinction between inside and outside, angels and women, the sacred and the profane, the visits to the exterior parlors that brides paid on their wedding day highlighted and underlined those boundaries. According to Francesco Sansovino, a patrician wedding began with the presentation of the bride to the groom's relatives and friends; she then leaves her husband's house and, "accompanied . . . by many noblewomen . . . enters a gondola . . . and, followed by a great number of other gondolas, she goes to visit the convents of nuns."[256] As numerous state ordinances suggest, those wedding processions upset the nuns considerably. In 1654, the Senate ordered:

> It is a licentious act of the young people to annoy the convents of nuns with hateful and vile disturbances, particularly during the solemn functions of the visits of novices [brides], when the limits of proper modesty . . . are transgressed by crowds of noblemen and other people in excessive confusion. . . . It shall be absolutely and entirely prohibited to all novices of whatever status and condition to visit the convents of nuns, accompanied by an entourage of noblewomen, during the solemn days of their wedding.[257]

After the "lay novice" officially completed her transferal from convent to husband's house on her wedding day, the "solemn function" of visiting her former convent marked the end of her transitional state. For the first time, the young bride confronted the nuns with whom she had grown up from beyond the grilles. Those triumphant processions to the exterior parlors dramatized the borderline separating the nuns who had been "wasted" and "sacrificed" to a life in perpetual seclusion from the women who had entered the realm of public exchange and circulation. At the same time, a girl's ritual return to the convent after her wedding ceremony was a form of homage she paid to her former home. Convent life—or, in general, a secluded lifestyle—was the norm for upper-class women, a concept that these wedding parades seemed to emphasize; a bride left the enclosure of her childhood and entered the sphere of circulation only to immediately pass into the seclusion of her husband's house. Every young woman was a "novice" before pronouncing either the three holy vows or the vow of matrimony. A wedding procession celebrated the bride's departure from her seclusion, while at the same time affirming the principle of confinement. The attraction these parades had for local youths, who transformed the "solemn" confrontation between bride and nuns into a *chiarivari*-like festivity, underlined the importance of this ritual.

In general, religious functions highlighting the nuns' enclosure—the dressing, profession, and consecration ceremonies—turned easily into neighborhood festivals. This was partially because of the distribution of wine and *bozzolai* (sweets),[258] but the popularity of those "dramas of confinement" among urban crowds exceeded the attraction of refreshments. The nuns' ceremonies were spectacular rites of sacrificial exclusion, in the course of which these offerings to Christ were

Giacomo Franco, *Brides on a Gondola Ride*, ca. 1600. From *Habiti delle donne veneziane.* (By permission of the Houghton Library, Harvard University.)

shielded against the contaminations of the world, and boundaries drawn around the sacred enclosures of virgin nuns. Convent functions separated order from chaos, ascetic purity from "the stench of carnal desires," women "wasted" (nuns) from women "spent" (brides). As "threshold dramas," monachization ceremonies attracted ridicule and laughter. Annoyed by the fact that carnivalesque reversals threatened to subvert the religious meaning of clausura ceremonies, state and church authorities tried to suppress these public festivities—without much success. The popularity of convents as centers of entertainment and the establishment of institutions of surveillance have to be seen as complementary, mutually reinforcing phenomena. Both developments demonstrate that the seclusion of upper-class women in the late sixteenth and early seventeenth centuries was a public procedure of political importance.

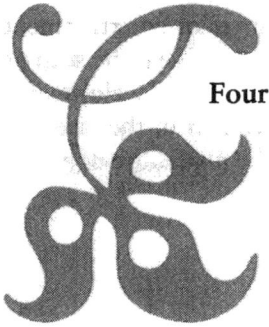

Four

THE ECONOMIC DIMENSIONS OF THE CONVENT-REFORM PROGRAM

The gradual implementation of strict encloisterment changed convent life irrevocably. Clausura not only encroached upon the nuns' comforts and ancient liberties, but drastically reduced their autonomy in convent administration. Isolating the nuns from families and friends in the name of spiritual renewal and disciplinary reform was instrumental in curtailing the decision-making powers of abbesses and the institutional independence of the convents. Once clausura laws had "freed" the nuns from outside pressures and distractions, eliminated individually granted papal privileges, and replaced the supervisory functions of monastic congregations with episcopal jurisdiction and state surveillance, reformers turned to intervening directly in convent management. The disciplinary measures weakened the nuns' power to resist further infringements on their status; but apart from the strategic importance of clausura in limiting convent autonomy, strict encloisterment was a measure to cut spending: in a society of reciprocal gift-giving, cultivating social relationships cost a great deal of money.

Starting in the early sixteenth century, Venetian state and church reformers collaborated in their efforts to eliminate the nuns' "waste" of convent resources and their "corruption" in property management.[1] Sumptuary laws were imposed to limit the amount of money nuns spent on celebrating dressing ceremonies, professions, and consecrations; distributions of "charities" to needy friends and bribes to servants were prohibited; abbesses were encouraged to not admit more "mouths to feed" than convent revenues could pay for; and government officials were elected to periodically audit the nuns' account books. The concern for limiting the nuns' "superfluous" expenses and reducing their debts was part of the government's strategy to turn convents into economically self-sufficient institutions. Because of the civic importance of convents as "safe-deposits" of the patriciate's purity and honor, the government had a strong interest in protecting their properties against loss due to corruption or lack of managerial skills. After the introduction of clausura, insufficiently endowed convents could no longer supplement their income through begging or work and had to rely on state subsidies for survival. While the government had a vested interest in containing the alienation of existing convent patrimonies, it also tried to limit the drain of taxable real estate resulting from private persons' testamentary legacies and donations of land to church institutions. Mortmain laws aimed at restricting the accumulation of ecclesiastical real estate in Venice (1536) and the entire *terraferma* (1605), but church patrimonies nonetheless grew steadily until the late eighteenth century. Acknowledging the impossibility of enforcing mortmain legislation, the government abolished the principles of tax exemption and non-alienation of church properties. In 1569, the pope granted the government the right to estimate ecclesiastic patrimonies in the entire republic and to levy a permanent tax. In 1605, first attempts were made to auction off illegally acquired church properties; this "experiment" proved unsuccessful, however, until repeated in a different political climate with more vigor and support by eighteenth-century Enlightenment reformers.[2]

While church authorities shared the government's interest in "rationalizing" and supervising convent management for the purpose of preserving the nuns' endowments, they obviously resisted any attempts to reduce further accumulations of convent patrimonies. Nonetheless, the collaboration between convent magistrate and curia in matters of clausura and financial administration continued undisturbed even when the Senate's reduction of "spiritual dowries" in 1604 seriously strained the government's relationship with Rome. There was a clear division of competences between patriarch and state magistrate in their ongoing efforts to reform unruly nuns. Since only the patriarch had the right to enter the nuns' clausura, he was in charge of issuing rules, communicating with the nuns, and executing details: the patriarch checked how many nuns disposed of independent income, asked for inventories of church properties, and taught treasurers the principles of double-entry bookkeeping. The convent magistrate, on the other hand, prosecuted corrupt proxies, authorized all expenses exceeding twenty-five ducats, and investigated violations of sumptuary laws. Because of the prestige the patriarch enjoyed among ecclesiastics, nuns were more likely to follow his orders than those issued by lay officials of possibly lower social standing. Despite the reformatory zeal of patriarchs such as Lorenzo Priuli, who was genuinely interested in improving monastic observance among Venice's many dissident nuns, the curia was generally reduced to implementing legislation passed by the government and to functioning as intermediary in conflicts among the republic, the nuns, and the papacy.

Just as strict encloisterment was never fully implemented but served to control and limit the nuns' social relationships with relatives, friends, and confidants by "disciplining" their bodies, thus establishing the capillary systems of power Foucault has identified as characteristic of modern societies, some convents survived until the end of the republic without ever introducing the principles of rational property management as defined by state and church. Only when individual abbesses and the nuns themselves decided to cut down on conspicuous consumption and other forms of "waste," to fire corrupt estate managers, supervise the collection of revenues, and economize their resources—as happened in Sant' Andrea de Zirada in the second half of the seventeenth century—were economic reforms successful. Laws that required all convent managers and superiors to seek government approval for major expenses, investments in private loans, and other monetary transactions were violated as often as sumptuary laws prohibiting the nuns' "superfluous" display of wealth on feast days and at convent celebrations.[3] Audits of convent account books by state officials, a practice initiated in the early sixteenth century, were similarly inefficient; only rarely did such checks lead to prosecutions of corrupt procurators and managers. As late as 1676, the Senate issued a law that made it mandatory for all convent managers and accountants to demonstrate their bookkeeping skills before obtaining a work permit, an indication that double-entry bookkeeping was still the exception rather than the rule.[4]

Mortmain laws were systematically violated as well, demonstrating the undiminished popularity of lay persons' bequests to the church, the government's lack of executive power to force ecclesiastic institutions to divest themselves of illegally acquired properties, and the privileged status monastic institutions enjoyed until the late eighteenth century. Church taxes were levied regularly after 1536, but only twice adjusted for inflation and property appreciation, in 1569 and 1768. The only "reform" the government adamantly pursued, and successfully implemented, was the reduction of spiritual dowries legislated in the early seventeenth century. Once the government gave up on issuing upper limits for bridal dowries—the last law to this effect was passed in 1575—the Senate insisted that access to convents had to be "equal" and "free" to the entire patriciate. Entrance fees were not to exceed eight hundred to one thousand ducats in cash, also payable in the form of a lifelong pension of sixty ducats annually. Convents and the papacy protested vehemently against this new provision, interpreting it—correctly—as a new mortmain law, which outlawed individual, competitive settlements of dowry payments at a time of peaking monachization rates, and drastically reduced the possibilities for further accumulations of capital. The government remained firm in its decision, however, issuing detailed executive measures: no candidate could be officially "dressed" until the ceremony was authorized by the convent magistrate upon her father's deposit of a spiritual dowry in the legally determined amount. Although nothing prevented a prospective nun's relatives from offering unaccountable "charities" in cash to the convent of their choice, the standardization of convent fees gradually caught on: in 1734, the convent magistrate required all monetary transactions between convents and lay persons to be publicly approved, "as is practiced with deposits of spiritual dowries."[5] The government's firm stance in fighting inflated monachization fees was of paramount importance to the entire patriciate, since rising spiritual dowries would have prevented the honorable withdrawal of unmarriageable women from circulation. The potlatch system would have collapsed had its costs not been contained by the government.

The introduction of a standard monachization fee was the most tangible result of the reformers' program to fight the alienation of convent properties without draining the laity's resources. The "rationalization" of accounting methods, the maximization of revenues, and the limitation of "waste" happened only gradually; the "modernization" of convent management was most efficient if introduced by reform-minded nuns themselves. The structurally most significant and long-lasting effect of the convent-reform movement was the establishment of state and church bureaucracies charged with supervising, correcting, and limiting the nuns' economic activities. Just as clausura was never fully realized but served to justify the surveillance of nuns by outside authorities and turned "discipline" from a spiritual disposition into normative compliance with monastic rules, so did the fight for financial self-sufficiency and rational property management serve broader political purposes. Essentially, the economic reforms were designed to support the patriciate's monachization practices by guaranteeing secure and predictable revenues to convents without endangering lay patrimonies, and to enable less well endowed nunneries to observe strict encloisterment. Although some abbesses took pride in maximizing their resources and rationalizing their spending policies for the benefit of their communities, and church authorities naturally supported all measures designed to protect the convents against debts and the loss of patrimonies, the economic interventions in convent management were primarily of civic importance. In order for the potlatch to function, convents had to be transformed into financially healthy institutions.

The Fight against Waste and Corruption

The emphasis on strict encloisterment and spiritual renewal necessarily had a financial dimension, because the nuns' efforts to maintain a network of friends from behind the grilles cost money. Since the nuns' relationships with outsiders other than their relatives had repeatedly been declared illegal, convent reformers naturally regarded any expense for the purpose of socializing as "waste." In order to meet and entertain friends, nuns employed go-betweens, who delivered their messages, kept them up to date on the latest gossip, and introduced them to potential friends and lovers. These services needed to be paid for. In 1568, the convent magistrate interrogated every single widow residing in the hospital of Sant' Andrea de Zirada to collect information on the spending habits of the nuns who oversaw the hospital.[6] According to Catarina, six women and a man of dubious reputation carried away baskets full of flour and other foodstuffs during their numerous visits to the convent parlor, while "we have to drink spoiled wine."[7] Although all of the nuns made significant gifts to visitors, Sisters Beatrice, Gabriela, Anna, Lena, and Augustina, who had particularly busy social lives, were the main sponsors of seven go-betweens. The giveaways happened despite the fact that during his visitation of Sant' Andrea two years earlier, Patriarch Giovanni Trevisan had explicitly ordered that "in the parlor, one cannot offer food and drink to anybody passing by."[8] This prohibition belonged to the standard repertoire of every patriarch who visited Venetian convents until 1620.

While Patriarch Trevisan had contented himself with admonishing the nuns that "they should not give away so many baskets and so many cakes, but only in modest amounts,"[9] his successors, Lorenzo Priuli and Francesco Vendramin, attacked the nuns' excessive "alms-giving" as a serious abuse. They ordered nuns to compile minute accounts of their income and expenses and severely reproached rich convents such as San Zaccaria for consuming 500 *staia* of wheat (for measures, see the appendix) per year, which was 200 staia more than they judged necessary.[10] This averaged 622 liters per capita, compared to an average per capita consumption of 250 to 330 liters of wheat annually in sixteenth-century Venice.[11] The residents of Santa Maria delle Vergini consumed even more—600 staia of wheat per year (49,986 liters total, or 746 liters per capita), most of it for the purpose of baking pastries.[12] But the rich convents were not the only ones to give away food in great quantities. The mendicant nuns of San Sepolcro and Santa Maria Maggiore also indulged in excessive hospitality, with the result that the nuns themselves did not have enough to eat.[13]

The economy of gift exchange was a vital part of the nuns' social relations. Many nuns depended on supplementary food supplies; they returned favors rendered by offering *bozzolai* (pastries), needlework, and other services. They nurtured friendships by making donations of

Francesco Guardi, *Parlor of Nuns* (Mari-Cha collection, Hong Kong)

any sort, and bribed go-betweens for their (illegal) services. While the patriarchs' attacks on the nuns' unauthorized donations to lay persons as a form of embezzlement and alienation of convent properties were largely motivated by their fight against "waste," spiritual consider-ations played a role as well: during his visitation of Santa Anna in 1609, Patriarch Vendramin pointed out that the convent's reputation was endangered because of the nuns' numerous relations with lay per-sons who provided them with wine and wheat.[14] It is impossible to decide whether it was the nuns' social contacts with outsiders or their spending habits that the authorities tried to correct more arduously. When the nuns of San Sepolcro, reproached by Patriarch Priuli for wasting their scarce resources, abolished gift-giving and developed a catering business instead, they were reprimanded again: "The abuse of cooking the food sent by parents and friends to the convent and of selling the prepared dishes outside the convent has to be abolished entirely."[15] In addition, state and church magistrates tried to suppress other services that were part of the nuns' elaborate system of exchange, such as washing the laundry of friends and relatives.[16]

While convent reformers seem to have been moderately successful in reducing the nuns' everyday traffic in alms, gifts, goods, and ser-vices, their plan to eliminate the "superfluous" expenses on feast days proved to be almost impossible to realize. Since the early sixteenth century, church and state laws had prohibited any pomp during the celebration of *sagre* (the nuns' consecration ceremonies), saints' days, and other religious festivities. In 1509, Patriarch Antonio Contarini outlawed banquets and the display of excessive church decor on feast days.[17] In 1524, Contarini's vicar prohibited elaborate concerts given in honor of the convent saints; no musicians other than four *psalma-dori* (psalm singers) were to be employed.[18] In 1547, the Council of Ten declared that *vestizioni* (dressing ceremonies), *professioni* (profes-sions), and *sagre* should not be celebrated by banquets; not even the nuns' relatives were supposed to be entertained.[19] During carnival, it was strictly forbidden to give dinner parties in the parlors.[20] Because these festivities caused the convents and the nuns' relatives to spend considerable sums of money, and because they attracted crowds of people to the nuns' sacred enclosures, any display of luxury was strictly forbidden. Both the government and the curia repeatedly issued corre-sponding sumptuary laws, only to acknowledge in 1644 that in Padua and Torcello, *sagre* were still celebrated in the form of neighborhood festivals.[21] Extravagant consecration ceremonies in several Venetian convents led the convent magistrate to start an inquiry in 1641. Asked how much they spent on the occasion of four recent consecration parties, the nuns of San Gerolamo produced several bills showing that their expenses for sugar, cinnamon, marzipan, and candles had not surpassed the legal amount of fifty ducats—about five months' wages for a skilled worker.[22] Sister Cecilia Campi, however, reported that "they spent much more than they admit," and the abbess frankly stated that the customary expenses for handkerchiefs, fruit juices, and coins to be offered to members of their congregation naturally exceeded the fifty ducats allowed by the Senate. Instead of producing fake bills, the nuns of San Zaccaria answered rather vaguely when asked how much their recent *sagre* had cost: "This is something one cannot know for sure, because one spends money here and there, and one cannot do without it." The nuns of Santi Biagio e Cataldo, on the other hand, claimed—rather unconvincingly—that their relatives had paid for everything. Since an audit of several spice vendors' account books did not produce any proof that the nuns had made purchases, the allegations against them and their families were finally dropped.[23]

The nuns' spending habits had preoccupied state and church officials since the beginning of the sixteenth century. In fact, the very first task of the newly founded convent magistrate in 1521 was the "limitation of the expenses of both observant and non-observant nuns in this city [Venice] and in Torcello."[24] According to Patriarch Gerolamo Querini, the financial situation of some convents was disastrous; he ordered that abbesses stop accepting novices if the convent's resources were too slim to provide for their livelihood.[25] Querini's decree also specified that novices be admitted only if a council of older nuns, the chapter, the abbess, and he himself approved it. In order to decide how many *bocche* (mouths) a convent could feed, he told every abbess to compile a list of her convent's revenues. Patriarch Querini's decree suggests that he blamed the abbesses' arbitrary rule for the mismanagement of their convents. The numerous orders issued by the Council of Ten between 1521 and 1534 relating to convents' finances affirm this assumption. In contrast to the late sixteenth and early seventeenth centuries, when the Provveditori sopra i Monasteri di Monache were busy containing the nuns' squandering of baskets full of flour, the early decades of the reform were dominated by a battle against a more serious form of corruption. In 1521, the Council of Ten asked the two Provveditori "to check carefully every *livello*[26] and lease contract" and gave them "the authority . . . to revoke and annul [them]. . . . In the future, no convent may close a lease or *livello* contract . . . with persons who have relatives in those convents."[27] In 1528, it was also specified that the convent magistrate and the patriarch should control the account books of convent agents and estate managers and force them to return any sums they might have embezzled.[28] Three years later, in 1531, the same officials were supposed to collect the credits owed to convents and make sure that neither agents nor estate managers closed lease contracts without the permission of the abbess.[29] In 1533 and 1534, these decrees were reissued.[30] None of them, however, was ever executed (see chapter 3). In the early decades of the reform, neither the convent magistrate nor the patriarch was endowed with enough authority and power to intervene in such a delicate affair as supervising the financial transactions between the city's foremost families and convents. The office of Provveditore sopra i Monasteri was therefore extremely unpopular: in 1522, one year after its foundation, the elected candidates refused to serve on this commission. As a consequence, the Council of Ten issued a decree forbidding elected officials to resign—a measure that secured the formal survival of this magistracy but showed how little political support it enjoyed.[31] The system of favoring private moneylenders through *livelli* contracts was obviously too widespread, the interests at stake too powerful, and the reform faction within the patriciate too weak for this commission to function properly. The early-sixteenth-century reform of what government and curia called the nuns' excessive spending habits, corruption, and mismanagement failed entirely. Between 1534 and 1558, no decree regarding the supervision of the convents' account books was reissued.

Revenues and Expenses according to the Tax Records of 1564

It was not until after the Council of Trent (1545–63) that the convent magistrate and the patriarch resumed their efforts to supervise the convents' finances.[32] By now, the political climate had changed: the republic's recognition in 1564 of the council's legislation marked a considerable—if short-lived—improvement in relations between Venice and Rome.[33] Only months earlier, Pope Pius IV had consented to have Venetian church patrimonies reappraised for the purpose of state taxation. This estimate was a major political breakthrough for the "lay" faction within the patriciate, because it enabled the government to collect church tithes on a more regular basis, adjust the tax rates to the increase in ecclesiastic properties since 1536, and gather important information regarding the composition and management of church patrimonies in general.[34] Among other things, it offered valuable insights into the problem of how much mismanagement, debt, and poverty there really was among Venetian convents. The tax law required that every piece of convent property and the annual income it generated in cash or in kind be listed separately, as well as the amount of wheat, wine, oil, firewood, soap, spices, and other items the nuns consumed yearly. Income from interest-bearing capital invested in *livelli* (private credits), *monti* (forced loans), and the *procuratie* (trust funds) was also reported; only government bonds were exempted.[35] The estimate of the *decima del clero* (ecclesiastic tithe) of 1564 thus gives a detailed picture of the distribution of wealth among Venetian convents, the structure and size of their patrimonies, and the amount of their yearly expenditures and debts (see appendix, table A4).

The distribution of taxable income among convents was extremely unequal. Revenues ranged from 7,467 ducats per year in the case of San Zaccaria to 42 ducats in the case of Santi Marco e Andrea (see table A6). The distribution of per capita income in particular shows that San Zaccaria was by far the richest among Venetian convents. It disposed of 187 ducats per nun, followed by Santa Maria della Celestia with 80 ducats and San Lorenzo with 57. One-fifth of the nunneries recorded a per capita income of less than 10 ducats per year; the nuns' average revenues amounted to 30 ducats. In the same period, a master in the construction trade earned an annual salary of 60 ducats.[36] The wealthiest convents were either Benedictine, Cistercian, or Augustinian convents of ancient foundation (see table A3). Of the poorest nunneries, many were founded in the late fifteenth or early sixteenth century, when mortmain laws prohibited large endowments of church institutions. Other poor convents belonged to the Franciscan order, which rejected the possession of real estate out of principle.

The differences in expenditures among convents are largely reflective of the differences in income distribution—that is, rich convents spent more than poor convents. In some cases, however, the estimate recorded remarkable discrepancies between revenues and expenditures (see table A6). While several wealthy convents recorded unbalanced budgets or debts (for example, Santa Croce della Giudecca, Santa Maria della Celestia, Santa Maria degli Angeli, and Sant' Alvise), a num-

ber of only modestly endowed convents disposed of disproportionately
high net revenues (for example, San Servolo, Sant' Antonio di Torcello,
San Mauro di Burano, and Santa Maria Valverde).

Among the convents' expenditures, church functions were the single most important entry. Even the underendowed convents reported
paying considerable sums for priests' salaries and for church furnishings such as linen, silverware, and candles (see table A7). The mendicant convents of Santa Croce di Venezia, Santa Maria dei Miracoli,
and San Sepolcro declared that everything they spent went for priests'
salaries and church decor. Among the convents with the highest total
expenditures, San Zaccaria, Santa Maria degli Angeli, Santa Maria
delle Vergini, and Santa Croce della Giudecca used 12 to 18 percent
of their budgets for church employees and furnishings (that is, between
463 and 670 ducats). Next to church functions, foodstuffs such as fish,
meat, cheese, and pasta occupied a prominent place in most of the
convents' budgets. Clothes, firewood, and oil were also important
items, followed by salaries for the nuns' *barcaruoli* (boatmen), bakers,
gardeners, and porters. Although two-thirds of the convents indicated
having considerable expenditures for bread, wine, and additional
foodstuffs *(companadego)*, food was apparently a dispensable part of
their budgets. Generally, only the wealthier convents declared buying
food in large quantities, while the poorer ones preferred spending what
little money they had on spices, clothes, oil, servants, and church functions.[37]

Paradoxically, the poor convents, which did not purchase food,
lacked income in kind as well—an indication that strict encloisterment
would have been difficult to introduce. Many of the rich nunneries,
in contrast, which disposed of a more than sufficient per capita supply
of basic foodstuffs, bought supplementary wheat and wine in large
quantities (see table A8). Those convents that reported neither income
in kind nor expenditures for food also lacked net revenues in cash.
The complete absence of data regarding the poorer nuns' food consumption suggests that their convents had other, nontaxable sources
of income in either cash or kind; that these nuns were provided for
individually by their families; or that they lived off state subsidies and
charitable donations. Also, the summaries of expenditures might have
been intended not to report the convents' actual budgets and consumption patterns, but to function as a proposal for itemized tax deductions. This would explain why rich convents reported paying disproportionately large amounts for "necessary" items such as food and

church functions but concealed any "superfluous" or "wasteful" expense for architectural embellishments or convent festivities. This assumption would also explain why underendowed convents did not give a full account of their actual expenditures.[38]

Regardless of how exact the tax records really were, they do confirm the assumption of Patriarchs Trevisan, Priuli, and Vendramin that the per capita consumption of wheat and wine in most convents surpassed the nuns' needs, thus indicating that much food was indeed given away or stolen. While average wheat consumption in sixteenth-century Venice (and Tuscany) lay between 250 and 330 liters and average wine consumption was approximately 225 liters,[39] the nuns' declarations showed that they consumed between 271 and 580 liters of wheat and 251 to 577 liters of wine per capita annually (see table A8). In many cases, it is not clear whether the nuns distinguished neatly between income in kind, consumption, and expenditure for supplementary wheat and wine. San Lorenzo, for example, reported a per capita consumption of wine of 299 liters, which was exactly the amount of wine the convent received from its tenants, but declared buying an additional 382 liters per capita on the market. San Giacomo, Santi Rocco e Margherita, and Spirito Santo, on the other hand, had very little income in kind but declared consuming several hundred liters of wheat and wine per capita, without indicating that any money was spent on supplementary food items. While some convents might have consumed their income directly (such as San Zaccaria), others probably sold their wheat when prices were high, buying whatever they needed for their own consumption on the market when prices were low. Santa Maria della Celestia, for example, had an income of 2,261 liters of wheat per capita but bought an additional 587 liters on the market, which suggests that the convent speculated with grain prices.

Apart from the more than generous consumption of wheat and wine by the wealthiest convents, the tax records give scarce evidence of the nuns' alleged waste and mismanagement. Although fifteen of the forty convents had debts and nearly half of them had unbalanced budgets, only some convents appeared to have suffered serious financial problems. San Matteo di Murano, for example, was hardly in a position to pay off its debts of over 2,300 ducats with a total yearly income of only 68 ducats. San Giacomo had revenues of 554 ducats, but expenditures two to three times that amount—plus 1,650 ducats in debts. Santa Croce di Venezia had only 800 ducats in debts, but its per capita income of barely 2 ducats made it unlikely that the nuns could pay off their obligations without outside financial aid. In contrast, Santi Biagio e Cataldo, with debts of almost 3,000 ducats but a net revenue of 413 ducats and a yearly income of 2,122, seemed less endangered. Unbalanced budgets—that is, disproportionately high expenditures—were worrisome only in those cases in which low yearly revenues were coupled with debts.

As already mentioned, the tax records give only an approximate account of the convents' revenues. The degree to which the declarations were manipulated for the purpose of tax evasion is impossible to estimate; moreover, they list only taxable wealth. They show neither that many nuns were supported by their families[40] or earned their living through work,[41] nor that large parts of the convents' income derived from tax-exempt spiritual dowries and pensions in the form of cash payments, *livelli,* or government bonds. Depending on how many residents a convent had, this additional cash income could be quite high. The dowries paid to Sant' Andrea de Zirada ranged between six hundred and twelve hundred ducats in 1570 and 1571;[42] the novices of Santa Croce di Venezia paid three hundred ducats in 1517 and four hundred in 1589;[43] the prestigious convent of San Lorenzo demanded eight hundred ducats in 1530 and twenty-five hundred in 1610.[44] Many of the property-less convents lived entirely off their residents' annuities, occasional donations, and state subsidies.[45] It is therefore plausible to assume that additional, tax-exempt revenues of various kinds made up for the budgetary imbalances and debts investigated above.[46] Poor convents, in particular, depended on spiritual dowries to pay off their debts. In 1564, the abbess of Santa Marta explained the vicious cycle in which an under-endowed convent such as hers was caught. It had recently accepted more nuns than it could provide for in order to pay off its debts, only to be forced to take out more loans afterward:

> In these miserable times our number has increased to 46, because we were recently forced to accept 8 nuns, whose dowries we needed to pay off some of our debts . . . for oil, wine, firewood, and many other things, in addition to an infinite number of other debts, amounting to 1,500 ducats. . . . Not only are our revenues insufficient to provide for our daily needs, we also had to borrow a large sum of money . . . to build a refectory, a kitchen, a dormitory, and a granary—rooms we needed to repair, having increased in number.[47]

Whatever the nuns' exact financial situation, government and church officials continued to insist that Venetian convents suffered from structural mismanagement and needed to be reformed. Five years after the estimate was compiled, the Council of Ten stated that "the revenues of several convents in this city . . . are poorly managed, mostly because their legal agents *(procuratori)* . . . who are not related to the nuns by blood, do not properly care for them."[48] As a consequence, the council ruled that each chapter should elect three legal representatives from among the male relatives of the nuns. Two months later, in August of 1569, another law was issued declaring that any contract concluded by abbesses would be invalid unless approved by two-thirds of the nuns, the three *procuratori,* the patriarch, and the convent magistrate. The preamble focused on abuse by convent governesses who allegedly alienated convent properties by taking out credits in the form of *livelli:*

> Although it has been established in many deliberations that ecclesiastical properties cannot be alienated, it has become the custom that the abbesses and prioresses of the convents of this city and Dogado take out loans from private persons as they please without notifying the chapters, concluding contracts in which they obligate the possessions of the convents, and in which they promise to pay every year six ducats per hundred in interest, or five staia of wheat, until the original sum is returned, and they do this under the pretext of paying debts, or to undertake unnecessary construction in the convents, or for other frivolous reasons, and when they lack the money to pay the interest and canons, they take out additional credits in the same fashion, so that the interest payments increase despite the fact that the convents have high revenues, and the poor nuns lack food and clothing, and the affairs of the convent go from bad to worse, so that a certain convent that has five thousand ducats annually has 5,000 ducats in debts at the moment, a problem that needs to be solved.[49]

According to the tax records of 1564, fifteen of the forty convents in Venice and Torcello were burdened with debts, but only San Matteo di Murano specified them as interest payments on *livelli.*[50] None of the convents reported debts of five thousand ducats. The government's attack on mismanagement and corruption seems therefore exaggerated; it was instrumental, however, in justifying the laws designed to eliminate the arbitrary powers of abbesses and prioresses. It reestablished the chapters as decision-making agents, though not without subjecting all future management decisions to the approval of state and church authorities.

While the government outlined the general direction of the economic reform of the convents, the Venetian curia adjusted the laws to the specific needs of individual convents. Supporting the state campaign against mismanagement and corruption, Patriarchs Trevisan, Priuli, and Vendramin issued detailed instructions for a more "democratic" and efficient administration in their visits to the convents. They ruled that abbesses must give a regular account of the convent's finances;[51] they instituted councils of older nuns and charged them with co-administering revenues and expenses;[52] they introduced the concept of double-entry bookkeeping;[53] they took an inventory of the money that many nuns received from their families and ordered that this money be kept in a "public" cash deposit box to which the abbess, the treasurer, and the secretary each had a key.[54] Those regulations were supposed to provide the infrastructure for a rationalization of the convents' financial management. Internal and external control mechanisms, it was hoped, would render the decision-making process more transparent, eliminate corruption and "waste," and result in a maximization of revenues.

The Management Reform of Sant' Andrea de Zirada

Although well-intentioned, state laws and patriarchal supervision had only a limited impact on how abbesses ran their convents. Without the commitment and courageous participation of the nuns themselves, no mismanaged convent was able to improve its situation. Ultimately, the impetus for financial reform had to come from within; government and church authorities could do little more than provide the legislative frame and external support. Mothers Elena Malipiero and Isabella Cornero, successive abbesses of Sant' Andrea de Zirada between 1651 and 1659, compiled detailed reports on how difficult it was to implement new managerial ideas in a centuries-old institution, in addition to their everyday activities of governing some one hundred involuntary nuns and a hospital whose residents refused to acknowledge their authority. The report that Mother Elena proudly wrote on "the liberation of the convent from 34 years of permanent debts, the increase of revenues, and the investment of a thousand ducats"—the composition of which recalled a saint's vita—documents that running a convent's business well under the condition of strict encloisterment was indeed an accomplishment comparable to saintly deeds.[55] It also is evidence that the rationalized, efficient, and frugal management that convent reformers had been dreaming about for more than a century was, in some cases, gradually becoming reality, thanks to the efforts of reform-minded nuns.

In the late sixteenth century, Sant' Andrea de Zirada was repeatedly accused of "wasting" its resources;[56] otherwise, it was considered a well-endowed, properly managed convent. It ranked among the ten richest convents in terms of total income; it had no debts, an annual surplus of 954 ducats in cash (see table A6), moderate expenditure patterns (table A7), and a sufficient per capita income in wheat and wine (table A8). A century later, Mother Elena described the convent's financial situation as disastrous. The obstacles she faced in governing the convent seemed insurmountable at first: the money box was empty, but she needed to pay tithes and buy firewood, oil, and wine. The convent, the church, and almost all of the convent's houses were dilapidated and needed to be repaired. The tenants refused to pay their outstanding rents, escaped without paying their debts, or occupied the convent's properties illegally. Several lawsuits were pending, but the documents and papers were in total disarray. The estate manager resigned without leaving account books or any other kind of information about the convent's state of affairs. Also, nobody could replace him quickly enough to oversee the harvest. This happened at a time when the convent was fighting unsubstantiated requests by the government for the payment of duties. All in all, the convent suffered from long-standing neglect and mismanagement: since 1619, it had been burdened with debts of 3,288 ducats and *livelli* payments of 650 ducats, even though 21,000 ducats in dowries had been received in the same period. "I confess," Mother Elena reported, "that more than once I was terrified." Considering, however, that the afflictions were sent by God, who "perhaps wanted to test our faith, and humiliate our human arrogance," she regained her strength and started her work of renewal. She first reformed the nuns' spiritual life, increased choir attendance, and improved the church service. She then turned to the convent's temporal affairs by appointing reliable *procuratori,* who retrieved outstanding rents and credits, decided which houses needed to be fixed, inspected the properties in the countryside, helped to draw up lease contracts, and loaned money. She also hired two new physicians, employed an inspector to supervise the tenants at harvest time, and replaced the fish buyer, since "shopping for fish requires an expert who knows on what day and at what hour good fish is cheap." Besides sifting through the convent archive, commissioning a new inventory, and compiling an index to existing cadastres, she minutely documented how she solved problems with tenants and renters, and which of the houses in Venice had been remodeled. Unafraid of taking resolute decisions, she decided to phase out the widows' hospital: not only did its residents refuse to acknowledge the authority of the convent's abbess, but their pension payments of two hundred ducats had long ago ceased to cover their expenses.

Mother Elena also devoted much attention to issues of housekeeping. She replenished the convent's drug supply, since "medicine is very important and can save lives." She insisted that tenants deliver the full amount of wheat and wine contractually agreed upon, and that the quality of the products be good: recently, several *botti* of wine (one *botte* equaled about 750 liters) had gone bad every year. She negotiated better prices on firewood, oil, cheese, salt, rice, salami, and *macheroni,* installed a new, energy-saving stove in the kitchen, and ordered new glass pitchers for wine. In order to perpetuate the memory of those women who—like her—had served or benefited the convent, she commissioned various chronicles listing the founders, donors, nuns, and abbesses by name. She also had portraits painted of the noblewomen who had founded the convent and hospital in 1331, as well as of several outstanding abbesses.

Lastly, she presented her accounts: the commemorative paintings, as well as the tableware and stove, were paid for with "private" money, that is, by donations from several nuns. The debts, construction costs, and supplies such as firewood were almost entirely covered by incoming dowries and pensions of boarders amounting to 7,484 ducats. The remaining deficit of 1,277 ducats was in her eyes of little concern, because "one can easily see that had there been no incoming dowries and pensions of boarders, nor [extraordinary expenses in the form of] old debts or construction costs, the convent could have easily sustained itself on the basis of its revenues." She proved, in other words, that the convent, if managed properly, was financially autonomous—a result that convent reformers had been waiting for since the early sixteenth century. At the same time, she insisted that additional income from dowries and pensions was crucial in order to cover extraordinary expenses for repairs and remodeling projects.

Elena Malipiero's government—as well as that of her equally reform-minded successor—was widely successful thanks to her courage and managerial talents; yet her report also testified to the fact that even the shrewdest businesswoman would have failed without the assistance of reliable *procuratori* who loaned money to the convent during temporary cash shortages, chastised tenants for embezzlement, and supervised maintenance works. In a certain sense, she demonstrated that state and church reformers were wrong to weaken the authority of abbesses and eliminate traditional networks of support: ultimately, a reform project required the assistance and collaboration of nuns and lay persons deeply committed to the convent's cause—a form of support that only a charismatic abbess could mobilize and coordinate.

"Spiritual Dowries" in an Age of Peaking Monachization Rates

As Elena Malipiero's report illustrates, the nuns' so-called spiritual dowries and the annual pensions that boarders paid for their education constituted a large part of Sant' Andrea's cash income, even though her convent was fairly wealthy. Poor convents practically lived off their boarders' annuities: "I hereby testify," the abbess of San Mauro di Burano added to her tax declaration of 1564, "that if I were not helped by some generous persons, and if we did not keep boarders in our convent, we certainly could not survive, and we . . . also contribute some money through our work, which keeps us awake day and night in addition to our daily services."[57] A century later, the abbess of San Giuseppe tried to dissuade the convent magistrate from initiating a possibly scandalous inquiry, asserting "for God's sake, we are all good nuns, and we keep a lot of young girls as boarders, and if it were not for them we could not survive."[58] Not every poor convent was concerned with safeguarding its reputation for economic reasons, however: the frequency with which the Franciscan nuns of San Sepolcro were involved in criminal investigations rather suggests the opposite.[59]

The patriarchs knew that income from dowries was vital for the survival of underendowed convents, and they devoted special attention to this issue during their visitations. While Giovanni Trevisan recommended that convents negotiate the highest dowry amount possible,[60] Francesco Vendramin had some abbesses compile inventories of their revenues from landed estates, houses in Venice, and interest-bearing investments, including dowries and pension payments. Vendramin's data unequivocally illustrate the importance of dowries and pensions, invested as interest-bearing capital in government bonds or private *livelli*: Sant' Alvise received 2,285 ducats from interest-bearing investments in 1612, Santa Caterina di Venezia reported 2,851 ducats in 1616, San Gerolamo listed 5,712 ducats in 1609, and San Giuseppe received 1,046 ducats in 1618 (see table A5). In contrast, the tax declarations of 1564, which omitted annuity payments as nontaxable wealth, showed interest income for these four convents—that is, interest on investments other than dowries and pensions—of only 8, 131, 576, and 84 ducats, respectively (table A4).

In order to provide poor convents with a regular income and render the nuns independent from their families' subsidies, Patriarch Priuli issued a decree "regarding the dowries . . . of daughters who enter convents" in 1593.

> Considering the state of convents in this city, which for the most part are very needy, able to provide neither clothes nor enough food for the nuns, so that each nun is forced to get many things from outside the convent with great danger for her soul, and since we know from experience that the dowries, or alms, that are given to the girls for their monachization in the form of cash are a great burden to private persons, but of only limited use to the convents who receive them . . . we order . . . that convents . . . should not receive . . . a single sum of money all at once . . . but an annual income sufficient to provide modestly but regularly for the food and clothes of one person.[61]

Priuli considered this decree to be crucial for the general introduction of strict encloisterment, the centerpiece of his convent-reform program. In his eyes, an annual pension of sixty ducats per nun would enable even propertyless convents to supply enough food and clothing, while an additional four hundred ducats in cash would cover the costs for the monachization ceremonies and the furnishing of a cell. At the same time, it would fight the inflation of spiritual dowries in prestigious convents, render all nunneries equally accessible to upper-class daughters, and enable larger numbers of girls from middle-income patrician families to take the veil. Priuli's decree directly supported the patriciate's potlatch game, which during his patriarchate reached the peak of its popularity. Consequently, his ruling was adopted by the Senate in 1602 in a slightly modified version as state law. In contrast to Priuli, whose intention was to provide all convents with a minimum income, the government complained that "the expenses for the monachization of daughters have grown so excessively . . . that a solution to this abuse . . . has to be found, in order to enable all the families of this city to accommodate the daughters equally [in convents] for the service of God."[62] Instead of defining a lower limit on spiritual dowries for the benefit of poor convents, the Senate set a general upper limit of fourteen hundred ducats for the benefit of poor patricians.

The government's limitation of convent dowries was extremely unpopular among prestigious convents; at a time of rising monachization rates and dowry inflation, spiritual dowries had become increasingly profitable for them. As a consequence, many prestigious convents that could afford to demand higher prices simply ignored the decree, backed by the tacit consent of the Venetian curia and the open resistance of papal representatives. According to Nuncio Offredo di Offredi, the bishop of Torcello "has little esteem for this dowry, and says that some of his convents, which have received dowries of more than two thousand ducats for quite some time, have debts."[63] In fact, less than three months after the law was passed, Monsignor Offredi triumphantly wrote to Rome that "in the diocese of Torcello, a girl has taken the veil a couple of days ago with a dowry of two thousand five hundred ducats, without any sign of protest so far."[64] The papal legate himself was outraged, not only because the law effectively diminished church properties, but principally because—from his point of view—it violated ecclesiastic jurisdiction. He pressured the Senate to accept formally the authority of Pope Clement VIII in this affair, whom he advised to recognize the decree retroactively.[65] The government insisted that no papal authorization was needed, since the law "commanded only the laity,"[66] and continued to issue legislation in this regard.[67] In 1603, the government increased the dowry by 150 ducats, for construction costs; this sum, however, was to be spent only if a convent was overcrowded and unable to pay for additional cells. In order to guarantee that the money was not spent for any other purpose, it was payable to the convent magistrate.[68] A year later, the convent magistrate was authorized to punish transgressors of the dowry law with a fine of twenty-five ducats.[69]

Nonetheless, some convents continued to ignore the dowry laws, taking advantage of the rapidly increasing demand for monachizations and forcing fathers to pay more than twice the legal amount. When in 1610, several patricians refused to pay the inflationary surcharge and successfully pressured the Senate to institute a commission to investigate possible solutions to the problem of rising convent dowries, the nuns of San Lorenzo flatly refused to obey the laws, and initiated what would become a decade-long fight against state and church authorities (see chapter 5). On 15 April 1610, the Senate passed a new law that defined the dowry as a lifelong usufruct of sixty ducats, plus two hundred ducats for the festivities, one hundred for the nun's trousseau, and two hundred for additional expenses the convent might have. This further reduction of convent dowries—insofar as the cash payment of a thousand ducats was replaced by the annual revenues such capital generated—was deemed necessary for the "conservation of the families, noble as well as non-noble."[70] In addition, the doge insisted on confirming and reissuing the law in the name of the patriciate as a whole. When confronted with the nuncio's argument that "to spend three or four thousand ducats for a nun should not be regarded as a burden, considering the tens of thousands of scudi spent in bridal dowries, jewelry, and clothes," the doge answered that "only very few [patricians] . . . give these high dowries for marriages, and those accommodate few daughters in convents. . . . some convents in Venice that dispose of eight to ten thousand scudi [in income per year] . . . shamelessly demand five thousand ducats for each girl."[71]

The nuns of San Lorenzo, however, did not conceive of their prestigious convent as a welfare institution for patrician families at risk. As the dowry commission reported to the Senate, the convent insisted that the thirty-five girls accepted as novices shortly before (and no doubt in anticipation of) the passage of the new law could not profess their vows unless their families paid the contractually agreed upon price. The twelve girls with no relatives in the convent, in particular, had to pay more than the legal amount, in order to cover expenses for the construction of new cells, the remodeling of dilapidated houses, and the repair of damaged dikes in convent-owned properties on the *terraferma*. Likewise, the nuns of Santa Caterina di Venezia were of the opinion that the daughters of Marco Dandolo and Nicolò Venier should pay the increased amount of twenty-five hundred ducats, as was customary for "unrelated" candidates. Patriarch Vendramin backed the nuns of Santa Caterina, suggesting to the girls' fathers that they officially pay the legal amount and deposit the remaining sum secretly in the alms box of the convent church.[72] Interrogated by the Senate on 5 May 1610, Marco Dandolo and Nicolò Venier confirmed having received this advice the previous day.[73] They refused to take it, however, because they knew that during the patriarchate of Lorenzo Priuli, the nuns of San Zaccaria and Santi Biagio e Cataldo had agreed to accept several girls with a dowry of sixty ducats annually, despite the fact that sums of two thousand to twenty-five hundred ducats had been negotiated earlier. Alvise Pisani told the investigating commission that he had already paid twenty-five hundred ducats to San Lorenzo, and he renounced the refund to which he was legally entitled "for the sole benefit of knowing that my girl was safe *[in salvo]*"; but the nuns had neither professed his daughter nor returned the money, "and so the girl is still at home and the money and her belongings are with the nuns."[74] Called before the Senate as witnesses from earlier conflicts, Battista Moro and Andrea Vendramin testified that in 1602, they had managed to accommodate their daughters in San Zaccaria and Santi Biagio e Cataldo, respectively, without surpassing the legal amount of fifteen hundred ducats, even though they had promised larger sums before the dowry law was passed. The other applicants (thirty-one in the case of San Zaccaria and fourteen in the case of Santi Biagio e Cataldo) had also been admitted at a reduced rate, though not without compensating the nuns individually for their "flexibility."[75] Asked why he changed his arrangements, Battista Moro answered that the convent magistrate had warned him under threat of penalty not to surpass the legal amount.[76]

On 6 May, a commission of the Venetian curia went to the convent of San Lorenzo in order to persuade the nuns to receive the girls they had already accepted and to refund the excess money that had been paid. The nuns answered that they could not possibly counteract their chapter's decisions, that they needed the money for urgent maintenance work, that they had also accepted a poor noble girl without any dowry at all, and that the parents of the "unrelated" girls had offered to pay higher sums than were finally agreed upon. And "although the patriarch continued to pressure them, showing signs of disgust and anger . . . the nuns were firm and determined not to receive any of the girls and to return the thirteen or fourteen thousand ducats they had received already. . . . [and] having said that, the Most Illustrious Monsignor Patriarch remained greatly annoyed and left."[77]

In reality, returning the fourteen thousand ducats already received and renouncing the outstanding ten thousand was out of the question for the nuns.[78] Both the financial loss and the political defeat were unacceptable to them. As the nuncio reported half a year later, "the nuns of San Lorenzo are busily distributing favors in order to remove any obstacle to receiving the dowries they fixed."[79] They finally succeeded in getting a commission of senators to inspect their convent to verify that several new cells needed to be built—an expense the twelve newcomers' higher dowries were supposed to cover. The patriarch was tacitly on the side of the nuns, as was evidenced by the investigations of the senatorial commission; yet his official role as mediator between Senate and convent forced him to demonstrate publicly his disapproval of the nuns' illegal actions. In December of 1610, the nuncio was pleased to report to Rome that the patriarch had "cleverly assisted the nuns, so that the affair will end quietly and as advantageously as possible for the nuns."[80] Finally, five years later, when the government was no longer paying attention to the case, a settlement was reached. As the patriarch had recommended to Marco Dandolo and Nicolò Venier earlier, the applicants each paid twelve hundred ducats publicly and the rest secretly as an offering for the new altar in the church of San Lorenzo.[81]

Poor convents also protested against the dowry law of 1610—which reduced the dowry to a lifelong usufruct—not only because it prevented them from negotiating higher amounts, but because it prevented them from accumulating capital at all. In addition, they were justly afraid that annual pensions would be hard to retrieve, especially after the death of the nuns' fathers or other original contractors. Some senators reassured the nuns, aware of the fact that relatives often neglected inherited obligations.[82] Trying to spare the nuns costly lawsuits, they proposed establishing a special fund in which parents would invest one thousand ducats for each novice and charging the convent magistrate with transferring the annual interest payments of 6 percent to the accounts of each convent. Probably because of the uproar it caused among the nuns as well as the "papal" faction of the patriciate, this proposal was quickly dropped. The nuncio especially lobbied against it, pointing out to the patriarch that "if a government fund is instituted, these gentlemen [i.e., the convent magistrates] can refuse payment to the convents whenever they find them disobedient on any imaginable issue."[83] In order to protect the nuns' interests, the law of 15 April 1610 required the convent magistrate to inquire about the security of any invested capital before it was assigned.[84] The mendicant convents in particular, however, continued to protest against the replacement of cash payments by lifelong annuities; six months later, the law was modified according to their wishes: "Because we have to find ways for the poor convents to sustain no greater damage . . . but to preserve the status they have preserved so far, and even to be able to improve their fortunes," these convents were allowed to demand a flat rate of eight hundred ducats instead of receiving annual pension payments.[85]

Despite those settlements, the battle surrounding the standardization of dowry payments continued. Not knowing how to combat the nuns' refusal to accept its laws other than by issuing new ones, the Senate proclaimed in 1620: "We have to find a way for our deliberations to be observed in all parts . . . and cannot allow a small number of nuns, as is publicly known . . . to practice undue disobedience."[86] This law was aimed at the nuns of San Lorenzo, who continued to ignore the government's and the patriarch's dowry legislation as an encroachment upon their traditional rights. In a memorandum "on the events that happened to our convent in 1620 and 1621 . . . because of some girls who had been accepted as nuns," the abbess of San Lorenzo explained and justified her convent's defiance of state and church authorities. In 1619, the daughters of Francesco Querini Stampalia, Agustin Contarini, and Pietro Badoer had been accepted with the permission of Patriarch Vendramin for two thousand ducats each.[87] In order to prevent the girls from officially entering the convent, the Senate reconfirmed the dowry laws of 1602, 1603, 1604, and 1610 on 9 July 1620; Vendramin's successor, Patriarch Giovanni Tiepolo, reissued Priuli's dowry decree of 1593 a month later.[88] Meanwhile, five novices took their vows; the legal maximum expense of fifty ducats per novice for convent functions was observed, except for the pistachio and marzipan pastries the girls received from their aunts. When he heard of these gifts, which—according to the abbess—"did not even cost 2 lire per nun," Patriarch Tiepolo punished the nuns by imposing a ban on confessions.[89] After three months without confessions, the nuns tried to smooth things out by inviting the patriarch to visit their convent; they stated that they had not intended to contradict his authority. Not satisfied with this oral declaration, Tiepolo demanded that the abbess and the oldest nuns sign a written statement of intent "always to obey his orders." Suspecting some "hidden trap," however, the nuns refused to sign any such declaration. They were confirmed in their decision by "other persons who saw through this affair . . . and doubted the legitimacy of such a request."[90] Although the nuns turned to the convent magistrate and many senators for support, Tiepolo's ban on confessions remained in force. The patriarch insisted he would not lift it unless the nuns received the three daughters of Francesco Querini Stampalia, Agustin Contarini, and Pietro Badoer as novices "in accordance with the rules," that is, under observance of the dowry decrees. In the eyes of the nuns, this demand was inadmissible. They let the ultimatum expire, though not without explaining "to the Most Illustrious Monsignor, that in accordance with the Holy Canons, and the customary right of our convent, we cannot obey his rules without a new chapter decision."[91]

Through the intervention of several senators, the ban on confessions was temporarily lifted a couple of days before Christmas. On Christmas Eve, the patriarch again imposed a general interdict; the convent magistrate would even have locked church and parlors had it not been for the intervention of some high-ranking senators who wanted to visit their relatives. All convent and church employees lost their license to enter the nuns' clausura: no Christmas mass was held, and the baker was barely allowed to deliver bread. The nuns responded to this offense by sending Tiepolo and the Collegio a legal report "written by a famous Theologian," of which neither the patriarch nor the government deigned to take note. The author of this treatise confirmed that "it is the opinion of the Palermitano, in his chapter *Ad Apostatas de Regularij,* that in the issue of accepting novices in all orders, one has to respect the customary right of every order, and also its traditions and privileges."[92]

By insisting on their "traditional" privileges and customary autonomy—thus openly criticizing and resisting the deliberations of the Council of Trent—the nuns of San Lorenzo provoked a politically precarious situation. Powerful politicians came to the convent parlor, trying to change the nuns' minds. Even the doge visited them, threatening that "parlor, windows, and doors would be walled up, their revenues confiscated, San Lorenzo closed down, the nuns scattered over other convents, and other similarly terrifying things."[93] During this time, neither the physician nor the estate manager was allowed to enter the convent, and tenants who came to pay their rents were sent home. Faced with the immediate danger of having their doors walled up, the nuns finally declared that they would receive the three girls within the following six days, reserving for themselves the right to take a new chapter decision on the dowry amount. This compromise was favored by Benedetto Bondumier, a member of the Council of Ten and one of the chief mediators in the conflict. The six-day ultimatum passed, however, and no progress was made until the patriarch presented another proposal: if the nuns deposited the three girls' dowries in the Zecca (government fund) and refunded them partially, the patriarch would respect their request to revise the dowry contracts in a formal voting procedure. This is how the conflict was finally resolved, and on the first day of Lent the interdict was lifted.

The nuns considered this compromise a victory. Although they partially refunded the dowries that had been contractually agreed upon—and thereby acknowledged the dowry decrees of the Senate and curia—both the patriarch and the government formally recognized the ultimate authority of their chapter decisions in matters of novices. In reality, it was a Pyrrhic victory that the nuns of San Lorenzo proudly recorded in their "Note on the accidents that happened in our convent in 1620 and 1621 . . . so that it can serve as a notice of what could happen again."[94] The nuns' main source of power had always been their widespread kinship ties with the most prestigious families in town. While those private connections enabled them to generate support among the highest-ranking politicians, the nuns' strategy ultimately backfired, in that it provoked strong resentment among those patricians who aimed to secure "equal access" to monachizations among rich and poor aristocrats alike. The church, for its part, reacted strongly against attempts to restore pre-Tridentine privileges, theories, and jurisdiction. In this respect, the conflict between San Lorenzo and the curia and government of Venice strengthened the convent-reform faction, despite the formal recognition of the convent's ancient traditions.

After 1620, the process of standardizing spiritual dowries and subjecting the management of convent patrimonies to state and church intervention continued more intensively than ever. On 27 August 1620, the Senate charged the Provveditori sopra i Monasteri with offering legal assistance to nuns and convents fighting for their annuity payments. The same law also defined spiritual and bridal dowries as being of equal legal status; that is, widows who remained single could dispose of their own dowries to contract pension payments for their daughters, and entailed patrimonies could be obligated to pay for the spiritual dowries of female relatives in case the paternal noncondi-tioned capital was insufficient.[95] Besides protecting the nuns from getting too little, the convent magistrate had to prevent the nuns from getting too much: in 1620, the Provveditori started to issue "monachization permits," certifying that the girl's guardians had sworn under oath that they had not paid more than the law of 1610 permitted. The Provveditori were also charged with soliciting denunciations and prosecuting offenders.[96]

The function of the convent magistrate as a court of first appeal in lawsuits over dowry payments was reconfirmed in 1637; this law also specified that convents should liquidate their debts by using 50 percent of their income deriving from annuity payments.[97] In 1622, the Provveditori resumed their task of reviewing convent accounts.[98] Beginning in 1628, they were occasionally charged with intervening in dowry conflicts on the mainland,[99] and in 1637 their authority was officially extended to all convents and monasteries on the Venetian *terraferma*.[100] In the second half of the seventeenth century, the main functions of the convent magistrate were to oversee the financial management of all monastic institutions, male and female, on the republic's territory and to implement state laws regarding ecclesiastic patrimonies—in contrast to the sixteenth and early seventeenth centuries, when the imposition of strict encloisterment was the focus of all reform measures.[101]

Mortmain Legislation and Its Effects (1605–1768)

The government's grasp on convent patrimonies became even tighter after a comprehensive mortmain law was issued in 1605. A long Venetian tradition of restricting the growth of monastic landed properties and subjecting ecclesiastic possessions to lay taxes culminated in this most radical of all mortmain laws, which prohibited the acquisition of real estate by ecclesiastic institutions anywhere in the republic.[102] In Venice, the first law of this kind dates back to 1258, when the Great Council subjected all pious bequests in the form of real estate to lay taxes. In 1333, the Great Council ruled that church institutions could keep their bequests and donations in the form of real estate situated in Venice for ten years only; after this period, these properties had to be sold, and the capital invested in government bonds. Fourteen years later, the government halted the foundation of new monastic and charitable institutions, and in 1353 the Procuratori di San Marco were charged with selling all real estate in their management retroactively and investing the money in government bonds.[103] In 1472, the Senate subjected all new acquisitions of Venetian real estate by ecclesiastic institutions to lay taxes.[104] In 1536, the law of 1333, which "was never observed," was reissued, since "one cannot permit all the real estate of this city to go to the church."[105] Between 1605 and 1610, the republic's mortmain legislation reached an unprecedented peak: the prohibition on acquiring land in conjunction with the standardization of the spiritual dowry as a lifelong annuity meant a total ban on further capital accumulations. The conversion of convent dowries into a sixty-ducat usufruct not only reduced many nuns' cash income and violated the decision-making autonomy of chapters, but also complemented the ban on economic growth proclaimed with the mortmain law of 1605.[106] At a time when the acquisition of landed estates among the nobility was at an all-time high and the entailment of patrimonies was becoming increasingly common, the elimination of church competition from the land market and the freeze on dowry expenses were complementary measures designed to protect patrician—and, more generally, lay—patrimonies, and to favor their growth to the detriment of ecclesiastic institutions.

It was precisely the mortmain law of 1605—in addition to the perennial problem of lay jurisdiction over criminal ecclesiastics—that provoked the crisis of the Interdict of 1606. According to Pope Paul V, the Venetian law constituted an attack on "the liberty of the church," which he sought to defend by excommunicating the Venetian Senate and by proclaiming a statewide ban on all church functions.[107] Instead of revoking the law, however, the government adamantly defended its attempts to contain the disproportionate growth of church patrimonies as a necessary measure to secure the welfare of its citizens. In an open letter to "the municipalities and subjects of the Most Serene Republic," the Senate blamed the "astuteness of the clergy, and the simplicity of the devout, and pious persons" for the alienation of up to a third of the republic's rural and urban real estate to the church, resulting in a massive reduction of the state's tax income. The government made a populist appeal for support against the pope, pointing out to its citizens that "you have to bear the continuous burden of taxation, while others idly enjoy the properties that have been acquired with the sweat and blood of your ancestors."[108] In the ensuing "war of the pamphlets," Andrea Querini even claimed that "the convents and monasteries . . . occupy half of the surface area of Venice," and Paolo Sarpi warned that the republic would turn into a "monstrous body" if the church, "ingesting more resources than is proper, damaged the other members by taking what is theirs, and, unable to digest the superfluous, were filled with bad humors, which would result first in the illness of this member [i.e., the church], and then in the corruption of the entire body." In Sarpi's opinion, the church was already stricken with an indigestion of gargantuan proportions, because it "constitutes about one percent of the population, but has attracted . . . a third [of the landed properties] in the Padovano, more than half in the Bergamasco, and at least a quarter everywhere else." The distribution of income between the clergy and the laity was all the more unhealthy because "three-quarters of the clergy live . . . off alms and donations, while the possessions and revenues [of the church] belong to a very small number of ecclesiastics . . . half of whom live outside of our state."[109] Sarpi's catastrophic scenario of the clergy's "bad humors" underlined the fierceness with which the government and its supporters were fighting—not for an egalitarian income distribution among all citizens, but for the patriciate's monopoly on the land market, at a time when investments in real estate were judged the most profitable and reliable economic resource.[110]

The government's convent-reform program thus intersected with its general church policy in a variety of ways. On the one hand, state (and church) authorities aimed to secure convent patrimonies against loss. The anticorruption laws of 1569, the introduction of a standard dowry in 1602, the insurance against creditors starting in 1620, and the rationalization of convent management encouraged by every post-Tridentine patriarch were measures in this direction. Mortmain and dowry laws, on the other hand, severely limited the prospects for increasing ecclesiastical patrimonies, while the imposition of lay and ecclesiastic taxes in the fifteenth century abolished the traditional immunity of church properties. The church tax *(decima del clero)*, granted by the papacy as a contribution to the republic's military expenses, was levied regularly from 1535 on.[111] As the estimate of 1564 illustrates, it encompassed the bulk of the convents' assets, in the form of real estate in Venice, landed possessions, and capital investments in *monti, livelli,* and *procuratie.* The lay tax *(decima del laico)* was levied beginning in 1472, when the government decided that any further acquisition of Venetian real estate by the church would be subject to the property tax citizens had to pay. Because the law of 1472 was supplanted by more restrictive prohibitions in 1536 and 1605, the lay tax covered only a tiny fraction of what the church really owned. Any piece of property acquired after 1536 in Venice and after 1605 on the mainland was supposed to be sold within a couple of years; therefore, the estimates of lay tithes compiled in 1566, 1582, and 1661 theoretically register nothing but the properties that church institutions legally acquired in the interim period, that is, between 1472 and 1536 or 1605 (see table A4).[112] The church, however, continued to acquire real estate despite the prohibition. Since the laws of 1472 and 1536 were mutually exclusive, legal ambiguities arose that made the lay tax difficult to collect.[113]

Both tax and mortmain laws were designed to stop the ongoing withdrawal of fixed capital from circulation; therefore, it was the tax collectors (Dieci Savij sopra le decime di Rialto) who were officially in charge of executing the mortmain laws. They sold at public auction the properties acquired by church institutions through donations and legacies when notaries informed them of those illegal property transactions.[114] This policy was highly inefficient: a survey conducted in the second half of the eighteenth century shows that only one-quarter of the mortmain possessions accumulated between 1605 and 1767 were returned to the market. As a result, the value of the illegally acquired possessions of the Venetian church had increased by 584,000 ducats in the same period, while illegal mortmain possessions statewide amounted to more than six million ducats, of which only about 5 percent was subject to taxation.[115] While the purpose of this survey was to determine the efficacy of the mortmain law of 1605, the government also inquired about the actual increase of taxable wealth in the hands of church institutions. In 1769, for the first time since 1564, a new estimate of possessions subject to the *decima del clero* was conducted. Because the growth of mortmain possessions had been outlawed in

Properties left to the church (1605–1767). From BNM, It. VII 1522 (8825), c. 694. (Courtesy of the Biblioteca Nazionale Marciana, Venice.)

1536 and 1605, the estimate of 1564 was long assumed to be appropriate for the collection of church property taxes—an assumption the tax declarations of 1769 widely contradicted.

According to the tax estimate of 1769, all of the convents in Venice and Torcello except for Corpus Domini had increased their yearly revenues over the previous two centuries. The increase ranged from fifty-eight ducats in the case of Santa Maria Maggiore to 16,103 ducats in the case of San Zaccaria (see table A11); the rate of growth ranged from 27 percent in the case of San Daniele to 4,662 percent in the case of San Matteo di Murano (table A12). While the increase in cash revenues might have been partially due to inflation,[116] most of the convents also recorded an increase in the amount of agricultural land and the production of wheat and wine. As already mentioned, the mortmain law of 1605, which required ecclesiastic institutions to sell the land they acquired through pious donations, was only partially enforced. Among the most successful landowners were the convent of Santa Maria degli Angeli, which expanded its rural real estate holdings by 71,334 ares, or 276 percent, and San Matteo di Murano, which acquired all of its 53,633 ares after 1564. The newly founded convent of Santa Teresa had also made astonishing gains: in the course of the seventeenth century, it accumulated rural estates of more than fifty thousand ares in the vicinity of Verona.[117] Because of the remote location of these properties, Santa Teresa's rural rents were paid exclusively in cash. Many other convents accumulated real estate in distant areas as well.[118] In contrast to Santa Teresa, Santa Maria degli Angeli and San Matteo di Murano received most of their rural rents in the form of wine. Their wine production rose by 150,442 liters and 48,219 liters, respectively. Since the two convents were located in the same neighborhood of Murano, their similar economic development hints at a common management, close familial ties, or other forms of administrative collaboration. The spectacular rise of San Matteo di Murano from a virtual have-not to the fourth largest landholder among Venetian convents would hardly have been possible without the sound financial or managerial assistance of a devoted patron.

Several convents sold or squandered parts of their rural estates, most notably San Giovanni Evangelista di Torcello, which lost approximately twelve thousand ares of its farmlands.[119] Its wheat and wine production declined by roughly five thousand liters each. As already discussed in chapter 3, San Giovanni Evangelista di Torcello was badly mismanaged; in 1652, one of the convent's *procuratori* complained about widespread corruption, embezzlement, and waste.[120] Also, the quality of its vineyards and farmlands was uneven; the estates located in Piave were subject to floods, which caused the convent to lose between one-third and one-half of its revenues from these areas in 1564.[121] The remote location of the convent created additional expenditures and made efficient management difficult, as the abbess explained to the tax collectors in 1564:

> We have faithfully recorded everything [we own] . . . and also described how many duties, expenses, and debts the convent has to pay so that Your Most Illustrious and Reverend Lordships . . . can take into consideration how much we need to have, given the number of nuns, but also our location . . . which forces us to endure many excessive and intolerable expenses that one does not have to bother about when living in Venice or closer in.[122]

The two convents with the largest increase in total revenues were San Zaccaria and San Lorenzo. They were, after San Giovanni Evangelista di Torcello and Santa Caterina di Mazzorbo, the oldest convents of the lagoon (see table A3), and had been unparalleled in wealth at least since the sixteenth century. In contrast to the more land-oriented convents, about 70 percent of their cash increase resulted from an increase in urban rents collected. Other convents with high shares of Venetian real estate were Sant' Andrea de Zirada and San Gerolamo (see table A10). In 1769, these were the four biggest real estate owners among Venetian convents, with annual rents of 15,910 ducats (San Zaccaria), 11,411 ducats (San Lorenzo), 3,125 ducats (San Gerolamo), and 3,114 ducats (Sant' Andrea de Zirada) (table A4). The four convents were already receiving large parts of their revenues from urban rents in 1564, but increased these shares significantly over the course of two hundred years. In 1564, revenues from Venetian houses, shops, and warehouses constituted 53 percent and 54 percent of the total income of San Zaccaria and San Lorenzo, respectively, compared with 67 percent and 64 percent in 1769 (tables A9 and A10). Sant' Andrea de Zirada and San Gerolamo similarly concentrated their investments in urban real estate, which made up 31 percent and 41 percent of their revenues in 1564, but 53 percent and 59 percent in 1769. A comparison with Daniele Beltrami's study of the estimate of properties subject to lay taxation in 1661 shows that the biggest rate of increase in real estate occurred between 1564 and 1661, when San Zaccaria's rental income rose by 144 percent, San Lorenzo's by 153 percent, San Gerolamo's by 254 percent, and Sant' Andrea de Zirada's by 117 percent.

The rate of increase in urban rents slowed down in the following century, when San Zaccaria, San Lorenzo, and Sant' Andrea de Zirada recorded increases of 66, 26, and 74 percent, respectively, and San Gerolamo showed a decline of 3 percent.[123]

In 1564, only six convents received more than half of their total revenues from urban rents. The most common forms of income were wheat and wine, especially among the wealthy convents; only Santa Maria degli Angeli derived more than half of its revenues from rural rents. The mendicant convents and other poor nunneries lived mainly off interest-bearing capital investments.

By 1769, the composition of revenues had changed significantly: taxable revenues from cash investments had declined sharply. This was mainly because of the replacement of forced loans *(monti)* by tax-exempt government bonds. While most convents still derived a considerable portion of their income from wheat and wine,[124] urban and rural rents constituted a larger share of their total revenues in 1769. The increase in rural rents was particularly large: ten convents increased their cash revenues from landholdings by more than 1,000 percent, while income in kind did not rise significantly (table A12). Urban rents grew by up to 914 percent. Apart from illegal acquisitions of Venetian real estate, the rise in rental revenues was mainly due to the extension of rental space through the improvement and remodeling of old houses and the construction of new buildings on existing real estate.

Replacing payments in kind with cash payments was extremely profitable, as the patrimonial development of Santa Maria degli Angeli suggests: the convent, which received 65 percent of its total income in rural rents in 1564—compared with 21 percent in kind—extended its landholdings by more than seventy thousand ares in the course of two centuries. Although by 1769 Santa Maria degli Angeli and its "twin" convent of San Matteo di Murano specialized in viticulture, other convents followed its earlier strategy of accumulating land by restructuring the rental system: Santa Maria della Celestia received 53 percent of its total income in 1769 from rural rents, compared with 13 percent in 1564, and increased its agricultural possessions by 14 percent (10,835 ares). By 1769, Santa Caterina di Mazzorbo had managed to increase its modest landholdings by 4,466 ares, or 33 percent, while deriving 93 percent of its revenues in the form of cash payments from agricultural possessions.

Replacing income in kind by cash rents was a trend followed by large and small landholders alike. Cash rents were a more predictable, more secure, and apparently more profitable form of income. As numerous postscripts to the tax declarations of 1564 show, income in kind was rarely delivered in the quantity and quality that was contractually agreed upon; a bad harvest, unreliable tenants, or corrupt estate managers could reduce a convent's revenues significantly.[125] Moreover, strict encloisterment posed serious obstacles to efficient management, as the report of Mother Elena Malipiero of Sant' Andrea de Zirada illustrated. Nunneries traditionally preferred to invest in Venetian real estate, because houses and shops, especially when located in the convent's neighborhood, were easier to manage than distant landholdings. In contrast, monasteries accumulated vast landed estates.[126] The replacement of income in kind by cash payments in the sixteenth, seventeenth, and eighteenth centuries was thus a way of avoiding the managerial difficulties posed by the nuns' clausura.

Despite the high rates of income growth in some convents, the distribution of income remained practically the same. With the exception of San Matteo di Murano, Santa Giustina, Santa Caterina di Venezia, and Sant' Alvise—all of which specialized in viticulture—no convent significantly improved its rank in amount of taxable wealth (see table A10). The six richest nunneries in 1564 remained the richest in 1769, despite relatively low growth rates of between 113 and 236 percent. The mendicant convent of San Sepolcro improved its position by one margin only, although it reported an 876 percent increase in total revenues. The five convents whose ranking dropped the most (San Daniele, Corpus Domini, Santa Caterina di Mazzorbo, San Giacomo, and Santi Rocco e Margherita) had significant losses in urban rents and in income from capital investments, as well as low growth rates in total revenues, which ranged from an actual decline of 7 percent to an increase of 81 percent.

Given the considerable growth of convent patrimonies, the results of the government's mortmain legislation are difficult to assess: while the law of 1605 might have slowed down further accumulation of real estate by convents, it certainly did not stop the growth of their landed possessions. As the survey on donations "ad pias causas" (to ecclesiastic institutions) of 1767 suggests, the law was only sporadically observed and did not prevent the convents from acquiring fixed properties. The specialization in viticulture and the introduction of new managerial strategies such as the replacement of income in kind by cash payments—which suggests a trend of concluding rent contracts with intermediate managers rather than small peasants—demonstrate the nuns' capacity to maximize profits and increase their patrimonies. With a few exceptions, all of the convents improved their economic situation, some of them considerably; even the poor convents had growth rates of up to 876 percent. The pyramid of income distribution remained unchallenged, however, despite the fact that ancient convents such as San Giovanni Evangelista di Torcello refused to modernize their management and lost vast portions of their estates. These losses, together with Mother Elena Malipiero's emphasis on liquidating outstanding debts, renovating dilapidated houses, retrieving the full amount of rent payments, and employing reliable *procuratori,* proved that convent reformers had been correct in proclaiming the elimination of corruption and the rationalization of the convents' financial management as necessary measures. Nonetheless, their legislative interventions aimed at reducing the nuns' alleged "waste" and debts, curtailing the power of abbesses, and introducing external control mechanisms did not have a sizable impact on the convents' economic recovery. Rather, it was reform movements from within— finally stressing profit maximization over conspicuous consumption, bribery, and generous alms-giving—that guaranteed the convents' economic survival. Neither the mortmain laws nor the economic reform programs of state and church left tangible traces in the convents' tax declarations from 1564 to 1769. The standardization of spiritual dowries in 1602 had had similarly ambiguous results: on the one hand, poor convents were provided with a secure, regular, and predictable source of income that the convent magistrate helped to retrieve and co-administer. On the other hand, the taming of inflationary trends at a time when monachizations were in high demand prevented the nuns from negotiating the highest dowry amount possible. Whether the introduction of a sixty-ducat annuity affected the rapid growth rates of poor convents between 1564 and 1769 favorably or unfavorably is another question the tax records leave unanswered.

While the economic impact of the government's convent-reform program and anticlerical policy is difficult to assess, the results on the level of politics are more tangible. The tax records of 1769 show, if anything, the inertia of the convents' wealth and the lack of decisive change. If the tax, mortmain, and dowry laws did not prevent the convents' patrimonies from growing, they certainly abolished the principle of the inalienability and immunity of church properties. While the very process of subjecting ecclesiastic patrimonies to state regulation demonstrated the government's determination to disregard ancient taboos and extend its jurisdiction, the particular importance that convents had assumed for the reproduction of the body politic translated the government's paternalistic interventions into a policy of "secularization." The government program to reestablish convents as economically independent and morally upright institutions was not an altruistic gesture toward the church: it had a precise political function in the context of the patriciate's reproduction patterns, in that monachization practices helped construct the patriciate as a "nobility" and temporarily stabilized a political system threatened by a lingering crisis of legitimation. Apart from its secular functions and ramifications, however, the government's convent-reform program could not but reestablish, strengthen, and protect convents as religious institutions. If convents were to be protected against moral disarray and financial ruin, the government had to assist the patriarch's attempts to exercise his jurisdiction over monastic institutions more efficiently and to strengthen the nuns' religious vocation and identity. The surveillance of the nuns' discipline and the supervision of their economic management—in other words, the elimination of the convents' relative jurisdictional autonomy by church and state officials—thus had secularizing as well as confessionalizing effects.[127] In the process of serving the vital interests of both the republic's self-proclaimed nobility and the post-Tridentine church, convents became hybrid institutions, while involuntary nuns performed patriotic acts by subjecting their bodies and souls to the rigor of monastic discipline.

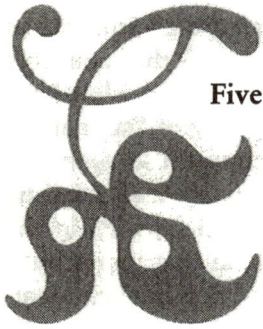

Five

Convents and the Question of State Sovereignty

Doge Sebastiano Ziani's Many Marriages

King Solomon . . . started to build the House of the Lord in Jerusalem on Mount Moriah, a site shown to David his father. . . . And adjacent [to this temple] he built the House of the Virgins in Jerusalem. This is where Saint Mary stood at the time of her Annunciation by the angel. And this is also where, some time afterward, Saint Peter founded the convent of the Holy Virgin Mary in Jerusalem. . . . In the same place, Saint Mark the Evangelist established the Order of the Canons and Canonesses.[1]

This impressive topography of holy sites forms the prelude to the chronicle of the convent of Santa Maria delle Vergini, written most likely by one (or several) of its nuns soon after the convent reform of 1519. According to the author, Santa Maria delle Vergini was established in Venice in 1177 as a refoundation of an ancient nunnery in Jerusalem that had been lost to the "infidel" during the Crusades. This original convent had allegedly been founded by Saint Peter. The chronicle linked the history of the convent and, by extension, the history of the city of Venice directly to events of eschatological significance such as the foundation of Israel, the Annunciation of the Virgin Mary, Saint Peter's activities as Christ's representative on earth, and the preachings of Saint Mark, patron saint of Venice. In terms of secular history, the chronicle affirmed the convent's political importance in sealing the peace settlement between Emperor Frederick Barbarossa and Pope Al-

Doge Sebastiano Ziani offers shelter to Pope Alexander III.
From "Cronica del Monastero delle Vergini di Venetia,"
MCC, Correr 317, c. 15r. (Courtesy of the Museo Civico Correr, Venice.)

Doge Sebastiano Ziani receives Emperor Frederick Barbarossa.
From "Cronica del Monastero delle Vergini di Venetia,"
MCC, Correr 317, c. 15r. (Courtesy of the Museo Civico Correr, Venice.)

exander III in 1177, which Doge Sebastiano Ziani helped to negotiate after Venice had offered shelter to the pope, defeated the imperial fleet, and captured the emperor's son. According to Venetian mythography, this victory put the republic on the map of world politics, resulting in Venice's formal independence from foreign rule. Ingeniously, the chronicle drew a connection between this seminal date in Venetian history, next in importance only to the "translation" (i.e., theft) of the relics of Saint Mark from Constantinople to the ducal chapel, and the foundation of Santa Maria delle Vergini as a sign of republican self-assertion.

In reality, the convent was founded much later, under Doge Pietro Ziani in 1222–24, as numerous historians of the fourteenth and fifteenth centuries reported.[2] Despite the sixteenth-century forgery of its foundation date, the convent was undeniably of special political significance: it belonged to the Order of the Canons of Saint Mark, and it was the only Venetian convent under ducal jurisdiction, that is, exempt from the supervision of episcopal and monastic authorities in its "temporal affairs." As a convent under the doge's direct rule, it enjoyed the same status as the ducal chapel itself and two of the city's oldest churches, San Giovanni Elemosinario and San Giacomo di Rialto. While the two parish churches were awarded the privilege of ducal jurisdiction by Popes Alexander VI and Clement VII only in 1493 and 1523, respectively, the chapel of Saint Mark had been granted independence from ecclesiastic control in 1177, on the very occasion of the peace settlement between Frederick and Alexander.[3] The chronicler of Santa Maria delle Vergini thus claimed the same event that elevated Saint Mark's Chapel to the status of a quasi-imperial church in the Byzantine tradition as the date of its own foundation. In predating the convent's origin to 1177, the chronicler interpreted the existing jurisdictional analogies between the convent and the ducal chapel as evidence that the two sacred sites had the same function: to constitute, contain, and enhance the doge's sacred powers as the head of a sovereign state.

The associations of Santa Maria delle Vergini with republican sovereignty were multiple and complex. The most vivid expression of the convent's symbolic significance during Venice's rise to power was the direct analogy between the doge's "marriage" to the abbess of Santa Maria delle Vergini on the occasion of her investiture, and the doge's annual "marriage" to the sea, celebrated on the day of the Feast of the Bucentaur (Bucintoro).[4] The chronicle's introductory narrative depicts the two "wedding" rites and the accompanying gift exchange as complementary in their function of sealing the peace treaty of 1177. Defeated by republican forces, Emperor Frederick reciprocated the doge's offer of peace by giving him his daughter Julia, destined to become the convent's first abbess, in "marriage." He also granted the republic unfettered sovereignty over the Adriatic Sea. Doge Sebastiano Ziani accepted Julia as a hostage in return for the release of the emperor's son and welcomed the formal recognition of his maritime dominion. Pope Alexander III, in return for the defeat of his enemy, the emperor, offered Ziani supreme jurisdiction over the ducal chapel, as well as over the new convent to be founded. He then performed the double wedding rites, investing the ducal "groom" with power over the Adriatic Sea and giving him both "the church of Santa Maria delle Vergini and the abbess as brides." The sapphire embellishing the ring with which the pope married Ziani to his many brides carried the likeness of Saint Mark the Evangelist, under whose ultimate authority and in whose name the various transferals of power took place.[5] The peace treaty was thus concluded in the form of a multiple exchange of symbolic brides—the most important gifts imaginable, if we remember Lévi-Strauss—and their lavish dowries. According to the chronicle of Santa Maria delle Vergini, the events of 1177 evolved as the republic's foundational potlatch, during which the emperor and the pope renounced their respective paternalistic claims to the Adriatic Sea, the city of Venice, the ducal chapel, and the newly founded convent. Julia's investiture as the first abbess of a convent under ducal jurisdiction sealed the trilateral agreement that represented Venice's victory over both emperor and pope.[6]

The beautifully illuminated chronicle of Santa Maria delle Vergini was composed as a vindication of the convent's prestige and political significance in the aftermath of the reform of 1519.[7] The author refers to the forced imposition of clausura, and the subsequent expropriation of the nuns who refused to practice it, as a "most painful event." In the eyes of the chronicler, the reform, during which "observant" nuns from convents of lesser prestige were endowed with the patrimony of Santa Maria delle Vergini, was planned and orchestrated by "this cruel traitor Octavian," the patriarch's vicar. Allegedly the son of a Jewish mother, he came to Venice to cause "such ruin as one encounters in the fire of hell. . . . Through his cunning and deception, he managed to have the Most Reverend Patriarch make this servant of the devil [i.e., himself] his vicar, and this sorcerer . . . through gain and simony

The pope marries the doge to the Adriatic Sea. From "Cronica del Monastero delle Vergini di Venetia," MCC, Correr 317, c. 15v. (Courtesy of the Museo Civico Correr, Venice.)

Investiture of Abbess Julia. From "Cronica del
Monastero delle Vergini di Venetia," MCC, Correr 317, c. 18v.
(Courtesy of the Museo Civico Correr, Venice.)

robbed the church of God and took the money of the poor nuns, observant as well as non-observant."[8] A detailed account of the reform and the nuns' attempts to resist it, interspersed with antisemitic diatribes against the vicar as its alleged mastermind, concludes the chronicle. The author's passionate polemic against the introduction of clausura, perceived by the nuns as an ignominious abolishment of ancient privileges, frames the chronicle's grandiose representation of the convent as an institution of prime political significance. Given the nunnery's prominent place in the context of both revelation history and Venetian mythology, the debasing events of 1519 could not be explained but through the work of the devil. The chronicler's many historical misrepresentations, such as collapsing the convent's foundation date with the events of 1177, served to render the implicit relevance of this unique institution explicit.

It was not until the end of the century, however, that the chronicle's ingenious forgeries were exploited as politically convenient. Doge Marino Grimani relied on the chronicle to officially justify the government's stance in one of the republic's most serious jurisdictional conflicts with the papacy before the crisis of the Interdict in 1606. In contrast to early-sixteenth-century historians, who unanimously declared that the convent was founded under Doge Pietro Ziani in 1222–24[9]— and not, as the chronicler had claimed, in 1177—Giovanni Stringa was the first to echo the nuns' false claims. In his updated edition (1604) of Sansovino's *Venetia città nobilissima et singolare* (Venice, most noble and unique city), Stringa points to an inscription above a portal inside the church of Santa Maria delle Vergini as proof of its foundation by Pope Alexander III in 1177.[10] It may have been his special affinity with the nuns as canon of the ducal chapel of Saint Mark that made him neglect sterile historical accuracy in favor of meaningful deception. Another indication of the chronicle's circulation and increasing public recognition was the publication of the *Breve trattato delle citta nobili del mondo* (Short treatise on the world's noble cities) in Florence in 1574, which copied—sometimes verbatim—the chronicle's fantastic accounts of the foundation of Milan and Venice.[11] Giovanni Botero even devoted several pages to reproducing Sister Aurelia Querini's Latin oration, given in honor of the election of Abbess Sofia Malipiero in 1598, in his *Relatione della Republica venetiana* (Report on the Venetian Republic; 1605). The speech was preceded by a brief, semi-accurate foundation account (Botero, always careful to pay homage to Venetian mythography without sacrificing intellectual integrity, declared the convent to have been founded by Frederick II, whose rule coincided with the tenure of Doge Pietro Ziani, but neglected to mention a precise date) and a description of the abbess's investiture ceremony.[12]

Botero's *Relatione* was dedicated to Doge Marino Grimani, under whose rule (1595–1605) the convent reached its peak of public recognition. In 1598, on the occasion of Abbess Maria Benetti's death, Grimani insisted on fully recovering his jurisdiction over Santa Maria delle Vergini, which had been seriously endangered by the protocol that was observed during her election in 1578. Representatives of both Saint Mark's Chapel and the curia had supervised that election; the presence of patriarchal legates—required by the Council of Trent—set a dangerous precedent that called into question the doge's ancient privilege of controlling the convent's "secular" affairs. Grimani's plot to exclude the patriarch from assisting the election in 1598 erupted into a major conflict between the doge and the government on the one hand, and Patriarch Priuli, Pope Clement VIII, and the nuns themselves on the other. The chapter of Santa Maria delle Vergini had unanimously aspired to introduce triennial terms for abbesses in accordance with the Tridentine reform and Clement's bull of 1583, but lost its fight for a more "democratic" form of convent management against Doge Marino Grimani and his advisers. Santa Maria delle Vergini became the showcase of republican sovereignty; for that purpose, its abbesses had to continue to "marry" the incumbent doge just as Julia was supposed to have done four centuries earlier. In 1612, the doge, government representatives, and an entourage of noblewomen visited the convent in honor of the feast of Santa Maria della Porziuncula. By reviving the tradition of entering the convent's clausura on the first of May to receive an indulgence, the government celebrated the preservation of a quasi-regal privilege.

The importance that Marino Grimani and his successors attributed to the recovery of ducal jurisdiction over Santa Maria delle Vergini at a time when a succession of Tridentine hard-liners in Rome were determined to extend ecclesiastic authority over secular governments was only one instance in a series of anticlerical measures taken during the so-called regime of the *giovani* ("young patricians").[13] Although Grimani belonged to the more conservative faction of *papalisti* (philoclericals), he was determined to recuperate and defend longstanding republican rights and privileges upon which the church had started to encroach. In Gaetano Cozzi's opinion, he not only took his role as "the state's highest priest" and "the celebrant of communal life" more seriously than had any of his predecessors, but aimed at "exalting the symbolic and spiritual values of his office."[14] He organized the most splendid civic festivities that Venice had ever seen, among which his wife's coronation ceremony and "investiture" with a golden rose offered by the pope was the most spectacular and politically controversial.[15] His main interest, however, was directed toward the chapel of Saint Mark, the ducal jurisdiction of which had come under serious attack not only by Tridentine reformers in Venice and Rome, but by the oligarchs among the Venetian patricians themselves. As Gasparo Contarini had already pointed out, "the ducal chapel of Saint Mark lent the doge a sacred connotation, the highest and most distinct of his authority, which also the *procuratori* regarded as something of their own."[16] A series of conflicts marked the growing tensions surrounding the governance of Saint Mark's Chapel between doge, patriarch, and high republican magistrates. In 1592, Patriarch Priuli started his campaign against the practice by the *primicerio* (primate) of Saint Mark's Chapel of licensing priests employed in one of the four Venetian churches under ducal jurisdiction. In 1599, both doge and patriarch claimed the right to prosecute a chaplain of Saint Mark's Chapel accused of rape. In 1605, the Collegio Minore decided that in case of a conflict, the salaried personnel of the ducal chapel had to appeal to the *procuratori* for mediation.[17] In all instances, Doge Grimani was able to defend his prerogatives, but not without causing serious protest among ecclesiastic authorities and his oligarchic competitors.

The continual jurisdictional conflicts over the ducal chapel and its twin institution, the convent of Santa Maria delle Vergini, were fought to reassert Venetian sovereignty in the face of the politics of expansion of post-Tridentine "papal princes."[18] The debate shows how intricately legal prerogatives were dependent on their symbolic expression. Wedding rites marking the republic's foundational potlatch, which Pope Alexander III and Emperor Frederick I allegedly celebrated to render homage to the victorious Doge Ziani in 1177, were of concrete legal and political significance to the republic for centuries to come. Under Grimani's tenure, rituals such as the doge's "marriage" to the abbess of Santa Maria delle Vergini were revived with the explicit purpose of defending the republic's status as an independent state against papal intrusion. After all, the convent and its abbess had been given to Doge Ziani as brides by Pope Alexander III, who, in a dual ceremony, had also invested him with power over the Adriatic Sea and the chapel of Saint Mark. Conflicts over convent jurisdiction in general played a significant part in the events leading to the standoff between Venice and Rome in 1606. At a time of peaking monachization rates, the patriciate was more than ever concerned with safeguarding the boundaries of its "depositories" of virgin blood and bodies against all forms of pollution—be they social and sexual relationships with lay persons or papal infringements on ancient rights of ducal jurisdiction.

Jurisdictional Conflicts

In the aftermath of the Council of Trent, jurisdictional conflicts between the "papal prince" and the Republic of Venice were the order of the day. In the many disputes over how—and whether—to divide authority over ecclesiastical persons and the government of church institutions, convents played a major role. Because of the extraordinary social, political, and representative functions that female cloisters had assumed for the governing patriciate, however, the popes' efforts to contest the nobility's paternalistic and protectionist attitude toward "its" convents remained largely unsuccessful. Although complying with the papacy's expansionist policy in other areas, the Venetian government was determined to defend its "traditional," that is, pre-Tridentine, rights to reform and govern the city's nunneries. While the Council of Trent ruled that convents were to be subject to the jurisdiction of bishops, who should "exhort the princes to help them, and command the [secular] magistrates" in implementing strict encloisterment,[19] the patriarchs of Venice continued to be executives of government orders. Faced with the republic's determination to prevent the Venetian and, by extension, the Roman curia from claiming supreme authority in convent affairs, the papacy hesitated to make blunt demands in this regard. No post-Tridentine pope ever officially tried to revoke the bull of Leo X, who in 1521 gave full authority to the Council of Ten and its newly founded magistrate, the Provveditori sopra i Monasteri di Monache, to reform the city's non-observant nuns.[20]

The only attempt to curtail the republic's "traditional" authority over its convents was made by Gregory XIII in 1580, who charged Nuncio Alberto Bolognetti with organizing a Borromeo-style apostolic visitation of the diocese of Venice.[21] After more than two decades of Venetian compliance with the papacy's new jurisdictional claims— during which time the government introduced the Inquisition, helped

to implement the Index of Forbidden Books, and refrained from prosecuting criminal ecclesiastics[22]—the Council of Ten vehemently opposed the visitation as an intrusion in the republic's domestic affairs.
As an influential senator confidentially told Nuncio Bolognetti, the
government would approve of the visitation "if one were to visit only
the priests and the monks, but not the nuns, because the majority [of
the councilors] thinks it very tough to prosecute the imperfections
of their women, that is, to disseminate things that one should rather
cover up."[23] In December of 1580, the nuncio informed Gregory of
the government's concern that "if one reformed the convents and reduced them to greater austerity, the patricians' daughters, who before
the visitation entered convents only reluctantly, would flatly refuse to
enter them afterward"; but in January he stated that it was rather the
hospitals, the *procuratie* (trust funds), and the *scuole* (confraternities)
that the government wanted to protect against foreign interventions.[24]
In fact, both the convents and the charitable institutions were, in the
opinion of the government, of special interest to lay society and traditionally exempt from Roman jurisdiction. On 19 January 1580 (m.v.),
the Senate instructed its ambassador in Rome to present the following
arguments against the planned apostolic visitation of the city's "pious
sites": the confraternities, the trust funds for ecclesiastical legacies, and
the hospitals of Venice had been founded and were endowed and governed by laymen; all of the city's parish churches were under state jurisdiction; and the reform of the convents had been, since Pope Leo's
approval, the combined task of the Provveditori sopra i Monasteri di
Monache and the patriarch. Moreover, "The convents are full of
daughters and sisters of our noblemen and citizens, of our own viscera
collected and preserved in those sacred sites as in a safe-deposit, for
the security of the religion and their [the nuns'] honor, to which we
attend with a diligence that is as great and universal as the interest
that the whole city has in them, because of their [the nuns'] blood and
kinship."[25]

The archaic imagery of the Senate's plea against a general visitation underlined the urgency of the government's protest. Because the
untouchability of the patrician virgins' enclaves was in the "universal
interest of the city," allowing the depositories of the nobility's (and
the citizenry's) flesh and blood to be subject to the scrutiny of outsiders
would tarnish the honor of the ruling class and the entire republic.
Symbolizing the link between the nobility's political power and the
immaculate preservation of its blood, the sacred enclosures of its "vis-

cera" were under the special care and vigilance of the government. Because of their civic importance at a time of peaking monachization rates, Venetian cloisters were taboo. Subjecting patrician nuns to the visitation of nonpatrician church officials would—as the Senate's discourse seems to suggest—lessen the constitutional legitimacy of the body politic. Faced with the government's dramatic rhetoric and determined stance, Gregory XIII gave in, contenting himself with the visitation of the city's parish churches and monasteries. He thereby acknowledged not only the secular nature of the city's charitable institutions and trust funds for legacies, but the hybrid character of Venetian convents as ecclesiastic institutions of supreme political significance to the patriciate.

In 1602, another Venetian-Roman conflict over convent issues arose when the Senate passed a law that limited the cost of monachizations to one thousand ducats, plus four hundred ducats for ceremonies and cell furnishings (see chapter 4).[26] While presented as a sumptuary law for upper-class citizens, the reduction of "spiritual dowries" was in reality the first of a series of mortmain laws that would become a major source of dissent during the Interdict of 1606. In the eyes of the pope, any restriction on the church's acquisition of properties violated his supreme authority in spiritual affairs. In the eyes of the government, the nuncio's (and the pope's) complaints were unsubstantiated, because the law "did not command anybody but the laity"— that is, it prohibited lay persons from paying money to the church, not the church from receiving it.[27] Faced with resistance to his arguments and aware of the determination with which the government traditionally defended its prerogatives in convent issues, Nuncio Offredi did not even try to have the Senate revoke its law; all he aimed for was a formal recognition of the pope's ultimate authority. His idea was to have the pope send a brief to the patriarch of Venice and the bishop of Torcello, telling them to accommodate the government by reducing the size of convent dowries. Explaining his "spin operation" to Clement VIII, Offredi pointed out that the retroactive authorization of the law of 1602 would not only save the pope's reputation, but subject the monastic orders to the authority of the ordinaries and imply that the pope did a favor to the government.[28]

The Collegio initially rejected this plan, complaining that "the demand to have the regulation of [spiritual] dowries depend on the authority of Our Lordship would abolish . . . [our] ancient power to govern . . . the convents."[29] The Senate, however, instructed the Venetian ambassador in Rome to downplay the more radical argument that mortmain laws were in the exclusive domain of secular governments—and therefore valid independently of the pope's approval—but to evoke once again the special importance of convents as "safe-deposits" of "our daughters and sisters" and to point out that "we know very well from experience, not only public but also private . . . the state of our convents, and nobody has a greater interest in them than we." In addition, the ambassador was to insist that the republic had always governed the convents, "either in collaboration with the patriarchs, and bishops of Torcello . . . or also alone," and had instituted a special magistrate to take care of the convents; and that it was precisely the collaboration between state officials and ordinaries that produced "those good results that everybody knows." [30] Unlike what happened in 1606, when the demand by Pope Paul V that the government revoke the mortmain law of 1605 provoked it to claim absolute sovereignty over both laity and clergy on republican soil, the dispute over the dowry law of 1602 was downplayed by both sides and quickly settled. As had already occurred in 1580, the pope recognized the special interest the patriciate had in governing its convents, and the Senate did not extend the conflict into a fight for principles. After all, convent issues needed to be dealt with discreetly. Five months after the dowry law was passed, Clement VIII addressed a brief to Patriarch Matteo Zane, ordering him to "provide . . . a remedy against those abuses and inconveniences [i.e., the inflation of spiritual dowries], and to do everything that is in your power to support . . . the pious intention of our beloved son, the nobleman Marino Grimani, Doge of Venice." [31]

The swift resolution of a potentially risky conflict shows that the papacy tacitly acknowledged not only the patriciate's "traditional" authority over its convents, but also the "good results" of the republic's convent-reform policy. Apart from their efforts to implement strict encloisterment, government officials more than once supported the Venetian curia in its efforts to subject monastic congregations to the patriarch's jurisdiction. As already mentioned, in 1556 Nuncio Aloysius Scorta asked the convent magistrate to investigate in the case of San Giovanni in Laterano, whose confessor not only cultivated illegal relationships with several nuns, but incited the abbess to disobey the patriarch's orders on the grounds that the convent was subject solely to its Roman congregation (see chapter 3). In 1594, two Franciscan convents went on "clausura strike," protesting the pope's decision to withdraw the friars from their government and subject the nuns to the jurisdiction of the patriarch. Only the Council of Ten and the convent magistrate were able to make the nuns leave the exterior churches and return to their clausura; as the nuncio admitted, "their authority, and *braccio* [executive organs] were needed to enforce obedience without unrest."[32] Nuncio Taverna was pleased with the government's intervention because "these blessed friars truly caused me a lot of trouble; it has never been possible to prevent them from socializing with the nuns or writing to them, despite all my efforts to prohibit it. I believe, though, that in the future they will restrain themselves out of fear of the government."[33]

Despite the papacy's de facto surrender of convent jurisdiction "in temporalibus" (in temporal affairs) to the Venetian government, the patriciate had to defend and reaffirm its prerogatives constantly—sometimes also against the nuns themselves. Even after the crisis of the Interdict—which by no means settled the jurisdictional disputes between Venice and Rome—conflicts over convent government abounded. When in January of 1609 (m.v.) the Senate instituted a commission to tighten the dowry law of 1602, Nuncio Berlinghiero Gessi immediately entered into feverish negotiations with Patriarch Vendramin, encouraging him to assert his authority against the government as best he could. In his monthly letters to Cardinal Scipione Caffarelli Borghese, however, the nuncio regularly reported that the patriarch "shows little inclination to resist," "does not dare to contradict the public will," or "thinks it better not to oppose himself publicly."[34] In this situation, the nuns were left without any support, "because it seems that the entire nobility is united; even the relatives and legal representatives of the convents are against them, demonstrating that they prefer the public interest and common welfare [to their cause]."[35] The nuns would shortly find ways to assert themselves, but the nuncio was helpless, confronted with a government that preferred the "public interest" over the interests of the patriciate's flesh and blood and the virgins' "sacred enclosures." Venice's firm stance during the Interdict had profoundly altered the political discourse: "The truth is that these gentlemen claim a great authority for themselves, and if the present matter was difficult in 1602 . . . it is more than difficult now, because of the doge, and [because] of the style that they have assumed in these ecclesiastical negotiations."[36] In fact, two days after a revised and tightened dowry law was issued, the Senate instructed the Venetian ambassador to represent the government's position to the pope by employing the radical arguments that members of the Collegio had already supported in 1602:

> Noticing the abuses, excesses, and great inconveniences that increased steadily, to the detriment of our noble and citizen families and other inhabitants of this city and the Dogado, because of the introduction of exorbitant dowries and of vain and superfluous expenses, we have declared it necessary to find a remedy, and to do what we have always done, that is, *command the laity* to abstain from such excesses and superfluous expenses by limiting their [the nuns'] dowries . . . something that could not be done by the Reverend Patriarch or the vicar of Torcello, *since this concerns transgressions of the laity*.[37] (My emphasis)

While the government plainly insisted on its sovereignty in issuing laws concerning the laity, thereby abandoning its usual plea for the recognition of the convents' special status, Nuncio Gessi picked up on the patricians' old rhetoric and tried to reverse it: he implored the doge not to infringe upon the liberties of the convents, "which serve the interests of the nobility and the commoners, and [are] the ornament of this city."[38] But since the government had redefined the city's "public interest" in opposition to the interests of the convents, and since the new rhetoric, stressing the exclusively lay character of the dowry law, obviated any need for another retroactive papal approval, the nuncio's diplomatic efforts were utterly unsuccessful. The only person other than the nuncio who dared to criticize the law was, ironically, Nicolò Contarini, an intimate friend of Doge Leonardo Donà and Paolo Sarpi and one of the republican hard-liners during the Interdict.[39] The reason one of the most intransigent *anti-papalisti* among the patriciate risked political estrangement in order to defend the nuns' financial independence—in essence, the papacy's interests—can only be guessed at. The nuncio would later point to Contarini's sense of obligation toward the nuns in his family,[40] but all he cared for at the moment was how the patrician could favor the ecclesiastic cause.[41] Because of the enormous pressure among the political elite to conform to the government's anticlerical policy—another legacy of the Interdict—minority positions were not discussed. Nicolò Contarini was quickly silenced, dashing the nuncio's hopes for an unusual collaboration.[42]

While the government managed to suppress any overt opposition among patricians and church officials against the new dowry law, some of the rich convents were determined to resist this further attempt to reduce their income. As discussed in chapter 4, the nuns of San

Lorenzo and Santa Caterina refused to admit thirty-seven novices in accordance with the dowry law, insisting that they would rather stop recruiting novices altogether than admit the girls with half the dowry amount previously agreed upon. The nuns' disobedience threatened to become an embarrassing test case for the government, which only a few years earlier had so magisterially defended its jurisdiction in temporal affairs against Rome and proudly proclaimed its absolute sovereignty on republican territory. In order to break the nuns' resistance, the Senate did not have any choice but to rely on collaboration with an ambivalent ally—the Venetian curia. Patriarch Vendramin declared himself to be loyal to the government, but his real interests lay elsewhere. Although he refrained from criticizing the dowry law publicly, he promised the nuncio that he would "support the nuns' cause discreetly, by way of friends, as best he could." In his opinion, any open opposition would only move the government to take more radical measures.[43]

When members of the government became aware of the patriarch's double role, they summoned him to the Collegio "to tell him that his negotiations with the nuns were not entirely satisfactory . . . and that they disapproved of the fact that he expressed opinions to the nuns . . . that differed from their own."[44] The Senate was especially annoyed with Vendramin after an investigating commission discovered that he had advised the rejected girls' relatives to pay whatever the nuns requested: the legal amount publicly, and the rest secretly as an offering for the construction of a new altar. The indignant patricians testified that Vendramin had told them that alms-giving was the easiest way to secure their daughters' quick and smooth monachizations.[45] The Collegio reproached the patriarch strongly for his disloyalty, but was unable to suppress his secret negotiations. In December of 1610, Vendramin assured the nuncio that the affair of San Lorenzo would soon be settled to the nuns' entire satisfaction; the case of Santa Caterina proved to be more difficult, because of the uncompromising stance of Nicolò Venier, brother of one of the novices. While the other girls' relatives gradually surrendered to the nuns' demands by following the patriarch's ingenious suggestion, Venier continued to insist on having his sister take the veil for the legal amount of twelve hundred ducats. He encouraged the government to force the nuns into obedience—if necessary, with violence. Venier encountered a powerful opponent in Nicolò Contarini, however, who, as the nuncio reported, "this time spoke up for the right cause." Contarini was opposed to the reduction of spiritual dowries from the beginning, but was especially dedicated to the convent of Santa Caterina, where several of his sisters and nieces were professed choir nuns. By mobilizing support among the nuns' relatives, Contarini and the patriarch succeeded in persuading the government to refrain from using violent means to break the nuns' resistance.[46] In 1615 the conflict ended in the manner Patriarch Vendramin had favored all along: while formally respecting the government's legislative authority, the girls' parents entirely satisfied the nuns financially by offering the outstanding sums in alms.[47]

The battle between the convents and the state was far from over, however: in 1620, the Senate reissued the dowry law of 1610 with the explicit purpose of rectifying the fact that "a small number of nuns, as is well known, practice undue disobedience, with great damage to this cause and to the public reputation." In a barely veiled attack against San Lorenzo and Santa Caterina, the preamble further stated that

> everybody knows very well that [spiritual dowries] would never have risen so excessively, to the detriment and damage of the entire city [*universale*], as is manifest to everybody, if the above-mentioned deliberations [of 1602, 1603, 1604, and 1610] had had their due and necessary execution; [this is] all the more [important] because they have no other goal than to [serve] equally the particular welfare of the nobility, the citizenry, and our other subjects, and the convenience and advantages of the convents in our city and Dogado.[48]

Determined to enable all upper-class families of even modest means to engage in the potlatch, the government declared those convents that opposed the introduction of a standard dowry to be enemies of the public interest and welfare. Unperturbed by this allegation, the nuns of San Lorenzo continued to defy the government's legislative authority. As they had done earlier, in 1619 they denied admittance with a reduced dowry to two novices, after two thousand ducats had been negotiated with their parents. This time the conflict took a different turn, mainly because the new patriarch, Giovanni Tiepolo, was less lenient and compliant with the nuns' demands than his predecessor had been. He not only confirmed the law by issuing a similar decree on his own,[49] but, in execution of the government's demands to enforce obedience, closed the parlors of San Lorenzo and imposed an interdict on the convent church. The nuns replied that no superior—lay or ecclesiastic—could force them to act against their chapter decisions. Instead of surrendering, they commissioned a legal report in support of their cause. Quoting Nicolas de Tudeschis, a fifteenth-century canonist and supporter of the conciliarist movement,[50] their expert witness stated that "in the issue of accepting novices in all orders, one has to respect the customary right of every order, and also its traditions and privileges."[51] Accordingly, the nuns insisted that a formal decision of their chapter was needed to revise the two girls' dowry contracts. In order to break the deadlock and facilitate the overdue monachizations, the patriarch finally gave in to the nuns' demands and lifted the ban on church functions.

In contrast to 1610, when the nuns of San Lorenzo gained an informal victory by receiving the outstanding dowry payments as a voluntary offering, the protest of 1620 was aimed at winning official recognition of their institutional independence. While eventually bowing to the patriarch's pressure and renouncing part of the money, the nuns maintained that any change in their admissions policy required a debate and official approval of the issue in a chapter meeting; neither the patriarch's orders nor the government's laws, but only a majority of the nuns themselves, could officially and rightfully modify existing dowry contracts.

The nuns' defense of their "traditional" rights to govern the convent's temporal affairs was in open contradiction to the government's long-standing anticlerical policy and its paternalistic attitude vis-à-vis the "sacred enclosures" of its "blood and viscera," but also to the attempts of the post-Tridentine papacy to disempower the intermediate authorities of monastic institutions. By quoting Nicolas de Tudeschis, the nuns of San Lorenzo bluntly questioned the legitimacy of both the government's and the papacy's policies to curb the customary rights of monastic self-government. Their protest was directed against the "absolute" power that both the Republic of Venice and the post-Tridentine papal monarchy aspired to exert over their subjects. In this sense, the nuns' attempt to assert what was left of their convent's institutional autonomy briefly disrupted the otherwise triumphant process of conceptualizing territorial sovereignty.

Apart from questioning the government's right to interfere in what the nuns perceived to be their internal affairs, the conflict also revealed the limited legislative and executive power of a state that had so vehemently defended its sovereignty against the pope and his powerful allies a decade earlier. The government failed to impose obedience on the nuns in 1610, and it achieved a partial success in 1620 only because of the support of Vendramin's successor, Patriarch Tiepolo. Without the reliable collaboration of episcopal authorities—who disposed of efficient means of coercion, such as banning confessions and other sacraments—the state was rather helpless when confronted with the resistance of wealthy and prestigious convents such as San Lorenzo and Santa Caterina. Because the nuns could usually count on support from their relatives, the government was rarely in a position to employ drastic measures on its own.

The refusal of the nuns of San Lorenzo and Santa Caterina to accept the reduction of monachization fees was particularly provocative to the government because it undermined the central arguments of the republic in its fight against Paul V in 1606. By defending their financial and administrative autonomy against the state, the nuns questioned the concept of the government's unrestrained and God-given authority over all its citizens and their properties in its dominion—as was claimed by Doge Leonardo Donà, Antonio Querini, Paolo Sarpi, and Marc'Antonio Capello during the Interdict.[52] In addition, the nuns protested against their disenfranchisement and the state's paternalistic protectionism by appropriating the same arguments that the government employed in its own disputes with Rome. In 1606, the doge declared that he would not suffer the pope's infringement upon those "most ancient customs and native privileges in applying our laws, which over the course of 1,200 years no power in the world dared to attack."[53] On similar occasions, the republic defended its authority over convents by reference to ancient privileges such as the bull of Pope Leo X of 1521. The nuns, however, maintained that they had traditions and privileges of their own, predating the convent-reform movement by more than half a millennium.

Of course, the nuns' resistance never seriously threatened the government's authority; at best, it illustrated that the "republican absolutism" that men such as Querini, Sarpi, and Capello conceptualized in their fight against the "papal monarchy" was far from becoming political reality. As a new element in the disputes between Venice and Rome over how to partition authority over the clergy, the convents' defense of their right to self-government only confirmed the opinion of Nuncio Anton Maria Graziani: in his eyes, jurisdictional conflicts were like "hydras that constantly grow twice the number of members that are cut off."[54]

Apart from the broader implications of the convents' unparalleled protest, the nuns' defiance of state authority raises the question to what extent they were accustomed to engaging in political activities. According to contemporary observers, nuns were a political force to be reckoned with. Church authorities often complained about the nuns' power in defending their privileges. In 1491, Patriarch Maffio Girardo attributed his failure to reform the convents to the fact that the nuns "solicit favors . . . sow disobedience . . . and . . . go to the Council of Ten where business is suspended and left unresolved to listen to them."[55] In 1502, chronicler Girolamo Priuli reported that the nuns resisted the government's attempts to curb their liberties by sending "a representative to Rome with a large sum of money to convince the pope not to approve the Senate's deliberation. . . . These nuns enjoy great favor in the Councils and Colleges of Venice."[56] Nuncio Alberto Bolognetti had an even more far-reaching theory regarding the difficulties of implementing strict encloisterment in Venetian convents. In 1580, he informed the pope:

> Since relatives and friends are more important than anything else in achieving the ranks and dignities of this republic, one greatly capitalizes on the nuns, who, in sending for fathers, brothers, and other relatives, and asking them favors for this and that person, can be of great help or damage. And this is the reason that the highest-ranking Senators press for satisfying the convents. As a consequence, it is extremely difficult to prohibit the nuns from seeing and talking to their relatives.[57]

According to Bolognetti, convents functioned as a kind of clearinghouse for political careers, because of the widespread kinship ties that communities of nuns could dispose of and mobilize. In recompense, the nuns demanded that the government protect their liberties. Bold enough to bribe the pope, Venetian nuns were well accustomed to manipulating the government, at least until the end of the sixteenth century; the growing intransigence of the antipapal faction at the turn of the century and the new emphasis on "public interests" and "public welfare" seem to have called for a change in strategy. While kinship ties continued to be a priceless asset, their importance declined when disagreements among the patriciate, and particularly the conflicts with Rome, became increasingly confrontational and ideological.

The crisis of the Interdict in 1606 deeply upset the republic's political culture, even if only temporarily, because it evolved as a public debate over fundamental principles. Given the change in political climate, the nuns of San Lorenzo and Santa Caterina also opted for an open confrontation in their fight against the limitation of monachization fees. How strongly they were influenced by the style and arguments of the most radical *anti-papalisti* becomes clear when one considers their close connection with Nicolò Contarini, Giovanni Marsilio, Michelangelo "zoccolante," and Fulgentio Micanzio, all of them friends of Paolo Sarpi and active promoters of the republican cause.[58] Father Giovanni Marsilio, a critic of Cardinal Bellarmino's anti-Venetian treatise[59] (and under close surveillance by the nuncio), "lives with a concubine in a house adjacent to the nuns of Santa Caterina, celebrates mass from time to time, converses with a great number of noblemen, and seeks to become the confidant of the members of the Collegio and the Council of Ten."[60] Paolo Sarpi also "often goes to the lane of the nuns of Santa Caterina."[61] Nicolò Contarini had multiple kinship ties with the nuns of the same convent; moreover, he was able to provide Friar Michelangelo with the pulpit of San Lorenzo.[62] The nuns of San Lorenzo also hosted Fulgentio Micanzio's highly provocative Lenten sermons of 1609.[63] Much to the indignation of Nuncio Gessi, Patriarch Vendramin was in no position to prevent Friar Fulgentio from being selected as official Lenten preacher, "because these gentlemen want him to deliver his sermons at any cost."[64] The widespread admiration for Fulgentio's evangelistic sermons deeply concerned the nuncio, as is evidenced by his weekly correspondence with Rome in the spring of 1609:

> Friar Fulgentio . . . continues to preach in front of a very numerous audience, [composed] particularly of Englishmen, Flemings, and Greeks, and . . . many noblemen.[65]

> The friar preaches the observance of the holy Scriptures and of the precepts of Christ, and with astuteness and malice diminishes the authority of Our Lord and of the holy church and of the interpreters of the holy Scriptures, and also of traditions.[66]

> He says often that the church has as its sole head Christ, or that there is no other head than Christ. . . . He preaches and glorifies contrition, so that it seems that he excludes confession. . . . He exalts greatly the faith in the blood of Christ and the grace of God for our salvation, and neglects or barely mentions works. . . . He says that the secular princes must have the cure of the religion.[67]

In the eyes of the nuncio, Fulgentio's reformist evangelism was, if not outright heretical, "erroneous and scandalous," to say the least. Gessi officially demanded that "in accordance with the Holy Council of Trent," Fulgentio be removed from his position. But the government, still confident after its success of 1606, gave its full support to Sarpi's friends. In his capacity as Venetian ambassador in Rome, Nicolò Contarini declared that the sermons did not contain "anything that did not conform to the ancient piety of his [the pope's] predecessors with regard to faith and religion"[68]—a position with which the pope did not entirely agree. In fact, Fulgentio's public demands for a spiritual reform of Catholicism and Sarpi's conciliarist ideals could hardly have seemed more unorthodox to a Tridentine hard-liner such as Paul V. In retrospect, the pope must have perceived the republic's fight for state sovereignty in 1606 to be an anything-but-innocent prelude to a much more far-reaching attack on his supreme authority in all things spiritual.

The short-lived but radical movement for a spiritual and institutional renewal of Catholicism had as its center the churches of San Lorenzo and Santa Caterina. As the nuncio's reports show in great detail, the nuns of these two convents actively supported the most prominent politicians and theologians of the republican cause during the Interdict. How much the nuns were influenced by Paolo Sarpi and his friends is also evidenced by their protest against the dowry laws in 1610 and 1620. The nuns appropriated some of the government's arguments during the Interdict, but applied them critically and exploited them for their own ends. For example, the confrontation between San Lorenzo and the state (and, by extension, the patriarch) in 1620 centered around the convent's defense of its ancient prerogatives, particular privileges, and institutional traditions—echoing the government's repeated demands for the pope's recognition of its special interests and authority with regard to convent issues. At the same time, the nuns' demands for autonomy and independence directly opposed the Sarpian concept of state sovereignty, insofar as it implied the government's "absolute" power over all persons and properties in its dominion. To what extent Sarpi's and Micanzio's ideas for religious reform, especially their attack on the infallibility of the pope and his supreme authority in spiritual affairs, as well as their quest for an evangelistic renewal, influenced the nuns' protests remains obscure. The fact is, however, that without the politicizing experience of the Interdict, and the close connection with the circle around Nicolò Contarini and Paolo Sarpi, the nuns' resistance against the dowry laws would have been unthinkable—at least in the way it actually evolved. Compared with the nuns' traditional forms of exerting political power through bribery and behind-the-scenes manipulations, the open fight for legal principles by the convent of San Lorenzo in 1620 was a rare case of collective political action aimed at asserting the nuns' institutional independence.[69]

The resistance of the nuns of San Lorenzo and Santa Caterina against the government was all the more disturbing to the patriciate because the "sacred enclosures" of its virgins were supposed to signify the "immaculacy" of the body politic, the territorial integrity of the state, and the untouchability of the constitution. In addition, the nuns' insistence on their ancient rights to self-government threatened to jeopardize the potlatch game, which required women to resign themselves to a silent and passive life behind convent walls and to focus their attention on the protection of their virginity as their most precious asset. The metaphorical connection between the protection of the patriciate's "blood and viscera" against outside contamination and the preservation of the nobility's legitimacy as a ruling class was a powerful rhetorical device in the republic's defense of its authority over convents as well as during its fight for absolute sovereignty over all of its citizens.

Among all the "depositories" of patrician women, the convent of Santa Maria delle Vergini gained special symbolic importance in the rivalry between Venice and Rome. Since its foundation in the early thirteenth century, this wealthy and prestigious convent had been under ducal jurisdiction. In the second half of the sixteenth century, the patriarch of Venice tried to impose his own authority, in accordance with the principles of the Council of Trent. In 1578, legates of both the ducal chapel of Saint Mark and the episcopal cathedral of Saint Peter supervised the election of Abbess Maria Benetti.[70] When she died and her seat became vacant in 1598, Doge Marino Grimani took the opportunity to reconfirm his patronage. His idea was to have her successor elected in the presence of his representatives only and to exclude the patriarchal legates. Far from being only a small formality, this change in protocol was a political statement with many implications. Before taking this significant step, Grimani discussed the issue with members of the Collegio on 8 July 1598. He also commissioned reports by legal experts, because if "one did not proceed cautiously and legally," the patriarch's attempts to encroach upon the doge's right of investiture would only increase.[71] The vicar of Saint Mark's Chapel assured the doge that the convent was undoubtedly under the government of the "Most Reverend Primates [Primicerij] of Saint Mark's" and that the patriarch "cannot pretend [to have] any jurisdiction either as ordinary or as apostolic legate in accordance with the ninth chapter of the twenty-fifth session of the Council of Trent."[72] Doctor Graziani, a law professor from Padua, principally endorsed that opinion, pointing to the many papal bulls and privileges the convent possessed; the only legal problem he saw was the precedent constituted by the presence of the patriarch's vicar at the last election. He therefore urged the doge to speed up the election process, and to preempt the nuns' likely protests by explaining that the procedures would be just like the ones observed prior to the election of Maria Benetti.[73] In fact, when Secretary Padavin, vicar of Saint Mark's Chapel, and Galeazzo Secco, head of the ducal administration (Cancelliere Inferiore), visited the nuns of Santa Maria delle Vergini on 9 July 1598, informing them of the doge's plan, they encountered considerable resistance. The nuns, eager to introduce triennial terms for the office of abbess,[74] insisted on waiting for the patriarch's imminent return, but finally gave in to Padavin's and Secco's pressure. Unable to win the government's approval for the abolition of lifelong tenure, they elected Sofia Malipiero as their new abbess under the old rule. Meanwhile, Secretary Massa went to see the patriarch's vicar, informing him that the nuns were at that moment choosing a new abbess "in accordance with the usual and ancient customs." Outraged, the vicar responded that he should have at least been given the opportunity to defend his point of view publicly; in his eyes, the election was invalid because the jurisdiction of Santa Maria delle Vergini was, since Maria Benetti's election in 1578, in the hands of the patriarch.[75]

The doge's coup was the beginning of a prolonged conflict with Cardinal Lorenzo Priuli, unfolding as yet another fight for independence and sovereignty in the period leading up to the Interdict. Upon his return to Venice a week later, the patriarch declared the election to be invalid; he informed the Senate that in 1583, Gregory XIII had abolished lifelong tenure for the position of abbess, ruling that abbesses could be elected for a three-year term only. Having hoped for this important reform, the nuns now felt betrayed by the precipitous election procedures.[76] When the Senate officially ordered the patriarch not to oppose the election but to "favor the preservation of the [doge's] patronage," Priuli gave in, but insisted that the investiture would remain illegal unless confirmed by the pope. Calmed by the cardinal's conciliatory attitude, the Senate agreed to having Clement VIII give his benediction; after Marino Grimani formally instituted Mother Sofia Malipiero on 20 July 1598, the Venetian ambassador in Rome was charged with soliciting the pope's consent.[77]

The doge's resistance to triennial terms for abbesses in the convent of Santa Maria delle Vergini was not motivated only by his efforts to exclude the Venetian curia from supervising the election procedures. Some time after the election of Sofia Malipiero, he summoned three legal advisers to debate the political consequences of such a change in convent management. A certain Paolo (Sarpi?) di Venetia advised him against abolishing lifelong tenure, because the symbolic significance of the rite of abbatial investiture would suffer enormously if repeated every three years; moreover, if any doge ever neglected to perform the "marriage" ceremony, such negligence could constitute a justification for the church to claim that the doge's jurisdiction had fallen into disuse.[78] The second counselor sustained the opposite position, arguing that frequent investiture ceremonies could not but reinforce the doge's jurisdictional rights. The rites could easily take place on the occasion of the doge's annual visit to the convent on the first of May. The third and least sophisticated legal recommendation rejected the introduction of novelties out of principle.[79] Needless to say, the doge opted for Paolo's proposal; reaffirming ancient prerogatives seemed to mix badly with the introduction of administrative novelties. Moreover, giving in to the nuns' wishes might have looked dangerously like surrendering to patriarchal and papal demands for an execution of Gregory's bull of 1583.

Lorenzo Priuli soon found a way to avenge the humiliation he had suffered in 1598. On 9 January 1599 (m.r.), Nuncio Offredi reported that the cardinal had issued a decree on the basis of which any ecclesiastic found in a whorehouse was to be immediately imprisoned. Not surprisingly, the first to be arrested was a canon of Saint Mark's Chapel, the parish priest of San Moisé. As soon as he heard of this incident, the doge summoned the patriarch's vicar and demanded the immediate release of the ecclesiastic, since the regulars of Saint Mark were under his, not the patriarch's, jurisdiction. Priuli protested this assessment, insisting that as the parish priest of San Moisé, the defendant fell under his authority. The doge threatened to have the patriarch's entire family exiled, whereupon Priuli took his cause to the Collegio. Without even listening to his arguments, Grimani simply warned him "that he was under the obligation not to violate the interests of the republic." According to the nuncio, the affair was relegated to the Senate for decision, while Patriarch Priuli was determined to stand firm at any price.[80]

The conflicts over who had the right to invest Mother Sofia Malipiero and who had the right to prosecute the parish priest of San Moisé were thus intricately intertwined. Pope Clement VIII did not take long to understand the situation. He warned Ambassador Mocenigo that he would never tolerate that "His Serenity [the doge] aimed to degrade the patriarch, and upgrade the status of the *primicerio* [primate of Saint Mark's Chapel]."[81] Meanwhile, the political pressure on Cardinal Priuli increased. A week after Mocenigo's audience with the pope, the patriarch gave in and requested to be relieved of the government of Santa Maria delle Vergini in order "to avoid further occasions of conflict with these gentlemen," as he explained to the nuncio. He wanted to be free of any supervisory function, even in matters of *clausura*. In return for Priuli's surrender, the senators agreed to stop accusing him of any wrongdoing and to hold the patriarchal vicar responsible for the recent jurisdictional conflicts instead.[82]

Once Priuli had officially renounced authority over Santa Maria delle Vergini, the negotiations concerning Mother Malipiero's papal confirmation were resumed. The Senate also wanted the pope to choose one among the four main bishops of the *terraferma* to substitute for Priuli as the nuns' superior "in spiritualibus" (in spiritual affairs). On this occasion, Ambassador Mocenigo was to explain to Clement VIII that the convent

> represents a most esteemed deed by the republic: its victory over Frederick Barbarossa, and having Pope Alexander III, who was held in Ancona, reinstituted in his pontifical see, who—after the daughter of the Emperor asked him to found a convent in Venice, and after our government donated this island [of Castello] for the purpose of constructing it—contented himself with founding it, and he consecrated the said daughter of the Emperor as its abbess, with the patronage belonging to our Most Serene Prince.[83]

The fictive foundation legend of Santa Maria delle Vergini had thus entered the discourse of high diplomacy. Lecturing the pope about what was for him a rather embarrassing historical episode had, of course, a concrete political purpose. The government, well on its way to winning the final battle for jurisdictional sovereignty, reminded Clement VIII that there had been a time when the papacy's fate was in Venetian hands, and, more specifically, that the birth of the republic's independence coincided with, even depended on, its victory over the papacy's most powerful enemy. According to Venetian historiographers, the republic's role as intermediary between empire and papacy formally affirmed its independence as a state. Collapsing this episode with the foundation of Santa Maria delle Vergini served to lend weight to the immediate demands of the Senate, which was determined not to surrender a privilege that was supposed to have sealed the emperor's and the pope's acknowledgment of Venice as an equal partner. As mentioned above, the convent's foundation myth was of relatively recent origin and would later be criticized by church historians such as Flaminio Corner, but for the time being it served its purpose.[84] On 13 March 1599, Clement VIII agreed to appoint a new superior to the convent and to confirm the election of Abbess Malipiero—not without complaining to the ambassador "that one should be very careful when augmenting the jurisdictional authorities of princes, who, if one offers them a small finger, demand the whole arm," and not without first investigating copies of the convent's bulls and privileges.[85] Also, revealing himself to be an astute diplomat, Clement VIII protracted the settlement with a final clever tactic. The brief he eventually sent to Venice affirmed Patriarch Priuli's authority over the convent "in accordance with the Council of Trent" but exempted him from his supervisory function at the request of the Venetian government, only to replace him with the bishop of Vicenza. The Senate was incensed. It charged the ambassador with renegotiating the issue and sent him a draft of a brief it would find acceptable. On 29 May, a final conclusion was reached that confirmed the republic's exclusive rights of patronage and investiture over the convent of Santa Maria delle Vergini.[86]

The government's revaluation of the convent as a symbol of Venetian sovereignty reached its peak in 1613, when the Senate decreed that a government delegation had to visit the convent of Santa Maria delle Vergini each year to receive the indulgence of Santa Maria della Porziuncula, conceded by Boniface VIII and declared to be permanent by Paul V in 1605.[87] After decades of non-observance, the first procession of this kind took place in 1612, when the ducal family and an entourage of noblewomen entered the nuns' clausura to celebrate the conferral of this indulgence.[88] On the occasion of the state visit to the convent in 1613, the nuns published an open letter to Doge Marc'Antonio Memmo, thanking him for this honor and declaring their perpetual loyalty to the government. In this letter, they also explained why their ancient prerogatives as "the doge's predilected and firstborn daughters" had not been observed until recently.[89] Although the convent's chronicle could "serve as the evident proof" that Santa Maria delle Vergini was founded by Alexander III to commemorate the peace settlement with Emperor Frederick in 1177, historians had obfuscated this truth, the nuns said, for a long time, mostly for political reasons.[90] Because the nuns themselves were unable to read the Latin chronicle, the circumstances of their foundation were forgotten until some of their relatives took the initiative to revive the remembrance of this important date and convinced the doge to reestablish his jurisdiction over their convent in 1598. In mentioning the glorious role Lauro Mastropietro played in the Venetian victory over the emperor, the letter indicates that it was most likely the Malipiero family who promoted the recovery of the duke's patronage. Coincidentally, "just as the convent had its origins in the virtue of a member of the Malipiero family, it regained the possession of its ancient privileges under the government of Abbess Malipiera."[91]

As a further "proof" of the convent's politically significant origins, the letter explained the symbolism of the rite of investiture of its abbesses. This ring ceremony, as it was called, during which each newly elected abbess of Santa Maria delle Vergini was invested by her ducal patron, was—according to the nuns—instituted by the convent's founder, Alexander III, who

> wanted that in his presence the Most Serene Ziani confirm Julia as abbess by putting two rings on her fingers, one with the image of Saint Mark, and the other with a sapphire, as a sign of doubled faith, the first signifying that this convent was instituted with the rule of Saint Mark, confirmed by the Blessed Peter, First of the Apostles; and the other, that this property of Saint Peter . . . should remain under the protection and perpetual dominion of the Most Serene Princes of Venice.[92]

The ring ceremony was observed by every doge until the end of the republic.[93] Its importance went beyond its significance as a rite of investiture, because it was perceived and performed as a complementary rite to the doge's "marriage to the sea." As the doge yearly renewed his power over the Adriatic Sea and the eastern Mediterranean by throwing a wedding ring into the lagoon, he "married" each newly appointed abbess of the convent whose foundation marked the origins of republican sovereignty and independence. The ring ceremony conferred the highest formal rank that any Venetian woman could possibly occupy on the abbess of Santa Maria delle Vergini, who, according to Gabriella Zarri, was thereby "elevated to the symbol of the city through a ceremony that . . . [was] connected to the rites that confer sacred value on the power of the doge."[94]

The numerous conflicts surrounding the excommunication of Venice show that the republic fought against the pope for the acknowledgment not only of its jurisdictional and legislative sovereignty, but of its distinct religious identity and traditions as well.[95] In an attempt to

Jacopo Tintoretto, *Venetia as Queen of the Adriatic Sea* (Hall of the Senate)

rival the special status of Rome as the holiest of Christian cities (next to Jerusalem), Venetian mythographers drew an analogy between the doge's chapel and the pope's cathedral, which housed, respectively, the shrine of Saint Mark and the relics of Saint Peter. In contrast to Rome, Venice was even under the special patronage of the Virgin Mary, because the city was founded on the day of Mary's Annunciation, the twenty-fifth of March. The particular grace Venice enjoyed, of which the republic's miraculous perfection was a living proof, provided the grounds for a republican critique of the pope's demand for supremacy in spiritual affairs. Giovanni Marsilio compared Venice to Rome by stating, "If Rome rightfully calls itself Civitas Petri, Venice . . . can rightfully call itself Civitas Virginis, for having always remained a virgin, in its religion as well as in its liberty."[96] Paolo Sarpi even proclaimed that God wished Venice and Rome to be of equal status: "It seems certain that according to God's architectural plan, the city of Venice should remain virginal, modest, and innocent, so that she, together with Rome, would be of support and assistance to Christendom, and of ruin to the persecutors of the faith."[97]

As shown by the government's revaluation of Santa Maria delle Vergini in particular and its paternalistic convent policy in general, nunneries were of crucial importance to the way the republic conceptualized and practiced state sovereignty. Multiple metaphorical connections linked the untouchability of the nuns' sacred enclosures to the legitimacy of patrician rule, the sovereignty of the republic, and the immaculacy of the city. Conceptions of political power were thus intricately intertwined with the notion of virginity. The ring ceremony, especially, symbolized how the doge's authority and the virgins' sacrality constituted each other.[98] Nonetheless, the degree to which nuns could capitalize on their symbolic status and exert political power for their own ends was limited. Like the doge, consecrated virgins represented authority and conferred it upon others, but they did not properly possess it. On the contrary, it was their very impotence as victims of a sacrificial rite, performed in order to maintain the "purity" and nobility of the body politic, that constituted the nuns' extraordinary importance as signifiers of that which they had to endure: the "absolute" power of a sovereign state.

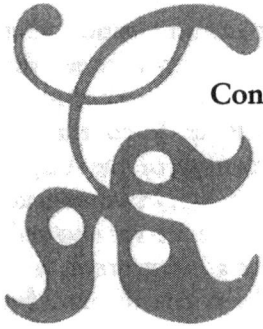

Conclusion

Clausura, noble magnificence, the potlatch, and the mythical perfection of virgin Venice: the chronicle of Santa Maria delle Vergini and its usage in political discourse in late Renaissance Venice neatly contains the major topics of this study. By declaring the convent reform of 1519 to be the result of a Jewish-Satanic conspiracy, the chronicle's author shows how significant a change the imposition of clausura brought about in a convent assumed to be under the doge's special protection. When in 1613 the Senate added an annual procession to Santa Maria delle Vergini to the government's already busy schedule of civic holidays, it gave ritual expression to an ancient ducal privilege and affirmed that religious ceremonies were part of the patriciate's conspicuous display of political magnificence. As the doge's "personal" convent, Santa Maria delle Vergini complemented the representative function of Saint Mark's as a government-run chapel in the imperial Byzantine tradition, signifying that the republic's sovereignty was as complete and "absolute" as that of any territorial monarchy in contemporary Europe. After all, its alleged first abbess was the emperor's daughter, in her time the most precious bride available to be sacrificed in exchange for peace and divine protection. In sixteenth-century political discourse, Doge Sebastiano Ziani's spectacular triple "marriage" to the sea, to Abbess Julia, and to the convent yet to be founded acquired the significance of the republic's foundational potlatch. Taking place under the patronage of Saint Mark the Evangelist, this multiple exchange of the most precious brides and wedding gifts ever to be received by a patrician groom established Venice's power and independence as the foundation for republican liberties in the making. The chronicle of Santa Maria delle Vergini located the origin and the secret of Venetian perfection in the conferral of imperial and sacral power on Doge Sebastiano Ziani in 1177 and thus served to obscure the long, and fairly recent, process of establishing the patriciate as a closed—that is, hereditary—ruling class. Virgin-like, the patriciate was, and always had been, the miraculously perfect embodiment of a state created under the guardianship of Saint Mark, and the only class qualified to rule a city such as Venice, immaculately conceived on the day of Mary's Annunciation. A nunnery of virgins from among the most prestigious families in town, Santa Maria delle Vergini manifested many of the attributes that Venice's "perfectly noble" body politic sought to assume in its rhetoric of self-fashioning.

While the adoption of specific marriage strategies designed to reproduce the patriciate in and as a closed system was downplayed in contemporary theories on nobility, the political character of marriage as a symbolically potent event of reciprocal gift-giving was highlighted in mythological descriptions and rites such as the chronicle of Santa Maria delle Vergini and the doge's annual marriage to the sea. Given the complexity of its metaphoric function for Venetian statehood and the legitimacy of patrician rule, the convent of Santa Maria delle Vergini became one of the battlegrounds in the republic's fight against post-Tridentine "papal princes." Not by coincidence, it was Doge Marino Grimani—a firm believer in the sacred character of his office and the powerful effects of conspicuous consumption—who renewed the republic's ancient prerogatives over the chapel of Saint Mark as well as the convent of Santa Maria delle Vergini. Civic festivities and religious processions were never more numerous, magnificent, and luxurious than under his tenure. Grimani's defiance of papal authority with respect to the election and investiture of Abbess Sofia Malipiero was a small but significant, and by no means isolated, event in the republic's politics of the late sixteenth and early seventeenth centuries.

Monachization rates peaked at the same time that state and church authorities implemented strict encloisterment, Venice and Rome fought over mortmain laws, virgin metaphors dominated political mythography, patricians transformed themselves into noblemen, and the republic's defense of ancient rights and prerogatives evolved as a fight over jurisdictional and ceremonial affairs. Only when, in the course of the sixteenth century, the display of a truly aristocratic consumption behavior became mandatory, when political theorists defined "nobility" in terms of purity and self-destructive displays of honor, and when the government declared the fortification of boundaries and enclosures to be of top priority in domestic as well as foreign affairs did the patriciate's concern with exclusive marriage strategies for its women intensify. By the year 1600, reciprocal gift-giving, spectacular waste, and the public display of political magnificence had turned into the kind of "total social phenomenon" Marcel Mauss identified in his study of archaic societies. Although intermarriage and forced vocations had been practiced for several centuries, patrician monachizations assumed their potlatch-like significance only in conjunction with those other cultural and social phenomena described above, all of which derived their political meaning from the dynamic of competitive gift-giving.

Without the ideological pressure to represent and enact the "nobility" of the body politic through intermarriage and conspicuous waste, the acceleration of the rate of forced monachizations at the end of the sixteenth century is hardly imaginable. The emphasis on virginal purity and noble exclusivity in political discourse not only required the potlatch as a way to implement aristocratic values, but gave it a central place in the context of Venetian mythography and thus made a painful social practice if not acceptable, at least intelligible to the women who were forced to act as its protagonists. Aside from endowing an essentially self-destructive practice with meaning and constructive purpose, the metaphoric value attached to the integrity of women's virginal bodies found concrete application on the level of institutional policy: strict encloisterment and the surveillance of convents by state and church authorities were necessary measures to guarantee the nuns' hymens pledged to Christ. Without the degradation and isolation that clausura reform brought about, the nuns might have more successfully obstructed the transformation of previously semi-autonomous convents into "safe-deposits" of patrician blood. The fight by the convents of San Lorenzo and Santa Caterina against the limitation of spiritual dowries shows how vigorously the government sought to eliminate any obstacle to a smooth functioning of the potlatch game. The "value" attached to virginity and the requirement to express a woman's intrinsic "worth" in monetary terms were instrumental in the treatment of persons as objects to be exchanged. How could brides have functioned as gifts were it not for the process of objectification all women had to endure, because of dowry inflation and the link between honor and

bodily integrity? An examination of the peak in patrician monachization rates at the end of the sixteenth and the beginning of the seventeenth century, then, unravels a host of interlocking historical phenomena—a "total social fact," as it were—for which an understanding
of marriage and monachization as conspicuous gift exchange and the
analysis of virginity as a ubiquitous metaphor in political discourse
provide the keys of interpretation.

What remains to be explained is whether and to what extent the
Venetian potlatch was unique, and why an essentially self-destructive,
paradoxical, and, in Arcangela Tarabotti's words, "tyrannical" practice was not given up before it became obsolete. The latter question
touches upon the capability of societies to clearly observe and, consequently, change the often paradoxical—according to Niklas Luhmann—foundations upon which they are built, a theoretical problem
exceeding the range of this study by far.[1] The former question, however, needs to be addressed. Monachization rates rose everywhere in
Italy, perhaps even all over Catholic Europe. Ruling classes fashioned
themselves as "truly noble" not just in sixteenth-century Venice, but
in other regions of Italy as well. Clausura reform was legislated by the
international Council of Trent. Virginity, as a master metaphor, ruled
a variety of political discourses. Patriarchy was ubiquitous. Aristocracies constitute themselves through intermarriage by definition. Competitive gift-giving is, if we follow Marcel Mauss, a trait common to
all archaic (or pre-modern?) societies.

The specificity of the Venetian potlatch, then, is the consequence
of an interplay of factors unique to sixteenth-century Venice. The dilemma of an ideally egalitarian ruling class whose reproductive behavior fostered "noble" distinctions contributed to the extraordinarily
high rates of forced vocations among patrician women. The virgin
metaphor and the image of Venus, its paradoxical counterpart, were
popular devices to express the myth of Venetian perfection. Government interventions in matters of clausura and convent management,
as well as the jurisdictional conflicts with Rome over spiritual dowries,
visitations, and the status of Santa Maria delle Vergini, were in line
with the republic's traditional antipapal policy. The Venetian potlatch
was therefore a unique, and perhaps the most spectacular, manifestation of a problem that to varying degrees plagued elite women all over
Catholic Europe at the end of the sixteenth century.

Appendix

The following notes on measures and prices explain how I dealt with the raw data used in the tables contained in this appendix.

Measures and Conversion Factors

Field measures	1 campo trevisano	52.04 ares	1.28 acres
	1 campo padovano	38.62 ares	0.95 acres
	1 campo friulano	35.05 ares	0.86 acres
	1 campo vicentino	38.62 ares	0.95 acres
	1 campo veronese	30.47 ares	0.75 acres
	1 campo di Rovigo	44.64 ares	1.10 acres
Grain measures	1 staio veneziano	83.31 liters	22.01 gal
	1 staio trevisano	86.81 liters	22.93 gal
	1 moggio padovano	347.80 liters	91.88 gal
	1 staio friulano	73.15 liters	19.32 gal
	1 sacco vicentino	108.17 liters	28.57 gal
	1 staio vicentino	27.04 liters	7.14 gal
	1 sacco veronese	114.65 liters	30.29 gal
	1 minale veronese	38.21 liters	10.09 gal
Wine measures	1 botte veneziana	751.17 liters	198.45 gal
	1 mastello veneziano	75.11 liters	19.84 gal
	1 conzo trevisano	77.98 liters	20.60 gal
	1 mastello padovano	71.27 liters	18.82 gal
	1 brento veronese	70.51 liters	18.62 gal
Oil measures	1 migliaio veneziano	631.59 liters	166.86 gal
	1 miro veneziano	15.79 liters	4.17 gal

Weight measures	1 libbra veneziana	0.47 kg	1.03 lb
	1 libbra trevisana	0.51 kg	1.12 lb
	1 libbra padovana	0.48 kg	1.05 lb

Most of the landed estates of Venetian convents were located in the Mestrino, Trevisano, and Padovano; by the eighteenth century, some convents also owned properties in the Friulano, Vicentino, Veronese, and Polesine (near Rovigo). Following Anna Pizzati, I have converted the measures for fields located in the Mestrino according to the measure of Treviso *(misura trevisana)* and calculated the surface of fields in the Friulano as 35.05 ares per campo.[1] All the other measures were identified and converted according to Angelo Martini's *Manuale di Metrologia ossia misure, pesi e monete* (Turin, 1883) and the *Atlante dei Centri Storici, Provincia di Venezia* and *Provincia di Treviso* (Padua, 1983). I have disregarded the smaller field measures *quarte* and *tavole,* because only very few convents listed them.

In general, I have converted the entries for wheat and wine according to the Venetian measures (i.e., 1 staio = 83.31 liters and 1 mastello = 75.11 liters) unless specified otherwise. The tax records often summarized wheat and wine in staia and mastelli, despite the fact that the products came from fields in different locations.[2] Frequently, wheat deriving from Treviso or Padua was explicitly measured in staia veneziani. I have calculated the income in kind from these areas in their local measures only if those measures were explicitly mentioned, such as *conzi,* the measure of Treviso for wine, or *moggia,* the measure of Padua for grain.[3] (The difference for wine is minimal in any case: 1 conzo trevisano = 77.98 liters; 1 mastello padovano = 71.27 liters; 1 mastello veneziano = 75.11 liters. The wheat measures of Treviso and Venice are also almost the same: 1 staio trevisano = 86.81 liters; 1 staio veneziano = 83.31 liters. Only the staio padovano deviates significantly: 1 staio padovano = 28.98 liters.)

Prices of Consumables

	1534	1564	1566	1582	1661	1769
1 staio of wheat	0.8	1.6	1	1	2.5	*4.3*
1 mastello of wine	0.23	1.23	0.37	0.4	1.3	*1.7*
1 staio of minor grains				0.375		*1.6*
1 staio of legumes				0.75		*3.2*
1 libbra of pork				0.0115		*0.0645*
1 carra of wood		0.26				
1 migliaio of soap		30.7				

Note: Prices are in ducats; italics indicate inferred numbers (see below).

1 ducat	= 6 lire and 4 soldi	
1 lira	= 20 soldi	= 240 denari
1 ducat	= 24 grossi	1 grosso = 24 piccoli

Appendix 243

I have calculated the value of income in kind on the basis of the average prices indicated in the tax records.

For 1534, the prices of wheat and wine listed above are recorded in the tax declaration of Santa Anna.[4]

For 1564, I have calculated the average prices of wheat, wine, wood, and soap on the basis of the prices listed in the tax records of fourteen convents.[5] The price of 1.6 ducats per staio of wheat roughly corresponds with the price of 1.45 ducats that Maurice Aymard calculated.[6]

For 1566, I calculated the prices based on the records of San Daniele.[7]

For 1582, the tax records set the "norm," or accounting, values listed above,[8] although, according to Maurice Aymard, the wheat price rose to 2.4 ducats in that year.

Since I lacked any price information for 1661, I based my calculations on the prices given in the cadastre of Santa Chiara di Venezia of 1667.[9]

For 1769, the only price indicated in the tax records is that of pork. For lack of a better alternative, I have calculated the prices for wheat, wine, minor grains, and legumes on the basis of the increase in meat prices between 1582 and 1769.[10]

The prices are not adjusted for inflation. Because all figures are rounded, some totals show discrepancies of plus or minus 1.

Sources of Data in Appendix Tables

ASV, Sopraintendenti alle Decime del Clero, busta 32, polizze 16, 20, 45, 50, 51, 52, 56, 60, 69, 70, 79, 81, 83, 85, 98; busta 33, polizze 6, 116, 121, 126, 131, 137, 149, 150, 151, 158, 161, 164, 171, 175, 180, 185, 189, 202, 204; reg. 241, polizze 124, 125, 138, 167, 168, 211; busta 77, polizze 10, 32, 37, 57, 80, 83, 88, 93, 95, 102, 104, 123, 136, 137, 139, 140, 166, 173, 174, 181, 182, 193, 214, 227, 251, one unnumbered polizza; busta 78, polizze 288, 316, 333, 335, 370, 388, 392, 393, 394, 395, 418, 420, 422, three unnumbered polizze.

ASV, Dieci Savij sopra le decime di Rialto, busta 127, polizza 658; busta 129, polizza 300; busta 158, polizza 903; busta 159, polizza 200; busta 160, polizze 529, 653, 748, 768; busta 161, polizza 1145; busta 163, polizza 775; busta 164, polizze 831, 1075; busta 167, polizze 174, 381; busta 168, polizze 463, 479, 480, 537, 539, 585, 686; busta 169, polizza 375; busta 170, polizze 437, 479; busta 172, polizza 1407; busta 214, polizza 990; busta 216, polizza 317; busta 217, polizze 441, 534, 535, 632, 727, 760; busta 218, polizze 840, 1006; busta 219, polizze 230, 232, 356, 365; busta 220, polizze 664, 767; busta 224, polizze 98, 111, 121, 126, 207, 259, 284, 297, 329, 376, 382; busta 225, polizza 596; busta 226, polizze 179, 243; busta 227, polizza 723; busta 228, polizze 916, 1058, 1110.

ASV, Santa Chiara di Venezia, busta 1/2, catastico 1550; catastico 1677; San Lorenzo, busta 1, catastico 1452; busta 9, Decima del Clero 1534; San Zaccaria, busta 73, Decima del Clero 1528, 1534, 1537.

APV, Visite Vendramin, Sant' Alvise 1612; Santa Caterina di Venezia 1616; San Gerolamo 1609; San Giuseppe 1618.

TABLE A1 Nuns per Convent, 1564–1680

Convents	All Nuns					Chapter Nuns				
	1564	1594–96	1600–18	1620–28	1624	1655–60	1661–65	1666–70	1671–75	1676–80
S. Alvise	84	40	105					44		
S. Andrea de Zirada	105		70					32		
S. Anna	60				66		22			
S. Antonio Abate	30									
S. Bernardo di Murano	30									
SS. Biagio e Cataldo	54		69		71			18		
S. Caterina di Mazzorbo	60									
S. Caterina di Venezia	65		120	111						
S. Chiara di Venezia	56		49						47	
S. Chiara di Murano		46							42	
Convertite					348		135			
Corpus Domini	80	70	50	56				38		
SS. Cosma e Damiano	54				59		26		27	37
S. Croce della Giudecca	118	103	100		124	38	44			
S. Croce di Venezia	84			79						
S. Daniele	87		74		99	36		42	35	31
S. Eufemia	26									
Gesu e Maria										
S. Giacomo di Murano	58							14	13	
S. Giovanni Evangelista	50									
S. Giovanni in Laterano					48					
S. Gerolamo	80	6		44			14	14	16	
S. Giuseppe	60	94	85	77	121		41	50	69	
S. Giustina		48			63		24	70	29	26
S. Lorenzo	115			167	138	42	38	28	28	
S. Lucia		81	76					35		

Convent	S1	S2	S3	S4	S5	S6	S7	S8	S9	S10
S. Matteo di Mazzorbo	66							18	23	22
S. Matteo di Murano	48									
SS. Marco e Andrea			49	43						
S. Maria Angeli di Murano	90						22	20	21	
S. Maria della Celestia	57					61	16			16
S. Maria Grazie di Burano			90				48			10
S. Maria Maggiore	64		44			44	30		57	53
S. Maria dei Miracoli						61	26		31	33
S. Maria Umiltà						26		19		
S. Maria Valverde	23									
S. Maria delle Vergini	65		67			65				
S. Marta			14	108		102	54		49	49
S. Martino di Murano	40									
S. Mauro di Burano	24									
Ognissanti	52		33	69		84	32	32	33	33
SS. Rocco e Margherita	80		72	46				27	28	28
S. Sepolcro	65		55			149	40	47		
S. Servolo	37		33	49		110		90	49	39
Spirito Santo										
SS. Vito e Cipriano	40			97						
S. Zaccaria			67	62		83	37		37	29
Total	2,107	1,015	1,108	747	142	1,896	649	678	634	345
Number of convents	34	17	14	9	4	20	17	19	18	11
Nuns per convent	62	60	79	83	36	95	38	36	35	31

Sources: APV, Visite Priuli (1592–96); Visite Vendramin (1609–18); Visite Tiepolo (1620–27); Elenchi Elezioni Abbadesse (1656–70); Decretorum et Mandatorum Monialium, c. 12r; Torcellania Criminalia Monialium (1600–89) (Tarli); ASV, Sopraintendenti alle Decime del Clero, buste 32, 33; reg. 241; Provveditori sopra Monasteri, busta 347, fascicolo 1; busta 268, fascicolo 36; busta 270, fascicolo 5; Corpus Domini, busta 8, fascicolo "Pro Ven.o Mon.o Corporis Christi, S. Lucretia Morosini"; Santa Croce di Venezia, busta 2, fascicolo 2; Volker Hunecke, "Kindbett oder Kloster: Lebenswege venezianischer Patrizierinnen im 17. und 18. Jahrhundert," *Geschichte und Gesellschaft* 18 (1992): 446–76.

TABLE A2   Patrician Nuns and Brides, 1590–1670

Family	Nuns	Brides	Family	Nuns	Brides
Alberti	3	4	Caotorta		1
Albrizzi		1	Capello	28	38
Altieri		1	*Carminati*	1	
Antelmi		1	Cassetti	2	1
Ariano		1	*Castelli*	1	
Arimondo	6	7	Cattaneo		2
Avanzago	1	3	Cavalli	2	11
Avogadro		8	Cavazza		1
Avonal	1	3	Celsi	1	3
Badoer	31	28	Cernovicchia	1	1
Baffo	2		Cibo		1
Baglioni	1		Cicogna		2
Balbi	22	42	Ciuran	5	8
Barbarigo	8	34	Cocco	7	7
Barbaro	17	23	Collalto		7
Baroni	1		Condumier	1	4
Barozzi	3	23	Contarini	79	128
Basadonna	20	17	Conti		1
Basegio	3	4	Coppo		2
Battagia	2	7	Corner	36	88
Belloni		2	Corregio	1	
Bellotto	1		Correr	8	16
Bembo	24	29	Cosazza		3
Benedetti	3	5	Crivelli	2	
Bentivoglio		1	Crotta		7
Benzon	2	5	Dalla Nave		1
Beregan		2	Da Lezze	5	7
Beregonzi	1	3	Da Mezzo		14
Berlendis	1		Da Mosto	12	13
Bernardo	16	17	Da Mula	3	8
Bianchi	1		Dandolo	8	27
Boldu		21	Da Ponte	3	4
Bollani	10	11	Dario	4	
Bon	19	17	Da Riva		1
Bonaldi	1		Diedo	12	22
Boncompagni		1	Dolce		1
Bondumier	12	6	Dolfin	22	47
Bonfadini		1	Donà	28	53
Bonhomo	1		Donado	7	
Bonvicini		3	Dondiorologio		1
Boninsegna	1		Dotto		2
Bonvieni	3		Duodo		7
Bragadin	31	45	Emo	8	8
Brandolin		2	Erizzo	7	3
Bressa		1	Fabrizii	1	1
Calbo	3	3	Falier	9	20
Calergi		12	Farsetti		1
Canal	11	19	Ferro	2	

TABLE A2   (*Continued*)

Family	Nuns	Brides	Family	Nuns	Brides
Flangini	3	7	Memmo	2	11
Fonseca		1	Miani	4	8
Foscari	5	14	Michiel	28	60
Foscarini	31	35	Minio	3	10
Foscolo		5	Minotto	5	9
Franco	1		Mocenigo	20	37
Gabrieli	13	9	Molin	16	37
Gallo		1	Moro	17	20
Gambara	2	3	Morosini	50	89
Garzoni	3		Muazzo	9	22
Gherardini		1	Nadal		5
Ghiberti	1		Nani	4	15
Giovanelli		1	Navagier		6
Girardi	16	2	Odescalchi		1
Giupponi	5		Orio	1	4
Giusto/Zusto	3	1	Ottobon		2
Giustinian	32	44	Pallavicini		1
Gonzaga		4	Papafava		1
Gozzi		1	Paruta		6
Gradenigo		28	Pasqualigo	16	29
Grego	3	3	Pellizzari	1	
Grimani	22	39	Pepoli		2
Grioni	3	4	Pesaro	5	14
Gritti	15	19	Piovene		1
Guera	1		Pisani	25	49
Gussoni	5	5	Pizzamano	8	6
Labia	2	4	Polani	2	14
Lando	1	10	Premarin	3	1
Leoni	1		Priuli	32	74
Lion	6	6	Querini	53	62
Lippamano	16	14	Renier	10	16
Lombardo		5	Riva	3	
Lombria		1	Robolini	1	
Longo	6	11	Rossi	4	2
Loredan	46	46	Rubini	5	1
Maffetti	1	2	Ruzzini		8
Magno	7	2	Sagredo	3	9
Malatesta	2		Salamo(n)	15	18
Malipiero	30	4	Sangiantofetti		1
Manin	5	1	Santasofia		17
Manolesso	1	3	Sanudo	6	7
Manzoni	2		Savoia		1
Marcello	16	34	Savorgnan		5
Marini	7	2	Semitecolo	1	8
Marioni	1		Sforza	1	
Martinelli		3	Soderini	2	2
Martinengo		7	Soranzo	13	30
Medici	1	1	Statio	1	

TABLE A2   (*Continued*)

Family	Nuns	Brides	Family	Nuns	Brides
Suriani	4	16	Vidali	4	2
Taiapietra	3	8	Vidman	2	1
Tasca	4	1	Vitturi	3	5
Tiepolo	10	24	Vizzamano		4
Torre	3	3	Volpe	2	
Trevisan	16	27	Zancani	1	
Tron	1	7	Zancarol	1	6
Valaresso	8	7	Zane	8	29
Valier	16	27	Zen	17	54
Valmarana		1	Zenobio		1
Van Axel		2	Zio	1	
Vendramin	8	14	Zon		2
Venier	52	29	Zorzi	14	45
Verdizotti		1	Zulian	7	
Viani	1		Total	1,434	2,440
Viaro	1	6			

Sources: ASV, Avogadori di Comun, G. Giomo, "Matrimoni patrizi per nome di donna"; APV, Visite Priuli (1592–96); Visite Vendramin (1609–18); Visite Tiepolo (1620–27); Elenchi Elezioni Abbadesse (1656–1670); Decretorum et Mandatorum Monialium, c. 12r; Torcellania Criminalia Monialium (1600–1689) (Tarli); ASV, Provveditori sopra Monasteri, busta 347, fascicolo 1; busta 268, fascicolo 36; busta 270, fascicolo 5; Corpus Domini, busta 8, fascicolo "Pro Ven.o Mon.o Corporis Christi, S. Lucretia Morosini"; Santa Croce di Venezia, busta 2, fascicolo 2.

Note: Families whose names appear in italics were accepted into the patriciate only after 1670. Volker Hunecke, *Der venezianische Adel am Ende der Republik (1646–1797): Demographie, Familie, Haushalt* (Tübingen, 1995).

TABLE A3   The Foundation of Convents in Venice and Torcello

Convent	Order	Year of Foundation
San Giovanni Evangelista di Torcello	Benedictine	640
Santa Caterina di Mazzorbo	Benedictine	783
San Zaccaria	Benedictine	827
San Lorenzo	Benedictine	853
Santa Eufemia di Mazzorbo	Benedictine	10th cent.
San Servolo	Benedictine	1109
Santa Maria degli Angeli di Murano	Augustinian	1187
Sant' Angelo di Ammiano	Benedictine	1195
Santi Apostoli Filippo e Giacomo	Benedictine	12th cent.
Sant' Adriano di Costanziaca	Benedictine	12th cent.
San Mauro di Burano	Benedictine	1214
Santa Maria delle Vergini	Augustinian	1222–24
Santi Biagio e Cataldo	Benedictine	1222
Santa Chiara di Venezia	Franciscan	1236
Santa Maria della Celestia	Cistercian	1237
San Antonio Abate di Torcello	Benedictine	1246
San Matteo di Murano	Benedictine	1280
Santa Maria Valverde	Cistercian	1281

TABLE A3 (*Continued*)

Convent	Order	Year of Foundation
Santa Caterina di Venezia	Augustinian	1288
Santa Anna	Benedictine	1297
San Matteo di Mazzorbo	Cistercian	1298
Eremite di San Giuseppe	*pizzochere*	13th cent.
Santa Chiara di Murano	Clares	ca. 1300
Santa Marta	Augustinian	1315
Santa Croce della Giudecca	Benedictine	1328
Sant' Andrea de Zirada	Augustinian	1329
San Giacomo di Murano	Augustinian	1330
San Bernardo di Murano	Augustinian	1362
San Gerolamo	Benedictine	1375
Sant' Alvise	Augustinian	1388
Corpus Domini	Dominican	1395
San Daniele	Augustinian	1437
Santa Giustina	Augustinian	1448
Santa Lucia	Augustinian	1459
Santa Croce di Venezia	Clares	1470
Ognissanti	Benedictine	1472
Santa Maria dei Miracoli	Clares	1481
Santi Cosma e Damiano	Benedictine	1481
Spirito Santo	Augustinian	1483
Santa Maria Maggiore	Franciscan	1483
Santi Rocco e Margherita	Augustinian	1488
San Sepolcro	Franciscan	1493
Santi Marco e Andrea di Murano	Benedictine	1496
San Martino di Murano	Augustinian	1501
San Giovanni in Laterano	Benedictine	1505
Santi Vito e Cipriano di Burano	Benedictine	1516
San Giuseppe	Augustinian	1525
Santa Maria Maddalena (Convertite)	Augustinian	1525
Santa Maria delle Zitelle		1558
Santa Maria del Soccorso		1578
Santa Maria delle Dimesse di Murano		1594
Santa Maria del Redentore	Capuchins	1605
San Giorgio dei Greci	Basiliane	1609
Santa Maria dell'Umiltà	Benedictine	1615
Santa Maria delle Grazie di Burano	Serviti	1619
Gesu e Maria	Augustinian	1623
Santa Teresa	Carmelites	1647
Santa Maria del Rosario	Dominican	1649
Santa Maria del Pianto	Serviti	1657
Santa Maria delle Grazie in isola	Capuchins	1669
Cappuccine di Castello	Capuchins	1672
San Giuseppe di Murano	Descalzed Carmelites	1736
Santa Maria delle Penitenti		18th cent.

Source: Flaminio Corner, *Notizie storiche delle chiese e monasteri di Venezia e di Torcello* (Padua, 1758).

TABLE A4 The Taxable Wealth of Venetian Convents, 1528–1769

Convent	Rents Urban (ducats)	Rents Land (ducats)	Other Cash (ducats)	Wheat (liters)	Wheat (ducats)	Wine (liters)	Wine (ducats)	Total (ducats)	Fields (ares)
Convertite									
Decima del Clero 1769	8	25	30					63	
Corpus Domini									
Decima del Clero 1564	1,301	407	273	19,495	374	14,857	253	2,609	3,171
Decima di Rialto 1582	189	31		7,081	85	4,039	22	327	4,801
Decima di Rialto 1661	415	31	249	5,368	161	3,534	64	920	14,482
Decima del Clero 1769	1,201	61	32	16,079	830	12,909	304	2,428	13,710
Gesu e Maria									
Decima di Rialto 1661	62		12	2,583	721	78	13	808	2,194
Ognissanti									
Decima di Rialto 1661	283	266	666	5,498	165	865	16	1,395	
Decima del Clero 1769	268	178	88	13,964	721	14,188	334	1,588	9,750
S. Alvise									
Decima del Clero 1564	924	74	8	22,827	438	4,327	74	1,518	14,926
Decima di Rialto 1582	550	19		24,973	300	12,549	70	938	10,317
Decima di Rialto 1661	2,699	147	16	24,160	725	13,414	242	3,829	17,373
Decima del Clero 1769	2,501	1,012		26,243	1,355	16,227	383	5,250	19,020
S. Andrea de Zirada									
Decima del Clero 1564	823	2	773	35,823	688	23,223	396	2,681	17,249
Decima di Rialto 1582	480			10,414	125	6,274	35	640	4,878
Decima di Rialto 1661	835			10,081	303	6,851	124	1,261	3,785
Decima del Clero 1769	3,114	144	14	38,739	2,000	27,189	641	5,912	20,916
S. Anna									
Decima del Clero 1534	112		168	12,330	124	5,108	16	420	8,432
Decima del Clero 1564	504	27	204	21,411	411	13,703	234	1,379	
Decima del Clero 1769	1,123		126	22,577	1,165	15,434	364	2,778	14,615

S. Antonio di Torcello									
Decima del Clero 1564	180	26		47,403	910	28,848	492	1,608	34,870
Decima del Clero 1769	110	200	481	39,072	2,017	18,174	428	3,236	38,719
S. Bernardo									
Decima del Clero 1564		103	100	1,833	35			238	3,285
Decima di Rialto 1661								64	
Decima del Clero 1769	313		190	19,328	998	12,631	298	1,798	10,209
S. Caterina di Mazzorbo									
Decima del Clero 1564	12	106	392	12,935	248	7,645	130	888	13,335
Decima del Clero 1769		100	1,295					1,395	17,801
S. Caterina di Venezia									
Decima del Clero 1564	547	131	50	34,407	661	23,078	394	1,783	25,244
Decima di Rialto 1582	556			4,166	50	4,327	24	630	2,863
Decima di Rialto 1661	1,256	553	1,361	3,957	119	4,188	75	2,003	3,487
Decima del Clero 1769	2,115	125		37,026	1,911	56,220	1,325	6,837	61,233
S. Chiara di Murano									
Decima di Rialto 1582	105	73	68	5,415	163	2,885		73	
Decima di Rialto 1661		170					52	558	
S. Chiara di Venezia									
Decima del Clero 1564	649	402	55	41,455	796	12,405	212	2,113	28,074
Decima di Rialto 1582	19			1,999	60	1,154	21	19	
Decima di Rialto 1661		307	265					388	
Decima del Clero 1769	1,422			49,694	2,565	27,117	639	4,891	35,084
S. Croce della Giudecca									
Decima del Clero 1564	1,011	661	36	41,238	792	18,391	314	2,814	17,189
Decima di Rialto 1582	341		341	19,328	232	10,097	74	988	
Decima del Clero 1769	2,025	269	829	41,072	2,120	28,315	667	5,910	34,905
S. Croce di Venezia									
Decima del Clero 1564		195						195	
Decima del Clero 1769		39	342	4,549	235	440	10	626	6,259

TABLE A4 (Continued)

Convent	Rents		Other Cash	Wheat		Wine		Total	Fields
	Urban (ducats)	Land (ducats)	(ducats)	(liters)	(ducats)	(liters)	(ducats)	(ducats)	(ares)
S. Daniele									
Decima del Clero 1564	237	20	792	42,405	814	21,636	369	2,232	30,545
Decima di Rialto 1566	145			15,121	309			453	10,836
Decima di Rialto 1582	119			16,037	193	7,068	39	351	10,210
Decima di Rialto 1661		4	563	24,077	723	8,150	147	1,436	10,573
Decima del Clero 1769		584		34,924	1,803	19,292	455	2,841	31,010
S. Eufemia									
Decima del Clero 1564	8	14	88	17,162	330	5,409	92	524	9,889
Decima del Clero 1769		139		15,370	793	10,429	246	1,186	9,523
S. Gerolamo									
Decima del Clero 1564	912	17	576	26,826	515	12,837	219	2,238	19,050
Decima di Rialto 1582	395			2,166	26			421	676
Decima di Rialto 1661	210	370		666	20			600	
Decima del Clero 1769	3,125	220	179	24,406	1,260	22,199	523	5,307	22,959
S. Giacomo di Murano									
Decima del Clero 1564	204		136	6,665	128	5,048	86	554	4,841
Decima di Rialto 1582	369	68		9,309	112	7,500	42	590	
Decima del Clero 1769	143	168	103	8,063	416	7,236	171	1,000	4,312
S. Giovanni Evangelista di Torcello									
Decima del Clero 1534	2,067	1,169	577	69,980	672	40,171	128	4,614	29,436
Decima del Clero 1564	395	79	168	82,227	1,579	47,383	808	3,029	44,164
Decima del Clero 1769	872	278	897	77,185	3,984	42,407	1,000	7,030	32,111
S. Giovanni in Laterano									
Decima di Rialto 1661		5		292	9			14	840
Decima del Clero 1769	356	15		15,662	808	6,707	158	1,338	7,881

S. Giuseppe									
Decima del Clero 1564	84	30	84						198
Decima di Rialto 1661	138	121	195						454
S. Giustina									
Decima del Clero 1564	284		224	30,242	581	6,000	102	1,191	
Decima di Rialto 1582	760		25	1,000	12			797	
Decima del Clero 1769	1,897	1,007	29	49,590	2,560	22,300	526	6,018	4,685
S. Lorenzo									
Decima del Clero 1534	1,885		562	18,357	176	6,719	21	2,644	19,022
Decima del Clero 1564	3,572	110	880	76,216	1,464	34,329	585	6,611	40,686
Decima di Rialto 1582	50		17	2,999	36	2,885	16	119	
Decima di Rialto 1661		23	3					27	
Decima del Clero 1769	11,411	612	301	83,615	4,316	47,971	1,131	17,770	49,942
S. Lucia									
Decima del Clero 1564	264	25	96	8,664	166	19,328	301	852	6,674
Decima di Rialto 1661	220	60	220	696	21	1,069	19	540	888
Decima del Clero 1769	510	614	22	24,077	1,243	16,804	396	2,785	21,006
S. Maria degli Angeli di Murano									
Decima del Clero 1564	344	2,125	440	33,990	653	2,164	37	3,254	
Decima di Rialto 1582, aggiunto		4	24					372	
Decima di Rialto 1661	579		310					889	
Decima del Clero 1769	786	3,846	262	47,278	2,440	152,606	3,597	10,932	25,891
S. Maria della Celestia									
Decima del Clero 1564	601	587		128,861	2,475	52,384	893	4,556	97,225
Decima di Rialto 1582	38		46					84	
Decima di Rialto 1661	59	12	81	1,083	33			184	
Decima del Clero 1769	950	7,957	49	89,688	4,629	56,258	1,326	14,911	86,702
S. Maria delle Grazie									
Decima di Rialto 1582				4,166	50	4,616	26	76	

253

TABLE A4 (Continued)

Convent	Rents Urban (ducats)	Rents Land (ducats)	Other Cash (ducats)	Wheat (liters)	Wheat (ducats)	Wine (liters)	Wine (ducats)	Total (ducats)	Fields (ares)
S. Maria Maggiore									
Decima del Clero 1564			50					50	
Decima di Rialto 1661	18	120	250					388	2,082
Decima del Clero 1769		108						108	2,082
S. Maria dei Miracoli									
Decima del Clero 1564			80					80	
Decima di Rialto 1661	272			3,982	120	3,462	62	454	
Decima del Clero 1769	403							403	2,047
S. Maria Valverde									
Decima del Clero 1564	50	104	21	10,664	205	4,976	85	465	8,380
Decima di Rialto 1661	250	14		2,734				264	1,562
Decima del Clero 1769	230	181		10,164	525	6,491	153	1,089	8,161
S. Maria delle Vergini									
Decima del Clero 1564	532	1,102	348	60,400	1,160	29,007	495	3,637	
Decima di Rialto 1582			117	2,749	33			150	
Decima di Rialto 1661	59	35	327	4,082	123			544	
Decima del Clero 1769	1,361	2,208		60,974	3,147	43,182	1,018	7,735	44,942
S. Marta									
Decima del Clero 1564	12	17	158	18,162	349	9,448	161	697	
Decima di Rialto 1661	32			3,499	105	2,596	47	187	2,290
Decima del Clero 1769	57	84		22,160	1,144	15,289	360	1,645	13,572
S. Martino									
Decima del Clero 1564			74					74	
Decima di Rialto 1661			1,343					1,343	

S. Matteo di Mazzorbo									
Decima del Clero 1564	405	8	134	30,825	592	18,030	308	1,446	33,833
Decima di Rialto 1582	14			854	10	721	4	28	521
Decima del Clero 1769	1,351	387	1	27,242	1,406	14,568	343	3,489	34,509
S. Matteo di Murano									
Decima del Clero 1564			68					68	
Decima di Rialto 1582		16	48	333	4	361	2	70	1,219
Decima di Rialto 1661		214	163					377	5,065
Decima del Clero 1769		603	50	21,311	1,100	48,219	1,137	2,889	49,112
Decima del Clero 1769, aggiunto		281	43	500	26			349	4,521
S. Mauro di Burano									
Decima del Clero 1564	14	16	26	14,912	286	8,654	148	490	11,347
Decima di Rialto 1661	52	56		14,931	448	13,257	239	795	10,358
Decima del Clero 1769	142	290	34	16,412	847	7,868	185	1,498	
S. Sepolcro									
Decima del Clero 1564	57	26	16					99	
Decima di Rialto 1661	296	264	124					622	
Decima del Clero 1769	576			6,523	196	7,212	130	964	3,228
S. Servolo									
Decima del Clero 1564	836		196	30,741	590	18,679	319	1,940	17,046
Decima di Rialto 1582				4,166	50	2,885	16	66	1,816
Decima di Rialto 1661		47		4,499	135	2,885	52	187	1,816
Decima del Clero 1769	1,075			30,491	1,574	20,194	476	3,172	13,327
S. Teresa									
Decima del Clero 1769	78	4,163						4,241	51,176
S. Zaccaria									
Decima del Clero 1528	2,367	257	328					2,952	
Decima del Clero 1534	2,416	368	425					3,209	
Decima del Clero 1537	2,668	333	364					3,365	
Decima del Clero 1564	3,923	482	571	91,911	1,765	42,601	727	7,467	1,473
Decima di Rialto 1661		109	153	1,666	50			312	
Decima del Clero 1769	15,910	1,478		98,184	5,068	47,295	1,115	23,570	47,389

255

TABLE A4 *(Continued)*

Convent	Rents		Other Cash (ducats)	Wheat		Wine		Total (ducats)	Fields (ares)
	Urban (ducats)	Land (ducats)		(liters)	(ducats)	(liters)	(ducats)		
Spirito Santo									
Decima del Clero 1564	79		113	1,691	32	1,298	22	167	2,225
Decima di Rialto 1582		571		417	5			655	
Decima di Rialto 1661	57	247	32	500	15			351	3,075
Decima del Clero 1769	173	220		750	39			431	1,286
SS. Biagio e Cataldo									
Decima del Clero 1564		529	131	52,373	1,006	26,726	456	2,122	33,573
Decima del Clero 1769		851		46,904	2,421	38,512	908	4,179	34,091
SS. Cosma e Damiano									
Decima del Clero 1564	723	85	132	54,443	1,046	28,451	485	2,471	23,081
Decima di Rialto 1582	267	23						290	
Decima di Rialto 1661	338	100	12					450	
SS. Marco e Andrea									
Decima del Clero 1564	12			1,583	30			42	
Decima di Rialto 1661				2,927	88	1,872	34	122	781
Decima del Clero 1769	11	50	25	2,041	105			191	260
SS. Rocco e Margherita									
Decima del Clero 1564	267	169	91	3,591	69	1,226	21	617	872
Decima di Rialto 1566	208	28	24	3,400	69	943		330	1,184
Decima di Rialto 1582	205	54		11,522	138	9,376	52	449	7,485
Decima di Rialto 1661	268	96		4,749	143	2,308	42	549	8,446
Decima del Clero 1769	217	415		3,680	190	2,885	68	890	8,569
SS. Vito e Cipriano									
Decima del Clero 1564	64							64	
Decima del Clero 1769	34	21	14	2,916	151	1,298	31	251	

TABLE A5 Additional Records of Convent Revenues, 1452–1677

Convent	Rents		Other Cash (ducats)	Wheat			Wine			Total (ducats)	Fields (ares)
	Urban (ducats)	Land (ducats)		(liters)	(ducats)		(liters)	(ducats)			
S. Alvise Visita Vendramin 1612	2,231	275	2,285							4,791	
S. Caterina di Venezia Visita Vendramin 1616	1,900		2,851	46,320			31,733			4,751	
S. Chiara di Venezia Catastico 1550	1,588	119	1,295	56,276	1,743		34,255	588		5,334	25,344
Catastico 1677											33,386
S. Gerolamo Visita Vendramin 1609			5,712							5,712	
S. Giuseppe Visita Vendramin 1618	199	158	1,046							1,403	
S. Lorenzo Catastico 1452	1,807	132		34,553			676			1,939	16,338

TABLE A6 Net Revenues of Venetian Convents, 1564 (in ducats)

Income Rank	Convent	Income Total	Income Per Capita	Expenditures Total	Expenditures Per Capita	Net Revenue	Debts
1	S. Zaccaria	7,467	187	4,192	105	3,275	
2	S. Lorenzo	6,611	57	3,756	33	2,854	
10	SS. Cosma e Damiano	2,471	46	1,152	21	1,319	
11	S. Gerolamo	2,238	28	1,228	15	1,011	1,348
8	S. Andrea de Zirada	2,681	26	1,727	16	954	
6	S. Giovanni Evangelista di Torcello	3,029	61	2,213	44	816	
15	S. Servolo	1,940	30	1,161	18	780	1,381
17	S. Antonio di Torcello	1,608	54	901	30	707	
4	S. Maria delle Vergini	3,637	56	3,091	48	545	1,600
13	SS. Biagio e Cataldo	2,122	39	1,709	32	413	2,916
28	S. Mauro di Burano	490	20	166	7	324	
29	S. Maria Valverde	465	20	141	6	324	880
9	Corpus Domini	2,609	33	2,344	29	265	291
25	SS. Rocco e Margherita	617	12	428	8	189	800
31	S. Giuseppe	198	3	24		174	
20	S. Anna	1,379	23	1,268	21	111	
30	S. Bernardo	238	8	162	5	76	
34	S. Sepolcro	99	1	83	1	16	

38	SS. Vito e Cipriano	64		51		13	
35	S. Maria dei Miracoli	80		86		−6	
19	S. Matteo di Mazzorbo	1,446	22	1,454	22	−8	1,752
12	S. Daniele	2,232	26	2,243	26	−11	
16	S. Caterina di Venezia	1,783	27	1,803	28	−20	800
32	S. Croce di Venezia	195	2	216	3	−21	
27	S. Eufemia	524	20	551	21	−27	
36	S. Martino	74	2	115	3	−41	
24	S. Marta	697		884		−187	
23	S. Lucia	852		1,046		−194	
7	S. Croce della Giudecca	2,814	24	3,057	26	−243	
3	S. Maria della Celestia	4,556	80	4,809	84	−252	
33	Spirito Santo	167	5	461	12	−294	
22	S. Caterina di Mazzorbo	888	15	1,268	21	−380	889
5	S. Maria degli Angeli	3,254	36	3,862	43	−608	
14	S. Chiara di Venezia	2,113	38	2,981	53	−868	1,600
18	S. Alvise	1,518	18	2,466	29	−947	1,733
26	S. Giacomo	554	10	1,507	26	−953	1,650
21	S. Giustina	1,191					
37	S. Matteo di Murano	68	1				2,306
39	S. Maria Maggiore	50	1				500
40	SS. Marco e Andrea	42					

TABLE A7 Expenditures, 1564

Convent	Total (ducats)	% Wheat	% Wine	% Add. Food	% Spices	% Medicine	% Soap	% Clothing	% Oil	% Firewood	% Church	% Servants	% Repairs	% Duties	% Misc.
S. Maria della Celestia	4,809	13	14	14	3			4	4	6	5	8	5	2	21
S. Zaccaria	4,192			38	4			5	1	9	16	9		4	14
S. Maria degli Angeli	3,862	16	16	10	2			6	10	13	12	4	5		6
S. Lorenzo	3,756		20		3		2	15	8	11	8	10	11	8	2
S. Maria delle Vergini	3,091			16	5			10	7	12	15	6	8	12	9
S. Croce della Giudecca	3,057			22		4	2	10	6	7	18	4	5	6	15
S. Chiara di Venezia	2,981			16		5	1	10		8	7	13	14	4	17
S. Alvise	2,466			11	4			4	9	11	21	5	12	21	4
Corpus Domini	2,344	3	8	22	2	4	4	17	8	7	9	7	6	4	1
S. Daniele	2,243			27	1	2	1	13	4	14	7	3	5	13	10
S. Giovanni Evangelista di Torcello	2,213			25	1	3	1	7	9		13	10	7	20	3
S. Caterina di Venezia	1,803		3	43	1		2	3	5		6	5	7	21	3
S. Andrea de Zirada	1,727			42	3		3	7		12	10	5	6		12
SS. Biagio e Cataldo	1,709			20	2			10	8	12	6	8			19
S. Giacomo	1,507			24	7			10	8	13	21	8		15	9
S. Matteo di Mazzorbo	1,454	10	10	38			2	3	11	21			2		3

S. Caterina di Mazzorbo	1,268	2	9	39			10				15	10	4	13	26
S. Anna	1,268		9	32			2				14	2	7	10	33
S. Gerolamo	1,228										8	44		8	4
S. Servolo	1,161			32				4	10	16	2	7		26	2
SS. Cosma e Damiano	1,152			41						13	20	8	5		5
S. Lucia	1,046			29				10		20	16	10		7	11
S. Antonio di Torcello	901			19		4		10	14	9	10	3	8	15	13
S. Marta	884		20	20	1		2		9	9	8	10	2	9	6
S. Eufemia	551		18	22	4		1	13	9	6	10	4	5	3	6
Spirito Santo	461			43	3				9	5	30	12	5		
SS. Rocco e Margherita	428			70					12	18					
S. Croce di Venezia	216										100				
S. Mauro di Burano	166								4		54	18			24
S. Bernardo	162				19				7		25	12	2		35
S. Maria Valverde	141								4		46	18	7		25
S. Martino	115				12						78	9			1
S. Maria dei Miracoli	86										100				
S. Sepolcro	83										100				
SS. Vito e Cipriano	51										90				10
S. Giuseppe	24														
S. Maria Maggiore															
S. Matteo di Murano															
S. Giustina															
SS. Marco e Andrea															

TABLE A8 Supply and Consumption of Wheat and Wine as Recorded in 1564

Convent	Income Per Capita		Consumption Per Capita		Supplements Per Capita		Net Revenue (ducats)
	Wheat (liters)	Wine (liters)	Wheat (liters)	Wine (liters)	Wheat (liters)	Wine (liters)	
S. Zaccaria	2,298	1,065			587		3,275
S. Maria della Celestia	2,261	919				679	−252
S. Giovanni Evangelista di Torcello	1,645	948	347	577			816
S. Antonio di Torcello	1,580	962					707
SS. Cosma e Damiano	1,008	527	540	401			1,319
SS. Biagio e Cataldo	970	495	540	294			413
S. Maria delle Vergini	929	446	577	355			545
S. Chiara di Venezia	740	222					−868
S. Lorenzo	663	299	580	299		382	2,854
S. Eufemia	660	208	522	499		226	−27
S. Mauro di Burano	621	361					324
S. Caterina di Venezia	529	355	487	300		54	−20
S. Daniele	487	249	383	497			−11
S. Servolo	473	287	418	399			780
S. Matteo di Mazzorbo	467	273	442	437	118	133	−8
S. Maria Valverde	464	216	333	251			324
S. Maria degli Angeli	378	24			347	391	−608

S. Anna	357	228					117	111
S. Croce della Giudecca	349	156						−243
S. Andrea de Zirada	341	221	397	343				954
S. Gerolamo	335	160						1,011
S. Alvise	272	52						−947
Corpus Domini	244	186	271	270	39	132		265
S. Caterina di Mazzorbo	216	127			23	117		−380
S. Giacomo	115	87	330	435				−953
SS. Rocco e Margherita	69	24	481	388				189
S. Bernardo	61							76
Spirito Santo	46	35	315	390				−294
S. Croce di Venezia								−21
S. Giuseppe								174
S. Giustina								
S. Lucia								−194
S. Maria Maggiore								
S. Maria dei Miracoli								−6
S. Marta								−187
S. Martino								−41
S. Matteo di Murano								
S. Sepolcro								16
SS. Marco e Andrea								
SS. Vito e Cipriano								13

TABLE A9 The Composition of Revenues, 1564

Cohort	Convent	Total (ducats)	Rents		Other Cash (%)	Wheat (%)	Wine (%)
			Urban (%)	Rural (%)			
1	S. Zaccaria	7,467	53	6	8	24	10
1	S. Lorenzo	6,611	54	2	13	22	9
1	S. Maria della Celestia	4,556	13	13		54	20
1	S. Maria delle Vergini	3,637	15	30	10	32	14
1	S. Maria degli Angeli	3,254		65	14	20	1
1	S. Giovanni Evangelista di Torcello	3,029	13	3	6	52	27
1	S. Croce della Giudecca	2,814	36	1	23	28	11
1	S. Andrea de Zirada	2,681	31		29	26	15
1	Corpus Domini	2,609	50	16	10	14	10
1	SS. Cosma e Damiano	2,471	29	3	5	42	20
2	S. Gerolamo	2,238	41	1	26	23	10
2	S. Daniele	2,232	11	1	35	36	17
2	SS. Biagio e Cataldo	2,122		25	6	47	21
2	S. Chiara di Venezia	2,113	31	3	19	38	10
2	S. Servolo	1,940	43		10	30	16
2	S. Caterina di Venezia	1,783	31	3	7	37	22
2	S. Antonio di Torcello	1,608	11		2	57	31
2	S. Alvise	1,518	61	5	1	29	5

2	S. Matteo di Mazzorbo	1,446	28	1	9	41	21
2	S. Anna	1,379	37	2	15	30	17
3	S. Giustina	1,191	24		19	49	9
3	S. Caterina di Mazzorbo	888	1	44	12	28	15
3	S. Lucia	852	31	3	11	20	39
3	S. Marta	697	2	2	23	50	23
3	SS. Rocco e Margherita	617	43	27	15	11	3
3	S. Giacomo	554	37		25	23	16
3	S. Eufemia	524		3	17	63	18
3	S. Mauro di Burano	490	3	3	5	58	30
3	S. Maria Valverde	465	11	22	5	44	18
3	S. Bernardo	238		42	43	15	
4	S. Giuseppe	198	42	15	42		
4	S. Croce di Venezia	195			100		
4	Spirito Santo	167			67	19	13
4	S. Sepolcro	99	58	26	16		
4	S. Maria dei Miracoli	80			100		
4	S. Martino	74			100		
4	S. Matteo di Murano	68			100		
4	SS. Vito e Cipriano	64	100				
4	S. Maria Maggiore	50			100		
4	SS. Marco e Andrea	42	28			72	

TABLE A10 The Composition of Revenues, 1769

Increase in Rank	Cohort in 1564	Convent	Total (ducats)	Rents		Other Cash (%)	Wheat (%)	Wine (%)
				Urban (%)	Rural (%)			
0	1	S. Zaccaria	23,570	67	6		22	5
0	1	S. Lorenzo	17,770	64	3	2	24	6
0	1	S. Maria della Celestia	14,911	6	53		31	9
1	1	S. Maria degli Angeli	10,932	7	35	2	22	33
−1	1	S. Maria delle Vergini	7,735	18	29		41	13
0	1	S. Giovanni Evangelista di Torcello	7,030	12	4	13	57	14
9	2	S. Caterina di Venezia	6,837	31	20	2	28	19
13	3	S. Giustina	6,018	32	17		43	9
−1	1	S. Andrea de Zirada	5,912	53	2		34	11
−3	1	S. Croce della Giudecca	5,910	34	14	5	36	11
0	2	S. Gerolamo	5,307	59	4	3	24	10
6	2	S. Alvise	5,250	48	19		26	7
1	2	S. Chiara di Venezia	4,891	29	5		52	13
n.a.	n.a.	S. Teresa	4,241	2	98			
−2	2	SS. Biagio e Cataldo	4,179		20		58	22
3	2	S. Matteo di Mazzorbo	3,489	39	11		40	10
20	4	S. Matteo di Murano	3,238		27	3	35	35
−1	2	S. Antonio di Torcello	3,236	3	15	6	62	13

−4	2	S. Servolo	3,172	34			50	15
−8	2	S. Daniele	2,841	18	1		63	16
2	3	S. Lucia	2,785	40	21	1	45	14
−2	2	S. Anna	2,778	49	22	5	42	13
−14	1	Corpus Domini	2,428	17	3	1	34	13
6	3	S. Bernardo	1,798	3	11		55	17
−1	3	S. Marta	1,645	17	5		70	22
n.a.	n.a.	Ognissanti	1,588	9	11	6	45	21
1	3	S. Mauro di Burano	1,498		19	2	57	12
−6	3	S. Caterina di Mazzorbo	1,395	27	93	7		
n.a.	n.a.	S. Giovanni in Laterano	1,338	1	1		60	12
−3	3	S. Eufemia	1,186	21	12		67	21
−2	3	S. Maria Valverde	1,089	14	17		48	14
−6	3	S. Giacomo	1,000	60	17	10	42	17
1	4	S. Sepolcro	964	24	27	13		
−9	3	SS. Rocco e Margherita	890		47		21	8
−3	4	S. Croce di Venezia	626		55	6	37	2
−1	4	S. Maria dei Miracoli	403	100				
−4	4	Spirito Santo	393	44	56		60	
0	4	SS. Vito e Cipriano	251	14	9	6	55	12
1	4	SS. Marco e Andrea	191	6	26	13		
−1	4	S. Maria Maggiore	108		100			
n.a.	n.a.	Convertite	63	13	40	48		

TABLE A11 Increase in Taxable Wealth, 1564–1769

Cohort in 1564	Convent	Total Income (ducats)	Rents (ducats)		Other Cash (ducats)	Fields (ares)	Production (liters)	
			Urban	Rural			Wheat	Wine
1	S. Zaccaria	16,103	11,987	996		-8,915	6,273	4,694
1	S. Lorenzo	11,159	7,839	502	-579	9,256	7,399	13,642
1	S. Maria della Celestia	10,355	349	7,370	49	10,835	-39,173	3,874
1	S. Maria degli Angeli	7,678	786	1,721	-178	71,334	13,288	150,442
2	S. Caterina di Venezia	5,054	1,568	1,311	-6	35,989	2,619	33,141
3	S. Giustina	4,826	1,613	1,007	-195		19,349	16,298
n.a.	*S. Teresa*	*4,241*	*78*	*4,163*		*51,176*		
1	S. Maria delle Vergini	4,098	829	1,107		7,518	574	14,175
1	S. Giovanni Evangelista di Torcello	4,001	477	199	729	-12,053	-5,042	-4,976
2	S. Alvise	3,732	1,577	938		4,093	3,416	11,900
1	S. Andrea de Zirada	3,231	2,291	142	-759	3,667	2,916	3,967
4	S. Matteo di Murano	3,170		883	25	53,633	21,811	48,219
1	S. Croce della Giudecca	3,096	1,014	793	-392	9,945	-167	9,925
2	S. Gerolamo	3,068	2,214	203	-397	3,909	-2,420	9,361
2	S. Chiara di Venezia	2,778	773	210		7,010	8,239	14,712
2	SS. Biagio e Cataldo	2,058		321		518	-5,469	11,786
2	S. Matteo di Mazzorbo	2,043	947	379	-133	677	-3,582	-3,462
3	S. Lucia	1,932	246	589	-74	14,331	15,412	-2,524
2	S. Antonio di Torcello	1,628	-70	481	174	3,849	-8,331	-10,674
n.a.	*Ognissanti*	*1,588*	*268*	*178*	*88*	*9,750*	*13,964*	*14,188*
3	S. Bernardo	1,560	313	90		6,924	17,495	12,631

2	S. Anna	1,399	620			−83	1,166	1,731
n.a.	*S. Giovanni in Laterano*	*1,338*	*356*	*15*	*−78*	*7,881*	*15,662*	*6,707*
2	S. Servolo	1,231	239	47		−3,719	−250	1,515
3	S. Mauro di Burano	1,008	128	274	7		1,500	−786
3	S. Marta	948	45	67		2,015	3,999	5,842
4	S. Sepolcro	865	519	238	108	3,228		
3	S. Eufemia	662	8	125		−366	−1,791	5,020
3	S. Maria Valverde	624	180	77		−219	−500	1,515
2	S. Daniele	609		564		465	−7,481	−2,344
3	S. Caterina di Mazzorbo	507		903	−6	4,466		
3	S. Giacomo	447	−61	168	−33	−528	1,399	2,188
4	S. Croce di Venezia	431		342	−156	6,259	4,549	440
4	S. Maria dei Miracoli	323	403					
3	**SS. Rocco e Margherita**	**273**	**−50**	**246**		**7,696**	**89**	**1,659**
4	**Spirito Santo**	**225**	**173**	**220**		**−939**	**−941**	
4	*SS. Vito e Cipriano*	*187*	*−30*	*21*	*14*		*2,916*	*1,298*
4	SS. Marco e Andrea	149	−1	50	25	−402	458	
n.a.	*Convertite*	*63*	*8*	*25*	*30*			
4	S. Maria Maggiore	58		108		2,082		
1	Corpus Domini	−181	−100	−346	−241	−669	−3,416	−1,947
4	**S. Martino**							
4	**S. Giuseppe**							
1	**SS. Cosma e Damiano**							

Note: Italics—no entry for 1564; bold—no entry for 1769.

TABLE A12 Percentage Increase in Taxable Wealth, 1564–1769

Cohort in 1564	Convent	Total Income	Rents		Other Cash	Surface Area of Fields	Production of	
			Urban	Rural			Wheat	Wine
4	S. Matteo di Murano	4,662			36			
4	S. Sepolcro	876	911	915	682			
3	S. Bernardo	655		90		211	955	
3	S. Giustina	405	568		−87		64	272
4	S. Maria dei Miracoli	404				−61	29	
4	SS. Marco e Andrea	351	−8					
4	SS. Vito e Cipriano	294	−46					
2	S. Caterina di Venezia	284	287	2,621	−5	143	8	144
2	S. Alvise	246	171	1,272		27	15	275
1	S. Maria degli Angeli	236		81	−40	276	39	6,953
1	S. Maria della Celestia	227	58	1,256	−77	14	−30	7
3	S. Lucia	227	93	2,356	−80	215	178	−13
4	S. Croce di Venezia	221						
1	S. Zaccaria	216	306	207		−16	7	11
3	S. Mauro di Burano	205	914	1,709	28		10	−9
1	S. Lorenzo	169	219	456	−66	23	10	40

2	S. Matteo di Mazzorbo	141	234	4,739	-99	2	-12	-19
2	S. Gerolamo	137	243	1,194	-69	21	-9	73
3	S. Marta	136	375	394		17	22	62
4	Spirito Santo	135				-42	-56	
3	S. Maria Valverde	134	360	74		-3	-5	30
1	S. Giovanni Evangelista di Torcello	132	121	251	434	-27	-6	-11
2	S. Chiara di Venezia	131	119	383		25	20	119
3	S. Eufemia	126		873		-4	-10	93
1	S. Andrea de Zirada	121	279	7,340	-98	21	8	17
4	S. Maria Maggiore	116						
1	S. Maria delle Vergini	113	156	100		20	1	49
1	S. Croce della Giudecca	110	100	2,204	-59	40		54
2	S. Anna	101	123		-38	-1	5	13
2	S. Antonio di Torcello	101	-39		681	11	-18	-37
2	SS. Biagio e Cataldo	97		61		2	-10	44
3	S. Giacomo	81	-30		-24	-11	21	43
2	S. Servolo	63	29			-22	-1	8
3	S. Caterina di Mazzorbo	57		230	-6	33		
3	SS. Rocco e Margherita	44	-19	146		882	2	135
2	S. Daniele	27		2,820		2	-18	-11
1	Corpus Domini	-7	-8	-85	-88	-5	-18	-13

Notes

Introduction

1. Herodotus, *The Histories,* ed. Walter Blanco and Jennifer Tolbert Roberts (New York, 1992), p. 142.

2. "Eglino [i nobili Veneziani] . . . sono lo stato medesimo." Marco Ferro, "Nobiltà," in *Dizionario del diritto comune e veneto,* 2d ed., vol. 2 (Venice, 1845), p. 325. Unless otherwise noted, all translations of quotations from works in foreign languages are my own.

3. Gerhard Rösch, *Der venezianische Adel bis zur Schliessung des Grossen Rats: Zur Genese einer Führungsschicht* (Sigmaringen, 1989), pp. 172–79. In contrast to the Florentine ruling class—a rather broad, open, and volatile elite, as Anthony Molho's recent study has shown—access to the Venetian patriciate was legally defined. Anthony Molho, *Marriage Alliance in Late Medieval Florence* (Cambridge, Mass., 1994).

4. Stanley Chojnacki, "Social Identity in Renaissance Venice: The Second *Serrata,*" *Renaissance Studies* 8, no. 4 (1994): 341–58.

5. From the perspective of the patriciate, marrying "out" was practically synonymous with marrying "down."

6. "Duemille e più Nobili . . . in questa Città vivono rinserite nei monasterij come quasi in publico deposito." Emilio Zanette translated "deposito" as "tomba" in his *Suor Arcangela monaca del Seicento veneziano* (Venice, 1960), p. 36. For the notion of nuns as "dead" to the world in particular, and the phenomenon of high monachization rates among Florentine upper-class women in general, see Anthony Molho, "Tamquam vere mortua: Le professioni religiose femminili nella Firenze del tardo Medioevo," *Società e Storia* 43 (1989): 1–44.

7. "Riflettendo in me stesso come esse siano nobili, allevate e nodrite con somma delicatezza et rispetto, che se fossero d'altro sesso ad esse toccarebbe il comandare e governare il Mondo . . . che si sono confinate fra

quelle mura, non per spirito di devotione ma per impulso dei loro, facendo della propria libertà . . . un dono non solo a Dio, ma anco alla Patria, al Mondo, et alli loro più stretti parenti." "Scriptura R.mi D.i Patriarchae," Museo Civico Correr (MCC), Codex Cicogna (CC) 2570, ff. 299–304; Zanette, *Suor Arcangela,* p. 36.

8. In a recent article, Gabriella Zarri has shown that forced vocations were by no means an exclusively female problem. Gabriella Zarri, "Gender, Religious Institutions, and Social Discipline: The Reform of the Regulars," in *Gender and Society in Renaissance Italy,* ed. Judith C. Brown and Robert C. Davis (Essex, 1998), pp. 193–212.

9. For a historical precedent of those "patriotic" sacrifices of virgin women to which Tiepolo might have been alluding, see Joan B. Connelly, "Parthenon and *Parthenoi:* A Mythological Interpretation of the Parthenon Frieze," *American Journal of Archaeology* 100 (1996): 53–80.

10. Among the most recent examples are Stanley Chojnacki, "Daughters and Oligarchs: Gender and the Early Renaissance State," in *Gender and Society in Renaissance Italy,* ed. Brown and Davis, p. 70; Molho, *Marriage Alliance,* p. 308; and Richard Trexler, "Celibacy in the Renaissance: The Nuns of Florence," in *Dependence in Context in Renaissance Florence,* ed. Richard Trexler (Binghamton, N.Y., 1994), p. 369.

11. In addition, women were accused of having caused the illegal growth of mortmain properties: since the dowry inflation forced many girls to enter convents, women's dowries contributed indirectly to the uncontrolled growth of church properties, that is, the withdrawal of real estate from the sphere of taxation and circulation—an obviously false allegation, because mortmain laws severely restricted the acquisition of real estate by the church, and because convent fees had been paid in the form of a yearly annuity since the beginning of the seventeenth century. Vettor Sandi, *Principj di storia civile della Repubblica di Venezia dalla sua fondazione sino all'anno di N.S. 1700,* pt. 3, vol. 2 (Venice, 1756), pp. 1086–87; Marino Berengo, *La società veneta alla fine del Settecento* (Florence, 1956), p. 90.

12. Stanley Chojnacki, "Dowries and Kinsmen in Early Renaissance Venice," *Journal of Interdisciplinary History* 5, no. 4 (1975): 571–600.

13. Diane Owen Hughes, "From Brideprice to Dowry in Mediterranean Europe," *Journal of Family History* 3 (1978): 262–96; James Q. Whitman, "The Lawyers Discover the Fall of Rome," *Law and History Review* 9, no. 2 (1991): 191–220.

14. Gene Brucker, ed., *Two Memoirs of Renaissance Florence: The Diaries of Buonaccorso Pitti and Gregorio Dati* (Prospect Heights, 1967).

15. On so-called clandestine marriages in pre-Tridentine Europe, see, among others, Gene Brucker, *Giovanni and Lusanna: Love and Marriage in Renaissance Florence* (Berkeley, 1986); and Ludwig Schmugge, *Kirche Kinder Karrieren* (Zurich, 1995), p. 192. For early modern England, see Lawrence Stone, *Uncertain Unions: Marriage in England, 1660–1753* (Oxford, 1992); and R. B. Outhwaite, *Clandestine Marriage in England, 1500–1850* (London, 1995).

16. Among the Germanic populations of early medieval Europe, the

morgengabe was paid by the groom to the bride in exchange for her virginity, while the brideprice went to the bride's father as compensation for his loss of legal authority over his daughter. Diane Owen Hughes, "Riti di passaggio nell'Occidente medievale," in *Storia d'Europa*, vol. 3, *Il Medioevo* (Turin, 1995), pp. 1014–17.

17. In this respect I disagree with Christine Klapisch-Zuber, who argued that the reciprocity of dowry exchange was constituted by the groom's gifts to the bride. Christine Klapisch-Zuber, "The Griselda Complex: Dowry and Marriage Gifts in the Quattrocento," in *Women, Family, and Ritual in Renaissance Italy* (Chicago, 1985), pp. 213–46.

18. Although the declining birthrate also reduced the number of grooms in the following generation, one cannot in the same sense speak of a "bride shortage," because patrician men were allowed to marry honorable nonpatrician women, while marriages between patrician women and citizens or commoners were extremely rare. See chapter 1.

19. Volker Hunecke, *Der venezianische Adel am Ende der Republik (1646–1797): Demographie, Familie, Haushalt* (Tübingen, 1995).

20. This first major *aggregazione* (addition) of new families into the patriciate since the late fifteenth century happened between 1646 and 1669. Ibid., app. 1, pp. 357–58, 383.

21. Hughes, "Riti di passaggio," p. 1018.

22. Marcel Mauss, *The Gift: The Form and Reason for Exchange in Archaic Societies* (New York, 1990; first ed. [in French]: 1925), p. 5.

23. See also Jacques Derrida's recent interpretation of a text by Baudelaire on the giving of alms, entitled *Given Time: I. Counterfeit Money* (Chicago, 1992).

24. Claude Lévi-Strauss, *The Elementary Structures of Kinship* (London, 1969; first ed. [in French]: Paris, 1949), p. 65.

25. Lévi-Strauss distinguished between prescriptive marriages—that is, systems in which the incest prohibition translates into the designation of a particular relative as spouse, such as matrilineal cross-cousins—and generalized exchange, that is, systems in which all unmarried women within a particular group who do not stand in a particular kinship relationship to the groom are available to him.

26. Lévi-Strauss hypothesized the following cycle of exchange (capital letters indicate male gender): A > b; B > c; C > a; a > B; b > C; c > A.

27. This phenomenon was reported as recently as 1966 by sociologists who investigated social mobility in Britain. Mary Douglas, *The World of Goods* (New York, 1979), pp. 86–87.

28. Nonetheless, I do not agree with Trevor Dean and Kate Lowe's assessment that Lévi-Strauss's structural analysis of the reciprocal giving of brides "both ignores and objectifies women." It is the practice of bridal exchange, not Lévi-Strauss's analysis of it, that has this effect. Introduction to *Marriage in Italy, 1300–1600,* ed. Trevor Dean and Kate Lowe (Cambridge, 1998), p. 19.

29. See, most recently, Joanne Ferraro, "The Power to Decide: Battered Wives in Early Modern Venice," *Renaissance Quarterly* 48, no. 3 (1995):

492–512; Virginia Cox, "The Single Self: Feminist Thought and the Marriage Market in Early Modern Venice," ibid., pp. 513–81; Stanley Chojnacki, "Nobility, Women, and the State: Marriage Regulation in Venice, 1420–1535," in *Marriage in Italy,* ed. Dean and Lowe, p. 136; Judith C. Brown, "Monache a Firenze all'inizio dell'età moderna: Un' analisi demografica," *Quaderni Storici* 85, no. 1 (1994): 117–52.

30. It was often remarked, for example, that Venice was the most stable and secure city of Europe, despite the fact that it was built in water and unprotected by city walls. See chapter 2.

31. *Squitinio della libertà veneta nel quale si adducono anche le raggioni dell'impero Romano sopra la Città & Signoria di Venetia* ([Mirandola?], 1612); Tommaso Campanella, *Antiveneti,* ed. Luigi Firpo (Florence, 1945; written in 1606).

32. On semi-secular institutes for women, see Luisa Ciammitti, "Quanto costa essere normali: La dote nel conservatorio femminile di Santa Maria del Baraccano (1630–1680)," *Quaderni Storici* 53, no. 2 (1983): 469–97; Lucia Ferrante, "L'onore ritrovato: Donne nella Casa del Soccorso di San Paolo a Bologna (sec. XVI–XVII)," ibid., pp. 499–527; idem, " 'Malmaritate' tra assistenza e punizione (Bologna, secc. XVI–XVII)," in *Forme e soggetti dell'intervento assistenziale in una città di antico regime: Atti del 4. colloquio, Bologna, 20–21 gennaio 1984,* vol. 2, ed. Paolo Prodi (Bologna, 1986), pp. 65–109; and Sherrill Cohen, *The Evolution of Women's Asylums since 1500* (New York, 1992). On similar institutes in Venice specifically, see Flaminio Corner, *Notizie storiche delle chiese e monasteri di Venezia e di Torcello* (Bologna, 1990; first ed.: Padua, 1758). On the Casa delle Zitelle in Venice, see Monica Chojnacka, "Women, Charity, and Community in Early Modern Venice: The Casa delle Zitelle," *Renaissance Quarterly* 51, no. 1 (1998): 68–91.

33. Judith Brown has shown that sex between women was rarely prosecuted, although it was defined as a serious crime in the Middle Ages and the early modern period. Judith C. Brown, *Immodest Acts: The Life of a Lesbian Nun in Renaissance Italy* (Oxford, 1986).

34. On Venetian convents, see Fernanda Sorelli, "Per la storia religiosa di Venezia nella prima metà del quattrocento: Inizi e sviluppi del terz'ordine domenicano," in *Viridarium Floridum: Studi di storia veneta offerti dagli allievi a Paolo Sambin,* ed. Maria Chiara Billanovich et al. (Padua, 1984), pp. 89–114; Maria Pia Pedani, "Monasteri di Agostiniane a Venezia," *Archivio Veneto,* 5th ser., 122–25 (1984–85): 35–78; idem, "L'osservanza imposta: I monasteri conventuali femminili a Venezia nei primi anni del cinquecento," ibid., 179 (1995): 113–25; and Francesca Medioli, ed. *L'inferno monacale di Suor Arcangela Tarabotti* (Turin, 1990).

Chapter One

1. Anthony Molho, "Tamquam vere mortua: Le professioni religiose femminili nella Firenze del tardo Medioevo," *Società e Storia* 43 (1989): 1–44; Richard Trexler, "Le célibat à la fin du Moyen Age: Les religieuses de Florence," *Annales E.S.C.* 27 (1972): 1329–50; idem, "Celibacy in the Re-

naissance: The Nuns of Florence," in *Dependence in Context in Renaissance Florence,* ed. Richard Trexler (Binghamton, N.Y., 1994), pp. 343–72.

2. Dante E. Zanetti, *La demografia del patriziato milanese nei secoli XVII, XVIII, XIX* (Pavia, 1972).

3. Volker Hunecke, *Der venezianische Adel am Ende der Republik (1646–1797): Demographie, Familie, Haushalt* (Tübingen, 1995); Anthony Molho, *Marriage Alliance in Late Medieval Florence* (Cambridge, Mass., 1994); Maria Antonetta Visceglia, *Il bisogno dell' eternità: I comportamenti aristocratici a Napoli in età moderna* (Naples, 1988); Gérard Delille, "Strategie di alleanza e demografia del matrimonio," in *Storia del matrimonio,* ed. Michela De Giorgio and Christine Klapisch-Zuber (Bari, 1996), pp. 283–303; idem, *Famille et propriété dans le Royaume de Naples* (Paris, 1985).

4. Gabriella Zarri, "Monasteri femminili e città (secoli XV–XVIII)," in *Storia d'Italia,* annali 9, *La Chiesa e il potere politico dal Medioevo all'età contemporanea,* ed. Giorgio Chittolini and G. Miccoli (Turin, 1986), pp. 357–429.

5. See also Kate Lowe, "Secular Brides and Convent Brides: Wedding Ceremonies in Italy during the Renaissance and Counter-Reformation," in *Marriage in Italy, 1300–1600,* ed. Trevor Dean and Kate Lowe (Cambridge, 1998), pp. 41–65.

6. Volker Hunecke, "Kindbett oder Kloster: Lebenswege venezianischer Patrizierinnen im 17. und 18. Jahrhundert," *Geschichte und Gesellschaft* 18 (1992): 446–76.

7. R. Burr Litchfield, "Demographic Characteristics of Florentine Patrician Families, Sixteenth to Nineteenth Centuries," *Journal of Economic History* 29, no. 2 (1969): 191–205; Zanetti, *La demografia del patriziato milanese.*

8. Hunecke, *Der venezianische Adel,* pp. 153–54.

9. Thomas H. Hollingsworth, "The Demography of the British Peerage," supplement to *Population Studies* 18, no. 2 (1964). Molho mentions that John Cannon calculated endogamy rates of 60 to 72 percent among the British peerage for the eighteenth century. Molho, *Marriage Alliance,* p. 14.

10. Molho, *Marriage Alliance,* p. 288.

11. Hollingsworth, "Demography of the British Peerage," p. 9, table 1; Molho, *Marriage Alliance,* p. 288.

12. Archivio Patriarchale di Venezia (APV), Archivio "Segreto," Santa Maria Formosa, registri di matrimoni, regg. 1–5 (1569–1640). My findings are in direct contradiction to Hunecke's opinion that "it was very common in the seventeenth and eighteenth centuries, but also earlier, for daughters of patricians to marry men who did not belong to their estate." Unfortunately, Hunecke does not provide any numerical evidence to support his claim. His lack of interest in the question of women's marriage behavior might result from his claim—erroneous, in my view—that "the frequency of patrician women's celibacy did not have the slightest influence on the size of the Venetian aristocratic population. For one became a Venetian patrician by birth only if one's creator belonged to this state; the mother's social status was for that matter absolutely irrelevant." Hunecke, *Der venezianische Adel,* p. 102.

13. Lorenzo Fabbri, *Alleanza matrimoniale e patriziato nella Firenze del '400* (Florence, 1991), p. 39.

14. Hunecke, *Der venezianische Adel,* p. 391, table 12.

15. Ibid., p. 34; p. 381, table 2. Aggregations on a smaller scale had continued until the late fifteenth century.

16. "I poveri nobili si moltiplicano, tutti si maritano, tutti figliano. Nei ricchi rarissime volte più d'uno per casa [si sposa?] per conservar indivisibile il patrimonio, per esser sempre potenti di ricchezze." Ibid., p. 11.

17. Visceglia, *Il bisogno dell' eternità,* p. 64; Delille, "Strategie di alleanza," p. 295; Litchfield, "Demographic Characteristics," p. 198.

18. Hunecke, *Der venezianische Adel,* pp. 267–68.

19. Ibid., p. 112; p. 391, table 12; p. 392, table 13. Fifteen percent of all marriages concluded by patrician men between 1646 and 1797 were not registered with the Avogadori di Comun (state attorneys). Most of these unregistered marriages were secret, and most of the secret marriages remained unregistered.

20. For an introduction to the rich historiography on "secret" and "clandestine" marriages and the contradictions between secular and ecclesiastical marriage law, see De Giorgio and Klapisch-Zuber, *Storia del matrimonio,* especially the contributions by Diane Owen Hughes and Daniela Lombardi.

21. APV, Archivio "Segreto," Matrimoni segreti, busta 1.

22. Fabbri, *Alleanza matrimoniale,* p. 117; Molho, *Marriage Alliance,* p. 226.

23. Fabbri, *Alleanza matrimoniale,* p. 195.

24. See Gene Brucker, ed., "The Diary of Gregorio Dati," in *Two Memoirs of Renaissance Florence: The Diaries of Buonaccorso Pitti and Gregorio Dati* (Prospect Heights, 1967).

25. Christine Klapisch-Zuber, "The Griselda Complex: Dowry and Marriage Gifts in the Quattrocento," in *Women, Family, and Ritual in Renaissance Italy* (Chicago, 1985), pp. 213–46; Isabelle Chabot, " 'La Sposa in Nero': La ritualizzazione del lutto delle vedove fiorentine (secoli XIV–XV)," *Quaderni Storici* 86, no. 2 (1994): 421–62.

26. Mario Biagioli, *Galileo, Courtier: The Practice of Science in the Culture of Absolutism* (Chicago, 1993); see also Paula Findlen, *Possessing Nature: Museums, Collecting, and Scientific Culture in Early Modern Italy* (Berkeley, 1996).

27. Marcel Mauss, *The Gift: The Form and Reason for Exchange in Archaic Societies* (New York, 1990; first ed. [in French]: 1925), p. 65.

28. "Percioche a gli honorati Cittadini, i quali hanno il governo della Città, giudico non solo esser convenevole, ch'essi habbiano le case & stanze commode, ma piu tosto palagi honorevoli ampi & magnifici, & ne i siti piu commodi & degni della Città: si per commodità loro, come per ornamento di questa. Siano adunque tai palagi piu magnifici & honorati, che si puo." *Dialogo del Magn. Cavaliere M. Gio. Maria Memmo, nel quale dopo alcune filosofiche dispute, si forma un perfetto Prencipe, & una perfetta Republica, e parimente un Senatore, un Cittadino, un Soldato, & un Mercatante* (Ven-

ice, 1563), p. 79. "Giudico degni di non poca riprensione quei Cittadini, che spendono il suo in ornamenti & pompe soverchie, cosi nel fabricare, & molto piu in altri ornamenti si delle case & camere loro, coprendo i cieli di finissime pitture, ornate di molto oro, fornimenti di letti, & tapezzarie di seta & d'oro, & d'altre vanità e peggio; spendendo in un convito quello che basteria a nutrir le famiglie loro per un'anno, con ruina di esse famiglie. Il che non solo è dannoso a' Cittadini, & famiglie private, ma corrompe le Città: percioche da tali essempi mossi molti, i quali non hanno il modo per poter fare il medesimo, & venire a tal segno, si fanno licito a fare ogni male per acquistar danari da poter sodisfar le voglie loro in simili cose, & finalmente tal corruttele sono la ruina non solo de' privati Cittadini, ma delle Città & Republiche, dove sono permesse tai cose." Ibid., p. 73.

29. "La Magnificenza . . . come è nobile virtù . . . non ha occasione di spesso dimostrarsi; ma in quelle cose solamente si adopera, le quali rare volte si fanno; come sono i conviti, le nozze, le fabriche; ove conviensi spendere senza havere consideratione alla spesa, ma solamente alla grandezza, & alla bellezza dell'opra." Paolo Paruta, *Della perfettione della vita politica* (Venice, 1599; 1st ed.: 1579), p. 282.

30. See Jacopo Morelli, *Delle solennità e pompe nuziali già usate presso li Viniziani, pubblicata nelle nozze di S. E. il Signor Giovanni Almorò Tiepolo con la nobile Signora Marianna Gradenigo* (Venice, 1793), p. 2.

31. The term *serrata* refers to the transformation of the members of the Great Council into a hereditary ruling class. It is commonly believed to have occurred, or begun, in 1297.

32. The *barbarella* was an annual lottery whose winners could enter the Great Council before they reached the legal age of twenty-five.

33. In my opinion, the many unsuccessful attempts to reduce dowries by imposing ceilings on spending might have had the opposite effect—of defining minimum amounts for what could pass as an appropriate patrician dowry.

34. Stanley Chojnacki, "Social Identity in Renaissance Venice: The Second *Serrata,*" *Renaissance Studies* 8, no. 4 (1994): 341–58.

35. Pompeo Molmenti, *La Dogaressa di Venezia* (Turin, 1884), pp. 110–13.

36. Chojnacki, "Social Identity," p. 350.

37. This development culminated in the marriage laws of 1506 and 1526, according to which every patrician marriage had to be registered with the Avogadori di Comun in the so-called Golden Book. Only sons of registered marriages had access to the Great Council, and the family background of nonpatrician brides was scrutinized closely by the Avogadori di Comun. See, among others, Hunecke, *Der venezianische Adel,* p. 31; and Stanley Chojnacki, "Marriage Legislation and Patrician Society in Fifteenth-Century Venice," in *Law, Custom, and the Social Fabric in Medieval Europe: Essays in Honor of Bryce Lyon,* ed. Bernard S. Bachrach and David Nicholas (Kalamazoo, Mich., 1990), pp. 163–84, esp. 170.

38. Dennis Romano, *Patricians and Popolani* (Baltimore, 1987), pp. 34–35.

39. As the most recent example, see Molho, *Marriage Alliance,* p. 308.

40. Ibid., p. 226; Fabbri, *Alleanza matrimoniale,* p. 117.

41. My proposal to analyze the rising rates of coerced monachization in late Renaissance Venice as a potlatch might answer the question Sharon Kettering posed in her article on reciprocal gift-giving in French patronage systems, where she wondered "in what other contexts and for what other purposes this behavior occurred." Sharon Kettering, "Gift-Giving and Patronage in Early Modern France," *French History* 2, no. 2 (1988): 151. See also the groundbreaking article by Natalie Zemon Davis, "Beyond the Market: Books as Gifts in Sixteenth-Century France," *Transactions of the Royal Historical Society,* 5th ser., 33 (1983): 69–87.

42. On sixteenth- and seventeenth-century theories of nobility, see Claudio Donati, *L'idea della nobiltà in Italia: Secoli XIV–XVII* (Bari, 1988).

43. Sara Cabibbo and Marilena Modica, *La Santa dei Tomasi: Storia di Suor Maria Crocefissa (1645–1699)* (Turin, 1989); Sara Cabibbo, "La santità femminile dinastica," in *Donne e fede: Santità e vita religiosa in Italia,* ed. Lucetta Scaraffia and Gabriella Zarri (Bari, 1994), pp. 399–418; Elisa Novi Chavarria, "Nobiltà di seggio, nobiltà nuova e monasteri femminili a Napoli in età moderna," *Dimensioni e Problemi della Ricerca Storica* 2 (1993): 84–111.

44. Cabibbo and Modica, *La Santa dei Tomasi.*

45. Silvio Tramontin, "La visita apostolica del 1581 à Venezia," *Studi Veneziani* 9 (1967): 480. Tramontin describes the conflict that arose between the papacy and the Republic of Venice after Nuncio Alberto Bolognetti insisted that Venetian convents had to be inspected by apostolic visitors in 1581.

46. Patriarch Giovanni Tiepolo, quoted in Emilio Zanette, *Suor Arcangela monaca del Seicento veneziano* (Venice, 1960), p. 36.

47. Hunecke, "Kindbett oder Kloster." With respect to age differences between spouses in Renaissance Florence, see David Herlihy and Christine Klapisch-Zuber, *Tuscans and Their Families* (New Haven, 1985).

48. Elisja Schulte van Kessel, "Virgins and Mothers between Heaven and Earth," in *A History of Women in the West,* ed. Georges Duby and Michelle Perrot, vol. 3, *Renaissance and Enlightenment Paradoxes,* ed. Natalie Zemon Davis and Arlette Farge (Cambridge, Mass., 1993), p. 155; Hunecke, "Kindbett oder Kloster."

49. Judith C. Brown, "Monache a Firenze all'inizio dell'età moderna: Un' analisi demografica," *Quaderni Storici* 85, no. 1 (1994): 117–52.

50. Katherine Gill, "Open Monasteries for Women in Late Medieval and Early Modern Italy: Two Roman Examples," in *The Crannied Wall: Women, Religion, and the Arts in Early Modern Europe,* ed. Craig A. Monson (Ann Arbor, Mich., 1992), pp. 15–47.

51. Claudia Opitz, *Frauenalltag im Mittelalter: Biographien des 13. und 14. Jahrhunderts* (Weinheim, Germany, 1985); Jane Tibbetts Schulenburg, "The Heroics of Virginity: Brides of Christ and Sacrificial Mutilation," in *Women in the Middle Ages and the Renaissance: Literary and Historical Perspectives,* ed. Mary Beth Rose (Syracuse, 1986), pp. 29–72.

52. See introduction, n. 6.

53. Because of this difficulty, the law was modified so that such no-blemen could be elected; but they were not supposed to intervene in convents where their daughters, sisters, nieces, or cousins were nuns. In such cases, members of the Magistrato contro la Bestemmia (Magistrate against Curs-ing) and the Magistrato sopra le Heresie (Magistrate against Heresies) were supposed to assist. "Et perche le leze per li quali è disposto circa quelli che si cazzano ut supra, sono state poste, quando essi sopra li Monasterij havev-ano la cura delli Monasterij riformati solamente nelli quali era facil cosa che non si trovassero Monache congionte a Nobeli Nostri eletti à tal carico, il che hora che ad essi Nobili per la parte ultima è stata data la cura de tutti li Monasterij della Città, et del Ducato, è quasi impossibile che sia." Council of Ten, 12 April 1553, Archivio di Stato di Venezia (ASV), Provveditori sopra i Monasteri di Monache (PsM), capitolari, reg. 1, c. 26r.

54. The category of *monache* as used in the censuses of 1581 and 1642 included *converse* (servant nuns), novices, and professed nuns. There was a separate category of *pizzochere*—third-order nuns, who lived in indepen-dent women's communities and were loosely affiliated with a parish priest who took care of their spiritual needs. *Pizzochere* took only "simple" vows; that is, they were not irrevocably bound to a life in perpetual seclusion and obedience to a formal monastic order. They typically entered a religious community at an older age than "professional" *monache da ufficio,* often as widows. *Converse* had, from the point of view of canonical law, a status similar to that of the *pizzochere*. They made up about one-quarter to one-third of the population of the convents, where they lived and worked as servants of the professed nuns. According to the Tridentine decrees, novices were allowed to take their holy vows at the minimum age of sixteen, after they had passed a year of probation. At age twenty-five, professed nuns be-came consecrated and were conceded the passive and active vote in the chapter.

55. The percentage of nuns who were patricians seems to have been highest between 1600 and 1650. Convents that were exclusively or predomi-nantly aristocratic recorded a remarkable "population increase" in the early seventeenth century—a trend that declined a generation later. According to my estimates, the percentage of patrician women who were nuns rose from 54 percent in 1581 to 82 percent in 1642. The latter figure, especially, is unrealistically high, but since both numbers are inferred from comparable source material, I use them to indicate a clear trend. It is probably safe to say that the percentage of nuns among patrician women lay well above 60 percent in the first half of the seventeenth century—especially if one consid-ers that the poorer noble families sent their daughters to convents on the *terraferma,* which are not included in my estimates. See Hunecke, "Kindbett oder Kloster." For Florence, R. Burr Litchfield came up with comparably high numbers; see Litchfield, "Demographic Characteristics." On nuns in Florence, see Molho, "Tamquam vere mortua"; and Trexler, "Le célibat à la fin du Moyen Age."

56. See the discussion earlier in this chapter. On female marriage behav-

ior in the fifteenth century, see Chojnacki, "Marriage Legislation"; for the later period, see Alexander Francis Cowan, *The Urban Patriciate: Lübeck and Venice, 1580–1700* (Cologne, 1986).

57. Note that the comparison is made between brides and nuns already living in convents, which distorts the comparison in favor of the number of nuns. Unfortunately, the records did not contain the information required for a comparison between brides and novices, or between wives and nuns.

58. See the discussion earlier in this chapter; see also Volker Hunecke, "Matrimonio e demografia del patriziato veneziano (secc. XVII–XVIII)," *Studi Veneziani* 21 (1991): 269–319, esp. 299.

59. Molho, "Tamquam vere mortua," p. 6.

60. Among others, see Zarri, "Monasteri femminili e città," pp. 357–429, esp. 361–65; and idem, "Aspetti dello sviluppo degli Ordini religiosi in Italia tra Quattro e Cinquecento: Studi e problemi," in *Strutture ecclesiastiche in Italia e in Germania prima della Riforma,* ed. Paolo Prodi and Peter Johanek (Bologna, 1984), pp. 207–58, esp. 232–35.

61. Most of the nunneries established between 1437 and 1505 were located in the city of Venice—in contrast to earlier centuries, when the preferred site for nunneries was the upper lagoon. Flaminio Corner, *Notizie storiche delle chiese e monasteri di Venezia e di Torcello* (Padua, 1758).

62. On the popularity of communities of *pizzochere,* or *bizzoche,* in fifteenth-century Italy, see Gill, "Open Monasteries"; and Jo Ann Kay McNamara, *Sisters in Arms: Catholic Nuns through Two Millennia* (Cambridge, 1996), pp. 385–418.

63. Among these institutions for women at risk, only Santa Maria Maddalena, also called Le Convertite, was founded as a proper convent, in 1525. It served as a refuge for former prostitutes. The other institutions for former prostitutes and spinsters were Santa Maria del Soccorso—whose foundation in 1578 was promoted by Veronica Franco, poet and famous courtesan—and Santa Maria delle Zitelle, founded in 1559. See Margaret F. Rosenthal, *The Honest Courtesan: Veronica Franco, Citizen and Writer in Sixteenth-Century Venice* (Chicago, 1992), p. 131.

64. On post-Tridentine female orders, see Joseph Grisar, " 'Jesuitinnen': Ein Beitrag zur Geschichte des weiblichen Ordenswesens von 1550–1650," in *Reformata Reformanda, Festschrift für Hubert Jedin zum 17. Juni 1964,* vol. 2 (Münster, 1965), pp. 70–113; idem, *Maria Wards Institut vor Römischen Kongregationen, 1613–30* (Rome, 1966); Anne Conrad, "Ordensfrauen ohne Klausur? Die katholische Frauenbewegung an der Wende zum 17. Jahrhundert," *Feministische Studien* 1 (1986): 31–45; idem, *Zwischen Kloster und Welt: Ursulinen und Jesuitinnen in der katholischen Reformbewegung des 16./17. Jahrhunderts* (Mainz, 1991); Elizabeth Rapley, *The Dévotes: Women and Church in Seventeenth-Century France* (Montreal, 1990); and Natalie Zemon Davis, "New Worlds: Marie de l'Incarnation," in *Women on the Margins: Three Seventeenth-Century Lives* (Cambridge, Mass., 1995), pp. 63–139.

65. On the foundation of convents in the dioceses of Venice and Torcello, see Flaminio Corner (Cornarus, Cornaro, Cornelius), *Ecclesiae Vene-*

tae antiquis monumentis nunc etiam primum editis illustratae ac in decades distributae, 13 vols. along with *Supplementa ad Ecclesiae Venetas et Torcellanas* (Venice, 1749) and the abbreviated version in Italian, *Notizie storiche delle chiese e monasteri di Venezia e di Torcello,* pp. 89–114; Fernanda Sorelli, "Per la storia religiosa di Venezia nella prima metà del quattrocento: Inizi e sviluppi del terz'ordine domenicano," in *Viridarium Floridum: Studi di storia veneta offerti dagli allievi a Paolo Sambin,* ed. Maria Chiara Billanovich et al. (Padua, 1984), pp. 89–114; Maria Pia Pedani, "Monasteri di Agostiniane a Venezia," *Archivio Veneto,* 5th ser., 122–25 (1984–85): 35–78; and Victoria Primhak, "Women in Religious Communities: The Benedictine Convents of Venice, 1400–1500" (Ph.D. diss., University of London, 1991). In my study, I have disregarded the nunneries in Chioggia and on the Lido, where some Venetian noblewomen might have lived, and concentrated on the city of Venice and the islands of the upper lagoon, that is, Murano, Burano, Mazzorbo, and Torcello.

66. The city's two most prestigious convents were San Zaccaria and San Lorenzo; in 1602 San Zaccaria accepted thirty-three novices, and in 1610 San Lorenzo accepted thirty-five. ASV, Senato Deliberazioni Roma Ordinaria, reg. 18 (1610–12), fascicolo 33; 3, 4, 6 May 1610.

67. During his visitation on 1 September 1565, Patriarch Giovanni Trevisan threatened the chapter of Santa Caterina with excommunication if it continued to reject citizen nuns: "We have heard . . . that you . . . have turned down applications from citizens who wanted . . . to place their daughters as nuns in your convent, for no other reason than that you only want to admit . . . patricians, . . . despite the fact that there have always been . . . citizens in your convent, and without considering that the major part of the revenues of your convent stem from citizens' legacies." "E pervenuto à notitia nostra . . . che nel vostro Monasterio sempre sijno state . . . figliuole de Cittadini . . . et voi nondimeno . . . le rechieste da alcuni Cittadini quali desideravano . . . metter le loro fig.le monache nel vostro Monastero le havete recusate non mosse da altra causa se non che non volete admetter ne accettar . . . senon nobile . . . non considerando che la maggior parte dell'entrade del monasterio vostro sijno state lassate da essi Cittadini." APV, Visite Trevisan, c. 17v, 1 September 1565.

68. Some of the "mixed" convents show a decreasing percentage of patricians in the second half of the seventeenth century.

69. For example, Santa Chiara di Venezia, San Matteo di Mazzorbo, Santa Maria dei Miracoli, and San Sepolcro.

70. "Caterina di Vieri, Charlotte de Bourbon, Arcangela Tarabotti, and hundreds of other coerced nuns were the victims of parents acting out of a kind of greed, there is no way around it; it was a greed so profoundly rooted in their social world as to be immune from moral scrutiny." Margaret L. King, *Women of the Renaissance* (Chicago, 1991), pp. 92–93. "The convent . . . became a painful prison for so many miserable women, often coerced to take the veil by the will of their fathers, who aimed at collecting the patrimony in male hands." Pompeo Molmenti, *La storia di Venezia nella vita privata,* vol. 2 (Bergamo, 1925), pp. 459–60. See also Romano Canosa, *Il*

velo e il capuccio: Monacazioni forzate e sessualità nei conventi femminili in Italia tra '400 e '700 (Rome, 1991).

71. "Other [girls] . . . were coerced [to enter a convent] by their relatives who aimed at preventing the patrimonies from declining through the endowment of a dowry compatible with their status or [who aimed at] reserving such a dowry for another sister." Pio Paschini, "I monasteri femminili in Italia nel '500," in *Problemi di vita religiosa in Italia nel Cinquecento: Convegno di storia della Chiesa in Italia, 1958, Bologna* (Padua, 1960), p. 37; see also Zarri, "Monasteri femminili e città," p. 365; and Francesca Medioli, ed., *L'inferno monacale di Suor Arcangela Tarabotti* (Turin, 1990), pp. 112–17.

72. Bolognetti told the pope why he thought the Venetian government tried to prevent the projected apostolic visitation: "L'una che riformandosi i Monasterij di Monache et riducendosi a maggior strettezza le figliuole de nobili che prima anco vi entravano mal volentieri, doppo la riforma non vi vorrebbero entrare in modo alcuno: et vien detto che già se ne vede l'effetto di alcune che ricusano arditamente di monacarsi doppo il romore di questa visita: il che dicono sarebbe causa della rovina di molte famiglie per l'eccessive doti che usano i nobili alle figliuole che si maritano." Quoted in Tramontin, "La visita apostolica," p. 466.

73. On the reemergence of the dowry system and on dowry inflation, see, among others, Diane Owen Hughes, "From Brideprice to Dowry in Mediterranean Europe," *Journal of Family History* 3 (1978): 262–96. For Florence, see Julius Kirshner and Anthony Molho, "Il Monte delle Doti a Firenze dalla sua fondazione nel 1425 alla metà del sedicesimo secolo: Abbozzo di una ricerca," *Ricerche Storiche* 10, no. 1 (1980): 21–48; idem, "The Dowry Fund and the Marriage Market in Early *Quattrocento* Florence," *Journal of Modern History* 50, no. 3 (1978): 403–38; Molho, *Marriage Alliance;* Julius Kirshner, "Pursuing Honor While Avoiding Sin: The Monte delle Doti of Florence," *Quaderni di Studi Senesi* 41 (1978): 1–82; and Christine Klapisch-Zuber, "The 'Cruel Mother': Maternity, Widowhood, and Dowry in Florence in the Fourteenth and Fifteenth Centuries" and "The Griselda Complex," in *Women, Family, and Ritual in Renaissance Italy*, pp. 117–32, 213–46. For Venice, see Stanley Chojnacki, "Dowries and Kinsmen in Early Renaissance Venice," *Journal of Interdisciplinary History* 5, no. 4 (1975): 571–600. On patrician women as testators, see idem, "Patrician Women in Early Renaissance Venice," *Studies in the Renaissance* 21 (1974): 176–203. Most recently, see Donald E. Queller and Thomas Madden, "Father of the Bride: Fathers, Daughters, and Dowries in Late Medieval and Early Renaissance Venice," *Renaissance Quarterly* 46, no. 4 (1993): 685–711.

74. "Nuovamente siam' tornate / Ale nostre cose antiche / Padri et Madri ci han scacciate / Come lor mortal nimiche / Dican che han troppe fadiche / A dotare l'altre sorelle." Benedetto Cingulano, "Barzelletta dele Monacelle," BNM, Classe It. IX, 369 (7203), Poesie varie, sec. XVI, c. 48v.

75. "Questa Dea che al mondo regna / Cieca, sorda, aspra e fallace: / A chi è madre, a chi matregna, / Tolle et da, come allei piace." Ibid., c. 49r.

76. "Se son piu sorelle, luna / Siede in grembo ala fortuna / L'altre son da lei scacciate / [Monacelle incarcerate] / Luna è sempre in doglia et pianto / L'altra è sempre in gioco et festa / Luna ha il vezzo, et ricco manto, / L'altra ha il negro; e'l velo in testa!" Ibid.

77. "Spesso chiuse in nostre celle / Tutte nude guardavamo / Nostre membra bianche et belle / Poi piangendo diciavamo / Dolce tempo che perdiamo / Quanto ben, quanto diletto / De segiuarmi quel santo detto / Cresciute et moltiplicate." Ibid., c. 49v. A similar song is transcribed by Guido Ruggiero, *The Boundaries of Eros: Sex Crime and Sexuality in Renaissance Venice* (Oxford, 1985), p. 77.

78. "Ogni forza, ingegno et arte / Usaremo ogni mestiero / Farem' prima ogni vil'arte / Che tornare al munistero / Noi haviam fermo el pensiero / In un viver cosi giocondo / Con mariti stare al mondo / Se adotar voi ci aiutate." Cingulano, "Barzelletta dele Monacelle," c. 50v.

79. On the *querelle des femmes* in Venice, see Patricia Labalme, "Venetian Women on Women: Three Early Modern Feminists," *Archivio Veneto,* 5th ser., 152 (1981): 81–109; and, more recently, Virginia Cox, "The Single Self: Feminist Thought and the Marriage Market in Early Modern Venice," *Renaissance Quarterly* 48, no. 3 (1995): 513–81.

80. "Ma l'ingiusta partialità de' genitori determina a suo piacere contro ogni raggione: la di costoro malvagità è tale e tanta che genera maraviglia e compassione in chi la considera." Medioli, *L'inferno monacale,* p. 44.

81. "Quei genitori che, nel maritar una figlia—sirocchia dell'insidiata e mal condotta—non hebbero riguardo a verun dispendio, in aggiunta d'una dotte esorbitante di multiplicar decine di migliaia di scudi, scialaquano in ogni occorenza per fare che la novella sposa pompeggi fra gl'ori e fra le gemme. . . . Il veluto, la felpa che non è d'opera più che humana è stimato indegno di coprir quelle membra che pur sono uscite da quel medemo ventre di dove nacque l'altra sfortunata che, al suo dispetto coperta d'una veste lugubre e semplice ed accompagnata da novecento a mile e dugento—secondo l'uso de' luoghi misserabili—ducati, o ver cento alle più ricche, con cinquanta di provissione all'anno per alimento, sente rimproverarsi dal genitore e parenti l'eccessiva e soverchia spesa. Nel riscuotere per questa povera annual provisione, l'abbandonate stillan sudori di sangue per ché, oltre l'esser trascurato il tempo, viene stentatamente in più volte sborsata." Ibid., p. 40. "Non si trova già legge per la quale habbiano più ragionevoli pretensioni le maritate che le monacate sopra le case de' loro parenti, essendo e l'un e l'altra legittime." Ibid., p. 44.

82. "Che i privati per loro interesse . . . commettano tal'enormità, è abuso detestabile; mà che i superiori, e prencipi il permettano, è cosa da far istupidir d'horrore la stessa insensibilità: quando l'occhio del Principe deve non solamente invigilare sopra la raggion di stato, ma etiamdio sopra alla salute dell' anime, e non lasciarne perir tante miseramente." Suor Arcangela Tarabotti, *La semplicità ingannata,* published posthumously under the pseudonym Galeana Baratotti ([Leiden?], 1654), pp. 40–41.

83. "Se stimate pregiudicar la multiplicità delle figliole alla Ragion di Stato, poi chè, se tutte si maritassero, crescerebbe in troppo numero la no-

biltà et impoverirebber le case col sborso di tante doti." Medioli, *L'inferno monacale,* p. 93.

84. "Il mondo pure è una scena piena d'inganni, ma li chiostri e l'habbitanti in essi, per le maligne prettensioni de gli huomeni che si fan lecito riempirli di donne tradite più d'ogni altra parte dell'universo, rappresentano un teatro in cui si reccitan funestissime tragiedie poi ché il fine di molte dell'imprigionate è il perdere forsi l'anima. . . . tutto è vanità, prospettiva ed ombra che inganna l'occhio." Ibid., p. 39.

85. "If you think that the high number of these girls does damage to the *ragion di stato*—for if all of them were married the nobility would grow too much, and the families would become impoverished through the expenses of so many dowries—*why don't you take the partner destined for you by God without the avarice of money*" (my emphasis). "Se stimate che l'numero grande d'esse figliuole pregiudichino alla ragion di stato, poiche se si maritassero tutte troppo crescrebbe la Nobiltà e s'impoverirebbero le case, con lo sborso di tanti doti, pigliate la compagnia che vi è stata destinata da Dio senza avidità di danari." Tarabotti, *La semplicità ingannata,* p. 92.

86. Memmo, *Dialogo,* p. 125; Giovanni Botero, *Della Ragion di Stato libri dieci, con tre Libri delle Cause della Grandezza, e Magnificenza delle Città* (Venice, 1589), p. 206.

87. "[P]erche con questo mezo si viene a levar quella mala, & dannosa usanza, che era introdotta tra li Nobeli, & Cittadini nostri di spender profusamente il danaro, & facoltà loro nel maritar le figliuole, il che alli padri apportava danno grande, & all'universale mala satisfattione." Preamble to the dowry law of 23 March 1551, *Volumen statutorum legum ac iurium DD Venetorum* (Venice, 1665), p. 300.

88. On the problems involved in enforcing sumptuary legislation, see Catherine Kovesi Killerby, "Practical Problems in the Enforcement of Italian Sumptuary Law, 1200–1500," in *Crime, Society, and the Law in Renaissance Italy,* ed. Trevor Dean and K. J. P. Lowe (Cambridge, 1994), pp. 99–120.

89. Brian Pullan, "Service to the Venetian State: Aspects of Myth and Reality in the Early Seventeenth Century," *Studi Secenteschi* 5 (1964): 137–38; Medioli, *L'inferno monacale,* pp. 113–14.

90. Quoted in Pullan, "Service to the Venetian State," p. 139.

91. See, among others, the serial analysis of Sienese wills by Samuel Cohn, *Death and Property in Siena, 1205–1800: Strategies for the Afterlife* (Baltimore, 1988); and Brian Pullan, *Rich and Poor in Renaissance Venice: The Social Institutions of a Catholic State* (Oxford, 1971). On charitable activities in seventeenth- and eighteenth-century France, see Colin Jones, *The Charitable Imperative: Hospitals and Nursing in Ancien Regime and Revolutionary France* (London, 1989).

92. Pullan, "Service to the Venetian State," p. 138; Chojnacki, "Marriage Legislation"; Romano, *Patricians and Popolani,* pp. 34–35.

93. See introduction, n. 7.

94. "Et acció, che tù . . . non vada susurrando le mie parole esser indrizzate contro il santo Concilio . . . mi protesto con alta voce di sapere, che

quei santi, & incorrotti Padri, adunati in sacro concistoro, inspirati dallo Spirito santo . . . stabilirono un' instituto più divino, che humano. . . . quando quei sacri Porporati rissolsero di ridurre à clausura i Monasteri, promulgarono un' editto, che quelle, che volontarie non acconsentissero di chiudersi per sempre, potessero liberamente partire, senza che loro fosse imputato ad errore, ò dishonore veruno." Tarabotti, *La semplicità ingannata,* pp. 128–30.

95. "Qui la mia penna vorrebbe volar troppo ardita nella censura de superiori Religiosi, come complici in simili affari . . . mà l'interesse di stato, padre di tutti gli errori, contamina anche questi supremi ministri, e per tal causa permettono, che si facciano monache." Ibid., p. 88.

96. "L' Rè de' cieli non gradisce, anzi abomina queste vittime sacrificategli, non volontarie, ma sforzate." Ibid., p. 82.

97. "Se havessero potuto o voluto altramente disponere di loro stesse, che confusione! che danno! che disordine! quali pericoli! quai scandali, et qual male conseguenze si sariano vedute per le case, e per la Città!" Quoted in Zanette, *Suor Arcangela,* p. 36.

98. "Padri e parenti di figlie tali . . . [sanno] pure quante di queste . . . habbiano dishonorate loro case, e anche quelle di Dio." Tarabotti, *La semplicità ingannata,* p. 89.

99. "[L]a é una buona zovene, mà Dio perdona à chi mette le fie in Monestier per forza." "[S]on stata tradita dalli miei proprij parenti." ASV, PsM, busta 347, fascicolo 5, 10 June 1604. "Vorrei piutosto esser nata da un fachin." Ibid., fascicolo 7, 19 June 1604.

100. Ibid., busta 263, fascicolo 6, cc. 1–2.

101. "Suor Chrestina non è partita qua per alcuna causa disonesta ma perchè la non voleva star à patto alcun et doppo la morte di suo padre et poi di suo fratello la non ha fatto altro che dir che la voleva andar via come sano tutte le monache." Ibid., c. 8r.

102. "I know that Sister Chrestina wanted to leave the convent for many years, even when her father was still alive, and she cursed soul and body of her father who put her in this convent, and she complained all day long . . . she never confessed and took communion except once a year out of desperation for being in this place." "Io so che sono molti anni che Suor Chrestina fino in vita di suo padre haveva voglia di uscir di questo monastero et la biastemmava l'anima et il corpo di suo padre che l'hanno messa in questo monastero et si doleva et canciava tutto 'l giorno . . . non si confessava et comunicava salvo una volta all'anno per desperation di star in questo luogo." Ibid., c. 5v.

103. Since the Tridentine order prohibiting novices from professing before age sixteen had not yet been instituted, it might well have been the case that she entered at age eleven.

104. Vincenzo de Lonzi, a baker in San Gregorio, testified: "I wished strongly that he [Ferraruol] would take her away, because she disturbed me a lot, because she is sick, and almost every day she suffers from spasms, [?] and I believe that she will die, because she is in a miserable state and has only skin over her bones." "Io desideravo grandemente che'l [Ferraruol] la

levasse via perche la mi [a] da[to] grandissimo disturbo perche lè amalata et quasi ogni giorno le vien alcuni parasismi che mi dubito che la debba morir essendo essa riduta che la non ha altro che la pelle su le osse." ASV, PsM, busta 263, fascicolo 6, c. 11r.

105. According to Lorenzo Fabbri, a girl's male relatives were among her most important resources—which means that orphans or only children such as Sister Laura would have had a hard time finding a marriage partner even with a substantial dowry. Fabbri, *Alleanza matrimoniale,* p. 34.

106. ASV, Archivio Notarile Testamenti, Atti Cigrini, busta 198, polizza 112, testament of Beatrice fo de Mes. Michiel Bataia consorte de Mes. Julio Quirini fo de Mes. Hier.o della contra de San Zuane Bragola, 25 February 1574 (m.v.). In Venice, the new calendar year started on the first of March, which means that according to our (Roman) calendar, this date would have been 25 February 1575. In order to remind the reader of this discrepancy, I have marked all January and February dates with either *m.v.* (more veneto) or *m.r.* (more romano).

107. Ibid., polizza 120, testament of 19 June 1579.

108. ASV, PsM, busta 265, fascicolo 2, cc. 3r–v.

109. "Io venivo in questo Monasterio putta piccola in tempo del contaggio, che le figlie venivano dentro in Monastero, et poi fui messa a spese nel Monastero di S. Vido de Buran, dove stetti cinque in sei anni fino che fui accettata Monaca in questo Monastero, che potevo haver intorno quindise anni, et fui vestita, et feci poi la professione con la bocca, ma non col cuore. Io son stata sempre tentata dal Demonio di romper mi il collo, et sempre ho havuto per il tempo passato diverse amicitie . . . et messami [?] per le mani di D.a Cipriana, che è morta, ma con queste amicitie io non ho mai fatto cosa cattiva, cio e non ho perso la mia virginità, et finalmente già sei anni mi fu fatto vedere da detta D.a Cipriana . . . un Zuane Cocco giovane all'hora di 20 anni in c.a, il quale è venuto qualche volta à vedermi nascostamente alli parlatorij, in maniera, che io m'inamorai in lui, et lo indussi ad amarmi, et usai ogni arte etiam Diabolica per indurlo ad amarmi, cioè sconguiri, et orationi superstitiose, invocando Diavoli, et hebbi queste cose da Donna Cipriana per forza de danari, et offersi al detto Cocco, che volendo venir a trovarmi." Ibid., cc. 9r–v.

110. On the age discrepancy between brides and grooms, see, among others, Herlihy and Klapisch-Zuber, *Tuscans and Their Families,* p. 87.

111. In 1627, Sister Lugretia Barbarigo di Zuan Alvise, a nun in Sant' Alvise for fourteen years, succeeded in getting her vows annulled by the Sacra Congregazione de' Cardinali sopra Vescovi e Regolari (the Holy Congregation of Cardinals over Bishops and Regulars). The Venetian government, however, put pressure on Sister Lugretia and her brother Sebastiano Barbarigo to renounce this privilege, "because one notices already the confusion that goes through this convent and that would be introduced also in others . . . our interest requires that a due and necessary remedy be found." "Già si conosce la confusione che passa nel medesimo Monasterio, et si verebbe ad introdurne in altri ancora . . . richiede il Servitio delle Cose Nostre che

vi si ponga il debito e neccessario rimedio." Senate and Pregadi, 2 October 1627, ASV, Compilazione Leggi (CL), busta 288, c. 596.

112. A "spiritual dowry" was the entrance fee a novice had to pay to the convent, either in the form of lifelong annuity payments of sixty ducats or as a cash payment or investment of one thousand ducats, which would stay with the convent after the nun's death. See the decrees of Patriarch Lorenzo Priuli and the Senate: Patriarch Lorenzo Priuli, "Ordini circa le Doti," 24 November 1593, MCC, CC 2583, cc. 127r–v; and "Parti prese in diversi tempi nell'Eccellentissimo Senato in materia della Dote delle Figliuole, che vogliono monacare," 26 July 1602, 6 October 1610, 9 July 1620, BNM, Misc. 2937 no. 14.

113. Although I am concentrating on patrician monachization strategies, wealthy citizen families were equally affected by dowry inflation and might have similarly engaged in "depositing" daughters in convents. Venetian citizens were a small, legally defined class of privileged families who often served as secretaries to the numerous government organs, magistrates, and courts. See Andrea Zannini, *Burocrazia e burocrati a Venezia in età moderna: I cittadini originari (sec. XVI–XVIII)* (Venice, 1993).

114. ASV, Archivio Notarile Testamenti, Atti Brinis, busta 32, c. 365, testament of 18 January 1606 (m.v.).

115. ASV, Corpus Domini, busta 6, 19 May 1626.

116. The exiled relative might have been Iseppo, the son of Zorzi's paternal cousin Piero. Ibid., 14 January 1628 (m.v.).

117. Ibid., 15 May 1629.

118. Ibid., 14 January 1629 (m.v.), 22 May 1629.

119. ASV, Notarile, Testamenti Non Pubblicati, buste 31–35, Notaio Girolamo Brinis, cedola 351, testament (unopened) of 9 July 1617.

120. Francesco Ercole, "L'istituto dotale nella pratica e nella legislazione statutaria dell'Italia superiore," parts 1 and 2, *Rivista Italiana per le Scienze Giuridiche* 45 (1908): 191–302; 46 (1908?): 167–257.

121. Ibid., part 1, p. 285; see also Marco Ferro, "Dote," in *Dizionario del diritto comune e veneto*, 2d ed. (Venice, 1845), p. 642.

122. Sometimes, men would force their sisters or nieces to sign a disadvantageous quitclaim, whereby the young girl renounced her share in the family patrimony in exchange for a dowry. In her testament of 1680, Countess Cecilia Trissino, daughter of Count Galeazzo Niero, insisted on bequeathing parts of her father's patrimony to her children, although she had legally renounced them in signing a quitclaim before her marriage. She declared the quitclaim legally invalid, since "I have never expressed my consent to this document, because only a very small part of it was read to me, because Signor Bernardin Bertoncelli [the notary] was interrupted in reading it by one of the Counts, my brothers, who said, 'What, are you going to read the entire thing?' whereupon another one of my brothers answered, 'No, it doesn't matter,' and then I also said that it did not matter; they then put the document in front of me on the table and showed me the place where I had to sign, which I did . . . although I was ignorant of the content of that

document, which I learned about only after my marriage, with great pain, because they neglected to read to me and point out that I renounced the paternal and maternal patrimonies as well as the legacies of my aunt Countess Maddalena from Vienna, and of my uncle Count Vincenzo Caldogna [?] . . . and therefore I do not intend to express my consent, as I have never consented [to the quitclaim]." "Io non ho mai prestato alcun assenso à quella scrittura perchè mi fu letto pochissima parte di quella, essendo stato interrotto nella lettura della medesima il Sig.r Bernardin Bertoncelli da uno de med.mi Sig.ri Co: Co: miei fratelli, col dir, che se ghe lezelo tutto? al che rispose un' altro degl'istessi, e non importa, e così anch'io dissi e non importa, il che detto fu posta la carta sopra un tavolino, dimostrandomi il loco ove dovevo in fine di essa fare la mia sottoscrittione, che fu da me . . . fatta . . . benchè ignara del contenuto della stessa scrittura, pervenutomi à notitia solamente doppo esser maritata, con tanto mio pregiudizio, essendo stato tralasciato di leggermi, e notificarmi, che io rinonciavo li beni paterni, e materni, e legati della Sig.ra Co: Madalena mia Zia da Vienna, e del Co: Vincenzo Caldogna [?] mio Zio . . . che percio non intendo prestare, nè d'haver mai prestato alcun assenso." Testament of Contessa Cecilia filia del q. Co: Galeazzo Niero, 17 August 1680, ASV, Corpus Domini, busta 8, fascicolo "Le Rev.de Monache . . . per li Testi [?] che rogano Conte Trisino."

123. Without the help of the convent magistrate, who acted as the legal representative of nuns fighting for their annual pension, women did not have the means to put pressure on their relatives. A letter of Sister Biancha Tosetti, abbess of Santa Chiara, to her nephew Alessandro, which was preserved among trial records, shows how desperately she tried to settle the matter informally before going to court: "Although it is of no use that I beg you to visit me, I ask you to send me some fish for next Monday, even if it is not extremely good, send whatever you can find—but this is not the service that I wanted to ask of you, and neither is it the one that I ask now. I want you to find me some particularly beautiful pears, either the Caravelli ones, or simply the best and most beautiful ones on the market, eight or ten of them . . . but I want to know the price before you buy them, and don't say anything to Donna Menega, write to me when you send the fish, as I greet you all, and ask you to come and visit me. I believe you forgot about me, because the more I send for you and ask that you come and see me, you will not do me that favor—my dear son, I beg you to come and see me, I really need to talk to you, and if I knew whom you loved, I would ask them to do me this favor, but because I don't know whom you love, I ask you by the soul of God, please come." "Già che non vale il pregarvi che venite a trovarmi, vi prego mandarmi un poco di pesce per lunedi prossimo, se bene non fosse tanto bello, mandi di quello, che trovi, mà questo non è il servitio, che desidero di dirvi, ne anche questo, che vi dico adesso. Vorrei, che mi trovassi un poco di peri particolari belli, che fosse, ò Caravelli, ò di quelli più boni, e belli, che si trovi, otto, ò dieci . . . mà vorrei sapere il costo avanti che li compra, mà non dica niente à Donna Menega, scrivetemi voi quando mi mandate il pesce, e vi saluto, voi e tutti, e prego venite à trovarmi.

Credo, che vi habbiate scordato di me, che più che mando à pregarvi, che
venite qui da me, e non posso havere questa gratia, caro mio caro fio, vi
prego à venire à trovarmi, ne ho gran necessità di parlare con voi, e se sapessi
à chi volete bene, pregherei quelli, che mi facessi questo servitio, mà perchè
non só che amate, vi prego per l'anima di Dio, che venite." Undated letter
(ca. 1680), ASV, Santa Chiara, busta 14, fascicolo 7, "Pro Reverendibus
Monialibus Sanctae Clarae Venetiarum contra Hereditates q.m q.m D. Ja-
cobi, et . . . D. Donati frum [fratellum] Tosetti, 1680, 31 Marzo," cc. 65v–
66r.

124. Chojnacki, "Patrician Women," p. 195.

125. Vettor Sandi, *Principj di storia civile della Repubblica di Venezia
dalla sua fondazione sino all'anno di N.S. 1700,* pt. 3, vol. 2 (Venice, 1756),
pp. 1086–87.

126. The role of the nun's "lucky brother" and family's universal heir
is reflected in popular literature. In Baltassare Sultanini's libertine "comical
satire" *Il novo parlatorio delle monache,* an involuntary nun complains
about having been cheated by her brother: "Damned brother . . . [he] promised mountains of gold to convince me to become a nun. . . . My father left
me six thousand ducats; my aunt another two thousand; my sister, who died
last year, another thousand; my mother would have given me the fourth part
of her dowry, so that I could have made a very good match. But in order
to accommodate him, I have inconvenienced myself." "Fratello maledetto
. . . [lui] promesse monti d'oro per farmi risolvere ad esser monaca. . . . Mio
padre m'ha lasciati sei mila Ducati; mia Zia due altri mila; mia sorella che
morì l'anno passato altre mille; mia Madre mi havrebbe data la quarta parte
della sua Dote, onde haverei potuto collocarmi bene, e benissimo. Pure per
accommodar lui, mi sono contenta[ta] di incommodar me stessa." Baltassare
Sultanini, *Il novo parlatorio delle monache, satira comica,* 2d ed. (Venice,
1677), pp. 238–39.

127. A *fidei commissum* (in Italian *fidecommesso*) was a legal instrument that allowed Venetian testators to prohibit the alienation of their patrimonies; in the absence of primogeniture, all of the heirs (mostly male) could
then inherit equal shares of the patrimony, but they could be forced to bequeath them to future male heirs of legitimate descent, that is, to their own
sons or to the sons of the brother who married. In other cases, one son would
inherit the whole patrimony while other sons (and daughters) would be entitled to equal amounts of an annual usufruct; in both cases, the effect was
similar, in that only one son was in a position to marry and produce male
heirs. Ferro, "Fedecommesso," in *Dizionario del diritto comune e veneto,*
1:704–16; Sandi, *Principj di storia civile,* p. 1083.

128. James Cushman Davis, "Entailing Land and Excluding Daugh-
ters," in *A Venetian Family and Its Fortune, 1500–1900: The Donà and the
Conservation of Wealth* (Philadelphia, 1975); Brian Pullan, ed., *Crisis and
Change in the Venetian Economy in the Sixteenth and Seventeenth Centuries*
(London, 1968).

129. ASV, Corpus Domini, busta 6, cc. 8r–10r; 6 January 1600 (m.v.).

130. Ibid., 9 January 1601 (m.v.).

131. Tax declaration found among convent records, ibid., polizza 319, Cannaregio.

132. Ibid., marriage contract of 27 January 1585 (m.v.). *Campo* is a measure for fields. In Padua, 1 *campo* equaled 38.62 ares (1 are = 100 square meters); in Treviso, 1 *campo* equaled 52.04 ares.

133. Ibid., testament of 2 March 1591.

134. Sisters were usually left out of an "equally" distributed inheritance of real estate when a sibling died; the deceased sibling's share was usually divided by the remaining brothers alone.

135. ASV, Corpus Domini, busta 6, 18 May 1605.

136. Ibid., 11 April 1628.

137. Ibid., 11 October 1625, 8 November 1627.

138. This means that Andrea Morosini must have assigned the house—which was part of the Morosini patrimony—to his wife, Laura Memmo, as part of a dowry recompensation. But this could not have become valid before the death of his siblings.

139. ASV, Corpus Domini, busta 6, 4 March, 2, 13 April 1639.

140. Ibid., 11 January 1651 (m.v.), 10 June 1654, 7 July 1656.

141. Paulina finally did get married, but not until she was at least forty-five years old. In a document of 1628, she was still called Paulina Morosini. A document dated 2 April 1639 mentioned her as widow of Andrea Contarini.

142. There is no testament of either their father, Piero Morosini, or their mother, Chiara Corner.

143. Elena got a substantial trousseau as well, as was customary for prospective nuns. Her *cassa* contained, among other things, a large crucifix, 4 large paintings, 17 small paintings, a pair of gilded angels, a mattress, 2 large pillows, 2 small pillows, chandeliers, other furnishing items, and a variety of fabrics. ASV, San Lorenzo, busta 19, cc. 34r–35v.

144. ASV, San Lorenzo, busta 19, 9 November 1596, 8 November, 6 September 1599.

145. There is no declaration by her father, Antonio; since he married only in 1584, he might not have been emancipated yet in 1582.

146. According to my calculations, his income amounted to only 590 ducats and 217 lire, plus about 175 *staia* of wheat, 120 *staia* of minor sorts of grain, and 362 *mastelli* of wine. One Venetian *staia* equaled approximately 0.83 hectoliters, and one Venetian *mastello* equaled 0.75 hectoliters. Since his fields lay in the territories of Padua and Treviso, where slightly different measures applied, these amounts are only approximate. The price for wheat was about two ducats per *staia* in 1582, so one can say that his total income far exceeded a thousand ducats annually. ASV, San Lorenzo, busta 19, condizione di decima, 1582; Maurice Aymard, *Venise, Raguse, et le commerce du blé pendant la seconde moitié du XVIe siècle* (Paris, 1966), p. 110.

147. In his testament of 1581, Marin Pesaro mentions a "ducal gown"

(veste ducal). ASV, Archivio Notarile Testamenti, Atti Ziliol, busta 1260, c. 688, testament of 10 October 1581. It is unclear what he meant by that term, since he does not seem to have been doge. Claudio Rendina, *I Dogi: Storia e segreti* (Rome, 1984).

148. ASV, Archivio Notarile Testamenti, Atti Ziliol, busta 1260, c. 688, testament of 10 October 1581.

149. ASV, San Lorenzo, busta 19, copy of the dowry contract dated 5 March 1584. The Monte Vecchio was one of the republic's private trust funds, administered by the Procuratori di San Marco. See Reinhold C. Mueller, *The Procuratori di San Marco and the Venetian Credit Market* (New York, 1977); and idem, "The Procurators of San Marco in the Thirteenth and Fourteenth Centuries: A Study of the Office as a Financial and Trust Institution," *Studi Veneziani* 13 (1971): 105–220.

150. ASV, San Lorenzo, busta 19, 28 April 1618.

151. Ibid., 8 August 1631.

152. Ibid., Giudici del Proprio, 14 December 1634.

153. Ibid., 22 June 1639.

154. Ibid., 17 March 1650.

155. Ibid., 9 June 1650.

156. Ibid., 7 March 1654.

157. Ibid., 23 June 1656.

158. Ibid., 28 July 1656. Tenants and farmers often refused to stop paying their annual rent to their landlords, probably out of fear of repercussions and because they felt the legal grounds were uncertain.

159. Ibid., 9 September 1655.

160. Ibid., 25 September 1656; 28 September 1657; 28 September 1658.

161. Ibid., 18 January 1662 (m.v.), 28 March, 12 September 1663.

162. Ibid., 17 August 1665.

163. Ibid., 26 March 1666.

164. Ibid., 17 August 1666.

165. In my usage, the expression "patrician reproduction patterns" refers to the legal as well as physical reproduction of the ruling class; I am interested in the problems patricians faced in reproducing the body politic as a social, cultural, and political entity. I am not concerned with patricians' illegitimate offspring, for example. "Patrician reproduction patterns" thus refers less to a biological than to a cultural phenomenon.

166. Although I do not want to suggest that the patriciate's demographic problems as discussed below could have been avoided by cooperation, the situation of the Venetian patriciate around 1600 is as paradoxical as the hypothetical setting of the two prisoners. Like the prisoners, the patriciate was caught between the mutually exclusive demands of two different rationales, as I will explain in the following. See, among others, G. Hardin, "The Tragedy of the Commons," *Science* 162 (1968): 1243–48; and James P. Kahan, "Rationality, the Prisoner's Dilemma, and Population," *Journal of Social Issues* 30, no. 4 (1974): 189–210.

167. On patrician marriages, see Cowan, *The Urban Patriciate.* Volker Hunecke shows that endogamous marriage practices were increasingly abandoned from about 1650 on. Hunecke, "Matrimonio e demografia."

168. On the increasing social differentiation among the patriciate, see Pullan, "Service to the Venetian State"; idem, "Poverty, Charity, and the Reason of State: Some Venetian Examples," *Bollettino dell'Istituto di Storia della Società e dello Stato Veneziano* (same as *Studi Veneziani*) 2 (1960): 17–60; and Chojnacki, "Marriage Legislation."

169. Social climbers were, for example, rich citizens or wealthy patricians of "recent" nobility—that is, families who were ennobled during the *serrata* of 1297—trying to acquire relatives of more ancient patrician descent. But the hierarchy within the highly differentiated patriciate offered incentives for social climbing to just about everyone. Stanley Chojnacki has shown that in the fifteenth century, the *case vecchie* (noble families allegedly descending from Roman senators) practiced "endogamy within an endogamous system." By limiting their marriages largely to their own circle, they enhanced their prestige and raised the price of marrying into that circle. Chojnacki, "Marriage Legislation," pp. 174–75. Cowan, however, states that by the late sixteenth century the "old houses" intermarried freely with the "new" ones. Cowan, *The Urban Patriciate,* pp. 163–64.

170. "In the eighteenth century, in fact, the senatorial aristocracy of Venice is constituted by ca. 150 families in whose circle the capital fluctuates, but never leaves: they [these families] can be more or less rich in a specified period of time, but, given that testaments, marriages, sales, and loans happen almost exclusively within this circle, a redistribution of patrimonies is always possible, which during the last decades of the republic often assumes the character of a true concentration of riches, because of the specific demographic contraction of this class." Giuseppe Gullino, *I Pisani dal Banco e Moretta* (Rome, 1984), p. 24.

171. See the preambles to the dowry laws mentioned above (e.g., in n. 87).

172. "Consideró in quel secolo e nella situazione di que' tempi il Governo quanto osservabile aggruppamento di male derivava dalle costituzioni di dote con eccesso date alle femmine nel collocarle: danno grave alle famiglie donde escono le donne se vengono collocate; impotenza in molti di collocar le donzelle per l'esempio delle doti eccedenti date a femmine di condizione eguale, ed inferiore . . . motivo nella eccedente dotazione di lusso dispendiosissimo alle famiglie, che ricevono le donne, dal cuor delle quali nell'alterezza regolarmente propria del sesso vibransi saette dalle doti grandi; consequenze di funestissima rovina ad esse famiglie che le ricevono, allorchè per viduità delle donne nascono quasi sempre i casi di restituir le doti avute, e restituirle intere, permettendo già il diritto Veneziano alla donna anche a discendenza sua esistente disporre a stranieri la dote, detratta solo minima porzione di lucro al marito per li corredi nuzziali." Sandi, *Principj di storia civile,* pp. 1086–87.

173. "Ed invero rari sono i casi . . . che ricca dote sollievo rechi alle famiglie, poichè consumandosi il pronto denaro, rimane . . . il peso di resti-

tuire con quell'apprezziamento assai vantaggioso alle femmine, alle quali deve restituirsi." Ibid., p. 1087.

174. "Ma non dee la prudente moglie istimar suo, dote, danari, bellezza, o nobiltà, ch'ella porti seco in casa del marito; ma la honestà, la castità, la bontà, la virtù, la obbedienza, la diligenza nel governo della famiglia, & si fatti thesori: de i quali s'ella é abbondevole, é riccamente dotata di ogni bene." Lodovico Dolce, *Dialogo della institution delle donne* (Venice, 1547), p. 53v.

175. "La Moglie non è padrona del corpo suo: ma quello è tutto in poter del Marito." Lodovico Dolce, "Ammaestramenti," in *Le Bellezze, le Lodi, gli Amori, & i Costumi delle Donne; Con lo Discacciamento delle Lettere, di Agnolo Firenzuola Fiorentino, Et di Alessandro Picolomini Sanese. Giuntovi appresso i Saggi Ammaestramenti che appartengono alla honorevole, e virtuosa vita Virginale, Maritale, e Vedovile, di Lodovico Dolce*, 2d ed. (Venice, 1622), p. 68.

176. Gaetano Cozzi, "Ambiente veneziano, ambiente veneto: Governanti e governati nel dominio di qua dal Mincio nei secoli XV–XVIII," in *Storia della cultura veneta*, vol. 4, part 2, *Il Seicento* (Vicenza, 1984), pp. 495–539.

177. "Conchiuse le nozze per terza persona, senza veder la fanciulla . . . fra i nobili molto grandi, lo sposo riduce la mattina seguente in Corte di Palazzo, dove si publica il parentado. . . . indi s'invitano gli amici a casa del padre della sposa . . . dove vanno a rallegrarsi . . . gli Avogadori, i Savi, i Capi del Consiglio de Dieci. . . . montati in sala, dove non si veggono altri che huomini, posti a sedere, il Paraninfo conduce fuori d'una stanza la sposa, vestita per antico uso di bianco, et con chiome sparse giù per le spalle, conteste con fila d'oro. Et fattesi le parole ceremoniali dello sponsalitio, viene condotta al suono di pifferi, di trombe et d'altri stromenti armonici attorno alla sala, tuttavia ballando placidamente et facendo inchini a i convitati. Et così mostrata et veduta da tutti, si ritorna dentro." Giulio Bistort, *Il Magistrato alle Pompe nella Repubblica di Venezia* (Venice, 1912), pp. 97–98. See also Lowe, "Secular Brides and Convent Brides"; and Patricia H. Labalme and Laura Sanguinetti White, "How to (and How Not to) Get Married in Sixteenth-Century Venice (Selections from Marin Sanudo)," *Renaissance Quarterly* 52, no. 1 (1999): 43–72.

178. "[mostrando ogniuno . . . segno di allegrezza] . . . per veder cosi bella & rara coppia a marital nodo congiunti. Venne finalmente . . . l'hora della magnifica cena, anzi d'un regal convito." Lodovico Domenichi, *La Nobiltà delle Donne* (Venice, 1551), p. 3r.

179. "Se una donna si marita, & habbia in dote cinquecento scudi, sei cento ne sorbisce nelle vesti, ne i fregi, ne gli ornamenti: e . . . perche le donne sono di natura pompose, nè mai à bastanza sono ornate." Giuseppe Passi, *I donneschi diffetti nuovamente riformati, e posti in luce . . . aggiuntovi in questa seconda impressione molte cose belle, á discorso, per discorso, degne d'esser lette da studiosi* (Venice, 1601), p. 175. See also Patricia Allerston, "Wedding Finery in Sixteenth-Century Venice," in *Marriage in Italy*, ed. Dean and Lowe, pp. 25–40.

180. "Non essendo poi altro le lamentationi degli ammogliati, che follie, anzi sceleraggini di coloro, che doppo haver con studiati mezzi procurata una ricca dote, si dolgono poi di dover far le spese necessarie per quelle, c'hanno fatto loro conoscere d'esser cosa pretiosa, portando seco quantità di tesori, se prima, ch'arrivassero ad ottenerle in mogli, se professavano di loro ardenti, & amanti, hora vorebbero, ch'elle vestissero all' uso della nostra prima Madre, per più agiatamente poter scialacquare in adornar le Meretrici, da che nascono quei lamenti, che così sovente assordano l'aria in detestatione degli habiti, e pompe donnesche." Arcangela Tarabotti, "Antisatira," in *Contro 'l Lusso Donnesco, satira menippea del Sig. Francesco Buoninsegni* (Venice, 1644), pp. 86–87.

181. James Cushman Davis, *The Decline of the Venetian Nobility as a Ruling Class* (Baltimore, 1962), p. 66.

182. *Livelli* were personal loans secured by real estate and income in grain. Gigi Corazzol, *Livelli stipulati a Venezia nel 1591,* Supplementi di Studi Veneziani (Pisa, 1986); idem, *Fitti e livelli a grano* (Milan, 1979).

183. According to Daniele Beltrami, the landed possessions of the Venetian patriciate rose dramatically during the course of the sixteenth century.

Year	1510	1537	1566	1582
Taxable worth of land (ducats)	33,279	41,685	93,326	133,706

Daniele Beltrami, *La penetrazione economica dei veneziani in terraferma: Forze di lavoro e proprietà fondiaria nelle campagne venete dei secoli XVII e XVIII,* Civiltà veneta studi 12 (Rome, 1961) p. 51. See also Gullino, *I Pisani dal Banco e Moretta,* p 28, n. 13; Angelo Ventura, "Considerazioni sull' agricoltura veneta e sulla accumulazione originaria del capitale nei secoli XVI e XVII," *Studi Storici* 3–4 (1968): 674–722, esp. 674–78; Ugo Tucci, "Les émissions monétaires de Venise et les mouvements internationaux de l'or," *Revue Historique* 527 (1978): 91–122; Carlo Livi, Domenico Sella, and Ugo Tucci, "Un problème d'histoire: La decadence économique de Venise," in *Aspetti e cause della decadenza economica veneziana nel secolo XVII: Atti del Convegno 27 giugno–2 luglio 1957, Venezia, Isola di San Giorgio* (Venice, 1961), pp. 287–317; Fernand Braudel, "La vita economica di Venezia nel XVI secolo," in *Storia della civiltà veneziana,* ed. Vittore Branca (Florence, 1979), 2:259–70; and Gino Luzzatto, "La decadenza di Venezia dopo le scoperte geografiche nella tradizione e nella realtà," *Archivio Veneto,* 5th ser., 89–90 (1955): 162–81.

184. See Giuseppe Gullino's case studies "I Loredan di Santo Stefano: Cenni storici," in *Palazzo Loredan e l'Istituto Veneto di Scienze, Lettere, ed Arti* (Venice, 1985), pp. 11–33; and *I Pisani dal Banco e Moretta.*

185. Cozzi, "Ambiente veneziano."

186. "[An economy dominated by] landed property . . . did not offer a chance for poor patricians to enter it, to extract from it some margin or space for their business, as usually happened in mercantile activities. Thus landed property divided the patriciate, or at least accentuated its inner divisions." Hunecke, "Matrimonio e demografia," p. 281. Hunecke also quotes

a contemporary observer: "Because of the loss of trade with Asia and because of the acquisitions of territories . . . on the mainland, the differences
in fortune and wealth among the Venetian nobility were rendered more visible than before." Ibid., p. 280. Hunecke refers to Cozzi, Pullan, and J. C.
Davis to show that the investments in land accentuated the social divisions
within the patriciate. Gaetano Cozzi, "Politica, società, istituzioni," in *Dalla
guerra di Chioggia al 1517*, vol. 1 of *La Repubblica di Venezia nell'età moderna*, by Gaetano Cozzi and Michael Knapton, Storia d'Italia, vol. 12 (Turin,
1986) p. 121; Pullan, "Poverty, Charity, and the Reason of State," pp. 38ff.;
J. C. Davis, *The Decline of the Venetian Nobility*.

187. For example, in 1577 a proposal was passed to liquidate the state
debt in order to stimulate commerce by redirecting capital back into the
economy. But instead of investing in trade, the patricians bought land on
the *terraferma*. In 1584 a new state fund was created to finance military
expenditures and to respond to the widespread demand for secure investment opportunities. Another example of the government's miscalculated
economic policy was the protectionist navigation act of 1602, which required that all goods bound for Venice be carried either in Venetian ships
or in ships belonging to the country from which the goods originated. Instead
of stimulating trade, the act strangled commercial activities. Ugo Corti, "La
francazione del debito pubblico della Repubblica di Venezia proposta da
Gian Francesco Priuli," *Nuovo Archivio Veneto*, n.s., 7 (1894): 331–64; D.
Beltrami, "Un ricordo del Priuli intorno al problema dell'ammortamento dei
depositi in Zecca del 1574," in *Studi in onore di Armando Sapori*, vol. 2
(Milan, 1957), pp. 1071–87; Domenico Sella, "Crisis and Transformation
in Venetian Trade," in *Crisis and Change*, ed. Pullan, pp. 88–105.

188. J. C. Davis is of the opinion that *fidecommessi* made a family's
wealth less flexible. "The fideicommissum would have made it more difficult
to obtain through the sale of land the large amounts of money which were
necessary for the enormous costs of weddings, for the construction of the
new palace which might be necessary if more than one brother married, or
for all the necessities of a family. It would also have made it more difficult
to raise the money for a dowry." J. C. Davis, *The Decline of the Venetian
Nobility*, p. 71.

189. "Il numero de' Gentilhuomini Venetiani arrivava in quei principii
a quattro mila, & cinquecento, hoggi essendo mancate molte famiglie, a
pena arriva à tre mila." Giovanni Botero, *Relatione della Republica venetiana* (Venice, 1605), pp. 29v–30r.

190. J. C. Davis, *The Decline of the Venetian Nobility*; Daniele Beltrami, *Storia della popolazione di Venezia dalla fine del secolo XVI alla
caduta della Repubblica* (Padua, 1954); Hunecke, "Matrimonio e demografia"; idem, *Der venezianische Adel*.

191. Gasparo Contarini, *Della republica, e magistrati di Venezia. Libri
cinque* . . . (Venice, 1678; first ed. [in Latin]: Venice, 1543).

192. Dorit Raines, "Pouvoir ou privilèges nobiliaires: Le dilemme du
patriciat vénetien face aux agrégations du XVIIe siècle," *Annales E.S.C.* 46,
no. 4 (1991): 827–47.

193. Historians differ as to how to evaluate specific aspects of this process. Giuseppe Gullino sees dowry inflation and *fidecommessi* as positive instruments enabling rich families such as the Loredan or the Pisani dal Banco and Moretta first to accumulate and then to consolidate their patrimonies. Gullino, *I Pisani dal Banco e Moretta;* idem, "I Loredan di Santo Stefano." Brian Pullan seems to privilege dowry inflation over investment in land as an explanation for the ongoing concentration of wealth. Pullan, "Service to the Venetian State." Alexander F. Cowan, on the other hand, downplays the importance of dowry inflation for the concentration of patrimonies. He instead emphasizes its social importance and shows that the *case vecchie* (old houses) either practiced strict endogamy within their circle or introduced super-rich brides from outside the patriciate. In his opinion, the *case nuove* (new houses) tried to marry into the *case dogali* (ducal houses) by means of high dowries. Cowan, *The Urban Patriciate.*

194. According to Lorenzo Fabbri, the dowry was the only variable among the various criteria in choosing a bride in fifteenth-century Florence; a girl was assumed to have beauty, family background, and connections, but the dowry amount could be raised or lowered depending on whether she was expected to attract a groom of higher status or to content herself with a husband of more modest position. In other words, dowries reflected the status of the future husband rather than that of the father. Fabbri, *Alleanza matrimoniale,* pp. 71, 78.

195. "The political status of individuals in the brotherhoods and clans, and ranks of all kinds [among the native inhabitants of the American Northwest], are gained in a 'war of property', just as they are in real war, or through chance, inheritance, alliance, and marriage." Mauss, *The Gift,* p. 37; see also the introduction to this book. "The purely sumptuary form of consumption (which is almost always exaggerated and often purely destructive), in which considerable amounts of goods that have taken a long time to amass are suddenly given away or even destroyed, particularly in the case of the potlatch, give such institutions the appearance of representing purely lavish expenditure and childish prodigality. . . . But the reason for these gifts and frenetic acts of wealth consumption is in no way disinterested, particularly in societies that practise the potlatch. Between chiefs and their vassals, between vassals and their tenants, through such gifts a hierarchy is established. To give is to show one's superiority, to be more, to be higher in rank, *magister.* To accept without giving in return, or without giving more back, is to become client and servant, to become small, to fall lower (*minister*)." Ibid., p. 74.

196. "Marriages are a most basic form of gift exchange, in which it is women who are the most precious of gifts." Gayle Rubin, "The Traffic in Women: Notes on the 'Political Economy' of Sex," in *Toward an Anthropology of Women,* ed. Rayna Reiter (New York, 1975), p. 173.

197. Klapisch-Zuber, "The Griselda Complex."

198. Lorenzo Fabbri mentions that "the paradoxical case could happen that a girl endowed with a relatively high sum risked, because of the scarcity of appropriate candidates, encountering greater difficulties [on the mar-

riage market than a less well endowed girl]." Fabbri, *Alleanza matrimoniale,* p. 77.

199. "Si è introdotto in alcune casate il costume de Prencipi più sublimi, cioè di non dare, o ricevere Donne, che dello stesso lor sangue. Il Procurator Cornaro della Casa grande di San Maurizio, quello che fu uno degli Ambasciatori di complimento all'Imperator Leopoldo . . . a marita[to] tre Figlie, una al Proc. Contarini dalli Scrigni del solaro di sopra suo parente molto congionto, un altra nel Cornaro di S. Polo, la terza nel Cornaro della Regina. . . . et a me, che allora investigai, se veramente fosse stata vocazione questo monacato, mi fu risposto da Persona informata, e confidente, che quella Figliola monaca si espresse aver voluto monacare per non sopportar la Sig.ria di uomo, mentre non trovava chi potessero meritar più, che il servirla. . . . Quest'altra adunque sorella, che di già era destinata alla vita celibe con feminile inconstanza a dichiarato volersi maritare, parve strano a fratelli questa nuovità, perche gia si credevano esenti dall'obbligo di questa dote; ma intesa la rissoluzione della sorella gl'anno fatto un assegnamento di 30.000 ducati . . . l'anno disegnata al Sagredo nepote del fu Dose, quale non a badato a qualsisia quantità . . . di dote; conoscendo, e confessando la maggioranza del sangue." *Distinzioni segreti che corrono tra le Casate Nobili di Venezia,* (1684), BNM, Classe It. VII 1531 (7638), no pagination. Another version of the event is told by G. Burnet, an English observer. In his eyes, the arrogance of the Cornaro daughters contrasted vividly with their meager fortune: "The Cornaros carry it so high, that many of the Daughters of the Family have made themeselves Nuns, because they thought their own Name was so noble, that they could not induce themselves to change it for any other: And when lately one of that Family married the Heir of the Sagredos, which is also one of the ancientest Families, that was extreme rich, and she had scarce any Portion at all (for the Cornaros are now very low;) some of their Friends came to wish them Joy of so advantagious a Match; but they very coldly rejected the Compliment, and bid the others go and wish the Sagredos Joy, since they thought the Advantage was wholly on their side." G. Burnet, *Some Letters Containing an Account of what seem'd most remarkable in travelling thro' Switzerland, Italy, some Parts of Germany, &c. In the Years 1685, and 1686* (London, 1724), pp. 145–46. For more on this branch of the Cornaro family, see Hunecke, *Der venezianische Adel,* pp. 172–73.

200. "Sono spinte [le figliuole] dal timore de' padri i quali . . . non potendole maritare a pari loro per non haver facultà bastanti et non volendole maritare ad altri inferiori per non diminuire con questo lo splendore delle famiglie loro." Nuncio Alberto Bolognetti, "Dello stato et forma delle cose ecclesiastiche nel dominio dei signori venetiani," in Aldo Stella, ed., *Chiesa e stato nelle relazioni dei nunzi pontifici a Venezia* (Vatican City, 1964), p. 191.

201. "La Politica di mio Padre ha voluto che io venga in salvo in questo luogo . . . perchè la sua nascita e la sua ambitione non permetteva di collocarmi in matrimonio con persona disuguale di conditione." Sultanini, *Il novo parlatorio,* p. 253.

202. "[P]ure se si volessero al quanto abbassare con dar la povera Gentildonna al ricco Cittadino, conforme li necessitosi Patritij volentieri pigliano l'opulenti Plebee si levarebbero l'occasioni de' Mali e di lamenti." *Discorso aristocratico sopra il governo de' Signori Venetiani come si portano con Dio, con sudditi, e con Prencipi* (Venice, 1675), p. 82.

203. Hunecke claims that "it was very common in the seventeenth and eighteenth centuries, but also earlier, for daughters of patricians to marry husbands who did not belong to their class." Hunecke, *Der venezianische Adel*, p. 102.

204. Cowan, *The Urban Patriciate*, p. 165.

205. See documents IV and V in the appendix of Gullino, *I Pisani dal Banco e Moretta*, pp. 420–23.

206. J. C. Davis, *A Venetian Family and Its Fortune*, p. 107.

207. Stanley Chojnacki's assessment that the second *serrata* helped to establish "uniformity within the patriciate and its differentiation from the rest of society" as essential characteristics of the Venetian nobility has to be approached with caution, since the dowry law of 1420 allowed citizen brides to transgress the limit placed on patrician dowries. Chojnacki, "Social Identity," p. 352.

208. According to Niklas Luhmann, every system of communication (for example, the society of Renaissance Venice or the nobility as a subgroup) is based on a foundational paradox that must be veiled in order for it to function. See, among others, Niklas Luhmann, *Ecological Communication* (Chicago, 1989); and idem, *Love as Passion: The Codification of Intimacy* (Cambridge, Mass., 1986).

209. ASV, San Lorenzo, busta 19, parchment, 4 April 1623.

210. Ibid., 6 June 1628.

211. Apparently, Cornelia and Isabetta were accepted in San Lorenzo for half price. Ibid., 6 January 1635 (m.v.), 30 May 1636.

212. Ibid., 6 February 1641 (m.v.).

213. Ibid., 17 June 1642.

214. Isabetta died in 1647, Cornelia in 1659.

215. ASV, San Lorenzo, busta 19, 9 January 1661 (m.v.), 25 August 1664.

216. ASV, Archivio Notarile Testamenti, Atti Beaciani, busta 152, polizza 75, testament of Gerolamo Corner di Giacomo, 17 March 1655.

217. Ibid., Atti Ziliol, busta 1242, c. 163, testament of 20 December 1600.

218. ASV, San Lorenzo, busta 19, fascicolo "Lite per li ducati sessanta annui de DD. Cornelia, et Isabeta Dolfine," 21 January 1614 (m.v.).

219. Ibid., 12 January 1622 (m.v.).

220. Ibid., 14 December 1622.

221. Ibid., 30 October 1627.

222. Ibid., 10 January 1628 (m.v.).

223. Ibid., 2 June 1622.

224. Ibid., 27 March, 22 May 1638.

225. Ibid., 9 December 1638. It may have been that the sales contract

of 1627 required him to invest the five hundred ducats for ten years only. His refusal seems to have been legally correct, because no court ever bothered him again.

226. Ibid., 31 July 1640 (?).

227. Ibid., 20 July 1643.

228. Given that a nun could easily spend more than fifty years in a convent, the amount her relatives had to pay—if they chose to pay annuities instead of a thousand ducats in cash—could reach up to 3,240 ducats, plus additional expenses for the nun's cell and the festivities when the girl became "dressed," professed, and consecrated. This was a considerable sum compared to the legal maximum of six thousand ducats for bridal dowries. Of course, paying a lifelong rent was qualitatively different from alienating a piece of property from the family compound. However, bridal dowries were also often paid as *livelli* or in installments; and an increase in the number of lawsuits against relatives in the seventeenth century who failed to pay nuns' pensions shows that many families lacked the money to pay the annual sixty ducats.

229. Gabriella Zarri and Susanna Peyronel Rambaldi have already pointed out that forced monachizations and inflated dowries have to be seen in the context of the sixteenth-century "process of aristocratization." Zarri, "Monasteri femminili e città," p. 367; Susanna Peyronel Rambaldi, *Speranze e crisi nel Cinquecento modenese: Tensioni religiose e vita cittadina ai tempi di Giovanni Morone* (Milan, 1979), p. 165. More recently, see Chavarria, "Nobiltà di seggio"; and Cabibbo and Modica, *La Santa dei Tomasi.*

230. Molho, "Tamquam vere mortua."

231. See, among others, Eva Sibylle Rösch and Gerhard Rösch, *Venedig im Spätmittelalter, 1200–1500* (Würzburg, 1991), p. 35.

232. See Paul Ricoeur, *The Rule of Metaphor* (Toronto, 1991).

233. See Peter Brown, *The Body and Society* (New York, 1988); and Schulenburg, "The Heroics of Virginity."

234. See the discussion of figurative thinking by Erich Auerbach, "Figura," in *Scenes from the Drama of European Literature* (Minneapolis, 1984), pp. 11–76.

235. Hunecke, "Matrimonio e demografia."

Chapter Two

1. James S. Grubb, "When Myths Lose Power: Four Decades of Venetian Historiography," *Journal of Modern History* 58, no. 1 (1986): 43–94; Edward Muir, "Images of Power: Art and Pageantry in Renaissance Venice," *American Historical Review* 78, no. 1 (1979): 16–52; idem, *Civic Ritual in Renaissance Venice* (Princeton, 1981); Franco Gaeta, "Venezia da 'stato misto' ad aristocrazia 'esemplare,'" in *Storia della cultura veneta,* vol. 4, pt. 2, *Il Seicento* (Vicenza, 1984), pp. 437–94; Felix Gilbert, "Venice in the Crisis of the League of Cambrai," in *Renaissance Venice,* ed. J. R. Hale (London, 1973), pp. 274–92; idem, "Venetian Diplomacy before Pavia: From Reality to Myth," in *The Diversity of History: Essays in Honor of Sir Herbert Butterfield,* ed. J. H. Elliott and H. G. Koenigsberger (Ithaca, N.Y.,

1970), pp. 81–116; Myron Gilmore, "Myth and Reality in Venetian Political Theory," in *Renaissance Venice,* ed. Hale, pp. 431–44.

2. On the dates of composition and publication, see Felix Gilbert, "The Date of the Composition of Contarini's and Giannotti's Books on Venice," *Studies in the Renaissance* 14 (1967): 183; on the influence of Plato's *Laws* and Polybius's *Histories,* see Felix Gilbert, "The Venetian Constitution in Florentine Political Thought," in *Florentine Studies: Politics and Society in Renaissance Florence,* ed. Nicolai Rubinstein (Evanston, Ill., 1968), pp. 463–500; and Quentin Skinner, "Political Philosophy," in *The Cambridge History of Renaissance Philosophy,* ed. Q. Skinner, E. Kessler, and J. Kraye (Cambridge, 1988), pp. 416ff.

3. Gasparo Contarini, *The Commonwealth and Government of Venice,* trans. Lewes Lewkenor (London, 1599; facsimile ed.: Amsterdam, 1969), p. 17. This is a translation of *Della republica, e magistrati di Venezia.* For Contarini's biography, see Elisabeth G. Gleason, *Gasparo Contarini: Venice, Rome, and Reform* (Berkeley, 1993).

4. Patricia Fortini Brown, "The Self-Definition of the Venetian Republic," in *City States in Classical Antiquity and Medieval Italy,* ed. Anthony Molho, Kurt Raaflaub, and Julia Emlen (Ann Arbor, Mich., 1991), p. 512; idem, *Venice and Antiquity: The Venetian Sense of the Past* (New Haven, 1996).

5. "On that day, as is testified by Holy Scripture, was our first father Adam formed, at the beginning of the creation of the world. On the same day also the Blessed Virgin Mary received the Annunciation from the Angel Gabriel, and the Son of God entered her belly, and then Christ was born, who brought about our Redemption. According to some theologians, Jesus Christ our Redeemer was crucified by the Jews on Mount Calvary on the same day. This is why this day is very noteworthy." "Nel qual giorno, *ut divinae testantur Literae,* fu formato il primo nostro padre Adamo al principio della creazione del Mondo. Nel quale etiam la Beata Vergine Maria dall'Angiolo Gabriello fu annunziata, e il Figliuolo di Dio nel suo ventre entrò, e poi nacque Cristo, che fu la Redenzione nostra. Ancora in questo giorno, secondo alcuni Teologi, Gesù Cristo nostro Redentore fu dagli Ebrei nel Monte Calvario crocefisso. Sicchè è giorno molto memorabile." Marino Sanuto [Sanudo], "Vitae Ducum Venetorum italice scriptae ab origine urbis, sive ab Anno CCCCXXI usque ad Annum MCCCCXCIII auctore Marino Sanuto, Leonardi Filio, Patricio Veneto," in *Rerum Italicarum Scriptores,* ed. Ludovicus Antonius Muratorius, vol. 22 (Milan, 1733), pp. 406–7. On the Jews' exodus from Egypt and other important events that had happened on the twenty-fifth of March, see Thomas Diplovatazio, "Tractatus de Venetae urbis libertate et eiusdem Imperij Dignitate: et Privilegijs, et an de Jure Dominium Venetorum habeat superiorem In temporalibus compositus per me Thomam Diplovatatium Melinghi Patritium Constantinopolitanum I. V. Doctorem" (Venice, ca. 1530), BNM, cod. lat. XIV 74 (4056), ff. 20v–22r. See also Gino Benzoni, "Una città caricabile di valenze religiose," in *La chiesa di Venezia tra riforma protestante e riforma cattolica,* ed. Giuseppe Gullino (Venice, 1990), pp. 37–61; Lionello Puppi, " 'Rex sum

justicie': Note per una storia metaforica del Palazzo dei dogi," in *I Dogi,* ed. Gino Benzoni (Milan, 1982), pp. 183–213; and Manfredo Tafuri, "La 'nuova Constantinopoli': La rappresentazione della 'renovatio' nella Venezia dell'Umanesimo (1450–1509)," *Rassegna* 9 (1982): 25–38. On prefiguration in Christian thought, see Erich Auerbach, "Figura," in *Scenes from the Drama of European Literature* (Minneapolis, 1984), pp. 11–76.

6. William J. Bouwsma, *Venice and the Defense of Republican Liberty: Renaissance Values in the Age of the Counter Reformation* (Berkeley, 1968), p. 197.

7. Gilbert, "The Venetian Constitution"; Skinner, "Political Philosophy."

8. J. G. A. Pocock, *The Machiavellian Moment: Florentine Political Thought and the Atlantic Republican Tradition* (Princeton, 1975), p. 100.

9. "This whole assembly . . . of citizens . . . this great councell representeth in this commonwealth the forme of a popular state. The Duke who hath no time of government limited unto him, but ruleth during life, beareth the shew of a kingly power, representing in all thinges the glory, gravitie and dignity of a king. . . . But the Senate, the tenne, the colledge of elders or chiefe councellors . . . carry with them a certaine shew of an Aristocracy of government of the nobilitie. . . . There is in this cittie of ours an excellent contrived mixture of the best and iustest governments." Contarini, *The Commonwealth and Government of Venice,* pp. 18–19, 33.

10. "Those that have learnedlyest written of the ordering of a commonwealth, iudged that in the government thereof there should be a temperature between the state of nobility & popular sort . . . with . . . wisedome it was ordayned by our auncestors, that the common people should not bee admitted to this company of citizens." Ibid., pp. 14, 16.

11. The ancestors' "wise" disregard of ancient writers' recommendations to grant non-nobles a certain amount of governmental representation also informed their refusal to concede political rights to the nouveaux riches, that is, "the very skum of the people, [who sometimes] do scrape together great wealth, as those that apply themselves to filthy artes." Ibid., pp. 17–18.

12. Ibid., pp. 10–15, 148.

13. Ibid., p. 34.

14. Ibid., p. 18.

15. Ibid., p. 15.

16. Pocock, *The Machiavellian Moment,* p. vii.

17. Ibid., p. 156.

18. "All states, all forms of government that have had and continue to have authority over men, have been and are either republics or principalities. And principalities are either hereditary . . . or they are new. And if they are new, they are either entirely new . . . or they are like limbs added on to the hereditary state of the ruler who acquired them. . . . Those dominions that are acquired by a ruler are either used to living under the rule of one man, or accustomed to being free; and they are either acquired with soldiers belonging to others, or with one's own; either through fortune or through

strength." Niccolò Machiavelli, *The Prince,* ed. and trans. David Wootton (Indianapolis, 1995), p. 6.

19. Niklas Luhmann, "Sthenographie und Euryalistik," in *Paradoxien, Dissonanzen, Zusammenbrüche,* ed. Hans Ulrich Gumbrecht and K. Ludwig Pfeiffer (Frankfurt am Main, 1991), p. 58.

20. "Just as those who paint landscapes set up their easels down in the valley in order to portray the nature of the mountains and the peaks, and climb up into the mountains in order to draw the valleys, similarly in order to properly understand the behavior of the lower classes one needs to be a ruler, and in order to properly understand the behavior of rulers one needs to be a member of the lower classes." Machiavelli, *The Prince,* p. 6.

21. "I have oftentimes observed many strangers, men wise & learned, who arriving newly at Venice, and beholding the beautie and magnificence thereof, were stricken with so great an admiration and amazement, that they woulde . . . confesse, never any thing which before time they had seene, to be thereunto comparable, either in glory or goodlinesse. Yet was not every one of them possessed with the like wonder of one same particular thing: for to some it seemed a matter of infinit marvaile, and scarcely credible to behold, so unmeasurable a quantity of all sorts of marchadise to be brought out of all realmes and countries into this Citie. . . . For it is seated in a remote and secrete place of the Adriatike sea . . . fortified with an admirable artifice of nature." Contarini, *The Commonwealth and Government of Venice,* pp. 1–3. "She [Venice] . . . is nothing but a Divine creation. . . . To me it seems a great thing, because I have seen the impossible in the impossible." "Ella [Venezia] . . . non è se non fattura Divina. . . . A me par gran cosa, perch'io hò veduto l'impossibile nell'impossibile." Nicolò Doglioni, *Le cose notabili, et maravigliose della città di Venetia* (Venice, 1692; first ed.: 1602), pp. 1–2.

22. My interpretation of Venetian political theory, and especially of Paolo Paruta's work, differs considerably from the thesis advanced by William Bouwsma in his study *Venice and the Defense of Republican Liberty.* In Bouwsma's opinion, Florentine historiography had a profound influence on Venetian intellectuals such as Paruta, whose writings represented what he calls a "deepening of Venetian historicism" (p. 223) that accompanied the revival of Renaissance values in government politics at the end of the sixteenth century. However, the treatises and other writings Bouwsma cites as a proof of "the changing mood" in the second half of the sixteenth century, such as Gianmichele Bruto's *Florentinae historiae libri VIII* and the reports of Venetian ambassadors to Rome (p. 270), did not have the Venetian republic as their subject matter. Also, most of the authors whose writings were of a more critical nature did not come from within the Venetian political system. Bouwsma himself points out that works of patrician writers such as Pietro Giustiniani's *Rerum venetarum historia* and Agostino Valier's *Dell'utilità che si puo ritrarre dalle cose operate dai Veneziani* displayed a certain "transitional" character (p. 194). Also, Bouwsma's analysis of Paruta's work, which he singled out as typical of the new style, contains many disclaimers (see his discussion of *Della perfettione della vita politica* on

pp. 216–23); and his concluding remarks on Paruta's *Historia Veneziana* underline the difference between Paruta's work and the work of the major Florentine historians: "He did not altogether abandon the static idealism of the earlier century" (p. 270). As late as 1590, panegyrics appeared that clearly showed that "not all Venetians participated" in the "return" to Renaissance values (p. 269). See also my discussion of Paruta below.

23. Gaetano Cozzi, "Venezia dal Rinascimento all'Età barocca," in *Storia di Venezia,* vol. 6, *Dal Rinascimento al Barocco,* ed. Gaetano Cozzi and Paolo Prodi (Rome, 1994).

24. Manfredo Tafuri, *Venezia e il Rinascimento: Religione, scienza, architettura* (Turin, 1985).

25. Manfredo Tafuri, " 'Renovatio urbis Venetiarum': Il problema storiografico," in *'Renovatio Urbis': Venezia nell'età di Andrea Gritti,* ed. M. Tafuri (Rome, 1984), p. 11; Edward Muir, "The Doge as Primus inter Pares: Interregnum Rites in Early Sixteenth-Century Venice," in *Essays Presented to Myron P. Gilmore,* ed. Sergio Bertelli and Gloria Ramakus (Florence, 1978), 1:145–60. On Gritti's charisma, see Contarini, *The Commonwealth and Government of Venice,* p. 113.

26. Tafuri, " 'Renovatio urbis Venetiarum,' " pp. 23, 29.

27. Cesare Vasoli, "Un 'precedente' della 'vergine veneziana': Francesco Giorgio Veneto e la clarissa Chiara Bugni," in *Postello, Venezia e il suo mondo,* ed. Marion Leathers Kuntz (Florence, 1988), pp. 206, 212.

28. See Bouwsma, who argues in *Venice and the Defense of Republican Liberty* that in the later sixteenth century, Venetian writers overcame the conservative, even regressive tendencies of the era of restoration after Agnadello.

29. Gaetano Cozzi, "Domenico Morosini e il 'De bene instituta re publica,' " *Studi Veneziani* 12 (1970): 449; Tafuri, "La 'nuova Constantinopoli,' " pp. 32–33.

30. Tafuri, " 'Renovatio urbis Venetiarum,' " p. 32.

31. "Per questo rispetto meritamente si chiamano hoggi magnifici i gentili huomini Vinitiani, i quali nella grandezza, & pompa de gli edifici & publici & privati vincono tutti i moderni & pareggiano gli antichi. E i medesimi sono ancho quei veri nobili, i quali voi m'havete si vivacemente dipinti, & mostrati." Lodovico Domenichi, *Dialoghi* (Venice, 1562), p. 73.

32. See chap. 1, n. 28.

33. See chap. 1, n. 29.

34. Cozzi, "Domenico Morosini," p. 425. The Collegio was the executive branch of the government, consisting of the doge along with his councilors and various ministers.

35. Cozzi, "Venezia dal Rinascimento all'Età barocca."

36. Quoted in Cozzi, "Domenico Morosini," pp. 430–31.

37. Cozzi, "Venezia dal Rinascimento all'Età barocca."

38. Claudio Donati, *L'idea della nobiltà in Italia: Secoli XIV–XVII* (Bari, 1988).

39. See, among others, Bouwsma, *Venice and the Defense of Republican Liberty.*

40. "Nobility generates several worthy virtues, that is, magnificence and magnanimity"; but "Virtue combined with honor gives birth to nobility." "Potrebbesi appresso dire da chi lodar volesse la nobiltà, che ella sia produttrice di alcune degne virtù, che sono quasi di lei proprie; cioè della magnificenza, & della magnanimità. . . . La virtù congiunta con l'honore partorisce la nobiltà." Paolo Paruta, *Della perfettione della vita politica* (Venice, 1599; 1st ed.: 1579), pp. 372, 375.

41. "Here . . . rises the city of Venice, with the appearance of something rather born than fabricated: which had its origin on the twenty-fifth of March, 421, at noon." "Quivi . . . sorge la città di Venetia, con sembianza di cosa più tosto nata, che fabricata: ch'hebbe la sua origine del 421 a venticinque di Marzo, sul mezo giorno." Giovanni Botero, *Relatione della Republica venetiana* (Venice, 1605), p. 6v.

42. As was mentioned in chapter 1, no foreign nobleman or Venetian citizen was "aggregated" to the patriciate between about 1500 and 1646. Volker Hunecke, *Der venezianische Adel am Ende der Republik (1646–1797): Demographie, Familie, Haushalt* (Tübingen, 1995), p. 31.

43. "Venetia città . . . gia mille e duecento anni si è franca vergine." Botero, *Relatione*, p. 7r.

44. "Il stupendo et mirabile sito della Veneziana città non solamente questa sommità di Stato ove ella è venuta, a quei primi edificatori da principio poteva promettere, ma a discendenti eziandio stabile, perpetuo et durevole imperio." Marc'Antonio Sabellico, *Del Sito di Venezia Città*, ed. G. Meneghetti (Venice, 1957; first ed.: 1502), p. 10.

45. *Dialogo del Gentilhuomo vinitiano cioè institutione nella quale si discorre quali hanno a essere i costumi del nobile di questa città, per acquistarsi gloria & honore* (Venice, 1576), no pagination.

46. "Questa sola fabricata in mezzo l'acque a niuna altra simile, rende a chi la mira & considera stupor, & admiration incredibile." Francesco Sansovino, *Delle Orationi recitate a principi di Venetia* (Venice, 1562), p. 26v.

47. "Sola tu Venetia . . . sei una nuova Venere nata ignuda nel mezo del mare." Speech by Luigi Groto, ibid., p. 65r.

48. "Percioche il proprio ufficio dell'huom magnifico si è edificare theatri, tempij, piazze, loggie, & palazzi; come si richiede alla dignità della città, & alla presenza, & grandezza di colui che edifica." Domenichi, *Dialoghi*, p. 73; Tafuri, *Venezia e il Rinascimento*.

49. "Thus a constant idea seems to govern the reflections, the discussions, the decisions on the *construction* and *extension* of the city during the entire sixteenth century and beyond: the idea, that is, of turning the very *urban form* into a mirror of the state; and of configuring the urban space, of defining the ways of its organization, of conceiving the architectural signs . . . as symbolic references and an image of the republic itself." Ennio Concina, "Ampliar la città: spazio urbano, 'res publica' e architettura," in *Storia di Venezia*, vol. 6, *Dal Rinascimento al Barocco*, ed. Cozzi and Prodi, p. 271.

50. David Rosand, "Venetia Figurata: The Iconography of a Myth," in *Interpretazioni Veneziane*, ed. David Rosand (Venice, 1984), pp. 177–96.

51. "The law was not exterior to the Venetian aristocracy, not imposed: it was a means of expression of themselves, of their own will, their own character, the highest and most typical expression, most connatural to their own political and civic reality, most indispensable to their own existence; it was the result of their collective will, accepted and applied by everybody as something of their own, something one subjects oneself to, knowing that only in virtue of this [law] can the equality of single individuals be preserved, and with it [i.e., that equality] the liberty of the republic. The body of the aristocracy was constituted by men who were at the same time sovereigns and subjects, judges and judged." Gaetano Cozzi, *Repubblica di Venezia e Stati italiani: Politica e giustizia dal secolo XVI al secolo XVIII* (Turin, 1982), p. 100.

52. Marc'Antonio Sabellico, the first state-employed historian, wrote: "Some say that where the golden church of Saint Mark now stands was the starting point for the building [of Venice], and nearly all agree that the beginning was on the twenty-fifth of March. Whatever the case, if we would just consider some of the excellent works which have been performed on that day, there will be no doubt that [there was] nothing established on that day which is not great and marvelous, [for as] the sacred letters affirm for the perpetual glory of mankind, on that same day the omnipotent God formed our first ancestor. Likewise, [on that day,] the son of God was conceived in the womb of the Virgin." Quoted in Muir, *Civic Ritual in Renaissance Venice*, pp. 71–72. The Latin original is as follows: "Non desunt qui eo loco, ubi nunc auream Divi Marci aedem conspicimus, primo aedificari coeptum non dubitent affirmare: in eo fere omnibus convenire video, VII. Calend. Aprilis primordia urbis coepisse. Quod si eximia quaedam naturae opera, quae eodem die edita dicuntur, considerare volumus, non absurdum erit dictum, nihil ea luce inchoari potuisse, quod non idem magnificum esset, amplum, perpetuum, humanarumque rerum fastigium superaturum. Divinae literae testantur, eodem die ipsum humani generis parentem a Deo optimo formatum: ipsum quoque Dei filium in Virginis utero conceptum." Marcantonio Coccio Sabellico, "Historiae rerum venetarum ab urbe condita libri XXXIII" (first ed.: 1487), in *Degl'istorici delle cose veneziane, i quali hanno scritto per pubblico decreto*, vol. 1 (Venice, 1718), p. 14; see also Benzoni, "Una città caricabile di valenze religiose," p. 46.

53. "Direi che Vinegia è *Venere*, ambe celesti, ambe madri, e nodrici di santissimo amore. . . . Vinegia si hà conservato sempre il fiore della sua virginità." *Le orationi volgari di Luigi Groto Cieco di Hadria da lui medesimo recitate* (Venice, 1593), pp. 108r, 109v.

54. "Questi vapori produssero veramente un nuvol d'oro, che scese poi in forma di pretiosa pioggia nel grembo di questa Vergine non già per corromperla, e darle macchia, come fè il nuvol d'oro sceso nel grembo di Danae per fingimento de' Poeti, ma si bene per conservarla, e darle pregio per testimonio di tutti gli historici." Pompeo Caimo, *Parallelo Politico delle Republiche Antiche, e Moderne* (Padua, 1627), pp. 140–41.

55. I am referring here to Paul Ricoeur's theory of metaphors, according to which a metaphor is a conflation of two *different* concepts on

the basis of their predicative similarities while preserving their substantial difference. See Paul Ricoeur, *The Rule of Metaphor* (Toronto, 1991), esp. pp. 80, 196.

56. "Now a unitie cannot well be contayned, unlesse one being placed in authoritie above . . . have authoritie to combine them together, being scattered & disioynted, and to bind them (as it were) all into one entire body." Contarini, *The Commonwealth and Government of Venice,* p. 38.

57. "Thus in a civil community composed of multiple individuals we consider two things, that is, matter and form, just as in an animal [we consider] the body [as divided into] soul and matter, and [we think of] the form of the city [of Venice] as its body, and of the republic, which perfects and embellishes the community mentioned above, as its soul." "Perochè in una communanza, e moltitudine civile noi consideriamo due cose, la materia, e la forma, quasi in un'animale il corpo, e l'anima, e la materia, e come corpo è la Città, la forma, e come anima è la Republica la quale perció come tale perfettiona & abbelisce la sudetta communanza." Caimo, *Parallelo Politico,* p. 82.

58. "Which other [city] is in terms of its site, its abundance in everything, its order of government, more marvelous than this one? . . . such a noble mother does not deserve less generous sons." "Qual altra [città] è per lo sito, per l'abondanza di tutte le cose, per l'ordine del governo più di questa meravigliosa? . . . a cosi nobil madre non conveniansi men generosi figliuoli." Paolo Paruta, "Orazione per i Nobili Veneziani morti a Lepanto" (19 October 1571), in *Orazioni scelte del secolo XVI,* ed. Giuseppe Lisio (Florence, 1957), p. 298. See also Rosand, "Venetia Figurata," p. 190: "Venice patiently and deliberately created its own visual persona, a heroic queen subsuming all virtue, political wisdom, and historical destiny in her handsome self."

59. Quoted in Margaret F. Rosenthal, *The Honest Courtesan: Veronica Franco, Citizen and Writer in Sixteenth-Century Venice* (Chicago, 1992) p. 46.

60. "E già la terra gonfia il ventre e 'l fianco / inutilmente gravida de' morti / Squarcian care d'amor donne e donzelle / con le candide man le treccie bionde / e l'interne e profonde / lor piaghe amaro pianto / scopre di perle rilucenti e belle / il crin, il viso insanguinato e 'l manto." Valnea Rudman, "Lettura della canzone per la peste di Venezia di Maffio Venier," *Atti dell'Istituto Veneto di Scienze, Lettere ed Arti, Classe di scienze morali e lettere* 121 (1962–63): 639.

61. "Ah povera Venetia! . . . Za tempo intata e verzene . . . Adesso sporca Femena." Antonio Pilot, "Di alcuni versi inediti sulla peste del 1575," *Ateneo Veneto* 26 (1903): 355.

62. See Paolo Preto's study of Venetian responses to the plague of 1575–77; he paraphrases an anonymous contemporary author who tried to explain the catastrophe: "The holy writings and secular history have affirmed . . . without the shadow of a doubt . . . that the Venetian plague is nothing but an angel sent by God to castigate the peoples 'that live like animals,' that is, the Venetians, who were deaf to all those 'holy messengers'

in the past, such as famines, wars, fires, the loss of Cyprus. . . . Everybody took those 'true prodigies' for 'fairy tales,' and thus the adulterer kept the woman that was not his, the usurer sucked the blood of his neighbor again, the sodomite persisted in his infamous sin. . . . The usual exaltation of 'Laconical' [i.e., Spartan] habits in the past, a literary topos taken up by the poet in a period of a rigorous moral and religious tension, is the obvious promise of an apocalyptic denunciation of the vices and sins of a city in which harmony within the families waned and where priests and nuns were immersed in sins. The means of salvation for Venice, the 'dirty woman,' . . . were not physicians from Padua, medicines and other 'superfluous things,' but 'fasting and vigils,' . . . prayers to the Virgin, and litanies to Saint Gregory." Paolo Preto, *Peste e società a Venezia nel 1576* (Vicenza, 1978), p. 80. See also Pilot, "Di alcuni versi inediti"; and Rudman, "Lettura della canzone."

63. See n. 21 above.

64. Quoted in Gino Benzoni, "Venezia, ossia il mito modulato," in *Crisi e rinnovamenti nell'autunno del Rinascimento a Venezia,* ed. Vittore Branca and Carlo Ossola (Florence, 1991), p. 47.

65. In a speech given in honor of the newly elected doge Girolamo Priuli in 1559, Luigi Groto called the city a virgin and a "nuova Venere nata ignuda nel mezo del mare," "senza mura di mura inespugnabili." Groto, *Le orationi volgari,* p. 18v; his speeches also appeared in Sansovino's *Delle Orationi recitate.*

66. "Chi si maraviglierà . . . s'ella, per favor del Cielo, già mille cento quaranta sei anni conservando una incorrotta virginità partecipa quasi della natura delle Sibille? . . . non è dunque senza mura, anzi è attorniata di triplicate muraglie questa Città." Groto, *Le orationi volgari,* p. 37r.

67. "Il non haver Vinegia ne mura materiali, che la circondino, ne porte, che la serrino, ne chiavi, che la ritengano, argomenta la sua ampia libertà, e la sua publica liberalità, fà fede, che ella è un publico mercato, una continua fiera, una patente corte, un'aperto theatro, un porto generale, & una madre universale di tutto il mondo." Ibid.

68. "Così la grandezza di Vinegia è, che in un Mare così amaro sia una Città cosi dolce, in un Mar cosi instabile sia una Republica cosi ferma." Ibid., p. 38r.

69. "Ell' [Venezia] è una imagine della terra, da ogni parte sciolta, & una figura del cielo, da ogni lato aperto." Ibid., pp. 37r–v.

70. Roland Barthes, "L'effet de réel," *Communications* 11, no. 1 (1968): 84–89; see also Stephen Greenblatt's discussion of the "marvelous" as a category in colonial discourse. Stephen Greenblatt, *Marvelous Possessions: The Wonder of the New World* (Chicago, 1991).

71. On Giorgione's *Tempest* and Titian's *Venus,* see Tafuri, "La 'nuova Constantinopoli,'" p. 36; and David Rosand, "Venereal Hermeneutics: Reading Titian's Venus of Urbino," in *Renaissance Society and Culture,* ed. J. Monfansani and R. G. Musto (New York, 1991), pp. 263–80.

72. Francesco Sansovino was the son of Jacopo Sansovino, the architect and sculptor to whom Andrea Gritti offered employment after the sack of

Rome and who designed San Francesco della Vigna, the Zecca, the library, and the loggia on Saint Mark's Square, among other edifices. Tafuri, *Venezia e il Rinascimento.*

73. Later editions were Francesco Sansovino, *Venetia città nobilissima e singolare* (Venice, 1581); Doglioni, *Le cose notabili* (1602); Giovanni Stringa, *Venetia città nobilissima, et singolare, descritta già in XIIII Libri da M. Francesco Sansovino: Et hora con molta diligenza corretta, emendata, e più d'un terzo di cose nuove ampliata dal M. R. D. Giovanni Stringa, Canonico della Chiesa Ducale di S. Marco* (Venice, 1604); Giustiniano Martinioni, *Venetia citta nobilissima, et singolare, descritta in XIIII Libri da M. Francesco Sansovino . . . con aggiunta di tutte le Cose Notabili della stessa Città, fatte, & occorse dall'Anno 1580 fino al presente 1663 . . . Dove vi sono poste quelle del Stringa; servato peró l'ordine del med. Sansovino,* 2 vols. (Venice, 1663).

74. Sabellico, *Del Sito di Venezia Città* (1502).

75. The complete title of the first edition was *Delle cose notabili che sono in Venetia. Libri due ne[i] quali ampiamente, e con ogni verità, si contengono Usanze antiche; Habiti & vestiti; Officii e Magistrati; Vittorie illustri; Senatori famosi; Huomini letterati; Principi e vita loro; Tutti i Patriarchi; Musiche di piu sorti; Fabriche e Palazzi; Scultori e loro opere; Pittori & pitture* (Venice, 1561).

76. Cesare Vecellio, *Habiti antichi et moderni di Diverse Parti del Mondo* (Venice, 1590; facsimile edition: Bologna, 1982).

77. "Questo Habito rappresenta veramente la felice, & bene principiata grandezza di questa Republica Christianissima, fondata sopra lo scoglio fermo della Santa Fede per conservatione, & ornamento di tutta l'Italia, come chiaramente si vede, che ella fino à questi nostri tempi si è conservata Vergine intatta. Lo Habito dunque sopraposto è di gran decoro, & grandezza di questa Serenissima Republica." Ibid., p. 27. There is a reproduction of Franco's engraving of this robe in Muir, *Civic Ritual in Renaissance Venice,* p. 297.

78. Giacomo Franco, *Habiti d'huomeni et donne venetiane con la processione della Ser.ma Signoria et altri particolari cioè trionfi feste et cerimonie publiche della nobilissima città di Venezia* (Venice, 1610), no pagination.

79. "Marin Grimani fù creato Doge l'anno 1595, & fù la sua creazione con tanto giubilio, & tal contento di tutta la Città in universale, che con estraordinario modo fù mostrata chiaramente questa allegrezza. . . . Et perche haveva esso prencipe Moglie, nominata Morosina di famiglia Morosini, ordinó che si dovesse coronare come Dogaressa, il che si fece con tante pompe, & apparati, quante giamai si facessero." Doglioni, *Le cose notabili,* p. 107.

80. Pompeo Molmenti, *La Dogaressa di Venezia* (Turin, 1884), pp. 217–22; Muir, *Civic Ritual in Renaissance Venice,* pp. 293–98.

81. "The essential point [of this ritual] . . . was that in marrying the sea the doge established his legitimate rights of domination over trade routes and over the lands lapped by the waters of the Adriatic." Muir, *Civic Ritual in Renaissance Venice,* p. 124.

82. Ibid., pp. 103–19.

83. On the dogaressa's coronation festivities, see also Gina Fasoli, "Liturgia e ceremonia ducale," in *Venezia e il Levante fino al secolo XV,* ed. Agostino Pertusi, vol. 1 (Florence, 1973), pp. 289–91; and, more recently, Bronwen Wilson, "'Il bel sesso, e l'austero Senato': The Coronation of Dogaressa Morosina Morosini Grimani," *Renaissance Quarterly* 52, no. 1 (1999): 73–139.

84. "Le quali a due à due vestite di bianco con'ventagli di penne bianchissime caminavano appoggiate sopra alcuni giovanetti nobilmente guarniti, & havevano un mazzeto di fiori con manico dorato il qual però era da quei Giovanetti portato, essendo elleno occupate le mani, l'una nell'appoggiarsi, & l'altra nel tenire il ventaglio. Et di tal forma se ne viddero in numero di cento quaranta due tutte giovani, belle, bene attilate, & con un vezzo di perle al collo per ciascuna, un cento d'oro, & catena a cui stava appesso il ventaglio di eccessivo valore, essendo prohibito per legge di portar altre giogie. Poi si viddero cinquanta di più età vestite parte di verde, & pavonazzo. . . . indi cinque mattrone vestite di nero con maniche larghe, la prima moglie del Cancelier grande, e l'altre de Procuratori di San Marco. . . . dietro poi si veniva la Dogaressa con manto d'oro Ducale, & il corno in testa nella guisa del Doge, ma più piccolo alquanto, & stava in mezzo di due Consiglieri." Doglioni, *Le cose notabili,* pp. 124–26.

85. According to some mythographers, Venice was founded on the site of a temple of Venus, where Aeneas worshipped the goddess and received the inspiration to found a city. *Breve trattato delle citta nobili del mondo, et di tutta Italia, con la lunghezza, & larghezza di essa, confini, sito, & provincie, & il principio del Regno de' Longobardi* (Florence, 1574), no pagination.

86. "O magnifica Vinegia per tutti soccorrere messati in mare; ò grembo aperto al commertio di tutti gli huomini; ò mondo nuovo, ò paradiso terrestre." Groto, *Le orationi volgari,* p. 18v.

87. See n. 67 above.

88. See Rosenthal, *The Honest Courtesan,* p. 9.

89. "Ma la puttana non la attacca né al monistero né al marito: anzi fa come un soldato che è pagato per far male, e facendolo non si tiene che lo faccia, perché la sua bottega vende quello che ella ha a vendere. . . . Gli ortolani vendono gli erbaggi, gli speziali le speziarie, e i bordelli . . . mal franciosi." Pietro Aretino, "Ragionamento della Nanna e della Antonia fatto in Roma sotto una ficaia," in *Ragionamento—Dialogo* (Milan, 1988; first ed.: Venice, 1534), p. 275.

90. The eighteenth-century editor of Speroni's works annotates this treatise in the following way: "The motives that the author had in writing this oration become apparent from the opening lines. It was just when he had gotten into trouble because of his first dialogues in Rome that he started to defend himself with this famous apology of his in 1575." "I motivi, che ebbe l'autore di compor questa orazione, appariscono dalle prime parole. E fu appunto allora, quando travagliando in Roma per li suoi primi dialoghi, mise mano a difendersi con quella sua celebre Apologia l'anno 1575." The

opening lines the editor refers to are "Some days ago it was politely suggested to me by a well-meaning gentleman that I should criticize the courtesans, in the hope, as I announce, that by bringing shame on these miserable women by portraying their reprehensible lives in my pages, they would change their behavior and customs." "Li dì passati sendomi imposto cortesemente da alcun signore amorevole, che io biasimassi le cortegiane, con speranza, come io avviso, che vergognando le miserelle, che la lor vita vituperosa fusse ritratta nelle mie carte, cangiasser modi e costumi." Sperone Speroni, *Opere,* vol. 3 (Venice, 1989), p. 191.

91. "Libera tu, signora tu, miserella? e non hai membro sulla persona, che non sia servo di tutto 'l populo. Forse ti vanti di dominarlo, che dì e notte ti viene a casa ad ognora con mani piene di ariento ed oro? o non men pazza, che scelerata. . . . l'oro e l'ariento . . . non è tributo, ma pagamento per comperarti: dunque tu servi, non signoreggi." Ibid., p. 238.

92. Quoted in Rosenthal, *The Honest Courtesan,* p. 133; Italian original in Veronica Franco, *Lettere,* ed. Benedetto Croce (Naples, 1949), p. 38.

93. "Voi sapete quante volte io v'abbia pregata e ammonita ad aver cura della sua virginità. . . . d'improvviso l'avete fatta comparer co' capegli inanellati . . . con tutti quegli altri abbellimenti che s'usano di fare perché la mercanzia trovi concorrenza nello spedirsi." Franco, *Lettere,* pp. 36–37.

94. Quoted in Rosenthal, *The Honest Courtesan,* p. 141.

95. She herself was active in founding the Casa del Soccorso, an asylum for young girls "at risk." See Rosenthal, *The Honest Courtesan,* pp. 131–32.

96. "This liberty of hers [Venice's] was never disturbed, because of the form of her excellent government. Because it [the government] was well balanced among the best kinds of public administration, composed harmonically, well proportioned and unified, it has lasted already for many centuries without civil unrest, without weapons [violence] and [the shedding of] blood among its Citizens, inviolate and immaculate." "La qual libertà non le [a Venezia] fu mai turbata, & ció per la forma del suo eccelso governo. Conciosia che temperato di tutti i modi migliori di qualunque spetie di publica amministratione, & composto a guisa di harmonia, proportionato & concordante tutto a se stesso, è durato già tanti secoli, senza seditione civile, senz'armi, & senza sangue fra i suo Cittadini, inviolabile e immaculato." Sansovino, *Venetia città nobilissima e singolare,* p. 3v.

97. The author claimed that his first edition saw three pirate editions in nine months. "Essendomi stata ristampata quell'opera in Vinetia tre volte in nove mesi, ella . . . m'è . . . lacerata . . . di scorrettioni." Agostino Gallo, "A I Lettori" (To the readers), in *Le tredici giornate della vera agricoltura & de' piaceri della villa,* 2d ed. (Venice, 1564).

98. "I often wonder why agriculture is esteemed and practiced by so few noblemen. For if we think of its ancient origin, which is the foundation of nobility, we find that God has instituted it." "Molto mi meraviglio, onde nasca che da cosi pochi nobili [l'agricoltura] sia stimata, & essercitata. Percioche se riguardiamo l'antica sua origine, ch'è il fondamento della nobiltà,

trovaremo Iddio haverla da principio instituita." Gallo, *Le tredici giornate*, p. 1.

99. The nobleman Giovan Battista Avogadro explains to another nobleman why he left the city: "As life [in the city] was a continuous hell for me, so this life seems to me to be like paradise." "Come quella vita [in città] mi era un'inferno continuo, cosi questa mi pare una vera sembianza del paradiso." Ibid., p. 259.

100. Ibid., pp. 259–67.

101. "Assai più si contentano di stare qui in vita positiva, col godersi gratiosamente con noi in questa sì pretiosa libertà, che di stare da matrone legate con tanti rispetti nella Città." Ibid., pp. 266–67.

102. "[Molte donne] . . . vogliono d'ogni hora poter'andare dove piace loro, & con piu modi ben vestite, imbellettate, profumate, & gonfie di mille vanità, accioche maggiormente siano rimirate, & vagheggiate da questo, & quello che le vede. Non pensando mai in altro, che di scorrere quà, & là secondo i loro capricci; presentandosi sempre dove si balla, si fanno comedie, tragedie, giostre, bagordi, & torniamenti, ó la maggior parte del giorno starsi in porta, & alle finestre a guisa di donne pazze, & senza punto di vergona; le quali sono poi, & saranno sempre scandalo a tutta la Città." Ibid., p. 267.

103. Avogadro represents the late-sixteenth-century ideal of the gentleman farmer, who retired from the world of politics and commerce to enjoy a contemplative, quiet lifestyle "in villa." See the discussions of Paruta's reaffirmation of civic values in Donati, *L'idea della nobiltà in Italia;* and Bouwsma, *Venice and the Defense of Republican Liberty.*

104. "Questo corpo mortale, è a guisa di Nave posta nel mare di molte sceleratezze: lequali perche non possano penetrar nella parte interna . . . in modo, che si sommerga in quelle, bisogna chiuder loro tutte l'entrate." Lodovico Dolce, *Dialogo della institution delle donne* (Venice, 1547), p. 9v.

105. "Io certamente non so, se maggior peccato commettano quei, che rovinano la patria loro, che distruggono le leggi: che occidono i padri, et profanano le cose sacre. Et come puo istimar la moglie impudica d'havere in sua difesa Dio, et amici gli huomini? Le leggi, la patria, il padre, i parenti, i figliuoli, et il marito la condannano, et puniscono acerbamente: Dio giusto giudice con giusta vendetta la castiga." Ibid., p. 40v.

106. "Ma peggio è, che ogn'hora piu cotal morbo và crescendo; mercè de' ciechi mariti, & sciocchi padri che sono cagione di questa si vituperosa usanza: Nè vi sarebbe maggior rimedio, per esterminare questa pestifera semenza, che l'essequir quella giusta sententia fatta pur solamente contra a tutte le male donne. Si come alla cattiva figliuola si debbe dar per dote la morte, per vestimenti i vermi, & per casa la sepoltura; cosi alla infame maritata, si debbono cavar gli occhi, tagliar la lingua, & troncare le mani; ó piu tosto . . . abrusciarla viva." Ibid., p. 267.

107. Ibid., p. 268.

108. "Città veramente donzella immaculata e inviolata, senza macchia d'ingiustizia, e non mai offesa in se stessa da forza nemica per incendio di guerra nè per combustion di mondo, in ogni revoluzione sola per miracolo

conservata non pur intiera ma nè ancor tentata da contrario impeto, sì come sola per miracolo fondata nel mezo dell'acque, e con maravigliosa tranquillità stata in piedi . . . per infinito spazio di tempo." Franco, *Lettere*, p. 12.

109. "Tito Livio, Cornelio Nipote, and Strabone affirm, in agreement with the majority of writers, that the Heneti of Paflagonia . . . settled in this province, which they then called Venetia, of which the most noble inhabitants . . . were made . . . citizens, and then Senators of Rome." "Afferma Tito Livio, Cornelio Nipote, & Strabone, con la maggior parte de gli Scrittori, che gli Heneti di Paflagonia . . . si fermarono in questa Provincia chiamata poi dal nome loro Venetia, i cui habitatori nobilissimi fra gli altri . . . furono . . . fatti prima cittadini, & poi Senatori di Roma." Sansovino, *Venetia città nobilissima e singolare*, p. 1r.

110. See Gaetano Cozzi, "Ambiente veneziano, ambiente veneto: Governanti e governati nel dominio di qua dal Mincio nei secoli XV–XVIII," in *Storia della cultura veneta*, vol. 4, pt. 2, *Il Seicento*, pp. 495–539.

111. "Our forefathers wisely ruled that the common people were not to be admitted among the citizens, in whose hands rests the power of the republic. . . . Because every city needs artisans, and mercenaries, and also private servants. . . . but none of these can be called citizen. For a citizen is a free man, and all of these people serve in a public or private servitude." "I nostri maggiori ordinarono saviamente, che la Plebe non fosse admessa à questa compagnia di Cittadini, nella quale è tutta la possanza della Republica. . . . Percioche ciascuna Città hà bisogno de gli artigiani, e di molti mercenari, & anco di servi privati. . . . ma nessuno di questi veramente si può dire Cittadino. Perche il Cittadino è huomo libero, e tutti questi servono ò servitù publica, ò privata." Gasparo Contarini, *Della republica, e magistrati di Venezia. Libri cinque* . . . (Venice, 1678; first ed. [in Latin]: Venice, 1543), p. 29.

112. "Our very wise forefathers . . . ruled that public reason should better be defined by the nobility of blood than by the abundance of riches." "I nostri antichi huomini savissimi . . . giudicarono, che fosse meglio che questa diffinitione della ragione publica si facesse dalla nobiltà del sangue, che dalla grandezza della robba." Ibid., pp. 30–31.

113. Ibid., p. 16.

114. "Cadeva la publica riputazione . . . oscuravasi l'antica gloria. . . . Ma noi che, illuminati del vero, più non versiamo nelle tenebre di quella ignoranza, saremo forse così ciechi, che non veggiamo lo splendore del favor divino, il quale, sceso in questi uomini per salvarne co'l mezzo della lor virtù, s'è fatto così chiaramente conoscere?" Paruta, "Orazione per i Nobili Veneziani," pp. 309–10.

115. "What do you think, asked Molino, nobility consists of? Nothing else, answered Monsignor of Ceneda, than virtue itself." "Che cosa dunque, soggiunse il Molino, parvi, che ella [la nobiltà] sia? Nient'altro, rispose il Monsignor di Ceneda; che la propria virtù." Paruta, *Della perfettione della vita politica*, p. 363; see also discussion above.

116. "Grandemente importano le ricchezze alla nobiltà, rispose l'Am-

basciator Ponte; peroche elle sono di grande aiuto, & alla buona dispositione interna, & all'esterna operatione della virtù: si nodrisce il ricco di cibi buoni, che la complessione rendono dilicata, & meglio disposta alle discipline. . . . il ricco provede à figliuoli d'ottimi maestri, perche con lo studio aiutino la buona inclinatione. . . . ricco stimo colui, il cui havere è tanto, che possa fare ufficio di buon padre di famiglia, & di buon cittadino: cioè à dire, che, senza bisogno havere dell'altrui possa con le proprie rendite allevare liberalmente la famiglia; & cessando d'ogni opera vile, attendere al governo della Republica, alle lettere, all'armi, ò ad altro honorato, & nobile essercitio." Paruta, *Della perfettione della vita politica*, pp. 389, 404.

117. "La virginità, et altre cosi fatte [virtù] . . . inalzano l'huomo sopra il proprio suo stato dell'humanità. . . . ma la terza [maniera di virtù, i.e., virginità] standosi quasi in luogo più eminente, non sente i tumulti, che nascer sogliono più à basso nell'infima parte della nostr'anima." Ibid., pp. 260–61.

118. "Potrebbesi appresso dire da chi lodar volesse la nobiltà, che ella sia produttrice di alcune degne virtù, che sono quasi di lei proprie; cioè della magnificenza, & della magnanimità. . . . La virtù congiunta con l'honore partorisce la nobiltà." Ibid., pp. 372, 375.

119. Paolo Paruta, *Discorsi politici* (Venice, 1599), pp. 537–39.

120. Ibid., p. 353.

121. "And although the Romans possessed a much greater empire, as is known to everybody, I do not regard our republic as less happy and content. Because the welfare of a republic does not consist of the greatness of the empire, but of [the possibility] to live in tranquility and universal peace." "E quantunque i Romani possedessero tanto maggiore imperio, quanto è noto a ciascuno, non peró giudico la repubblica nostra meno beata e felice. Perciocchè la felicità d'una repubblica non consiste nella grandezza dell'imperio, ma sì ben nel vivere con tranquillità e pace universale." Donato Giannotti, "Della Repubblica e Magistrati di Venezia," in *La Repubblica Fiorentina e la Veneziana di Donato Giannotti* (Venice, 1840), p. 265.

122. "Sono adunque i nostri gentiluomini d'eccellente nobiltà, prima perchè sono discesi da quelli nobili e ricchi i quali, rifuggiti in questi luoghi paludosi, costituirono il corpo della nostra città. Secondariamente perchè hanno il sangue loro mantenuto incorrotto, per non aver patito la nostra città quelle cose che alterano e rinnovano gli abitatori." Ibid., pp. 283–84.

123. In describing the three steps of Venice's ascent to its position as a powerful state, Giannotti distinguishes the period of monarchical rule under the doges from later republican developments. He stresses the *serrata* of 1297 as the de facto birthdate of the patriciate. "The time when our [forefathers] started to rise in greatness and reputation in the handling of public affairs was [the period] between the foundation of the Great Council and its closure." "Da che l'ordine del gran Consiglio fu trovato, insino a che egli fu serrato, nel qual tempo i nostri cominciarono per trattare delle cose pubbliche a salire in grandezza e riputazione." Ibid., p. 285.

124. "E veramente parmi, che si possa osservare una bella somiglianza frà le Republiche e li corpi naturali, che si come frà questi, quelli che non

hanno mescolanza di materia, e non sono partecipi della feccia materiale, come avviene de' corpi celesti per dottrina di Aristotele nel primo del Cielo, e di Aueroe nel libro della sua sostanza, sono esenti di ogni alteramento, e liberi di ogni pericolo di corrottione, ma quelli, che sono materiali, e non hanno potuto fuggire il commercio della materia, cagione di ogni imperfetto, sono soggiacenti a mille varietà. . . . così le Republiche formate di nobili soli senza lasciar loco alla gente popolaresca, sono si ben fondate, che non ricevono quasi alcuna sorte di alteratione, e sono in certo modo perseveranti in eterno, ma quelle, che si veggono d'huomini parte patritij, parte popolani composte mille mutationi sortiscono, dalle quali sono al suo fine finalmente condotte." Caimo, *Parallelo Politico,* pp. 121–22.

125. James Howell, *A Survay of the Signorie of Venice, of Her admired policy, and method of Goverment, &c. with a Cohortation to all Christian Princes to resent Her dangerous Condition at Present* (London, 1651).

126. "And in the name of the Prince, the Senat and peeple of Venice, with humble devotion and in most supplicant maner we pray, beseech and implore that you wold vouchsafe to behold with the countenance of compassion our most afflicted condition, and to apply som comfortable remedy unto them: All the Laws of peace that you shall impose upon us, we will embrace, we shall obey all just, honest and equitable comands not swarving from reason; But haply we deserve that we lay a necessity upon our self, that all things may return to you as tru and lawfull Prince that which our progenitors took from this sacred Empire, and the Dukedom of Austria, which that it may be don more handsomly, we add whatsoever we possesse in the continent, we yeeld, notwithstanding any rites we can clayme unto them. Moreover we are willing to pay every yeer to your Majesty, and the lawfull successors of the Empire 500 weight of Gold in lieu of tribut, and we are ready to obey all Decrees. . . . Defend us therefore from those, we beseech you, with whom we lately joyned our armes, who we find now to be most cruell enemies. . . . Being preserved by this your clemency we shall call you our father, and parent, our protector and founder, and we shall digest these your mighty benefits into our annalls. . . . And truly this will be no small accession of glory to you, that you were the first before whom the Republic of Venice did present her self, to whom she layed down her neck, whom she adores, and reverenceth as som God decended from Heaven." Ibid., p. 43.

127. Ibid., p. 44.

128. Piero Del Negro, "Forme e istituzioni del discorso politico veneziano," in *Storia della cultura veneta,* vol. 4, pt. 2, *Il Seicento,* pp. 407–36.

129. Gaeta, "Venezia da 'stato misto' ad aristocrazia 'esemplare.'"

130. "E sappiate che i nostri senatori molto acconciamente somigliano quelle giovani pulzelle, che caste di animo e vergini di corpo vanno a marito; perché così come i trascurati mariti con mandarle a tutte le feste le pongono ne' balli dei puttanesimi, così le patrie libere co' premi delle memorie pubbliche, che altrui acquistano l'aura populare e il sèguito della vil plebe, imprudentissimamente mettono gli animi civili e ben composti de' senatori loro

ne' salti delle tirannidi." Traiano Boccalini, *Ragguagli di Parnaso,* ed. Luigi Firpo, vol. 1 (Bari, 1948; first ed.: Venice, 1612), p. 294.

131. Tommaso Campanella was imprisoned as a heretic by Spanish authorities in 1599; in his writings, composed while he was in prison, he tried to convince the authorities and judges of his Catholic orthodoxy.

132. This is a pun on Saint Mark's being called the son of Saint Peter. "Now I tell you that a girl remains a virgin as long as she remains under the care of her father." "Ora ti dico, che tanto è vergine la donzella, quanto sta sotto la cura del padre." Tommaso Campanella, *Antiveneti,* ed. Luigi Firpo (Florence, 1945; written in 1606), p. 11.

133. "Are you going to conclude an alliance with the Turk? . . . How will the Turk maintain your liberty and virginity, who has raped and [ridden?] old women, widows, wives, and vile cows?" "Farai lega col Turco? . . . Come il Turco manterrà in te la tua libertà e la tua virginità, il quale ha stuprato e cavalcato le vecchie e vedove e maritate e le vacche vili?" Ibid., p. 19.

134. "You will see then how your vassals will rebel against you and make you a slave, sold and despised, deflowered and in pain, as you despise your father." "Vederai poi tutti i tuoi vassalli ribellarsi a te e farti schiava, venduta e sprezzata, svirginata e dolorosa, come tu sprezzi il padre tuo." Ibid.

135. Cozzi, "Venezia dal Rinascimento all'Età barocca."

136. "La libertà è Signoria della Republica, risede nella sola nobiltà, restandone privi tutti gli altri habitanti, che sono non gia servi ma sudditi." *Squitinio della libertà veneta nel quale si adducono anche le raggioni dell'impero Romano sopra la Città & Signoria di Venetia* ([Mirandola?], 1612), p. 75.

137. Bouwsma, *Venice and the Defense of Republican Liberty.*

138. Quoted in Dorit Raines, "Pouvoir ou privilèges nobiliaires: Le dilemme du patriciat vénetien face aux agrégations du XVIIe siècle," *Annales E.S.C.* 46, no. 4 (1991): p. 836.

139. "The introduction of new noblemen has created another grotesque phenomenon in this Council." "Un altro lavoro a grottesco in questo Consiglio ha fatto l'introduzione de Nobili novi." "Relazione della Serenissima Republica di Venezia con la quale si descrivono i modi del suo Governo, i mezzi per tener a freno la Nobiltà; Le massime de Privati; La Politica che adopra con i Sudditi; il gienio, e le preteze co' Prencipi; Le sue forze ordinarie con che possa operare in un straordinario Armamento; L'abbondanza del Dinaro, e La sicurezza, ò il dubbio alla permanenza, di Cesareo Della Torre" (1682), BNM, Classe It. VII, 1533 (8826), c. 25.

140. "But such a monster is growing nowadays also in Venice, especially after the lengthy oriental war. . . . after the door was opened wide because of the need for money during the war, 55 families of vile persons were admitted to the body of the nobility. . . . Because the new noblemen, neglected by the ancient ones, have formed an alliance with the poor nobility, which is excluded from honorable offices . . . and with the nobility from

Crete, which suffers the same disgrace, they have formed out of three factions a mighty body, so that they can dominate the Great Council." "Ma un tal mostro oggi va crescendo anche in Venezia, massime doppo la guerra ostinata d'Oriente. . . . doppo che aperta amplamente la porta dal bisogno dell'oro nella guerra corrente, si è ammesso al corpo della nobiltà numero di 55 case d'ignobili persone. . . . Perochè, osservandosi i nobili nuovi affatto negletti da' vecchi, si sono congiunti colla nobiltà povera, che . . . vien tenuto lontana dalli onori, e colla nobiltà candiotta, che corre la medesima sventura; onde formano di tre sette un corpo sì possente, che nel Magior Consiglio fanno prevalere quella parte che essi favoriscono." Anonymous author, "Relazione dell' anonimo" (1665–69?), in Pompeo Molmenti, *Curiosità di storia veneziana* (Bologna, 1919), pp. 367–69.

141. "E considerabile ancora, come la Nobiltà antica sij fatta adoratrice della loro maniera . . . per procurarsi il favore de loro voti, perche costoro, come prattici della Mercatura non vogliono venderlo, che a caro prezzo d'Offizii, e di lusinghe." "Relazione della Serenissima Republica di Venezia," c. 25.

142. "Ecco due mali scandalosi, il far la grazia, quando si doverebbe far la giustizia, ed il far la grazia per prezzo . . . e far apparire una prostituta meretrice quella che doverebbe esser una Donzella." Ibid., c. 113.

143. "On voit quelquefois dans une mesme maison un Gentil-homme Venitien logé au premier estage, & une Courtisane . . . au second, sans que le Noble s'en mette beaucoup en peine: voilà en quoy Venise fait consister l'essence de sa liberté. . . . La fameuse liberté de Venise y attire les étrangers en foule, les divertissemens, & les plaisirs les y arrêtent, & épuisent leur bourse." Alexandre-Toussaint Limojon de Saint-Didier, *La Ville et République de Venise,* 3d ed. (Amsterdam, 1680; first ed.: 1670), pp. 328–29.

144. "Dans un pareil déréglement, & dans une corruption si generale, il ne faut pas s'étonner si la maladie, qui suit ordinairement ce vice, est si generalement répanduë; je ne dis pas seulement parmy les Courtisanes, qui en sont presque toutes perduës, mais encore parmy les femmes mariées, dont j'excepte moins les Gentil-Donnes, que les femmes du commun: & la raison est, que . . . non seulement la jeunesse, mais aussi les Nobles mariés, sont presque tous également plongez dans la débauche . . . il arrive que la corruption est presque universelle." Ibid., p. 337.

145. Luhmann, "Sthenographie und Euryalistik."

146. "Pour ce qui est de la vente de la Noblesse, elle est absolument necessaire, veu que les Anciennes Familles s'éteignent de jour en jour, & que si l'on n'en substituoit par d'autres en leur place, le Gouvernement tomberoit bientost en Oligarchie." Amelot de la Houssaie, *Histoire du gouvernement de Venise* (Paris, 1676), 1:127.

147. "[Giacomo Marcello] said that the basis of the Aristocracy was for centuries the number of Patricians, and their harmony; it [the republic] could not exist with few patricians, because of the offices, and because of the elections, which, if one wants them to be free and good, have to be held among many [candidates]. . . . the number of noblemen was already restricted for various reasons . . . and also Rome became great in conceding

citizenship to entire peoples, even defeated ones." "Dicera [Giacomo Marcello], che la base dell' Aristocrazia da secoli essere stato il numero de' Patrizj, e la concordia loro; sopra pochi non poter ella sussistere, nè per cagion degli impieghi, nè per la scelta, che volendosi libera, e buona deve farsi tra molti. . . . il numero de' Nobili già da qualche tempo esser ristretto per varj casi . . . anche l'antica Roma esser divenuta grande col donar la Cittadinanza ai popoli intieri anche vinti." Vettor Sandi, *Principj di storia civile della Repubblica di Venezia dalla sua fondazione sino all'anno di N.S. 1700*, pt. 3, vol. 2 (Venice, 1756), p. 1057.

148. The last addition of new members to the Great Council prior to 1646 had occurred in the late fifteenth century; if one takes the marriage legislation of 1413–22 as a point of departure, the period of "immaculacy" lasted more than two centuries.

Chapter Three

1. Francesca Medioli, "La clausura delle monache nell'amministrazione della Congregazione Romana Sopra i Regolari," in *Il monachesimo femminile in Italia dall'alto medioevo al secolo XVII: A confronto con l'oggi. Atti del Convegno del Centro di studi farfensi: Santa Vittoria di Mantenano, 21–24 settembre 1995*, ed. Gabriella Zarri (Verona, 1997); James R. Cain, "Cloister and the Apostolate of Religious Women," parts 1–4, *Review for Religious* 27, no. 2 (1968): 243–80; no. 4:652–71; no. 5:916–37; 28, no. 1 (1969): 101–21.

2. Raimondo Creytens, O.P., "La giurisprudenza della Sacra Congregazione del Concilio nella questione della clausura delle monache (1564–1576)," *Apollinaris* 37 (1964): 252–85; idem, "La Riforma dei monasteri femminili dopo i Decreti Tridentini," in *Il Concilio di Trento e la riforma tridentina: Atti del convegno storico internazionale, Trento, 2–6 settembre 1963* (Rome, 1965), 1:45–84.

3. "Bizzoche," in *Dizionario degli istituti di perfezione*, ed. Guerrino Pelliccia and Giancarlo Rocca, vol. 1 (Rome, 1974), columns 1476–77.

4. Katherine Gill, "*Scandala:* Controversies Concerning Clausura and Women's Religious Communities in Late Medieval Italy," in *Christendom and Its Discontents*, ed. Scott Waugh and Peter Diehl (Berkeley, 1996), pp. 177–203.

5. Graciela S. Daichman, *Wayward Nuns in Medieval Literature* (Syracuse, 1986); Gabriella Zarri, *Le sante vive: Profezie di corte e devozione femminile tra '400 e '500* (Turin, 1990); Katherine Gill, "Open Monasteries for Women in Late Medieval and Early Modern Italy: Two Roman Examples," in *The Crannied Wall: Women, Religion, and the Arts in Early Modern Europe*, ed. Craig A. Monson (Ann Arbor, Mich., 1992), pp. 15–47.

6. Jane Tibbetts Schulenburg, "Women's Monastic Communities, 500–1100," *Signs* 14, no. 2 (1989): 261–92.

7. Letizia Arcangeli, "Ragioni politiche della disciplina monastica: Il caso di Parma tra Quattro e Cinquecento," in *Donna, disciplina, creanza cristiana dal XV al XVII secolo*, ed. Gabriella Zarri (Rome, 1996), pp. 165–87.

8. Jo Ann Kay McNamara, *Sisters in Arms: Catholic Nuns through Two Millennia* (Cambridge, Mass., 1996), pp. 385–418.

9. Gill, "*Scandala*"; Maria Pia Pedani, "L'osservanza imposta: I monasteri conventuali femminili a Venezia nei primi anni del cinquecento," *Archivio Veneto*, 5th ser., 179 (1995): 113–25.

10. Gabriella Zarri, "Monasteri femminili e città (secoli XV–XVIII)," in *Storia d'Italia*, annali 9, *La Chiesa e il potere politico dal Medioevo all'età contemporanea*, ed. Giorgio Chittolini and G. Miccoli (Turin, 1986): 357–429.

11. Lucia Ferrante, "L'onore ritrovato: Donne nella Casa del Soccorso di San Paolo a Bologna (secc. XVI–XVII)," *Quaderni Storici* 53, no. 2 (1983): 499–527; Luisa Ciammitti, "Quanto costa essere normali: La dote nel conservatorio femminile di Santa Maria del Baraccano (1630–1680)," ibid., 469–97; Sherrill Cohen, *The Evolution of Women's Asylums since 1500* (New York, 1992); idem, "Convertite e malmaritate: Donne 'irregolari' e ordini religiosi nella Firenze rinascimentale," *memoria* 5 (1982): 46–63; Lucia Ferrante, Maura Palazzi, and Gianna Pomata, eds., *Ragnatele di rapporti: Patronage e reti di relazione nella storia delle donne* (Turin, 1988); Angela Groppi, *I conservatori della virtù: Donne recluse nella Roma dei Papi* (Bari, 1994).

12. Michel Foucault, *The Birth of the Clinic: An Archaeology of Medical Perception* (New York, 1973; first ed. [in French]: 1963); idem, *Madness and Civilization: A History of Insanity in the Age of Reason* (New York, 1988; first ed. [in French]: 1965); idem, *Discipline and Punish: The Birth of the Prison* (New York, 1977; first ed. [in French]: 1975); McNamara, *Sisters in Arms*, p. 472.

13. McNamara, *Sisters in Arms*, p. 475.

14. Wolfgang Reinhard, "Disciplinamento sociale, confessionalizzazione, modernizzazione: Un discorso storiografico," in *Disciplina dell'anima, disciplina del corpo e disciplina della società tra medioevo ed età moderna*, ed. Paolo Prodi (Bologna, 1994), p. 109.

15. Ibid., pp. 111–13, 123.

16. Dilwyn Knox, "Disciplina: Le origine monastiche e clericali del buon comportamento nell'Europa cattolica del Cinquecento e del primo Seicento," in *Disciplina dell'anima*, ed. Prodi, pp. 63–99; also published as "'Disciplina': The Monastic and Clerical Origins of European Civility," in *Renaissance Society and Culture, Essays in Honor of Eugene F. Rice Jr.*, ed. J. Monfasani and R. G. Musto (New York, 1991), pp. 107–35. Knox argues for a revision of Norbert Elias's model of the process of civilization, locating its origins in medieval monasticism as opposed to court culture.

17. Gabriella Zarri, "Disciplina regolare e pratica di coscienza: Le virtù e i comportamenti sociali in comunità femminili (secc. XVI–XVIII)," in *Disciplina dell'anima*, ed. Prodi, p. 262.

18. In 1593, a community of Dimesse was founded in Murano. See chap. 1, n. 65.

19. Zarri, "Disciplina regolare," p. 264.

20. McNamara, *Sisters in Arms*, pp. 452–525; Anne Conrad, *Zwischen*

Kloster und Welt: Ursulinen und Jesuitinnen in der katholischen Reformbewegung des 16./17. Jahrhunderts (Mainz, 1991); idem, "Ordensfrauen ohne Klausur? Die katholische Frauenbewegung an der Wende zum 17. Jahrhundert," *Feministische Studien* 1 (1986): 31–45; Elizabeth Rapley, *The Dévotes: Women and Church in Seventeenth-Century France* (Montreal, 1990); Joseph Grisar, " 'Jesuitinnen': Ein Beitrag zur Geschichte des weiblichen Ordenswesens von 1550–1650," in *Reformata Reformanda, Festschrift für Hubert Jedin zum 17. Juni 1964,* vol. 2 (Münster, 1965), pp. 70–113; idem, *Maria Wards Institut vor Römischen Kongregationen, 1613–30* (Rome, 1966).

21. McNamara, *Sisters in Arms,* pp. 489–525, esp. 507. On the phenomenon of "false saints" and their prosecution by the Inquisition, see Anne Jacobson Schutte, " 'Piccole donne', 'grandi eroine': Santità femminile 'simulata' e 'vera' nell'Italia della prima età moderna," in *Donne e fede: Santità e vita religiosa in Italia,* ed. Lucetta Scaraffia and Gabriella Zarri (Bari, 1994), pp. 277–302; and idem, "Inquisition and Female Autobiography: The Case of Cecilia Ferrazzi," in *The Crannied Wall,* ed. Monson, pp. 105–14.

22. Gabriella Zarri, "Recinti sacri: Sito e forma dei monasteri femminili a Bologna tra '500 e '600," in *Luoghi sacri e spazi della santità,* ed. Sofia Boesch Gajano and Lucetta Scaraffia (Turin, 1990), pp. 381–96.

23. Zarri, *Le sante vive;* idem, "Dalla profezia alla disciplina (1450–1650)," in *Donne e fede,* ed. Scaraffia and Zarri, pp. 177–226; Gill, "Open Monasteries"; Karen Scott, "Women's Networks, and the Lay Apostolate in the Siena of Catherine Benincasa," in *Creative Women in Medieval and Early Modern Italy: A Religious and Artistic Renaissance,* ed. E. Ann Matter and John Coakley (Philadelphia, 1994), pp. 105–199; Caroline Walker Bynum, "Corpo femminile e pratica religiosa nel tardo medioevo," in *Donne e fede,* ed. Scaraffia and Zarri, pp. 115–56; idem, *Holy Feast and Holy Fast: The Religious Significance of Food to Medieval Women* (Berkeley, 1987); idem, *Jesus as Mother: Studies in the Spirituality of the High Middle Ages* (Berkeley, 1982).

24. Craig A. Monson, *Disembodied Voices: Music and Culture in an Early Modern Italian Convent* (Berkeley, 1995); idem, "The Making of Lucrezia Orsina Vizzana's Componimenti Musicali (1623)," in *Creative Women,* ed. Matter and Coakley, pp. 297–323; Robert Kendrick, *Celestial Sirens: Nuns and Their Music in Early Modern Milan* (Oxford, 1996); idem, "Four Views of Milanese Nuns' Music," in *Creative Women,* ed. Matter and Coakley, pp. 324–42; Elissa B. Weaver, "Suor Maria Clemente Ruoti, Playwright and Academician," ibid., pp. 281–96; idem, "The Convent Wall in Tuscan Drama," in *The Crannied Wall,* ed. Monson, pp. 73–86; idem, "Le muse in convento: La scrittura profana delle monache italiane (1450–1650)," in *Donne e fede,* ed. Scaraffia and Zarri, pp. 253–76; idem, "Spiritual Fun: A Study of Sixteenth-Century Tuscan Convent Theater," in *Women in the Middle Ages and the Renaissance: Literary and Historical Perspectives,* ed. Mary Beth Rose (Syracuse, 1986), pp. 173–205.

25. Danilo Zardin claims, however, that nuns continued to collect and read religious and, to a certain extent, even secular books published before

the Index. Danilo Zardin, *Donna e religiosa di rara eccellenza: Prospera Corona Bascapè, i libri e la cultura nei monasteri milanesi del Cinque e Seicento* (Florence, 1992); idem, "Mercato librario e letture devote nella svolta del Cinquecento tridentino: Note in margine ad un inventario milanese di libri di monache," in *Stampa, libri e lettura a Milano nell'età di Carlo Borromeo,* ed. Nicola Raponi and Angelo Turchini, Biblioteca di storia moderna e contemporanea, vol. 3 (Milan, 1992), pp. 135–246.

26. Gabriella Zarri, "Donna, disciplina, creanza cristiana: Un percorso di ricerca," in *Donna, disciplina, creanza cristiana,* ed. Gabriella Zarri, pp. 5–19. Her article is the introduction to a collection of works on the history of female religious life and identity formation in the sixteenth century, followed by an inventory of contemporary books on devotion addressed to a female readership; this catalogue is a most useful tool for future research on the subject. See also Anne Jacobson Schutte, *Printed Italian Vernacular Religious Books, 1465–1550: A Finding List* (Geneva, 1983); and Gabriella Zarri, "Note su diffusione e circolazione di testi devoti (1520–1550)," in *Libri, idee e sentimenti religiosi nel Cinquecento italiano, 3–5 aprile 1986* (Modena, 1987), pp. 131–54.

27. Marilena Modica Vasta, "La scrittura mistica," in *Donne e fede,* ed. Scaraffia and Zarri, pp. 375–98; Katherine Gill, "Women and the Production of Religious Literature in the Vernacular, 1300–1500," in *Creative Women,* ed. Matter and Coakley, pp. 64–104.

28. "Andono a la Celestia perchè quelle monache Conventual molto disoneste portano caveli longi etc. E . . . loro visto una fia . . . Taiapiera con drezuole in testa di cavelli, il Patriarca l'aferó e di soa man li taió li cavelli." Marino Sanuto [Sanudo], *I diarii, 1496–1533* (Venice, 1879–1902), 25 August 1525, vol. 39, col. 345.

29. "Che [le monache] . . . non possino portar Vardacuori, scarpe, over scarpette alla Romana, Cassi duri, camise increspate, et lavorate alla condizione, et al modo delle mondane, fazzoletti lavorati, che si portano in mano, et altre vanità, come capelli biondi, rizzi, e bende stoccate." Patriarch Giovanni Trevisan, "Ordini generali," 24 November 1578, MCC, CC 2570, c. 242.

30. Patriarch Giovanni Trevisan, 23 September 1579, APV, Visite Trevisan (1560–89), c. 54v.

31. "Tutte le Monache debbono vestire con habiti honesti, et modesti tanto di sopra quanto di sotto talmente che non sia visto . . . nè il petto, nè altra parte scoperta non portino capelli, et portino le bende basse sul fronte." Patriarch Lorenzo Priuli, visitation of Sant' Andrea de Zirada, 9 April 1592, APV, Visite Priuli (1592–96), cc. 38r–v.

32. *Fonghi* or *fonghetti* (literally, "little mushrooms") was the name of a fashionable hairstyle that covered the forehead. Antonio Pilot, "Frottola vernacola inedita contro le monache e capitolo in risposta," *Luceria* 1, no. 7–8 (1910): 6, n. 4.

33. "[I vestimenti] . . . non siano di colore ne di estraordinaria finezza, li capelli bassi senza fonghi nelle tempie, ne zuffi in capo le bende . . . bassi, schietti, non gretolati; ne si porti habito nissuno di seta, l'habito sia alto, li veli abondanti, che coprirono tutto il petto, et le spalle. . . . li si prohibisce

totalmente il portar cassi, e zoccoli differenti." Patriarch Francesco Vendramin, visitation of Sant' Andrea de Zirada, 12 November 1609, APV, Visite Vendramin (1609–18), no pagination.

34. "Peró debbano le Monache [. . . ?] col capo velato in maniera che niente si veda dei capelli. . . . Li veli delle spalle siano tanto copiosi et ampli che coprano tutta la carne, siano sottili ma non trasparenti." Patriarch Francesco Vendramin, visitation of San Zaccaria, 19 October 1609, ibid.

35. "Prohibendo . . . l'uso de maneghetti di telle sottili . . . o di calce a gucchia, di scarpe alla Romana con cordelle di seda, et cose simili. . . . Prohibendo al tutto . . . Recchini . . . aghi d'argento e doro, o con altra sorte di ornamenti come di smalti, di perle, et di cose simili. . . . dalle tempie non si veggano fuori [capelli] longhi, o in forma di rizzi di sopra la fronte in forma di fonghetti, et monticelli." Patriarch Francesco Vendramin, 4 January 1619 (m.r.), MCC, CC 2570, c. 288. Illustrations of some of the nuns' dresses are reproduced in Pompeo Molmenti, *La storia di Venezia nella vita privata,* vol. 3 (Bologna, 1908), pp. 408–10.

36. "Two nuns may not sleep in one bed, nor in one room together." "Le monache non dormino doi in un letto, ne meno due in una cella." Patriarch Lorenzo Priuli, visitation of Sant' Andrea de Zirada, 9 April 1592, APV, Visite Priuli, c. 37r. "You should eat in the common refectory." "Si viva in comune Refettorio." *Constitutioni, et decreti approvati nella sinodo diocesana, sopra la retta disciplina monacale sotto L'illustrissimo, & Reverendissimo Monsignor Antonio Grimani Vescovo di Torcello. L'anno della Natività del Nostro Signore. 1592. Il giorno 7. 8. & 9. d'Aprile* (Venice, 1592), p. 37r.

37. "[The nuns] should refrain from writing [letters]." "S'astenghino dallo scrivere." Grimani, *Constitutioni,* p. 45r. "You may not learn to sing *canto figurato,* nor to play any kind of instrument." "Non possiate, ne debbiate imparar a cantar canto figurato, n'a sonar alcuna sorte d'instrumento." Patriarch Giovanni Trevisan, "Mandatum generale," 1575, APV, Visite Trevisan, c. 48r.

38. "The windows, air shafts, or any other site that . . . offers a view over the street, or other public sites . . . shall be walled up." "Le fenestre, luminali, & qual si voglia altro luogo, che . . . havesse la vista sopra la strada, ò altri luoghi publici . . . siano murati." Grimani, *Constitutioni,* p. 25r. "No nun should dare to possess a thing as her own with sensual affection, nor even desire to have it." "Nessuna Monaca ardisca di possedere cosa alcuna come propria con sensuale affettione, nè anco desiderare di haverla." Ibid., p. 32r (36r?).

39. Marcel Mauss, "Techniques of the Body," *Economy and Society* 2 (1973): 70–87.

40. "The observance of silence . . . the guarding of the exterior senses . . . [and] the guarding of the eyes [are necessary]. . . . [The nun] should restrain her sense of hearing . . . [and] restrain her sense of taste. . . . She has to . . . refrain from touching herself and others, and should also shun embraces and kisses." "[L']osservanza del silentio . . . la custodia de' sensi esteriori . . . [e] la custodia de gli occhi [sono necessarie]. . . . Bisogna che

[la monacha] raffreni l'udito . . . raffreni il gusto. . . . Debbe . . . raffrenare il tatto in se stessa, & in altri, fugga ancora gli abbracciamenti & basci." "Dialogo del divino Dionisio Certosino della Riforma delle Monache tradotto in volgare dal Reverendo Don Iacomo Mariabonna," in *Avvertimenti monacali, et modo di viver religiosamente secondo Iddio per le vergini, et spose di Giesu Christo di diversi eccellentissimi auttori antichi et moderni nuovamente posti insieme, & mandati in luce aggiuntovi lo stadio del Cursor Christiano, tradotto di Latino in Volgare da M. Lodovico Dolce. Leggano le Religiose i presenti trattati perche sono molto utili à superare le difficultà di questa vita, & acquistare la palma della promessa Virginità* (Venice, 1576), p. 70.

41. "One sin follows the next." "Un peccato tira ad un'altro." Ibid., p. 69.

42. "Nelle vostre Celle non possiate tenir tapedi, spaliere, panni rossi, nè d'altri colori a torno li muri, letti sontuosi, e superbi cioè con sponzette . . . copertari lavorati, e ricamati, e medesimamente li lenzuoli, o coscini, e coscinelli, nè banchaletto da letto." Patriarch Giovanni Trevisan, "Ordini generali," 24 November 1578, MCC, CC 2570, c. 242. At the beginning of the sixteenth century, the nunnery chest of a wealthy novice could easily contain items such as "a gold jewel . . . an embroidered veil for the hair . . . 2 headrests, 2 cushions . . . a pair of green serge curtains . . . 6 lengths of satin for hose." Quoted in Victoria Primhak, "Women in Religious Communities: The Benedictine Convents of Venice, 1400–1500" (Ph.D. diss., University of London, 1991), p. 151. Despite the convent reformers' concerted efforts to reintroduce collective dormitories, most nuns continued to live in lavishly furnished individual cells up until the late seventeenth century. Silvia Evangelisti, " 'Farne quello che pare e piace . . .': L'uso e la trasmissione delle celle nel monastero di Santa Giulia di Brescia (1597–1688)," *Quaderni Storici* 88, no. 1 (1995): 85–110.

43. "[Virginitas] repraesentat integritatem Ecclesiae triumphantis." Francesco Pellizzari, *Manuale Regularium*, vol. 2 (Lugduni [Lyons], 1653), para. 80, p. 801.

44. "Vedendo i Progenitori Nostri nel primo governo della Nostra Città esser stà imposto debite pene a i delinquenti di ogni qualità di delitto, eccetto il nefando vizio, et peccato del sacrilegio, cioè contamination delle vergini sacre a Dio [de]dicate, attestarono . . . perchè non si havendo tal scelerità per centinaia d'anni . . . mai sentita nella terra nostra hebbero preso constanti quelli santi primi Padri della Rep.ca essere impossibile che pensino non che effetto tanto abominevole, quanto è violar le spose di X.o Sig. Dio nostro, potesse mai cader in mente de homo christian.—Tanta reputarono esser la horibilità et abomination del peccato.—Ma sentendosi da poi molti anni tal peste come rara pullullar et . . . accrescere, furono fatte diverse provisioni per estirparla, la qual tenendo ut plurimum alla punition dell'effetto." Council of Ten, 9 August 1514, ASV, PsM, capitolari, reg. 1, c. 1v, in Innocenzo Giuliani, O.F.M, "Genesi e primo secolo di vita del Magistrato sopra monasteri," *Le Venezie Francescane* 28, no. 3–4 (1961): 148.

45. "Eum, qui copulam habet carnalem cum Moniali, illaqueari tribus criminibus, nempé sacrilegio . . . adulterio spirituali (quatenus violat sponsam Christi) & incestu (cum Monialis sit sponsa Dei, qui est pater noster, & consequenter consanguinea nostra, cum omnes sumus filij Dei)." Pellizzari, *Manuale Regularium,* p. 817.

46. René Girard, *Violence and the Sacred* (Baltimore, 1977).

47. "The exact connotation of the association of incest with fornication with nuns . . . became a commonplace in the rhetoric of such cases in the fifteenth century." Guido Ruggiero, *The Boundaries of Eros: Sex Crime and Sexuality in Renaissance Venice* (Oxford, 1985), pp. 73–74.

48. "Signori, vui fate serar le chiesie per paura di la peste: fate prudentemente; ma se Dio vorrà, non vallerà a far serar le chiesie. Se voria remediar a le cause che induce la peste, ch'è li peccati orendi che si fa; e biasmar Dio e santi; le scole di le sodomie; li infiniti contrati usurarii si fa a Rialto; e per tutto el vender di la justicia et far in favor del richo et contra il povero. Et pezo: quando vien qual che signor in questa terra, li mostrate li monasteri di monache, non monasterii ma prostibuli e bordelli publici. Serenissimo principe! io so che non sete ignorante, e che tutto sapeti meglio cha mi. Provedete, provedete, e provedereti a la peste." Quoted in Sanuto, *I diarii,* 24 December 1497, vol. 1, col. 836.

49. "[P]er purgar la terra nostra da cusi horendo vitio." Council of Ten, 9 August 1514, in Giuliani, "Genesi," p. 149.

50. "Non sia alcuna persona . . . che ardisca . . . parlar con Monache Sacre o non sacre . . . salvo Padri, fratelli, barbani, zermani zoè fradelli, et fioli de fradelli et de sorelle de Padri et de Madri et cugnadi et questi tutti alle grade solamente dei parlatorii deputadi et non altramente." Ibid.

51. "Giardino chiuso tu sei, sorella mia, sposa, giardino chiuso, fonte sigillata." Saint Jerome, Letter to Eustachium, in *Avvertimenti monacali,* pt. 2, quoted from Saint Jerome, *Lettere,* ed. Claudio Moreschini (Milan, 1989), p. 147.

52. "La prima [è] dele cenobite cioe d[i] quelle le quali habitano neli monasterii . . . la seconda: he dele anachorite zoe heremite: le quale . . . vano al deserto . . . sole . . . la terza sorte pessima e dele sarabaite le quale . . . facendo opere mondane . . . Et non serate neli seralgi de Dio: ma nele proprie stantie: hano per leze li sui desiderii: & la sua propria voluna . . . la quarta sorte de monache vien chiamata vagabonde per che tuto el tempo de la vita sua per diverse provintie alozano . . . sempre discorando: e non mai stabile: & compiacendo ale proprie volonta & a piaceri dela gola." *Questa sie la regula del glorioso confessore miser Sancto Benedeto in vulgare ad instantia de le venerabile monache de la celestia observante novamente stampata* (Venice, 1527), pp. 4r–v.

53. "Le Monache . . . abbandonati i loro Conventi, e Monasteri sotto pretexto de Brevi . . . vanno vagando et per la città, et de fuori, come li piace, cum scandalo suo, et murmuration universale." Pregadi, 22 March 1501, ASV, CL, busta 288, c. 239r.

54. "Che i luoghi sacri, dove si rinchiudeno Vergini dedicate à servire

à sua Divina Maestà, & elle stesse ancora fossero preservate, e custodite dalle profanità, & contaminationi del Mondo." Council of Ten, "Deliberatione dell'Eccelso Conseglio di X," 7 February 1604 (m.v.), ibid., c. 421r.

55. According to the Benedictine rule, for example, a nun was to be expelled from the convent after she had left the convent three times: "The sister who, because of her vices, leaves the convent or is expelled and then wants to return should first promise to refrain from that vice because of which she had left. Then she can be accepted into the lowest rank [among the nuns], so that she may prove her humility. And if she leaves the convent once again, she can be accepted again in the same way, up to three times. But after the third time, she should know that she will not be allowed to return to the convent." "Quella sorela la quale per proprio vicio usira o ver sara cazata fuor de monasterio: se la vora retornare, prima prometa & desponsasse ad ogni emendation del vicio per el quale lei e uscita fora: & cosi sia recevuta nel ultimo grado: azo che per questo sia provato la sua humilita: & se ancora una altra volta usira [?] del monasterio: per quel medesimo modo sia recevuto fina la terza volta: ma dapoi la terza volta: sapia che ogni retorno nel monasterio li sara negato." *Questa sie la regula*, p. 14r. In his preface to the *Constitutioni, et decreti approvati* of 1592, Bishop Antonio Grimani tried to convince his readers that "we do not intend to derogate ... from any rule of any convent, nor from the particular constitutions that we gave you during the visitation, nor from our decrees and rules, nor from the religious and praiseworthy customs that are in vigor in our well-ordered and devout convents." "Non intendiamo di derogare ... alle regole di ciascheduno Monasterio, ne all'altre particolari constitutioni lasciate da noi in visitatione, & altri decreti, & mandati nostri; ne meno alle religiose, & laudabili consuetudini, che sono in uso nelli bene ordinati, & divoti Monasteri nostri" (p. 1v).

56. See Creytens, "La giurisprudenza della Sacra Congregazione del Concilio;" and idem, "La Riforma dei monasteri femminili."

57. Patriarch Lorenzo Priuli, *Ordini, & avvertimenti, che si devono osservare ne' Monasteri di Monache di Venetia: Sopra le visite, & clausura* (Venice, 1591).

58. Patriarch Lorenzo Priuli, visitation of San Daniele, 29 November 1592, APV, Visite Priuli, cc. 59r–62r.

59. "We order that the doors of the cells should have no locks, so that [the nuns] cannot lock themselves in, and prevent the abbess from entering suddenly and spontaneously, and visiting them during the day, and night as she pleases." "Ordiniamo che sù le porte delle Celle non si tengano serrature, ne catenacci, acció [le monache] non possino serrarsi dentro, & per levare la facilità all'Abbadessa di potere subito, & all'improviso entrare, & visitarle di giorno, et di notte à suo beneplacito." Grimani, *Constitutioni*, p. 31v.

60. This novelty provoked resistance in the convent of Santa Lucia; see the letter of Nuncio Marcello, Archbishop of Otranto, to the Cardinal of Montalto, 10 February 1590 (m.r.), Archivio Segreto del Vaticano (AV), Nunziature di Venezia, reg. 27, c. 18r.

61. Council of Ten, 10 June, 31 August 1569, in Giuliani, "Genesi," pp. 162–63.

62. See Zarri, "Monasteri femminili e città," p. 401.

63. "You should not tolerate or allow that in your parlors unruly things happen, like cooking, or [the] serving [of] food . . . to anybody." "Non dobbiate admetter, ne permetter che nelli Parlatori vostri se faccino simili disordini di far mangiar, nè dar da mangiar a . . . persona alcuna." Patriarch Giovanni Trevisan, "Mandatum generale," 10 January 1565 (m.r.), MCC, CC 2570, c. 171; see also his "Mandatum generale," 29 October 1582, APV, Visite Trevisan, c. 62r. "We hereby notify all Reverend Mother Abbesses, Prioresses, Vicaresses, and nuns of our convents that since the time of Patriarch Trevisano it has been prohibited for anybody . . . to eat . . . in the parlors . . . and [that] the Abbesses, Prioresses, Vicaresses, Secretaries, and the other nuns who allowed, or consented to, or participated in, or assisted in, the offering of favors such as distributing wine, pastries, and other things would be deprived of their offices, and of their active and passive right to vote, and of the possibility of entering the parlors for one year." "Per tanto notifichiamo a tutte le RR. Madri Abbadesse, Priore, Vicarie, e Monache de Mon.rij nostri esser stato fino dal Patr.ca Trivisano pia, e santamente prohibito a qualsivoglia persona . . . a mangiare . . . nei parlatori . . . et le Abbadesse, Priore, Vicarie, et Camerlenghe, et altre Monache che permettessero, o fossero consentienti, o partecipi, o che prestassero aiuto, favore con ministrar vino, bozzolai, et altre cose . . . caschino in privatione dell' Abbadessato, Priorato, Vicariato, et di voce attiva, e passiva, et di poter andar in parlatorio per anno uno." Patriarch Francesco Vendramin, "Mandatum generale," 12 February 1609 (m.r.), MCC, CC 2570, c. 277.

64. Laws of the Senate, 31 June 1472, ASV, Senato Terra, reg. 6, cc. 166r–v; 22 December 1536, Senato Terra, reg. 29, cc. 83v–84r; 26 March 1605, Senato Terra, reg. 75, cc. 19r–v.

65. "Essendo interdette, et serrate le Chiese di due Monasterij di Moniche franciscane sottoposte ultimamente al governo di Mons.r Patriarcha per la loro ostinatione di non voler obbedire al Breve di N. S.re otto giorni sono rotto il muro della clausura entrar[o]no nella Chiesa esteriore apersero le porte, e stettero un giorno intiero passegiando in essa, siche per minaccie del Principe ritornar[o]no nella Clausura . . . [le monache] si sono levate alle Badesse, et Vicarie delli sodd.ti due Monasterij, e carcerate in altri Monasterij. Quest' essecutione è stata fatta d'ordine di Monsig.r Patriarcha et mio dalli Capi del Cons.o de dieci e Senatori Deputati sopra li Monasterij, essendovi bisognato la loro autorità, e Braccio per esser obbediti senza tumulto." Letter of Monsignor Taverna, Bishop of Lodi, to Monsignor Cinthio Aldobrandino, 21 October 1594, AV, Nunziature di Venezia, reg. 30, c. 292v.

66. "Ho trovato . . . che alcune Monache . . . andavano nei parlatorij . . . con permettere anco ad altre Donne parente, et massime putte allevate in Monastero l'ingresso dentro le porte della clausura, non peró à mal fine, nè con scandalo, anzi più presto per ignoranza, o cativo uso de questi paesi." 25 June 1588, ibid., reg. 28, c. 213r.

67. 10 June 1590, ibid., reg. 27, cc. 127r–v.

68. "[Le monache] non hanno mai voluto obedire al Pat.ca, ne temere le censure ecclesiastiche, per poter vivere in tutto et per tutto à suo piacere." 19 March 1588, ibid., reg. 28, c. 47r.

69. "Giudicai conveniente, che il N. S.re sapesse il stato, nel quale si trovava gran parte di quella gente miserabile di Aquileia, la quale insciente-mente erano entrati nella clausura delle monache." Ibid., cc. 47r–v. On 20 May 1588, the patriarch of Aquileia asked to resign, following a suggestion by Cardinal Montalto and the coadjutor of Aquileia, Monsignor Francesco Barbaro.

70. In 1588, "the Most Illustrious Taddea Cicogna, granddaughter of the Most Serene Prince of Venice, who was educated in the convent of San Giacomo di Murano since she was of a tender age, and who was married this year . . . wanted to see the nuns with whom she grew up, and went to visit them and inadvertently entered the seclusion, not knowing of the prohibition." "La Clar.ma Taddea Cicogna Nipote del Ser.mo Prencipe di Venetia è stata allevata da tenera età nel Mon.o delle Monache di San Gia-como di Murano, et essendo questo anno 1588 stata maritata . . . desiderosa di rivedere quelle Monache, con le quali è stata allevata, andó à visitarle, et inavvertemente entró nella Clausura, non sapendo la prohibitione." 2 April 1588, ibid., reg. 26, c. 179r.

71. "Io non ho mancato . . . di proveder alli molti abusi disordini, et scandali, che sono avenuti, et giornalmente succedono nelli Monasterij delle Monache. . . . ne ho parlato più volte nell'Ecc.mo Collegio, più volte anco à Sua Ser.ta con la Ill.ma Signoria . . . con l'intervento delli Clar.mi tre Sig.ri Diputati sopra detti Monasterij, et del mio Vicario, dove ho scoperto le molte piaghe, e ricordato, che mi si dia il braccio [secolare] a poter provedersi. . . . li castighi particolari, sebene giovano, nondimeno non rimediano al bisogno per non esservi veramente clausura nelli Monasterij . . . [la] quale . . . e facile a esseguire quando vi sia una certa deliberazione dell'Eccelso Cons. X. . . . altramente succedendo Io mi scarico . . . et mi dole, che li particulari scandali . . . vengano . . . scritti . . . per tutto, e particolarmente in Roma, dove forsi Io sono reputato negligente in questo, se bene senza colpa alcuna." 20 February 1588 (m.r.), ibid., reg. 28, cc. 565r–566r.

72. In 1592, the Senate wrote to the Venetian ambassador in Rome that he should tell the pope "how honest and reasonable the [nuns'] wish is to be able to continue . . . going to the exterior churches . . . out of devo-tion, and for spiritual consolation, and also in order to embellish and prepare them for the festivities." "Quanto sia onesto, e ragionevole il desiderio loro di poter . . . andar nelle loro Chiese . . . per devozione, e consolatione spiritu-ale, e per adonarle, e preparar sollennità." Pregadi, letter to the Ambassador in Rome, 29 February 1591 (m.v.), ASV, CL, busta 288, c. 389r.

73. "[La Verginità] è un thesoro preciosissimo . . . ascosto in vaso frag-ile . . . Peró [lo] si deve con grandissima diligenza custodire." "Trattato del divino Dionisio Certosino: Della lodevol vita delle Vergini," in *Avvertimenti monacali,* pt. 1, p. 19.

74. Prete Bernardino Scardeone, "Alle Venerande Madri, Madonna l'Abbadessa, et Monache di Santo Stefano di Padova," ibid., p. 5.

75. "Molti, & lunghi tempi inanzi lui erano le monache serrate, ma per alcuni anni inanzi esso Bonifacio erano cascate da quella clausura." Certosino, "Dialogo," p. 53.

76. Emilio Zanette translated "deposito" in a quotation from Patriarch Tiepolo ("duemille e più Nobili . . . vivono rinserite nei monasterij come quasi in publico deposito") variously as "tomb" and "warehouse." Emilio Zanette, *Suor Arcangela monaca del Seicento veneziano* (Venice, 1960), p. 36. See also Stanley Chojnacki, "Daughters and Oligarchs: Gender and the Early Renaissance State," in *Gender and Society in Renaissance Italy,* ed. Judith C. Brown and Robert C. Davis (Essex, 1998), p. 70.

77. "Observantia clausurae sit convenientissima statui Religioso foeminarum . . . ex alia parte nulla lege Ecclesiastica determinatum est de ratione intrinseca status Religiosi Monialium esse clausuram . . . sicque dicendum est eam non esse necessariam ad statum Religiosum Monialium." Pellizzari, *Manuale Regularium,* p. 769.

78. "[C]onstat clausuram Monialium inductam fuisse, non iure naturali, aut divino, sed humano positivo Ecclesiastico." Ibid., p. 828.

79. "Observantia clausurae sit convenientissima statui Religioso foeminarum . . . prout nunc est in usu Ecclesiae veritatem hanc satis confirmante: idque ex naturali conditione, ac fragilitate sexus foeminei." Ibid., p. 769.

80. "Clausura autem Monialium est moraliter necessaria ad puritatem status . . . [non solum] ad observandam castitatem." Ibid., p. 828.

81. *Claustro* is the term Pellizzari used to describe the space enclosed by the hymen. The same term also signifies "convent."

82. "Intelligi spatium illud, quod continetur intra ianuam Conventus semper clausam." Pellizzari, *Manuale Regularium,* p. 827.

83. "An violet clausuram Monialis, si ascendens arborem positam in horto monasterij procedat ad ramum omnino prominentem extra murum clausurae, ibique causa recreationis . . . consistat. Respondeo violare." Ibid., p. 842.

84. "An faciat contra legem clausurae Monialis, si magicis artibus curet ferri per aërem supra proprium monasterium. Respondeo non facere, si eo modo feratur solum intra ambitum clausurae . . . si deambularet supra tectum proprij monasterij: sicut ergo in isto eventu non diceretur violare clausuram, nisi excederet terminos tecti pertinentis ad proprium monasterium . . . ac si deambularet supra tectum alienae domus, quod forte continuaretur cum tecto proprij monasterij . . . in isto casu censeretur violare clausuram. . . . Tunc autem Monialis censetur violare clausuram per nimiam elevationem supra proprij monasterij tectum, quando elevatio est talis, ut vires humanas omnino excedat; ita ut nec auxilio scalae, nec alia industria artis humanae ad illam pertingi posset." Ibid.

85. "Tum quia in consecratione Virginum non attenditur, an culpa praecesserit, sed an subsistat virginitas, etiam corporalis, seu materialis, quae sic per ipsam consecrationem significatur . . . ac repraesentat integritatem Ecclesiae triumphantis." Ibid., p. 801.

86. "An possit consecrari Monialis, quae per voluntarium seminis effusionem polluta est, integro tamen remanente claustro." Ibid.

87. "Tum quia Ecclesia ad recipiendum velum consecrationis solum requirit integritatem carnis . . . non dicitur Monialem debere interrogari de aliqua contaminatione. . . . est virgo, non virtute, sed statu." Ibid.

88. "An possit consecrari Monialis, quae vel fuit carnaliter cognita à viro in vase praepostero; vel sodomitice à foemina. Respondeo posse. . . . Responsio tamen haec non procedit in casu, quo Monialis sodomitice cognita fuisset ab alia foemina medio aliquo instrumento, sive ligneo, sive vitreo in vase naturali . . . quod idem procederet in casu, quo Monialis in vase naturali fuisset cognita ab alia foemina habente nimphium magnum in vulva, idest, carunculam quamdam sic excrescentem, ut . . . reddat . . . foeminam potentem ad deflorendam aliam foeminam." Ibid., pp. 801–2.

89. "Si violatio sit occulta, poterit violata tuta conscientia recipere consecrationem." Ibid., p. 801.

90. "[S]i . . . capiant delectationem morosam de rebus venereis . . . si . . . obscoenos habeant sermones, aut ex aliis audiant, librosque turpes, & amatorios legant: si retineant obscoenas imagines . . . si carnaliter delectentur osculis, amplexibus & aliis tactibus obscoenis . . . si . . . si detineant in occasione proxima violandi votum castitatis." Ibid., p. 818.

91. "An Hermaphroditi possint recipi in Religione Monialium, & quando. Respondeo posse, si in iis iudicio medicorum aut peritarum, ac honestarum matronarum praevaleat sexus foemineus." Ibid., p. 774. "An teneat professio facta inter Moniales ab hermaphrodito, etiam postquam erupit in virum. Respondeo . . . non tenere . . . sequitur illum . . . posse manere in saeculo, ac inire matrimonium." Ibid., p. 791.

92. "Desiderando . . . che il regolato stato monacale vada tuttavia acquistando merito nella essemplarità del progresso suo, & camini . . . di perfettione in perfettione." Grimani, *Constitutioni,* preface.

93. Kate Lowe, "Secular Brides and Convent Brides: Wedding Ceremonies in Italy during the Renaissance and Counter-Reformation," in *Marriage in Italy, 1300–1600,* ed. Trevor Dean and Kate Lowe (Cambridge, 1998), pp. 41–65.

94. Convent churches were usually divided into an exterior part for the lay audience and an interior part connected to the convent; barred windows permitted the nuns to communicate with the priests while they were holding mass at the exterior main altar. See Marcia B. Hall, "The Tramezzo in Santa Croce, Florence, Reconstructed," *Art Bulletin* 56, no. 2 (1974): 325–41.

95. *Ordo rituum et caeremoniarum suscipiendi habitum Monialem, & emittendi Professionem ad Venetae Dioecesis usum olim iussu Illustrissimi & Reverendissimi D. D. Francisci Vendrameni Patriarchae Venetiarum, &c Editus nunc vero Curantibus Sororibus Theupolis Degentibus in Monasterio S. Luciae* (Venice, 1694), p. 1; André Campra (1668–1733), "Quemadmodum desiderat cervus," Psalm 42:1–4, 11.

96. "Non debbano . . . entrare pomposamente, nè con vestimenti di seta nè ornamenti di ori gioe, perle, nè accompagnate da molte persone." Grimani, *Constitutioni,* p. 15r.

97. "Si fanno insegnare alcuni versi da i Capellani . . . per recitarli nel giorno del suo vestire . . . spendendo il tempo di molti mesi in questa inutilissima vanità. . . . alle volte si perdono nel recitarli con vergogna loro . . . convertendo un'attione sacra, & divota . . . in una vana rappresentatione." Ibid., p. 17r.

98. Among others, see the "Mandatum generale" of Patriarch Giovanni Trevisan: "Non possiate nè dobbiate imparar Canto figurato . . . nè cantar tali canti nelle vostre Chiese." 24 November 1578, MCC, CC 2570, c. 243. The nuns were allowed to sing only the so-called *canto fermo,* i.e., rather plain melodies. On recitals of nuns in Bologna, see Craig A. Monson, "Disembodied Voices: Music in the Nunneries of Bologna in the Midst of the Counter-Reformation," in *The Crannied Wall: Women, Religion, and the Arts in Early Modern Europe* (Ann Arbor, Mich., 1992), pp. 191–209; idem, *Disembodied Voices.*

99. "Quid quaeris filia? . . . Unam petij à Domino, hanc requiram, ut inhabitem in domo Domini omnibus diebus vitae meae. . . . voluntariè sacrificabo Domino." *Ordo Rituum,* p. 6.

100. "Apostolus muliebrem sexum in signum subiectionis, humilitatis, & honestatis velamen super caput suum, propter Angelos, habere praecepit." Ibid., p. 10.

101. "Demum turpissimae mortis tuae dulcis sponsi sui memoriam hoc viduitatis inditium saepè mentis eius oculis repraesentent." Ibid.

102. "Accipe Cingulum super lumbos tuos . . . in signum temperantiae, & castitatis. . . . Praecingat Dominus lumbos corporis mei, ut circumcidat vitia cordis mei." Ibid., p. 12.

103. "Oremus . . . Dominum nostrum Iesum Christum pro hac famula sua; quae, ad deponendam comam capitis sui, pro eius amore, festinat." Ibid.

104. "Succingat crinem tuum modestia, sobrietas, continentia." Ibid., p. 13.

105. "Tuere, quaesumus, ancillam tuam . . . ut, quasi in horto clauso, & fonte signato, teneat claustra pudicitiae, signacula veritatis." Ibid.

106. "Surge Filia, & orna lampadem tuam, ecce sponsus venit, exi obviam ei." *Ordo Rituum,* p. 24.

107. "Ecce venio ad te dulcissime Domine, quem amavi, quem quaesivi, quem semper optavi." Ibid., p. 25.

108. "Me totam in hostiam viventem offero, & sacrifico." Ibid., pp. 26–27.

109. "Posuit signum in faciem meam, ut nullum praeter eum amatorem admittam." Ibid., p. 27.

110. The liturgy of the ceremony of profession of the second order of the Carmelites, for example, was worded similarly: "As you, Jesus Christ, eternal Father, offered yourself as a sacrifice on the Altar of the Cross for my salvation, so I will offer and sacrifice myself as a living host to you, with a humble and contrite heart." "Sicut tu Dne Jesu Christe aeterno Patri pro mea salute in sacrificium super Altare Crucis, te obtulisti, ita ego tibi hodie, humili, & contrito corde, me totam in hostiam viventem offero, & sacri-

fico." Biblioteca del Seminario Patriarchale di Venezia (BSP), ms. 23 (Sala Monice), f. 189. Another example is the eighteenth-century "Sermon sur les avantages de la vie religieuse pour une vêture," addressed to "a young virgin, ready to break away from us, determined to sacrifice for a consecration without limits every pleasure, every expectation . . . led to the altars, in order to begin the holocaust by putting on the somber gown of her sacrifice." "Une jeune vièrge, prête à s'arracher du milieu de nous, résolue d'immoler pour une consécration sans bornes tous les plaisirs, toutes les espérances . . . [est] conduite aux pieds des autels, pour y commencer l'holocauste par l'imposition des vêtements lugubres de son sacrifice." BSP, Mss 644 = 717, III 11, pp. 6–7.

111. "[Le vere Religiose] . . . legano le mani all'ira Divina, poiché se queste non trattenessero i flagelli dovuti alle colpe del Mondo, si vedrebbero le fiamme di fuoco stendersi per l'Universo à incenerir gli huomini, l'acque sormontar le più alte torri, e i più sublimi Monti." Arcangela Tarabotti, *Il Paradiso Monacale* (Venice, 1663), p. 200.

112. Quoted in Primhak, "Women in Religious Communities," p. 257.

113. "On avoit jadis de coustume d'esgorger les victimes, & puis les sacrifier à Dieu: d'autant peut estre que le principal siege des affections corporelles consistant au sang, on ne jugeoit pas qu'il fust convenable d'offrir à sa Majesté divine aucun holocauste qui n'eust esté premierement purifié de toute passion terrienne par l'effusion du sang: mais nos peres & meres n'ont point d'esgard à cela en nostre endroit. Nous sommes consacrées à Dieu avec toutes nos affections, & avec toutes nos passions. Or comment pouvons nous croire que Dieu nous ait agreables?" Ferrante Pallavicino, *Le divorce céleste, causé par les dissolutions de l'Espouse Romaine* (Ville Franche, 1649), p. 99.

114. Apart from Pietro Aretino's well-known *Ragionamento*, see, for instance, the "Frottola che dise mal delle Muneghe" and the "Capitolo in risposta," edited by Antonio Pilot in "Frottola vernacola inedita"; and the poem translated by Victoria Primhak in "Women in Religious Communities" (p. 256):

> My mother wished me to become a nun
> To fatten the dowry of my sister
> And I to obey my Mama
> Cut my hair and became one
> Yet the first night that I slept in a cell
> I heard my lover's footsteps below
> And rushed down to open the door
> But the mother Abbess caught me
> And asked: 'Little sister
> Do you have a fever or are you in Love?'

115. See Bartolomeo Cecchetti, "Disciplina, doti, clausura, governo dei conventi," in *La republica di Venezia e la corte di Roma,* ed. Bartolomeo Cecchetti (Venice, 1874), 1:200–211; see also Francesco Gregolin, "Saggio

di statistica di alcuni processi per malcostume, nei conventi di Venezia e dello Stato Veneto, sec. XVII e XVIII," ibid., 2:99–113; Molmenti, *La storia di Venezia nella vita privata* (Bergamo, 1925), 2:459–61; Zanette, *Suor Arcangela;* Fiamma Lussana, "Rivolta e misticismo nei chiostri femminili del Seicento," *Studi Storici* 28 (1987): 243–60; Francesca Medioli, ed., *L'inferno monacale di Suor Arcangela Tarabotti* (Turin, 1990), pp. 111–92; Romano Canosa, *Il velo e il capuccio: Monacazioni forzate e sessualità nei conventi femminili in Italia tra '400 e '700* (Rome, 1991); and Giovanni Spinelli, "I religiosi e le religiose," in *La Chiesa di Venezia nel Seicento,* vol. 5, edited by Bruno Bertoli, pp. 173–209 (Venice, 1992), esp. 189–98. On convent reform, see Pio Paschini, "I monasteri femminili in Italia nel '500," in *Problemi di vita religiosa in Italia nel Cinquecento: Convegno di storia della Chiesa in Italia, 1958, Bologna* (Padua, 1960), pp. 31–60; Giuliani, "Genesi"; Creytens, "La giurisprudenza della Sacra Congregazione del Concilio"; idem, "La Riforma dei monasteri femminili"; Franco Molinari, "Visite pastorali dei monasteri femminili di Piacenza nel sec. XVI," in *Il Concilio di Trento e la riforma tridentina,* 1:679–731; Massimo Marcocchi, "La riforma dei monasteri femminili a Cremona: Gli atti inediti della visita del vescovo Cesare Speciano (1599–1606)," *Annali della Biblioteca Governativa e Libreria Civica di Cremona* 17 (1966); Carla Russo, *I monasteri femminili di clausura a Napoli nel secolo XVII* (Naples, 1970); and Gabriella Zarri, "I monasteri femminili a Bologna tra il XIII e il XVII secolo," *Atti e Memorie della Deputazione di Storia Patria per le Provincie di Romagna,* n.s., 24 (1973): 133–224.

116. "L'imposizione della clausura alle monache rientra infatti in un più generale processo di repressione dei movimenti religiosi. . . . La clausura appare così, ad uno stesso tempo, provvedimento di polizia, di repressione di idee religiose sospette, di disciplinamento dei culti e, più in generale, una prima applicazione in forma metodica e capillare di quel criterio di "renfermement" successivamente volto verso le frange marginali della società." Zarri, "Monasteri femminili e città," p. 404.

117. According to Zarri, imposing clausura went hand in hand with an "economic rehabilitation of the convents" aimed at an "abolition of private property, [and the] reduction of the power of [individual] families over monastic institutions through a regulation of access to the offices of abbess and prioress." "Risanamento economico dei conventi ai fini di eliminare la proprietà privata; diminuzione del potere familiare sugli istituti monastici tramite una regolamentazione dell'accesso agli uffici abbaziali e priorali." Ibid. See also Gabriella Zarri, "Aspetti dello sviluppo degli Ordini religiosi in Italia tra Quattro e Cinquecento: Studi e problemi," in *Strutture ecclesiastiche in Italia e in Germania prima della Riforma,* ed. Paolo Prodi and Peter Johanek (Bologna, 1984), pp. 207–58, esp. 215. For Florence, see Arnaldo D'Addario, *Aspetti della Controriforma a Firenze* (Rome, 1972), pp. 132–45, 284–94.

118. 28 September 1462: the Senate asks the pope to revoke certain privileges so that the patriarch can visit the convents; ASV, CL, busta 288, c. 190r. 30 May 1486: the Great Council orders the patriarch to hand over

trials against *muneghini* (i.e., men having sex with nuns) to the Avogadori di Comun and rules that the pope be asked to revoke privileges enabling the nuns to leave their convents; ibid., c. 218r. 22 March 1501: the Senate asks the pope to revoke exemptions from clausura and prohibits private persons from gaining new privileges for convents; ibid., c. 239r. 21 August 1504: the patriarch revokes the licenses to leave the clausura of eight Venetian convents; MCC, CC 2570, c. 68.

119. 6 June 1469: the Senate asks that the convent of San Matteo di Mazzorbo be subjected to the patriarch; ASV, CL, busta 288, c. 196r. 24 September 1489: the Senate asks the pope to subject certain non-observant convents to the authority of the patriarch, so that they can be reformed; ibid., c. 228r. 29 June 1509: the Senate rules that nuns who leave their clausura are to be sentenced by the patriarch; ibid., c. 248r.

120. Council of Ten, 9 August 1514, in Giuliani, "Genesi," pp. 148–50.

121. The decrees of the late seventeenth century focus on the parlor rules; violations of clausura or sexual relationships with nuns are no longer explicitly mentioned. See, for example, Council of Ten, 4 January 1695 (m.v.), ASV, PsM, capitolari, reg. 2, cc. 66v–67v. In the eighteenth century, decrees "in materia di spese, rinfreschi, ed apparati" (on expenses, refreshments, and decorations) abound, but some also aim at reaffirming the parlor rules of the sixteenth and seventeenth centuries. ASV, PsM, 10 May 1710, 18 August 1732, 11 September 1744, 20 September 1745, 11 August 1749, 9 March 1763, 6 February 1777 (m.v.); Santi Biagio e Cataldo, busta 3, fascicolo "Filza Proclami, Parti, e Decreti in varj propositi," decrees 16, 21, 25.

122. Priuli, *Ordini, & avvertimenti;* Patriarch Francesco Vendramin, 12 November 1609, "Sommario degli ordini cavati dalla visita fatta . . . della chiesa, et Monasterio delle Rev.de Monache di Santo Andrea," ASV, Sant' Andrea de Zirada, busta 10, cc. 72r–83r, esp. 75r–77r. See also APV, Visite Vendramin.

123. Maria Pia Pedani, "Monasteri di Agostiniane a Venezia," *Archivio Veneto,* 5th ser., 122–25 (1984–85): 35–78, esp. 58–65; idem, "L'osservanza imposta"; Primhak, "Women in Religious Communities," pp. 281–87.

124. The nuns of Santa Maria delle Vergini complained that it "is very hard to be thrown out of one's own house." "É dura cossa esser cazade da la sua caxa." Sanuto, *I diarii,* 25 June 1519, vol. 27, col. 407.

125. Ibid., 25, 28 June 1519, cols. 407, 409.

126. "Havendo le monache di San Zacharia otenuto a Roma citation, per la qual vien citato il Patriarcha in Rota a veder *di jure* si pol far novità alcuna in quel monasterio." Ibid., 31 July 1519, col. 450.

127. Ibid., 26 August 1519, col. 593.

128. "Eleger si debbano tre honoratissimi . . . zentilhomini . . . quali insieme con ditto Rev.mo Patriarcha habbino ad udir, et intender le lamentationi et querelle di queste Monache conventuale circa il viver suo." Council of Ten plus Zonta, 17 September 1521, in Giuliani, "Genesi," p. 155.

129. "Dicendo di san Zacaria dove erano tutte nobele, hora sono poste monache . . . bastarde greche e populari." Sanuto, *I diarii,* 21 August 1521, vol. 31, col. 276.

130. Pope Leo X, 18 October 1521, in Giuliani, "Genesi," pp. 156–57.

131. "Havendo refudà quelli zentil'homeni nostri che ultimamente sono eletti et deputati per questo Cons. sopra la limitazione delle spese delle Monache si conventuali, come osservanti di questa città nostra e di Torcello . . . et restando ancora molte cose da esequir in questa materia di Monache . . . sia fatta elettion di tre savii zentil homini nostri in loco da i ditti che hanno refutado." Council of Ten plus Zonta, 29 October 1522; ibid., p. 157.

132. "Et riveder debbano li conti, et amministration delli Gastaldi, et fattori delli predetti Monasteri, e trovando che alcun de loro sia in mancamento insieme con il Rev.mo Patriarca, habbino li sopradetti . . . libertà circa l'amministration delle entrade delli detti Monasterii." Council of Ten plus Zonta, 30 October 1528, in Giuliani, "Genesi," p. 159. Since the existing convent archives do not contain any evidence that the convent magistrate actually interfered with the convents' finances during the lengthy period from roughly 1520 to 1650, government ordinances adopted between 1528 (when the Provveditori sopra i Monasteri di Monache became a permanent institution) and 1536 were probably never enforced. This "negligence" might have been due to—among other things—the fierce controversies generated by the reform of 1519: the hostilities it caused within the affected religious communities were still alive in the second half of the sixteenth century. "A very bad corruption has been introduced that disgraces . . . the convents of nuns . . . observant as well as non-observant . . . who talk publicly about the secret affairs of their convents to secular persons and complain . . . and, what is worse, they inform on each other, and dishonor each other, an intolerable thing in the eyes of the authorities." "É introducta una pessima et chativa corruptela in vituperio . . . de li Mon.rij de le Donne monache . . . si observante, come conventual . . . le qual vanno publicando le cose occulte de loro Mon.rij, et lamentandose con laici . . . et quod peijus est se vanno informando luna et laltra, et tolandese lhonor, cosa non tolerabile a li Superiori." Patriarch Gerolamo Querini, 8 July 1528, MCC, CC 2570, cc. 161–62. "We have wanted to admonish you . . . that you must not offend each other, nor say offensive, dishonest, and infamous words to each other, mentioning things past to each other." "Havemo voluto farvi la presente intimatione . . . che non debbiate ingiurarvi, ne dirvi parole ingiuriose, deshoneste, et de infamia con numerando le cose passate l'una contra l'altra." Patriarch Giovanni Trevisan, 22 August 1569, APV, Visite Trevisan, c. 29r. Exacerbated by the power struggle between "papal" and "antipapal" factions among the patricians, the debate over convent (and church) properties might have been too precarious for anybody to risk his political career over it. In 1558, the Council of Ten ruled that a new accountant should be elected, since the convents' account books had not been checked for twenty-five years. According to this decree, the last audit had occurred in 1533; but since no account books have survived from the first half of the

sixteenth century, it is impossible to tell what these accountants actually did. Council of Ten, 27 April 1558, ASV, PsM, capitolari, reg. 1, cc. 27r–v.

133. Council of Ten, 15 November 1531: the convent magistrate has to check the accounts of the convents' agents and estate managers; ASV, PsM, capitolari, reg. 1, cc. 10r–v. PsM, 28 February 1531 (m.v.): the convent magistrate requests permission to hire an accountant; Giuliani, "Genesi," p. 159. Council of Ten plus Zonta, 17 October 1533: the PsM have to check the convents' revenues and accounts; also, they have to delegate cases of sex with nuns to the Avogadori di Comun; ibid., p. 160. Zonta, 23 June 1536: the PsM are allowed to hire a paid accountant; ibid., p. 159.

134. "La experientia ... mostra, che le Ven.di Abbadesse ... recipiendo Moniales de novo ad libitum hanno redutto, et reducono in extremo necessità i loro Mon.rij et Monache, non abbastando li frutti de quelli alla substentatione de le donne." Patriarch Gerolamo Querini, 15 November 1530, MCC, CC 2570, c. 163.

135. Senate, 22 December 1536: no real estate located in Venice or the Dogado can be bequeathed, donated, or permanently leased to ecclesiastic institutions for more than two years; after that time, the Dieci Savij sopra le decime di Rialto (tax collectors) have to sell the property and have the Procuratori di San Marco administer the money belonging to these ecclesiastic institutions. ASV, Senato Terra, reg. 29, cc. 83v–84r.

136. See law of the Council of Ten plus Zonta, 17 October 1533, in Giuliani, "Genesi," p. 160.

137. On the development of regular taxation of church properties, see Luciano Pezzolo, *L'oro dello Stato: Società, finanza e fisco nella Repubblica veneta del secondo '500* (Treviso, 1990); Giuseppe Del Torre, *Venezia e la terraferma dopo la guerra di Cambrai: Fiscalità e amministrazione (1515– 1530)* (Milan, 1986); and idem, "La politica fiscale della Repubblica di Venezia nell'età moderna: La fiscalità," in *Fisco religione stato nell'età confessionale,* ed. H. Kellenbenz and P. Prodi (Bologna, 1989), pp. 387–426.

138. Pregadi, "Accettazione del Concilio di Trento da parte della Repubblica," 6 October 1564, BSP, Mss 1044.44.

139. Fornication with nuns was now punished by ten years' exile at least, as opposed to two years according to the law of 1514. Council of Ten, 29 March 1566, MCC, CC 2570, cc. 143–45.

140. Council of Ten, 31 August 1569, in Giuliani, "Genesi," pp. 163– 64.

141. "Although it was repeatedly forbidden to alienate church properties, it has become the custom that abbesses and prioresses ... without notifying the chapters take loans from private persons, obligating the convents' patrimonies ... and they do so under the pretext of liquidating debts or paying for restorations ... and, lacking the money to pay the interest, they take out more loans, so that interest payments rise daily, and despite the convents' rich revenues, the poor nuns generally lack food and clothing, and the convents' affairs go from bad to worse." "Se ben per molte deliberationi sia stà proveduto che li beni ecclesiastici non si possino alienar, nondimeno da certo tempo in quà è introdotto che le Abbadesse, over Priore de Monas-

terii . . . senza saputo del suo Capitolo, toglioni denari . . . ad imprestito da particolar persone . . . obligando li beni del Monasterio . . . e ciò fanno sotto coperta di convenire pagar debiti, per far fabriche . . . et non havendo poi modo di pagar li interessi . . . togliono delli altri denari ad interesse . . . di modo che se bene li Monasterii hanno buonissima entrata, crescendo ogni di più li interessi, le povere Monache generalmente patiscono del viver, et vestir, e le cose del Monasterio vanno di mal in peggio." Council of Ten, 31 August 1569; ibid., pp. 162–63.

142. Visitation of Santi Cosma e Damiano, 21 April 1561, APV, Visite Trevisan, cc. 8r–9r.

143. "The nuns should not make gifts to their friends who occupy offices, nor to anybody else inside or outside [of the convent], and during the feast of Corpus Domini they should not give away so many baskets [full of food] and cakes, but only a few of them." "Non se debbia ne possi far presenti alle compagne, che sono nelli officij, ne a niune altre dentro, ne di fuori, et che dalla festa del Corpus Domini non si mandi fuori tanti cesti, et tante torte, ma mediocramente." Visitation of Corpus Domini, 1560, ibid., c. 2v. "In the parlors, the nuns should not give food or drinks to anybody passing by." "Che nelli parlatorij non si possano dar da mangiar e bever ad alcuno passando." Visitation of Sant' Andrea de Zirada, 13 March 1566, ibid., c. 25r.

144. "The daughters who are to be received as nuns should be admitted with the highest amount of alms [i.e., fees] possible." "Le figliuole che saranno accettate monache sijno accettate con più elemosina che si potrà." Visitation of Sant' Alvise, 26 September 1565, ibid., c. 14r.

145. Visitations of Santi Biagio e Cataldo and Santa Maria della Celestia, 26 September 1565 and 7 September 1569, ibid., cc. 15v, 30r.

146. Visitations of San Lorenzo and Corpus Domini, 16 October 1568 and 11 March 1569, ibid., cc. 27r–28v; "Mandatum generale," 17 April 1573, ibid., cc. 42r–43r.

147. Visitation of Santa Marta, 21 May 1561, ibid., c. 11r.

148. "Commettemo alle R.de camerlenghe over cellerarie, che rendino conto della loro administratione di anno in anno alla detta R.da Abbadessa e Capitolo." Visitation of San Matteo di Mazzorbo, 15 April 1589, ibid., c. 85r.

149. "We order . . . that you should discuss all things that regard the management and governance of the convent with the mothers listed below . . . we order that all [the nuns] mentioned above should check the accounts of your convent every month, that is, income and expenses, and at the end of each month give a [financial] report to the chapter." "Vi ordiniamo . . . che tutte le cose, che aspettano al manizzo, et governo di esso vostro monasterio, debbiate consigliarle con le infrascritte madre [list of 10 names] . . . ordiniamo che tutte le sopraditte debbano ogni mese veder li conti di esso vostro monasterio, cioè il scosso, et il speso, et in capo di esso mese rifferire el tutto in capitolo." Visitation of Sant' Andrea de Zirada, 26 April 1570, ibid., c. 33r.

150. Among many others, see visitation of Santi Biagio e Cataldo, 26 September 1565, ibid., cc. 14v–15r.

151. In 1570, he severely reproached some nuns of Santa Maria della Celestia for having left their convent: "We understand that some nuns of this convent have been so temerarious and presumptuous that they left the convent, without any respect for, even in [direct] offense of, our Lord, dishonoring the convent, against our mandates, and in disregard of their religious state and profession, and [that] they, dressed in lay clothes, went to the convent that is under construction at the Celestia, [which is] a thing of great scandal, and gossip in the entire city." "Havemo inteso, che alcune monache de questo Monasterio sono state cosi temerarie, et presuntuose, che senza rispetto, anzi in offesa del Signor Iddio, et dishonor del Monasterio, contra i nostri mandati, et in disprezzo della sua religione, et profession sono uscite dal Monasterio, et in habito laical vestite andate al monasterio, che si fabbrica alla Celestia, cosa di grandissimo scandolo, et mormoratione di tutta questa città." 9 September 1570, ibid., c. 38v.

152. "Mandatum generale," 7 September 1569, ibid., c. 30r.

153. "Mandatum generale," 23 January 1572 (m.r.), ibid., c. 40v.

154. Doing the laundry for friends was a constant source of conflict between the patriarch and the nuns, who performed this service either in exchange for payment or as a favor. The authorities tried to suppress the practice not only because it violated the rule that nuns should not talk to any ecclesiastic person except their father confessor, but also because washing consumed costly resources such as soap and firewood. Visitation of San Servolo, 26 January 1581 (m.r.), ibid., c. 56r.

155. Visitation of San Gerolamo, 26 August 1583, ibid., cc. 70v–71r.

156. See, for example, visitation of Santi Cosma e Damiano, 22 April 1561, ibid., c. 5v.

157. Council of Ten, 29 March 1566, MCC, CC 2570, cc. 144–45.

158. ASV, CX (Council of Ten), Criminal, reg. 10, cc. 88v–94r, 7 January 1567 (m.v.).

159. Ibid., reg. 15, cc. 145r–170v, 27 January 1587 (m.v.) to 30 May 1588.

160. Why there are no cases between 1566 and 1618 is hard to tell.

161. ASV, PsM, busta 263, fascicolo 17.

162. Ibid., fascicolo 9.

163. Ibid., busta 265, fascicolo 22.

164. "[C]on quella vita piu austera, che fosse piu possibile, credendo, che questa mortificatione del corpo potesse esser piu grata al S.re." Ibid., fascicolo 34, 15 October 1618.

165. For example, Sister Francisca Lazari conversa was found "guilty of sensuality" by the Council of Ten, and Sister Ottavia Cadorini conversa denied being "guilty of [having a] close friendship with Alban Cicogna" and "of open sensuality and scandalous license." "Le scandalose attioni vostre [di Suor Francisca Lazari] come rea di sensualità, e dissolutezze hanno mosso l'Ecc.so Cons.o di X à motivare à Mons.r Ill.mo Vescovo le vostre colpe." "Sete liquidata rea [Suor Ottavia Cadorini] di streta amicitia col predetto Padre Alban Cigogna. . . . Voi sete stata posta prigione per? li motivi? portati? dall'Ecc.so Cons.o di X à Mons.r Ill.mo Vescovo di quelle vostre aperte

sensualità, et scandolose dissolutezze." APV, Fondo Torcellano, Torcellania Criminalia Monialium (1600–1689), busta 23, fascicolo Santi Vito e Modesto, 14 May 1652, cc. 69r, 70r.

166. ASV, PsM, busta 263, fascicolo 8, 10 January 1556 (m.v.?) to 6 March 1556.

167. Ibid., busta 347, fascicolo 1.

168. Ibid., fascicolo 2, c. 7r.

169. Ibid., fascicolo 4, cc. 1r, 2r.

170. "L'Ecc.so C.X., che, come dovete sapre, ha auttorità suprema, et l'ha sopra tutte le creatture, che vivono sotto l'ombra di questo Ser.mo Dominio, è restato molto maravegliato, et scandelizzato, che voi . . . deputata per il buon governo di questo santo luogo, et per rimovere quelli scandali . . . che possono machiar l'honor del Monasterio . . . inluogo di scoprir al vostro Principe Natural le piaghe, et gl'errori, affine che si possino, et curar, et correggere, nascondete il tutto, et negate non pur quelli disordini et delitti, che sono stati commessi secretamente, ma li palesi ancora. . . . essendo le lor S.rie Ecc.me sicure, che hora che siette sagramentata, et che sapete meglio la ressoluta volontà del sudd.to Ecc.so Cons.o, vi rissolverete de dire . . . tutto quello che sapete, per non danar l'anima v.ra et dar causa a questi S.ri Ecc.mi di servirsi de altro mezzo per saperla." Ibid., fascicolo 4, cc. 4r–v.

171. "Non voglio morir da morte subitanea." Ibid., c. 12v.

172. This might have been the brief obtained by the Council of Ten on 21 April 1604, which subjected the nuns to the patriarch.

173. "Postessi tutte le Monache con li ginochi in terra, sospirando, et molte gemendo, e lacrimando, dissero, che erano pronte di obedir alli commandamenti di sua Santità, ma che suplicavano bene, che le fussero dati confessori fratti, et che . . . cedesse Mons.r R.mo Patriarca farle gratia, che'l loro confessor della carità le reconciliasse, et admoniasse." Ibid., fascicolo 5, cc. 1r–v (2r–v?).

174. "Questa è la quinta volta, che questi S.ri Ec.mi di ord.e et commissione dell'Ecc.so C.X. sono venuti a questo Monasterio." Ibid., fascicolo 7, c. 1r.

175. "I would rather let my head and tongue be cut off than say anything. . . . it is said that you keep records of this trial, and that it will be known who said something and who did not say anything, I say this out of fear for my life. . . . crying, and sighing, she said . . . [that] in those incidents and animosities . . . one should call the nuns one by one, starting from the first and calling them one by one to the last, because the strategy you have followed so far will not get you anywhere ever." "Me lassero tagliar la testa e la lengua più tosto che dir niente de nissuna. . . . vien detto, che le haverà li processi nelle mani, et che le saverà chi ha ditto, et non ha ditto, el timor della mia vita mi ha fatto parlar cosi. . . . piangendo, e sospirando, disse . . . in questi accidenti e rancori . . . bisognerasse chiamar tutte le monache ad una, ad una incominciando dalla prima, et cosi de una in una fino all'ultima che per la via, che le ha osservato fin'hora, non saverà mai niente." Ibid., cc. 9r–v.

176. Ibid., c. 9v.

177. The trial proceedings of the Provveditori sopra i Monasteri followed the "secret rite" of the Council of Ten reserved for capital crimes, which meant that the defendants were not informed of the charges and had to prepare their defense without the help of a lawyer.

178. ASV, CX, Criminal, reg. 21, cc. 60r, 62v, 65v, 83r?.

179. Sister Serafica was not surprised to find out that she had been betrayed. After being asked about her relationship with Giulio da Molin, she said to herself, "Since I have been betrayed by my own relatives, it is no wonder that others should also attack me." "Se son stata tradita dalli miei proprij parenti non è maraveglia che sia assassinata anco da altri." ASV, PsM, busta 347, fascicolo 5, c. 12v.

180. Ibid., busta 263, fascicolo 19.

181. "Non posso[no] però Ecc.mi SS.ri se non credere, che q.a sia una impostura di quelli forse, che maneggiano le entrate del Mon., poiche forse disgustati, ch'io habbi in mano tali affari, e dubitando non gli levi li suoi utili, et civanzi, non gli è bastato di soggerire per il passato à Mons.r Ill.mo Vescovo, ch'io capitassi al Mon. frequentemente." Ibid., busta 13, 16 May 1652.

182. APV, Torcellania Criminalia Monialium, busta 23, San Vito di Burano, 9 September 1607 to 28 July 1608, cc. 1r–30r (pagination of fascicolo discontinuous).

183. Ibid., 17 October 1612, no pagination.

184. "Lo riprendevo acerbamente. . . . Lui era in camisa, con una camisa da donna indosso, et haveva in mano un paro di braghezze rosse, perchè havendo io la lume in mano lo vedevo. Et lui volendosi metter quelle braghezze io per modestia me partij. . . . Mi ha detto altre volte haver 36 anni in circa, ma credo habbia manco età, lui è un bel giovine, rosso, bianco, rizzo, grassotto, ma bassotto." Ibid., 8 November 1621.

185. "[I Provveditori sopra li Monasterij] . . . debbano almeno due volte alla settimana ridursi insieme con il Rev.mo Patriarca per proveder . . . che si vengha a fuger quei grandissimi inconvenienti che seguirebbero quando venisse de qui in tal materia visitator Apostolico." Council of Ten, 19 December 1584, in Giuliani, "Genesi," p. 161.

186. Council of Ten, 27 February 1583 (m.v.), 6 April 1589, ASV, PsM, capitolari, reg. 1, cc. 31r, 33v.

187. San Daniele was the focus of the trial of 1604; Santa Anna was the convent involved in the big trial of 1608, which resulted in the punishment of fifteen noblemen and three commoners. ASV, CX, Criminal, reg. 37, 26 November, 27 January 1608 (m.v.).

188. Council of Ten, 7 February 1604 (m.v.), in Giuliani, "Genesi," pp. 166–68.

189. "È di tanta importanza il carico delli Provveditori sopra Monasteri . . . che vi siano sempre de' principali senatori della nostra Repubblica." Council of Ten, 4 December 1608, ASV, PsM, reg. 1, c. 45v.

190. Council of Ten, 27 January 1608 (m.v.), ASV, CX, Criminal, reg. 25 (1608), c. 121v.

191. "Detti Signori Laici havevano fatto mettere in prigione molte per-

sone, e niuno più voleva entrare, ma . . . le monache . . . minacciavano d'uscire dal Monasterio." AV, Nunziature di Venezia, reg. 38A, 25 April 1609, c. 388r.

192. APV, Visite Priuli.

193. Patriarch Matteo Zane (1600–1605) neither visited convents nor issued decrees.

194. Vendramin's introduction to his "Mandatum generale" of 1609 shows that patriarchal rules and decrees, once issued, had to be executed with constant supervision and vigilance: "This is why so many good and healthy orders for the correct monastic discipline, given by the faithful inspiration [?] of the Most Illustrious Cardinal and Patriarch Priuli, our predecessor, with much zeal and profit, have been neglected, because of the long vacancy of the two seats [i.e., bishoprics]. Therefore, we intend, out of obligation for our pastoral office, to revive them gradually, and enforce their observance." "Di qui è che tanti buoni, e salutiferi ordini per la retta disciplina Monacale dati dalla fe[de?] me[desima?] dell'Ill.mo Sig.r Card. Priuli Patriarca pre[de]cessore nostro con molto zelo, et profitto, sono dalla longa vacatione di due sedi vacanti iti del tutto in desuetudine; onde per il debito nostro Pastorale officio siamo tenuti a poco a poco revivificarli, e ridurli in osservanza." MCC, CC 2570, c. 277.

195. Patriarch Lorenzo Priuli, 4 July 1597, ASV, Sant' Andrea de Zirada, busta 10, cc. 56r–58v.

196. "Considerando Noi lo stato dei Mon.rij de Monache di questa Città li quali per la maggior parte si trovano in gran bisogno, non havendo il modo di somministrare alle Monache non pur il vestito, ma ne'anco il sufficiente vitto, talmente che ogni Monaca é necessitata provedersi di molte cose fuori di Mon.rio con pericolo e pregiudizio dell'anima sua . . ." Patriarch Lorenzo Priuli, 24 November 1593, MCC, CC 2583, cc. 127r–128r.

197. In the past, the Tridentine clausura decree had proved to be inapplicable to mendicant nuns. See, for example, the Senate's letter to the Venetian ambassador in Rome regarding exemptions from the clausura rule that he was supposed to request for some nuns in Padua. Senate, 6 December 1586, ASV, CL, busta 288, c. 379r.

198. Council of Ten, 7 February 1604 (m.v.), in *Deliberatione dell'Eccelso Conseglio di X. e terminationi, et ordini delli Eccelentissimi signori proveditori sopra li Monasterij di Monache di Venetia, e Dogado* (Venice, 1625).

199. Council of Ten, 9 August 1611; ibid.

200. Council of Ten, 2 September 1611; ibid. All throughout the sixteenth century, prostitutes were banned from churches on holidays or whenever the churches were crowded, so that they would not mix with the noblewomen, who apparently dressed very similarly. See Antonio Barzaghi, *Donne o cortigiane? La prostituzione a Venezia: Documenti di costume dal XVI al XVIII secolo* (Verona, 1980).

201. Council of Ten, 30 January 1612 (m.v.); *Deliberatione dell'Eccelso Conseglio di X.*

202. Council of Ten, 23 January 1614 (m.v.); ibid.

203. Council of Ten, 18 December 1625; ibid. In 1647, the law of 1625 was reissued, which subjected married women living temporarily in convents to the nuns' clausura rules; shortly afterward, two women escaped from the convent of Santi Rocco e Margherita. ASV, CL, busta 288, cc. 778r–782r, 24, 29 October 1647. See also P. Renée Baernstein, "In Widow's Habit: Women between Convent and Family in Sixteenth-Century Milan," *Sixteenth Century Journal* 25, no. 4 (1994): 787–807.

204. Pregadi, 2 September 1628: the PsM are charged with helping the nuns of Cividale in Friuli to retrieve their credits and revenues; ASV, CL, busta 288, c. 608r.

205. Pregadi, 30 June 1637, ASV, PsM, capitolari, reg. 2, c. 1r.

206. In some Italian cities, such as Naples, the reform started much later; see Russo, *I monasteri femminili.*

207. ASV, PsM, busta 264, fascicolo "S. Vido de Buran contra Prete Iseppo Tagiapiera," 14 March 1611.

208. Ibid., fascicolo "Santa Anna contra Battista Murer," 2 April 1611.

209. Ibid., fascicolo "Convertide contra Camillo Barcaruol," 27 April 1611.

210. Ibid., fascicolo "Santa Marta contra D. Veronica da S.ta Marta," 29 May 1611.

211. Ibid., fascicolo "Santa Cattarina contra Francesco Rivoltela Murer," 18 April 1611.

212. Ibid., fascicolo "Corpus Domini contra Lazaro de Mazo, et Iseppo Finzi Ebrei," 2 May 1611. Although I have not seen a law in this respect, Jews were apparently prohibited from going to convents; they were prosecuted for doing so from about 1601 on.

213. Ibid., fascicolo "Santa Anna contra Battista fruttaruol," 23 June 1611.

214. Ibid., fascicolo "Santa Marta. D. Veronica fà servitij à quelle Monache," 23 July 1611.

215. Ibid., fascicolo "Contra Pasqualin Sonador," 11 August 1611.

216. Ibid., fascicolo "Sant' Andrea contra Novella meretrice," 30 November 1611.

217. Ibid., fascicolo "San Gerolamo contra Z. Antonio, ó Pier' Antonio Ciola, Medico," 15 February 1611 (m.v.).

218. See particularly the trial proceedings initiated by the vicar of Torcello in 1651 in which eleven nuns from various convents and nine men (ecclesiastics as well as seculars) were accused of having sexual relationships and other transgressions. The interrogation of thirty-eight lay men and women, twelve priests and monks, and thirty nuns gave the impression that corruption, lack of discipline, and mutual calumnies were dominant features of convent life in the diocese of Torcello. APV, Torcellania Criminalia Monialium, busta 23, proceedings starting 13 August 1651.

219. Zuane Raimondo was exiled in 1658 for having fathered Sister Degnamerita's child; he was denounced by Alban Minio, who had had a relationship with the nun for more than ten years. Sister Degnamerita died

shortly after giving birth. "They [the Council of Ten] wish that the above-mentioned Ser Zuanne Rimondo be deprived of his nobility and that his name be immediately canceled from the book of noblemen [kept by] the Avogaria di Comun, and also from the Golden Book of the Great Council. He should also consider himself banned from this City and the Dogado of Venice, and from all the other cities, territories, and places of our domain— on land, on water, as well as on armored ships—and disarmed in perpetuity." "Vogliono, che il sopradetto Ser Zuanne Rimondo sia privo di Nobiltà et il suo nome immediatemente depennato dal libro de Nobili della Avogaria di Comun, et anco dal libro d'oro del Maggior Consiglio. Sia in appresso, e s'intenda bandito da questa Città di Venezia e Dogado, e da tutte le altre Città, Terre, e luoghi del Dominio nostro terrestri, e maritimi, navilij armati, e disarmati in perpetuo." ASV, CX, Criminal, reg. 75 (1658), c. 34r, 9 July 1658. See also PsM, busta 270, fascicoli 18, 28; and APV, Torcellania Criminalia Monialium, busta 23, Santa Maria Valverde, 24 June–14 July 1658.

220. ASV, CX, Criminal, reg. 39, c. 196v, 14 February 1622 (m.v.).

221. Ibid., reg. 50, cc. 167v–168r, 9 January 1633 (m.v.).

222. The upper lagoon was part of the Dogado and therefore under the jurisdiction of the convent magistrate from the beginning. The inconveniences of long-distance gondola trips, however, made the close supervision of convents in Burano, Mazzorbo, and Torcello difficult. Therefore, the state of the convent reform in the upper lagoon was in practical terms comparable to that in the mainland cities, over which the convent magistrate was granted authority only in the middle of the seventeenth century.

223. *Avvertimenti monacali,* pt. 1, pp. 35–36.

224. ASV, PsM, busta 265, fascicolo without title, 31 July 1617. A love poem by Father Gerolamo is inserted in the sheet containing his sentence:

Since when is there so much pain
After [?] having enjoyed my love?
Because my life and death depends on you,
Bow to my prayers, to my desire
So that I will never feel bad again and languish
So that this sweet desire
To serve you, my Heart, [is satisfied]
And see to it that my misery
Is changed into joy and happiness.

Che gradito mio bene
Sin quando tante pene?
Se'n voi sta la mia vita, l'mio morire
Ch'io non prov'altro mal, altro languire
Che quel dolce desire
Di servir voi Cor mi[o]
Piegatevi a' miei preghi, al mio desio
E fate si che la mestitia mia
Mutata in gioia, et in Letitia sia.

225. "In tempo della messa grande fa[ce]va molti chiassi con diverse monighe." Ibid., busta 267, fascicolo "Ogni Santi contra Felice Romana sta' alli Crosechieri," 3 November 1625. The records of the Provveditori abound with denunciations of prostitutes, who, despite repeated prohibitions by the Council of Ten, frequented convent parlors and churches.

226. Ibid., fascicolo "Convertide contra Francesco Zachìa," 9 September 1625. Jews were denounced for visiting nuns as frequently as were prostitutes.

227. Ibid., busta 268, fascicolo "San Maffio de Muran contra Gasparo Rigo mercante da Chiodi," 13 November 1627.

228. Ibid., fascicolo "San Vido contra Piero Barbier," 29 May 1627.

229. Ibid., fascicolo "San Lorenzo," 21 August 1642.

230. Ibid., busta 269, fascicolo "Musica à San Lorenzo," 29 July 1653.

231. Ibid., busta 270, fascicolo 16, 7 March 1658.

232. Ibid., fascicolo 26, 18 July 1658.

233. APV, Torcellania Criminalia Monialium, busta 23, Santi Marco e Andrea, 18, 20 October 1622.

234. "Si serrano dentro [il parlatorio piccolo] persone à parlar con le monache à hore prohibite, facendo portar avanti, e indietro tutto il giorno drappi, et altre robbe per recitar tragedie, overo dimostrazioni con gran confusione nel monasterio e gran scandalo di fuori." APV, Visite Priuli, c. 398v, 12 February 1596 (m.r.). Regarding theater performances in Tuscan convents, see Weaver, "Spiritual Fun"; and idem, "The Convent Wall in Tuscan Drama."

235. Grimani, Constitutioni, p. 45v.

236. ASV, PsM, busta 271, fascicolo 4, 24 March 1660.

237. APV, Torcellania Criminalia Monialium, busta 23, fascicolo San Mauro di Burano, cc. 39r–49v, 24 January 1652 (m.r.).

238. "Non poteva esser altra monaca stravestita." Ibid., San Vito di Burano, 4 March 1608, c. 16r (erroneously marked 17; pagination discontinuous).

239. APV, Visite Priuli, visitation of Sant' Andrea de Zirada, 9 April 1592, c. 37r; visitation of Corpus Domini, 27 November 1595, c. 558r; Visite Vendramin, visitation of San Gerolamo, 4 November 1609; visitation of Sant' Andrea de Zirada, 12 November 1609; visitation of San Daniele, 21 April 1610; visitation of Santa Chiara, 13 January 1611 (m.r.).

240. "Le putte a spese sono di gran disturbo al monastero. . . . Sono anco tenute alcune di loro nelle celle delle medesime monache à dormire, e vanno per il dormitorio e dove più le piace vagando senza alcuna regola et giocano alle carte la notte con scandolo. Vi sono anco innamoramenti d'importantia tra Suor Lorenza Capello, et Orsetta Zorzi, e tra Suor Marina Bragadin, e Andriana Corner di modo che si doverà provede[re] che non vadano nè in choro, nè in dormitorio nè in altri luoghi communi senza le debbite guardie." Visitation of Santa Marta, 16 May 1594, APV, Visite Priuli, c. 184v.

241. Sister Julia Thiepolo: "Suor Chiara del Calice . . . porta zuffo, si

pella le ceglie, tien acqua da viso, dorme ogni notte con Suor Fiorenza, et non vuol obbedire, et alle volte Suor Lucietta Zen dorme anco con essa. . . . Portano odori, e muschi. . . . Suor Bianca è amica con Suor Perpetua, et tutta una cosa con essa, si serra in cella con essa." APV, Visite Tiepolo (1620–27), fascicolo 9, 23 September 1620.

242. "[Siano interrogate . . . le portinere . . . che sanno . . . che] più e più volte sia stato trovato monache nei parlatorii con le cozele alte et dei gentil homeni con le mani in seno et le monache con le mani nelle brachesse delli homeni et altre cose." Undated letter of denunciation, ibid.

243. Undated letter of denunciation, found among the records of Patriarch Giovanni Tiepolo's visitation of San Giuseppe, 1625–26, APV, Visite Tiepolo.

244. "Soleva [essere] publica meretrice, la qual è anche à spese . . . e pur è tanto scandalosa in quel Monastero andando vestita pomposamente di colar, sempre a Parlatorio con preti, frati somaschi, e mondani, essendo tutta intrinseca della madre Veniera." ASV, PsM, busta 270, fascicolo 5, 17 March 1656.

245. A law of 1621 prescribed that the introduction of married women into the convents had to be approved by two-thirds of the chapters, to minimize "the reticence that one finds ordinarily among the nuns [in accepting them]." "[E]t di far che si accomodino . . . le differenze, et . . . la renitenza, che s'incontra per ordinario delle monache, che . . . non senza molto disgusto, si lasciano persuadere à riceverle." Council of Ten, 15 February 1621 (m.v.), ibid., reg. 1, c. 67r.

246. Patriarch Lorenzo Priuli, "Ordini per le figliuole a spese," 2 November 1592, MCC, CC 2583, cc. 125v–126r. Regarding *donne a spese,* see PsM, 24 October 1647, ASV, CL, busta 288, cc. 778r–781r.

247. "Considerando noi quanta incommodità aporti al vostro Monastero di Sant'Andrea il tener fiole à spese dentro la clausura . . . . [Questo] anco . . . causa confusione nelli parlatorij." Patriarch Giovanni Trevisan, 28 April 1589, APV, Visite Trevisan, cc. 85r–v.

248. AV, Nunziature di Venezia, reg. 19, c. 22r, 25 January 1578 (m.r.).

249. "Andarono l'altr' hieri alcuni de' Consiglieri, et altri Senatori principali dentro il Monastero, per vedere, se è vero quello, che dicono le Monache, che gli bisogni per dette Zitelle fare nuove Celle." Ibid., reg. 40, c. 699v, 4 December 1610.

250. Ibid., reg. 42, cc. 532v–534r, 1 September 1612.

251. Patriarch Lorenzo Priuli, visitation of Santa Maria Maggiore, 21 November 1594, APV, Visite Priuli, c. 282v.

252. "Alcune monache vorrano che [le converse] fossero ridotte di dentro per manco spesa del monasterio, e maggior agiuto di esse monache, le quali fanno tutte le fattiche." Visitation of Santa Maria dei Miracoli, ibid., c. 368v, 9 January 1595 (m.r.).

253. "Mandamus . . . aliquo modo puellas, et mulieres, ut vulgo dicitur Novitias ante earum desponsationem, et transductionem vestimentis, et in-

dumentis nuptialibus indutas in Parlatorijs, et locis Monasteriorum vestrorum admittere." Patriarch Francesco Contareno, 25 November 1554, MCC, CC 2570, cc. 164–65.

254. "Non si possino far Sponsalitij in alcuna chiesa di essi Monasterij, nè trattar de contrazzer Matrimonj nelli parlatori, over alle Finestre di Chiesa, nè mostrar le Novizze per contrazer essi Matrimoni." Patriarch Giovanni Trevisan, "Ordini generali," 24 November 1578, MCC, CC 2570, c. 243.

255. "Le figliuole che saranno per tempo a spese fatte che sono novizze siano mandate a casa loro, et non si permetta, che stiano . . . vestite da maridate, nè li mariti le venghino à visitare con scandalo alle finestre." Patriarch Francesco Vendramin, visitation of San Servolo, 10 September 1610, APV, Visite Vendramin; see also Grimani, *Constitutioni,* pp. 13r–v.

256. "Accompagnata . . . da diverse gentildonne . . . monta in gondola . . . e si pone a sedere sopra un seggio alquanto rilivato . . . seguendola un gran numero d'altre gondole et se ne va a visitar i monasteri delle monache." Giulio Bistort, *Il Magistrato alle Pompe nella Repubblica di Venezia* (Venice, 1912), pp. 98–99.

257. "Trascorre troppo oltre una licentiosa libertà della gioventù à sturbare li Monasterij di Monache con detestande insidiose molestie in particolarmente nelle fontioni solleni delle Visite di Novizze, ove col seguito numeroso di Nobiltà, et d'ogni altro grado in confusioni eccedenti . . . si trappassa i limiti della dovuta modestia. . . . Sia peró preso che resti assolutamente, et intieramente proibito à tutte le Novizze sia di che grado, e conditione si voglia il capitar nei giorni solenni delle loro nozze, o in qualsisia altro con accompagnamento, ó seguito di Donne à Monasterij di Monache." Pregadi, 18 September 1654, ASV, CL, busta 289, cc. 21r–v.

258. See, among many others, the rules of 1620 and 1644 limiting expenditures for music and refreshments on the occasion of *sagre* (consecration ceremonies). In Padua and Treviso, these religious functions had got out of hand and turned into neighborhood festivals. Pregadi, 31 August 1644, ASV, CL, busta 288, cc. 731r–735r.

Chapter Four

1. For a discussion on the loss of ecclesiastic properties in the fifteenth and sixteenth centuries, see Carlo Cipolla, "Une crise ignorée: Comment s'est perdue la propriété ecclesiastique dans l'Italie du Nord entre le XIe et le XVIe siècle," *Annales E.S.C.* 2 (1947): 317–27; Giorgio Chittolini, "Un problema aperto: La crisi della proprietà ecclesiastica fra quattro e cinquecento," *Rivista Storica Italiana* 85 (1973): 353–93; Aldo Stella, "La proprietà ecclesiastica nella Repubblica di Venezia dal secolo XV al XVII," *Nuova Rivista Storica* 42 (1958): 50–77; and Enrico Stumpo, "Problema di ricerca: Per la storia della crisi della proprietà ecclesiastica fra Quattrocento e Cinquecento," *Critica Storica* 1 (1976): 62–80.

2. Dieci Savij sopra le decime de Rialto, 8 June 1709, 22 April 1766, ASV, Santi Biagio e Cataldo, busta 3.

3. Council of Ten, 10 June 1569, in Innocenzo Giuliani, O.F.M., "Gen-

esi e primo secolo di vita del Magistrato sopra monasteri," *Le Venezie Francescane* 28, no. 3–4 (1961): 162; PsM, 31 August 1734; Senate and PsM, 21 March 1747, ASV, Santi Biagio e Cataldo, busta 3.

    4. Senate and PsM, 4 January 1676 (m.v.), ibid.

    5. PsM, 31 August 1734, ibid.

    6. Sant' Andrea de Zirada was an Augustinian convent founded for the purpose of sheltering widows and other needy women in an adjacent hospital.

    7. "E noi beviamo vin guasto." ASV, PsM, busta 263, fascicolo "Santo Andrea di Venetia contra Z: Gaglarda, e sua fia. . . ," 9 July 1568.

    8. "Nelli parlatori non si possano dar da mangiar e bever ad alcuno passando." Visitation of Sant' Andrea de Zirada, 13 January 1566, APV, Visite Trevisan (1560–89), c. 25r.

    9. "Non se mandi fuori tanti cesti, et tante torte, ma mediocramente." Visitation of Corpus Domini, 1560, ibid., c. 2v.

    10. Visitation of San Zaccaria, 13 March 1596, APV, Visite Priuli (1592–96), c. 577r. See a repetition of this complaint by Patriarch Francesco Vendramin; APV, Visite Vendramin (1609–18), 19 October 1609.

    11. Maurice Aymard, *Venise, Raguse, et le commerce du blé pendant la seconde moitié du XVIe siècle* (Paris, 1966), p. 17. The per capita consumption of wheat in late-sixteenth-century Tuscany amounted to 292 liters annually. Judith C. Brown, *In the Shadow of Florence: Provincial Society in Renaissance Pescia* (New York, 1982), p. 70.

    12. Visitation of Santa Maria delle Vergini, 15 July 1596, APV, Visite Priuli, c. 588r. The per capita figures are based on the convent population figures from table A1.

    13. Visitation of San Sepolcro, 27 October 1597, ibid., c. 404r; visitation of Santa Maria Maggiore, 8 October 1610, APV, Visite Vendramin.

    14. "If they kept their food in common, as they are supposed to, there would be abundance instead of shortage in the convent; furthermore, the nuns, in order to provide themselves with wine and grain, have to frequent various lay persons, so that the reputation of the convent suffers." "Perché quando tutte ponessero in commune, come sono tenute non sarebbe strettezza nel Monastero, ma abbondanza, oltreché per provedersi in particolare di vino, et formenti li conviene alle volte passare per mano di diverse persone laiche con poca reputatione del Monastero." Visitation of Santa Anna, 18 November 1609, APV, Visite Vendramin.

    15. "Si levi totalmente l'abuso di cucinare in monastero le robbe che vengono mandate da parenti e altre persone per venderle cucinate fuori del monastero." Visitation of San Sepolcro, 11 March 1610, ibid.

    16. Letter of the abbess of San Sepolcro to Patriarch Vendramin: "The abuse of washing the laundry of lay people is worse than ever . . . which will be the ruin of this poor place because of the consumption of fire wood and water." "Si fano pelgio che mai circa . . . del lavar drapi di secolari . . . che sono la rovina de questo povero loco con consumar legne e acqua." Visitation of San Sepolcro, 29 May 1610, ibid. In 1570, the convent magistrate took action against the nuns of Corpus Domini and San Servolo be-

cause of their close friendships with several monks of San Salvatore. Among other things, the nuns regularly washed and cared for their friends' clothes. ASV, PsM, busta 263, fascicolo "Processus . . . formatus per Reverendissimum d. d. Patriarcham Venetiarum contra . . . Canonicos Regulares S. Antonij, et Sancti Salvatoris," 9 October 1570, c. 5r.

17. Patriarch Antonio Contareno, "De Apparati Ecclesiarum Monialium," 22 July 1509, MCC, CC 2570, c. 264.

18. Cesar Bacconus, Prothonotarius Apostolicus, "Musiche interdette," 11 August 1524, MCC, CC 2570, c. 160.

19. ASV, PsM, capitolari, reg. 1, c. 24v, 22 June 1547.

20. Patriarch Giovanni Trevisan, "Non si facciano pasti nei Parlatori," 10 January 1565 (m.r.), MCC, CC 2570, c. 170.

21. Pregadi, *Parte presa . . . in materia di monache*, 31 August (Venice, 1644).

22. ASV, PsM, busta 268, fascicolo "Inquisitio di trasgressori," 14 March 1641. According to Richard T. Rapp, a master in the construction industry earned 66 soldi a day between 1620 and 1629; 1 ducat equaled 6 lire and 4 soldi, or 124 soldi. Richard T. Rapp, *Industry and Economic Decline in Seventeenth-Century Venice* (Cambridge, 1976), p. 135.

23. ASV, PsM, busta 268, fascicolo "Inquisitio," 14 March 1641.

24. "Il Nobil Homo Ser Battista Erizzo . . . et NH Domenigo Trivisan . . . erano deputati, et eletti per questo Consiglio sopra la limitazion delle spese delle Monache, si conventual, come osservanti di questa Nostra Città, et Torcello." ASV, PsM, capitolari, reg. 1, c. 7v, 30 July 1522.

25. "Experience . . . has shown that the Reverend Abbesses of our convents of Venice, in admitting nuns again as they please, have reduced, and continue to reduce, their convents and nuns to extreme poverty, because their revenues are not sufficient to sustain the women, and [they accept] many persons unfit for a religious life, who disturb the peace and other good customs. This is the reason why I have decided to issue the present decree, and constitution, that no abbess . . . shall furthermore accept and receive girls in their convents, if not under observation of the following rule: three examiners shall be elected per chapter in every convent, mature and sufficiently [experienced] women, who, when it comes to receiving girls, are being charged with examining them, and if they think that it would be expedient and useful to admit them, [that is], if it seems to them [a good idea], or to the majority of them, with the intervention of the abbess, said girls shall be introduced not without our consent and [the consent of] the congregated chapter, and they will be admitted, and accepted as nuns, by a majority vote. Otherwise they are to be expelled, but when the majority [of nuns] think that they should be admitted, we will also examine, and carefully judge, whether the revenues of the convent are sufficient to feed the newcomers together with the others who already live in the convent. And because they [the abbesses] should know, to the advantage of the nuns who already live in the convents, how many novices they should introduce, and receive, we wish and order that within one month each convent, and abbess, should give us notice of the sum of their revenues and income of their convents,

because once we have seen and examined them, we will easily know how many women and mouths each convent can support." "La experientia . . . mostra, che le Venerande Abbadesse de li Monasterij nostri de Venetia recipiendo Moniales de novo ad libitum hanno redutto, et reducono in extrema necessità i loro Monasterij, et Monache, non abbastando li frutti de quelli alla substentatione de le donne, et multiplicati suppositi non apti a Religione, e destruttivi de la pace, et altri bon costumi, per la qual cossa semo mossi a far lo presente Decreto, et Constituzione che niuna Abbadessa . . . de cetero debbia admettere, et recever fie in loro Monasterij, nisi servata certa forma infrascribenda. Che per Capitolo debbiano esser elette tre Examinatrici in cadauno Mon.rio, done mature, et sufficiente, alle quale quando si hano a ricever fie se li commetta la examination de quelle, et pensino si sarà cossa expediente, et utile ad admetterle, et sì a quelle parerà, o alla maggior parte de esse, interveniente etiam la Abbadessa, alhora non tamen senza consentimento nostro [e quello del] Congregato Capitolo, se introducano ditte fie, quale si maiori parti videbitur, siano admesse, et introdutte in Monache. Aliter se li debba dar ripulsa, et quando de majori consensu parerà che debbiano esser admesse, volemo anchora Noi examinar, et veder diligentemente, se li frutti di quel Mon.rio bastino commodamente [per] dar lo viver a quelle Introducende con le altre se retrovano in Monasterij. Et perche debbiano saper per utile de quelle si trovano in Mon.rio, quante da novo si haveranno ad introdur, et recever, volemo, et ordenemo, che frà termine de un mese cadauno Monasterio, et Abbadessa ne debbia dar notitia de la quantità de frutti, et intrate de ditti loro Monasterij, perche illis habitis et consideratis de facili sapremo quante donne, et bocche potrà supportar cadaun Mon.rio." Patriarch Hieronimus Quirino, MCC, CC 2570, cc. 163–64, 15 November 1530.

26. A *livello* contract in this context was a veiled credit transaction, which often led to the alienation of church properties. There were two basic forms of *livello* contract. The first can be described as the concession of a piece of land in exchange for a renewable, perpetual lease: the convent would "sell" a piece of property to a lay person, who in turn would lease the same property to the convent in the form of an *enfiteusi*, i.e., a "perpetual," or twenty-nine-year-long, rent contract. If the convent failed to pay the annual rent, the "buyer" would become the legal owner of the property. The second type of *livello* was contracted with a so-called *promissio francandi*; the "buyer" obligated himself to return the piece of property if the convent, in addition to paying the annual rent, was able to put up the sum of money for which it had "sold" the property in the first place. *Livello* contracts were credit transactions, because the annual canon that the effective owner had to pay depended on the sum of money originally received by the convent; the "price" did not necessarily reflect the value of the property exchanged. *Livelli* were frequently contracted by convents and monasteries in need of cash. Problems derived from the fact that many abbots and abbesses closed *livello* contracts with relatives; corruption thus led to a gradual alienation of church properties. Gigi Corazzol, *Fitti e livelli a grano* (Milan, 1979); idem, "Sulla diffusione dei livelli a frumento tra il patriziato veneziano nella

seconda metà del '500," *Studi Veneziani,* n.s., 6 (1982): 103–28; idem, *Livelli stipulati à Venezia nel 1591.* Supplementi di Studi Veneziani (Pisa, 1986).

27. "Siano tenuti . . . a veder con diligentia tutte le livellation, et affitti fatti . . . di essi Monasterij. . . . [Loro] habbino auttorità, et libertà . . . di revocar, et anullar[li]. . . . Ne si possi praeterea dar ad affitto, ne etiam à livello cosa alcuna de i detti Monasterij . . . à persone che ad esse fussino conzonte con parentella." Council of Ten, ASV, PsM, capitolari, reg. 1, cc. 7r–v, 12 September 1521.

28. Council of Ten and Zonta, 30 October 1528, in Giuliani, "Genesi," pp. 158–59.

29. Council of Ten and Zonta, 15 November 1531, ASV, PsM, capitolari, reg. 1, cc. 10r–v.

30. Council of Ten and Zonta, 17 October 1533, 23 June 1534, in Giuliani, "Genesi," pp. 159–60.

31. Council of Ten and Zonta, 29 October 1522, in Giuliani, "Genesi," p. 157.

32. As the surviving archival documentation shows, the Provveditori sopra i Monasteri di Monache conducted numerous criminal investigations between 1555 and 1571, and Patriarch Giovanni Trevisan visited the convents in his diocese in roughly the same period (1560–89). See chap. 3.

33. Pregadi, "Accettazione del Concilio di Trento da parte della Repubblica," 6 October 1564, BSP, Mss 1044.44. In 1568, Pope Pius V reaffirmed his claims to tax exemption and ecclesiastical jurisdiction in his bull "In coena dominis"; see *La chiesa di Venezia tra riforma protestante e riforma cattolica,* ed. Giuseppe Gullino (Venice, 1990), p. 202. For a brief overview of the relationship between the Republic of Venice and the papacy after the Council of Trent, see Gaetano Cozzi, "L'intrecciarsi della vita religiosa ed ecclesiale con la vita politica (1565–1606)," in *Dal 1517 alla fine della Repubblica,* vol. 2 of *La Repubblica di Venezia nell'età moderna,* by Gaetano Cozzi, Michael Knapton, and Giovanni Scarabello, Storia d'Italia, vol. 12 (Turin, 1992), pp. 69–77.

34. The last estimate had been compiled in 1536. Regarding the development of the *decime del clero,* or state-owned church tithes, see Giuseppe Del Torre, *Venezia e la terraferma dopo la guerra di Cambrai: Fiscalità e amministrazione (1515–1530)* (Milan, 1986); Luciano Pezzolo, *L'oro dello Stato: Società, finanza e fisco nella Repubblica veneta del secondo '500* (Treviso, 1990); and Anna Pizzati, "La proprietà terriera dei monasteri benedettini veneziani nella seconda metà del cinquecento" (master's thesis, University of Ca' Foscari, Venice, Department of Literature and Philosophy, 1986), pp. 1–33.

35. On the Venetian *procuratie,* see Reinhold C. Mueller, *The Procuratori di San Marco and the Venetian Credit Market* (New York, 1977); and idem, "The Procurators of San Marco in the Thirteenth and Fourteenth Centuries: A Study of the Office as a Financial and Trust Institution," *Studi Veneziani* 13 (1971): 105–220.

36. Brian Pullan, "Wage-Earners and the Venetian Economy, 1550–

1630," in *Crisis and Change in the Venetian Economy in the Sixteenth and Seventeenth Centuries,* ed. Brian Pullan (London, 1968), p. 158.

37. San Bernardo and San Martino, for example, spent 19 and 12 percent, respectively, of their budgets on spices.

38. Although it is unclear exactly how the *decima del clero* was assessed, underendowed convents were usually exempted. Since the nuns were asked to report the number of *bocche* of each convent, one can assume that the per capita consumption of basic food items played a role in assessing deductions.

39. J. C. Brown, *In the Shadow of Florence,* p. 71.

40. See the lists of private revenues that Patriarch Priuli compiled during his visitations: APV, Visite Priuli, Sant' Alvise, 10 April 1595, cc. 426r–v; Santa Croce della Giudecca, 25 October 1595, cc. 495r–v; San Giuseppe, 9 November 1595, c. 515v; Santa Lucia, 20 November 1595, c. 538r; Santa Maria Maggiore, 21 November 1594, c. 284r; Santa Marta, 16 May 1594, c. 185r; Santi Rocco e Margherita, 27 July 1594, c. 238r; San Zaccaria, 13 March 1596, c. 579r.

41. Many nuns did needlework. Sister Diodata, for example, a nun in San Giuseppe, was excellent not only at baking pastries, but at making handkerchiefs, shirts, collars, and *maneghetti* (cuffs?); according to the prioress, she also made "stupendous hats embroidered with gold and silver, because she works miraculously with pearls and jewelry." Unfortunately, "she has never worked for the convent in thirteen years, consuming all her earnings on her own and investing them in [the production of] the things mentioned above." "[La ghe ha cusido] . . . [dei] capelli stupendissimi con recami d'oro, arzento soprarizzo, perche lei lavora miracolosamente con perle et con zogie. . . . l'é stata 13 anni, che la non ha mai lavorato per el monastero, et tutto quel che ha guadagnato l'ha messo in suo uso, et speso ogni cosa in le cose che ho ditto." ASV, PsM, busta 263, fascicolo "Copia processus Sancti Josephi Venetiarum contra il Confessor et Gasparo suo fratello," 13 August 1571, c. 2v. Before the convent of Sant' Adriano di Torcello was abolished and its possessions transferred to San Gerolamo, the nuns of San Gerolamo earned their living through the production of *ballotte* (pellets used in the Great Council for election procedures). In the first half of the sixteenth century, the nuns repeatedly petitioned the Senate for a pay raise. ASV, CL, busta 288, cc. 294r–v, 2 March 1522; c. 308r, 31 March 1534; c. 314r, 28 March 1544; c. 322r, 29 September 1547. The nuns of Santa Maria Maddalena (Le Convertite) printed books.

42. ASV, Sant' Andrea de Zirada, busta 7, reg. "Doti, Procure, Mansionarie, Commissarie," cc. 2r–12r.

43. ASV, Santa Croce di Venezia, busta 3, fascicolo "Doti di monache, 1517–1661," 17 September 1517, 7 January 1589 (m.v.).

44. ASV, San Lorenzo, busta 19, fascicolo 12, "Cessioni de livelli per l'alimento d'alcune Monache," parchment, 25 October 1530; Senato Deliberazioni Roma Ordinaria, filza 33, investigation of Alvise Pisani di Marc'Antonio, 5 May 1610.

45. On 22 March 1564, the Senate decided that the Provveditori alle

Biave (grain office) should buy 456 staia of grain (37,989 liters) and distribute it to the poor convents. ASV, Senato Terra, reg. 45, c. 7v. Unfortunately, the poor convents are not specified by name; cash subsidies are listed, however, for the convents of Santa Maria dei Miracoli (26 August 1564), San Sepolcro (28 September 1564), San Giuseppe (21 December 1565), Santa Chiara di Murano (24 March 1565), Ognissanti (13 December 1565), and Le Convertite (12 August 1564). Ibid., cc. 51v–52r, 67r, 201r, 109r, 200v, 50r. The last three convents did not file a tax return in 1564.

46. The visitation protocols of Patriarch Vendramin show that income from dowries could be quite high; see the column "Other Cash" in table A5.

47. "In questi tempi calamitosi siamo cresciute nui sole observanti al n.o di 46 per esserci state forza[te?] di tuorne di questi ultimi giorni monache n. 8 de la dota dele quale ne a bissognato pagare alcuni nostri debiti . . . di olgi vini legne et molte altre cose, oltra ch' siamo state cariche de infiniti altri debiti per la suma de ducati 1500. . . . oltra che il viver nostro cotidiano al qual non bastano le nostre intrade ne è stato forzza tuor molti danari ne è stato forzza anco tuorne per fabricar un refetorio una cusina e un albergo e granaro luogi tutti che non si poteva far di meno di refarli per esser cresciute." Tax declaration of Mother Maria Contarini, abbess of Santa Marta, ASV, Soprintendenti alle Decime del Clero, busta 32, polizza 45.

48. "Intendendosi, in diversi monasterij di monache di questa Città . . . non vi è quel buon governo delle Intrade, che bisognaria, et questo proceder principalmente, perche li Procuratori di quelli . . . non havendo alcuna Monaca parente di sangue, poco si curano di consigliarle, & aiutarle." Council of Ten, 10 June 1569, in Giuliani, "Genesi," p. 162.

49. "Se ben per molte deliberationi sia stà proveduto che li beni ecclesiastici non si possino alienar, nondimeno da certo tempo in quà è introdotto che le Abbadesse, over Priore de Monasterii de Monache di questa Città, et Dogado senza saputo del suo Capitolo, togliono denari che summa le piace ad imprestito da particolar persone, facendo scritti di mano, over instrumenti, et obligando li beni del Monasterio, et promettendoli di risponderli ogni anno ducati sei per cento, over stara cinque di formento all'anno, sino che le siano restituiti li denari del cavedal, e ciò fanno sotto coperta di convenir pagar debiti, per far fabbriche nelli Monasterii forse poco necessarie, et per altri lievi bisogni, et non havendo poi modo di pagar li interessi, et fitti sopraditti, togliono delli altri denari ad interesse ut supra, di modo che se bene li Monasterii hanno buonissima entrata, crescendo ogni di più li interessi, le povere Monache generalmente patiscono del viver, et vestir, e le cose del Monasterio vanno di mal in peggio, a tal che qualche Monasterio che ha d'entrata circa ducati cinque mille all'anno, si ritrova al presente debitor di duc. 5000, al qual inconveniente dovendosi proveder." Council of Ten, 31 August 1569, ibid., pp. 162–63.

50. ASV, Soprintendenti alle Decime del Clero, busta 33, polizza 202. Other convents might have concealed the fact that they had debts resulting from *livelli*—the abbesses and their notaries knew, of course, that state and church were critical of those credit transactions. On the other hand, it is

equally plausible that the abbesses exaggerated the amount of expenses and debts in order to qualify for tax exemptions. In any case, on the basis of the estimate of 1564, the government's complaint cannot be verified.

51. See, for example, Priuli's visitation of Santa Lucia, 16 February 1596 (m.r.), APV, Visite Priuli, c. 539v.

52. See, for example, Trevisan's visitation of San Lorenzo, 16 October 1568, APV, Visite Trevisan, cc. 27r–28r.

53. Unfortunately for the historian, this practice was not widespread before the late seventeenth century.

54. See, for example, Priuli's visitation of Santi Biagio e Cataldo, 17 February 1593 (m.r.), APV, Visite Priuli, cc. 113v–114v.

55. ASV, Sant' Andrea de Zirada, busta 12, fascicolo 48, "Relatione di Suor Elena Malipiero intorno al Priorato suo in Santo Andrea di Zirada," 1651–53, no pagination. All quotations in the following discussion are from this report.

56. See the investigation of Sant' Andrea de Zirada by the convent magistrate in 1568 and the protocols of the visitations of Sant' Andrea de Zirada by Patriarchs Trevisan and Vendramin; APV, Visite Trevisan, 13 March 1566, cc. 22v–25r; Visite Vendramin, 12 November 1609.

57. "Prometto . . . che si non fosse Io agiuto di qualche bonissima persona et il tenir de fie in Monasterio certo non potressimo viver et scoverimo [?] anco sustentarssi con li lavorieri che si fanno a diversi per giornata stando in piedi zorno et notte oltra li quotidiani officij." ASV, Sopraintendenti alle Decime del Clero, busta 32, polizza 20.

58. "Per gratia del Signor Dio sono tutte buone Monache, et habiamo delle figlie assai a spese, che se non fossero queste non si haverebbe da viver." ASV, PsM, busta 269, fascicolo "Sant' Iseppo," 18 April 1653.

59. Francesco Gregolin, "Saggio di statistica di alcuni processi per malcostume, nei conventi di Venezia e dello Stato Veneto, sec. XVII e XVIII," in *La republica di Venezia e la corte di Roma,* ed. Bartolomeo Cecchetti (Venice, 1874), 2:109–10.

60. Visitations of Sant' Alvise and Santi Biagio e Cataldo, 26 September 1565, APV, Visite Trevisan, cc. 14r, 15v.

61. "Considerando Noi lo stato dei Monasterij de Monache di questa città, li quali per la maggior parte si trovano in gran bisogno, non havendo il modo di somministrare alle Monache per il vestito, ma nè anco il sufficiente vitto, talmente che ogni Monaca è necessitata provedersi di molte cose fuori di Monasterio con pericolo e pregiudizio dell'anima sua. Et essendosi per esperienza conosciuto che le Doti, overo Elemosine, che si danno alle figliuole per monacar in danari contanti tutto che siano di grande pesa a particolari, riescono nondimeno per molti rispetti a Monasterij di poco utile. . . . ordiniamo . . . che [i monasterij] . . . non ricevino . . . in una sol volta una somma di danari . . . ma [una] annua entrata sufficiente al modesto, et regolato vitto e vestito d'una persona." MCC, CC 2583, pt. 1, c. 127r, 24 November 1593.

62. "Sono accresciute à tanto eccesso le spese, che si fanno nel Monacar figliuole . . . che . . . devesi provedere à questi abusi . . . si che possano

egualmente le famiglie di questa Città accommodar le figliuole al servitio del Signor Dio." Pregadi, 26 July 1602, ASV, CL, busta 288, c. 405r.

63. "Mons. di Torcello stima poco questa dote, e dice, che in alcuni suoi Monasterij, dove per tanto tempo s'è usato anche passar i due mila, sono le debiti." Nuncio Monsignor Offredo di Offredi, Bishop of Molfetta, to Cardinal S. Giorgio (the future Clement VIII), 31 August 1602, AV, Nunziature di Venezia, reg. 33, c. 262r.

64. "Nella Diocesi di Torcello s'è vestita questi giorni una figliuola con due mila cinque cento scudi di dote senza che sin hora se ne senta strepito." Offredi to Giorgio, 5 October 1602, ibid., c. 277v.

65. "I believe that one could issue a brief to Mons. Patriarch and another one to the Bishop of Torcello, in which one could say that since the Signoria told His Holiness of some disorders that arise because of the excess of dowries, and of other expenses when introducing and professing the nuns, His Beatitude, inclining to satisfy the republic as much as possible, is inclined to give jurisdiction to the above-mentioned Mons. Patriarch, and to the Bishop of Torcello, to reduce and moderate the above-mentioned dowries as they think is best. . . . Mons. Patriarch is of the opinion that it would be very reasonable to define the dowries in conformity with the decree of the Signoria, as also the other expenses of the families, [but] he wants to add that when daughters have to enter a convent, the parents . . . should be obligated to pay for the construction of the cell." "Io crederei che si possa fare un Breve à Mons. Pat.ca et un altro à Mons. . . . di Torcello, ne' quali si narrasse, c'havendo la Signoria fatto esporre à Sua Santità alcuni disordini, che nascono per il grave eccesso delle doti, e spese d'introdurre, e far professione le Monache, Sua Beatitudine inclinando à dar sodisfattione quant'è in lui alla Repubblica ha pensato di dar facoltà à detti Mons. Pat.ca, e Vescovo di Torcello, di ridurre, e moderare secondo essi giudicaranno meglio le predette Doti. . . . Mons. Pat.ca sarebbe d'opinione, che lo stabilir le doti conforme alla parte della Signoria fosse cosa ragionevole, come le altre spese della casa, vorria ben aggiongere, che dovendo entrar figlie in un Monastero, i parenti . . . fussero obbligati, à far la fabbrica per le celle." Offredi to Giorgio, 31 August 1602, ibid., cc. 261v–262r. On 28 December 1602, the papal brief was published; MCC, CC 2570, cc. 203–4.

66. "Il Collegio è stato diviso . . . havendo qualch'uno d'essi ancor opinione, che, non havendo se non commandato ai laici quel, che stimano servitio della Repubblica non habbiano hora che far più in questo negotio." AV, Nunziature di Venezia, reg. 33, c. 271r, 21 September 1602.

67. "Si che possano egualmente le famiglie di questa città accommodar le figliuole al servitio di Dio, senza esser astrette à spese maggiori di quelle, che ricerca . . . il commodo universale." Pregadi, 26 July 1602, ASV, CL, busta 288, c. 405r.

68. Pregadi, 3 June 1603, ibid., c. 410v.

69. Pregadi, 29 June 1604, ibid., c. 411r.

70. Pregadi, 15 April 1610, ibid., cc. 411r–v.

71. "Se si tollerava . . . per le doti, gioie, et acconci, le decine di migliaia di scudi, non doveva parer grave, che per una Monaca si spendessero tre,

o quattro mila scudi. . . . il Principe non ha mostrato d'aggradire molto il mio discorso. . . . ha detto . . . che sono molti pochi . . . che danno le doti cosi grosse per gli matrimonij, e che questi mettono poche figlie ne' Monasterij. . . . et che alcuni Monasteri di Venetia, ricchi di otto e dieci mila scudi . . . non si vergognano [di] dimandare 5000 ducati per qualch'una." AV, Nunziature di Venezia, reg. 40, cc. 481v–483r, 17 April 1610.

72. ASV, Senato Deliberazioni Roma Ordinaria, reg. 18 (1610–12), fascicolo 33, 3 May 1610.

73. Ibid., 4, 5 May 1610.

74. "Mi contentavo . . . [di] ricever questo solo sollevamento di haver la mia putta in salvo. . . . Et cosi la putta è ancora in casa mia et i soldi et la robba sono dalle Muneghe." Ibid., 5 May 1610.

75. Andrea Vendramin said that each of the fifteen girls paid six to seven ducats to each of the thirty-nine nuns of Santi Biagio e Cataldo. Ibid., 6 May 1610. For the number of nuns at the time, see the protocol of Vendramin's visitation of 22 September 1610, APV, Visite Vendramin.

76. ASV, Senato Deliberazioni Roma Ordinaria, reg. 18, fascicolo 33; 5, 6 May 1610.

77. "Et seben S. S. Ill.ma tornó a replicarle altre cose, mostrando segno di disgusto, et di gran risentimento, stettero nondimeno sempre ferme, et risolute di non voler ricever figliuole di alcuna sorte, et di esser pronte a restituire le tredesi, over quattordesi mille ducati. . . . Con che detto Mons. Ill.mo Patriarca restandone con molto risentimento si partì." Ibid., 6 May 1610.

78. This is the money the twelve "new" novices were supposed to pay; the other twenty applicants, who had sisters, cousins, or aunts in San Lorenzo, were admitted at a lower price that apparently did not surpass the legal amount.

79. "Le Monache di San Lorenzo si affaticano co' i loro favori per rimuovere ogni ostacolo del riscuotere le limosine dotali già stabilite con le Zitelle." AV, Nunziature di Venezia, reg. 40, c. 699v, 4 December 1610.

80. "Con destrezza va aiutando, acciò la cosa si finisca quietamente et quanto più utilmente si può per le Monache." Ibid., cc. 699v–700r.

81. In 1615, the nuncio wrote to Rome: "I have talked to Monsignor Patriarch of Venice about the affair of the nuns of San Lorenzo, which will end without damage to the convent because the nuns will have the 25,000 scudi agreed upon with the ten [?] girls, i.e., twelve hundred scudi each publicly, and the rest secretly under the pretext of the construction of the new altar." "Ho discorso con Mons. Patr.a di Venetia nel negotio delle Monache di San Lorenzo, il quale si terminerà senza danno del Monastero perche le Monache per le dieci Zitelle accettate havranno li 25,000 scudi convenuti, cioe mille due cento scudi per ciascuna palesemente et gli altri poi secretamente col pretesto della fabrica dell'Altare." Ibid., reg. 42C, c. 344r, 28 November 1615.

82. The nuncio made the following comments on the discussions surrounding the proposed pension decree three weeks before it was passed: "The deliberation . . . did not please the senators . . . without any doubt,

there will be difficulties in issuing it [the decree], but even more in executing it, because if lifelong annuities are being assigned with the obligation for parents to pay them, [the nuns] will never be able to retrieve them, and the convents will suffer extremely from this." "La rissolutione . . . non piacque a' Senatori . . . senza dubio vi saranno delle difficoltà nello stabilirla, ma più nell'esseguirla; perchè [se] s'assegnano crediti annui per la vita della Monaca con l'obbligo da pagarseli da' parenti, non li potranno mai risucuotere, et i Monasteri ne patiranno estremamente." Monsignor Gessi, Bishop of Rimini, to Cardinal Borghese, secretary of state, 20 March 1610, AV, Nunziature di Venezia, reg. 40, cc. 429r–v.

83. "Se sarà un monte eretto dalla Repubblica potranno questi Signori negare il pagamento a' Monasteri ogni volta, che non habbino l'intiera ubbidienza in quello, che gli piace." AV, Nunziature di Venezia, reg. 40, c. 404r, 27 February 1610 (m.r.).

84. "In order for the capital of those 60 ducats to be easier [to assign] and more secure, specific inquiries *[stride]* should be made [in order to find out whether the capital to be assigned was already burdened with a mortgage, *livello,* or any other form of credit], as is usual, about those goods that are to be assigned, and the assignment should only be regarded as valid after those inquiries have been concluded satisfactorily, and, if necessary, those capitals to be assigned should also be entailed in the form of a *fidecommesso* by [the nuns'] fathers." "Accioche il capitale per detti ducati 60 sia più facile, & sicuro, siano fatte particolari stride, secondo il solito, de' tali beni, che saranno assignati, ne s'intendi fatto l'assignamento, se non saranno passate quietamente esse stride, & per questi assignamenti siano anco date, dove occorresse dalli Padri, & altri, com'è predetto, fideiussioni idonee." Pregadi, 15 April 1610, ASV, CL, busta 288, c. 411v.

85. "Dovendosi provedere, che li detti poveri Monasterij non ricevino maggior danno, & incommodo: ma si conservino nello stato, nel quale si sono conservati fino à questo tempo, & possino anco migliorare la loro fortuna." Pregadi, 6 October 1610, ibid., c. 412r.

86. "Peró dovendosi ritrovar modo, che siano esse deliberationi in tutte le sue parti essequite, come è conveniente, nè permettere, che da un poco numero di Monache, come è benissimo noto, derivi . . . la indebita inobedienza." Pregadi, 9 July 1620, ibid., c. 412v.

87. ASV, San Lorenzo, busta 2, reg. A, "Monasterio S. Lorenzo n. 18, Cod. E," "Nota delli accidenti occorsi al Monasterio nostro l'anno 1620, et 1621 in tempo dell' Abbadessa Madona Eletta Vitturi per causa d'alcune figliuole che furono accettate Monache, et cio si fà perche servi per avertimento di quello, che possi occorrer nell'avenire," c. 1r.

88. Pregadi, 9 July 1620, ASV, CL, busta 288, cc. 412r–v; Patriarch Tiepolo, "Circa Dotes Monacandarum," 26 August 1620, MCC, CC 2570, cc. 290–93.

89. A ban on confessions greatly disturbed convent life, because confessions were mandatory before each convent function, apart from the emotional deprivation it meant for the nuns.

90. ASV, San Lorenzo, "Nota delli accidenti occorsi al Monasterio

Nostro l'anno 1620, et 1621 in tempo dell'Abbadessa Madona Eletta Vitturi per causa d'alcune Fig.le che furono accettate Monache, et cio si fà per che servi per avertimento di quello, che possi occorrer nell'avvenire," c. 1v.

91. "[C]i venne portato di ordine di esso Mons.r Ill.mo un mandato, che sara registrato perche dovessimo far ritornar nel Monasterio, et Vestire le sopradette Figliuole conforme alli sopradetti ordeni ... al che non potendo noi obedire lasciassimo senza far altro uscir il tempo del mese statuito, ma in tanto facessimo intendere a esso Mons.r Ill.mo che ... per la consuetudine del nostro Monasterio non potessimo senza nova balottatione adempire li suoi comandamenti." Ibid.

92. Ibid., c. 10r.

93. Ibid., c. 2v.

94. Ibid., c. 1r.

95. Pregadi, 27 August 1620, ASV, CL, busta 288, cc. 567r–568v.

96. Pregadi, 9 July 1620, ibid., cc. 412r–v.

97. Pregadi, 18 November 1637, ibid., cc. 681r–687v.

98. Council of Ten, 8 March 1622, ibid., cc. 581r–582r.

99. A convent in Cividale, Friuli, had problems retrieving rents and *livelli;* Pregadi, 2 May 1628, ibid., c. 606r. The dowry laws were reconfirmed on the occasion of the foundation of a convent in Bergamo; Pregadi, 31 March 1632, ibid., c. 626r. The nuns of Ceffalonia had difficulties in retrieving their income; Pregadi, 9 April 1633, ibid., cc. 638r–v. The dowries in Treviso needed to be limited; Pregadi, 30 April 1633, ibid., c. 640r.

100. Pregadi, 30 June 1637, ASV, PsM, reg. 2, c. 1r.

101. See the capitularies of the convent magistrate; ibid., regs. 1–4.

102. "Nobody in this city or in our state may under any pretext whatsoever sell, donate, or in any other way alienate any kind of immobile possessions to ecclesiastic persons, unless authorized to do so by a majority decision of this Council." "Alcuno cosi in questa città, come nel nostro stato, non possa sotto qual si voglia colore, o pretesto vender, donar, o quovis modo alienar alcuna sorte di stabili, possessioni, o altri simili beni a persone Ecclesiastiche, se non con licentia di questo Consiglio proprosta per la maggior parte di tutti li ordini." Pregadi, 26 March 1605, ASV, Senato Terra, reg. 75, cc. 19r–v.

103. Mueller, *The Procuratori di San Marco.*

104. Senate, 31 June 1472, ASV, Senato Terra, reg. 6, cc. 166r–v.

105. Senate, 22 December 1536, ibid., reg. 29, cc. 83v–84r.

106. In 1610, the nuncio pressured the patriarch "to consider the indemnity of the convents, which otherwise [i.e., after converting the dowry payments into lifelong pensions] will no longer have alms to invest. . . . I have the impression that [the patriarch] . . . is trying . . . to see that . . . the nuns get the capital." "Consideri l'indennità de' Monasteri, i quali in tal modo non havranno la limosina da investire. . . . à me pare, che [il Patriarca] . . . tenti . . . di vedere, che . . . le Monache habbino il capitale." AV, Nunziature di Venezia, reg. 40, cc. 369r–v, 28 January 1610 (m.r.).

107. On the Interdict of 1606, see the brief overview by Gaetano Cozzi, "La questione dell'Interdetto (1606–1607)," in Cozzi, Knapton, and Scara-

bello, *Dal 1517 alla fine della Repubblica,* pp. 87–91. See also William J. Bouwsma, *Venice and the Defense of Republican Liberty: Renaissance Values in the Age of the Counter Reformation* (Berkeley, 1968).

108. "Intendendosi con maggior disordine essere introdotto [l'alienare beni stabili in persone Ecclesiastiche] . . . nelle altre terre, & luoghi del suo Dominio, ove per l'accortezza delli Ecclesiastici, & per la semplicità delle devote, & pie persone, si sono alienati il quarto, & ancora il terzo delli terreni, & altri stabili delle Città istesse. Peró, come legge giustissima . . . [il governo] ha ordinato che . . . sia osservata la sopradecta prohibitione, stimando cosa indebita, che dovendo voi sopportare le continue fattioni, & gravezze, altri . . . otiosamente godano i beni acquistati col sudore, & col sangue de' vostri progenitori." "Lettera della Serenissima Republica, e Senato di Venetia, alle lor communità, e sudditi," in *Raccolta degli scritti usciti fuori in istampa, e scritti a mano, nella causa del P. Paolo V. co' signori venetiani secondo le stampe di Venetia, di Roma, & d'altri luoghi,* vol. 1 (Coira [Chur], 1607), p. 9.

109. "Così potrà fare il Senato altra legge . . . accioche un membro non cresca più del dovere, si che faccia il corpo mostruoso, & prendendo più alimento del conveniente dannischi le altre membra togliendo loro il suo debito; & per se stesso non potendo digerire il superfluoso si riempia di mali humori, onde nasca prima infirmità in lui, & poi corrottione di tutto il corpo. Ma lo stato de gli Ecclesiastici in questo Dominio è un membro, che puó essere una centesima parte di tutto il numero delle persone, & hà tirato in se non una portione delli beni à questo corrispondente; ma nel Padoana più d'un terzo: nel Bergamasco più della metà, & non vi è luogo, dove almeno non habbia un quarto delli beni. . . . tre quarti delli religiosi non vivono sopra le rendite Ecclesiastiche, ma di limosine, & oblatione de' secolari; essendo le possessioni, & entrate in un picciolissimo numero di Clerici, il quale appena arriva alla quarta parte di essi. Et quello, che più importa è, che di questi la metà habita fuori dello Stato." Paolo Sarpi, "Considerationi sopra le censure della Santità di Papa Paolo V. contra la Serenissima Republica di Venetia," in *Raccolta degli scritti,* p. 47. Up until the eighteenth century, contemporaries complained about the illegal increase of mortmain possessions: the *podestà* of Brescia, Domenico Ruzzini, reported in 1628 that he had "discovered massive violations of the law of 1605 in this city [Brescia] and its territory. . . . after the law was issued, real estate with a value of more than 50,000 ducats has been registered as having passed into the hands of the church." Quoted in Daniele Beltrami, *La penetrazione economica dei veneziani in terraferma: Forze di lavoro e proprietà fondiaria nelle campagne venete dei secoli XVII e XVIII,* Civiltà veneta studi 12 (Rome, 1961), p. 19, n. 2. The Deputazione straordinaria aggiunta al Collegio dei X Savi (extraordinary deputies added to the College of the Ten collectors of the ecclesiastic tithe on Rialto), which investigated the illegal growth of ecclesiastical patrimonies between 1605 and 1767, attributed the increase of mortmain possessions to the fact that "the convents of the consecrated virgins continuously raised the prices of placing the women of divine vocation." Marino Berengo, *La società veneta alla fine del Settecento* (Florence, 1956), p. 90.

110. Daniele Beltrami's study of the colonization of the *terraferma* by Venetian investors shows that it was mostly the Venetian patriciate that profited from the sales of communal properties and of the estates of dissolved monasteries in the seventeenth and eighteenth centuries. In Beltrami's eyes, the mortmain laws of 1605 were very effective. Beltrami, *La penetrazione economica,* esp. p. 107.

111. Del Torre, *Venezia e la terraferma,* p. 95.

112. ASV, Dieci Savij sopra le decime di Rialto, *condizioni di decima* 1566, 1582, 1661.

113. Tax evaders seem to have taken advantage of the legal uncertainties of the law of 1472. In 1639, for example, the convents of San Lorenzo, San Zaccaria, and Santi Cosma e Damiano refused to pay lay taxes on remodeled houses. Pregadi, 29 June 1639; Collegio, 28 June 1666, ASV, San Lorenzo, busta 9, fascicolo 9 (D), "Per Gravezze. San Lorenzo, San Zaccaria, SS Cosmo e Damian." In 1544, San Lorenzo won a lawsuit against the Dieci Savij sopra le decime di Rialto (lay tax collectors), insisting that the houses in question had been acquired before 1472. Ibid., fascicolo 10 (E), "Per Gravezze. San Lorenzo, San Zaccaria, SS Cosmo, e Damian," 28 June 1544. In 1585, San Zaccaria was acquitted of a tax debt of 165 ducats after it was proved that certain possessions were indeed exempt from lay property taxes. ASV, San Zaccaria, busta 74, reg. "Gravezze," vol. 2, c. 22r.

114. Between 1582 and 1630, the Dieci Savij sold thirty-three pieces of mostly urban real estate on behalf of the convents of Santa Maria Maddalena (Le Convertite), Santa Caterina di Venezia, Santa Croce di Venezia, San Daniele, San Giuseppe, Santa Lucia, Santa Maria degli Angeli, Santa Maria Maggiore, Santa Maria dei Miracoli, Santa Maria Valverde, San Matteo di Murano, San Sepolcro, Spirito Santo, and Santi Rocco e Margherita. ASV, Dieci Savij sopra le decime di Rialto, busta 1773.

115. Between 1605 and 1767, the church had acquired real estate worth 8,915,645 ducats through legacies and pious donations statewide, of which about one-quarter (worth 2,204,264 ducats) was auctioned off. A small fraction of the acquired properties (worth 416,356 ducats) were exempted from the mortmain law by the government, so that a capital of 6,295,025 ducats remained to be sold. Only about 5.2 percent of the real estate acquired (worth 325,078 ducats) was effectively subject to taxation. BNM, Classe It. VII 1522 (8825), c. 694, table "Beni . . . lasciati ad pias causas . . . dall'anno 1605."

116. Silver money in Venice was devalued by roughly 50 percent between 1520 and 1620. See Giuseppe Parenti, "Prezzi e salari à Firenze dal 1520 al 1620," in *I prezzi in Europa dal XIII secolo a oggi,* ed. Ruggiero Romano (Turin, 1967), p. 251, table 14. According to Parenti, grain prices in Siena doubled between 1564 and 1765. Giuseppe Parenti, *Prezzi e mercato del grano a Siena (1546–1765)* (Florence, 1942), pp. 27–28. According to Fernand Braudel and Frank Spooner, wheat prices in Udine, Siena, and Naples rose rapidly in the course of the sixteenth century but remained relatively stable from 1600 to 1760. F. Braudel and F. Spooner, "Prices in Europe from 1450 to 1750," in *The Cambridge Economic History,* vol. 4

(Cambridge, 1967), pp. 474–75, table, "Wheat Prices in Money of Account." A similar stabilization of general consumer prices in the seventeenth and eighteenth centuries is indicated in Henry Phelps Brown and Sheila V. Hopkins, "Seven Centuries of the Prices of Consumables, Compared with Builders' Wage-Rates," in *A Perspective of Wages and Prices*, ed. Henry Phelps Brown and Sheila V. Hopkins (London, 1981), p. 16, fig. 1. For Venice, no price study could be found that covers the whole period between 1564 and 1769. According to Richard Rapp, however, the wages of Venetian construction workers more than doubled between 1550 and 1629. Rapp, *Industry and Economic Decline*, p. 135, table 4.7. Maurice Aymard shows that grain prices in Venice and Ragusa rose steadily in the second half of the sixteenth century, reached a peak between 1590 and 1600, and dropped again in the first half of the seventeenth century. Aymard, *Venise, Raguse, et le commerce du blé*, pp. 120–21, table "Prix du blé à Venise."

117. Part of the farmland of Santa Teresa formerly belonged to the suppressed monastery of San Giorgio in Braida di Verona. ASV, Sopraintendenti alle Decime del Clero, busta 78, polizza 393.

118. The tax records of 1581, 1661, and 1769 in particular show that many convents acquired farmland in remote areas, such as the Friulano (Ognissanti), Polesine (Santa Anna, Spirito Santo, Santa Maria delle Grazie, San Sepolcro, Santa Croce della Giudecca, San Daniele), and Veronese (San Giacomo, Santi Rocco e Margherita, Santa Caterina di Venezia).

119. The recorded loss of about nine thousand ares of farmland in the case of San Zaccaria is inconsistent with its increase in wheat and wine production by 6,273 and 4,694 liters, respectively.

120. San Giovanni Evangelista di Torcello was the oldest convent in the lagoon; it had been founded in 640. The *procuratore*, who was in charge of transcribing thousands of medieval parchments documenting its ancient possessions, was falsely accused of violating the clausura laws by the convent's estate managers, who feared a loss of their influence. ASV, PsM, busta 13, 16 May 1652. In 1667, the Senate ordered a thorough review of the convent's accounts because of its tax debts and illegal *livelli* contracts. Pregadi, 5 April 1667, ASV, CL, busta 289, cc. 65–67r. In 1689, the convent magistrate decided to continue supervising the financial administration of the convent, which was close to a "total dissolution of its revenues." Council of Ten, 21 March 1689, ASV, PsM, reg. 2, cc. 50r–v.

121. In their tax declaration of 1769, the nuns inserted a testimony by Podestà Francesco Longo, who confirmed that the territories of Noventa di Piave had been damaged by floods. ASV, Sopraintendenti alle Decime del Clero, busta 32, polizza 56.

122. "Habbiamo il tutto fidelmente esposto nel presente volume, et parimente descritti li gravami spese et debiti che ha il povero nostro monasterio accioche le Illustrissime et Reverendissime Signorie Vostre col suo sapientissimo intelletto considera[n?]o quanto si deve havere in consideratione si per il numero de noi monache come per il sito in che si attroviamo da che sforzatamente siamo astrette a supportar molte piu eccessive et intolerabile spese

di quello che forsi essendo in Venetia o piu propinque facilmente si potrebbe schiffare." Ibid.

123. In absolute numbers, the increases in urban rental income (in ducats) are as follows:

	1564	1661	1769
San Zaccaria	3,923	9,562	15,910
San Lorenzo	3,572	9,022	11,411
San Gerolamo	912	3,228	3,125
Sant' Andrea de Zirada	823	1,785	3,114

Figures for 1564 and 1769 are from table A4; figures for 1661 are from Daniele Beltrami, *Storia della popolazione di Venezia dalla fine del secolo XVI alla caduta della Repubblica* (Padua, 1954), table 23. Beltrami must have based his survey on an analysis of the tax declarations of all Venetian citizens, who usually indicated where they lived and how much rent they paid. The tax records compiled by Venetian convents list only the few properties subject to the lay tithe (table A4, entries for 1566, 1582, and 1661).

124. It is possible that the importance of wheat and wine for individual convents actually declined; the composition of revenues in 1769 was calculated on the basis of inferred prices that might have been too high. I estimated the price of wheat at 4.3 ducats per staio and the price of wine at 1.7 ducats per *mastello.* See the appendix.

125. "We who are locked up in here very often do not get our rents, and we have a lot of trouble in retrieving our annual income, and especially in recent years, when we barely received all of our wheat and wine." "A noi che semo qui dentro serate et assai volte ne vie portado via el fito delle chase, et tanti fastidii et travalgii se anno a scuoder lintrade, et massime in questi anni che a pena si scuode tutto formento et vin." Tax declaration of Santa Maria delle Vergini, ASV, Sopraintendenti alle Decime del Clero, busta 32, polizza 79. "Your Most Reverend Lordships will consider very well our great misery, and how we will be able to provide for such a huge number of persons in these times of want with so many famines, especially because we did not even retrieve half of the amount of wine and not much more of the wheat." "Puol molto ben considerar Vostre Signorie Reverendissime la nostra grandissima calamita et miseria, et come potremo sustentare tanto numero di persone in questi tempi cosi penuriosi con tante carestie, et massime non havendo scosso questo anno circa mezza el fitto del vino et pocco piu del formento." Tax declaration of Prioress Zuana Contarini of Corpus Domini, ibid., polizza 70. Postscripts like these abound.

126. Beltrami, *Storia della popolazione,* table 23. In 1564, the nine Benedictine monasteries in Venice owned as much farmland as the twenty-one Venetian convents of the same order. Pizzati, "La proprietà terriera," p. 59.

127. On the intricate connections between the temporal and spiritual realms in both state and church, see Paolo Prodi, *The Papal Prince: One Body and Two Souls: The Papal Monarchy in Early Modern Europe*

(Cambridge, 1987); idem, "La Chiesa di Venezia nell'età delle riforme," in *La chiesa di Venezia,* ed. Gullino, pp. 63–75, esp. 64; and Gaetano Cozzi, "Venezia regina," in *Crisi e rinnovamenti nell'autunno del Rinascimento a Venezia,* ed. Vittore Branca and Carlo Ossola (Florence, 1991), pp. 1–9.

Chapter Five

1. "Rex Salamon . . . cepit edificare Domum Dominj in Hyerusalem in Monte Moria qui demonstratis fuerat David patri suo. . . . Et ibi contigue fecit edificare Domum Virginum in Hyerusalem. Et ibi steti Sancta Maria Virgo ubi fuit per angelum Annuntiata. Et ita in tempore Sanctus Petrus constituit Monasterum Sancte Marie Virginis in Hyerusalem. . . . Ita Sanctus Marchus Evangelista fundavit ordinem Canonicorum et Canonissarum." "Cronica del Monastero delle Vergini di Venetia," MCC, Correr 317, ff. 10v–11r.

2. Andrea Dandolo, "Andreae Danduli Venetorum Ducis Chronicon Venetum a Pontificatu Sancti Marci ad Annum usque MCCCXXXIX," in *Rerum Italicarum Scriptores,* vol. 12, ed. Ludovicus Antonius Muratorius (Milan, 1728), p. 343; Marino Sanuto [Sanudo], "Vitae Ducum Venetorum italice scriptae ab origine urbis, sive ab Anno CCCCXXI usque ad Annum MCCCCXCIII auctore Marino Sanuto, Leonardi Filio, Patricio Veneto," in *Rerum Italicarum Scriptores,* ed. Muratorius, vol. 22 (Milan, 1733), p. 407; Marcantonio [Marc'Antonio] Coccio Sabellico, "Historiae rerum venetarum ab urbe condita libri XXXIII" (first ed.: 1487), in *Degl'istorici delle cose veneziane, i quali hanno scritto per pubblico decreto,* vol. 1 (Venice, 1718), p. 160; Thomas Diplovatazio, "Tractatus de Venetae urbis libertate et eiusdem Imperij Dignitate: et Privilegijs, et an de Jure Dominium Venetorum habeat superiorem In temporalibus compositus per me Thomam Diplovatatium Melinghi Patritium Constantinopolitanum I. V. Doctorem" (Venice, ca. 1530), BNM, cod. lat. XIV 74 (4056), ff. 235r, 239r; Flavio Biondo, *Blondi Flavii Forliniensis de Origine & Gestis Venetorum ad Franciscum Foscari Serenissimum Ducem: Inclytumq Senatum: caeterosque Venetae Reipublicae Patritios* (Venice, 1503; written in 1454), no pagination; Flaminio Corner (Cornarus, Cornaro, Cornelius), *Ecclesiae Venetae antiquis monumentis nunc etjam primum editis illustratae ac in decades distributae,* vol. 4 (Venice, 1749), pp. 2–6; Edward Muir, *Civic Ritual in Renaissance Venice* (Princeton, 1981), pp. 127–28.

3. Gaetano Cozzi, "Giuspatronato del Doge e prerogative del primicerio sulla cappella ducale di San Marco (secc. XVI–XVIII): Controversie con i procuratori di San Marco de supra e i Patriarchi di Venezia," *Atti dell'Istituto Veneto di Scienze, Lettere, ed Arti* 151 (1992–93): 11, 14–16.

4. Gabriella Zarri, "Monasteri femminili e città (secoli XV–XVIII)," in *Storia d'Italia,* annali 9, *La Chiesa e il potere politico dal Medioevo all'età contemporanea,* ed. Giorgio Chittolini and G. Miccoli (Turin, 1986), p. 375.

5. There is some uncertainty as to whether the likeness of Saint Mark was imprinted on the sapphire, or whether two different rings were used to affirm Venetian sovereignty and to invest the abbess, respectively. See also the *Lettera delle RR. Monache di S. Maria delle Vergini, al Sereniss.*

Marc'Antonio Memmo, Principe di Venetia. Per la rinovatione della solenne visita alla lor Chiesa il primo giorno di Maggio. A ricever l'Indulgenza di Papa Alessandro III (Venice, 1613), no pagination.

6. "[The pope] said: O Ziano with my authority I will make the sea subject to you with this pawn [the golden ring with the incision of Saint Mark] . . . you and your successors shall marry the sea every year . . . as the wife to the husband, so the sea shall be subject to your dominion. . . . Then . . . the most holy pope together with the emperor and the Most Serene Prince Sebastiano Ziano laid the sacred stone in the church of Santa Maria delle Vergini in Jerusalem recently remade. . . . After a few days he [the pope] dressed the most serene Julia, daughter of the emperor, as nun, and made her abbess and had the Most Serene Prince invest her with the possession [of the church and convent] and wished that with the ring of Saint Mark's likeness he married the abbess. Then . . . the Most Serene Prince . . . married her with the Sapphire as is still observed today. Then the highest pontifex gave Prince Sebastiano Ziano the church of Holy Mary of the Virgins and the abbess as brides. The pope said [when he gave him] the sapphire as a sign of the consecration of the marriage: O Ziano through my authority these two marriages of double faith are yours and those of your successors . . . perform this ceremony of taking possession with the ring of Saint Mark, in memory of the divine Evangelist Mark, who founded this blessed order and rule, [which was] confirmed by Saint Peter the Apostle." "[Il pontefice] disse: O Ziano per mia auctorita cum questo pegno [lanello doro cum la prompta di Santo Marcho] te fazo el mar obligato . . . ti e li toi successori ogni anno habij spoxar il mar . . . como la moglie del marito cossi el mar al vostro imperio sia subiecto. . . . Da poi . . . El sanct.mo PP. Insieme cum limperator et el S.mo principo Sebastiano Ziano messe la pietra sacra nella giesia di Sancta Maria dele Vergine de Yerusalem novamenti facta. . . . Dali pocho giorni el messe lhabito alla serenissima Julia filia Imperatoris & fecella Abbadessa & fece che Ser.mo principo li desse el posseso e volse che cum lanello di San Marcho promptado el spoxasse la abbadessa. Da poi . . . el Sereniss.o Principo . . . la spoxa con el Saphyro come si observa usque in hodiernum diem. Alhora el summo pontifice dete per spoxa al principo Sebastiano Ziano la giesia de Sancta Maria delle Vergine et la Abbadessa. El pontifice al segelo sponsalizio del saphyro dela sua consecration disse o Ziano per mia auctorita queste do desponsatione de Duplicata fede son [di?] ti e de li toi successori . . . che in tal possesso con lanello di San Marcho faci tal cerimonia In memoria del divo Evangelista Marcho el qual a facto questo Benedeto ordine et regula confirmata per San Pietro Apostolo." "Cronica del Monastero delle Vergini di Venetia," ff. 1r–v; see also Muir, *Civic Ritual in Renaissance Venice*, p. 128, n. 62.

7. Maria Pia Pedani, "L'osservanza imposta: I monasteri conventuali femminili a Venezia nei primi anni del cinquecento," *Archivio Veneto*, 5th ser., 179 (1995): 117.

8. "Poi le venuto qua in Venetia & a posto tanta ruina quanto si trova alinfermal fucine. . . . Cum suo Inzegno et Arte a facto tanto Chel R.mo Monsignor Patriarcha la tolto questo artifice diabolico per suo vicario el

qual Malefico . . . per guadagno e symonia ha robar la Chiesia de dio et tirar li denari dalle povere monache si conventuale come observante." "Cronica del Monastero delle Vergini di Venetia," f. 57v.

9. See n. 2 above.

10. Giovanni Stringa, *Venetia città nobilissima, et singolare, descritta già in XIIII Libri da M. Francesco Sansovino: Et hora con molta diligenza corretta, emendata, e più d'un terzo di cose nuove ampliata dal M. R. D. Giovanni Stringa, Canonico della Chiesa Ducale di S. Marco* (Venice, 1604), p. 126v.

11. *Breve trattato delle citta nobili del mondo, et di tutta Italia, con la lunghezza, & larghezza di essa, confini, sito, & provincie, & il principio del Regno de' Longobardi* (Florence, 1574), no pagination.

12. Giovanni Botero, *Relatione della Republica venetiana* (Venice, 1605), pp. 103r–104r.

13. William J. Bouwsma, *Venice and the Defense of Republican Liberty: Renaissance Values in the Age of the Counter Reformation* (Berkeley, 1968), pp. 232–93.

14. Cozzi, "Giuspatronato del Doge," p. 5.

15. Matteo Casini, *I gesti del principe: La festa politica a Firenze e Venezia in età rinascimentale* (Venice, 1996), p. 45.

16. Contarini, paraphrased by Cozzi in "Giuspatronato del Doge," p. 23. The office of Procuratore di San Marco was reserved for the richest and most influential patricians.

17. Cozzi, "Giuspatronato del Doge," pp. 38, 42, 50.

18. This expression refers to the popes' "absolutist" rule after the Council of Trent. Paolo Prodi, *The Papal Prince: One Body and Two Souls: The Papal Monarchy in Early Modern Europe* (Cambridge, 1987).

19. "Che li vescovi abbino cura di restituir e conservare la clausura delle monache, esortando li prìncipi e comandando alli magistrati, in pena di scomunica, a prestarli aiuto." Paolo Sarpi, *Istoria del Concilio Tridentino,* vol. 2 (Florence, 1982), p. 1029.

20. Innocenzo Giuliani, O.F.M., "Genesi e primo secolo di vita del Magistrato sopra monasteri," *Le Venezie Francescane* 28, no. 3–4 (1961): 156–57.

21. Silvio Tramontin, "La visita apostolica del 1581 à Venezia," *Studi Veneziani* 9 (1967): 453–533.

22. Gaetano Cozzi, "L'intrecciarsi della vita religiosa ed ecclesiale con la vita politica (1565–1606)," in *Dal 1517 alla fine della Repubblica,* vol. 2 of *La Repubblica di Venezia nell'età moderna,* by Gaetano Cozzi, Michael Knapton, and Giovanni Scarabello, Storia d'Italia 12 (Turin, 1992), pp. 37–38.

23. "[I veneziani si sarebbero acquietati] . . . se si havesse a visitare solamente i Preti et Frati, et non le Monache, parendo alla maggior parte cosa dura, che delle imperfettioni delle loro Donne si habbino da far processi, con propalare quelle cose che più tosto si dovriano coprire." Quoted in Tramontin, "La visita apostolica," p. 459.

24. "L'una che riformandosi i Monasterij di Monache et riducendosi

a maggior strettezza le figliuole de nobili che prima anco vi entravano mal volentieri, doppo la riforma non vi vorrebbero entrare in modo alcuno." Ibid., p. 466.

25. "Li monasterij delle Monache sono ripienî di figliole, et sorelle delli proprij nobeli, et cittadini nostri, et le viscere nostre proprie collocate et riposte in quelli lochi sacri, come in sicuro deposito, per sicurtà della Religione et della pudicitia loro: alla quale si attende con tanta diligentia, quanto é grande, anzi universale l'interesse che ha in esse, per il parentado et per il sangue suo, tutta questa città." Ibid., p. 480.

26. Pregadi, 26 July 1602, ASV, CL, busta 288, c. 405r.

27. Nuncio Offredi to Cardinal S. Giorgio, 21 September 1602, AV, Nunziature di Venezia, reg. 33, c. 271r.

28. "It seems to me that it [i.e., the pope's retroactive authorization given to the Patriarch of Venice and the Bishop of Torcello to reduce spiritual dowries] would save the reputation of Our Lordship, force the monastic orders under the authority of the ordinaries, and suggest to them [the patricians] that we have satisfied the government." "Questo par à me, che salvi la riputatione di Nostro Signore, riduca questi ordini sotto l'ubbidienza degl' Ordinarij, e anche lasci à loro il pensiero di dar sodisfattione alla Signoria." Nuncio Offredi to Cardinal S. Giorgio, 31 August 1602, ibid., cc. 261v–262r.

29. "[Q]uesto voler far dipendere l'accomodamento delle Doti dall'auttorità di N.ro Sig.re sia un levarsi dall'antico possesso, c[he] hanno [i membri del Collegio] di governare . . . questi Monasteri." Quoted in Nuncio Offredi to Cardinal S. Giorgio, 12 October 1602, ibid., c. 279r.

30. "In tutti i tempi la Repubblica ha voluto conservar in se stessa la protettione et sopraintendenza del governo dei monasteri fondati particolarmente in questa città, et nel Dogado, et sempre, ò unitamente colli Patriarchi, et Vescovi di Torcello, overo anco separatamente secondo il bisogno, si sono andate regolando da noi le cose loro . . . perche in somma sono figliole, e sorelle nostre, nate dell'istesso sangue . . . essendo colocate, et riposte, come in sicuro deposito per sicurtà della religione, et pudicitia delle figliuole de nobili, et cittadini nostri; bisogna ben credere, che la cura, et protettione loro ci sia sopra ogni altra cosa à cuore, et che vi si attenda con tanto maggior diligenza, quanto è più grande l'interesse universale di tutta la città per sangue, et per parentado; onde vengono per ció deputati da noi cotidianamente tre Senatori per età, per intelligenza, et per auttorità principali, li quali tengono questa cura spetiale, insieme con Monsignor Reverendissimo Patriarca, e co'l Vescovo di Torcello. Da questa unione, et buona intelligenza sono seguiti quei buoni effetti, che ben si sa, et si vegono. . . . noi sapemo benissimo per esperienza, non solo publica, ma privata di cadauna famiglia lo stato de monesterij di monache, et nissuno é più interessato de noi medesimi, così in quelle, che già sono vestite, come in quelle, che doveranno vestirsi, perche tutte sono d'un istesso sangue." ASV, Senato Deliberazioni Roma Ordinaria, reg. 13 (1600–1602), cc. 161r–162r, 24 August 1602.

31. "Ut . . . abusibus, et incommodis . . . providas, totumque ea in re adiuves quantum poteris . . . piam intentionem dilecti filij Nobilis Viri Marini

[Grimano] Venetiarum Ducis." "Breve Apostolico intorno le Doti delle Monache," 28 December 1602, MCC, CC 2570, c. 203.

32. "Quest' essecutione è stata fatta d'ordine . . . del Concilio de dieci e Senatori Deputati sopra li Monasterij, essendovi bisognato la loro auttorità, e Braccio per essere obediti senza tumulto." Letter of Monsignor Taverna, Bishop of Lodi, 21 October 1594, AV, Nunziature di Venezia, reg. 30, c. 292v.

33. "Veramente questi benedetti frati m'hanno dato gran travaglio, non essendo mai stato possibile levare affatto la lor pratica, né con ogni diligenza che habbi usato prohibire che non li [alle monache] scrivessero. Credo peró che per l'avvenire se ne asterranno per paura del vigore di questi Signori." Letter of Monsignor Taverna, Bishop of Lodi, 26 October 1594, ibid., c. 296r.

34. Nuncio Gessi to Cardinal Borghese, 28 January 1610 (m.r.), 27 February 1610 (m.r.), 20 March 1610, ibid., reg. 40, cc. 369v, 404r, 451v.

35. "Le Monache si dogliono assai di questa nuova provisione, ma non hanno alcuno che l'aiuti; perché si scopre che tutta la Nobiltà é unita, et i Parenti loro, et i Protettori degli Monasterii gli sono anch'essi contrarij, mostrando di preferire l'interesse, e ben publico." Nuncio Gessi to Cardinal Borghese, 27 February 1610 (m.r.), ibid., cc. 404v–405r.

36. "La verità è, che questi Signori si pigliano una grande auttorità, et se era difficile la presente materia dell'anno 1602 . . . adesso è più, che difficilissima per rispetto del Principe, et dello stile, che hanno preso in questi negotij Ecclesiastici." Nuncio Gessi to Cardinal Borghese, 20 March 1610, ibid., c. 452r.

37. "Vedendo noi gli abusi, gli eccessi, et l'inconvenienti grandi, che sempre si facevano maggiori, con grave detrimento delle fameglie de' nostri nobili, cittadini, et altri habitanti in questa città, et nel dogado, per la introdottione de' doti essorbitanti, et di spese vane, et superflue, habbiamo convenuto necessariamente provedervi, et far quello, che si è sempre fatto, di commandare a' laici, che si astengano da tali eccessi, et superfluità, limitando loro la dote . . . cosa, che non poteva essere fatta da Monsignor Reverendissimo Patriarca, né dal Vicario di Torcello, concorrendovi la transgressione de' nostri laici." ASV, Senato Deliberazioni Roma Ordinaria, reg. 18 (1610–12), c. 39v, 17 April 1610.

38. "[N]on pareva à Sua Santità che fosse necessaria, ò utile tale riforma; poiché con essa si pregiudicava à Monasteri che servono per commodo della Nobiltà, et del Popolo, e per ornamento della Città." Nuncio Gessi to Cardinal Borghese, 17 April 1610, AV, Nunziature di Venezia, reg. 40, c. 481v.

39. On Contarini's political career, see Gaetano Cozzi, *Il Doge Nicolò Contarini: Ricerche sul patriziato veneziano agli inizi del seicento* (Venice, 1958). On Paolo Sarpi, see Gaetano Cozzi, *Paolo Sarpi tra Venezia e l'Europa* (Turin, 1979).

40. "Sir Nicoló Contarini . . . has this time intervened for the right side, because he has sisters and nieces in this convent." "Signor Nicoló Contarino . . . questa volta ha parlato per la buona parte, per haver sorelle, e nipoti

in quel Monastero." Nuncio Gessi to Cardinal Borghese, 4 June 1611, AV, Nunziature di Venezia, reg. 42, cc. 143v–144r. Also, in his testament of 1630 Contarini stressed that on his scale of obligations, the respect due to the nuns among his family members came right after his fear of God and the love of his fatherland *(patria)*. "I want to remind you of three things: first, the fear of God, which is the basis of every good, then the love of the fatherland to which we belong, and third, the satisfaction of the nuns who have left our house." "E tre cose gli arricordiamo, primieramente il timor di Dio, ch'el fondamento di ogni bene, doppo questo l'amor della Patria, a cui tanto siamo tenuti, e per terzo la sodisfattione delle monache uscite dalla nostra casa." Quoted in Cozzi, *Il Doge Nicoló Contarini,* p. 304.

41. "[Contarini] has expressed his opposition, so that if he persists in it, he could be useful to the [cause of] ecclesiastic jurisdiction." "[Contarini] ha fatte queste oppositioni, nelle quali, se durerà, potria giovare alla giurisdizione Ecclesiastica." Nuncio Gessi to Cardinal Borghese, 3 April 1610, AV, Nunziature di Venezia, reg. 40, cc. 460v–461r.

42. "The Collegio summoned him [Contarini] yesterday, and told him that everybody agreed on the law that they wanted to propose in the Senate, and they wished that he also would bring himself to agree, and remain silent, so that they would not have to quarrel publicly, but it was not possible, for the moment, to silence him." "Il Collegio l'altr' hieri lo [Contarini] fece chiamare, et gli disse, che tutti erano d'accordo nella Parte, che volevano proporre in Pregadi, et desideravano, che anco lui si facesse capace, et restasse quieto, acció non si havesse da oppore in publico, ma non fu possibile, che per all'hora lo quietassero." Ibid. "Procurator Contarini was summoned to the Collegio; he was the only one who was openly opposed, and after various arguments, he remained either confused or defeated." "Fu chiamato in Collegio il Procuratore Contarino, che solo alla scoperta s'opponeva, et è restato dopò varij discorsi, ò smarrito, ò vinto." Nuncio Gessi to Cardinal Borghese, 17 April 1610, ibid., c. 479v.

43. "Dice, ch'egli tiene per certissimo, che se fosse andato in Collegio à dire espressamente che non appartiene alla Repubblica simile negotio [di ridurre le doti spirituali], et che lascino il pensiero à lui di provederci, nel giorno istesso havriano passata la Parte, et che essendo egli prattico per tanti anni del governo di questa Città, ha giudicato meglio mostrare di non volersi opporre . . . et poi copertamente per via d'amici cercare d'avantaggiare l'interesse delle Monache quanto più havesse potuto." Nuncio Gessi to Cardinal Borghese, 20 March 1610, ibid., c. 451v.

44. "L'habbiamo per ció fatto venir qui, per dirle, che non essendo stato di nostra compita sodisfattione l'ufficio, che ella ha fatto ultimamente con le Monache . . . nè piacendoci, che con dette Monache, et con altri ella parli diversamente dal nostro concetto." ASV, Senato Deliberazioni Roma Ordinaria, reg. 18, c. 41r, 7 May 1610.

45. Investigation protocols of 3, 4, 5 May 1610, ibid., busta 18 (?), fascicolo 33, no pagination.

46. "With the help of his friends and of the relatives of the nuns of Santa Caterina, Monsignor Patriarch has tried to prevent Venier from getting the

government to execute the decree with force, after he wanted to have his sister, who had been admitted with the promise to pay 2,500 ducats, enter this convent against the will of the nuns with a dowry of twelve hundred ducats; and as a result of his efforts the affair has remained suspended, and the support with which the Collegio [initially] undertook this policy is vanishing, after the opposition of many noblemen was heard, among them Nicolò Contarini, who this time spoke up for the right cause, because he has sisters and nieces in this convent." "Monsignor Patriarcha di Venetia si è molto aiutato, per il mezo de gli amici suoi, et de' Parenti delle Monache di Santa Catherina per provedere, che il Veniero, il quale contra volontà di esse Monache voleva con la limosina dotale di scudi mille e duecento fare entrare in quel Monastero la sua sorella già accettata con la promissione di [duc.] 2500 non ottenga ordine violento da questi Signori e con i detti mezzi tanto si è operato, che la cosa resta sospesa, et il favore, con che il Collegio commandava questa recettione si è allentato, havendo sentite l'instanze di molti Nobili in contrario, fra' quali é stato il Signor Nicolò Contarino che questa volta ha parlato per la buona parte, per haver sorelle, e nipoti in quel Monastero." Nuncio Gessi to Cardinal Borghese, 4 June 1611, AV, Nunziature di Venezia, reg. 42, cc. 143v–144r.

47. AV, Nunziature di Venezia, reg. 42C, c. 344r, 28 November 1615.

48. "Molto ben si conosce, che con detrimento, e travaglio grandissimo universale non sarebbero passate à tanto eccesso, quanto à cadauno è manifesto, mentre havessero le sudette deliberationi ricevuta la debita, & necessaria essecutione; tanto più, che non hanno altro fine, che, con uguale mediocrità, il particolare beneficio de Nobili, Cittadini, & altri sudditi nostri, & il conveniente commodo de Monasterij di Monache di questa Città, & Dogado; Peró dovendosi ritrovar modo che siano esse deliberationi in tutte le sue parti essequite, come è conveniente, ne permettere, che da un poco numero di Monache, come è benissimo noto, derivi, con tanto deservitio di questo negotio, & della publica riputatione, la indebita inobedienza." Pregadi, 13 July 1620, ASV, CL, busta 288, cc. 412r–v.

49. Patriarch Giovanni Tiepolo, "Ordini intorno le doti, overo elemosine, et altre spese, che si haveranno à fare per le Figliuole, che entreranno ne i Monasterij per monacare," 26 August 1620, BNM, Misc. 2937 no. 16.

50. On Nicolas de Tudeschis, also known as Panermitano, see *Dictionnaire de droit canonique*, vol. 6 (Paris, 1957), cols. 1195–1215.

51. ASV, San Lorenzo, busta 2, reg. A, Monasterio S. Lorenzo n. 18, cod. E, "Nota delli accidenti occorsi al Monasterio Nostro l'anno 1620, et 1621 in tempo dell'Abbadessa Madona Eletta Vitturi per causa d'alcune figliuole che furono accettate Monache, et cio si fa perche servi per avertimento di quello, che possi occorrer nell'avenire," c. 10r.

52. "We, who have the obligation to preserve the state that God has given us to govern in peace and tranquility, and to maintain the authority of the Prince, who in temporal affairs does not recognize any superior under the Divine Majesty . . . protest." "Ritrovandosi in obligo di conservare in quiete, & tranquillità lo Stato datoci da Dio in governo, & mantenere l'auttorità di Prencipe, che non riconosce nelle cose temporali alcun superiore

sotto la Divina Maestà . . . protestiamo." "Lettera del Duce di Venetia agli Ecclesiastici del Dominio della Republica. Leonardo Donato per gratia di Dio Duce di Venetia," 6 May 1606, in *Raccolta degli scritti usciti fuori in istampa, e scritti a mano, nella causa del P. Paolo V. co' signori venetiani secondo le stampe di Venetia, di Roma, & d'altri luoghi,* vol. 1 (Coira [Chur], 1607), p. 8. "The prince is the patron of the entire . . . area contained in his dominion. . . . the prince . . . has a more absolute dominion over the land possessed by him than the private or particular person." "Il Prencipe è patrone di tutto lo spatio, & come essi dicono, di tutta l'Area contenuta nel suo Dominio. . . . [il] Prencipe . . . ha più assoluto dominio sopra le Terre da lui possedute, che non ha il privato, ó particolare." Antonio Querini, "Aviso delle ragioni della Serenissima Republica di Venetia intorno alle difficultà che le sono promosse dalla Santità di Papa Paolo V.," ibid., pp. 19–20. Marc'Antonio Capello argued that the prince "has greater dominion over their goods than the subjects have," and Paolo Sarpi was of the opinion that "the prince has ordinary and extraordinary rights of tribute over lay property, and in addition the personal services of the possessor; furthermore goods, while they belong to the laity, are subject to confiscation." Quoted in Bouwsma, *Venice and the Defense of Republican Liberty,* p. 439.

53. "E stato persuaso . . . Paolo V. . . . a volere . . . interrompere l'antichissime consuetudini, & nativi privilegi, con regolare il corso delle nostre giustissime leggi, quel che per lo spatio di 1200 anni potenza alcuna del mondo non ardì tentare." "Lettera della Serenissima Republica, e Senato di Venetia, alle lor communità, e sudditi," in *Raccolta degli scritti,* p. 10.

54. Quoted in Bouwsma, *Venice and the Defense of Republican Liberty,* p. 333.

55. Victoria Primhak, "Women in Religious Communities: The Benedictine Convents of Venice, 1400–1500" (Ph.D. diss., University of London, 1991), p. 247.

56. Ibid., p. 253.

57. "Vedo che nell'ottenere i gradi, et le dignità di questa Repubblica importando le parentele, et amicitie quasi il tutto, si fa grandissimo capitale delle Monache, le quali con mandarsi à chiamare Padri, et fratelli, at altri parenti, et pregargli à favore di questo, et di quello, possono giovare, et nuocere assai; et per questo anche [?] i Senatori principalissimi premono molto in gratificare i Monasterij di Monache. Da questo seguita, che il prohibir l'adito, et colloquio delle Monache a' parenti, è cosa difficilissima." Nuncio Bolognetti to the Cardinal of Como, 10 September 1580, AV, Nunziature di Venezia, reg. 21, cc. 351v–352r.

58. Friar Michelangelo and Friar Fulgentio Micanzio were among the authors of the "Trattato dell'interdetto della Santità di Papa Paolo V. nel quale si dimostra, che egli non è legitimamente publicato, & che per molte ragioni non sono obligati gli Ecclesiastici all'essecutione di esso, ne possono senza peccato osservarlo," in *Raccolta degli scritti,* pp. 77–96. Paolo Sarpi was listed as a co-author.

59. "Difesa di Giovanni Marsilio a favore della Risposta dell' Otto Proposizioni, contra la quale ha scritto L'Illustrissimo e Reverendissimo

Signor Cardinal Bellarmino," in *Opere del P. M. Paolo Sarpi Servita, Teologo e Consultore della Serenissima Repubblica di Venezia*, vol. 7 (Verona, 1768), pp. 223–364.

60. "Padre Giovanni Marsilio tien una Casa presso alle Monache di Santa Catherina insieme con una sua femina detta Cecilia, celebra qualche volta, conversa con gran numero della Nobiltà, e cerca quanto più può intrinsecarsi con i Nobili, che sono del Collegio, ò del Consiglio dei Dieci." AV, Nunziature di Venezia, reg. 38, c. 402r, 21 June 1608.

61. "Fra' Paulo Servita . . . per lo più và in Vicolo presso alle Monache di Santa Catherina." Ibid., cc. 401v–402r.

62. Ibid., c. 273v, 1 March 1608.

63. Pietro Savio, "Per l'epistolario di Paolo Sarpi," part 1, *Aevum* 11 (1937): 66, n. 2; 7 March 1609.

64. "Perche questi Signori in ogni modo vorriano che predicasse." Nuncio Gessi to Cardinal Borghese, 3 January 1609 (m.r.), AV, Nunziature di Venezia, reg. 38A, c. 326r.

65. "Frate Fulgentio . . . continua le sue prediche con assai numerosa audienza, et particolarmente d'inglesi, fiamenghi et greci, et . . . di molti nobili." Savio, "Per l'epistolario di Paolo Sarpi," part 1, p. 66, n. 2; 14 March 1609.

66. "Il frate predica l'osservatione della sacra Scrittura et di precetti di Christo, et con astutia et malitia diminuisce l'auttorità di Nostro Signore et della santa chiesa et degli interpreti sopra la sacra Scrittura, et così delle traditioni." Ibid., pp. 67–68, n. 2; 21 March 1609.

67. "Dice frequentemente che della chiesa è solo capo Christo, o che non habbiamo altro capo che Christo. . . . predica et essalta grandemente la contritione, talché pare che secluda la confessione. . . . essalta grandemente la fede nel sangue di Christo et la gratia di Dio per la salute nostra, et tralascia o nomina poco le opere. . . . dice che li principi secolari debbono havere cura della religione." Ibid., p. 68, n. 2; 4 April 1609.

68. "Affermando che non comporterebbe cosa non conveniente et non conforme all'antica pietà dei suoi maggiori in materie di religione et di fede." Nuncio Gessi to Cardinal Borghese, 11 April 1609, quoted in Savio, "Per l'epistolario di Paolo Sarpi," part 2, *Aevum* 13, no. 4 (1939): 576–77, n. 3.

69. Another example of open defiance of government orders by a convent was the case of the nuns of San Bernardo di Murano, who were on the side of the pope during the Interdict and wanted to suspend their church functions. The Dimesse, a lay community of religious women, also supported the papacy. The nuns of San Bernardo gave in only after the government had their doors and windows walled up; the community of Dimesse was dissolved. Bouwsma, *Venice and the Defense of Republican Liberty*, pp. 385–86. See also the protocols of the Senate's secret deliberations published by Enrico Cornet in his article "Paolo V e la Republica," *Archivio Veneto*, ser. 1, 6 (1873): 83–101, 108, 115–18.

70. ASV, Ceremoniale, reg. 1, cc. 63v–64r, 24 January 1577 (m.v.).

71. While Grimani was reading in the *ceremoniale* (book of ceremonies), "he was interrupted by the two vicars of Saint Mark's Chapel and of

the Cathedral in Castello, who were present at the election in order to count the nuns' votes, and they voiced the concerns and the protest of the Most Reverend Patriarch Trevisan, and talked of other events, which currently present a certain obstacle to his jurisdiction, and therefore he [Grimani] wondered whether even greater problems [in the enforcement of his jurisdiction] might arise, if in this new election of an abbess one did not proceed cautiously and legally." "Vi intervenero li doi Vicarij di San Marco, et di Castello presenti alla eletione, come scruttatori dei voti delle Monache, et che seguirono diversi protesti, et remotioni del Reverendissimo Patriarca Trivisan, et altri accidenti, li quali sicome all'hora apportarono qualche preiuditio alla giuriditione del Dogado nel suo giuspatronato, cosi dubitva, che potessero nascerne de maggiori, quando in questa nuova elettione di Abbadessa non si procedesse cautamente et giuridicamente." ASV, Cancelleria Inferiore, Archivio del Doge, busta 203, reg. "Iuspatronato sopra il Monasterio delle Monache delle Vergini à Castello," c. 1v, 8 July 1598.

72. "Il Monasterio delle Vergini de iure patronatus indubitato delli Serenissimi Principi, raccommandato alla loro protettione, é stato governato dalli Serenissimi suoi precessori mediante la persona delli Reverendissimi Primicerij di San Marco. . . . Monsignor Illustrissimo Patriarca non può, nè come ordinario, nè come delegato Apostolico in virtù del capitolo nono della 25. sessione del Concilio di Trento de Regularibus pretender, nè ingerirsi in alcun atto pertinente à giuridittione contra le ragione publiche." Ibid., c. 2r.

73. "Espose in voce il Dottor Gratiani in sostanza, che . . . nessun' altra cosa si poteva addur in contrario, se non il preiuditio, che si riceve nell'elettione dell'Abbadessa ultima, quando si lasciò intervenire al scrutinio il Vicario di Monsignore Illustrissimo Patriarca . . . et aggionse . . . che saria stato a preposito che le Monache devenissero quanto prima all'elettione di nuova Abbadessa; et che Sua Serenità le facesse sapere in questa nuova elettione si osservasse quello era stato osservato in tutte le altre elettioni precedenti a quella del 1578." Ibid., cc. 3v–4r.

74. See the petition of the nuns addressed to "Serenissimo principe e padre nostro," ASV, Cancelleria Inferiore, Archivio del Doge, busta 204, no pagination, no date.

75. Ibid., busta 203, reg. "Iuspatronato," cc. 4v–7v.

76. Ibid., cc. 10r–13v, 15 July 1598. See also Willibald M. Plöchl, *Geschichte des Kirchenrechts,* vol. 3 (Vienna, 1959), p. 514.

77. ASV, Cancelleria Inferiore, Archivio del Doge, busta 203, reg. "Iuspatronato," cc. 13v–17v.

78. "Essequendo il commandamento di Vostra Serenità," letter to the doge, ibid., busta 204, no pagination, no date.

79. "Le raggioni per far l'Abbadessa nel Monasterio delle Vergini per tre anni, et non in vita" and "Essendo stato proposto da alcunj," letters to the doge, ibid., no pagination, no date.

80. Nuncio Offredi to Cardinal Aldobrandini, 9 January 1599 (m.r.), AV, Nunziature di Venezia, reg. 34, cc. 32v–34v.

81. "Il papa . . . cominció à dire . . . che la Serenità pensava di abbassare il Patriarca, et ellevare in riputatione il Primocerio, cosa, che non poteva

apportar." Ambassador Mocenigo to the Senate of Venice, ASV, Cancelleria Inferiore, Archivio del Doge, busta 203, reg. "Iuspatronato," cc. 46r–v, 16 January 1599 (m.r.).

82. "Fui secondo l'ordine di Vostra Signoria Illustrissima dal Signor Cardinale Priuli per intendere la sua intenzione circa il governo delle Monache delle Vergini, e da Vostra Signoria Illustrissima mi fù risposto, ch'egli desidera, che li sia levato questo peso per levare l'occasione di disgusto con questi Signori. . . . Vorrebbe etiandio esser libero da ogni sopraintendenza etiam di clausura, perché non li restasse con auttorità limitata questo peso. . . . fra questi Signori é concetto generale, che tutti i disturbi, che nascono per la giurisdizione habbiano principio dal Vicario." AV, Nunziature di Venezia, reg. 34, cc. 43r–v, 23 January 1599 (m.r.).

83. "[Il convento] rappresenta l'attione tanto stimata dalla Repubblica nostra della Vittoria contra Federico Barbarossa, et dell'haver rimesso nella Sede Ponteficia, che condotto in Ancona Papa Alessandro Terzo, al qual havendo la figlia dell'Imperator dimandato la erettione di un Monastero in Venetia, et la Signoria nostra donato quell'istessa isola per questa edificatione si contentó di ereger questo Monasterio, et consecró la detta figlia dell'Imperatore Abbadessa in esso, co'l giuspatronato al Serenissimo Principe nostro." Senate of Venice to Ambassador Mocenigo, 20 February 1598 (m.v.), ASV, Cancelleria Inferiore, Archivio del Doge, busta 203, reg. "Iuspatronato," c. 55r.

84. Corner, Ecclesiae Venetae, 4:2–6.

85. "[B]isognava, che guardasse molto bene quello che faceva in non accrescere l'auttorità, e giuriditione a' Prencipi . . . [i] quali, che ne dava un dito, ne volevano poi un brazzo." ASV, Cancelleria Inferiore, Archivio del Doge, busta 203, reg. "Iuspatronato," cc. 57v–65v.

86. Ibid., cc. 42r–43v, 68v–73r, and the following unnumbered pages.

87. Flaminio Corner, Notizie storiche delle chiese e monasteri di Venezia e di Torcello (Padua, 1758), p. 99.

88. AV, Nunziature di Venezia, reg. 42, cc. 532v–534r, 1 September 1612.

89. Lettera delle RR. Monache di S. Maria delle Vergini.

90. See n. 2 above.

91. "[S]i come dalla virtù d'uno di casa Malipiero trasse il nostro Monasterio l'origine sua; cosi sotto la presente Abbadessa Malipiera siamo rimesse nel primiero possesso de gli Antichi nostri privilegi." Lettera delle RR. Monache di S. Maria delle Vergini.

92. "Volse, che alla sua presenza il Serenissimo Ziani confirmasse l'istessa Giulia in Abbadessa, mettendole due anelli in dito. L'uno con l'impronto di San Marco; e l'altro con un Zaffiro, in segno di duplicata fede. Il primo, per significar, che questo Monasterio era instituito con la regola di San Marco, confirmata dal Beato Pietro Prencipe de gl'Apostoli; & il secondo, che tale proprietà dell'istesso San Pietro . . . rimanesse sotto la protettione, e perpetuo Dominio delli Serenissimi Prencipi di Venetia." Ibid.

93. See, for instance, the account of the investiture of Abbess Maria Benetti in 1578, ASV, Ceremoniale, reg. 1, cc. 63v–64r, 24 January 1577

(m.v.). Doge Grimani refers to this ceremony in his discussion with the Collegio; ASV, Cancelleria Inferiore, Archivio del Doge, busta 203, c. 1r, 8 July 1598. See also the various protocols of investiture rites up to 1736 in ASV, Cancelleria Inferiore, Archivio del Doge, busta 204.

94. Zarri, "Monasteri femminili e città," p. 375.

95. Gaetano Cozzi speaks of a rivalry between Venice and Rome. Gaetano Cozzi, "Venezia Regina," in *Crisi e rinnovamenti nell'autunno del Rinascimento a Venezia,* ed. Vittore Branca and Carlo Ossola (Florence, 1991), pp. 1–9.

96. "Se Roma meritamente si chiama Civitas Petri; questa [città] ancora per esser fondata il giorno della sua Santissima Annunziazione, e . . . per esser sempre nella Religione e nella libertà stata Vergine, meritamente si può chiamare Civitas Virginis." "Difesa di Giovanni Marsilio," pp. 226–27.

97. "Certo pare, che l'architettrice mano di Dio abbia ordinato, che la Città di Venezia fosse Vergine, Pudica, ed Innocente, affinché insieme con Roma fosse il sostengo, e l'ajuto de' Cristiani, e la rovina de' Persecutori della Fede." Paolo Sarpi, "Risposta data . . . a Paolo V. Sommo Pontefice sopra l'interdetto da esso fulminato contro la Serenissima Repubblica di Venezia," in *Opere di F. Paolo Sarpi,* 6:150.

98. "The ceremony that accompanies the election of the abbess, apart from referring to the Venetian tradition of the 'marriage with the sea,' inserts itself in the symbolism of the mystic marriage, which a widespread iconography connects with the unification of Christ with the holy virgins; through this symbolism the rite acquires a more profound signification: the sacrality of ducal power is confirmed by the sanctity of the virginal brides, and at the same time the abbess who represents it [the brides' sanctity] is invested with the authority of the political power with which she is—together with the other nuns—symbolically and perpetually united." Zarri, "Monasteri femminili e città," p. 375.

Conclusion

1. See, for example, Niklas Luhmann, *Ecological Communication* (Chicago, 1989).

Appendix

1. Anna Pizzati, "La proprietà terriera dei monasteri benedettini veneziani nella seconda metà del cinquecento" (master's thesis, University of Ca' Foscari, Venice, Department of Literature and Philosophy, 1986), pp. ii, 54.

2. See the tax records of 1564 for Santa Anna, Sant' Antonio di Torcello, and San Giovanni Evangelista di Torcello. ASV, Sopraintendenti alle Decime del Clero, busta 32, polizze 81, 98, 56.

3. See the tax records of 1564 for Santa Chiara di Venezia, Santa Maria della Celestia, Santa Maria delle Vergini, San Zaccaria, and Santi Cosma e Damiano. Ibid., busta 33, polizze 164, 161; busta 32, polizza 79; reg. 241, polizza 168; busta 33, polizza 151.

4. ASV, Sopraintendenti alle Decime del Clero, busta 32.

5. Why the ratio between the prices of grain and wine in 1564 is differ-

ent from the price ratios of the same products in 1543, 1566, 1582, 1661, and 1769 still needs to be explained. Ibid., busta 32, polizze 45, 56, 60, 69, 70, 81, 83, 98; busta 33, polizze 149, 185, 204; reg. 241, polizze 124, 138, 167.

6. Maurice Aymard, *Venise, Raguse, et le commerce du blé pendant la seconde moitié du XVIe siècle* (Paris, 1966), p. 120.

7. ASV, Dieci Savij sopra le decime di Rialto, busta 129, polizza 300.

8. Ibid., busta 158, polizza 903; busta 160, polizze 529, 748; busta 163, polizza 775.

9. ASV, Santa Chiara di Venezia, busta 1/2, cadastre 1677.

10. ASV, Sopraintendenti alle Decime del Clero, busta 77, polizze 6, 88, 95.

Glossary

agnatic: patrilineal

Avogadori di Comun: state attorneys

bocca: mouth (to feed)

botte: a wine measure (see appendix)

Bucintoro: the Venetian republic's ceremonial galley

campo: a field measure (see appendix)

Cancelliere Inferiore: a high-ranking government bureaucrat; this office was
    reserved for "originary citizens"

canto figurato: melodic singing

cittadini: citizens; a legally defined class of Venetians enjoying special privi-
    leges but no political rights, ranking just below the patriciate. Some au-
    thors, such as Gasparo Contarini and Giovan Maria Memmo, referred
    to patricians as "citizens" in an effort to underline the republican char-
    acter of the body politic.

clausura: encloisterment

Collegio: the entire executive branch of the government, consisting of the
    doge, his six councilors, the three heads of the Quarantia (Council of
    Forty), six Savij Grandi (chief ministers), five Savij di Terraferma (minis-
    ters of war of the mainland), and five Savij agli Ordini (ministers of
    maritime affairs)

Collegio Minore: the inner government circle, also called the Signoria, con-
    sisting of the doge, his six councilors, and the three heads of the Quaran-
    tia (Council of Forty)

companadego: food in addition to wine and bread

conversa: servant nun; takes only simple vows

Council of Ten: the most powerful executive organ of the republic; originally
    founded to protect the republic from a coup d'état, complementing and
    at times supplanting the Collegio

decima del clero: ecclesiastic tithe

decima del laico: lay tithe

Dieci Savij sopra le decime di Rialto: tax collectors

Dogado: the Venetian dukedom

dogaressa: the doge's wife

doge: the republic's highest elected official (and the only one with a lifelong tenure); his function was mainly representative

donna a spese: married woman boarding in a convent

educanda: convent boarder to be educated

endogamy: marriage between partners of the same social or geographic origin

exogamy: marriage beween partners of different social or geographic origin

fidecommesso: entailment

fiola a spese: unmarried woman boarding in a convent

fonghi, fonghetti: a hairstyle popular in the sixteenth century; literally, "(little) mushrooms"

fortuna: goddess of fortune

fraterna: joint ownership of a family patrimony by all or several brothers

giovani: faction of "young patricians" of anticlerical attitude

Giudici del Mobile: one of the oldest civil law courts in Renaissance Venice

Giudici del Proprio: civil law court

Great Council (Maggior Consiglio): the full assembly of all Venetian noblemen over age twenty-five

hypergamy: upward marriage

interdict: excommunication (in 1606, of the entire Republic of Venice)

livello: lease contract functioning as a credit transaction

monte: government fund of forced loans

monticelli: hairstyle; literally, "little mountains"

nuncio: papal ambassador

Offizio sopra Datij: office for the collection of customs and excise duties

papalisti: papal faction among the patriciate

pares: men of equal status

patriarch: archbishop of Venice

patriciate: hereditary ruling class of Venice; here referred to also as "nobility" and "aristocracy."

pizzochere (also *bizzoche*): third-order nuns, Beguine nuns

popolani: commoners

Pregadi: enlarged Senate

Primicerio di San Marco: primate of Saint Mark's Chapel

procuratia: trust fund

procuratore: legal agent, proxy

Procuratori di San Marco: managers of trust funds and executors of testaments; one of the republic's most ancient and prestigious offices

professione: ceremony during which the holy vows are pronounced

Provveditori sopra i Monasteri di Monache: convent magistrate

putta a spese: boarder to be educated; also *educanda*

quietanza: quitclaim

ragion di stato: reason of state

Rota: papal court
ruota: revolving drawer through which things could be passed in and out
of convents
sagra: consecration ceremony
scuola: confraternity
serrata: literally, "closure"; refers to the transformation of the Venetian ruling class into a hereditary elite
Signoria: the Collegio Minore
Sopraintendenti alle Decime del Clero: collectors of the ecclesiastic tithe
staia: a grain measure (see appendix)
terraferma: republican territories on the Italian mainland
vestizione: ceremony during which aspiring nuns were "dressed" as novices
Zecca: the mint; also, a government fund
zuffi: bangs

References

Archival and Manuscript Sources

Archivio Patriarchale di Venezia (APV)
  Decretorum et Mandatorum Monialium
  Elenchi Elezioni Abbadesse (1656–70)
  Matrimoni segreti, busta 1
  Santa Maria Formosa, registri di matrimoni, reg. 1–5 (1569–1640)
  Torcellania Criminalia Monialium (1600–1689) (Tarli)
  Visite Priuli (1592–96)
  Visite Tiepolo (1620–27)
  Visite Trevisan (1560–89)
  Visite Vendramin (1609–18)

Archivio di Stato di Venezia (ASV)
  Avogadori di Comun, G. Giomo, "Matrimoni patrizi per nome di donna"
  Cancelleria Inferiore, Archivio del Doge, buste 203, 204
  Ceremoniale, reg. 1
  Compilazione Leggi, buste 288, 289
  Corpus Domini, buste 6, 8
  CX, Criminal, reg. 10, 15, 21, 37, 39, 50, 70, 75
  Dieci Savij sopra le decime di Rialto, buste 127, 129, 158, 159, 160, 161,
    163, 164, 167, 168, 169, 170, 172, 214, 216, 217, 218, 219, 220, 224,
    225, 226, 227, 228, 1773
  Notarile Testamenti, Atti Beaciani, busta 152; Atti Brinis, buste 31–35;
    Atti Cigrini, busta 198; Atti Ziliol, buste 1242, 1260
  Provveditori sopra i Monasteri di Monache, capitolari, reg. 1, 2; buste
    13, 263, 264, 265, 267, 268, 269, 270, 271, 347
  Sant' Andrea de Zirada, buste 7, 10, 12
  San Lorenzo, buste 1, 2, 9, 19

San Zaccaria, buste 73, 74
Santa Chiara di Venezia, buste 1/2, 13
Santa Croce di Venezia, buste 2, 3
Santi Biagio e Cataldo, busta 3
Senato Deliberazioni Roma Ordinaria, reg. 13 (1600–1602), 18 (1610–12), fascicolo 33
Senato Terra, reg. 6, 29, 45, 75
Sopraintendenti alle Decime del Clero, buste 32, 33, 77, 78, reg. 241

Archivio Segreto del Vaticano (AV)
Nunziature di Venezia, reg. 19, 21, 26, 27, 28, 30, 33, 34, 38, 38A, 40, 42, 42C

Biblioteca Nazionale Marciana (BNM)
Classe IX Cod. CCCLXIX (7203)
Classe It. VII 1522 (8825)
Classe It. VII 1531 (7638)
Classe It. VII 1533 (8826)
Cod. lat. XIV 74 (4056), Thomas Diplovatazio, "Tractatus de Venetae urbis libertate et eiusdem Imperij Dignitate" (ca. 1530)
Misc. 2937 no. 14, 16

Biblioteca del Seminario Patriarchale di Venezia (BSP)
Mss 644 = 717
Mss 1044.44

Museo Civico Correr (MCC)
Codex Cicogna 2570, 2583
Correr 317, "Cronica del Monastero delle Vergini di Venetia"

Published Sources

Allerston, Patricia. "Wedding Finery in Sixteenth-Century Venice." In *Marriage in Italy, 1300–1600,* edited by Trevor Dean and Kate Lowe, pp. 25–40. Cambridge, 1998.
Arcangeli, Letizia. "Ragioni politiche della disciplina monastica: Il caso di Parma tra Quattro e Cinquecento." In *Donna, disciplina, creanza cristiana dal XV al XVII secolo,* edited by Gabriella Zarri, pp. 165–87. Rome, 1996.
Aretino, Pietro. "Ragionamento della Nanna e della Antonia fatto in Roma sotto una ficaia." In *Ragionamento—Dialogo.* Milan, 1988. First edition: Venice, 1534.
Atlante dei Centri Storici: Provincia di Venezia; Provincia di Treviso. Padua, 1983.
Auerbach, Erich. "Figura." In *Scenes from the Drama of European Literature,* pp. 11–76. Minneapolis, 1984.
Avvertimenti monacali, et modo di viver religiosamente secondo Iddio per le vergini, et spose di Giesu Christo di diversi eccellentissimi auttori

antichi et moderni nuovamente posti insieme, & mandati in luce aggiun-tovi lo stadio del Cursor Christiano, tradotto di Latino in Volgare da M. Lodovico Dolce. Leggano le Religiose i presenti trattati perche sono molto utili à superare le difficultà di questa vita, & acquistare la palma della promessa Virginità. Venice, 1576.

Aymard, Maurice. *Venise, Raguse, et le commerce du blé pendant la seconde moitié du XVIe siècle.* Paris, 1966.

Baernstein, P. Renée. "In Widow's Habit: Women between Convent and Family in Sixteenth-Century Milan." *Sixteenth Century Journal* 25, no. 4 (1994): 787–807.

Barthes, Roland. "L'effet de réel." *Communications* 11, no. 1 (1968): 84–89.

Barzaghi, Antonio. *Donne o cortigiane? La prostituzione a Venezia: Documenti di costume dal XVI al XVIII secolo.* Verona, 1980.

Beltrami, Daniele. *La penetrazione economica dei veneziani in terraferma: Forze di lavoro e proprietà fondiaria nelle campagne venete dei secoli XVII e XVIII.* Civiltà veneta studi 12. Rome, 1961.

———. "Un ricordo del Priuli intorno al problema dell'ammortamento dei depositi in Zecca del 1574." In *Studi in onore di Armando Sapori*, 2: 1071–87. Milan, 1957.

———. *Storia della popolazione di Venezia dalla fine del secolo XVI alla caduta della Repubblica.* Padua, 1954.

Benzoni, Gino. "Una città caricabile di valenze religiose." In *La chiesa di Venezia tra riforma protestante e riforma cattolica,* edited by Giuseppe Gullino, pp. 37–61. Venice, 1990.

———. "Venezia, ossia il mito modulato." In *Crisi e rinnovamenti nell'autunno del Rinascimento a Venezia,* edited by Vittore Branca and Carlo Ossola. Florence, 1991.

Berengo, Marino. *La società veneta alla fine del Settecento.* Florence, 1956.

Biagioli, Mario. *Galileo, Courtier: The Practice of Science in the Culture of Absolutism.* Chicago, 1993.

Biondo, Flavio. *Blondi Flavii Forliniensis de Origine & Gestis Venetorum ad Franciscum Foscari Serenissimum Ducem: Inclytumq Senatum: caeterosque Venetae Reipublicae Patritios.* Venice, 1503. Written in 1454.

Bistort, Giulio. *Il Magistrato alle Pompe nella Repubblica di Venezia.* Venice, 1912.

Boccalini, Traiano. *Ragguagli di Parnaso.* Vol. 1. Edited by Luigi Firpo. Bari, 1948. First edition: Venice, 1612.

Botero, Giovanni. *Della Ragion di Stato libri dieci, con tre Libri delle Cause della Grandezza, e Magnificenza delle Città.* Venice, 1589.

———. *Relatione della Republica venetiana.* Venice, 1605.

Bouwsma, William J. *Venice and the Defense of Republican Liberty: Renaissance Values in the Age of the Counter Reformation.* Berkeley, 1968.

Braudel, Fernand. "La vita economica di Venezia nel XVI secolo." In *Storia della civiltà veneziana,* edited by Vittore Branca, 2:259–70. Florence, 1979.

Braudel, F., and F. Spooner. "Prices in Europe from 1450 to 1750." In *The Cambridge Economic History*, vol. 4. Cambridge, 1967.

Breve trattato delle citta nobili del mondo, et di tutta Italia, con la lunghezza, & larghezza di essa, confini, sito, & provincie, & il principio del Regno de' Longobardi. Florence, 1574.

Brown, Henry Phelps, and Sheila V. Hopkins. "Seven Centuries of the Prices of Consumables, Compared with Builders' Wage-Rates." In *A Perspective of Wages and Prices,* edited by Henry Phelps Brown and Sheila V. Hopkins. London, 1981.

Brown, Judith C. *Immodest Acts: The Life of a Lesbian Nun in Renaissance Italy.* Oxford, 1986.

———. *In the Shadow of Florence: Provincial Society in Renaissance Pescia.* New York, 1982.

———. "Monache a Firenze all'inizio dell'età moderna: Un' analisi demografica." *Quaderni Storici* 85, no. 1 (1994): 117–52.

Brown, Patricia Fortini. "The Self-Definition of the Venetian Republic." In *City States in Classical Antiquity and Medieval Italy,* edited by Anthony Molho, Kurt Raaflaub, and Julia Emlen, pp. 511–48. Ann Arbor, Mich., 1991.

———. *Venice and Antiquity: The Venetian Sense of the Past.* New Haven, 1996.

Brown, Peter. *The Body and Society.* New York, 1988.

Brucker, Gene. *Giovanni and Lusanna: Love and Marriage in Renaissance Florence.* Berkeley, 1986.

———, ed. *Two Memoirs of Renaissance Florence: The Diaries of Buonaccorso Pitti and Gregorio Dati.* Prospect Heights, 1967.

Burnet, G. *Some Letters Containing an Account of what seem'd most remarkable in travelling thro' Switzerland, Italy, some Parts of Germany, &c. In the Years 1685, and 1686.* London, 1724.

Bynum, Caroline Walker. "Corpo femminile e pratica religiosa nel tardo medioevo." In *Donne e fede: Santità e vita religiosa in Italia,* edited by Lucetta Scaraffia and Gabriella Zarri, pp. 115–56. Bari, 1994.

———. *Holy Feast and Holy Fast: The Religious Significance of Food to Medieval Women.* Berkeley, 1987.

———. *Jesus as Mother: Studies in the Spirituality of the High Middle Ages.* Berkeley, 1982.

Cabibbo, Sara. "La santità femminile dinastica." In *Donne e fede: Santità e vita religiosa in Italia,* edited by Lucetta Scaraffia and Gabriella Zarri, pp. 399–418. Bari, 1994.

Cabibbo, Sara, and Marilena Modica. *La Santa dei Tomasi: Storia di Suor Maria Crocefissa, 1645–1699.* Turin, 1989.

Caimo, Pompeo. *Parallelo Politico delle Republiche Antiche, e Moderne.* Padua, 1627.

Cain, James R. "Cloister and the Apostolate of Religious Women." Parts 1–4. *Review for Religious* 27, no. 2 (1968): 243–80; no. 4:652–71; no. 5:916–37; 28, no. 1 (1969): 101–21.

Campanella, Tommaso. *Antiveneti.* Edited by Luigi Firpo. Florence, 1945. Written in 1606.

Campra, André. "Quemadmodum desiderat cervus." Psalm 42:1–4, 11.

Canosa, Romano. *Il velo e il capuccio: Monacazioni forzate e sessualità nei conventi femminili in Italia tra '400 e '700.* Rome, 1991.

Casini, Matteo. *I gesti del principe: La festa politica a Firenze e Venezia in età rinascimentale.* Venice, 1996.

Cecchetti, Bartolomeo, ed. *La republica di Venezia e la corte di Roma.* Venice, 1874.

Chabot, Isabelle. " 'La Sposa in Nero': La ritualizzazione del lutto delle vedove fiorentine (secoli XIV–XV)." *Quaderni Storici* 86, no. 2 (1994): 421–62.

Chavarria, Elisa Novi. "Nobiltà di seggio, nobiltà nuova e monasteri femminili a Napoli in età moderna." *Dimensioni e Problemi della Ricerca Storica* 2 (1993): 84–111.

Chittolini, Giorgio. "Un problema aperto: La crisi della proprietà ecclesiastica fra quattro e cinquecento." *Rivista Storica Italiana* 85 (1973): 353–93.

Chojnacka, Monica. "Women, Charity, and Community in Early Modern Venice: The Casa delle Zitelle." *Renaissance Quarterly* 51, no. 1 (1998): 68–91.

Chojnacki, Stanley. "Daughters and Oligarchs: Gender and the Early Renaissance State." In *Gender and Society in Renaissance Italy,* edited by Judith C. Brown and Robert C. Davis, pp. 63–86. Essex, 1998.

———. "Dowries and Kinsmen in Early Renaissance Venice." *Journal of Interdisciplinary History* 5, no. 4 (1975): 571–600.

———. "Marriage Legislation and Patrician Society in Fifteenth-Century Venice." In *Law, Custom, and the Social Fabric in Medieval Europe: Essays in Honor of Bryce Lyon,* edited by Bernard S. Bachrach and David Nicholas, pp. 163–84. Kalamazoo, Mich., 1990.

———. "Nobility, Women, and the State: Marriage Regulation in Venice, 1420–1535." In *Marriage in Italy, 1300–1600,* edited by Trevor Dean and Kate Lowe. Cambridge, 1998.

———. "Patrician Women in Early Renaissance Venice." *Studies in the Renaissance* 21 (1974): 176–203.

———. "Social Identity in Renaissance Venice: The Second *Serrata.*" *Renaissance Studies* 8, no. 4 (1994): 341–58.

Ciammitti, Luisa. "Quanto costa essere normali: La dote nel conservatorio femminile di Santa Maria del Baraccano (1630–1680)." *Quaderni Storici* 53, no. 2 (1983): 469–97.

Cipolla, Carlo. "Une crise ignorée: Comment s'est perdue la propriété ecclesiastique dans l'Italie du Nord entre le XIe et le XVIe siècle." *Annales E.S.C.* 2 (1947): 317–27.

Cohen, Sherrill. "Convertite e malmaritate: Donne 'irregolari' e ordini religiosi nella Firenze rinascimentale." *memoria* 5 (1982): 46–63.

———. *The Evolution of Women's Asylums since 1500.* New York, 1992.

Cohn, Samuel. *Death and Property in Siena, 1205–1800: Strategies for the Afterlife.* Baltimore, 1988.

Concina, Ennio. "Ampliar la città: Spazio urbano, 'res publica' e architettura." In *Storia di Venezia*, vol. 6, *Dal Rinascimento al Barocco*, edited by Gaetano Cozzi and Paolo Prodi. Rome, 1994.

Connelly, Joan B. "Parthenon and *Parthenoi*: A Mythological Interpretation of the Parthenon Frieze." *American Journal of Archaeology* 100 (1996): 53–80.

Conrad, Anne. "Ordensfrauen ohne Klausur? Die katholische Frauenbewegung an der Wende zum 17. Jahrhundert." *Feministische Studien* 1 (1986): 31–45.

————. *Zwischen Kloster und Welt: Ursulinen und Jesuitinnen in der katholischen Reformbewegung des 16./17. Jahrhunderts.* Mainz, 1991.

Contarini, Gasparo. *The Commonwealth and Government of Venice.* Trans. Lewes Lewkenor. London, 1599. Facsimile edition: Amsterdam, 1969.

————. *Della republica, e magistrati di Venezia. Libri cinque di Gasparo Contarini, che fù poi Cardinale. Con un ragionamento intorno alla medesima di Donato Giannotti fiorentino, colle annotazioni sopra i due suddetti autori di Nicolo Crasso, et i discorsi de' governi civili di Sebastiano Erizzo, e XV discorsi di Bartolomeo Cavalcanti, aggiontovi un discorso dell'eccellenza delle Republiche.* Venice, 1678. First edition (in Latin): Venice, 1543.

Corazzol, Gigi. *Fitti e livelli a grano.* Milan, 1979.

————. *Livelli stipulati à Venezia nel 1591.* Supplementi di Studi Veneziani. Pisa, 1986.

————. "Sulla diffusione dei livelli a frumento tra il patriziato veneziano nella seconda metà del '500." *Studi Veneziani*, n.s., 6 (1982): 103–28.

Corner, Flaminio. *Ecclesiae Venetae antiquis monumentis nunc etiam primum editis illustratae ac in decades distributae.* 13 vols., along with *Supplementa ad Ecclesiae Venetas et Torcellanas.* Venice, 1749.

————. *Notizie storiche delle chiese e monasteri di Venezia e di Torcello.* Bologna, 1990. First edition: Padua, 1758.

Cornet, Enrico. "Paolo V e la Republica." *Archivio Veneto*, 1st ser., 6 (1873).

Corti, Ugo. "La francazione del debito pubblico della Repubblica di Venezia proposta da Gian Francesco Priuli." *Nuovo Archivio Veneto*, n.s., 7 (1894): 331–64.

Cowan, Alexander Francis. *The Urban Patriciate: Lübeck and Venice, 1580–1700.* Cologne, 1986.

Cox, Virginia. "The Single Self: Feminist Thought and the Marriage Market in Early Modern Venice." *Renaissance Quarterly* 48, no. 3 (1995): 513–81.

Cozzi, Gaetano. "Ambiente veneziano, ambiente veneto: Governanti e governati nel dominio di qua dal Mincio nei secoli XV–XVIII." In *Storia della cultura veneta*, vol. 4, pt. 2, *Il Seicento*, pp. 495–539. Vicenza, 1984.

————. *Il Doge Nicoló Contarini: Ricerche sul patriziato veneziano agli inizi del seicento.* Venice, 1958.

————. "Domenico Morosini e il 'De bene instituta re publica.'" *Studi Veneziani* 12 (1970): 405–58.

————. "Giuspatronato del Doge e prerogative del primicerio sulla cappella ducale di San Marco (secc. XVI–XVIII): Controversie con i procuratori di San Marco de supra e i Patriarchi di Venezia." *Atti dell'Istituto Veneto di Scienze, Lettere, ed Arti* 151 (1992–93): 1–69.

————. *Paolo Sarpi tra Venezia e l'Europa.* Turin, 1979.

————. *Repubblica di Venezia e Stati italiani: Politica e giustizia dal secolo XVI al secolo XVIII.* Turin, 1982.

————. "Venezia dal Rinascimento all'Età barocca." In *Storia di Venezia,* vol. 6, *Dal Rinascimento al Barocco,* edited by Gaetano Cozzi and Paolo Prodi. Rome, 1994.

————. "Venezia regina." In *Crisi e rinnovamenti nell'autunno del Rinascimento a Venezia,* edited by Vittore Branca and Carlo Ossola, pp. 1–9. Florence, 1991.

Cozzi, Gaetano, and Michael Knapton. *Dalla guerra di Chioggia al 1517.* Vol. 1 of *La Repubblica di Venezia nell'età moderna.* Storia d'Italia, vol. 12. Turin, 1986.

Cozzi, Gaetano, Michael Knapton, and Giovanni Scarabello. *Dal 1517 alla fine della Repubblica.* Vol. 2 of *La Repubblica di Venezia nell'età moderna.* Storia d'Italia, vol. 12. Turin, 1992.

Creytens, Raimondo, O.P. "La giurisprudenza della Sacra Congregazione del Concilio nella questione della clausura delle monache (1564–1576)." *Apollinaris* 37 (1964): 252–85.

————. "La Riforma dei monasteri femminili dopo i Decreti Tridentini." In *Il Concilio di Trento e la riforma tridentina: Atti del convegno storico internazionale, Trento, 2–6 settembre 1963,* 1:45–84. Rome, 1965.

D'Addario, Arnaldo. *Aspetti della Controriforma a Firenze.* Rome, 1972.

Daichman, Graciela S. *Wayward Nuns in Medieval Literature.* Syracuse, 1986.

Dandolo, Andrea. "Andreae Danduli Venetorum Ducis Chronicon Venetum a Pontificatu Sancti Marci ad Annum usque MCCCXXXIX." In *Rerum Italicarum Scriptores,* vol. 12, edited by Ludovicus Antonius Muratorius. Milan, 1728.

Davis, James Cushman. *The Decline of the Venetian Nobility as a Ruling Class.* Baltimore, 1962.

————. *A Venetian Family and Its Fortune, 1500–1900: The Donà and the Conservation of Wealth.* Philadelphia, 1975.

Davis, Natalie Zemon. "Beyond the Market: Books as Gifts in Sixteenth-Century France." *Transactions of the Royal Historical Society,* 5th ser., 33 (1983): 69–87.

————. *Women on the Margins: Three Seventeenth-Century Lives.* Cambridge, Mass., 1995.

Dean, Trevor, and Kate Lowe, eds. *Marriage in Italy, 1300–1600.* Cambridge, 1998.

De Giorgio, Michela, and Christine Klapisch-Zuber, eds. *Storia del matrimonio*. Bari, 1996.

Deliberatione dell'Eccelso Conseglio di X. e terminationi, et ordini delli Eccelentissimi signori proveditori sopra li Monasterij di Monache di Venetia, e Dogado. Venice, 1625.

Delille, Gérard. *Famille et propriété dans le Royaume de Naples*. Paris, 1985.

———. "Marriage, Faction, and Conflict in Sixteenth-Century Italy: An Example and a Few Questions." In *Marriage in Italy, 1300–1600*, edited by Trevor Dean and Kate Lowe, pp. 155–73. Cambridge, 1998.

———. "Strategie di alleanza e demografia del matrimonio." In *Storia del matrimonio*, edited by Michela De Giorgio and Christine Klapisch-Zuber, pp. 283–303. Bari, 1996.

Del Negro, Piero. "Forme e istituzioni del discorso politico veneziano." In *Storia della cultura veneta*, vol. 4, pt. 2, *Il Seicento*, pp. 407–36. Vicenza, 1984.

Del Torre, Giuseppe. "La politica fiscale della Repubblica di Venezia nell'età moderna: La fiscalità." In *Fisco religione stato nell'età confessionale*, edited by H. Kellenbenz and P. Prodi, pp. 387–426. Bologna, 1989.

———. *Venezia e la terraferma dopo la guerra di Cambrai: Fiscalità e amministrazione, 1515–1530*. Milan, 1986.

Derrida, Jacques. *Given Time: I. Counterfeit Money*. Chicago, 1992.

Dialogo del Gentilhuomo vinitiano cioè institutione nella quale si discorre quali hanno a essere i costumi del nobile di questa città, per acquistarsi gloria & honore. Venice, 1576.

Dictionnaire de droit canonique. Paris, 1957.

Discorso aristocratico sopra il governo de' Signori Venetiani come si portano con Dio, con sudditi, e con Prencipi. Venice, 1675.

Doglioni, Nicoló. *Le cose notabili, et maravigliose della città di Venetia*. Venice, 1692. First edition: 1602.

Dolce, Lodovico. "Ammaestramenti." In *Le Bellezze, le Lodi, gli Amori, & i Costumi delle Donne; Con lo Discacciamento delle Lettere, di Agnolo Firenzuola Fiorentino, Et di Alessandro Picolomini Sanese. Giuntovi appresso i Saggi Ammaestramenti che appartengono alla honorevole, e virtuosa vita Virginale, Maritale, e Vedovile, di Lodovico Dolce.* 2d ed. Venice, 1622.

———. *Dialogo della institution delle donne*. Venice, 1547.

Domenichi, Lodovico. *La Nobiltà delle Donne*. Venice, 1551.

———. *Dialoghi*. Venice, 1562.

Donati, Claudio. *L'idea della nobiltà in Italia: Secoli XIV–XVII*. Bari, 1988.

Douglas, Mary. *The World of Goods*. New York, 1979.

Ercole, Francesco. "L'istituto dotale nella pratica e nella legislazione statutaria dell'Italia superiore." Parts 1 and 2. *Rivista Italiana per le Scienze Giuridiche* 45 (1908): 191–302; 46 (1908?): 167–257.

Evangelisti, Silvia. " 'Farne quello che pare e piace . . .': L'uso e la trasmissione delle celle nel monastero di Santa Giulia di Brescia (1597–1688)." *Quaderni Storici* 88, no. 1 (1995): 85–110.

Fabbri, Lorenzo. *Alleanza matrimoniale e patriziato nella Firenze del '400.* Florence, 1991.

Fasoli, Gina. "Liturgia e ceremonia ducale." In *Venezia e il Levante fino al secolo XV,* edited by Agostino Pertusi, 1:261–93. Florence, 1973.

Ferrante, Lucia. " 'Malmaritate' tra assistenza e punizione (Bologna, secc. XVI–XVII)." In *Forme e soggetti dell'intervento assistenziale in una città di antico regime: Atti del 4. colloquio, Bologna, 20–21 gennaio 1984,* vol. 2, edited by Paolo Prodi, pp. 65–109. Bologna, 1986.

———. "L'onore ritrovato: Donne nella Casa del Soccorso di San Paolo a Bologna (sec. XVI–XVII)." *Quaderni Storici* 53, no. 2 (1983): 499–527.

Ferrante, Lucia, Maura Palazzi, and Gianna Pomata, eds. *Ragnatele di rapporti: Patronage e reti di relazione nella storia delle donne.* Turin, 1988.

Ferraro, Joanne. "The Power to Decide: Battered Wives in Early Modern Venice." *Renaissance Quarterly* 48, no. 3 (1995): 492–512.

Ferro, Marco. *Dizionario del diritto comune e veneto.* 2d ed. Venice, 1845.

Findlen, Paula. *Possessing Nature: Museums, Collecting, and Scientific Culture in Early Modern Italy.* Berkeley, 1996.

Foucault, Michel. *The Birth of the Clinic: An Archaeology of Medical Perception.* New York, 1973. First edition (in French): 1963.

———. *Discipline and Punish: the Birth of the Prison.* New York, 1977. First edition (in French): 1975.

———. *Madness and Civilization: A History of Insanity in the Age of Reason.* New York, 1988. First edition (in French): 1965.

Franco, Giacomo. *Habiti delle donne veneziane intagliate in rame.* Edited by Ferdinando Ongania. Facsimile edition: Venice, 1877. First edition: Venice, 1610.

———. *Habiti d'huomeni et donne venetiane con la processione della Ser.ma Signoria et altri particolari cioè trionfi feste et cerimonie publiche della nobilissima città di Venezia.* Venice, 1610.

Franco, Veronica. *Lettere.* Edited by Benedetto Croce. Naples, 1949.

Gaeta, Franco. "Venezia da 'stato misto' ad aristocrazia 'esemplare.' " In *Storia della cultura veneta,* vol. 4, pt. 2, *Il Seicento,* pp. 437–94. Vicenza, 1984.

Gallo, Agostino. *Le tredici giornate della vera agricoltura & de' piaceri della villa.* 2d ed. Venice, 1564.

Giannotti, Donato. "Della Repubblica e Magistrati di Venezia." In *La Repubblica Fiorentina e la Veneziana di Donato Giannotti.* Venice, 1840.

Gilbert, Felix. "The Date of the Composition of Contarini's and Giannotti's Books on Venice." *Studies in the Renaissance* 14 (1967): 172–84.

———. "The Venetian Constitution in Florentine Political Thought." In *Florentine Studies: Politics and Society in Renaissance Florence,* edited by Nicolai Rubinstein, pp. 463–500. Evanston, Ill., 1968.

———. "Venetian Diplomacy before Pavia: From Reality to Myth." In *The Diversity of History: Essays in Honor of Sir Herbert Butterfield,* edited by J. H. Elliott and H. G. Koenigsberger, pp. 81–116. Ithaca, N.Y., 1970.

———. "Venice in the Crisis of the League of Cambrai." In *Renaissance Venice*, edited by J. R. Hale, pp. 274–92. London, 1973.

Gill, Katherine. "Open Monasteries for Women in Late Medieval and Early Modern Italy." In *The Crannied Wall: Women, Religion, and the Arts in Early Modern Europe*, edited by Craig A. Monson, pp. 15–47. Ann Arbor, Mich., 1992.

———. "*Scandala*: Controversies Concerning Clausura and Women's Religious Communities in Late Medieval Italy." In *Christendom and Its Discontents*, edited by Scott Waugh and Peter Diehl, pp. 177–203. Berkeley, 1996.

———. "Women and the Production of Religious Literature in the Vernacular, 1300–1500." In *Creative Women in Medieval and Early Modern Italy: A Religious and Artistic Renaissance*, edited by E. Ann Matter and John Coakley, pp. 64–104. Philadelphia, 1994.

Gilmore, Myron. "Myth and Reality in Venetian Political Theory." In *Renaissance Venice*, edited by J. R. Hale, pp. 431–44. London, 1973.

Girard, René. *Violence and the Sacred*. Baltimore, 1977.

Giuliani, Innocenzo, O.F.M. "Genesi e primo secolo di vita del Magistrato sopra monasteri." *Le Venezie Francescane* 28, no. 1–2 (1961): 42–68; no. 3–4:106–69.

Gleason, Elisabeth G. *Gasparo Contarini: Venice, Rome, and Reform*. Berkeley, 1993.

Greenblatt, Stephen. *Marvelous Possessions: The Wonder of the New World*. Chicago, 1991.

Gregolin, Francesco. "Saggio di statistica di alcuni processi per malcostume, nei conventi di Venezia e dello Stato Veneto, sec. XVII e XVIII." In *La republica di Venezia e la corte di Roma*, 2:99–113. Venice, 1874.

Grimani, Bishop Antonio. *Constitutioni, et decreti approvati nella sinodo diocesana, sopra la retta disciplina monacale sotto L'illustrissimo, & Reverendissimo Monsignor Antonio Grimani Vescovo di Torcello. L'anno della Natività del Nostro Signore. 1592. Il giorno 7. 8. & 9. d'Aprile*. Venice, 1592.

Grisar, Joseph. " 'Jesuitinnen': Ein Beitrag zur Geschichte des weiblichen Ordenswesens von 1550–1650." In *Reformata Reformanda, Festschrift für Hubert Jedin zum 17. Juni 1964*, edited by Erwin Iserloh and Konrad Repgen, 2:70–113. Münster, 1965.

———. *Maria Wards Institut vor Römischen Kongregationen, 1613–30*. Rome, 1966.

Groppi, Angela. *I conservatori della virtù: Donne recluse nella Roma dei Papi*. Bari, 1994.

Groto, Luigi. *Le orationi volgari di Luigi Groto Cieco di Hadria da lui medesimo recitate*. Venice, 1593.

Grubb, James S. "When Myths Lose Power: Four Decades of Venetian Historiography." *Journal of Modern History* 58, no. 1 (1986): 43–94.

Gullino, Giuseppe. "I Loredan di Santo Stefano: Cenni storici." In *Palazzo Loredan e l'Istituto Veneto di Scienze, Lettere, ed Arti*, pp. 11–33. Venice, 1985.

———. *I Pisani dal Banco e Moretta*. Rome, 1984.

———, ed. *La chiesa di Venezia tra riforma protestante e riforma cattolica*. Venice, 1990.

Hall, Marcia B. "The Tramezzo in Santa Croce, Florence, Reconstructed." *Art Bulletin* 56, no. 2 (1974): 325–41.

Hardin, G. "The Tragedy of the Commons." *Science* 162 (1968): 1243–48.

Helyot, Pierre. *Histoire des ordres monastiques, religieux et militaires*. Vol. 6. Paris, 1714–19.

Herlihy, David, and Christine Klapisch-Zuber. *Tuscans and Their Families*. New Haven, 1985.

Herodotus. *The Histories*. Edited by Walter Blanco and Jennifer Tolbert Roberts. New York, 1992.

Hollingsworth, Thomas H. "The Demography of the British Peerage." Supplement to *Population Studies* 18, no. 2 (1964).

Houssaie, Amelot de la. *Histoire du gouvernement de Venise*. Vol. 1. Paris, 1676.

Howell, James. *A Survay of the Signorie of Venice, of Her admired policy, and method of Goverment, &c. with a Cohortation to all Christian Princes to resent Her dangerous Condition at Present*. London, 1651.

Hughes, Diane Owen. "From Brideprice to Dowry in Mediterranean Europe." *Journal of Family History* 3 (1978): 262–96.

———. "Riti di passaggio nell'Occidente medievale." In *Storia d'Europa*, vol. 3, *Il Medioevo*, pp. 985–1037. Turin, 1995.

Hunecke, Volker. "Kindbett oder Kloster: Lebenswege venezianischer Patrizierinnen im 17. und 18. Jahrhundert." *Geschichte und Gesellschaft* 18 (1992): 446–76.

———. "Matrimonio e demografia del patriziato veneziano (secc. XVII–XVIII)." *Studi Veneziani* 21 (1991): 269–319.

———. *Der venezianische Adel am Ende der Republik (1646–1797): Demographie, Familie, Haushalt*. Tübingen, 1995.

Jones, Colin. *The Charitable Imperative: Hospitals and Nursing in Ancien Regime and Revolutionary France*. London, 1989.

Kahan, James P. "Rationality, the Prisoner's Dilemma, and Population." *Journal of Social Issues* 30, no. 4 (1974): 189–210.

Kendrick, Robert. *Celestial Sirens: Nuns and Their Music in Early Modern Milan*. Oxford, 1996.

———. "Four Views of Milanese Nuns' Music." In *Creative Women in Medieval and Early Modern Italy: A Religious and Artistic Renaissance*, edited by E. Ann Matter and John Coakley, pp. 324–42. Philadelphia, 1994.

Kettering, Sharon. "Gift-Giving and Patronage in Early Modern France." *French History* 2, no. 2 (1988): 131–51.

Killerby, Catherine Kovesi. "Practical Problems in the Enforcement of Italian

Sumptuary Law, 1200–1500." In *Crime, Society, and the Law in Renaissance Italy,* edited by Trevor Dean and K. J. P. Lowe, pp. 99–120. Cambridge, 1994.

King, Margaret L. *Women of the Renaissance.* Chicago, 1991.

Kirshner, Julius. "Pursuing Honor While Avoiding Sin: The Monte delle Doti of Florence." *Quaderni di Studi Senesi* 41 (1978): 1–82.

Kirshner, Julius, and Anthony Molho. "The Dowry Fund and the Marriage Market in Early *Quattrocento* Florence." *Journal of Modern History* 50, no. 3 (1978): 403–38.

———. "Il Monte delle Doti a Firenze dalla sua fondazione nel 1425 alla metà del sedicesimo secolo: Abbozzo di una ricerca." *Ricerche Storiche* 10, no. 1 (1980): 21–48.

Klapisch-Zuber, Christine. *Women, Family, and Ritual in Renaissance Italy.* Chicago, 1985.

Knox, Dilwyn. " 'Disciplina': The Monastic and Clerical Origins of European Civility." In *Renaissance Society and Culture: Essays in Honor of Eugene F. Rice Jr.,* edited by J. Monfasani and R. G. Musto, pp. 107–35. New York, 1991.

———. "Disciplina: Le origine monastiche e clericali del buon comportamento nell'Europa cattolica del Cinquecento e del primo Seicento." In *Disciplina dell'anima, disciplina del corpo e disciplina della società tra medioevo ed età moderna,* edited by Paolo Prodi, pp. 63–99. Bologna, 1994.

Labalme, Patricia. "Venetian Women on Women: Three Early Modern Feminists." *Archivio Veneto,* 5th ser., 152 (1981): 81–109.

Labalme, Patricia H., and Laura Sanguinetti White. "How to (and How Not to) Get Married in Sixteenth-Century Venice (Selections from Marin Sanudo)." *Renaissance Quarterly* 52, no. 1 (1999): 43–72.

Lettera delle RR. Monache di S. Maria delle Vergini, al Sereniss. Marc'Antonio Memmo, Principe di Venetia. Per la rinovatione della solenne visita alla lor Chiesa il primo giorno di Maggio. A ricever l'Indulgenza di Papa Alessandro III. Venice, 1613.

Lévi-Strauss, Claude. *The Elementary Structures of Kinship.* London, 1969. First edition (in French): Paris, 1949.

Litchfield, R. Burr. "Demographic Characteristics of Florentine Patrician Families, Sixteenth to Nineteenth Centuries." *Journal of Economic History* 29, no. 2 (1969): 191–205.

Livi, Carlo, Domenico Sella, and Ugo Tucci. "Un problème d'histoire: La decadence économique de Venise." In *Aspetti e cause della decadenza economica veneziana nel secolo XVII: Atti del Convegno 27 giugno–2 luglio 1957, Venezia, Isola di San Giorgio,* pp. 287–317. Venice, 1961.

Lowe, Kate. "Secular Brides and Convent Brides: Wedding Ceremonies in Italy during the Renaissance and Counter-Reformation." In *Marriage in Italy, 1300–1600,* edited by Trevor Dean and Kate Lowe, pp. 41–65. Cambridge, 1998.

Luhmann, Niklas. *Ecological Communication.* Chicago, 1989.

————. *Love as Passion: The Codification of Intimacy*. Cambridge, Mass., 1986.

————. "Sthenographie und Euryalistik." *Paradoxien, Dissonanzen, Zusammenbrüche,* edited by Hans Ulrich Gumbrecht and K. Ludwig Pfeiffer, pp. 58–82. Frankfurt am Main, 1991.

Lussana, Fiamma. "Rivolta e misticismo nei chiostri femminili del Seicento." *Studi Storici* 28 (1987): 243–60.

Luzzatto, Gino. "La decadenza di Venezia dopo le scoperte geografiche nella tradizione e nella realtà." *Archivio Veneto,* 5th ser., 89–90 (1955): 162–81.

Machiavelli, Niccoló. *The Prince.* Edited and translated by David Wootton. Indianapolis, 1995.

Marcocchi, Massimo. "La riforma dei monasteri femminili a Cremona: Gli atti inediti della visita del vescovo Cesare Speciano (1599–1606)." *Annali della Biblioteca Governativa e Libreria Civica di Cremona* 17 (1966).

Marsilio, Giovanni. "Difesa di Giovanni Marsilio a favore della Risposta dell' Otto Proposizioni, contra la quale ha scritto L'Illustrissimo e Reverendissimo Signor Cardinal Bellarmino." In *Opere del P. M. Paolo Sarpi Servita, Teologo e Consultore della Serenissima Repubblica di Venezia,* 7:223–364. Verona, 1768.

Martini, Angelo. *Manuale di Metrologia ossia misure, pesi e monete.* Turin, 1883.

Martinioni, Giustiniano. *Venetia citta nobilissima, et singolare, descritta in XIIII Libri da M. Francesco Sansovino . . . con aggiunta di tutte le Cose Notabili della stessa Città, fatte, & occorse dall'Anno 1580 fino al presente 1663 . . . Dove vi sono poste quelle del Stringa; servato peró l'ordine del med. Sansovino.* 2 vols. Venice, 1663.

Mauss, Marcel. *The Gift: The Form and Reason for Exchange in Archaic Societies.* New York, 1990. First edition (in French): 1925.

————. "Techniques of the Body." *Economy and Society* 2 (1973): 70–87.

McNamara, Jo Ann Kay. *Sisters in Arms: Catholic Nuns through Two Millennia.* Cambridge, Mass., 1996.

Medioli, Francesca. "La clausura delle monache nell'amministrazione della Congregazione Romana Sopra i Regolari." In *Il monachesimo femminile in Italia dall'alto medioevo al secolo XVII: A confronto con l'oggi. Atti del Convegno del Centro di studi farfensi: Santa Vittoria di Mantenano, 21–24 settembre 1995,* edited by Gabriella Zarri. Verona, 1997.

————, ed. *L'inferno monacale di Suor Arcangela Tarabotti.* Turin, 1990.

Memmo, Giovan Maria. *Dialogo del Magn. Cavaliere M. Gio. Maria Memmo, nel quale dopo alcune filosofiche dispute, si forma un perfetto Prencipe, & una perfetta Republica, e parimente un Senatore, un Cittadino, un Soldato, & un Mercatante.* Venice, 1563.

Molho, Anthony. *Marriage Alliance in Late Medieval Florence.* Cambridge, Mass., 1994.

———. "Tamquam vere mortua: Le professioni religiose femminili nella Firenze del tardo Medioevo." *Società e Storia* 43 (1989): 1–44.

Molinari, Franco. "Visite pastorali dei monasteri femminili di Piacenza nel sec. XVI." In *Il Concilio di Trento e la riforma tridentina: Atti del convegno storico internazionale, Trento, 2–6 settembre 1963*, 1:679–731. Rome, 1965.

Molmenti, Pompeo. *Curiosità di storia veneziana.* Bologna, 1919.

———. *La Dogaressa di Venezia.* Turin, 1884.

———. *La storia di Venezia nella vita privata.* Bergamo, 1925.

Monson, Craig A. *Disembodied Voices: Music and Culture in an Early Modern Italian Convent.* Berkeley, 1995.

———. "Disembodied Voices: Music in the Nunneries of Bologna in the Midst of the Counter-Reformation." In *The Crannied Wall: Women, Religion, and the Arts in Early Modern Europe,* pp. 191–209. Ann Arbor, Mich., 1992.

———. "The Making of Lucrezia Orsina Vizzana's Componimenti Musicali (1623)." In *Creative Women in Medieval and Early Modern Italy: A Religious and Artistic Renaissance,* edited by E. Ann Matter and John Coakley, pp. 297–323. Philadelphia, 1994.

Morelli, Jacopo. *Delle solennità e pompe nuziali già usate presso li Viniziani, pubblicata nelle nozze di S. E. il Signor Giovanni Almoró Tiepolo con la nobile Signora Marianna Gradenigo.* Venice, 1793.

Mueller, Reinhold C. *The Procuratori di San Marco and the Venetian Credit Market.* New York, 1977.

———. "The Procurators of San Marco in the Thirteenth and Fourteenth Centuries: A Study of the Office as a Financial and Trust Institution." *Studi Veneziani* 13 (1971): 105–220.

Muir, Edward. *Civic Ritual in Renaissance Venice.* Princeton, 1981.

———. "The Doge as Primus inter Pares: Interregnum Rites in Early Sixteenth-Century Venice." In *Essays Presented to Myron P. Gilmore,* edited by Sergio Bertelli and Gloria Ramakus, 1:145–60. Florence, 1978.

———. "Images of Power: Art and Pageantry in Renaissance Venice." *American Historical Review* 78, no. 1 (1979): 16–52.

Opitz, Claudia. *Frauenalltag im Mittelalter: Biographien des 13. und 14. Jahrhunderts.* Weinheim, Germany, 1985.

Ordo rituum et caeremoniarum suscipiendi habitum Monialem, & emittendi Professionem ad Venetae Dioecesis usum olim iussu Illustrissimi & Reverendissimi D. D. Francisci Vendrameni Patriarchae Venetiarum, & c Editus nunc vero Curantibus Sororibus Theupolis Degentibus in Monasterio S. Luciae. Venice, 1694.

Outhwaite, R. B. *Clandestine Marriage in England, 1500–1850.* London, 1995.

Pallavicino, Ferrante. *Le divorce céleste, causé par les dissolutions de l'Espouse Romaine.* Ville Franche, 1649.

Parenti, Giuseppe. *Prezzi e mercato del grano a Siena, 1546–1765.* Florence, 1942.

————. "Prezzi e salari à Firenze dal 1520 al 1620." In *I prezzi in Europa dal XIII secolo a oggi,* edited by Ruggiero Romano. Turin, 1967.

Paruta, Paolo. *Della perfettione della vita politica.* Venice, 1599. First edition: 1579.

————. *Discorsi politici.* Venice, 1599.

————. "Orazione per i Nobili Veneziani morti a Lepanto" (19 October 1571). In *Orazioni scelte del secolo XVI,* edited by Giuseppe Lisio. Florence, 1957.

Paschini, Pio. "I monasteri femminili in Italia nel '500." In *Problemi di vita religiosa in Italia nel Cinquecento: Convegno di storia della Chiesa in Italia, 1958, Bologna.* Padua, 1960.

Passi, Giuseppe. *I donneschi diffetti nuovamente riformati, e posti in luce . . . aggiuntovi in questa seconda impressione molte cose belle, á discorso, per discorso, degne d'esser lette da studiosi.* Venice, 1601.

Pedani, Maria Pia. "Monasteri di Agostiniane a Venezia." *Archivio Veneto,* 5th ser., 122–25 (1984–85): 35–78.

————. "L'osservanza imposta: I monasteri conventuali femminili a Venezia nei primi anni del cinquecento." *Archivio Veneto,* 5th ser., 179 (1995): 113–25.

Pelliccia, Guerrino, and Giancarlo Rocca, eds. *Dizionario degli istituti di perfezione.* Vol. 1. Rome, 1974.

Pellizzari, Francesco. *Manuale Regularium.* Vol. 2. Lugduni [Lyons], 1653.

Pezzolo, Luciano. *L'oro dello Stato: Società, finanza e fisco nella Repubblica veneta del secondo '500.* Treviso, 1990.

Pignatti, Terisio. *Pietro Longhi: Paintings and Drawings.* London, 1969.

Pilot, Antonio. "Di alcuni versi inediti sulla peste del 1575." *Ateneo Veneto* 26 (1903): 350–58.

————. "Frottola vernacola inedita contro le monache e capitolo in risposta." *Luceria* 1, no. 7–8 (1910): 1–17.

Pizzati, Anna. "La proprietà terriera dei monasteri benedettini veneziani nella seconda metà del cinquecento." Master's thesis, University of Ca' Foscari, Venice, Department of Literature and Philosophy, 1986.

Plöchl, Willibald M. *Geschichte des Kirchenrechts.* Vienna, 1959.

Pocock, J. G. A. *The Machiavellian Moment: Florentine Political Thought and the Atlantic Republican Tradition.* Princeton, 1975.

Preto, Paolo. *Peste e società a Venezia nel 1576.* Vicenza, 1978.

Primhak, Victoria. "Women in Religious Communities: The Benedictine Convents of Venice, 1400–1500." Ph.D. diss., University of London, 1991.

Priuli, Patriarch Lorenzo. *Ordini, & avvertimenti, che si devono osservare ne' Monasteri di Monache di Venetia: Sopra le visite, & clausura.* Venice, 1591.

Prodi, Paolo. "La Chiesa di Venezia nell'età delle riforme." In *La chiesa di Venezia tra riforma protestante e riforma cattolica,* edited by Giuseppe Gullino, pp. 63–75. Venice, 1990.

————. *The Papal Prince: One Body and Two Souls: The Papal Monarchy in Early Modern Europe.* Cambridge, 1987.

Pullan, Brian. "Poverty, Charity, and the Reason of State: Some Venetian Examples." *Bollettino dell'Istituto di Storia della Società e dello Stato Veneziano* (same as *Studi Veneziani*) 2 (1960): 17–60.

———. *Rich and Poor in Renaissance Venice: The Social Institutions of a Catholic State.* Oxford, 1971.

———. "Service to the Venetian State: Aspects of Myth and Reality in the Early Seventeenth Century." *Studi Secenteschi* 5 (1964): 95–148.

———. "Wage-Earners and the Venetian Economy, 1550–1630." In *Crisis and Change in the Venetian Economy in the Sixteenth and Seventeenth Centuries,* edited by Brian Pullan, 146–74. London, 1968.

Puppi, Lionello. "'Rex sum justicie': Note per una storia metaforica del Palazzo dei dogi." In *I Dogi,* edited by Gino Benzoni, pp. 183–213. Milan, 1982.

Queller, Donald E., and Thomas Madden. "Father of the Bride: Fathers, Daughters, and Dowries in Late Medieval and Early Renaissance Venice." *Renaissance Quarterly* 46, no. 4 (1993): 685–711.

Questa sie la regula del glorioso confessore miser Sancto Benedeto in vulgare ad instantia de le venerabile monache de la celestia observante novamente stampata. Venice, 1527.

Raccolta degli scritti usciti fuori in istampa, e scritti a mano, nella causa del P. Paolo V. co' signori venetiani secondo le stampe di Venetia, di Roma, & d'altri luoghi. Vol. 1. Coira (Chur), 1607.

Raines, Dorit. "Pouvoir ou privilèges nobiliaires: Le dilemme du patriciat vénetien face aux agrégations du XVIIe siècle." *Annales E.S.C.* 46, no. 4 (1991): 827–47.

Rambaldi, Susanna Peyronel. *Speranze e crisi nel Cinquecento modenese: Tensioni religiose e vita cittadina ai tempi di Giovanni Morone.* Milan, 1979.

Rapley, Elizabeth. *The Dévotes: Women and Church in Seventeenth-Century France.* Montreal, 1990.

Rapp, Richard T. *Industry and Economic Decline in Seventeenth-Century Venice.* Cambridge, 1976.

Reinhard, Wolfgang. "Disciplinamento sociale, confessionalizzazione, modernizzazione: Un discorso storiografico." In *Disciplina dell'anima, disciplina del corpo e disciplina della società tra medioevo ed età moderna,* edited by Paolo Prodi, pp. 101–23. Bologna, 1994.

Rendina, Claudio. *I Dogi: Storia e segreti.* Rome, 1984.

Ricoeur, Paul. *The Rule of Metaphor.* Toronto, 1991.

Romano, Dennis. *Patricians and Popolani.* Baltimore, 1987.

Rosand, David. "Venereal Hermeneutics: Reading Titian's Venus of Urbino." In *Renaissance Society and Culture,* edited by J. Monfansani and R. G. Musto, pp. 263–80. New York, 1991.

———. "Venetia Figurata: The Iconography of a Myth." In *Interpretazioni Veneziane,* edited by David Rosand, pp. 177–96. Venice, 1984.

Rösch, Eva Sibylle, and Gerhard Rösch. *Venedig im Spätmittelalter, 1200–1500.* Würzburg, 1991.

Rösch, Gerhard. *Der venezianische Adel bis zur Schliessung des Grossen Rats: Zur Genese einer Führungsschicht.* Sigmaringen, 1989.
Rosenthal, Margaret F. *The Honest Courtesan: Veronica Franco, Citizen and Writer in Sixteenth-Century Venice.* Chicago, 1992.
Rubin, Gayle. "The Traffic in Women: Notes on the 'Political Economy' of Sex." In *Toward an Anthropology of Women,* edited by Rayna Reiter, pp. 157–210. New York, 1975.
Rudman, Valnea. "Lettura della canzone per la peste di Venezia di Maffio Venier." *Atti dell'Istituto Veneto di Scienze, Lettere ed Arti, Classe di scienze morali e lettere* 121 (1962–63): 599–641.
Ruggiero, Guido. *The Boundaries of Eros: Sex Crime and Sexuality in Renaissance Venice.* New York, 1985.
Russo, Carla. *I monasteri femminili di clausura a Napoli nel secolo XVII.* Naples, 1970.
Sabellico, Marc'Antonio. *Del Sito di Venezia Città.* Edited by G. Meneghetti. Venice, 1957. First edition: 1502.
———. "Historiae rerum venetarum ab urbe condita libri XXXIII" (first edition, 1487). In *Degl'istorici delle cose veneziane, i quali hanno scritto per pubblico decreto,* vol. 1. Venice, 1718.
Saint-Didier, T. L. E. D. M. S. [Alexandre-Toussaint Limojon] de. *La Ville et Republique de Venise.* 3d ed. Amsterdam, 1680. First edition: 1670.
Saint Jerome. *Lettere.* Edited by Claudio Moreschini. Milan, 1989.
Sandi, Vettor. *Principj di storia civile della Repubblica di Venezia dalla sua fondazione sino all'anno di N.S. 1700.* Pt. 3, vol. 2. Venice, 1756.
Sansovino, Francesco. *Delle cose notabili che sono in Venezia.* Venice, 1561.
———. *Delle Orationi recitate a principi di Venetia.* Venice, 1562.
———. *Venetia città nobilissima e singolare.* Venice, 1581.
Sanuto [Sanudo], Marino. *I diarii,* 1496–1533. Venice, 1879–1902.
———. "Vitae Ducum Venetorum italice scriptae ab origine urbis, sive ab Anno CCCCXXI usque ad Annum MCCCCXCIII auctore Marino Sanuto, Leonardi Filio, Patricio Veneto." In *Rerum Italicarum Scriptores,* edited by Ludovicus Antonius Muratorius, vol. 22. Milan, 1733.
Sarpi, Paolo. *Istoria del Concilio Tridentino.* Vol. 2. Florence, 1982.
———. "Risposta data . . . a Paolo V. Sommo Pontefice sopra l'interdetto da esso fulminato contro la Serenissima Repubblica di Venezia." In *Opere di F. Paolo Sarpi Servita, Teologo e Consultore della Serenissima Repubblica di Venezia.* Vol. 6. Verona, 1768.
Savio, Pietro. "Per l'epistolario di Paolo Sarpi." Parts 1 and 2. *Aevum* 11 (1937): 13–74, 275–322; 13, no. 4 (1939): 558–622.
Schmugge, Ludwig. *Kirche Kinder Karrieren.* Zurich, 1995.
Schulenburg, Jane Tibbetts. "The Heroics of Virginity: Brides of Christ and Sacrificial Mutilation." In *Women in the Middle Ages and the Renaissance: Literary and Historical Perspectives,* edited by Mary Beth Rose, pp. 29–72. Syracuse, 1986.
———. "Women's Monastic Communities, 500–1100." *Signs* 14, no. 2 (1989): 261–92.

Schulte van Kessel, Elisja. "Virgins and Mothers between Heaven and Earth." In *A History of Women in the West*, edited by Georges Duby and Michelle Perrot, vol. 3, *Renaissance and Enlightenment Paradoxes*, edited by Natalie Zemon Davis and Arlette Farge. Cambridge, Mass., 1993.

Schutte, Anne Jacobson. "Inquisition and Female Autobiography: The Case of Cecilia Ferrazzi." In *The Crannied Wall: Women, Religion, and the Arts in Early Modern Europe*, edited by Craig A. Monson, pp. 105–14. Ann Arbor, Mich., 1992.

———. "'Piccole donne', 'grandi eroine': Santità femminile 'simulata' e 'vera' nell'Italia della prima età moderna." In *Donne e fede: Santità e vita religiosa in Italia*, edited by Lucetta Scaraffia and Gabriella Zarri, pp. 277–302. Bari, 1994.

———. *Printed Italian Vernacular Religious Books, 1465–1550: A Finding List*. Geneva, 1983.

Scott, Karen. "Women's Networks, and the Lay Apostolate in the Siena of Catherine Benincasa." In *Creative Women in Medieval and Early Modern Italy: A Religious and Artistic Renaissance*, edited by E. Ann Matter and John Coakley, pp. 105–99. Philadelphia, 1994.

Sella, Domenico. "Crisis and Transformation in Venetian Trade." In *Crisis and Change in the Venetian Economy in the Sixteenth and Seventeenth Centuries*, edited by Brian Pullan, pp. 88–105. London, 1968.

Skinner, Quentin. "Political Philosophy." In *The Cambridge History of Renaissance Philosophy*, edited by Q. Skinner, E. Kessler, and J. Kraye, pp. 389–452. Cambridge, 1988.

Sorelli, Fernanda. "Per la storia religiosa di Venezia nella prima metà del quattrocento: Inizi e sviluppi del terz'ordine domenicano." In *Viridarium Floridum: Studi di storia veneta offerti dagli allievi a Paolo Sambin*, edited by Maria Chiara Billanovich et al., pp. 89–114. Padua, 1984.

Speroni, Sperone. *Opere*. Vol. 3. Venice, 1989.

Spinelli, Giovanni. "I religiosi e le religiose." In *La Chiesa di Venezia nel Seicento*, vol. 5, edited by Bruno Bertoli, pp. 173–209. Venice, 1992.

Squitinio della libertà veneta nel quale si adducono anche le raggioni dell'impero Romano sopra la Città & Signoria di Venetia. [Mirandola?], 1612.

Stella, Aldo. "La proprietà ecclesiastica nella Repubblica di Venezia dal secolo XV al XVII." *Nuova Rivista Storica* 42 (1958): 50–77.

———, ed. *Chiesa e stato nelle relazioni dei nunzi pontifici a Venezia*. Vatican City, 1964.

Stone, Lawrence. *Uncertain Unions: Marriage in England, 1660–1753*. Oxford, 1992.

Stringa, Giovanni. *Venetia città nobilissima, et singolare, descritta già in XIIII Libri da M. Francesco Sansovino: Et hora con molta diligenza corretta, emendata, e più d'un terzo di cose nuove ampliata dal M. R. D. Giovanni Stringa, Canonico della Chiesa Ducale di S. Marco*. Venice, 1604.

Stumpo, Enrico. "Problema di ricerca: Per la storia della crisi della proprietà ecclesiastica fra Quattrocento e Cinquecento." *Critica Storica* 1 (1976): 62–80.

Succi, Dario. *Francesco Guardi: Itinerario dell'avventura artistica.* Milan, 1993.

Sultanini, Baltassare. *Il novo parlatorio delle monache, satira comica.* 2d ed. Venice, 1677.

Tafuri, Manfredo. "La 'nuova Constantinopoli': La rappresentazione della 'renovatio' nella Venezia dell'Umanesimo (1450–1509)." *Rassegna* 9 (1982): 25–38.

———. "'Renovatio urbis Venetiarum': Il problema storiografico." In *'Renovatio Urbis': Venezia nell'età di Andrea Gritti,* edited by M. Tafuri, pp. 9–55. Rome, 1984.

———. *Venezia e il Rinascimento: Religione, scienza, architettura.* Turin, 1985.

Tarabotti, Suor Arcangela. "Antisatira." In *Contro 'l Lusso Donnesco, satira menippea del Sig. Francesco Buoninsegni.* Venice, 1644.

———. *Il Paradiso Monacale.* Venice, 1663.

———. *La semplicità ingannata.* Published posthumously under the pseudonym Galeana Baratotti. [Leiden?], 1654.

Tramontin, Silvio. "La visita apostolica del 1581 à Venezia." *Studi Veneziani* 9 (1967): 453–533.

Trexler, Richard. "Celibacy in the Renaissance: The Nuns of Florence." In *Dependence in Context in Renaissance Florence,* edited by Richard Trexler, pp. 343–72. Binghamton, N.Y., 1994.

———. "Le célibat à la fin du Moyen Age: Les religieuses de Florence." *Annales E.S.C.* 27 (1972): 1329–50.

Tucci, Ugo. "Les émissions monétaires de Venise et les mouvements internationaux de l'or." *Revue Historique* 527 (1978): 91–122.

Vasoli, Cesare. "Un 'precedente' della 'vergine veneziana': Francesco Giorgio Veneto e la clarissa Chiara Bugni." In *Postello, Venezia e il suo mondo,* edited by Marion Leathers Kuntz, pp. 203–25. Florence, 1988.

Vasta, Marilena Modica. "La scrittura mistica." In *Donne e fede: Santità e vita religiosa in Italia,* edited by Lucetta Scaraffia and Gabriella Zarri, pp. 375–98. Bari, 1994.

Vecellio, Cesare. *Habiti antichi et moderni di Diverse Parti del Mondo.* Venice, 1590. Facsimile edition: Bologna, 1982.

Ventura, Angelo. "Considerazioni sull' agricoltura veneta e sulla accumulazione originaria del capitale nei secoli XVI e XVII." *Studi Storici* 3–4 (1968): 674–722.

Visceglia, Maria Antonetta. *Il bisogno dell' eternità: I comportamenti aristocratici a Napoli in età moderna.* Naples, 1988.

Volumen statutorum legum ac iurium DD Venetorum. Venice, 1665.

Weaver, Elissa B. "The Convent Wall in Tuscan Drama." In *The Crannied Wall: Women, Religion, and the Arts in Early Modern Europe,* edited by Craig A. Monson, pp. 73–86. Ann Arbor, Mich. 1992.

———. "Le muse in convento: La scrittura profana delle monache italiane (1450–1650)." In *Donne e fede: Santità e vita religiosa in Italia*, edited by Lucetta Scaraffia and Gabriella Zarri, pp. 253–76. Bari, 1994.

———. "Spiritual Fun: A Study of Sixteenth-Century Tuscan Convent Theater." In *Women in the Middle Ages and Renaissance: Literary and Historical Perspectives*, edited by Mary Beth Rose, pp. 173–205. Syracuse, 1986.

———. "Suor Maria Clemente Ruoti, Playwright and Academician." In *Creative Women in Medieval and Early Modern Italy: A Religious and Artistic Renaissance*, edited by E. Ann Matter and John Coakley, pp. 281–96. Philadelphia, 1994.

Whitman, James Q. "The Lawyers Discover the Fall of Rome." *Law and History Review* 9, no. 2 (1991): 191–220.

Wilson, Bronwen. "'Il bel sesso, e l'austero Senato': The Coronation of Dogaressa Morosina Morosini Grimani." *Renaissance Quarterly* 52, no. 1 (1999): 73–139.

Wolters, Wolfgang. *Der Bilderschmuck des Dogenpalastes*. Wiesbaden, 1983.

Zanette, Emilio. *Suor Arcangela monaca del Seicento veneziano*. Venice, 1960.

Zanetti, Dante E. *La demografia del patriziato milanese nei secoli XVII, XVIII, XIX*. Pavia, 1972.

Zannini, Andrea. *Burocrazia e burocrati a Venezia in età moderna: I cittadini originari (sec. XVI–XVIII)*. Venice, 1993.

Zardin, Danilo. *Donna e religiosa di rara eccellenza: Prospera Corona Bascapè, i libri e la cultura nei monasteri milanesi del Cinque e Seicento*. Florence, 1992.

———. "Mercato librario e letture devote nella svolta del Cinquecento tridentino: Note in margine ad un inventario milanese di libri di monache." In *Stampa, libri e lettura a Milano nell'età di Carlo Borromeo*, edited by Nicola Raponi and Angelo Turchini, pp. 135–246. Biblioteca di storia moderna e contemporanea, vol. 3. Milan, 1992.

Zarri, Gabriella. "Aspetti dello sviluppo degli Ordini religiosi in Italia tra Quattro e Cinquecento: Studi e problemi." In *Strutture ecclesiastiche in Italia e in Germania prima della Riforma*, edited by Paolo Prodi and Peter Johanek, pp. 207–58. Bologna, 1984.

———. "Dalla profezia alla disciplina (1450–1650)." In *Donne e fede: Santità e vita religiosa in Italia*, edited by Lucetta Scaraffia and Gabriella Zarri, pp. 177–226. Bari, 1994.

———. "Disciplina regolare e pratica di coscienza: Le virtù e i comportamenti sociali in comunità femminili (secc. XVI–XVIII)." In *Disciplina dell'anima, disciplina del corpo e disciplina della società tra medioevo ed età moderna*, edited by Paolo Prodi, pp. 257–78. Bologna, 1994.

———. "Donna, disciplina, creanza cristiana: Un percorso di ricerca." In *Donna, disciplina, creanza cristiana dal XV al XVII secolo*, edited by Gabriella Zarri, pp. 5–19. Rome, 1996.

————. "Gender, Religious Institutions, and Social Discipline: The Reform of the Regulars." In *Gender and Society in Renaissance Italy,* edited by Judith C. Brown and Robert C. Davis, pp. 193–212. Essex, 1998.

————. "I monasteri femminili a Bologna tra il XIII e il XVII secolo." *Atti e Memorie della Deputazione di Storia Patria per le Provincie di Romagna,* n.s., 24 (1973): 133–224.

————. "Monasteri femminili e città (secoli XV–XVIII)." In *Storia d'Italia,* annali 9, *La Chiesa e il potere politico dal Medioevo all'età contemporanea,* edited by Giorgio Chittolini and G. Miccoli, pp. 357–429. Turin, 1986.

————. "Note su diffusione e circolazione di testi devoti (1520–1550)." In *Libri, idee e sentimenti religiosi nel Cinquecento italiano, 3–5 aprile 1986,* pp. 131–54. Modena, 1987.

————. "Recinti sacri: Sito e forma dei monasteri femminili a Bologna tra '500 e '600." In *Luoghi sacri e spazi della santità,* edited by Sofia Boesch Gajano and Lucetta Scaraffia, pp. 381–96. Turin, 1990.

————. *Le sante vive: Profezie di corte e devozione femminile tra '400 e '500.* Turin, 1990.

Index

Abbesses, triennial terms for, 116, 120, 128, 213, 229–30
aggregation. *See* sellout
Agnadello, 76, 77, 109, 125, 305n. 28. *See also* War of League of Cambrai
agnatic inheritance. *See* inheritance patterns
agriculture, 56, 99–100, 101, 102. *See also* land holdings
Alexander III: founding of Santa Maria delle Vergini and, 16, 164, 209, 212, 214–15, 231, 232, 233; Venetian sovereignty and, 95, 206, 208, 209
alms ("charities"), 128–29, 146–47, 170, 174–76, 204
annuities (pensions), 289n. 112, 301n. 228; of boarders, 187; vs. bridal dowries, 32, 43, 301n. 228; financial management and, 186; lawsuits regarding, 40–41, 43, 44–46, 49, 65–66, 67–68, 301n. 228; mortmain laws and, 196–97, 274n. 11; standardized at sixty ducats, 155, 188, 190, 196;

tax records and, 182, 188. *See also* spiritual dowries
Annunciation of Virgin Mary, 72, 84, 206, 235, 237
anti-papalisti, 220, 225
antisemitism, 209, 212, 236
architecture, 76, 77, 83
Aretino, Pietro, 97, 99, 140
aristocracy. *See* patriciate
Aristotelian philosophy: body images and, 87, 107; Contarini's use of, 72; dowry inflation and, 54; women's place and, 100

Badoer, Francesco, 149, 150, 151
Badoer, Pietro, 193
Balbi, Raphaela, 148, 161
Balbi, Serafica, 36, 149, 150, 151
barbarella, 22
Barbarigo, Lugretia, 288n. 111
Barbaro, Francesco, 73
beguines. *See* third-order nuns
Bellarmino (Cardinal), 226
Beltrami, Daniele, 201
Benedictine rules, 127, 326n. 55
Benetti, Maria, 213, 228, 229

tive, 148; hairstyles of, 120–23, 141, 161; literary and artistic activities of, 119, 124, 160–61, 162; male clothes worn by, 148, 160, 161, 162, 163; patrician percentage of, 26–27, 281n. 55, 282n. 57; political power of, 224–25, 235; social relationships of, 14, 157, 174–76 (*see also* parlors); total numbers of, 26; ungendered state of, 162–63; voluntary, 25, 140. *See also* mendicant nuns; servant nuns; sexual relationships of nuns; third-order nuns; virginity of nuns

Offredi, Offredo di, 189, 217, 230
oligarchy, 79, 80, 82; intermarriage and, 1, 3
orphans, 39–41, 41, 117, 288n. 105
Ottobon, Innocentia, 150

Pagano, Antonio, 118
Pallavicino, Ferrante, 140
papacy: collaboration with state on clausura, 142, 143, 146–47; nuns' private connections to, 146; vs. reformist evangelism, 226–27; vs. Venetian jurisdiction over convents, 16, 25, 214–17. *See also* Interdict of 1606; state sovereignty; Tridentine reforms
papalisti, 213
parlors, 14, 158–61; boarders in convents and, 164; bridal visits to, 166–67; government restrictions, 144, 146, 155–56, 167, 176, 334n. 121; marriage contracts negotiated in, 166; patriarchs' restrictions, 147, 160, 174–75
Paruta, Paolo: anti-myth and, 109; on aristocratic virtue, 103–5,

107, 113; Florentine historians and, 304n. 22; on magnificence, 22, 79, 80; on nobility, 82, 104, 105; noble mother metaphor of, 87; on peace and stability, 106; perfection myth and, 76; virgin metaphor and, 105–6
Passi, Giuseppe, 54, 55
patriarchal rule, 3, 6, 239
patriarchs. *See* Contarini, Antonio; Priuli, Lorenzo; Tiepolo, Giovanni; Trevisan, Giovanni; Vendramin, Francesco; Venetian curia
patriciate: addition of families to (*see* sellout); anti-myth and, 108, 109–10; aristocratic rule justified, 73, 82, 103, 104; closure of (see *serrata);* clothing of, 93–94, 95–96; convent reform and, 205; convents' political significance to, 216–17; decline of (*see* demographic decline of patriciate); egalitarian ideal, 2, 55, 83; financial independence of, 104; foundation myth and, 237; land investments of (*see* land holdings); metaphorical relationships of, 107; monachization rates, 17, 18–19, 26–29, 58–59, 71; mythical qualities of, 69–70; old houses of, 294n. 169, 298n. 193; paradoxical female images of, 83; perfection myth and, 2, 13, 106–7; political corruption of, 110–11, 112; reproduction of, 11, 17, 50, 64, 237, 293n. 165; social differentiation within, 24, 51, 55, 56, 57, 62–63, 294n. 169, 296n. 186; virgin metaphor and, 11, 12, 69, 105, 228; virtue of, 103–4. *See also* body politic

www.ingramcontent.com/pod-product-compliance
Lightning Source LLC
Chambersburg PA
CBHW022130020426
42334CB00015B/833